BIBLICAL MYTH AND RABBINIC MYTHMAKING

Biblical Myth and Rabbinic Mythmaking

MICHAEL FISHBANE

OXFORD
UNIVERSITY PRESS

OXFORD
UNIVERSITY PRESS
Great Clarendon Street, Oxford OX2 6DP

Oxford University Press is a department of the University of Oxford.
It furthers the University's objective of excellence in research, scholarship,
and education by publishing worldwide in

Oxford New York

Auckland Cape Town Dar es Salaam Hong Kong Karachi Kuala Lumpur
Madrid Melbourne Mexico City Nairobi New Delhi Shanghai Taipei Toronto

With offices in

Argentina Austria Brazil Chile Czech Republic France Greece
Guatemala Hungary Italy Japan South Korea Poland Portugal
Singapore Switzerland Thailand Turkey Ukraine Vietnam

Oxford is a registered trade mark of Oxford University Press
in the UK and certain other countries

Published in the United States
by Oxford University Press Inc., New York

First published 2003

First published in paperback 2005

British Library Cataloguing in Publication Data

Data available

Library of Congress Cataloging in Publication Data

Data applied for

ISBN 0-19-826733-9
ISBN 0-19-928420-2 978-0-19-928420-2

1 3 5 7 9 10 8 6 4 2

Typeset by Kolam Information Services Pvt. Ltd, Pondicherry, India
Printed in Great Britain on acid-free paper by
Biddles Ltd,
King's Lynn, Norfolk

for
Eitan and Elisha
בני עליה, מאורי אור

PREFACE

THIS book has been many years in the making, though indeed the phenomenon of mythopoesis is one of my oldest and most enduring intellectual passions—undergoing metamorphosis after metamorphosis. Research and thinking for the present work is evidence of that, as the project has been rethought afresh at several junctures. As the work developed, I determined to set midrashic mythmaking in a larger context, and this led to expansions and remouldings of various sorts. The present three-tiered schema is the result, with each part presented in its own right but also as part of a wider and continuous phenomenon—this being monotheistic myth and its exegetical dimensions. An early interest in the term *kivyakhol* proved problematic on several counts, and ultimately too restrictive; the larger themes of rabbinic myth overtook it in the end. A monograph-length study of the term and its exempla is found in Appendix 2.

My work on the subjects of this book benefited considerably from two occasions when I was a Fellow of the Institute for Advanced Study at the Hebrew University of Jerusalem. The first of these was in 1989–90, when the subject was 'Jewish Hermeneutics'; the second was in 1998–9, when the subject was 'The Book of Zohar and its Study'. My thanks to my friends and colleagues, Professor Moshe Idel and Professor Yehuda Liebes, who were the conveners of the two study groups, respectively. Seminar presentations and on-going conversations stimulated my thinking or sharpened my formulations on several issues. I happily record my thanks to the Institute and its staff for the congenial atmosphere provided. I also wish to thank my students Laura Lieber and Steven Sacks for ably assisting me in the pursuit of articles, books, and manuscripts; and special thanks to Steven Sacks for his assiduous and devoted work on the thematic and textual indices.

In this study, Hebrew transliterations have been simplified for the benefit of non-specialists. Thus the letter *b* represents *bet* in all circumstances, except where more well-known terms are used (e.g. *Ṭov*); and *q* represents *qof*, except for some standard formulations (e.g. *Pirkei*). Similarly *ḥ* represents *ḥet*, except for specific names (e.g. Simeon bar Yochai). Vowel length for Hebrew is unmarked; but vowel length for Greek is marked, since different letters are involved.

As I complete my present studies on this subject, I give heartfelt thanks to my dear wife Mona, for her love and life-long companionship and support. Among many memorable conversations on the theme of myth, I joyfully recall some musings on mythopoesis in a snowstorm so many years ago. And it is with a heart full of love and gratitude that I dedicate this book to our two sons, Eitan and Elisha. Their overflowing love and intellectual energy have contributed in so many ways to this book. I am a most blessed of fathers.

M. Fishbane

September 2002/Rosh Hashana 5663

CONTENTS

GENERAL ABBREVIATIONS

A	Amora
AB	Anchor Bible
AcOr	*Acta Orientalia*
AfO	*Archiv für Orientforschung*
AJSL	*American Journal of Semitic Languages*
AJS Rev.	*Association for Jewish Studies Review*
Akk.	Akkadian
AnOr	Analecta Orientalia
AnSt	*Anatolian Studies*
AO	Der Alte Orient
AOAT	Alter Orient und Altes Testament
AS	Assyriological Studies
BA	Babylonian Amora (followed by generation number)
BA	*Biblical Archaeologist*
BASOR	*Bulletin of the American Schools of Oriental Research*
Ber.	*Berakhot*
Bib.	*Biblica*
BJS	Brown Judaica Studies
BKAT	Biblischer Kommentar: Altes Testament
BO	*Bibliotheca Orientalis*
BT	Babylonian Talmud
BWANT	Beiträge zur Wissenschaft vom Alten und Neuen Testament
CAD	*The Assyrian Dictionary of the Oriental Institute of the University of Chicago*
CBQ	*Catholic Biblical Quarterly*
CBQM	Catholic Biblical Quarterly Monograph Series
CH	*Church History*
CT	Cuneiform Texts from Babylonian Tablets in the British Museum
CTA	*Corpus des tablettes en cunéiformes alphabétiques à Ras Shamra-Ugarit de 1929 à 1939* (ed. A. Herdner)
EI	*Eretz Israel*
Erub.	*Erubin*
GCS	Die Griechischen Christlichen Schriftsteller
Ḥag.	*Ḥagigah*
HDR	Harvard Dissertations in Religion

Horovitz–Rabin	*Mechilta D'Rabbi Ismael*, ed. H. S. Horovitz and I. A. Rabin (Jerusalem: Bamberger & Wahrman, 1960) = *Mekhilta de-Rabbi Ishmael*
HR	*History of Religions*
HSM	Harvard Semitic Monographs
HSS	Harvard Semitic Studies
HTR	*Harvard Theological Review*
HUCA	*Hebrew Union College Annual*
IOS	*Israel Oriental Studies*
Ish Shalom	*Pesikta Rabbati*, ed. M. Ish Shalom (Vilna: J. Kaiser, 1880)
JAAR	*Journal of the American Academy of Religion*
JANESCU	*Journal of the Ancient Near Eastern Society of Columbia University*
JAOS	*Journal of the American Oriental Society*
JBL	*Journal of Biblical Literature*
JCS	*Journal of Cuneiform Studies*
JJS	*Journal of Jewish Studies*
JJTP	*Journal of Jewish Thought and Philosophy*
JNES	*Journal of Near Eastern Studies*
JQR	*Jewish Quarterly Review*
JRAS	*Journal of the Royal Asiatic Society*
JSJ	*Journal for the Study of Judaism in Late Antiquity*
JSJT	*Jerusalem Studies in Jewish Thought*
JSOT	*Journal for the Study of the Old Testament*
JSOTMS	*Journal for the Study of the Old Testament Monograph Series*
JSQ	*Jewish Studies Quarterly*
JSS	*Journal of Semitic Studies*
JT	Jerusalem (Palestinian) Talmud
JTS	*Journal of Theological Studies*
KAR	E. Ebeling, *Keilschrifttexte ans Assur religiösen Inhalten*
Kidd.	*Kiddushin*
KS	Kleine Schriften
KTU	M. Dietrich, O. Loretz, and J. Samartin, *Die Keilalphabetischen Texte aus Ugarit*
Meg.	*Megillah*
Men.	*Menaḥot*
MGWJ	*Monatsschrift für Geschichte und Wissenschaft des Judentums*
MT	Masoretic Text
MVAG	*Mitteilungen der Vorasiatischen und Ägyptischen Gesellschaft*

NJPS	New JPS Translation of the Bible (1985)
OBO	Orbis biblicus et orientalis
OECT	Oxford Editions of Cuneiform Texts
OIP	Oriental Institute Publications (Chicago)
Or.	*Orientalia*
PAAJR	*Proceedings of the American Academy for Jewish Research*
PEQ	*Palestine Exploration Quarterly*
PG	*Patrologiae cursus completus: Series Graeca*, ed. J.-P. Migne, 161 vols. (Paris: J.-P. Migne, 1857–66).
RA	*Revue d'Assyriologie et d'Archéologie Orientale*
RB	*Revue Biblique*
RdHR	*Revue d'Histoire des Religions*
REJ	*Revue des Études Juives*
RS	signature for texts from Ras Shamra
SAA	State Archives of Assyria
Sanh.	*Sanhedrin*
SBLMS	Society of Biblical Literature Monograph Series
SEL	*Studie Epigrafici e Linguistici sul Vicino Oriente antico*
SFSHJ	South Florida Studies in the History of Judaism
Sheb.	*Shebuʿot*
StudOr	Studia Orientalia (Fennica)
SVT	Vetus Testamentum Supplements
Theodor–Albeck	*Midrash Bereshit Rabba*, ed. J. Theodor and C. Albeck (2nd printing; Jerusalem: Wahrmann Books, 1965) = *Bereishit Rabba*
TJ	Targum Jonathan
TLZ	*Theologische Literaturzeitung*
TO	Targum Onkelos
Tos.	*Tosephta*
TZ	*Theologische Zeitschrift*
UBL	Ugaritic and Biblical Literature
UF	*Ugaritische Forschungen*
Ug.	*Ugaritica*
UT	C. H. Gordon, *Ugaritic Textbook* (AnOr 38; Rome: Pontificium Institutum Biblicum, 1965)
VAT	tablets in collection of Staatliche Museen Berlin
VC	*Vigiliae Christianae*
VT	*Vetus Testamentum*
ZA	*Zeitschrift des Assyriologie*
ZAW	*Zeitschrift für die Alttestamentliche Wissenschaft*
ZDMG	*Zeitschrift der Deutschen Morgenländischen Gesellschaft*
ZDPV	*Zeitschrift des Deutschen Palästina-Vereins*

Zohar	*Sefer Ha-Zohar*, ed. Reuven Margoliot (4th edn., with corrections and additions; Jerusalem: Mosad Ha-Rav Kook, 1964)
ZTK	*Zeitschrift für Theologie und Kirche*

Introduction

A. THINKING ABOUT THE SUBJECT

Myth is that most elusive of cultural forms—forever avoiding the constraints of definition and analysis; yet always attesting, through its protean persistence, to an indomitable grip upon the human imagination. Call myth what you will, others will certainly put it differently and claim good grounds for their standpoint. For those bred in the West, the ancient Greek patrimony casts a long shadow over the mind, particularly through its well-known juxtaposition of myth to other forms of thought or creativity. The most characteristic contrast is between *mythos* and *logos*. The early occurrence of such words as *mythologia* or *mythologeuein* (also *mythoeomai* and *mythēsasthai*) indicates that originally *mythos* (as a formulated speech) was a type of articulation of a plan or story—even a fabulation about the gods or heroes in archaic times or in the course of culturally formative events. However, the sources vary as to whether *mythos* or *logos* is the preferred term or value. Thus, quite contrary to common presumption, the term *logos* often appears in Hesiod and Homer as a negative, untrustworthy, and even crafty form of speech; whereas *mythos* in its varieties is 'an assertive discourse of power and authority that represents itself as something to be believed and obeyed'.[1] Gradually, from the sixth and fifth centuries BCE on, in the period sometimes referred to as the first sophistic enlightenment, *mythos* and *logos* marked different valences—with great and long-standing cultural consequences.

For Plato, when myth was just being itself, whether the 'greater' myths of the poets or the 'lesser' ones of grandmothers and nurses, it produced marvellous imaginative fictions (*mythōdēs*) about reality—well-suited to oral genres or poetry, and even leading to persuasion and insight, but hardly conducive to rigorous dialectic or truthful discourse (*alēthinos logos*).[2] It thus had to be rejected for its distortions and illusions, but especially for the

[1] Bruce Lincoln, *Theorizing Myth: Narrative, Ideology, and Scholarship* (Chicago: The University of Chicago Press, 1999), 17; and overall, chs. 1–2, for much evidence. For *mythos* as a speech of power in Homer, see also the discussion and statistics in Richard Martin, *The Language of Heros: Speech and Performance in the Iliad* (Cornell, NY: Cornell University Press, 1989), 10–26.

[2] See *Republic*, 377c and 522a; *Timaeus* 26e; *Gorgias* 527a. For a full conceptual and contextual analysis, see now Luc Brisson, *Plato the Myth Maker* (Chicago: University of Chicago Press, 1999), with a complete bibliography.

morally harmful content of these inventions, as Xenophanes had observed years earlier, when he lambasted Homer and Hesiod for having 'attributed to the gods all that is shameful and disgraceful among men: they steal, commit adultery, and deceive one another'.[3] Aristotle widened the breach between *mythos* and *logos* even more when he counselled that 'into the subtleties of the mythologists it is not worth our while to inquire seriously', and urged his listeners to turn rather to those who reason by demonstration and 'use the language of proof'[4]—and his influence has been considerable. Nevertheless, even the master acknowledged that myth is a valid expression of wonder and the love of Wisdom; and even observed (with respect to speculations on substances) that 'Our forefathers . . . have handed down to their posterity a tradition, in the form of a myth', and added that the 'rest of the tradition has been added later in mythical form with a view to the persuasion of the multitude and to its legal and utilitarian expediency'.[5] Myth in its own right may thus be of positive and propaedeutic value.

Another response to the character of the ancient Greek myths was to claim that myth is not what it appears to be, but rather something 'other'—an allegory, in fact, of underlying truths entirely compatible with the logic of reason. In this way, myth was purged of its apparently harmful content and character, and judged to be a more fanciful way of presenting the truth.[6] The (intellectual) *logos* is now not juxtaposed to some instance of (imaginary) *mythos*, but absorbed into it, so that all that is required for its proper understanding is the interpretative key to the marvellous code. According to a Porphyrian scholium on the battle of the gods in *Iliad* 20.67, this approach to the myths of Homer had already been undertaken by Theagenes of Rhegium (sixth century BCE).[7] A century or so later Plato firmly rejected this tactic, and dismissed the offensive Homeric material 'whether composed with underlying meanings (*en hyponoiais*) or without them'.[8] Nevertheless, an allegorical solution found favour with sundry Stoics (like Heraclitus),[9]

[3] *Die Fragmente der Vorsokratiker*, Greek text and German trans. Hermann Diels, 10th edn., ed. Walther Kranz (Berlin: Wiedmann, 1960–1), 21 B 11.

[4] *Metaphysics* III, 1000^{a} 18–23; the translation follows *The Complete Works of Aristotle*, ed. Jonathan Barnes (Bollingen Series LXXXI:2; Princeton: Princeton University Press, 1995), ii. 1580.

[5] See *Metaphysics* III, 1074^{b} 1–5; and cf. 982^{b}12–22; ibid., pp. 1698, 1554, respectively. My thanks to Prof. Joel Kraemer, for recalling these discussions.

[6] Jean Pépin, *Mythe et allégorie: Les Origines grécques et les contestations judéo-chrétiens* (2nd edn.; Paris: Études augustiniennes, 1976).

[7] See *Quaestionum Homericarum ad Iliadem/Odysseam Reliquae*, ed. Hermann Schrader (Leipzig: Teubner, 1880–90), i. 240–1; and also Diels–Kranz, *Die Fragmente* 8 A 2. For a review of the evidence, see Robert Lamberton, *Homer the Theologian: Neoplatonist Allegorical Reading and the Growth of the Epic Tradition* (Berkeley: University of California Press, 1989), 32.

[8] *Republic* 378d. For Plato's attitude to allegory, see J. Tate, 'Plato and Allegorical Interpretation', *Classical Quarterly*, 23 (1929), 142–54.

[9] *Homeric Allegories* 34. 2 (commenting on *Iliad* 5. 392–4). See *Heraclite: Allegories d'Homère*, ed. Felix Buffière (Paris, 1962).

as well as with middle Platonists (like Clement and Origen) and Neoplatonists in the Plotinian tradition (like Proclus and Porphyry).[10]

Greek-inspired cultures are thus marked by diverse strategies with respect to myth, variously increasing or obscuring the difference between *mythos* and *logos*. Of particular interest are modern arguments that have an evolutionary bias, and regard the mythic imagination as a primitive form of thought—a harbinger or muddled precursor of reason and scientism. Nothing so much signals this triumphant attitude as the title of Wilhelm Nestle's influential book, *Vom Mythos zum Logos*;[11] and this orientation to myth as a form of thinking on the way to reason, has also not been absent from the academic study of religion. Indeed, it has been astutely observed that the nineteenth-century interpretation of myths as disguised observations of natural phenomena, propagated by Max Müller and his circle,[12] is in effect a species of physical allegoresis.[13] By this means, the rough and seemingly outlandish features of certain myths are domesticated as inchoate or befuddled thought, and the mythmakers themselves rehabilitated as primitive philosophers—of sorts. In our own day, Lévi-Strauss has taken up the cudgels of this conviction in his polemical proclamation that 'the purpose of myth is to provide a logical model capable of overcoming a contradiction'; and that 'prevalent attempts to explain alleged differences between the so-called "primitive" mind and scientific thought' must be rejected, 'for the kind of logic which is used by mythical thought is as rigorous as that of modern science'.[14] The end result is the revealment of a *logos* within the *mythos*—a comforting enterprise for those concerned with 'deep structures' and 'rationality', but a procedure that elides the autonomous and inherent value of mythic imagery and displaces its immediate effects.

B. RETHINKING JEWISH MYTH

The Greek purgation or taming of myth—as a fund of dramatic images about the gods—has also been the inheritance of those in Jewish culture, since late antiquity, who have been influenced by one form or another of Greek rationality. In a manner appropriate to their purpose, a genealogy of interpreters has attempted to qualify, filter, or otherwise reinterpret the anthropomorphic

[10] For the latter, see the extensive discussion and evaluation of Lamberton, *Homer the Theologian*, 78–232.

[11] The subtitle is *Die Selbstenfaltung des griechischen Denkens von Homer bis auf die Sophistik und Sokrates* (Stuttgart: A. Kröner, 1940).

[12] See Müller's *Lectures on the Science of Language*, 2nd ser. (New York: Scribner, Armstrong, 1873).

[13] So, Fritz Graf, *Greek Mythology: An Introduction* (Baltimore: Johns Hopkins University Press, 1993), 197.

[14] See Claude Lévi-Strauss, 'The Structural Study of Myth', in Thomas Sebeok (ed.), *Myth: A Symposium* (Bloomington: Indiana University Press, 1958), 105 f.

and anthropopathic depictions of God in the Hebrew Bible, and thus save Scripture from the merest taint of mythic irrationality and its so-called imaginative excesses. The hermeneutical achievements of Philo, Saadia Gaon, Maimonides, and Hasdai Crescas, among others, mark a chain of culture that seeks to distance itself from the felt theological mischief and danger of *mythologoumena* as much as possible, out of the conviction that the Bible in its deep and true sense is a book of philosophical reason, revealed by a rational God who may best be understood and loved intellectually.[15] And if this truth is often obscure to the naked eye, then that is due to the artful cunning of God Himself, who revealed His wisdom in normal human language, so that it might be for the benefit of all—commoner and philosopher alike.[16] From this perspective, the mythic imagery of Scripture is a rhetorical accommodation to time and circumstance, and especially to the addressees of the revelation in antiquity; however, the rational core is its eternal truth, disclosed by the exegetical devices of philosophical allegory.

I

A quite different negation of myth and mythic imagery is not the adopted child of Athena, but something altogether native in character—the putative result of a monotheistic revolution at the very origin of ancient Israelite existence. For those who adopt this position, the issue is not so much the purification of theological thought but its original purity. Parties to this view stress an essential contrast between polytheism and monotheism, with the former presumed to have a certain set of traits deemed characteristic of myth (concrete, anthropomorphic images of divinities, who personify diverse natural forces in a vast chain of being), and the latter the result of a breakthrough to a more abstract and transcendental religious perception (reflected by a greater purity of literary expression and belief).[17] Indeed the core differences between these two religious types are deemed so fundamental as to mark a deep conceptual caesura, for which no evolutionary development could reasonably be posited.[18] This monotheistic innovation is variously

[15] Cf. Simon Rawidowicz, 'Saadya's Purification of the Idea of God', in E. I. J. Rosenthal (ed.), *Saadya Studies in Commemoration of the One-Thousandth Anniversary of the Death of R. Saadya Gaon* (Manchester: Manchester University Press, 1943), 139–65; and Zeev Harvey, 'She'elat 'Iy-Gashmi'ut ha-'El 'Etzel Rambam, Ra'bad, Qresqes, ve-Shpinozah', in Sara Heller Wilensky and Moshe Idel (edd.), *Meḥqarim be-Hagut Yehudit* (Jerusalem: The Magnes Press, 1989), 63–78. See also the discussion of J. Samuel Preus, 'Anthropomorphism and Spinoza's Innovations', *Religion*, 25 (1995), 1–8.

[16] See Moses Maimonides, *The Guide of the Perplexed*, III. 32; trans. Shlomo Pines (Chicago: University of Chicago Press, 1963), 525–8; and also Pines's discussion, pp. lxxii–lxxiv.

[17] For this overall characterization, we may mention the phenomenological-typological orientation of Gustav Mensching, *Die Religion: Erscheinungsformen, Structurtypen und Lebensgesetze* (Stuttgart: Curt E. Schwab, 1959), 177 f.

[18] In broad terms, see the influential position formulated by Raffaele Pettazzoni, 'The Formation of Monotheism', in his *Essays on the History of Religions* (Leiden: E. J. Brill,

ascribed to the transformative effect of a national or divine will, depending on the writer's orientation.[19]

A striking feature of contemporary attempts to differentiate ancient Israel from myth thus often depends upon constructions that first define myth in terms of polytheistic paganism, and then juxtapose this definition to features of biblical monotheism—concluding thereby that 'myth' is absent from the latter. For example, on the argument that an essential variable of ancient Near Eastern paganism is the origin of the gods in a cosmic *plenum*, from which substance they emerge as differentiated personalities, but upon whose elemental character they are necessarily and inherently dependent, the figure of a singular God with a transcendent will, who is (apparently) distinct from the natural world to which He gave created form, is of a fundamentally different sort.[20] Hereby, myth is linked with the nature gods of polytheism and totally dissociated from supernatural monotheism. Accordingly, it is presumed that any hints of myth as recognizable from the ancient Near East (in terms of divine action, imagery, or personality) can only be harmless vestiges of a figurative (or metaphorical) sort—and thus neither true nor living myth.[21]

But this is a self-serving and fallacious line of argument. Whether or not these characterizations of polytheistic paganism or monotheism are in any way accurate, the exclusive identification of a literary phenomenon (myth) with a specific religious or cultural form (natural polytheism) is both

1954), 1–10 (monotheism denoted 'the negation of polytheism' and 'takes shape by means of revolution'; p. 9). This position was already formulated in his article on 'Monotheismus und Polytheismus I. Religionsgeschichte', in H. Gunkel and L. Zscharnack (edd.), *Die Religion in Geschichte und Gegenwart* (Tübingen, 1930), iv. 188: 'Aus dem P[olytheismus] entwinckelt sich der M[onotheismus] nicht durch Evolution, sondern durch Verneinung, was ebenso viel heisst wie Revolution'. Also cf. G. Ernest Wright, *God Who Acts: Biblical Theology as Recital* (London: SCM Press, 1952), 20 f.: 'It is impossible on any empirical ground to understand how the God of Israel could have evolved out of polytheism'.

19 H. and H. A. Frankfort, in *The Intellectual Adventure of Ancient Man: An Essay on Speculative thought in the Ancient Near East* (Chicago: University of Chicago Press, 1946), 369 f., formulate the matter from both angles: 'Hebrew thought... created... myth of the Will of God' and 'history had become a revelation of the dynamic will of God'. Further on this perspective, see next note.

20 On this matter, Frankfort, *Intellectual Adventure*, 367–71; and the extended discussion of Yeḥezkel Kaufmann, *Toledot ha-ʾEmunah ha-Yisraʾelit* (1937; 6th printing, Jerusalem and Tel Aviv: Mosad Bialik & Devir, 1964), pt. 1, bk. 2, 221–416. The subtitle of one of the chapters says it all: 'There is no myth in Israel' (p. 422). Kaufmann's depiction of the will of God 'as a force divorced from the natural tendencies of a divine personality', has been properly criticized by Moshe Halbertal and Avishai Margalit, *Idolatry* (Cambridge, Mass.: Harvard University Press, 1992), 71–2. See also Kaufmann's entry, 'Dat Yisraʾel', in *Encyclopedia Biblica* (Jerusalem: Mosad Bialik, 1965), ii, cols. 729 f. This issue shall be taken up below. It may be noted that Kaufmann's notion of the divine will and national creativity was influenced by the neo-Kantianism of Hermann Cohen. See the analysis of Eliezer Schweid, 'Bein Ḥoqer le-Mefaresh Filosofi shel ha-Miqra", in Michal Oron and Amos Goldreich (edd.), *Massuʾot: Studies in Kabbalistic Literature and Jewish Philosophy in Memory of Prof. Ephraim Gottlieb* (Jerusalem: Mosad Bialik, 1994), 414–28.

21 See next note.

tendentious and tautological: the first, because the definition is arbitrary and selective; and the second, because the identification is always self-confirming, and without any means of checking its circular or redundant character. Such argumentation is also based on certain essentialist views regarding polytheism and monotheism, though it generally avoids this stigma through the pretence of comparative historical study, and conceals an old cultural animus against brute 'myth' (the heir of Hellas) under the cover of an analytical phenomenology of religion.[22] Nevertheless, such intellectual practices reveal just how much the category of myth still serves as a container for all the cultural forms or ideologies that one has purportedly transcended (like irrationality, polytheism, and paganism)—for the sake of others assumed to be superior in kind (like reason, monotheism, or historical inquiry) and with which one identifies.[23] The result is a lamentable impoverishment of the notion and nature of myth, and its formulations within biblical monotheism; but it is also a schematization of monotheism that equally impoverishes its inherent and complex features. Indeed, the upshot of much recent writing is to claim differences between monotheism and polytheism that are arguably more polemical than propaedeutic, and that need to be thoroughly reconsidered.[24]

Equally tendentious is the presumptive dismissal of certain apparently mythic features of biblical language (its unabashed and pervasive depictions of God in anthropomorphic and anthropopathic terms) that blatantly occur in the monotheistic canon of Scripture—as if these were merely due to 'the inadequacy of human language' and 'limitation of human thought', or to some sort of necessarily 'indirect grasp' of 'spiritual concepts' by 'images . . . that emphasize the sensual'.[25] But on what grounds are such assertions

[22] But sometimes even this methodological mask is dropped, as in the remark by Yeḥezkel Kaufmann that 'Biblical religion is in essence non-mythological; the myth is demolished and suppressed, existing only in shredded remnants.' See his 'The Bible and Mythological Polytheism', *JBL* 70 (1951), 182.

[23] For a discussion of how myth stakes out borderlands between one cultural sphere and another, see Marcel Detienne, *The Creation of Mythology* (Chicago: University of Chicago Press, 1986).

[24] For the larger problematic, see the considerations of Gregor Ahn, '"Monotheismus"—"Polytheismus": Grenzen und Möglichkeiten einer Klassifikation von Gottesvorstellungen', in Manfried Dietrich and Oswald Loretz (edd.), *Mesopotamia-Ugaritica-Biblica: Festscrhift für Kurt Bergerhof* (Kevelaer and Neukirchen-Vluyn: Butzon & Bercker and Neukirchen, 1993), 1–24. The difficulty is further evident from the admirable analysis of Burkhard Gladigow, 'Strukturprobleme polytheistischer Religionen', *Saeculum*, 34 (1983), 292–304, since a number of the 'constitutive elements' he detects in polytheism (like pantheon; hierarchy; strife) have their monotheistic correlates, which suggests that external types need to be supplemented by internal phenomenological differences. See further below, and in the conclusions to Part I.

[25] These phrases are taken from the lengthy and learned discussion by M. Zobel, entitled 'Anthropomorphismus', produced for the *Encyclopedia Judaica* (Berlin: Verlag Eschkol, 1928), ii. 886. Similar formulations occur; cf. the entry 'Anthropomorphism and Anthropopathism' by Louis Ginzberg, in *The Jewish Encyclopedia* (New York and London: Funk & Wagnells, 1901), 621 f., esp.

made? Surely there is nothing in Scripture itself that would point in this direction, or suggest that the representations of divine form and feeling in human terms are anything other than the preferred and characteristic mode of depiction.[26] Moreover, on what basis should one assume that the plain sense of Scripture is some (quasi-allegorical) approximation of a more spiritual or purely metaphorical content? And what would that content be, we may well ask, and is it even possible to get past the thick immediacy of biblical language and its concrete and sensible accounts of God?[27] One can only conclude that the evasions of the direct sense of Scripture that such attitudes represent are attempts to save Scripture from itself—for oneself, and must thus be considered a species of modern apologetics.[28]

II

The modern study of Midrash has fallen under a similar spell in its evaluation of the mythic language and imagery that abound in this literary corpus. The roots of such an apologetic approach are arguably embedded in the late Geonic period, in the comments of such sages as Hai Gaon of Babylonia and Rabbeinu Ḥananel of North Africa (eleventh century CE);[29] but it is the influence of Maimonides' subsequent treatment of biblical language that seems most directly to have affected the judgement of contemporary interpreters—particularly their claims that a concern to qualify bold predications

[26] Cf. the judicious concern of James Barr, 'Theophany and Anthropomorphism in the Old Testament', *Congress Volume, Oxford* (SVT 7; Leiden: E. J. Brill, 1960), 33, who urges the interpreter to shift from the question 'Is God conceived of as essentially in human form?' to 'When he does appear in a form at all, is it thought that the human form is the natural or characteristic one for him to assume?'

[27] See the even more sharply formulated comments of Franz Rosenzweig, in *Franz Rosenzweig: Der Mensch und sein Werk: Gesammelte Schriften*, vol. iii: *Zweistromland: Kleinere Schriften zu Glauben und Denken* (Dordrecht: Martinus Nijhoff Publishers, 1984), 735–41. Rosenzweig's note on anthropomorphism was written in response to the Encyclopedia article cited above (n. 25), and published in *Der Morgen*, 4.5, 1928. On the whole matter, see Barbara Galli, 'Rosenzweig Speaking of Meetings and Monotheism in Biblical Anthropomorphisms', *JJTP* 2 (1993), 219–43.

[28] Particularly striking is the study of Margo Korpel, *A Rift in the Clouds: Ugaritic and Hebrew Descriptions of the Divine* (UBL 8; Münster: Ugarit-Verlag, 1990). After documenting over 700 close linguistic and conceptual correlations between the two cultures, she remarkably concludes that, despite the clear 'representation of God' in 'corporeal' terms, Israel broke with its environment, and its anthropomorphisms are 'merely a way of speaking' (p. 627) and not significant features—the result of a certain demythologizing of nature (pp. 628–31). The obviously tendentious nature of this move speaks for itself.

[29] For example, Hai Gaon interprets the image of divine tears in *Ber.* 59a as a parable; see Benjamin M. Lewin (ed.), *ʾOtzar ha-Geʾonim: Thesaurus of the Geonic Responsa and Commentaries* (Haifa and Jerusalem, 1928–43), *Berakhot*, 2. Rabbeinu Ḥananel understood the same passage docetically—as an appearance but not a reality; cf. *Peirushei Rabbeinu Ḥananel bar Ḥushiel le-Masekhet Berakhot*, ed. R. David Metzger (Jerusalem: Lev Sameaḥ Institute, 1990), 130. I have treated this passage in my *The Exegetical Imagination: On Jewish Thought and Theology* (Cambridge, Mass.: Harvard University Press, 1998), 24–6; and the discussion below.

about God in Scripture may already be found in the ancient Midrash.[30] One text often adduced in this connection is the comment found in *Genesis Rabba* 27. 1, 'Great is the power of the prophets; for they liken a form (*tzurah*) to its Creator'. According to the traditional interpretation, first articulated in an authoritative manner by Maimonides himself, this remark conveys the idea that the forms by which the prophets imagined God are themselves created by the Creator for purposes of communication or effect.[31] On this view, the *tzurah* mentioned above indicates any one of the many imaginative figures through which divinity is boldly conceived by the prophets, through the inspiration of God. But this interpretation is not certain, and a quite different understanding may be proposed on the basis of two important considerations. The first of these is the observation that the various biblical proof-texts adduced in *Genesis Rabba* 27. 1 to support the aforenoted teaching actually refer to the human-like figure on the heavenly throne (mentioned in Ezek. 1: 26 and elsewhere), so that the key word *tzurah* in the rabbinic dictum must rather be understood as a human representation of God—and not just any mimetic figure.[32] A second consideration reinforces this point, since the very word used here to indicate form (*tzurah*) is also an ancient technical term for a divine form, recurring throughout later medieval Jewish philosophy.[33] Taking both points together, we may conclude that the rabbinic passage in question is best understood as an assertion about the power of the ancient prophets to envision the figure of God upon His throne of glory in the very form (human) which He himself created in His own (divine) image.[34] Thus, far from being some ancient apology, the midrashic comment is rather a bold encomium concerning anthropomorphic figures of God in Scripture. Hence the taint of apologetics must be attributed to its latter-day receptors only, not the ancient formulators of the dictum.[35]

[30] For the ensuing example, see Ginzberg, 'Anthropomorphism', 622.

[31] See Maimonides, *The Guide of the Perplexed*, 1.46; in the Pines trans., (above, n. 16), 103. A recent study of the passage has been undertaken by Zeev Harvey, '"Gadol Kokhan shel Nibi'im", 'Iyyun be-Moreh Nebukhim Ḥeleq I Pereq 46', *Daat*, 37 (1996), 53–61.

[32] For the proof-texts and textual variants, see *Midrash Bereshit Rabba*, ed. Juda Theodor and Chanoch Albeck (2nd edn.; Jerusalem: Wahrmann Books, 1965), 255 and notes. (Hereinafter: Theodor–Albeck.)

[33] See my discussion of the passage and its terminology, in 'Some Forms of Divine Appearance in Ancient Jewish Thought', in Jacob Neusner, Ernest Frerichs, and Nahum Sarna (edd.), *From Ancient Israel to Modern Judaism. Essays in Honor of Marvin Fox* (Atlanta: Scholars Press 1989), ii. 261–70, with related literature.

[34] For another discussion of divine forms in the Midrash, see my *The Exegetical Imagination*, ch. 4.

[35] The well-known rabbinic dictum 'to break open the ear in its capacity to hear' (*Mekilta de-Rabbi Ishmael*, ed. Jacob Lauterbach (Philadelphia: Jewish Publication Society, 1953), ii. 221) has also been interpreted as a qualification of certain bold biblical imagery; but again, the passage and the proof-texts belie this. See also David Stern, *Midrash and Theory: Ancient Jewish Exegesis and Contemporary Literary Theory* (Evanston: Northwestern University Press, 1996), 75. On the phrase 'to break open (*le-shaber*) the ear', see Ḥanokh Yalon, *Pirkei Lashon* (Jerusalem: Mosad Bialik, 1971), 304–7, with textual variants.

Other examples of this orientation to rabbinic imagery can be found in a wide spectrum of modern statements about Midrash, that range from hard to soft forms of distantiation from the idea of myth in this corpus. At one extreme we can find a sweeping judgement regarding 'the tendency of the classical Jewish tradition to liquidate myth as a central spiritual power'—a tendency 'not diminished by' the preservation of 'quasi-mythical vestiges transformed into metaphors'.[36] Such an assessment is both conceptual and literary, and conceives the primary process of monotheism to be a break with myth, such that any figures which appear in that guise are drained of their vitality and force. Less radical, but of a similar spirit, is the view that acknowledges that '[r]emnants of myths and legends ... gained currency in various circles' of ancient Judaism, but contends that they were variously 'Judaized and deprived of their hurtful mythological characteristics'.[37] In this way the dangerous features of polytheistic paganism are presumed to have been transformed into 'soulless myth', or otherwise nativized through some sort of *interpretatio judaica*.[38] Such activist tendencies of rabbinic reformulation are modulated at the other end of the spectrum, where we find the more moderate claim that the mythic images preserved in the sources are merely 'faded fragments' of non-Jewish antiquity and devoid of any real mythic valence.[39]

However, these and other similar generalizations will not suffice, and fly in the face of numerous midrashic figures of sea monsters and primordial battles, of independent princes of darkness and death, and any number of examples of divine sympathy and wrath—often enacted with concrete and dramatic physical gestures, and always presented in the context of normative theology or religious history. Indeed, there is no way to isolate these mythic tropes from the domain of rabbinic instruction as a whole, or presume that these are merely marginal gaffes. Their recurrence and stability suggest otherwise. Moreover, the assumption that these sometimes terse or elliptical mythic images have either been neutralized of their vital or noxious (polytheistic) effects, or that they surface as dead metaphors or empty figures (in the context of rabbinic monotheism), needs to be thoroughly reconsidered and subjected to careful contextual and comparative analysis. We shall study such matters in due course.[40] For the present, it may suffice to observe that such blanket assessments conceal any number of assumptions about the

[36] Gershom Scholem, 'Kabbalah and Myth', in *On the Kabbalah and its Symbolism* (New York: Schocken Books, 1960), 88.

[37] Ephraim E. Urbach, *The Sages* (Cambridge, Mass.: Harvard University Press, 1987), 228. See also his comment on p. 230, *ad fin.*

[38] For a striking example of this phenomenon, see Gerard Mussies, 'The Interpretatio Judaica of Serapis', in M. J. Vermaseren (ed.), *Studies in Hellenistic Religions* (Leiden: E. J. Brill, 1979), 189–214, with earlier literature cited. See also David Flusser and Shua Amorai-Stark, 'The Goddess Thermuthis, Moses, and Artapanus', *JSQ* 1 (1993/4), 217–33.

[39] Thus Louis Ginzberg, *On Jewish Law and Lore* (New York and Philadelphia: Meridian & Jewish Publication Society, 1962), 63.

[40] See in Part II, below.

nature of Jewish myth, and reinforce the presumption that classical Judaism not only extends the monotheistic revolt of ancient Israel against its pagan environment, but that its cultural forms are autonomous entities able to resist foreign features incompatible with its monotheistic or spiritual nature.[41] Such an idealized perspective may serve personal and cultural ideologies, but it flattens out the textual evidence and reduces it to a one-dimensional and often tendentious caricature.[42]

III

The complex question of the relationship between monotheism and myth recurs at a later point in Jewish culture, and bears upon our present concern in several ways. For when viewed against its own literary and cultural patrimony, the mythic features which abound in the major Kabbalistic works that appear in medieval Provence and Castile in the twelfth and thirteenth centuries CE (notably the book of *Bahir* and the book of *Zohar*), certainly mark a *novum* in Jewish literature—since in these works there is visible, in full force and without notable restraint, a vigorous mythic reality that covers a wide range of themes and theologies, along with a protean exegetical energy that turns biblical verses in every conceivable direction in order to reveal their esoteric truth. Given all this, the question must be asked, Is such activity a new birth or a rebirth of older processes?; and, Is this the return or invasion of alien pagan elements, or the recrudescence and reformulation of inner-Jewish images and topics? In my view, this is the real cultural issue at hand, and to answer it one must first come to terms with the biblical and midrashic evidence.

Two preliminary considerations may nevertheless be noted at this point—the one literary, the other conceptual in nature.

The literary issue to be observed here is the fact that the Kabbalistic traditions found in the book of *Zohar* (and earlier in Spanish and Provençal sources) are developed exegetically,[43] and both echo and extend the mythic

[41] Cf. Urbach, *The Sages*, 37: 'From the Bible the Sages acquired their supermythological and supernatural conception of God... All possibility of representing God by means of any creature upon the earth or the hosts of heaven is completely negated.'

[42] The cultural stakes involved are quite evident in the polemical tone and (neo-Maimonidean) (mis-) treatment of midrashic sources by Shalom Rosenberg, in 'Miṭos ha-Miṭosim', *Jewish Studies*, 38 (1998), 145–79; answered by Yehuda Liebes, pp. 181–5. See also, in this regard, the remarkable generalization made by Alexander Altmann, 'Symbol and Myth', *Philosophy*, 20 (1945), 171, who goes so far as to say that 'the whole history of the Jewish religion and of Jewish philosophical and mystical speculation represents a continuous struggle against the mythical elements from Babylonia, later from the Gnostic world, which tended to overlay its monotheistic and ethical structure'. This excessive formulation may be understood, in part, as a response to the *Kulturkampf* that had just concluded.

[43] See the discussion of Zoharic materials in Part III, preceded by a consideration of some Catalonian evidence found in the commentary on the Song of Songs by R. Ezra of Gerona, and in R. Azriel's commentary on selected midrashic teachings.

themes developed in midrashic literature, though now under the sign of theosophical truth. If there were a mythic gap between the Scriptures of ancient Israel and certain circles in medieval Spain, the blatant and often self-conscious mythic features found in the later literature, produced without any trace of apology, would be hard to explain. In fact—and here the conceptual issue comes into play—were there a cultural break of the nature or magnitude presumed by certain scholars, it would be equally difficult to understand how theological material of such a presumably alien and dangerous nature (with stark emotional and erotic valences) could have entered the conservative mentality of rabbinic Judaism, have been thoroughly absorbed into its ritual life, and have been presented publicly as a most sacred and primordial truth to scholars and lay persons alike. Is it really conceivable that the circles responsible for the creation and diffusion of the *Zohar* could have passed off an utterly non-existent mythic tradition as the most authentic truth of Judaism, were there no precedent and no continuity to support the claim?[44]

Such queries seem sufficient to justify a rethinking of myth and mythmaking in the Hebrew Bible and rabbinic Judaism, and to support the proposal that, alongside the philosophical trajectory of Jewish thought outlined earlier (from Philo to Crescas), another cultural sequence may be highlighted. Different from the first, this one is rooted in the anthropomorphic and anthropopathic imagery of Scripture, and was variously developed and intensified by its midrashic and kabbalistic inheritors, who also received the mythic figures of antiquity and extended them through bold and innovative exegetical strategies. In order to avoid essentialist or tendentious characterizations of this vast mythic phenomenon, it is necessary to provide a definition of myth that is at once conducive to broad comparative possibilities, while also in tune with the technical sense of myth used or assumed by modern historians or anthropologists of religions.[45] Toward this end, *we shall understand the word 'Myth' to refer to (sacred and authoritative) accounts of the deeds and personalities of the gods and heroes during the formative events of primordial times, or during the subsequent historical interventions or actions of these figures which are constitutive for the founding of a given culture and its rituals.*[46] Such a broad characterization has always constituted the

[44] Note also the point of Moshe Idel, 'Rabbinism versus Kabbalism: On G. Scholem's Phenomenology of Judaism', *Modern Judaism*, 11 (1991), 290, that '[s]uch an organic explanation would more easily explain why Kabbalah emerged on the historical scene in the most important center of Rabbinic learning and not in a marginal area of Jewish culture'. The assertion of a mythic gap and revival is the point of Gershom Scholem's classic essay, 'Kabbalah and Myth', in *On the Kabbalah and its Symbolism*.

[45] The literature is legion. I have found the essay by Percy Cohen, 'Theories of Myth', *Man*, 4 (1969), 337–53 quite helpful. See next note.

[46] I intentionally avoid defining myth in terms of a specific genre, agreeing entirely with the observation that 'A myth is a peculiar kind of story. It does not coincide with a particular text or literary genre.' Cf. Graf, *Greek Mythology*, 2. For a definition and discussion of myth along the

core of world mythology, and it shall serve here as a touchstone for the ensuing treatment of biblical and later rabbinic myth.

Given the extraordinary diversity of definitions and conceptions of myth, any delimitation of the phenomenon (such as the foregoing) naturally runs the risk of arbitrariness or exclusion;[47] but to conclude from this variety that myth is best regarded only as a narrative of power, with its meaning or nature to be signified case by case, effectively delimits the study of 'myth' to the taxonomies and ideologies of these narrative accounts.[48] Such an orientation may seem reasonable and justified given the evidence, or the desire to develop a comprehensive meta-theory for the history of religions. But such a position is, in my view, both too broad and too narrow, and is in any case not directly conducive to the more immediate cultural task that is required—namely, to reconsider certain biblical and rabbinic evidence in the light of related comparative phenomena, and thereby to determine their nature and meaning *sine ira et studio*.

Given the presumptive dismissal of much of this material as non-mythic for one or another reason, with the result that its meaning is trivialized or rejected without further ado, I see no alternative but to provide a preliminary and propaedeutic focus on the evidence at hand by means of definitions and comparisons that can be debated from different points of view. Hence I have proposed the foregoing definition in the hope that its broad and neutral scope may allow us, in the first instance, to consider textual features about the gods and their actions found in the Hebrew Bible or other cultural contexts (like the ancient Near East and ancient rabbinic literature) that might otherwise be overlooked or dismissed as having no relevance for the study of myth. But this identification of external correlations must then be supplemented by more nuanced evaluations of their respective meanings and functions in context.[49] Such a procedure will allow us to consider the nature and vitality of the imagery involved—aided by an analysis of the modes of discourse involved and the cultural strategies that the specific topics encode. Certainly no definition of myth will give a fixed Archimedian point, agreeable to all; but it may provide something of a wobbling pivot around which we may analyse certain cultural data from a comparative

lines taken here, see the remarks of Lauri Honko, 'Der Mythos in der Religionswissenschaft', *Temenos*, 6 (1970), esp. 40–5.

[47] Something of the immensity of the subject can be sensed from the survey produced by Axel Horstmann, 'Der Mythosbegriff vom Frühen Christentum bis zur Gegenwart', *Archiv für Begriffsgeschichte*, 23 (1979), 7–54, 197–245.

[48] This is the conclusion of Lincoln, *Theorizing Myth*, 147, who variously executes this approach to myth.

[49] This corresponds to what Carsten Colpe, in 'Zur Neubegründung einer Phänomenologie der Religionen und der Religion', in Hartmut Zinser (ed.), *Religionswissenschaft: Eine Einfüring* (Berlin: Dietrich Riemer, 1988), 139 f., has distinguished as the 'inner' (phenomenological) and 'outer' (typological) perspectives on religion and its subject matter.

and even more universal perspective. And just that is the aim of my present task.

C. THE CHARACTER AND SCOPE OF THIS INQUIRY

I. Monotheistic Myth and its Study

In light of the preceding discussion and definition, let me now specify the purpose of this book as an attempt to retrieve, study, and even reconstruct the phenomenon of monotheistic myth over the course of two millennia—focusing on its first literary articulations in the Hebrew Bible and continuing through the increasingly intensified process whereby mythmaking occurs in classical rabbinic Midrash and the medieval Kabbalistic book of *Zohar*, by means of hermeneutical reformulations of scriptural myths and language. As the acts (both physical and emotional) of the God who is the dominant subject of these myths are many, and these are diversely presented in a multitude of historical and literary strata, a narrowing of focus is necessary. In what follows, I shall adopt a typological approach that will isolate several paradigmatic configurations overall, and use these types to explore the varied character and construction of monotheistic myth in the sources, as well as its patterns of thematic continuity and transformation. Such a methodological strategy will permit a synchronic analysis of central topics in each separate period (with due attention to the diversity of motifs and structures), and facilitate their diachronic correlation and comparison in different corpora.[50]

The following myths and mythologems (or isolated mythic figures and motifs) shall be deemed exemplary, and shall be taken up, each in terms of its particular content, context, and structure.

1. Divine Combat. In our sources, an exemplary type of myth dealing with divine power and pre-eminence has to do with strife and battle against other forces. These are characteristically myths of divine combat and occur primarily against the Sea in primordial times—both before and during the creation; at the time of the exodus from Egypt and exile; and in various prophecies of the future or end of days. In certain cases this battle is between God (or His agent) and a clearly demarcated deity, as in similar ancient Near Eastern myths of this type; while in other instances, the antagonistic figure is

[50] While the analyses do not have a formal analytical purpose, they do nevertheless fit into a broad folkloristic framework in terms of functions and classifications. I have found flexible and productive the approach of Yoav Elstein, 'Liqra't Ṭematologia shel Sifrut ʿAm Yisraʾel: Perespeqṭivot u-Baʿayot', *Proceedings of the Tenth World Congress of Jewish Studies* (Jerusalem: World Union of Jewish Studies, 1990), ii. D, 51–8; and also Yoav Elstein and Avidor Lipsker, 'The Homogeneous Series in the Literature of the Jewish People: A Thematological Methodology', in Frank Trammler (ed.), *Thematics Reconsidered: Essays in Honor of Horst S. Daemmrich* (Amsterdam: Rodapi, 1995), 87–116. For the broader background, see Lubomír Doležel, 'From Motifemes to Motifs', *Poetics*, 4 (1970), 55–90.

a personified power or monster of some sort. In all cases, however, the figure of the Sea (or its thematic variant) represents a force or power of chaos, rebellion, or evil, and the recurrence of the combat motif in numerous texts during two thousand years marks a paradigm of divine power that is celebrated (as an event past) or anticipated (as an event to come). Through our treatment of this 'event' it will be possible to consider cultural similarities and differences in the use of myth, and the way different realizations of the scenario express different theologies of history and evil. The recurrence of this motif in a vast variety of contexts, and in the guise of various transformations, attests to its remarkable vitality.

2. Divine Wrath and Sorrow. The emphasis here is not on outward acts but inner valences—on emotional structures or poles of the divine personality, particularly the psychological patterns of anger and compassion. For its part, the modality of anger is expressed primarily in terms of violent acts of destruction and judgement (planned or performed), and directed primarily against Israel itself, as the rebellious nation of God, but also against foreign peoples for various reasons (in both cases, God's wrath may be expressed through the agency of natural or historical events). By contrast, the modality of compassion is conveyed largely through a state of divine sorrow or remorse at the catastrophe wrought by such acts of doom.

These polarities of the divine personality vary in terms of the sources and periods involved, so that, for example, in the biblical period God's wrath can also be expressed by a withdrawal of engagement, and not just an overt manifestation of anger. Similarly, His compassion can involve the suspension of angry judgement before or after the due date (including its vicarious transfer), and not merely the expressions of remorse over the violence unleashed.[51] In certain other instances, characteristic of the later rabbinic sources, the two poles (of anger and compassion) may be articulated or even activated by one and the same word, as for example where the verb *sha'ag* conveys both God's 'roar' of anger in certain biblical sources, but also His 'groan' of despair and sorrow in their midrashic transformations.[52] In rabbinic texts this polarity characteristically revolves around the destruction of the Temple and its ritual or social consequences. In other cases the polar states are expressed by means of dramatic physical actions, like fiery fury or lonely tears. Through these figures the actions of God are related to states of pathos, and portray images of great mythic boldness regarding His active involvement in human history. An immense imaginative creativity

[51] Overall, see the valences considered by Yochanan Muffs, *Love and Joy: Law, Language and Religion in Ancient Israel* (New York: The Jewish Theological Seminary of America, 1992), ch. 1; and dynamics considered below.

[52] Note the difference in the function of this verb in Jer. 25: 30, and its rabbinic employment in *BT Ber.* 3a; cf. my discussion in *The Exegetical Imagination*, 26f.

and theological assertiveness thus characterize our sources, even where some rabbinic ones seem hedged by literary hestitations or probity.[53]

The mythologems conveying the advent of God in judgement utilize images widespread in ancient Near Eastern polytheism, and often pivot around the characteristic features of a storm god come to battle. Recognizing this factor will allow us to explore the phenomenon of myths and motifs shared by Israel and its neighbours, and the distinctiveness of Israel's monotheistic formulations. In this regard, grand mythic images depict God's enthronement upon a celestial chariot on His way to war, led and supported by a host of divine powers. During these theophanies, the supernatural God is manifested in the natural order robed in the garments of myth. The force of the biblical images must be scrutinized in each case, in order to assess their different nuances and tone. Our midrashic sources build on these images in various ways. Manifestations of divine salvation, on the other hand, often involve bold rereadings of biblical passages; and it is here that the rabbinic texts are sometimes marked by comments on their status or function. Evaluative terms like 'as if' or 'a difficult (theological) matter' or 'were it not written' variously recur in the Midrash, and invite special scrutiny.

3. Sympathetic Identification. Characteristic of the mythic theology of the Hebrew Bible is the relative separation of the divine and human realms, and of divine and human action: the one is heavenly and transcendent, the other earthly and historical. This does not mean that the two spheres are absolutely impenetrable from either side (for in fact the divine can intervene or appear concretely in the human plane, and some humans do ascend to the heavenly court);[54] nor does it mean that there is no correlation between the two realms (for the covenant does establish a bond linking the will and action of God to the will and action of Israel, such that divine anger or disappointment is in response to human sin or misdeed). Nevertheless, there is no case of *imitatio hominis* in biblical literature, where divine actions are said to imitate or identify with human ones—or of God performing actions in a divine sphere, related to or in response to human actions. But just this is remarkably what occurs repeatedly in midrashic mythopoesis, and numerous terms and behaviours concretize a variety of examples repeated in numerous cultural contexts. In this way, not a bond of will but a bond of pathos links the divine and human subjects, and the behaviour of the divine is dramatized in bold mythic figures centred around physical actions and gestures.

[53] Cf. Cohen, 'Theories of Myth', 337, who astutely observes that some events in myth exist only in the world portrayed by the myth. An assessment of various so-called terms of qualification will be considered in due course, and especially in Appendix 2.

[54] Notably, Micaiah ben Imlah in 1 Kings 22: 19–23 and Isaiah ben Amoz in Isaiah 6; the former seems entirely visionary in nature, while the latter conveys a sense of bodily participation. See the discussion in the conclusions below.

The interpenetration of the divine and human realms is rendered more audacious, dramatic, and complete in Zoharic myths, and the correlation between human and divine actions or feelings is a central feature of the whole 'chain of being' imagined in this literature. Indeed, as we shall see, throughout the *Zohar* the divine myths of Scripture and Midrash are raised to cosmic proportions, and their mythologems serve to depict theosophical dramas in the supernal realms. The various mythic figures associated with divine acts of sympathetic identification have a poignant and recurrent place in this constellation. No hesitation or qualification hides the vigour of mythic expression—a fact impressed upon the reader who is challenged by the authorial assertion *mamash* ('really!') or *vada'i* ('truly!'), after an already astonishing statement of divine act or feeling is given.

All told, the preceding thematic configurations reinforce our salient point (to be demonstrated at great length throughout this book) that the categories of monotheism and myth are not mutually exclusive or incompatible; but rather, the evidence shows that the nature and content of biblical and rabbinic myth were shaped by the topics and concerns of the different periods of monotheistic religion reflected in Hebrew Scripture, the Midrash, and the book of *Zohar* (primarily). Indeed, such myths are a positive and vital feature of this vast monotheistic literature, and the carrier of some of its most powerful and poignant theological topics. Just how this is so brings us to the next subject.

II. Mythopoesis, or the Making of Myth

We earlier characterized monotheistic myth as the product of an artful mythmaking, and as employing various hermeneutical strategies developed over many years and realized in numerous forms. Given their complex and often dense or elliptical formulations in the sources available to us, it is often a matter of hard judgement as how best to assess and ascertain the meaning of the images. I shall therefore now set forth a number of principles of evaluation and analysis that shall guide the present study.

1. Context and Meaning. A first principle of analysis to be employed is that there is no abstract myth, but rather the focus is on this or that mythic expression in this or that text and context. Hence the form and content of the myths are concrete features of specific settings, and occur in specific acts of literary discourse or fabulation at a specific point within them. The given myth is therefore cited or recited in the context of a given literary genre, and serves to evoke certain topics involving (primarily) divine actions or nature in the past or the future to come. In the Hebrew Bible, for example, certain mythic topics (like the divine combat) are cited in specific psalms, prophecies, and wisdom pieces, where they may serve as paradigms of primordial or hoped-for acts of power. The topics are thus contextualized differently (in

different genres and in different ways within those genres); and it is precisely in and through these specific settings that these topics affect the reciter or receiver of the text, and where the validity of any given myth is made manifest. In another setting or form, all this would change.

Such methodological considerations cannot be sufficiently emphasized, and to ignore them would be to make textual judgements based on specious semantic criteria and generalized notions of the mythic language and ideas expressed. Hence, let us agree that 'syntactical relations ... and groupings of words' are of fundamental importance 'for the bearing of significance' or meaning in given passages as one moves beyond 'the more purely lexicographical aspects of the single word'.[55] This being so, we may also note that 'the linguistic bearer' of mythic references or accounts is 'usually the sentence and the still larger literary context'. It therefore follows that one can derive valuable and distinctive clues for determining the sense or meaning of the myths from these particular narrative settings.[56] Inner-cultural and cross-cultural comparisons further extend the literary context and provide new frameworks for the determination of similarity and difference.[57]

Whether the particular mythic references or accounts in biblical and rabbinic literature are extensive or brief, direct or merely allusive, their understanding presupposes several wider considerations, not always kept in mind. The first of these may be called the *principle of parsimony*. That is to say, a mythic topic (like the divine combat) known from a certain cultural sphere, like the ancient Near East, should be assumed to have that same literary effect or value (whether literal or figurative) in all its various occurrences unless there is a marked reason for thinking otherwise. On this basis, we should not assume two different mental universes when we come across a similar image in Mesopotamian, Canaanite, and biblical literature. Rather, following the principle of parsimony, one should start with the assumption that the topic conveys a similar content if it bears the same or similar imagery in the same or similar contexts. It is an entirely biased attitude that uses the image of gods eagerly smelling the savour of sacrifices after the flood in *Gilgamesh* XI. 161 as evidence for the concreteness of pagan mythology, and then goes on to distinguish it from the post-diluvian scene found in Genesis 8: 21—especially

[55] See James Barr, *The Semantics of Biblical Language* (Oxford: Clarendon Press, 1961), 222.

[56] Ibid. 269 f.; Barr's principle focus here is with biblical theology, but his concerns have a wider applicability. Instructive in this regard is a consideration of the literary contexts of ancient Egypt myth; see John Baines, 'Myth and Literature', in Antonio Loprieno (ed.), *Ancient Egyptian Literature: History and Forms* (Leiden: E. J. Brill, 1996), 361–77.

[57] An analytical review of this large topic, with all pertinent literature can be found in Fitz John Porter Poole, 'Metaphors and Maps: Towards Comparison in the Anthropology of Religion', *JAAR* 54 (1986), 411–57. Among many stimulating studies by Jonathan Z. Smith, note especially his essay 'In Comparison a Magic Dwells', repr. in his *Imagining Religion: From Babylon to Jonestown* (Chicago: University of Chicago Press, 1982), ch. 2; and the many reflections on comparison and its contexts in *Drudgery Divine: On the Comparison of Early Christianities and the Religions of Late Antiquity* (Chicago: University of Chicago Press, 1990).

insofar as that text simply states (with no further ado or suggestion of metaphorical intent) that 'YHWH smelled the sweet-smelling aroma' of Noah's huge sacrifice of birds and animals (v. 20), 'and YHWH said in his heart: "I shall never again curse the earth because of earthlings . . . nor smite all living beings, as I have done" '. Equivalent treatment of such apparent similarities should be a guiding principle, and will have notable consequences for our study of monotheistic myth. To proceed otherwise would be to court the spectre of apologetics, in one form or another.

By the same token, uses of a certain mythic topic in another cultural sphere, like the reuse of a biblical theme in the rabbinic Judaism of Roman Palestine, should similarly be assumed to have a meaning similar to its cross-cultural cognates if the thematics and language of that topic stay the same or similar. Hence a mythic topic in Hebrew Scripture like divine combat can undergo a recontextualization in the exegesis of rabbinic Midrash but still remain the same mythic topic overall, if the terms remain the same and if there is no wholesale theological or literary transformation. This granted, it must nevertheless be stressed that every new occurrence of a mythic topic (in its new context) produces a new myth overall, insofar as the concerns and purposes of the latter varies. The principle of parsimony does not therefore mean that a myth or mythologem in its various renditions is always one and the same, by any means, but only that similar images should be assumed to be the same and have the same semiotic value unless there are good textual reasons to conclude differently. Thus a priori assumptions that rabbinic images of a certain type are merely metaphors or drained of their mythic force, and merely serve some 'higher' monotheistic purpose, violate this essential hermeneutical principle. Upholding it, we may recognize mythologems for what they are—in all their concrete variety.

Another hermeneutical consideration to be noted is the *principle of charity*, which introduces a method of reading that begins with the assumption that every text makes or conveys sense and that one should therefore construe it in the best possible light, taking account of all its factors.[58] We take this principle to be crucial for understanding the language and phenomenon of biblical and rabbinic myth, primarily because of the often condensed or obfuscated nature of its transmission, and the fact that the myths often occur within genres or contexts where one might, in an uncharitable or prejudicial spirit, construe them as mere metaphors (living or dead). Hence one should first presume that a mythologem is textually invoked to represent

[58] See W. V. O. Quine, *Word and Object* (Cambridge, Mass.: MIT Press, 1960), 58 f., where the principle is used in a limited sense; a broader application, along the lines to be taken here, is given by Ronald Dworkin, *Law's Empire* (Cambridge, Mass.: Harvard University Press, 1985), 53–65. For reflections on the use of this hermeneutical instrument with respect to biblical and rabbinic legal texts, see Moshe Halbertal, *Mahapeḥot Parshaniyot Be-Hithavutan* (Jerusalem: Magnes Press, 1997), 185–93.

or depict some actual reality, unless there are specific markers or reasons to indicate otherwise. Thus, to anticipate some ensuing discussions, it would be uncharitable to presume that the biblical citation of a divine combat in a given prayer (for example Ps. 74: 12–14) does not refer to a real mythic event, or is not intended to convey a mythic truth of divine power—especially since the speaker invokes God's remembrance of this past deed as a prelude to his petitioning the recurrence of a similar manifestation of divine might in the present (vv. 10–11, 20–3); and also since the very language and drama found there is similar to ancient Near Eastern combat scenes with sea monsters.[59] In a similar vein, it would be uncharitable and presumptuous to assume that the words 'YHWH roars (*yish'ag*) from on high, He makes his voice heard (*yitten qolo*) from His holy dwelling' in Jer. 25: 30 is a mere metaphor and not a mythologem conveying the onset of divine wrath—given its 'evidentness' as a mythic reality in the biblical text;[60] and given the occurrence of similar phraseology in Akkadian sources, where one would be hard pressed to deny its mythic valence.[61] Starting with a positive regard for the evidentness of mythic figures in the Hebrew Bible and Midrash, one may begin to appreciate their different literary and hermeneutical constructions.

These and many other cases are considerably enriched through a comparative consideration of the structures, terms, and images involved. Such a concern differs markedly from approaches that try to hunt down the influence or filiation of one literature upon another, or where the meaning of one text is imposed upon another in disregard of either context or content. By contrast, by this method I shall hope to retrieve lost biblical and rabbinic meanings or semantic valences by correlating their language with forms found in the ancient Near East and elsewhere. This procedure will be of particular value where an extended mythic text from a non-Israelite context, like a Ugaritic or Mesopotamian account of a battle with a sea monster, is related to a version or digest of this battle (with similar or cognate terms) within the Hebrew Bible.

It will also be of interest where a given mythic image in one biblical genre (like Jeremiah's oracular reference to YHWH's roar) is similar to other ones

[59] Cf. my discussion in *The Exegetical Imagination*, 89–92; and also below, in Part I.

[60] The term is adapted from Hans Blumenberg, *Work on Myth* (Cambridge, Mass.: MIT Press, 1985), 136, where he states that 'Docetism is the ontology appropriate to myth. It suggests a level of evidentness that does not depend on the distinction between appearance and reality.'

[61] Cf. the phrase 'who set his voice (*ša iddin rigmašu*) in the heavens like Adad, and all the earth trembles at his voice', in Johannes Knudtzon, *Die El-Amarna-Tafeln* (Leipzig: Hinrichs, 1915), no. 147:14–15; and also, 'as when Addu bellows (*šagimešu*), the mountains tremble', in W. G. Lambert, 'Three Unpublished Fragments of the Tukulti-Ninurta Epic', *AfO* 18 (1957–8), 50f. (l. 6). For the identity of Addu and Baʿal in a list of divinities at Ugarit, see *RS* 20.2 and *RS* 1929.17, examined by Jean Nougayrol, in Jean Nougayrol *et al.*, *Ugaritica, v: Nouveaux textes accadiens, hourites et ugaritiques des Archives et Bibliothèques privées d'Ugarit, commentaires des textes historiques* (Mission de Ras Shamra, 16; Paris: Imprimerie Nationale/P. Geuther, 1968), 44–5, 47–8.

found in quite different Akkadian genres (like the references to Adad's roar found in historical texts or inscriptions)—and where these latter occurrences would normally be assumed to convey a mythologem or mythic allusion.[62] Indeed, such comparisons across genres can be of much help in assessing the living vibrancy of various myth-like phrases in biblical texts, especially where our cognitive distance or presumptions, or the particular stylistic or rhetorical setting, might lead one to suppose that the formulation in question is only a literary trope or figure of divine action. Not least of all, our study of such comparative structures and terms will highlight ongoing mythic conventions and traditions, and their use in non-mythic contexts.

2. Exegesis and Reuse. In the transmission and creation of biblical and rabbinic myth, two features stand out. The first is that myth is kept alive by its uses and reuses, as it moves from context to context and serves different cultural or individual needs. This mutant vitality of the myths in our sources sometimes appears as a strategic reference to a given mythologem, that evokes an event or theme particularly suited to a given discourse or topic. The use of certain images of divine might in various personal prayers or prophetic diatribes in Scripture may thus function to convey a certain rhetorical effect or pathos. In a similar manner, mythic images also occur in the Midrash in ways that redirect or reshape the biblical reference to a new issue, or otherwise provide a particular theological resonance to the topic at hand.

Mythmaking is also a learned and literary act that, far from being a feature of degeneration or decreased spontaneity, is often a key factor in the revitalization of earlier sources and a sign of ongoing cultural creativity. It is particularly important to stress this point, since it is so often ignored or disregarded in favour of the naive or fabulous character of archaic mythology, and the assumption that only the earliest or most 'primitive' manifestations of myth are the most authentic and the door to the mysteries of 'mythic thought'. But such a Romantic view will not serve us well in many respects, and least of all in understanding the highly literate and even scholarly nature of mythopoesis in the ancient Near East,[63] whose components

[62] Cf. the examples in the preceding note; and see also the reference to Adad's roar in the inscription of Nebuchadnezzar I, published by Franz M. Th. de Liagre Bohl, 'Eine zweisprachige Weiinschrift Nebukadnezars I', *BO* 7.2/3 (1950), 42–6; esp. pp. 43–4, ll. 7–10. See also the references in 'The Kurba'il Statue of Shalmaneser', published by J. V. Kinnier Wilson, *Iraq*, 24 (1961), esp. p. 93, ll. 5–7.

[63] Many examples show the scholarly nature and character of Mesopotamian mythopoesis, as well as its accumulative growth and intertextual character. For such matters, see, for example, W. G. Lambert, 'The Cosmology of Sumer and Babylon', in Carmen Blacker and Michael Loewe (edd.), *Ancient Cosmologies* (London: George Allen & Unwin, 1975), 42–62; and idem, 'Ninurta Mythology in the Babylonian Epic of Creation', in Karl Hecker and Werner Sommerfeld (edd.), *Keilschrift Literaturen: Ausgewälte Vorträge der XXXII Rencontre Assyriologique Internationale (1985)* (Berliner Beiträge zum Vorderen Orient, 6; Berlin: Dietrich Reimer Verlag, 1986), 55–60. Another instructive case is found in the neo-Babylonian tablet published by

were transmitted to the mythmakers of ancient Israel and Greece in their own sophisticated forms.[64] Even less will such a prejudice benefit the study of myth in the Midrash and book of *Zohar*, where an ancient literary thesaurus was remoulded by learned acts of textual exegesis.

Such acts make myth happen again and again—in a manner that looks on Scripture with an uncommonly concrete eye and reworks its linguistic components to produce a great variety of mythic forms and topics. The means of production may be to invert the sense of an adverb or preposition, find an opening in one text in order to insert another (appropriately reinterpreted), or to concretize a stylistic feature like 'the sea saw and fled' in Ps. 114: 3—thereby transforming the personified sea into a mythic personality with will and character, and inventing a fabulation that narrates what or whom the sea saw that inspired such fear at the exodus. The God who is presented as its antagonist walks onto the pages of Midrash with a marvellous mythic vitality.[65]

It is one of the goals of this book to valorize the whole phenomenon of literary and exegetical mythopoesis, as it finds expression in the textual culture of ancient Israel and classical and medieval Judaism. A complex symbiosis exists here between the mythic themes themselves and their diverse realization in literary form; and it is in just this complexity that one will find the compositional elements that give each mythic invention its peculiar tone and effect. The modalities of myth are thus never the same, even where a similar theme or topic may be present; for in one case you may find stylistic restraint or reserve in the depiction of God or His acts, while elsewhere the imagery is marked by greater boldness or graphic detail. As a symbolic form of the imagination, these literary elements bring myth into being and mark its character across the textual strata. Such matters are part and parcel of the acts of mythmaking to be studied here and, if one may say so, of its artifice as

Werner Mayer, 'Ein Mythos von der Erschaffung des Menschen und des Königs', *Or.* 56 (1987), 55–68. Some aspects of this account echo both the Sumerian narrative of *Enki and Ninmaḫ* and the Akkadian *Atraḫasis* epic. Mayer points to various verbal correspondences with other mythic texts (like *Enuma elish*).

[64] Much evidence has been accumulated to indicate that Hesiod knew closely related Hittite and Babylonian myths. Cf. P. Walcot, *Hesiod and the Near East* (Cardiff: University of Wales Press, 1966), and Walter Burkert, *The Orientalizing Revolution: Near Eastern Influence on Greek Culture in the Early Archaic Age* (Cambridge, Mass.: Harvard University Press, 1992), ch. 3. For a consideration of this topic with due attention to methodological considerations, see idem, 'Oriental and Greek Mythology: The Meeting of Parallels', in Jan Bremmer (ed.), *Interpretation of Greek Mythology* (London: Routledge, 1988), 10–40; and esp. Robert Mondi, 'Greek Mythic Thought in the Light of the Near East', in L. Edmunds (ed.), *Approaches to Greek Myth* (Baltimore: Johns Hopkins University Press, 1990), 142–98.

[65] On this biblical prosopopoeia and its reinterpretation in the *Mekhilta de-Rabbi Ishmael, Beshalaḥ 4*, see in the edition of H. S. Horovitz and I. A. Rabin (*Mechilta D'Rabbi Ismael* (Jerusalem: Bamberger & Wahrman, 1960)), 103 (hereinafter: Hororitz–Rabin), see the discussion of Daniel Boyarin, 'Midrash and the (Psycho)Dynamics of Intertextuality', *Poetics Today*, 10 (1989), 664–7, esp., and in Part II below.

well. The theology (not to mention the drama) of the mythic product is unthinkable except in these terms. Indeed, as I have already noted, there is no abstract myth, but only and always its concrete manifestation in numerous shapes and styles.

3. Multiplicity of Variants. Mythmaking has a protean quality, reformulating its content with every new fabulation and transmission. This is clearly evident in the configurations and topics noted earlier: the combat with the sea; the acts of divine wrath and compassion; and God's sympathetic identification with the life and fate of Israel. It is therefore, to my mind, utterly egregious to construct or posit a hyper-myth out of the variants of any given myth—on the assumption that such a composite macroform will fill in the lacunae of the individual cases, or that each microform is somehow only a variant of the master-myth and only worthy of analysis in these terms.[66] To proceed in such a manner would be completely to ignore the particular mythologems themselves in the literary form in which they appear, in favour of some hypothesized whole. It would be similarly tendentious to posit a quite different type of hyper-myth, on the assumption that it is the deep structure of a series of paradigmatic elements that is of main importance—and not the actual cases of the myth.[67] But the very notion that these variants are superposable features of a certain mythic type ignores the syntax of images in any rendition of a myth and the way it constructs meaning.[68] These elements are the irreplaceable components of its performative particularity.[69]

By contrast, the approach to be adopted here will be to take seriously each version of a myth and understand its meaning within the specific fabulation or setting in which it occurs.[70] It is to be hoped that this procedure will respect the concrete cases and their contexts, and return us in each instance to the mythopoeic factor, by which I mean the creative construction of myth and its formulation within different literary genres. To my mind, it is just here

66 This attitude is reflected in the attempt of Umberto Cassuto to reconstruct the ancient Hebrew myth of the sea from the various references to it in Scripture; see his 'The Israelite Epic', in *Biblical and Oriental Studies* (Jerusalem: Magnes Press, 1975), ii. 80–102, esp. In the process, he abstracts the references and treats them as components of a hypothetical structure or composition.

67 This is, of course, one of the tenets of the mythological method of Claude Lévi-Strauss, as evidenced most classically in his essay on Oedipus in *Structural Anthropology* (New York and London: Basic Books, 1963), and in many monographs.

68 Cf. the critique of Lévi-Strauss and the proposal offered by Jean-Pierre Vernant, *Myth and Society in Ancient Greece* (New York: Zone Books, 1988), 246–60.

69 See also the critique of Lévi-Strauss and the valuable remarks of Pierre-Ives Jacopin, 'On the Syntactic Structure of Myth, or the Yukuna Invention of Speech', *Cultural Anthropology*, 3 (1988), 131–59.

70 I have greatly benefited from the essay of Terrence Turner, 'Narrative Structure and Mythopoesis', *Arethusa*, 10 (1977), 103–64, and his penetrating rethinking of the œuvre of Lévi-Strauss.

that the hierarchies and value concepts of the myths are evident in all their diversity, and may serve as an index of changing cultural or theological concerns.[71] These factors bring us to the topic of tradition.

III. Tradition and the Transmission of Myth

As the foregoing discussion of mythopoesis makes clear, myth itself (which is to say 'the myths') has a history and changes from one formulation to another. Indeed, the materials to be studied in the following parts of this book span nearly three millennia in some cases, if we take into consideration that the Hebrew Bible draws on a fund of Near Eastern myths that in turn has its own history. Over this span of time the content and forms of the myths naturally change, though it is also the case that each successive stage makes use of the accumulating bundles of tradition of the culture. Most remarkably, as we shall see, this cultural thesaurus is not simply limited to the mythic motifs themselves. For although the mythologems of Scripture draw on the bundles of mythic tradition derived from ancient Canaan and Mesopotamia, midrashic mythopoesis draws on the entirety of Scripture for its content, and the *Zohar* makes use of both of these earlier layers—and much more.[72]

1. Content and Continuity. We may thus supplement our earlier observation that all myths are made, and say that myths are received as well. Stated more formally, let us note that each mythic invention produces a mythic *traditum* (or body of tradition) that is received as a living *traditio* (or transmission of that tradition).[73] The dialectics of *traditum-traditio* are thus fundamental features of the mythmaking imagination to be presently examined, as also of most other aspects of culture-building in ancient Israel and rabbinic Judaism. In this regard, the mythmaker stands in an axial position: receiving, making, and thus transmitting the myths, he also makes those who receive this material participants in the overall traditionary process.

2. Metamorphosis. The interplay of *traditum* and *traditio* allows us to shift the focus from the factors that affect the making of myth, or mythopoesis, to its changes of form and content, or metamorphosis. This category will help us to conceptualize (and thus analyse) several aspects of these changes. Three of them may be mentioned at this point. The first may be called 'the genetic-diachronic factor', since it focuses on the temporal sequence of any mythic

[71] Cf. Marcel Mauss, *Oeuvres: Representations collectives et diversité des civilisations* (Paris, 1969), ii. 195–242, and his notion that myths provide a classificatory collection of cultural norms and attitudes.

[72] It is in this setting that one must think about the issue of influence and related matters. On this thorny subject, see the ruminations of Ihab Hassan, 'The Problem of Influence in Literary History: Notes Towards a Definition', *Journal of Aesthetics and Art Criticism*, 14 (1955), 66–76.

[73] I made extensive use of these categories in my *Biblical Interpretation in Ancient Israel* (Oxford: Clarendon Press, 1985), introd. and *passim*.

type and tries to trace such matters as origins and influences over time.[74] It also seeks to correlate changes at different points along a given morphological spectrum, and considers the factors that make for the differences. For any number of reasons (whether the vagaries of creativity or survival) there is no necessarily clear or straight line of development among the various forms, and, what is more, some of the processes may not even be represented at the textual level. Nevertheless, the diachronic factor is of particular value for understanding the history of myths—especially when, as in this book, the myths are carried or conserved in vastly different bodies of literature and produced for different cultural circles over the course of several millennia.

Another of the changes marked by the metamorphosis of myth is 'the acculturation factor', by which I mean the process whereby certain myths were nativized or otherwise differentiated from their pagan allomorphs, and in the process adapted to biblical or Judaic values and ideas. As noted earlier, many writers who have discussed biblical or rabbinic myth have been quick to point out that many of the myths deriving from the surrounding pagan cultures were depleted of their hurtful or dangerous qualities.[75] This approach is apologetic and blatantly prejudicial. Much more productive, I argue, is a positive attitude to the inner-cultural processes of adaptation. After all, the mythic topics taken over by biblical and rabbinic monotheism were stimulating and attractive to the tradents themselves, or they would have been completely ignored or suppressed; and it is this very fascination that underlies their reformulation or re-creation, guided by a different religious spirit and different literary universe. One must add that the process of acculturation may include inner-cultural dynamics, as well, insofar as the myths in any one theological stratum (like the Midrash) may need to be significantly changed to fit into another, quite different conceptual or intellectual universe (like that found in the *Zohar*). It is precisely here, moreover, that some of the protean vitality of mythmaking is most visible, and the inevitable tendency towards routinization in the creation or role of myth is checked and challenged.

A final issue bearing on the metamorphosis of myth may be called 'the fabulation factor'. The concern here is to focus on the processes of mythmaking, whereby each recitation or account of the myths is a reshaping of both

[74] This positivist and chronological approach was given classical expression by Otto Gruppe, 'Geschichte der klassischen Mythologie und Religionsgeschichte, während des Mittelalters im Abenland und während der Neuzeit', in *Lexicon der griechischen und römischen Mythologie*, ed. W. H. Roscher, suppl. (Leipzig: B. G. Teubner, 1921).

[75] In addition to the earlier citations, cf. the remark of Cassuto, in 'The Israelite Epic', 101, where he says that 'among the Israelites' the 'original mythological garb' of the old myths of the sea were 'cast off' and 'assumed a form more in keeping with the national ethos'. Where nevertheless 'alien' elements still remained, he claims that they were treated in an 'unsympathetic way'.

meaning and form. Thus, for example, the citations of myth of divine combat in the psalms and prophecies of Scripture are fabulated entirely differently in midrashic exegesis, where different literary patterns and hermeneutical strategies are evident. The mythic fabulations found in the *Zohar* are different yet again—with more extensive narrative forms, and featuring mythic discourses set within a structure of mystical study and interpretation. Given such diversity, it will be a concern of successive chapters to examine the ways different genres transform or otherwise appropriate earlier mythic content. In the process, different hierarchies of religious ideas and values emerge, attesting to the dynamic and living character of mythopoesis.

It should be added here that each stage in the fabulation and growth of a mythic *traditum* is characterized by a different type of 'modelling system'.[76] By this category I mean to stress the fact that the constructions of myth shape and reshape different models of reality and theology. We may even say that mythopoesis (as a symbolic form of the imagination) brings a kind of narrative world into being. Indeed, such literary constructions have the character of fictive realities—these latter being the dimension of truth which the mythmaker (and his disciples or heirs) inhabits through his hermeneutical inventions, and which may be accepted or transformed by successive stages of mythopoesis. This topic will occupy us in each part of this book, and will be the subject of an independent reflection in the final conclusions.

IV. The Role of Scripture

I have saved until last a discussion of the place of myth in biblical Scripture and the role of that Scripture in Jewish myth and mythmaking. With this topic we turn from method and orientation to the sources themselves.

1. From Myth to Mythmaking. Prior to its canonization in ancient Judaism, the biblical corpus was an open collection of texts and traditions, containing many mythic references and allusions to divine acts in the archaic past or during the founding events of the culture. It is with reference to these models that present and future divine actions were requested or anticipated. And while it is not always easy to date these materials, the occurrence of much myth in various genres of the later post-exilic strata of Scripture shows that this form remained alive and was used creatively. However, it should be added that these examples do not extend beyond their specific or isolated occurrences, and there is no attempt to construct a unified collection of myths. Accordingly, in our study we shall focus on each text separately, understanding the given myth within its given literary context.

[76] For this notion, see Jurij Lotman, *The Structure of the Artistic Text* (Michigan Slavic Contributions, 7; Ann Arbor: University of Michigan, 1977), 14, 18.

By contrast, the myths and mythopoesis found in the Midrash are based on a closed, canonical Scripture, whose every word and phrase can serve as the basis of new mythic inventions. Thus the older biblical mythologems are expanded and correlated with other passages that are read mythically; and the central topics of primordial and sacred history in the biblical text (the creation; exodus; revelation at Sinai; destruction of the Temple; exile of the people; and national restoration) are all given new mythic resonance through exegetical fabulations of God's role in sacred history. In addition, one can also find traces of an emerging mythology in the narrative expansions and collations of related mythologems that appear in the rabbinic collections.[77] This feature has antecedents in ancient Mesopotamia (in such mythic sources as *Atraḫasis* and *Enuma elish*), as well as in ancient and classical Greece (notably, Hesiod's *Theogony* and the *Library* of Apollodorus).[78]

The full emergence of a mythological corpus from the myths and language of Scripture can be found in the *Zohar*. In it, the vast *traditum* of Judaism is taken over as a resource for a powerful and protean mythopoesis built out of the language of Scripture. There is now virtually no word or image in the Hebrew Bible that is not a potential myth, encoding in symbolic forms the esoteric theosophy of the supernal powers that constitute the Godhead. The new fabulations draw upon all the natural images, personalities, and reports found in the scriptural source and transform their meaning and essence. Not merely figures of this world, the various images are revealed as ontological and hypostatic forms; and the syntactic interaction of words and images in a sentence are shown to conceal arcane dynamics in the heavenly worlds. Who could anticipate the profound mythic fabulations about the emanation of divine Being that could be wrought from a narrative snippet like 'And Benayahu the son of Yehoiada, the son of a valiant man, of Qabtziel, who had done many valiant acts, he slew two lion-hearted men of Moab; and he went down and slew the lion in the midst of a pit in a time of snow' (2 Sam. 23: 20)?[79] For the latter-day mythoplasts, the very structure of this report, and its sequence of names and images, provide the template for its remarkable symbolic transvaluation into a code for revealing cosmic and intra-divine processes. I shall develop these matters below.

Particularly important for the phenomenon of mythmaking in this corpus is the fact that many myths are produced as peripatetic discourses among the personalities in the *Zohar*, or in the course of a conclave and dialogue among them. Through their symbolic fabulations (often enriched by the riddling

[77] See, for example, my discussion of the mythemes collected in *BT Baba Batra* 74b-75a, in *The Exegetical Imagination*, ch. 2, and the extended discussion below.

[78] On the author of the *Library*, see M. van der Valk, 'On *Apollodori Bibliotheca*', *Revue des Études Grecques*, 71 (1958), 100–68.

[79] See *Zohar* I. 6a/b. Citations follow *Sefer Ha-Zohar*, ed. Reuven Margoliot (4th edn., with corrections and additions; Jerusalem: Mosad Ha-Rav Kook, 1964). (Hereinafter: *Zohar*.)

narratives spoken by odd characters encountered on the road; or by the happenstance of history or nature), Hebrew Scriptures are revealed as a collection of myths dealing with the divine Being itself—in all its emanational permutations. With some justice, one may even call this transformed Scripture a mega-myth about God and His inmost reality.

2. The Changing Surface of Scripture. The three stages of myth and myth-making being treated here (the Hebrew Bible, rabbinic Midrash, and the book of *Zohar*), represent three readings of Scripture and its traditions, whereby the signs at one level may serve as the signifiers at another. Thus the mythic signs in the Bible (like the paradigms of divine combat) may signify aspects of a cosmic and even preternatural mythology in the *Zohar* (becoming the paradigms of divine Being); and the non-mythic signs of Scripture (its lexical thesaurus) may, in turn, signify entirely new mythic signs for rabbinic Midrash or the later mystical tradition. At each stage in the process, the transformation of signs and signifiers is realized through hermeneutical devices that invent different types of myth. The canon of myth may thus widen to embrace the entirety of Scripture, even as the mythic figures may mutate from the domain of fantastic realism in the texts of the Hebrew Bible to the realistic phantasms found in the book of *Zohar*. At the mystical level, the surface of Scripture is the elusive symbolic code of Divinity—revealed and concealed at the same time.

We now turn to a study of the myths themselves, transmitted and received for millennia. The modern interpreter is a further link in this chain of reception. Indeed, to analyse or reconstruct the myths of Hebrew Scriptures and Judaism is to add a new chapter to the cultural work of enlivening and formulating myth in contemporary terms. Such a process does not ensure the historical or analytical validity of the conclusions drawn in any given case; but it does emphasize the fact that the old myths are also revealed and revived anew by the work of scholarship—an intriguing and intricate case of *logos* in the service of *mythos*.

I
Biblical Myth

1
Introduction

The attempts of modern scholarship to understand the religion and culture of ancient Israel within its Near Eastern context have focused as much on features of continuity and similarity as on topics of difference and distinction. Notable forebears of this academic genealogy include Spinoza and Michaelis, followed by their intellectual progeny. A decisive turning point in this enterprise was the publication of Friedrich Delitzsch's *Babel und Bibel*, and the vigorous debate that ensued.[1] Soon a plethora of parallels was advanced, documenting undeniable similarities. Comparisons between such texts as the flood narrative in the *Gilgamesh Epic* and Genesis 6: 9–9: 7, or the legal code of Hammurapi and Exodus 21–3, caused initial interest. In due course, many authorities also pointed out significant differences. Among these, phenomena such as monotheism, prophecy, and the role of God in history were regarded as evidence for Israelite uniqueness within this larger cultural milieu. But even these matters have been variously qualified, and the isolation of surface parallels was replaced by more nuanced and culture-specific analyses.[2]

Central to this whole discussion is the phenomenon of myth, which was presumed to mark a caesura between the cosmic religions of Near Eastern polytheism and the covenantal nomism of ancient Israelite monotheism.

[1] The first two lectures on the subject appeared early in the century; see Friedrich Delitzsch, *Babel und Bibel: Ein Vortrag* (Leipzig: J. C. Hinrichs, 1903), and *Zweiter Vortrag über Babel und Bibel* (Stuttgart: Deutsche Verlags-Anstalt, 1903). All three lectures soon appeared in English, together with criticisms and the author's replies; see *Babel and Bible* (Chicago: The Open Court Publishing Company, 1906).

[2] The question of ancient Israelite monotheism and its Egyptian forerunners, has recently been taken up again, and in a striking manner, by Jan Assmann, *Moses the Egyptian* (Cambridge, Mass.: Harvard University Press, 1997), with earlier literature cited. For its part, the phenomenon of biblical prophecy must also be studied against the background of ancient Mesopotamian oracles and prophecy. See, for example, the studies of Armin Schmitt, *Prophetischer Gottesbescheid in Mari und Israel* (BWANT 114; Stuttgart, 1982); Helga Weippert, Klaus Seybold, and Manfred Weippert, *Beiträge zur prophetischen Bildsprache in Israel und Assyrien* (OBO 64; Freiburg and Göttingen, 1985); and Martii Nissinen, 'Der Relevanz der neuassyrischen Prophetie für die alttestamentliche Forschung', in Manfried Dietrich and Oswald Loretz (edd.), *Mesopotamia-Ugaritica-Biblica: Festschrift für Kurt Bergerhof* (Kevelaer: Butzon & Bercher, 1993), 217–58. On the issue of sacred history as a unique feature of ancient Israel, see Bertil Albrektson, *History and Gods: An Essay on the Idea of Historical Events as Divine Manifestations in the Ancient Near East and Israel* (Coniectanea Biblica, Old Testament Series 1; Lund: C. W. K. Gleerup, 1967), and the review of Wilfred G. Lambert, in *Or.* 39 (1970), 170–7. See also the overview of these topics by H. W. F. Saggs, *The Encounter with the Divine in Mesopotamia and Israel* (London: Athlone Press, 1978).

After all, there is arguably a fundamental difference between religions in which the personal powers or gods of nature and the celestial order are formed (or emerge) from a common substance, which ritual behaviour tries to maintain or utilize, and a religion that radically differentiates one true God from the natural or cosmic order, which He has formed and brought into being, and to whom alone human obedience is due and whose revealed law contains the only valid ritual prescriptions.[3] Myth is commonly presumed to be a feature of the former phenomenon only, not the latter.[4] But such estimations use the themes or structures of religion (especially an 'other' religion) to define the nature of myth, and thus turn on self-fulfilling or circular arguments.[5] A more promising approach would be to focus on content and context.

Given the diversity and tendentiousness associated with the term 'myth', James Barr has introduced a significant shift in the discussion. His programmatic suggestion is that one should always understand myth within its specific cultural ambience, so that, for the purposes of Biblical Studies, myth would be taken to mean 'the sort of thing we find in Ugarit, or in *Enuma elish*, or in other expressions of culture which in fact impinged upon Israel with some directness'.[6] I regard this as wise counsel and shall, on its merits, consider two thematic constellations of much importance for understanding myth and mythmaking in the Hebrew Bible. The first of these features involves reference to a paradigmatic divine action—specifically, to a divine battle (theomachy) against the sea (as a natural and often personified element), adduced or evoked in conjunction with the origin of the world or subsequent acts of divine power.[7] The second focuses on the divine personalities themselves, who provide sustenance, protection, or military assistance to their faithful human subjects, and who may be coaxed and praised for these benefits—but who may also withdraw their favour or abandon their worshippers or shrines in moments of wrath.[8] If the sea battle is one of the

[3] For a related phenomenology, see Yehezkel Kaufmann, *Toledot ha-ʾEmunah ha-Yisraʾelit* (1937, 6th printing; Jerusalem and Tel Aviv: Mosad Bialik & Devir, 1964), pt. 1.2, 221–416; and my discussion in *The Garments of Torah: Essays in Biblical Hermeneutics* (Bloomington: Indiana University Press, 1989), ch. 3.

[4] In his valuable and insightful study, Johannes Hehn, *Die biblische und die babylonische Gottesidee* (Leipzig: J. C. Hinrichs, 1913) noted different modalities of monotheism in the ancient Near East, and comparable modalities of divine personal powers; but he ultimately distinguishes ancient Israel and its God from the mythic civilizations roundabout. His argument turns on the point that 'Dem A. T. fehlt die wesentliche Voraussetzung des Mythos, die personifikation der Naturerscheinungen' (p. 315); also cf. p. 283.

[5] See my earlier discussion, in the general Introduction.

[6] See his 'The Meaning of "Mythology" in Relation to the Old Testament', *VT* 9 (1959), 2.

[7] It would appear that the first comparative study is that of George A. Barton, *JAOS* 15 (1893), 1–27; it was followed by the more extensive work of Hermann Gunkel, *Schöpfung und Chaos in Urzeit und Endzeit: Eine Religionsgeschichtliche Untersuchung über Gen 1 und Ap Joh 12* (Göttingen: Vandenhoeck & Ruprecht, 1895). The present treatment will attempt a new approach to the whole issue.

[8] This focus on divine deeds and affects follows my definition of myth; see above, p. 11.

most common and dramatic mythologems in ancient Near Eastern literature,[9] the relationship between worshippers and their gods has been identified as a common religious pattern throughout the region.[10]

A divine battle against a sea dragon or serpent is found as early as a Mesopotamian cylinder seal from Tell Asmar in the Akkad dynasty (*c.*2400 BCE), which features two gods in combat with a monster with seven heads (four are slain, three remain aggressive).[11] Further evidence is found in diverse literary sources. A recent attestation of our mythologem occurs in a letter found at Mari (eighteenth century, BCE), that refers to the slaying of the goddess Tiʾamat by the West Semitic god Addu, lord of Aleppo.[12] This early record of the theomachy is all the more significant insofar as it pre-dates the predominant Canaanite and Babylonian evidence, and uses terminology recurring in the later Ugaritic and biblical texts.[13] The subsequent Ugaritic myths from the Cassite period show a diffusion of the sea battle among various gods, most notably referring to Baʿal, who slays the monster Lotan (Leviathan), 'the mighty one of the seven heads (*šlyṭ. d. šbʿt. rʾašm*)', and to Anat, who does the same to Tunnanu.[14] This scenario is thus contemporaneous with, or slightly earlier than, the great battle portrayed in the Babylonian epic of *Enuma elish*,[15] where the hero Marduk kills the sea monster Tiʾamat, and out of her bisected body forms the upper and lower world.

9 See below.

10 See the extensive evidence adduced by Morton Smith, 'The Common Theology of the Ancient Near East', *JBL* 71 (1952), 135–47.

11 See the plate and discussion in Henri Frankfort, 'God and Myths on Sargonid Seals', *Iraq*, 1 (1934), 8 (and plate 1*a*); the seal was found in the temple. In many other images, however, a dragon or serpent serves the gods in one way or another, or is subservient to them; overall, see E. Douglas Van Buren, 'The Dragon in Ancient Mesopotamia', *Or.* 15 (1946), 1–45, and earlier in L. Heuzey, 'Dragons sacrés de Babylone et leur prototype chaldéen', *RA* 6 (1906), 95 ff.

12 See the edition and discussion of text A.1968 from *Archives Royales de Mari* XXXVI/3, by Jean-Marie Durand, 'Le Mythologeme du Combat entre le Dieu de l'Orage et la Mer en Mésopotamie', *MARI, Annales de Recherches Interdisciplinaires*, 7 (1993), 41–61, esp. pp. 43–5. In the key passage (ll. 3′–4′), the god has given to the king the weapons *ša itti temtim amtaḫṣu* ('with which I smote Tiʾamat').

13 An apparently earlier fragment has been discussed by A. Westenholz, in *AfO* 25, p. 102. The Akkadian verb *maḫaṣu* noted above (n. 12) occurs in the Ugaritic myths to be mentioned below, and in Job 26: 12.

14 See André Herdner, *Corpus des tablettes en cunéiformes alphabétiques* (Paris: Imprimerie Nationale, 1963), 5. 1.1–5 and 3. 3.35–9, respectively. On Anat's strife, see Samuel Loewenstamm, 'Anat's Victory over the Tunnanu', *JSS* 20 (1975), 27. The occurrence of two theomachies has been much discussed, and ably defended by Edward Greenstein, 'The Snaring of Sea in the Baʿal Epic', *Maarav*, 3 (1982), 195–216, with references to the earlier literature. The different references to the monster have led to various identifications, as in John Day, *God's Conflict with the Dragon and the Sea* (Cambridge: Cambridge University Press, 1985), 13–14; but see the critique of Nicolas Wyatt, 'Killing and Cosmogony in Canaanite and Biblical Thought', *UF* 17 (1986), 377 f., and his proposal of four dragon-slayers. For the rendering of the monster as 'tunnanu' in the Ugaritic polyglot, see John Huenergard, *Ugaritic Vocabulary in Syllabic Transcription* (HSS 32; Atlanta: Scholars Press, 1987), 72, 185 f.

15 A post-Cassite dating of the epic to the reign of Nebuchadnezzar (1125–1104 BCE) was proposed by Wilfred G. Lambert, 'The Reign of Nebuchadnezzar I: A Turning Point in the

For over a century, Genesis 1 has been read in the light of this Mesopotamian account of creation and the many similar sequences of action and style shared between them.[16] While the parallels could not be ignored, it has also been observed that this biblical passage was without any account of a theogony or theomachy; and this notable absence has led to the frequent assertion that such matters had been expunged by the writer, who even introduced certain features which, to the discerning eye, also attested to the polemical nature of the chapter.[17]

But this line of argument is not universally accepted;[18] and, in any case, it bears recalling that the creation account in Genesis 1 was not always the opening or foundational narrative of a 'Bible'. In fact, many other accounts and apostrophes of the creation circulated in ancient Israel, and some of them were even recited in prayers preserved in the book of Psalms. Among these, there are several examples in which a divine combat against the sea is featured as one of the valorous acts of God in primordial times. Accordingly, the complete biblical evidence seems rather to indicate two different models of the creation. One of these we shall designate the '*logos* model', since it particularly or primarily emphasizes a verbal creation, though physical formations are not excluded.[19] Genesis 1 is the pre-eminent example of this

History of Ancient Mesopotamian History', in W. S. McCollough (ed.), *The Seed of Wisdom: Essays in Honor of T. J. Meek* (Toronto: University of Toronto, 1964), 3–13. Against this dating, see Stephanie Dalley, *Myths from Mesopotamia: Creation, the Flood, Gilgamesh, and Others* (New York: Oxford University Press, 1989), 228–30.

[16] See already the point made by F. Delitzsch in *Bibel und Babel*, 34f. Similarities were culled by Alexander Heidel, *The Babylonian Genesis* (Chicago: Phoenix Books, 1963), 129, and taken over and expanded by Ephraim A. Speiser, *Genesis* (Anchor Bible, 1; Garden City, NY: Doubleday & Company, 1964), 9–11. Among recently noted parallels, one may note the striking affinity between the phrase *nibnima ṣalam ṭiṭṭi* ('let us create an image of clay'), spoken by Belet-ili to Ea in a Mesopotamian myth dealing with the creation of man and king, and the expression *naʿaseh ʾadam be-ṣalmeinu* ('let us make man in our image') found in Gen. 1: 26 (2: 7 refers to the material of clay). For the text, see Werner Mayer, 'Ein Mythos von der Erschaffung des Menschen und des Königs', *Or.* 56 (1987), 56 (obv. l. 8′); the observation was made by Victor Hurowitz, *JQR* 87 (1997), 414.

[17] Cf. Umberto Cassuto, *Peirush ʿal Sefer Bereiʾshit* (3rd edn.; Jerusalem: Magnes Press, 1959), i. 12–13, 30–1; and Arvid Kapelrud, 'Mythological Features in Genesis Chapter 1 and the Author's Intentions', *VT* 24 (1974), 183–4, esp. Nevertheless, one may wonder whether the phrase *toledot ha-shamayim veha-ʾaretz* ('generations of heaven and earth') in Gen. 2: 4a may betray some trace of a theogonic tradition (qualified by v. 4b), since the word *toledot* suggests the siring of generations (cf. Gen. 5: 1–5, etc.). An anti-mythological tendency in Genesis was also noted by F. M. T. de Liagre Bohl, 'Babel und Bibel, 1', *Jaarbericht van het Vooraziatisch-Egyptisch Genootshap 'Ex oriente Lux'*, 16 (1959–62), 106.

[18] See the evaluation of the evidence by W. G. Lambert, 'A New Look at the Babylonian Background of Genesis', *JTS*, NS 16 (1965), 285–300. Moreover, one cannot ignore intriguing features of similarity between Genesis 1 and myths of creation in ancient Egypt; for which, see Siegfried Hermann, 'Die Naturlehre des Schöpfungsberichtes: Erwägungen zur Vorgeschichte von Genesis 1', *TLZ* 86 (1961), 413–24.

[19] For a re-evaluation of earlier discussions and new proposal of the strata of a 'Wort- und Tatbericht' in Genesis 1, see Werner H. Schmidt, *Die Schöpfungsgeschichte der Priesterschrift* (Neukirchen-Vluyn: Neukirchener Verlag, 1964), 73–159; but this does not contradict my

mythic type, with its theology of an absolutely sovereign creator who speaks and shapes dormant or unresistant matter into effective (viable) existence and order. Over against this type we may place the '*agon* model', which gives dominant emphasis to acts of strife and subjugation at the beginning of the world; and particularly since it is God's victory over antagonistic creatures of the sea that marks His great sovereignty and might.

One can best appreciate the difference between these two types of creation when they are aligned with other topics. For its part, the *logos* model underscores the authority of divine speech and its superiority to the words and plans of His creatures. This point is particularly marked in Psalm 33. The prayer opens with a call to the righteous and 'upright (*yesharim*)' to give praise to the Lord in song and sound (v. 1), 'because the word (*dabar*) of the Lord is right (*yashar*)' and 'His every deed is faithful' (v. 4). Moreover, the speaker adds that God 'loves what is right and just', and that 'the earth is full of His faithful care (*ḥesed*)' (v. 5).[20] This account of divine providence leads to a celebration of the divine act of creation above and below: 'By the word (*dabar*) of YHWH the heavens were made, and by the breath of His mouth, all their hosts. He gathers up the waters like a mound, stores the deep in vaults' (vv. 6–7). What is particularly notable here is the verbal character of the creation of the heavens and their hosts, and the gathering and storing of the ocean waters in the lower realm without any combat or violence.

The psalmist reinforces the theme of divine creation through speech when it calls upon 'all the inhabitants of the world' to fear the Lord, 'for He spoke, and it was; He commanded, and it endures (*va-yaʿamod*)' (v. 9). This point is further developed by extending God's creative power into the realm of history: 'YHWH ruins the plans of nations'—since 'What YHWH plans endures (*yaʿamod*) forever, (and) what He designs (lasts) for generations on end' (vv. 10–11). The striking parallelism between the endurance of God's creative word and His historical will projects a certain continuity of divine power upon which humans can rely, and that forms a basis of hope for the psalmist as well. We may furthermore note that, in the sequel, the psalmist twice refers to God's 'faithful care (*ḥesed*)' (vv. 18, 22), thereby extending divine concern for the earth to all those who put their trust in him. It is important to stress this thematic link between God's creative word and His

present point, based on a phenomenology of the final redaction. Two notable earlier studies are by Friedrich Schwally, 'Die biblischen Schöpfungsberichte', *Archiv für Religionswissenschaft*, 9 (1906), 159–75; and M. Lambert, 'A Study of the First Chapter of Genesis', *HUCA* 1 (1924), 3–12.

[20] The psalmist has taken over the common covenantal triad of righteousness, justice, and faithfulness and applied it to God's role as creator and caretaker of the earth. For the triad, see Jer. 9: 23 and Hos. 2: 21. On these elements, see Moshe Weinfeld, *Social Justice in Ancient Israel and in the Ancient Near East* (Jerusalem and Philadelphia: Magnes Press and Fortress Press, 1995).

providential rule, since it shows the living application that a *logos* theology could take in ancient Israel.[21]

An inter-textual perspective reinforces this point, since just this combination of themes occurs in a post-exilic prophecy of Deutero-Isaiah, whose polemical purpose is to stress the power of the divine word to create the world and fulfil prophecies. Note that after YHWH states that it is He alone who 'made everything' (Isa. 44: 24), He immediately adds that He annuls 'the omens of diviners' (v. 25) but 'confirms the word of My servant and fulfils the prediction of my messengers' (v. 26).[22] And in a climactic exemplification of this verbal power to shape nature and realize prophecies, YHWH adds: 'It is I who say of Jerusalem, "It shall be inhabited", and of the towns of Judah, "They shall be rebuilt" . . . ; (And it is I) who said to the watery deep, "Be dry; I shall dry up your rivers" ' (v. 27).

On the basis of these two examples, from different genres, we can see how the *logos* model of creation marks a mythic perspective entirely different from the one that sees in God's suppression of sea monsters in ancient days a paradigm of His power to destroy the historical enemies of Israel, or otherwise bring to pass an act of salvation. Such a combative model gives a different type of hope to the faithful, while it at the same time shows a theological parallelism between a formative act of origins and ongoing expressions of divine sovereignty. Whereas one model emphasizes effective speech in the past and present, the other underscores strife and physical victory at both temporal poles.

[21] It may be added that various texts in Deutero-Isaiah show a connection between a theology of creation and an emphasis on God's prophetic word. Both are deemed to be expressions of an incomparable divine power. Cf. Isa. 44: 24–8; 45: 11–12; 46: 9–11. Rolf Rendtorff, 'Die Theologische Stellung des Schöpfungsglaubens bei Deuterojesaja', *ZTK* 51 (1954), 12, has rightly noted that creation is mentioned in the context of disputations of salvation oracles. For a comparison of two types of *logos* theology, see Klaus Koch, 'Wort und Einheit des Schöpfergottes in Memphis und Jerusalem', *ZTK* 62 (1965), 251–93.

[22] This combined function is found throughout this collection, also through the juxtaposition of creation and prophecy; cf. 40: 12–31 and 41: 1–7, or 41: 17–20 and 21–4.

2

Combat Myths and Divine Actions: Prayers and Prophecies of Divine Might

A. IN THE PSALMS

A situation of personal or national crisis characterizes the psalms and prophecies in which God's victory over primordial sea monsters is recalled or invoked. For although the precise historical situation involved cannot always be identified in our sources, they all palpably reflect (or refer to) some concrete occasion of suffering or distress when the lack of divine presence was keenly felt. Indeed, it is just the tangible pathos of a human outcry that gives these texts their tone of urgency, and marks the mythic acts adduced therein as real and significant events *in illo tempore*. To think that the speakers who recall to God His own past acts of power and salvation, in order to induce their repetition in the present, would cite mere metaphors or fables strains credulity and all literary sense. In the ensuing analyses, the standpoint of the speaker and the urgency of the appeal shall be deemed crucial for appreciating how each recitation of (or reference to) the combat myth renews its actuality and truth in the present.

Of related importance for our study of the mythologems and their function will be attention to matters of genre and form, as well as language and imagery. This focus will facilitate a comparative analysis of the different texts, after the inherent features of each of them have been separately considered. In this way we may hope to penetrate the religious consciousness that pervades these texts, and the mythic theology that is variously expressed thereby.

We begin with Psalm 74, since it sets forth most of the issues with paradigmatic completeness. This prayer has a tripartite structure: (1) an opening lament (vv. 1–11); (2) a central hymnic recitation (vv. 12–17); and (3) a concluding plea (vv. 18–23). The lament speaks directly to God on behalf of the community, expressing despair at the ongoing divine wrath through a series of queries and appeals. The opening cry, 'Why (*lamah*), O YHWH, do You reject (*zanaḥta*) Your flock?' establishes the emotional tone of despair, and is echoed by other questions throughout the first part—twice using the form 'how long' (*ʿad mah*; *ʿad matay*; vv. 9–10), and the word *lamah* again at the end (v. 11). Each query raises a different issue. At the beginning the psalmist asks why God remains angry with His special flock, described as the nation He redeemed from Egypt and 'made' His own at Sinai 'long ago (*qedem*)' (v. 2); he then shifts the issue to divine honour, and wonders why God allows the enemy that has destroyed the Temple (vv. 3–8) to 'blaspheme' and 'revile' His holy name (v. 10);[1] and finally, the divine absence is marked by an inquiry about God's withdrawn hand, because of which the enemy is now dominant. For the speaker each of these lamentable concerns feels as if it has endured 'forever (*netzaḥ*)'—a word that is repeated three times in the prayer (vv. 1, 3, 10). By contrast, the speaker's only sense of God's presence is the fury which he says 'fumes' or 'smokes (*yeʿeshan*) in Your nose' (v. 1), and that is actualized on earth by the 'fire' set by the enemy in the sanctuary (v. 7). This mythic trope leads the psalmist to counterpoint his queries of despair with imperatives exhorting immediate divine action: 'remember (*zekhor*) Your flock' (v. 2); 'raise Your feet' on behalf of the destroyed Temple (v. 3); and finally, 'draw forth Your right hand from Your bosom' (v. 11).

All of these issues are intensified in the concluding petition. Echoing the beginning of his prayer, the psalmist again appeals to God to 'remember (*zekhor*)' that the enemy 'blasphemes' and 'reviles' His 'name' (v. 18), and not 'forget forever (*netzaḥ*)' His faithful 'dove' that praises His 'name'. Indeed, the Lord is strongly implored to 'arise' against those who 'rise' against Him (v. 22), against those whose roar 'ascends all the time (*ʿoleh tamid*)' (v. 23). With this striking image, the speaker evokes a powerful pun on the 'daily burnt offering (*ʿolah tamid*)' of the Temple which has ceased through the fires of divine fury. Through this allusion, the absence of true worship evokes the presence of doom.

Between the opening lament and concluding petition is the voice of praise for things past. Turning from the query as to why God has withdrawn His saving arm, the psalmist now speaks directly about earlier acts of divine power; and echoing the earlier reference to God having made Israel His covenant people 'of old (*qedem*)', he now addresses Him as 'my God from of old (*mi-qedem*), who works salvation in the midst of the earth' (v. 12). These wondrous acts are then enumerated.

> You it was who smashed Sea (*Yam*) with Your might,
> Who battered the heads of (the) (*tanninim*) monsters in the waters;
> You it was who crushed the heads of Leviathan,
> Who left them for food for the denizens of the desert;
> You it was who cut springs and torrents,
> You made the rivers run dry;
> Yours is the day, and also the night;
> You established the moon and sun;

[1] This refers presumably to the Temple of Zion, destroyed in 587/586 BCE. The use of the image of God's withdrawn arm in v. 11 and in Lam. 2: 3 (on which see below) lends some support to this view. It would thus be part of the varied post-destruction literature bemoaning divine wrath and its effects.

You fixed the boundaries of the earth;
Summer and winter—You made them. (vv. 13–17)

Repeatedly (seven times) the psalmist addresses God as 'You' (*ʾattah*), and extols primordial acts in which He was victorious over sea monsters and gave the world its order and divisions. This combination of an account of God's mighty deeds and a direct personal address is also found in ancient Near Eastern laments and hymns from different periods.[2] In the present instance, the biblical battle scenes are expressed in violent terms and serve as a prelude to the more benign descriptions of God's establishment of diurnal and seasonal rhythms, and formation of the boundaries of the earth. The contrast is notable, and leads one to the sense that the seas (variously personified and named) are primordial forces of disorder; and that the cutting of springs and river beds is a form of management of the waters made possible by their physical containment. Thus the structure of world governance presupposes a mythic model in which a theomachy precedes the work of creation.

The many-headed creatures of the deep (the *tanninim* and Leviathan) suggest some beastly aspect—comparable to the seven-headed sea dragon pictured on a third-millennium seal impression from Akkad.[3] A similar image occurs in a Canaanite myth depicting Baʿal's victory over the sea god Yam, which refers to the smashing of Lotan (a dialectal variant of the Hebrew name *livyatan*, Leviathan) and the defeat of a monster with seven heads.[4] What is more, in this same text the serpent Lotan is described as both 'slant' and 'twisted' (*brḥ* and *ʿqlṭn*)—apostrophes exactly like those used of Leviathan in Isa. 27: 1 (who is called both *bariaḥ* and *ʿaqalaṭon*);[5] and the verb that is used to describe the smashing (*tmḫṣ*) of Lotan is identical to that used in Job 26: 12 (*maḥatz*) when it depicts the defeat of the sea monster Rahab.[6] Such battle scenes also recall the account of the lord Marduk's battle against Tiʾamat in Babylonian mythology, where we learn that 'He

[2] For a broad range of sources, see esp. the materials collected by Friedrich Stummer, *Sumerisch-akkadische Parallelen zum Aufbau alttestamentlicher Psalmen* (Paderborn: Verlag von Ferdinand Schoeningh, 1922); and note esp. the Hymn to Marduk (IV R 29, no. 1), which combines cosmic epithets and a personal address (*atta*), pp. 51 f. For this text, see J. Hehn, *Hymnen und Gebete an Marduk* (Leipzig, 1905 (= Beiträge zur Assyriologie und semitischen Sprachwissenschaft, 5: 279–400), no. 7.

[3] See above, Ch. 1, n. 11.

[4] Cf. Herdner, *CTA* 5.1. 1–5. For the term for the dragon, see John Emerton, 'Leviathan and *ltn*: The Vocalization of the Ugaritic Word for the Dragon', *VT* 32 (1982), 327–31. The motif of a multi-headed sea monster had a long afterlife; cf. Rev. 12: 3, *drakon megas*... *echon kephalas hepta* ('great monster... having seven heads'), and *BT Kidd.* 29b, *ʾidamei leih ke-taninaʾ de-shivʿah reishvateih* ('it (the demon) appeared to him (R. Aḥa bar Jacob) in the guise of a seven-headed dragon'). Cf. Rashi (ad loc.), *teninaʾ de-shivʿah reisheih*.

[5] Regarding the depiction of Lotan, see Herdner, *CTA* 5.1. 1–5.

[6] For the verb, see Moshe Held, '*mḫṣ*/**mḫš* in Ugaritic and Other Semitic Languages (A Study in Comparative lexicography)', *JAOS* 79 (1959), 159–76. The verb *mḫṣ* occurs in Herdner, *CTA* 3. 3. 35, 37—a context that describes Anat's victory over Yam in ways similar to the defeat by Baʿal.

smashed (her) skull with his merciless staff' (*ina mittišu la padi ulatti muḫḫa*; *Enuma elish* IV. 130).[7]

All these cross-references and shared depictions suggest that ancient Israel drew upon a bundle of mythic traditions that circulated throughout the Syro-Palestinian region, and used them in order to depict battles against sea dragons—albeit for its own purposes and in its own ways.[8]

The mythologems used by the author of Psalm 74 come alive as paradigms and proofs of divine might, and as a way to coax YHWH into saving action. They function as the speaker's own faithful recollection of all God's deeds 'in the earth', even as God is called upon to remember His covenant with His people, and to arise on their behalf and His own.[9] A central passage in this regard is the verse: 'Why do You hold back Your hand (*yadkha*)? Draw Your right hand (*yeminkha*) out of Your bosom!' (v. 11).[10] For it condenses the despair over divine withdrawal and the hope in divine salvation around one anthropomorphic figure. The choice of this mythic image was rooted in native tradition. On the positive side, there is the recurrent reference to the exodus from Egypt as the product of God's 'outstretched arm' (Exod. 6: 6); and He is extolled on this account with the words 'Your right hand (*yeminkha*), O YHWH, is awesome in strength' (Exod. 15: 16). The same topos is also found in other psalms, as in the request 'send forth Your hand (*yadkha*) from heaven, rescue me and save me from the mighty waters' (Ps. 144: 7), as well as in many prophetic passages to be considered below. On the negative side, the sense of divine impotence is referred to as a 'short' (rather than extended) hand (Isa. 50: 3), or as a 'withdrawn right hand' (Lam. 2: 3) that allows the enemies to triumph—exactly as in our psalm. The hand of the Lord thus serves as a mythic metonym for divine power, its extension or withdrawal being the dramatic counterpart to the emotions of favourable

[7] In IV. 129, it is stated that Marduk strode over the back of Ti'amat (*ikbusma . . . išidsa*). This phrase recalls the image in Job 9: 8, in which YHWH, the creator, is described as *dorekh ʿal bamatei yam*, as having 'trod upon the back of Yam' (understanding *bamatei* in the light of Ugaritic *bmt*, 'back'). The mythic background of the image is further assured from v. 13, which states that 'God does not restrain His fury, the warriors (*ʿozrei*) of Rahab sink beneath Him' (understanding *ʿozrei* in the light of Ugaritic *ǵzr*, 'warrior'. For this term, cf. A. G. Vaughan, '*il ǵzr*—An Explicit Epithet of El as Hero/Warrior', *UF* 23 (1993), 423–30.

[8] Cf. the remarks of H. Donner, 'Ugaritischen in der Psalmforschung', *ZAW* 79 (1967), 344. Samuel Loewenstamm, 'Miṭos ha-Yam be-Kitbei 'Ugarit ve-Ziqato 'el Miṭos ha-Yam ba-Miqra'', *EI* 9(1969), 101, correctly observes that in the Hebrew Bible the seasonal battle between the storm and the sea has a cosmogonic application, thus suggesting a common West Semitic source for both patterns.

[9] The statement *habeiṭ la-berit* ('look to the covenant') in Ps. 74: 20 may not refer to the events of Sinai (alluded to in v. 2) but to the divine attributes of mercy listed in Exod. 34: 6–7.

[10] The verb *khalleih* is difficult. An old tradition, first found in the Targum (followed by Rashi) renders it 'take out' or 'draw forth'—presumably giving a more figurative rendition to the sense 'make an end' (cf. Ps. 59: 14); but this latter sense could also yield a sense parallel to the first stichos. This approach seems to be the basis for the emendation *keluʾah* ('held back'), suggested by Hans-Joachim Kraus, *Psalmen*, 2: *Psalmen 60–150* (BK; Neukirchen-Vlyun: Neukirchener Verlag, 1961), ad loc. Thus the speaker refers doubly to God's withdrawn or restrained hand.

regard or fury. For the speaker of our psalm especially, it would hardly make sense to reduce the divine hand to a mere metaphor or the sea monsters to allegorical figures—as if these images are simply the product of an inability to speak abstractly.[11] Within the literary and religious framework of the prayer, both images partake of a vivid mythic realism whose facticity the speaker hardly doubts. This is, in fact, a core element of the psalmist's hope that God will re-actualize His ancient acts of victory for him in the present.

This conclusion allows us to reconsider the old question of myth and history. On the basis of the assumption (both cultural and religious) that myth refers to the events of the gods, and is thus a feature of pagan polytheism, whereas history is the central feature of biblical monotheism and the sphere where God's covenant and providence are actualized, the two categories have been kept apart. This prejudice has obscured a more accurate perception of their correlation and interrelation. For as we have just seen, the speaker of Psalm 74 refers to the mythic events of combat and creation as paradigmatic acts of divine power whose like he hopes to evoke in his own time. This suggests that there is a sense that all of God's mighty acts are correlated, from the earliest victories over archaic monsters down to and including the salvations wrought for the people of Israel past and present. To call one type of act mythic and the other historical because of the sphere or type of action that is described, misses the more important emphasis on divine acts of power and victory at all times. In ensuing discussions we shall see how the splitting of the sea at the exodus, and the hope for other moments of divine aid for the nation or individual, are also depicted in the language of mythic strife with sea monsters—thereby reinforcing the present contention that, for the ancient Israelite, God's effective power was the real issue, and that the report or imagery of ancient divine battles was invoked in order to vivify or concretize the speaker's claim. The so-called dichotomy between myth and history is thus the product of a quite different cultural consciousness, and the presumptions of divine action its heirs wish to perpetuate. But such a perspective distorts the actual testimony of ancient biblical literature.[12]

Other psalms reinforce this picture. Particularly notable is Psalm 89, which provides another celebration of divine might in primordial time. For all that, the psalm also stems from a moment of national crisis, when the absence of divine power is lamented and its return beseeched.[13] The movement from

[11] Ibn Ezra refers to the hand as a *mashal* (parable); and both Rashi and Ibn Ezra allegorize the sea monsters. This tactic is already found in the Targum.

[12] Further reflections on the relationship between myth and history in the Hebrew Bible will be given in the Conclusions, after the separate cases have been presented.

[13] The specific occasion that lies behind this psalm is uncertain, and this has led to various proposals. Among them we may mention the crisis of the Syro-Ephraim invasions of Judah,

praise to petition spans the three parts of the psalm. Part 1 (vv. 1–19) rings with praise, centred around the words *ḥesed* ('steadfast love') and *ʾemunah* ('faithfulness'). Repeatedly the psalmist intones these words (vv. 1–2, 6, 9, 15), and stresses that he together with the divine council sing God's praise, whose great faithfulness is also established in the heavens above. This initial hymnic unit (vv. 1–3, 5–12) is interrupted by a promise spoken by God Himself, who proclaims that He will establish His covenant for His servant David (v. 4). The second half of the praise-unit is of particular interest for the present inquiry, since among the divine actions celebrated there the psalmist gives special emphasis to God's power over the sea:

> You rule over the upsurge of the sea;
> When its waves rise up, You subdue them.[14]
> You crushed Rahab like a corpse;
> With Your mighty arm You scattered Your enemies.
> Yours is the heaven, the earth as well;
> The world and all it holds—You established them.
> North and south—You created them;
> Tabor and Hermon sing forth Your name.
> Yours is an arm (*zeroʿa*) endowed with power;
> Your hand (*yadkha*) is mighty,
> Your right hand (*yeminkha*) exalted. (vv. 10–14)

Part 2 of the psalm (vv. 20–37) returns to the theme of God's faithfulness to David and cites the royal covenant established in 2 Sam. 7: 1–17.[15] Particularly noteworthy with regard to the mythic themes considered here, is God's word of assurance to the scion of David: 'My hand shall be constantly with him, and My arm shall strengthen him' (v. 22); and 'I shall set his hand upon the sea, his right hand upon the rivers' (v. 26)—promises not found in the original royal covenant but resonant with the imagery of mythic combat and hegemony found in vv. 10–11, in which subjugation of the sea monsters was achieved by YHWH's mighty hand. Indeed, this figure establishes the Judaean regent as God's cosmic viceroy—a topos that recalls the ancient Mari document cited earlier, in which the king is told that his divine patron is depositing in the shrine the very weapons with which he subdued Tiʾamat in battle.[16] A further confirmation of this relationship between a king and divine hero occurs in a neo-Assyrian ritual commentary, virtually

suggested by Nahum Sarna, 'Psalm 89: A Case of Inner-Biblical Exegesis', in Alexander Altmann (ed.), *Biblical and Other Studies* (Cambridge, Mass.: Harvard University Press, 1963), 43–5; and the subjugation of one of the successors of Josiah to the sovereignty of Egypt or Babylon, noted by Kraus, *Psalmen*, ad loc. There is no way to know.

[14] Hebrew *tishabbeḥeim* seems difficult, and has often been emended to *tishabbereim* in light of Ps. 74: 13 and the similar context of physical suppression. However, cf. Ps. 65: 7.

[15] See the analysis of Sarna, 'Psalm 89', 36–9 for a discussion of the reuse of 2 Sam. 7: 1–17 in this psalm; and cf. my comments in *Biblical Interpretation in Ancient Israel* (Oxford: Clarendon Press, 1985), 466 f.

[16] See above, Ch. 1, n. 12.

contemporary with our psalm. We read there that 'The king, who wears on his head a golden tiara from the inside of the temple and sits on a sedan chair, while they carry him and go to the palace, is Ninurta, who avenged his father. The gods, his fathers, gave him the scepter, throne and the staff...'.[17] Here again, there is no break between human history and mythic paradigms.

The prevalent hand imagery in the first two parts also recurs in Part 3 (vv. 39–53). Now the psalmist rebukes God for having broken His faithfulness with His human steward (vv. 39–40) and allowing the 'right hand' (*yamin*) of His enemies to prevail (v. 43). He cries out: 'How long (*ʿad mah*), O YHWH, will You forever (*la-netzaḥ*) hide Your face, Your fury blaze like fire?' (v. 47). Without waiting for an answer, the speaker immediately appeals to God to 'remember (*zekhor*)' His suffering servant (vv. 48, 51) and restore the 'steadfast love' and 'faithfulness' He swore to David (v. 50). The historical crisis being alluded to is clearly the motivation for the psalm, which (as noted earlier) led to the insertion of a reference to God's faithfulness to David into an earlier hymn of praise concerning God's cosmic faithfulness (v. 4)—thereby serving as a prelude to this account of its repudiation (v. 40). In a comparable manner, God's great deeds against the sea serve as a prolepsis of His support for His regent's 'hand' over the sea (v. 26), and this in turn serves to counterpoint the lament that God has now given the king's enemy the upper hand (v. 43).

The mythic theme of divine combat seems to have been deliberately introduced into Part 1 in order to dramatize the theme of divine power; for upon examination, one will note that this unit (vv. 10–14) splits up the words of praise found in vv. 9 and 15. After the words 'Who is mighty like You, O YHWH, Your faithfulness surrounds You?' (v. 9), one would have expected the clarifying phrase 'Righteousness and justice are the base of Your throne, steadfast love and faithfulness stand before You' (v. 15)—as heavenly hypostases around the divine throne.[18] Instead of this vision of glory, the query is followed by references to mythic battles in primordial time. These are rendered as a series of praises directed to God through a repeated use of the pronoun 'You' (*ʾattah*)—just as in Psalm 74; and also like that psalm, there is a shift in Psalm 89 from the direct pronoun *ʾattah*, when describing the battles, to the more indirect phrase *lekha...ʾaf lekha* ('Yours...Yours too') when depicting the establishment of the cosmic order after the cosmic battles. Such similarities indicate that Pss. 74: 12–17 and 89: 10–14 derive

[17] *KAR* 307 (VAT 8917), r 20–23, published with the foregoing translation, by Alasdair Livingstone, in *Court Poetry and Literary Miscellanea* (SAA III; Helsinki: Helsinki University Press, 1989), 102; cf. also v 25 (p. 100), for the identification of the king with Ninurta. For an earlier case, where the enemy is demonized as a raging flood, see Stefan Maul, '"Wenn der Held (zum Kampfe) auszieht"... Ein Ninurta-Eršemma', *Or.* 60 (1991), esp. pp. 313, 328. See further, below.

[18] See further, below.

from a common type of mythic recitation. A further link lies in the fact that the praise in Psalm 89 is joined to words of lament that ask God 'how long (*ʿad mah*)' He will reject (*zanaḥta*) His faithful servant; and finally, both prayers call upon YHWH to remember (*zekhor*) His earlier covenantal commitments to the people, and come to their rescue.

For the psalmist and tradition represented in Psalm 89, there is no gap between myth and history—both because the sources of God's historical faithfulness to Israel are personified by heavenly hypostases around His throne, and because of the parallelism between the reference to God's mighty arm against the sea (in days of yore) and the assertion of His support for His royal regent (in history) through the figure of His placing the king's arm over the seas. The intensity of the crisis that calls forth these mythic features, and the vividness of the language, make it unlikely in this instance (as also in Psalm 74) that mere metaphors are involved. Rather, it seems, that the speaker recalls the ancient battles of God's as paradigms of divine power, which he recites in the hope that the divine warrior will again act with a great arm and save His royal servant from his enemies. With such divine help the scion of David would again act with the cosmic power endowed to the founder of the dynasty and promised to his successors 'forever' (v. 29).

Psalm 77 presents a different conjunction of myth and history, with its portrayal of God's power during the exodus. This theophany is featured in the second section of the psalm. Part 1 (vv. 2–11) opens with a great personal cry and lament, in which the speaker describes his endless suffering and the absence of divine favour. Using fixed forms of lament, the psalmist asks, 'Will the Lord reject (*yiznaḥ*) forever? . . . Has His faithfulness disappeared forever (*la-netzaḥ*)? . . . Has He in anger repressed compassion?'[19] These questions (like earlier examples) display the despair that characterizes the speaker's situation. Particularly poignant, is the withdrawal of divine compassion and care—a state epitomized by the statement that 'the right hand of the Most High has changed (*shenot*)' or 'turned' (v. 11).[20]

This mythic figure counterpoints the recitation of God's wondrous acts 'of old (*mi-qedem*)' in Part 2 (vv. 12–21)—in which God's mighty arm plays a formidable role as an agent of salvation.

> By Your arm (*zeroʿa*) You redeemed Your people,
> The children of Jacob and Joseph. *Selah*
> The waters saw you, O God, the waters saw You and shook,
> Even the very deeps convulsed violently.
> Clouds streamed with water, the heavens thundered forth,
> Even Your arrows flew about.

[19] Hebrew *qafatz be-ʾaf raḥamav* is difficult. I follow Rashi, who understands *qafatz* as 'close', on the basis of the usage in Deut. 15: 7.

[20] Following the Targum, Rashi, and Ibn Ezra.

The sound of Your thunder was in the wheels (of Your chariot);
Lightning brightened the world;
The earth convulsed and shook. (vv. 16–18)

The prayer concludes with a glorification of God's mysterious role on behalf of the people. Having struck the sea with terror, He guided His flock unseen and unmarked through the waters—by the hand of Moses and Aaron.

Central to the second part of this psalm is the manifestation of YHWH as a storm god blasting against the sea below. The whole depiction brims with mythic tropes common throughout the ancient Near East, particularly the sound of thunder that shakes the earth and the rumbling of the divine chariot with the advent of the god. Special attention may be given in this context to hymnic depictions reporting the appearance of storm gods. For example, it is said of Adad, 'that at the sound of his voice the heavens convulse, the earth shakes, the mountains tremble';[21] and similar praise is preserved from the West Semitic sphere itself, which says 'who sets his voice in the heavens like Adad, and all the earth shakes at his voice'.[22] The Canaanite god Baʿal is also depicted in this manner, when a mythic account says that 'Ba[ʿal gives] forth his holy voice... (and) the high places of the earth totter'.[23] Another parallel portrays Baʿal's thunderous voice among other meteorological phenomena: '(He) gives forth his voice in the clouds, sends forth lightning bolts to earth'.[24] This tradition is also found in Egyptian sources.[25]

The appearance of warrior and storm gods on their heavenly chariot is another common Near Eastern element, found in various forms of mythic representation. For example, on a seal from the Akkadian period (late third millennium BCE), the weather god appears on his four-wheeled chariot drawn by a lion-griffin, with a goddess on its back holding bundles of rain or

[21] *ša ina sikir pišu šamu irubu, erṣetu inerrutu, itarru ḫurani*, Erich Ebeling, *Akkadische Gebetserie 'Handerhebung'* (Deutsche Akademie der Wissenschaften zu Berlin, Institut für Orientforschung, 20; Berlin: Akademie-Verlag, 1953), p. 104: 8–9. See also in Stephen Langdon, *Babylonian Penitential Psalms* (Oxford Edition of Cuneiform Texts, 6; Paris: Librairie Orientaliste Paul Guethner, 1927), 32, ll. 16–20 (here, at Adad's roaring, the gods of heaven ascend into heaven and the gods of earth descend into the earth).

[22] *ša iddin rigmašu ina šame kima Addi u tarkub gabbi mati ištu rigmišu*, in J. A. Knudtzon, *Die El-Amarna-Tafeln* (Leipzig: Hinrichs, 1915), p. 147: 14–15; and similarly in the Tukulti Ninurta Epic, see W. G. Lambert, *AfO* 18 (1957–8), p. 50: 6. On these various traditions, and others describing other types of gods, see Samuel Loewenstamm, 'Raʿadat ha-Tebaʿ be-Shaʿat Hofaʿat YHWH', in *ʿOz le-David* (David Ben-Gurion Festschrift), pub. by the Israel Bible Society and the World Jewish Bible Society (Jerusalem: Kiryat Sepher, 1964), 508–20; and Moshe Weinfeld, '"Min ha-Shamayim Nilḥamu": Hitʿarbut Gufim Shamaymiyim be-Qerab ʾim ha-ʾOyeb be-Yisrael ube-Mizraḥ ha-Qadum', *EI* 14 (1968), 23–30.

[23] See in Herdner, *CTA* 4. 7. 29, 31, *qlh.qdš[.]b[ʿl.y]tn.... bmt.ʾa[rs].tttn.*

[24] Ibid. *4. 5. 70–1, w[y]tn.qlh.bʿrpt slḥ.lʾarṣ̈.brqm.*

[25] Cf. Wolfgang Helk, *Die Beziehungen Ägyptens zu Vorderasien im 3. und 2. Jahrtausend v. Chr.* (Wiesbaden: Harrassowitz, 1962), 482–5.

lightning.[26] About a millennium later, Marduk, in his battle against the sea monster Ti'amat, 'mounted the storm-chariot (*narkabta*)...(and) harnessed to it a team of four' (*Enuma elish* IV. 50–1); whereas in a recension of the *Atraḫasis* epic we read that 'Adad rode on the four winds...the chariot of the gods'.[27] A related depiction is also reported of Baʿal in Canaanite sources.[28] And finally, in light of the depiction of the roar of Ninurta on his advent upon his chariot,[29] it seems reasonable to conclude that the reference in Ps. 77: 19 to God's thunderous voice 'in the *galgal*' should also be interpreted as the din arising from the wheels of His chariot.[30] An explicit depiction of YHWH riding a horse-drawn chariot (*merkabah*) in His battle against the sea is found in Hab. 3: 8.[31]

The bundles of thematic tradition found in the foregoing sources compress their mythopoeic intuitions into somewhat stereotypic formulas; but these renditions do not in any way neutralize the sensibilities that engender them, or the experiences of the divine that they represent. Psalm 77 must be seen in this light; for while it uses conventional storm imagery to depict the theophany of YHWH at the exodus, the psalm retains a dramatic and living quality. It does so on two accounts. On the level of imagery, the portrayal of the flight of the sea before the presence of God introduces a numinous dimension into the complex of meteorological effects. In so doing, the author leaves the depiction of the divine warrior to the imagination, which is therefore more restrained than the bold anthropomorphisms found in Hab. 3: 10–11.[32] At the same time, the depiction in Psalm 77 retains an aura of mythic realism that is lost in the more artful rendition of the flight of the sea found in Ps. 114: 3–8, where the metaphor of dancing mountains weakens the effect of the sea that views God and flees.

The vitality of the mythopoesis also occurs on the level of narrative voice. Most obviously, the personal crisis of the speaker and his sense of

[26] See in James Pritchard, *Ancient Near Eastern Pictures* (Princeton: Princeton University Press, 1955), 221, no. 689, and p. 322. For an analysis, see E. Douglas Van Buren, *Symbols of the Gods in Mesopotamian Art* (AnOr 23; Pontificium Institutum Biblicum, 1945), 68.

[27] See W. G. Lambert and A. R. Millard, *Atrahasis: The Babylonian Story of the Flood* (Oxford: Clarendon Press, 1969), 122–4, rev. 5, 12 (an Assyrian recension).

[28] The god is told to take his clouds, his winds, his *mdl*, and his rains; see Herdner, *CTA* 5. 5. 6–8. Elsewhere, the word *mdl* occurs parallel to *ṣmd* ('yoke') in the context of harnessing; see Jonas Greenfield, 'Ugaritic mdl and its Cognates', *Bib.* 45 (1964), 537 f. It is therefore reasonable to assume that Baʿal hitched up a storm chariot as well. It is also notable, in this regard, that the expression used of Marduk's act of hitching up his chariot is *iṣmissima*... *naṣmadi*. On these matters, see Moshe Weinfeld, '"Rider of the Clouds" and "Gatherer of the Clouds"', *JANESCU* 5 (1973), 422–4.

[29] See F. Hronzný, 'Sumerisch-babylonische Myth von dem Gotte Ninrag (=Ninib)', *MVAG* 8.5 (1903), 10 (Tablet II, rev. 2–4).

[30] This observation is also noted in Loewenstamm, '*Raʿadat*', 513 n. 14. In Ezekiel's opening vision, the wheels are called *'ofanim* (Ezek. 1: 16); but in a later vision the term *galgal* is used (Ezek. 10: 2).

[31] See further, below.

[32] See the discussion below, where some common features are noted.

divine abandonment undergo an abrupt transformation through his decision to celebrate God's redemption of the nation by the battle waged on their behalf with His mighty arm and weapons of war. On closer examination, one can see that the author has bound the two levels of the psalm into one stylistic whole—by virtue of his repetition of key terms for new purposes. Thus the speaker begins by saying that he will raise up his 'voice' (*qoli*) (v. 1) in prayer, and will 'call God to mind (*ʾazkirah*)' in his sorrow (v. 4), thinking of days 'of old (*mi-qedem*)', and years 'long past' (v. 6); and he goes on to say that he will 'recall (*ʾazkirah*)' his sufferings and 'commune (*ʾasiḥah*)' with himself concerning the absence of divine favour (vv. 7–8). With dramatic intensity, this scene of despair shifts to a celebration of God's deeds, and with it a new use of these terms. The psalmist now says that 'I shall recall (*ʾazkirah*) the mighty acts of YHWH; indeed, I recall (*ʾezkerah*) Your wonders of old (*mi-qedem*), (and) recount (*ʾasiḥah*) all Your works' (v. 11)—when he delivered his people and appeared in the 'sound (*qol*)' of thunder on their behalf.[33]

The narrative voice of the psalm will be even more appreciated through a consideration of other compositional considerations. For example, there is a marked difference in both style and content between the mythic portrayal of the storm scene and divine advent in Ps. 77: 17–20, and the recitation of God's deeds at the exodus presented in vv. 12–16 and 21.[34] This difference suggests that the storm scene has been incorporated secondarily into a celebration of the redemption by the arm of the Lord, and His guidance of the people by the hand of Moses and Aaron (vv. 16, 21). But with this mythopoeic complex in place, the whole depiction of divine victory is altered. In the primary stratum, the speaker evokes God's arm as a mythic metonym for the power of His redemptive act—but without that arm serving any concrete role in the account. The static nature of this figure changes dramatically in the final composition, where the arm functions as one of the active elements in the divine triumph over the sea. The presentation of this entire unit in the voice of the psalmist is thus a creative act of mythopoesis—a dramatic account of God's power in mythic terms. Moreover, in this process, the literary tradition of an ancient storm scene has been re-actualized as living myth. For the speaker of the psalm, there is no separation between myth and history. The two are thoroughly integrated in his mind and, we may add, part of a continuum of divine actions that extend from the past to his own situation. In this respect, the victory myth is not simply an event long ago, *in illo tempore*, but a reality that can and may be realized in the present.

[33] One may also note that the psalmist raises his 'hand' in supplication (v. 3), and celebrates the work of God's 'arm' (v. 16).

[34] It has often been observed that virtually all of the first part of the psalm (except v. 3), including the celebration of the exodus in vv. 12–16 and 21 are all bi-cola, whereas vv. 17–20 has tri-cola.

The mythopoeic tone I am seeking to delineate can be put into a comparative context. The prayer in Isa. 63: 7–19 offers a point of departure. It opens in general praise of 'the kind acts of YHWH' to Israel in the past, when He took them as His people and redeemed them from Egypt (vv. 7–9). These acts are specified at a later point through a series of laments in which the speaker asks: 'Where is He who brought them up from the sea...? Where is He who put in their midst His holy spirit, who made His glorious arm (*zeroʿa*) march at the right hand (*liymin*) of Moses, who divided the waters before them to make Himself a name for all time, who led them through the deeps so that they did not stumble?' (vv. 11–13). For all their pathos and intensity, these indirect queries break up the narrative of redemption and report it as a set of isolated images. The stylistic effect is thus both more rhetorical and more reflective than the recitation in Psalm 77, and this diminishes its mythopoeic immediacy.

Another striking difference is the complete absence of storm imagery in the Isaianic prayer, a factor that considerably reduces its mythic drama and puts the full weight of action on God's arm. At the same time, we may observe that this focus on one feature of the divine action gives the arm a mythic character of a unique sort. Indeed, the phrase 'who made His glorious arm march at the right hand of Moses' (*ha-molikh liymin Moshe zeroʿa tifʾarto*) indicates that for the speaker God's mighty arm functions as a hypostatic reality that endows the right hand of Moses with divine power. When Moses acts, God is acting; and when God is acting, Moses' arm is seen. One can hardly imagine a more mythic dimension of heroic action, for in this case the divine world and the human world completely intersect. It may be supposed that this bold figure is the product of inner-biblical mythopoesis. Faced with the phrase 'Then Moses extended his hand over the sea, and YHWH drove back (*va-yolekh*) the sea with a mighty east wind' (Exod. 14: 21), a later reader would have been puzzled by the two actions portrayed here.[35] Not wanting to assume that Moses initiated an act that God then executed, he took a different hermeneutical turn and filled in the narrative gap by fusing the two actions. Drawing upon the earlier language, the prophet now states that Moses' human hand marks the presence of God's own arm in human history.

B. IN PROPHETIC LITERATURE

We spoke earlier of the situations of crisis that characterize the psalms referring to the divine combat with the sea. Whether that crisis is personal (Psalm 77), national (Psalm 74), or royal (Psalm 89), ancient acts of mythic

[35] For the later, rabbinic treatment of this duality in *Mekhilta de-Rabbi Ishmael* (Horovitz–Rabin, 102 f.), see Daniel Boyarin, *Intertextuality and the Reading of Midrash* (Bloomington: Indiana University Press, 1990), 95 f.

power are recalled before God, in the hope that the speaker may induce a re-manifestation of His redemptive power on earth. As remarked, the pathos of the appeals makes it unlikely that the precedents mentioned are either fable or metaphor, since such an assumption would empty the prayers of the very claims upon which they depend. The prophetic evidence to which we now turn deepens and extends these points. Here too, the drama of a divine combat against the sea betokens a manifestation of divine power sufficient to terminate a problematic situation of one sort or another. In these cases, as well, the concrete realism of the images provides an objective correlative for the intense hopes that underlie them; and it is just this quality of the images that suggests that we are in the presence of living myth—and not effusions of poetic embellishment.

The prophetic prayer in Isa. 51: 9–11 is a striking example of the way the evocation of mythic precedents serves to intensify and give dramatic focus to the people's expectations. Speaking among the nation in the Babylonian exile, and comforting them with the imminence of God's saving arm (Isa. 51: 5), the prophet suddenly cries out:

> Awake, awake, clothe yourself with might, O arm of YHWH!
> Awake as in days of old, as in ages past!
> Was it not you that smote Rahab, that pierced Tanin?!
> Was it not you that dried up Yam,
> The waters of the great deep,
> That made the depths of the sea a road for the redeemed?!
> So let the ransomed of YHWH return,
> And come to Zion with shouting, crowned with eternal joy.
> Let them attain joy and gladness, and may sorrow and sighing flee.[36]
> (Isa. 51: 9–11)

In this prayer, the arm (*zeroʿa*) of the Lord is addressed as an animate reality capable of responding to human entreaty. Indeed, in distinct contrast to the mythic sequence in Ps. 74: 13–15, where God is repeatedly addressed as the 'You' (*ʾattah*) who performed the great deeds of the past, it is now the arm itself that is called 'you' (*ʾat*) and beckoned to be aroused as an active and saving divine power—again in the present, as formerly in the past.

Two ancient events are evoked. The first is the primordial battle and slaying of the sea monster: 'Was it not you that smote (*ha-maḥtzebet*) Rahab, that pierced (*meḥolelet*) Tannin?' This narrative epitome echoes older Canaanite versions. As noted earlier, Baʿal 'smashed (*tmḥṣ*)' the sea serpent Lotan, and Anat destroyed Tunnanu. Moreover, in a late Israelite reflex of the battle scene, we read that God 'smashed (*maḥatz*) Rahab' and

[36] This appeal appears to precede the decree of Cyrus in 538 BCE, permitting Judaeans to return to their homeland—and thus is also prior to the celebration of Cyrus as YHWH's anointed one in Isa. 45: 1. The prayer is in the context of intense expectation (note the term *qarob*, 'near'; cf. Ezek. 12: 23), when God's arms (*zeroʿay*) would judge and rescue the nations (v. 5).

that 'His hand (*yado*) pierced (*ḥolelah*) the slant serpent' (Job 26: 12–13).[37] The use here of the verb *ḥalal* with the motif of a piercing hand, clearly links the Joban version of the myth with that in Isa. 51: 9;[38] and the use of the verb *maḥatz* in that context and in Baʿal's own victorious battle against the sea dragon in Ugaritic mythology, gives strong reason to presume that the verb *ha-maḥtzebet* in Isa. 51: 9 should be emended to *ha-moḥetzet*; and the occurrence of just this latter reading in the large Isaiah scroll from Qumran confirms the point.[39] It may be added that the verbs in this passage are participial in form, thus underscoring the agency of the arm and its fame as 'the smasher' of Rahab, and 'the piercer' of Tannin.

Participial verbs also occur in the second event depicted, the exodus from Egypt. Here, too, the arm of YHWH is portrayed as the active power in drying up the waters, so that the people might cross over. And further, just as the sea monsters mentioned in the first episode occur in their nominal form (Rahab, Tannin), it deserves emphasis that the victory of the arm in the second event was against Yam—and not the generic 'sea'. This being so, one may suppose that the parallel reference to 'the waters of the great deep (*tehom rabbah*)' actually conceals the mythic epithet Tehom Rabbah ('Mighty Tehom'). If this reconstruction is correct, we may find in Isa. 51: 10 an otherwise unattested West Semitic variant of the monster Tiʾamat.[40]

The epitomization of the hand of YHWH as the vanquisher of Yam during the exodus invites comparison with the song of Moses in Exodus 15, where the divine victory is twice praised with reference to the right hand of the Lord. The first instance is a general laudation: 'Your right hand, O YHWH, is glorious in strength / Your right hand, O YHWH, crushes the foe'—and sunk them 'like a stone (*ke-ʾeben*)' (v. 6); whereas the second celebrates the

[37] Given the nominal references to Rahab and Naḥash Bariaḥ here, one should prefer the reading 'in His strength he suppressed Yam' to *ha-yam* ('the sea') in Job. 26: 12. Further evidence for an old battle scene has been obscured by later scribes in Job 26: 13, whose impossible *be-ruḥo shamayim shifrah* ('by whose wind the heavens were calmed'; NJPS) should be restored to *be-ruḥo sam yam shifrah* ('by whose wind he put Yam into a snare'), as noted already by Naftali H. Tur-Sinai, *The Book of Job* (Jerusalem: Kiryat Sepher, 1957), 383–4. He correctly pointed to the fact that Marduk caught Tiʾamat in a net (*saparu*), in *Enuma elish* IV. 95 (*ušparirma belum saparašu ušalmeši*, 'the lord spread his net, he enfolded her'). It may be added that the noun *shifrah* occurs in parallel to *noʾd*, and thus also refers to a bag of some sort. On the latter point, see Greenstein, 'The Snaring of Sea in the Baʿal Epic', *Maarav*, 3 (1982), 208 n. 67; and also his attempt to find a Ugaritic parallel for the snaring motif, pp. 208–16.

[38] The piercing motif also occurs in Ps. 89: 11, 'You pierced (*dikkʾita*) Rahab like a corpse (*ḥalal*)'.

[39] It has often been assumed that *maḥtzebet* is a popular or accidental combination of the verbs *maḥatz* and *ḥatzab* ('hew'). Notably, the two verbs are parallel in Ugaritic passages (V AB B 5–7, 19–20, 29–30).

[40] Cf. the title [^{d}*A*] .*AB.BA.GAL* (i.e. [*ta*]*mtu rabitu*]) found in an Akkadian text from Ugarit (RS 17.33 obv. 4'); this deified sea serves as a witness in a treaty between the Hittite king Mursilis and his Ugaritic vassal Niqmepa. See Jean Nougayrol, *Le Palais royale d'Ugarit, 4: Textes accadiens des Archives Sud (Archives internationales)* (Mission de Ras Shamra 12; Paris: Imprimerie Nationale, 1956), 85.

destruction of the enemy, which had boasted that it would raise its sword and destroy the Israelites with 'my hand' (v. 9): 'You (YHWH) extended Your right hand and the earth swallowed them up' (v. 12). These references are noteworthy on two accounts. First, the praise is directed to the Lord of battles, whose right hand worked wonders, and not to the hand itself; and second, the victory that is highlighted and repeatedly emphasized in this song is the one wrought against human enemies (the charioteers of Egypt) and not the sea *per se*. Accordingly, even where the hymnist does refer to the congealing of the waters by the blast of divine fury (v. 8), this reference plays a relatively minor role overall. The combined result is therefore to diminish the mythic effect of the account.

Another mythic aspect of Exodus 15 should be mentioned in this context. For just like Isa. 51: 9–10, which links a primordial divine victory against the sea to another one in historical time, so also in Exodus 15 two moments of divine victory are correlated. This point can be corroborated by observing that the thematic continuation of the reference to God bringing the nation 'in might to your holy sanctuary' (v. 13) is the exultation 'You will bring them and plant them in Your own mountain, the place You made to dwell in, O YHWH' (v. 17). In their present form, however, these two passages are disrupted by a reference to the terror of the Canaanite nations at the news of God's great deeds (vv. 14–16).[41] Significantly, in that interpolation it is stated that when God's arm was empowered (*bi-gdol zeroʿakha*; v. 16) the trembling peoples became as 'still as stone (*nidmu ke-ʾeben*)' (v. 15). Set within the context of the exodus tradition, this imagery serves to link the hostile nations in Canaan (metonymically) with the congealed waters (*ned nozlim*) at the exodus, and thereby mythicize the conquest—insofar as the Canaanite enemy is now rendered helpless by God's mighty arm, like the waters years before, when the nation of Israel 'passes' through them into the promised land. The editorial result is to establish a mythic parallelism between the two events.[42]

A further development in this direction appears in Josh. 4: 13–17, where the crossing of the Jordan is depicted in terms of the crossing of the sea during the exodus: when the priests entered the river with the holy ark, the flowing waters immediately congealed 'like a wall (*ned*)' (v. 16), thus allowing the people to cross into Canaan on dry land.[43] This depiction echoes

[41] The reference to the terror of the nations is similar to that found in Josh. 2: 9–10. In both cases the Canaanites 'hear' (*shameʿu*; *shamaʿnu*) the news of God's victory, and 'melt' (*namogu*) out of 'fear' (*ʾeimatah*; *ʾeimatkhem*). Cf. this topos in Deut. 2: 25.

[42] I agree with Samuel Loewenstamm, *Masoret Yitziʾat Mitzrayim Be-Hishtalshelutah* (Jerusalem: Magnes Press, 1967),113, that v. 17 refers to the Temple of Solomon; but it does not follow that the 'only possible' way to view the conquest of Canaan depicted in this hymn is in the light of David's military victories.

[43] On the issue of typologies in the Hebrew Bible, see my *Biblical Interpretation in Ancient Israel* (Oxford: Clarendon Press, 1985), 350–79.

the mounting of the sea into a 'wall (*ned*)' (Exod. 15: 8), when the ancient Israelites fled their Egyptian pursuers. To be sure, the narrative of the crossing of the Jordan also shows signs of a miracle tale; but this feature notwithstanding, its more dominant effect lies in the common chord it strikes with the exodus paradigm, and in what it reveals of the complex fusion of the mythic imagination and historical memory in ancient Israel.

The striking description in Exod. 15: 16 of the empowering or 'lengthening' of God's arm (*bi-gdol zeroʿakha*) provides a concrete counterpoint to the mythic statement in Isa. 50: 2. In this case it is not the prophet who beseeches the arm of God to be aroused, but God Himself who complains of the people's lack of confidence in His saving might. 'Why, when I came, was no one there; why, when I called, did no one respond?[44] Is My arm too short (*ha-qatzor qatzrah yadi*) to redeem, have I not the power to save? Behold, when I roar (*be-gaʿarati*) I dry up [the] sea (*yam*), and turn rivers (*nehorot*) into desert.' In the light of the motif of God's arm, and the use elsewhere of the divine roar in connection with his blast against the waters at creation (Ps. 104: 6–7) and the exodus (Ps. 106: 19), it is apparent that Isa. 50: 2 utilizes the old mythologem of battle in connection with God's present work of redemption.[45] In other cases, the mythic motifs of storm and battle are used to depict the advent of God to avenge evil. In Nahum 1: 3–6, we read that 'YHWH travels in a whirlwind, clouds are the dust of His feet. He roars at the sea and dries it up... The earth heaves before Him... and the mountains melt... Who can stand before His fury? His anger pours out like fire.' Of even greater mythic intensity and violence is the apocalyptic tone sounded in Isa. 30: 27–8, 30–3, when God comes to destroy Assyria.

> Behold, YHWH comes from afar, with blazing nose the Name of God comes;[46]
> His lips full of fury, His tongue like a consuming fire;
> And His breath like a raging flood,
> Reaching halfway up the neck...
> Surely YHWH will make His thunderous voice heard,[47]
> And display the sweep of His arm in raging fury,[48]
> In a consuming blaze of fire,
> In tempest, and rainstorm, and hailstones...;

[44] It is striking that the interrogative *lamah* ('why?') used commonly to express a cry of human lament before God (cf. Pss. 44: 24–5; 74: 1, 11), is used here to express a divine lament and reproach to the people.

[45] For the figure of God's short hand, the people's lack of response, and the manifestation of the saving hand, see Isa. 59: 1, 16–19; and cf. 63: 1–6.

[46] This use of a divine Name in the context of God's advent (v. 27) is difficult, and its use may be a later attempt to qualify the bold anthropomorphisms. The term is absent in v. 30.

[47] Reading *hed qolo* (lit. 'the reverberation of his voice') for *hod qolo*, 'His majestic voice' (v. 30), with Arnold Ehrlich, *Randglossen zur Hebraïschen Bibel* (Leipzig: Hinrichs, 1912), ii. 111.

[48] For this sense of *ve-naḥat zeroʿo* (v.30), as meaning that God sets forth his arm against the enemy, see Rashi and Kimḥi.

His fire pit has been made both deep and wide, Stoked with fire and wood,
And with the breath of YHWH burning in it like a stream of sulphur.

Such depictions of divine wrath combine diverse images of volcanic and tempestuous fury. Their unrestrained anthropomorphic concreteness—focused on nostrils, lips, tongue, breath, and voice—produces an iconographic cluster of a terrifying sort. Of equal length and quality is the advent of YHWH as a god of storm and battle pictured in Habakkuk 3. However, this advent does not occur in an oracle, but constitutes a theophany set within an opening petition and concluding response. The petition (v. 2) recalls other petitionary prayers, since the speaker first turns to God and says: 'I have heard (*shamaʿti*) of Your renown' and 'deeds', and then requests that He turn from 'wrath' (*rogez*) and once again manifest His salvation as of old (cf. Pss. 44: 2–8, 27; 77: 12–13; 143: 5–12).[49] The final unit harks back to the beginning with the words, 'I heard (*shamaʿti*) and my being quaked (*vatirgaz*)', though its reference is to the preceding vision and its effect upon the speaker (vv. 16–19).[50]

The intervening section begins with an announcement of God's advent from his abode on Mount Paran in a blaze of light (vv. 3–4; cf. Deut. 33: 2), causing the nations and surrounding nature to tremble at the sight (vv. 5–7).[51]

His majesty covers the heavens,
His splendour fills the earth;[52]
Its effulgence is like light,
Emitting rays from His hand—
And therein is hidden His might.
Pestilence goes before Him, plague follows behind.
When He stands, the earth shudders;
When He glances, nations tremble,
Primeval mountains burst apart, ancient hills cave in,
His ways are primordial.[53] (vv. 3–6)

[49] Cf. above for this motif in Exod. 15: 8; Deut. 2: 25; and Josh. 2: 9–10. Psalm 44 will be considered more carefully below.

[50] For this reference to the hearing in v. 16, cf. Ehrlich, *Randglossen*, ii. 455. One should note that the verb *ragaz* is also used regarding the quaking of the nations in v. 7, thus serving as a theme word that integrates various levels of the text. The structure of Habakkuk 3, and its sequence of actions, has been frequently studied. Cf. Theodore Hiebert, *God of My Victory: the Ancient Hymn in Habakkuk 3* (HSM 38; Atlanta: Scholars Press, 1986), with a full bibiography.

[51] In light of the fear motif in v. 7, I am inclined to accept the emendation of *taḥat ʾavon* to *taḥat ʾOn* ('On [Heliopolis] will be frightened'), proposed by Felix Perles, *Analekten zur Textkritik des Alten Testaments* (Munich: Theodor Ackermann, 1895), 66. The juxtaposition of Cushan and On causes no difficulty, since Cush is often linked to Egypt (Gen. 10: 6; Isa. 20: 3–5).

[52] The word *tehillato* is from the root *h-l-l*, and means 'splendour' here, as also in Job 29: 3 (see Kimḥi).

[53] I follow Yitzhak Avishur, *Studies in Hebrew and Ugaritic Psalms* (Jerusalem: Magnes Press, 1994), 170, who suggests that the word *halikhot* here and in Ps. 68: 25 does not refer to

Such a theophany is a manifestation of that brilliant radiance frequently reported of divinities in Mesopotamian sources,[54] and which surrounds YHWH here as a garment of light, concealing His inner glory, just as in other theophany accounts His presence is enclosed within a cloud (cf. Exod. 40: 34–7). In this account the great light of the manifestation also reveals an anthropomorphic presence: light streams from God's hand; and He stands and glances. Moreover, in this appearance YHWH is surrounded by the destructive powers of *deber* and *reshef* ('pestilence' and 'plague'). These powers are among the divine elements or spirits that surround God's heavenly throne, and do His earthly bidding ('He makes the winds His messengers, fiery flames His servants'; Ps. 104: 4). For example, in one depiction of the upper world, we read that 'cloud (*ʿanan*) and thick mist surround Him, righteousness and justice are the base of His throne; fire is His vanguard, burning His enemies on every side' (Ps. 97: 2–3).

The mythic nature of these depictions of the divine entourage should not be overlooked, or reduced to mere literary figures. Indeed, it bears mention that the reference to 'righteousness and justice (*tzedeq u-mishpaṭ*)' in Ps. 97: 2 as the supports of the heavenly throne is not to some kind of moral hyperbole—but to actual divine powers or beings, like the gods Kettu and Mešaru in Mesopotamian sources,[55] and the pair Sdq and Mšr who appear in lists of the Canaanite pantheon.[56] The latter deities are also referred to as Sydyk and Misor in later Greek sources that preserve the old Phoenician traditions of Philo of Byblos.[57] Moreover, among other attendants, *ʿnn ʾilm* ('cloud of the gods') is recorded as an emissary of Baʿal in Canaanite sources;[58] and

'processions' of God, but rather to his behaviour and conduct. He also notes the similar Akkadian expression, *alakki ili* (cf. *CAD* A, p. 297).

[54] See A. Leo Oppenheim, 'Akkadian pul(u)ḫ(t)u and melammu', *JAOS* 63 (1943), 31–4; and more fully, Elena Cassin, *La Splendeur divine: Introduction à l'étude de la mentalité mésopotamienne* (Civilisation et Société, 8; Paris and The Hague: Mouton & Co., 1968). Moshe Weinfeld, 'Ha-ʾEl ha-Boreiʾ be-Bereiʾshit 1 ube-Nebuʾat Yeshayahu ha-Sheini', *Tarbiz*, 37 (1967–8), 131–2, has shown the relationship between Akkadian *melammu* and Hebrew *kabod* ('glory').

[55] See in Erich Ebeling, *Beiträge zur Kenntnis der babylonischer Religion* (Leipzig: Hinrich, 1886–1901), 96 ff., where these gods appear in a ritual text with Shamash and Adad. Cf. also in F. Thureau-Dangin, *Rituels accadiens* (Paris: E. Leroux, 1921), 93, l. 26, where Mešaru is worshipped with Adad at Uruk.

[56] See Johannes C. de Moor, 'The Semitic Pantheon of Ugarit', *UF* 2 (1970), 196, 225.

[57] See in Eusebius, *Praeparatio Evangelica* 1, 10, 13. See now the critical text and translation of Harold W. Attridge and Robert A. Oden, *Philo of Biblos: The Phoenician History* (CBQM 9; Washington, DC: Catholic Biblical Association of America, 1981), 44–7. Cf. the earlier edition and discussion of Carl Clemen, *Die Phönikische Religion nach Philo von Byblos* (*MVAG* 42.3; Leipzig: J. C. Hinrichs, 1939), par. 14, 25, 38 (pp. 24, 28, 31), and p. 55; and also note the remarks of Samuel A. Loewenstamm, 'Philon mi-Gebal', *Peraqim*, 2 (1971), 319.

Eusebius, ibid. 1, 10, 25 also says that Sydyk bore Asklepios. Notably, Damascius, in *Vit. Isid.* (in *PG*, 103, col. 1304 c) states that Esmunos (Phoenician Ešmun) is the son of Sadykos.

[58] See *CTA* 3. D. 4. 76, and the discussion of Johannes C. de Moor, *The Seasonal Pattern in the Ugaritic Myth of Baʿlu* (AOAT 16; Neukirchen–Vlyn: Neukirchner Verlag, 1971), 129–30.

Resheph is also known as a Canaanite deity of pest and plague.[59] His role as one of the attendants in YHWH's entourage in Hab. 3: 5 shows that he also had a place among the heavenly host in ancient Israel. A striking near-contemporary example of the role of divinities in the military service of a chief god occurs in the annals of the Assyrian king Ashurbanipal, where it is said that 'Ishtar rains fire, Erra smashes the enemy, Ninurta cuts the neck of the enemy, and Nusku, who goes at the command of Ashur and Ninlil, takes his place at the head of the army and smites the enemy'.[60] Speaking of the imminent destruction of Assyria, the prophet Nahum reflects all these mythic realities when he says that 'YHWH takes vengeance upon His enemies, He rages against His foes... He travels in whirlwind and storm, and a cloud (*ʿanan*) is the dust of His feet. He rebukes the sea and dries it up, and He makes all rivers fail' (Nahum 1: 2–4).

Accordingly, it is evident that Habakkuk describes YHWH's advent in the common language of ancient Near Eastern myth, having asked Him to 'renew' His great deeds of old in the present. The Lord makes good this request, quite precisely; for as the prophet envisions YHWH's overwhelming military approach, it reminds him of ancient battles against the seas.

> Are You angry, O YHWH, with Neharim;
> Do You fume against Neharim, or rage against Yam—
> That You are driving Your steeds, Your victory chariot?
> Your bow is bared and drawn;...[61]
> You cleave the earth into streams.
> The mountains see You and quake, waters gush torrents;[62]
> Tehom roars aloud, raising its hand aloft.
> Sun (and) moon stand still,

[59] See the comprehensive discussion of Diethelm Conrad, 'Der Gott Reschef', *ZAW* 83 (1971), 157–83. It also seems that Resheph may have been a helper of Baʿal when he destroyed Tannin. See *KTU* 1.82.1–3 (*UT* 1001.1–3), and the discussion of John Day, 'New Light on the Mythological Background of the Allusion to Resheph in Habakkuk iii 5', *VT* 29 (1979), 353–5; and also in *God's Conflict with the Dragon and the Sea* (Cambridge: Cambridge University Press, 1985), 106. In line 1 of the text the verb *mḥṣ* is again used.

[60] See M. Streck, *Annals of Ashurbanipal*, ii, IX: 79 f. This text is adduced by M. Weinfeld, 'Min ha-Shamayim Nilḥamu', 28, also with reference to Hab. 3: 5. Also note the statement regarding Marduk: 'before him (goes) Enlil, and behind (him) Nergal' (*ša panušu Enlil, kutallašu Nergal*); see in E. von Weiher, *Der babylonischer Gott Nergal* (AOAT 11; Neukirchen-Vluyn: Neukirchner Verlag, 1971), 67.

[61] The phrase *shebuʿot maṭṭot ʾomer* is a notorious crux. The suggestion by H. St John Thackery, 'Primitive Lectionary Notes in the Psalm of Habakkuk', *JTS* 12 (1910–11), 195–202, that the words refer to readings in the triennial cycle of Scriptural readings, remains a brilliant and intriguing hypothesis. Umberto Cassuto, 'Chapter iii of Habakkuk and the Ras Shamra Texts', in *Biblical and Oriental Studies* (1st pub. 1938; Jerusalem: Magnes Press, 1975), ii. 12 proposed that MT *ʾomer* is, in this battle context, the mace called *ʾaymr* and wielded by Baʿal in his battle against Yam (see *CTA* 2. 4. 19). But this sense does not fit easily into the present setting.

[62] The words *zerem mayim* can mean a torrential flow, as in Isa. 28: 2; but perhaps read *zarmu mayim ʿabot*, 'the clouds pour rain', with Ps. 77: 18.

Moving by the light of Your arrows, by the splendour of Your flashing spear.
You stride the earth in fury, crushing nations in rage. (vv. 8–12)

The text goes on to describe the brutal destruction of the human enemies with verbs (*maḥatzta*, 'You smashed'; *naqabta*, 'You pierced') resonant with mythic overtones of combats with the sea (cf. Job 26: 12–13, *maḥatz rahab... ḥolelah yado naḥash bariaḥ*, 'He smashed Rahab... His hand pierced slant Nahash'). In this way, the mythic and historical realities are completely interfused. Indeed, for the prophet, who invokes an ancient battle between YHWH and the sea monsters Neharim and Yam,[63] there is no gap between primordial and contemporary acts of divine power: they are part of one continuum of *magnalia dei*—the ancient deeds of God remembered and invoked in the present, when God's saving presence was felt to be absent.

Phenomenologically speaking, however, there is a significant difference between these human petitions to God which focus on the past, and divine prophecies to humans which focus on the future. Two instances may be noted. The first of these is exemplified by Isa. 11: 11–16, where YHWH promises that He will 'again' send forth 'His hand' to redeem His people from their far-flung dispersion (v. 11). 'YHWH will dry up the tongue of the Egyptian sea.—He will raise his hand over the river (Euphrates): His wind will split the sea,[64] and break it into seven streams, so that it can be trodden with shoes. Thus there shall be a highway for the other part of His people out of Assyria, just as there was for Israel when it left Egypt' (vv. 15–16). In this description, it is hard to miss the typological comparison of the new redemption with the old—a veritable new exodus—and the presentation of God's work of salvation in terms of a mythic combat with the sea. As in other cases, He manifests His hand, blasts with His wind, and splits the sea.[65] As an event to come, it conjoins the mythologems of the past with those of the future. The

63 The battle between Baʿal and Naharu and Yammu is a central aspect of Canaanite myth; see esp. *CTA* 2. 4. 12–13, and 19–20. It is also important to note that in other Hebrew versions of Habakkuk 3 there was apparently a reference to a battle against Mot, the god of death, since instead of MT *maḥatzta roʾsh mi-beit rashaʿ* ('you smashed the head of the enemy's house'; v. 13) the LXX reads 'you smashed the head of wicked Death (*thanaton*)'. This presumes a reading *be-mot* ('against Mot'), instead of *mi-beit* ('from the house'). I have no doubt that the LXX preserves an authentic tradition. Earlier, Cassuto, 'Chapter iii of Habakkuk', 12, simply emended *mi-beit* to *mavet*; but it is possible that some scribe heard *mavet* (*mvt*) and transcribed *mbt*, which led to the present vocalization of the grapheme. For other uses of *thanatos* that suggest a divinity, see *Wisdom of Solomon* 1: 16 and 2: 24, and the discussion of Yehoshua Amir, 'The Case of the Death of Death in the *Wisdom of Solomon*', *JSS* (1979), 157ff. Other biblical reflexes of Mot shall be considered in the conclusions, below.

64 Reading *baqaʿ yam*, 'split the sea', instead of the faulty MT *baʿayam*. The verb *baqaʿ* occurs regularly in biblical accounts of the exodus (cf. Exod. 14: 16; Isa. 63: 12; and Ps. 78: 13, which reads *baqaʿ yam*); and in accounts of theophany, like Hab. 3: 9. Cf. already in my *Biblical Interpretation*, 355 n. 100.

65 The splitting of the water into seven streams echoes the Canaanite theme of Baʿal killing Lotan of 'seven heads' (*šbʿt.rʾašm*); cf. *CTA* 5. 1. 1, and the discussion above.

people are promised a new occurrence in the mythic events of yesteryear. Accordingly, myth now articulates the shape of hope, not just its ancient memory.

Of a similar kind is the prophecy in Isa. 27: 1—though its promise that 'In that day YHWH will punish,[66] with His cruel, great, (and) mighty sword, Leviathan the slant serpent (*naḥash bariaḥ*), Leviathan the twisting serpent (*naḥash ʿaqalaṭon*); He will slay the dragon (*tannin*) in the sea' makes no reference to past battles. The entire mythic portrayal is here cast towards the future, as a great event to come. Precisely what this drama could mean as a promise to people living in historical time is unclear, since there is no correlation between the mythic battle to come and Israel's life among the nations. Moreover, it is also not stated whether the slaying of 'the dragon in the sea' is the same act as the preceding promise of punishing Leviathan, or is another and different one. Nor can one determine from this oracle whether or not these monsters are related to those slain by YHWH in primordial time (cf. Isa. 51: 9)—or, indeed, what such a mythic recurrence might mean. All that one may conclude from the language of this text is that the creatures mentioned are somehow real embodiments of evil and chaos, and not just symbols of historical kingdoms or powers.[67] As for the mythic events of the past, or those to come: these constitute mythic gaps that the later rabbinic sages sought to fill.[68]

[66] Translating *yifqod* as 'punish', as in Exod. 20: 5 and 34: 7. The verb *paqad* is a theme word recurring in the oracular anthology leading up to Isa. 27: 1 (see Isa. 26: 14, 16, 21; also 27: 3).

[67] There is no internal reason to assume that the text is using symbols or allegory here; hence all such attempts, beginning with the Targum and including medieval commentators (cf. Kimḥi, who refers to Leviathan as a 'parable' for 'strong pagan kings'), are external projections, seeking to demythologize or historicize the prophecy. For a modern example, see Day, *God's Conflict*, 112, where he says that 'Leviathan in Isa. 27: 1 most probably denotes Egypt but it could be Babylon or Persia'. It is hard to know what is learned from such speculations, and on what basis it proceeds.

[68] See below, Part II.

3
Personalization and Historicization of the Combat Motif: In Prayer and Prophecy

In the preceding discussion, the main subject was the myth of the divine combat with the sea—both in the *Urzeit* of world origins, and in the *Endzeit* to come for the nation in travail. In all cases, this myth was repeatedly revised and incorporated into prayers and prophecies to meet the needs of changing circumstances or concerns. But however varied the voice of the speaker who refers to these mythic events, or who is invested in their reality and recurrence, the concern is with communal crises, and not a difficulty in the life of any specific individual or personality. Moreover, the *magnalia dei* referred to serve as mythic prototypes for the divine power and aid requested for the nation. The events in time past thus have their own independent status separate from the contexts in which the speaker exists. The cases wherein God prophesies a new iteration of victory confirm this point.

Quite different are the cases of mythopoesis where these mythic exemplars are variously personalized or historicized. On these occasions, features of the mythic trope of combat are applied to an individual or nation and produce a complex metaphor of identity; and it is just this fusion of differences (of a person with a dragon, for example) that is rhetorically exploited by the speaker.[1] Accordingly, for all their fantastical qualities, these metaphors concretize a correlation perceived between a given person or nation and the mythologem, and in so doing they not only reactualize the myth in dramatic ways, but give human life an ironic dimension. This process of ironization through mythic attribution saves the image from veering into the absurd or from totally encumbering the rhetoric. Hence whereas myths derive their effect precisely because they narrate something ancient and believed true, these mythic metaphors open up an ironic space between the image (the dragon or the sea) and its vehicle (the person or the nation) and are effective

[1] Cf. Douglas Berggren, 'The Use and Abuse of Metaphor, I', *Review of Metaphysics*, 61 (1962), 237: '[M]etaphor constitutes the indispensable principle for integrating diverse phenomena and perspectives, without sacrificing their differences'. See also Ian G. Barbour, *Myths, Models and Metaphors: A Comparative Study of Science and Religion* (San Francisco: Harper & Row, 1974), 12–13: 'A metaphor proposes analogies between the normal context of a word and the new context into which it is introduced...There is a tension between affirmation and negation, for in analogy there are both similarities and differences'; and 'a metaphor is not a useful fiction, a mere pretense, a game of make-believe without relation to reality; it asserts that there are significant analogies between the things compared'.

precisely because they are perceived to be both true and not true at the same time.

Job 7: 12 provides a concise example of this mythopoeic process. Exasperated by the false comfort of his friends, Job turns to God and complains without restraint: 'Am I Yam or Tannin that You have set a guard (*mishmar*) upon me?' The queries here are obviously ironical, just like the rhetorical questions posed in Hab. 3: 8, where the prophet envisions God's awesome advent and asks if it is with Neharim or Yam that He is angry, since He now rides upon the seas in His heavenly chariot.[2] In both cases, the speaker uses mythic images to express his great astonishment at the display of divine force against humans;[3] but the difference is that whereas the prophet stays within the frame of a mythic depiction begun with the description of God's approach, Job shifts conceptual frames as he underscores his private torment by asking God if He thinks that He is battling ancient sea monsters when He punishes him with such unchecked power.

This correlation is clearly paradoxical and pulls in opposite directions. On the one hand, by personalizing the old mythologem, Job is not asking for a literal answer—since at the level of fact he is certainly not a sea dragon that could threaten or challenge God, and that requires active restraint; whereas, on the other hand, by thus posing an ironic identification with this monster, Job actually succeeds in suggesting a certain analogy between his own embattled plight and the subjugation of the ancient sea serpents at God's hand. Indeed, it is just this identification—at once absurd and real—that actualizes the ancient mythologem on the personal plane and gives Job's query its particular power.[4] At the same time, one must emphasize that the whole rhetorical purpose of this act of mythopoesis is to undermine its own plausibility (i.e. that Job is Yam), and thereby convince God to curtail the violence that evoked the imagery in the first place.

The mythopoesis in Psalm 44 is different in form and function. On the one hand, the prayer harks back to the laments and petitions found in Psalms 74 and 77, examined earlier, since here too the speaker makes importuning references to having 'heard (*shamaʿnu*)' of God's great 'deeds (*poʿal paʿalta*)'

[2] For this and related types of rhetorical questions, see Moshe Held, 'Rhetorical Questions in Ugaritic and Biblical Hebrew', *EI* 9 (1969), 71–9.

[3] The image of a guard against the sea is not otherwise known in biblical mythic sources, and the old comparison of this text with *Enuma elish* IV. 139–40, in which the waters of defeated Tiʾamat are held in check, has been rightly rejected insofar as the image in Job 7: 12 indicates an active divine restraint of sea monsters; cf. David Diewert, 'Job 7; 12: *Yam, Tannin* and the Surveillance of Job', *JBL* 106 (1987), 204. Canaanite parallels of the subjugation of Tannin by a muzzle are not certain (see ibid. 206 f., with literature); and thus J. Gerald Janzen, 'Another Look at God's Watch over Job (7: 12)', *JBL* 108 (1989), 110 f., has proposed comparing *Enuma elish* IV. 41–2, 110–14 (where winds hem Tiʾamat in) with our passage, and translating *mishmar* in an active combative sense (as a 'siege guard').

[4] Paul Weiss, *Nine Basic Arts* (Carbondale: University of Illinois Press: 1961), 164–6, argues that any metaphor is implicitly akin to a counterfactual statement.

in 'days of old (*qedem*)' (Ps. 44: 2); and personally addresses Him as his 'king' (*'attah ... malki*) who performed these acts with 'Your hand (*yadkha*) ... Your right hand and Your arm (*yeminkha u-zeroʿakha*)' (vv. 3–4). The notable difference is that, in the other retrospectives, God's victory over the sea in primordial times or at the exodus was praised, whereas now the marked achievement is His dispossession of the nations and the planting of Israel in their homeland (v. 3; cf. Exod. 15: 17). Moreover, like these other petitions, the speaker also emphasizes that God has 'rejected (*zanaḥta*)' His people, and left them prey to 'taunting revilers (*meḥaref u-megaddef*)' (vv. 9, 17). For this reason, the psalmist concludes the prayer by calling upon God to 'arise (*qumah*)' to power, so that His people may be saved as befits 'Your faithfulness (*ḥasdekha*)' (v. 27).

At first sight, this prayer seems to omit any reference to the theme of divine combat. However, the close affinity between the language of this psalm and others of the same type, where the theme does in fact occur, urges a careful inspection of the prayer; and this reveals a striking subjectivization of the mythologem that we have been tracking. Indeed, in a bold trope, the speaker stresses the ongoing steadfastness of the nation to God—even 'though You have pierced us (*dikkiʾtanu*) instead of Tannim,[5] and covered us over with darkest gloom' (v. 19). One can hardly miss the allusion to the theomachy motif here—a matter reinforced by the similar formulation of the strife in Ps. 89: 11, where YHWH's power is praised because 'You pierced (*dikkiʾta*) Rahab like a corpse with Your mighty arm.' The difference between the two passages is that now the sea monster is replaced by the covenant nation, and the ancient victory over chaos is portrayed as an act of divine injustice. The ironic extension of the motif is thus doubly paradoxical: it creates a metaphoric identification of the sea monster with Israel, in order to dramatize the people's suffering at divine hands; and it evokes God's ancient strife with Tannim, in order to stress the present case of misplaced divine aggression. The result is an inverted actualization of the old mythologem and a singular act of theological effrontery—in the hope of a restoration of God's might.

Such personalizations of the combat motif demonstrate the living power of the mythologem in religious consciousness, and the collapsing of the boundaries between myth and personal experience. The conjunction of myth and history takes a different expression in those cases where there is a clear historicization of the motif. Particularly instructive are Ezek. 29: 2–6 and its variant in 32: 1–8, where the Pharaoh of Egypt is portrayed as a

[5] Tannim is like Tannin; cf. Ezek. 29: 3 and 32: 2. This term may be based on a false construal of the ending *-in* in Tannin as an Aramaic masculine plural, which was then changed to the regular Hebrew form. Many interpreters propose reading 'in the place of (*ba-maqom*) Tannin' (namely, in the sea) instead of MT 'in place of (*bi-mqom*) Tannin'; but this change is unnecessary, and only serves to deflate the mythic image.

Tannim-dragon.[6] Like other oracles of this type, in which the king of Babylon is banished 'from heaven' (Isa. 14: 3–16), and the ruler of Tyre is doomed to derision 'in the pit' (Ezek. 28: 1–11), the Pharaoh is also condemned here for his divine pretensions and overweening pride.[7] Thus in the first oracle, YHWH says: 'Behold! I am greater than you, O Pharaoh king of Egypt, mighty Tannim, sprawling in his (Nile-) streams, who says, "Mine is my Nile, I made [it] for me".[8] I shall put hooks in your jaws, . . . and shall haul you up from your streams . . . and fling you into the desert . . . Then all the inhabitants of Egypt shall know that I am YHWH' (29: 3–6).

The metaphoric identification of Pharaoh with the sea dragon, and his boast of creative powers, transforms the divine oracle into a contestation of sovereignty and power, and alludes to the combat myth of YHWH with sea monsters. But since it is also obvious that the Pharaoh is not literally a dragon of the deep, and that his boast cannot be taken at face value, the account of the subjugation and defeat of the Tannim never breaks the bounds of metaphor to become living myth. The king and the dragon remain distinct entities, despite their figurative fusion in the prophecy—and this gives the new mythic image its ironic edge. Significantly, just this edge is lost in the version of the oracle found in Ezek. 32: 2–8, where the Pharaoh is said to be 'like the Tannim'. The use of a simile here, instead of a metaphor, highlights the difference between the person and the dragon, and reveals the artifice of the trope and its rhetorical character. It further reduces or circumscribes the mythopoeic nature of the piece.[9]

These examples, and many others of the same type,[10] reveal the different modalities that the scenario of mythic combat assumed in the religious life and thought of ancient Israel. Central to its dynamics is the celebration or

[6] The Pharaoh is in fact Hophra; the first oracle dates from June 587, a year after the beginning of the siege of Jerusalem; the second from March 586, after the fall of the city. For the term Tannim, see n. 5.

[7] Note esp. the expression in which the royal figure dares to imagine himself a divinity (Isa. 14: 13–14; Ezek. 28: 2). For structural features of these units, and other considerations, see below.

[8] Supplementing 'it' with the Samaritan version; LXX has 'them', i.e. the streams. Literally, MT reads 'I made myself'.

[9] Theodore Lewis, '*CT*. 33–34 and Ezekiel 32: Lion Dragon Myths', *JAOS* 116 (1996), 28–47, has sought to emphasize the 'mythological backdrop' of the chapter and its link to a combat myth featuring the deity Tishpak, who is designated as both a dragon and a lion. Lewis notes this fusion in Ezek. 32: 2, and explains it against this literary and other iconographic evidence. Rashi and many moderns (see Lewis, 40 n. 96) regard the *vav* of *ve-ʾattah* in Ezek. 32: 2 as disjunctive or adversative, thus splitting the two images and putting the dragon in the inferior position. My point is more literary, and focuses on the effect of the simile upon the mythopoeic character of the text.

[10] For another case of historicization, see Isa. 17: 12–13, where the nations are identified with the roar and upsurge of 'mighty waters', and their subjugation achieved by God's shout (*ve-gaʿar bo*), which causes them to flee. Such a mythic scene and vocabulary is found elsewhere; cf. Nahum 1: 2–6 and Ps. 104: 6. Further on the verb *gaʿar*, see A. A. Macintosh, *VT* 19 (1969), 471–9. It is also used in Canaanite myth; cf. *CTA* 2. 1. 24 and 2. 4. 2

invocation of divine power and victory—whether against primordial or contemporary enemies, and whether against natural or human forms; and central to its pathos is the depiction of divine might and fury—whether displayed through such anthropomorphic images as a mighty hand and terrifying roar, or through such natural effects as a thunderstorm and lightning. In diverse combinations, this cluster of images was reworked, reused, and reshaped for new circumstances. The adaptive power of this mythic complex can also be seen through its role in the theophany at Sinai, where YHWH's advent is depicted upon a cloud, and His appearance is accompanied by thunder and lightning and fire (Exod. 19: 9, 16, 18). A more hymnic version of this episode, replete with the old mythic images, occurs in Ps. 68: 8–11.[11]

This last example is instructive for the way it confirms our earlier discussions regarding the role of genre in the re-actualization and expression of myth in the Hebrew Bible. In particular, we may note the more restrained depiction of the theophany in the historical narratives as compared with their more poetical renditions. In the latter cases, the mythopoesis is bolder and more compact, and much more dramatic in its use of a variety of images. Rabbinic exegesis will add a new dimension to this material, as we shall see, when it extends these depictions, along with God's activities, and combines the various images into new complexes and bundles of tradition. In this respect the ancient Midrash had a keen eye for the mythic figures of Scripture, even as it reread them for its own mythopoeic purposes.

[11] See the comparative analysis of Édouard Lipiński, 'Juges 5, 4–5 et Psaume 68, 8–11', *Bib.* 48 (1967), 185–206. The mythic scene is also applied to the conquest; see vv. 16–18.

4
Conclusions and Other Considerations

A. MYTHIC COMBAT IN ANCIENT ISRAEL

Throughout the ancient Near East there were two particularly dominant structures of divine power and creativity: the one was a theology of the effective word, which we have called the *logos* model;[1] the other was a theology of combat against the forces of chaos or disorder, which we have called the *agon* model. The *logos* model was presumably derived, in part, from the precedent of royal edicts or the evocative word of magicians and oracles; whereas the *agon* model seems to have been inspired by meteorological phenomena, and especially by the seasonal clash between the heavenly powers in the thunderstorm and the divine powers in the earthly waters. The containment and domestication of the Tigris and Euphrates rivers certainly made an impression on the composers of *Enuma elish*,[2] even as the gathering of the lower waters in oceans and rivers impressed the authors of Psalms 74 and 104, and appeared to them as the result of the defeat or subjugation of the primeval waters by the high creator god.

Our analysis of biblical myth and mythmaking has focused on this *agon* model, because it allows us to see how the common ancient Near Eastern topos of divine combat with the sea was realized in Israelite sources. Careful analysis shows that, at the level of imagery and terminology, there is no disjunction between the pagan and monotheistic texts, and in fact many of the nominalizations of the sea (Yam, Leviathan, Naḥash) and its attributes (*bariaḥ* and *ʿaqalaṭon*) comport with common Canaanite prototypes. At the same time, there is no indication in the biblical materials that the sea is a fully distinct divine personality with its own biography, as we can know it from Canaanite texts, or that the theomachy is a recurrent seasonal phenomenon. Rather, in a distinctive manner, the biblical versions link the prototypical conflict at the beginning of the world order (*Urzeit*) with its recurrence within the sacred history of Israel during the exodus from Egypt, and its anticipated recurrence in new forms thereafter, up to and including the final defeat of the sea in the future (*Endzeit*).

[1] For a wide-ranging and still valuable investigation, see Lorenz Durr, *Die Wertung des Göttlichen Wortes im Alten Testament und im Antiken Orient* (MVAG 42. 1; Leipzig: J. C. Hinrichs Verlag, 1938).

[2] See Tablet v, esp.

This typologization of occurrences in most of the versions establishes a certain mythic structure to time, in which the significant events of order and salvation are modelled on the primordial victory over the sea monster *in illo tempore*. As we have observed, this structuring of time in terms of the manifestation of divine power collapses any simple division between myth (as events of the past) and history (as the events of the present and future). Indeed, it is precisely the sense that all acts of divine salvation are modelled upon the great mythic precedents of origins (whether of the world or the nation) that explains the invocation of these deeds by psalmists and prophets, when they sense the withdrawal of divine favour and power because of anger or rejection. Thus the myth of recurrence in ancient Israelite theology is one of divine salvation or victory in time, and not of the repetition of seasonal cycles in nature. It is within this mythic consciousness that the seeds of apocalyptic eschatology are sown, already in prophetic sources.

The different expressions of the combat myth in biblical sources are not full-scale narrations of mythic events, recounting a complete series of occurrences. They are rather highly condensed epitomes or evocations of these events, set within another (non-mythic) literary context or genre. What is more, this surrounding context is determinative for understanding the role of the mythic citation or allusion for the speaker. In this regard, three literary observations can be made. The first is that it is precisely the intensity and immediacy of the mythologems that shows their *ontological veracity* or reality for the human speaker. For example, the prayers in Psalms 74, 77, and 89 are addressed to God, who is asked to hear the plea of His supplicant and be aroused to manifest new acts of power like the olden ones in bygone times. Such petitions would be utterly meaningless if the *magnalia dei* recited to God were deemed mere fable or fiction. The prophecies of a future manifestation of divine power over the sea in Isa. 11: 11–16 and 27: 1 also presuppose this conviction for the other end of the temporal spectrum. Similarly, the direct appeal to the arm of the Lord in Isa. 51: 9–10, or the depiction of God's advent to battle, reflect scenes of great mythic immediacy and religious conviction. There is nothing about them which remotely suggests that they are stylistic fictions or conventions; rather, the mythic imagery conveys a truth of divine being, without qualification.

The second point to be made is that a striking number of these narrative epitomes bear traces of their *composition*, and thus reveal something of the mythopoeic processes whereby ancient precedents were re-actualized or linked to contemporary concerns. Thus in our analysis of Psalms 74, 77, and 89, we noted how the imagery of a theophany or divine combat was interpolated into the petitions, so as to establish a prototype which the speaker then invokes in support of his petition. In a comparable manner, the conquest of Canaan and the fear of its kings were given a mythic dimension and incorporated into the surrounding hymn of Exodus 15. The result of such redaction or combination is that myth and history are complexly interfused in ancient Israelite thought, so that any valid analysis of their correlation must begin with this textual evidence—and not with ancient or contemporary notions of myth and assertions of their incomparability with the events of history.[3]

My third observation brings to the foreground the fact that the different examples of biblical mythopoesis are carried by *diverse genres* for new purposes. For example, they occur within petitionary prayers (Psalms 74, 77, and 89); prophetic petitions (Isa. 51: 9–11) and promises (Isa. 27: 1); supernatural visions (Hab. 3: 3–13); oracles against foreign nations (Ezek. 29: 1–6; 32: 1–8); and in various types of discourse within wisdom literature (Job 7: 12; 9: 4–13; and 26: 1–14). Inevitably, the way the mythopoesis is formulated covers a broad rhetorical spectrum—from direct statements to God (Ps. 77: 13–22), to indirect statements of His great deeds (Isa. 63: 10–13); from ironic questions that personalize the imagery (Job. 7: 12), to ecstatic accounts of God's transcendent majesty (Hab. 3: 3–13); and from descriptive accounts of divine manifestation (Isa. 30: 27–30) to personalized identifications of the speaker with the mythic content (Ps. 44: 20).

In all these contexts, the vividness of the biblical imagery changes, as does the degree of its expansion. Thus the Leviathan may be obliquely depicted in minimal terms, as a monster with various heads (Ps. 74: 14), or as a slant or twisting serpent (Isa. 27: 1); whereas, in other cases, there is an almost epical expatiation on the nature of the beast, enlarging at length upon his terrifying and massive features, and transforming the theme of his defeat or containment into a rhetorical device to mock the puny powers of human beings (Job 40: 25–41: 26). The effect is to transform Leviathan into something more like a mythic emblem of awesome might, than a character in a real mythic drama.[4] Inevitably, Job must fall silent to such questions as 'Have you an arm (*zeroaʿ*) like God's? Can you thunder (*tarʿem*) with a voice (*qol*) like His?'; or to such divine challenges as 'Clothe yourself with glory and majesty. Scatter wide your fuming anger—see every proud man and bring him low... then even I shall praise you, for your right hand (*yeminkha*) has won you victory' (Job 40: 9–11, 14).

These queries and challenges allude to various depictions of YHWH, the mighty lord of battles, and thereby mock the limited powers of human beings.[5]

[3] In addition to the reasons or assertion noted earlier, one should also include such more benign differences as those that see myth as something that can be repeated or replicated, and history that is something that is unique and differentiated. For this characterization, see Karin Andriolo, 'Myth and History: A General Model and its Application to the Bible', *American Anthropologist*, 83 (1981), esp. 261–8.

[4] For an analysis of the passage in light of Canaanite myth, see André Caquot, 'Le Leviathan de Job 40, 25–41, 26', *RB* 99 (1992), 40–62.

[5] The image of God's thunder and voice is well known, and is echoed in Ps. 18: 14, 'YHWH thunders (*va-yarʿem*) from heaven; yea, the Most High gives forth His voice (*qolo*)' (cf. Ps. 104: 6);

Among the mythic presentations of YHWH in the psalms, however, the situation is entirely different; for the anthropomorphic imagery of divine majesty and power used there is not for the purpose of mocking human impotence, but rather to show the utter dependence of the supplicant upon God's might. The most dominant physical expression of this topic is the image of God's arm, and its ability to conquer the sea dragon and save Israel. In Isa. 51: 9, this arm even appears as a hypostatic power that may be invoked or addressed in personal terms. Accordingly, the figure of the withdrawn or inactive arm condenses the worshipper's sense of divine abandonment (Pss. 74: 11; 77: 11), and this leads to the repeated appeals that YHWH again manifest His saving might.

Stated differently, we may say that the divine arm functions in the myths of combat as a metonym for YHWH's physical presence—whether manifest or hidden—for punishment and woe. When turned against Israel, God's fury and forgetting result in the people's suffering at the hands of other nations, without divine intervention or rescue (Pss. 44: 10–23; 74: 1–10, 17–23); and when turned against foreigners, the fury expresses a divine advent to battle and revenge, without restraint or mercy (Isa. 63: 1–64: 11; Nah. 1: 2–6; Hab. 3: 3–16). In these cases, there is evinced a demonization of the historical enemy and its depiction in mythic terms.[6] Moreover, just as the anthropomorphic figure of the divine arm is marked by the binary structure of revealment–concealment (or long–short; and extension–withdrawal), the anthropopathic state of YHWH's relationship to Israel is marked by the polarity of forgetting–remembrance (or abandonment–rescue; hiddenness–manifestation; and anger–mercy). These physical and emotional counterpoints are variously correlated, and their different configurations constitute the pathos and hope of the prayers.[7]

It is instructive to compare the anthropopathisms of divine remembrance in priestly traditions with their occurrence in the prayers and prophecies dealt

the depiction of YHWH as robed in glory and splendour (*hod ve-hadar labashta*) is found in Ps. 104: 1; and the image of God's right hand saving him is literally echoed in Ps. 98: 2 and Isa. 59: 16. On the possible effect of the psalms on late Isaianic passages dealing with the divine arm, see H. L. Ginsberg, 'The Arm of YHWH in Isaiah 51–63 and the Text of Isa 53: 10–11', *JBL* 77 (1958), 153 f. Cf. the discussion of Y. Kaufmann, *Toledot*, II/2 (= part 5), 717–18, 723–5.

6 An interesting depiction of this type arguably occurs in Ps. 92: 10, where the tri-cola depiction of YHWH's defeat of the enemy (*hinneh ʾoybekha YHWH*, 'Behold, your enemy, O YHWH', etc.) is remarkably like the depiction of Baʿal's defeat of his enemy (*ht. ʾbk. bʿl*, 'Behold, your enemy, O Baʿal', etc.) in *CTA* 2. 4. 8–9; see Nahum M. Sarna, 'The Psalm for the Sabbath Day (Psalm 92)', *JBL* 81 (1962), 160–2. On this issue of depicting an enemy in mythic terms; see above, Maul, ' "Wenn der Held (zum Kampfe) auszieht" ', *Or.* 60 (1991), 328 f., and also Volkert Haas, 'Die Dämonisierung des Fremden und des Feindes im Alten Orient', *Rocznik Orientalistyczny*, 41.2 (1980), 37–44 (anniversary vol. dedicated to Rudolf Ranoszek).

7 While his main concern is with the theme of the turning away of the divine face, Samuel E. Balentine, in *The Hidden God: The Hiding of the Face of God in the Old Testament* (Oxford: Oxford University Press, 1983) has noted some of these various theological and semantic fields in ch. 5; but he has not focused on mythic features or the dialectical dimensions involved.

with earlier, since they show markedly different mythic modalities. In the first category we note how various signs or objects serve to arouse YHWH's remembrance and favourable regard: the appearance of the rainbow will remind God (*ve-zakharti*) of His convenant with humankind, so that he would not go forth again with His bow and bring a destructive storm upon the earth (Gen. 9: 11–17);[8] the names of the tribes of Israel, which the high priest Aaron is instructed to bear 'on the breast piece of judgement over his heart, when he enters the sanctuary' shall serve 'as a (token of) remembrance (*le-zikkaron*) before YHWH' (Exod. 28: 29); the half-sheqel which the Israelites gave as expiation money following the census in the desert, was to be given 'to the service of the Tent of Meeting', and thus 'it shall serve the Israelites as a reminder (*le-zikkaron*) before YHWH, as expiation for your persons' (Exod. 30: 16)—for otherwise a plague would kill them off (v. 12);[9] and in addition, at dangerous moments before battle, two special silver trumpets were to be blown (by Aaron's sons) so 'that you may be remembered (*ve-nizkartem*) before YHWH, your God, and be delivered from your enemies' (Num. 10: 9); and finally, 'on your joyous occasions—your fixed festivals and new moon days—you shall sound the trumpets over your burnt offerings and your sacrifices of well-being: they shall be a reminder (*le-zikkaron*) of you before your God' (v. 10).

As these examples show, the accounts of divine remembrance in the priestly literature are marked by considerable descriptive restraint; but these are also, for all that, texts of considerable mythic power and tension. Thus, on the one hand, God says that when He will look upon the rainbow (no mere natural object, but His own weapon of battle in the storm), He will remember humankind and never again destroy it; while, on the other, He says that certain cultic objects (the breastplate of judgement and the product of the half-sheqel poll tax) or performances shall serve as a reminder of the people before Him. Such statements are as remarkable for what they say as for what is left unsaid; namely, that the God who is worshipped in the shrine (the Tent of Meeting) and who even comes from heaven to dwell therein, is not always attentive or mindful of His people, and that, without these tokens of sight and sound, danger or disfavour could result. In the case of the rainbow and the objects built from the poll money, the signs serve explicitly to restrain the outburst of divine wrath; whereas in the case of the trumpet blasts in times of military danger, the sounds are intended to arouse divine

[8] The image is quite mythic, for the rainbow is God's own weapon of battle, now hung in the sky; cf. the drawn bow in Hab. 3: 9, and the arrows that are the rain he casts earthward along with lightning. Marduk also fights with a bow and other weapons (*Enuma elish* IV. 35–49).

[9] For a discussion of this passage, and its transformation in rabbinic exegesis, see my 'Census and Intercession in a Priestly Text (Exodus 30: 11–16) and in its Midrashic Transformation', in David P. Wright, David Noel Freedman, and Avi Hurvitz (edd.), *Pomegranates and Golden Bells: Studies in Biblical, Jewish, and Near Eastern Ritual, Law, and Literature in Honor of Jacob Milgrom* (Winona Lake, Ind.: Eisenbrauns, 1995), 103–11.

favour and aid (and surely the arousal of favour is the purpose of the blasts on joyous occasions, linked to various phases of the moon).

By contrast with these priestly instructions, the prayers in which the combat motif appears are marked by explicit statements of God's anger and rejection, and the repeated appeal that He remember His supplicants and not forget them. Particularly poignant is the direct petition: 'Remember (*zekhor*) Your flock that You made Yours long ago' (Ps. 74: 2); and the concern to align Israel's suffering with a maligning of YHWH Himself: 'Remember this (*zekhor zo'ṭ*) ... how base people revile Your name ... Look to the covenant ... Remember (*zekhor*) that You are blasphemed ... all day long' (vv. 18, 20, 22; cf. Ps. 89: 51). In other cases, the appeal is that God turn from His anger by remembering mercy (Hab. 3: 2, 'In anger remember (*tizkor*) mercy'; cf. Ps. 25: 6). These and related petitions recall the intercessory appeal to YHWH by Moses after the sin of the golden calf, that He relent of His great wrath and 'remember (*zekhor*)' His promise to the patriarchs (Exod. 32: 13; Deut. 9: 27)—so that the people are not destroyed.

Such petitionary attempts to assuage divine wrath, by urging God to remember various subjective and objective considerations (His past care for the nation; His sense of indignation at being blasphemed; His commitment to covenantal promises), are instructive parallels that help elucidate the statements of worshippers who say that *they* now 'remember' YHWH's great acts of victory and salvation in the past, and in reciting these deeds hope to induce Him to turn from his state of wrath or rejection to one of mercy (see Ps. 77: 12; cf. Pss. 44: 2–5; and 74: 12). Isa. 63: 7–19 brings together most of these themes, and gives poignant expression to the use of human memory as a mode of piety and act of supplication. The speaker opens by stating that 'I shall recall (*'azkir*) the kind acts of YHWH ... for all that YHWH has done for us ... according to His mercy (*raḥamav*) and great kindness' (v. 7). He then recounts how the nation was delivered by Him and became His people; but when they later rebelled, He turned into their enemy (vv. 8–10)—until the people 'remembered (*va-yizkor*) the ancient days' and how He saved them from the sea with 'His glorious arm ... at the right hand of Moses' (vv. 11–14). Now in suffering, and with the sanctuary destroyed, the supplicant cries out: 'Look down from heaven and see: ... Where (*'ayeh*) is Your mighty zeal? Your compassion and mercy (*raḥamekha*) are withheld from us! Surely You are our Father ... Why (*lamah*), YHWH, do you make us stray from You?[10] Relent for the sake of Your servant, the tribes of your

[10] The anguished queries *'ayeh* ('where?') and *lamah* ('why?') are found repeatedly in the pattern of prayers we have been analysing, along with much shared terminology. See Pss. 44: 25; 74: 1, 11; 89: 50; and cf. Exod. 32: 11 and Lam. 5: 20. On these interrogatives, and a tabulation of occurrences, see Balentine, *The Hidden God*, esp. 116–21. Another query, *'ad mati* ('until when?'), found in Ps. 74: 10 (also Pss. 79: 5; 84: 3; and 94: 3), is like Akkadian *adi mati*, found frequently in laments of various types. Note, for example, the supplication to Ishtar to overcome

inheritance... O, if You would but tear back the heavens and descend—even the mountains would quake before You!' (vv. 15–19).

The evocative tone of these appeals, together with the more neutral priestly texts, allow us to penetrate somewhat into the mythic sense of the divine personality reflected thereby—as well as to the role of human action or speech in moving the divine from a pole of impassiveness, hiddenness, withdrawal, rejection, or anger, to a pole of attentiveness, manifestation, engagement, assuagement, and mercy. In all cases, the religious concern of the worshipper is to ensure or activate divine care and protection. The polarity of divine forgetfulness and human remembrance is thus central to this complex, for it appears that the activation of human memory is not only a sign of restored piety, but that it is also a liturgical means for inducing divine favour through the restoration of His mighty arm of salvation. YHWH's subjugation of the sea in the past serves as the paradigmatic expression of this positive might; and thus, correspondingly, in the psalms we have examined, the occlusion or withdrawal of the divine arm serves as a physical expression of the emotional states of divine rejection that are variously bemoaned by the worshipper. In this way, the anthropomorphisms and anthropopathisms we have examined form two parts of the same mythic complex: of divine actions and feelings, both positive and negative. The anguish or urgency of the speaker indicates just how much the figurative representations of God found in the preceding texts are grounded in a concrete mythic realism of a vital and continuously renewed kind.

B. THE MYTHIC HIERARCHY OF ANCIENT ISRAEL

In the various mythologems discussed above, we have repeatedly referred to God's advent to earthly battle on a heavenly throne, surrounded by divine powers or aides, and borne on a cloud in a nimbus of radiant light, which surrounds His apparently anthropomorphic shape. As variously noted, virtually all of this biblical imagery is found in one way or another in the surrounding Near Eastern civilizations, and constitutes part of their mythic depictions and traditions of storm and warrior gods with their retinue. The occurrence of the ancient Israelite data in fragmentary or abbreviated forms, and in diverse genres by different authors or schools, might lead to the supposition that they are merely idiosyncratic features of some mythic mentality or mentalities, but without any value for understanding the ancient Israelite religious world. Such a judgement may derive from scholarly caution at the risks of drawing inferences from data spread over a long period of

her wrath, in Leonard W. King, *The Seven Tablets of Creation* (London: Luzac & Co., 1902), i. 234f. (ll. 93–4); and also the use of the term *aḫulap*, pp. 226–9 (ll. 27–30, 45–50). Also cf. F. Stummer, *Sumerisch-akkadische Parallelen Zum Aufbau alttestamentlicher Psalmen* (Paderborn: Verlag von Ferdinand Schoeningh, 1922), 90f.

time and taken from different genres; but it may also derive from a failure of nerve, or from even less noble presuppositions regarding the absence of a mythic mentality in ancient Israel. We have already cast our intellectual judgement in the opposite direction, on the basis of the conceptual and analytical reasons put forward at length. Moreover, the occurrence of these similar Near Eastern types also in fragmentary and abbreviated forms, where one would hardly doubt their concrete mythic force, is significant. On the basis of the principles of parsimony and charity enunciated earlier,[11] we should thus be ready to concede the likelihood that the similar forms of occurrence in ancient Israel should also be taken as mythically alive. Such an argument from comparative Near Eastern contexts supplements the analysis of mythic features within the specific rhetorical contexts of the biblical texts themselves.

We shall now take a further step in our attempt to provide an understanding of biblical myth through a presentation of the hierarchy of powers that constitute Israel's mythic universe—without implying that we can infer the unknown (or unstated) from the known (or stated) in any given period or group of traditions, but also without avoiding the clear thematic and conceptual continuities that are evident in a great variety of biblical sources. For by refraining from this attempted reconstruction, we would err on the other side, and leave the quite unwarranted impression that nothing unified or systematic can be said of the material. I choose to run this risk of reconstruction in the conviction that it will bring some structural order into our understanding of ancient Israelite religion and its mythic mentalities, and also provide a conceptual framework for the post-biblical religious universe that succeeded ancient Israel—and that not only expanded its mythic theology and structures, but also transformed them in many remarkable ways.

I. A Fourfold Hierarchy

A fourfold hierarchy of powers may be mapped, moving from high heaven down to the netherworld. This vertical perspective does not mean that there is always or inevitably a diminution of power from above to below, or that the various zones of power are uniform and without their own sub-hierarchies. Moreover, the existence of diverse spheres of power or personality does not mean that these realms are mutually impermeable, since there are cases where the zones are crossed in different directions, through one or another form of physical or spiritual metamorphosis of beings between the spheres—these changes being of various durations and types. This said, we shall map this hierarchy spatially from above to below, from the God YHWH, the chief lord of life and the created order, who rules from His throne in heaven; to the divine host that surrounds Him and is at His service; to the chthonic or

[11] See above, in the General Introduction.

earthly realm, which is dominated (in part) by human beings (who are nevertheless dependent upon the upper powers for their sustenance and safety); and down to the netherworld, which is populated by the shades and powers of death.

1. The Throne World. According to a variety of liturgical and prophetic sources, the throne of YHWH is a complex in heaven (Pss. 11: 4 and 103: 19; Isa. 57: 15) that is surrounded by a 'council (*sod*)' or 'retinue (*qahal*)' of divine powers (Ps. 89: 6–7), known variously as 'holy beings (*qedoshim*)', 'divine beings (*benei ʾelim*)', or 'mighty powers (*gibborei koaḥ*)' (Pss. 89: 6–7; 103: 20), and who, among other things, engage in praise of YHWH or His attributes (Ps. 89: 6).[12] According to two different testimonies, 'righteousness and justice (*tzedeq u-mishpaṭ*)' serve as bases for the throne (Pss. 89: 15; 97: 3); and similar to other ancient Near Eastern traditions, they are actual divine hypostases (of some sort) and not simply moral hyperboles.[13] According to Ps. 85: 14, *tzedeq* goes before YHWH and makes smooth His way;[14] and the same source also refers to *tzedeq* as an element that 'looks down from heaven' (v. 12). In addition, we are also informed that the throne was enveloped by various dense clouds, and that fire went before it as a vanguard (Pss. 97: 2–3; 104: 4).

Confirming these heavenly realities, the prophet Isaiah reports an experience in which the Lord was seen seated upon an exalted throne, with winged 'fiery beings (*seraphim*)' standing in attendance and reciting a litany of praise, 'Holy, holy, holy, is YHWH of Hosts! His *kabod* (presence) fills all the earth' (Isa. 6: 1–3).[15] And in an even more awesome spectacle, Ezekiel perceived the 'likeness of the appearance a man' radiating with the likeness of 'the image of the *kabod* of YHWH' seated upon a throne, borne upon the firmament by a quaternary of winged beings of anthropomorphic appearance (some of

[12] Among other terms, the divine council is called the *ʿadat ʾel* ('assembly of El') in Ps. 82: 1. The MT *be-har moʿed* ('in the mountain of meeting') of Isa. 14: 13, which the pagan speaker says is above the 'stars of El' has been emended by H. L. Ginsberg to *paḫar mo ʿed* ('assembled gathering') in the light of Ugaritic *pḫr mʿd*, a term for the divine assembly; see his 'Isaiah in the Light of History', *Conservative Judaism*, 22 (1967), 14 and n. 10. For the Ugaritic idiom *pḫr ilm*, see RS 1929: 17, line 7; and for *mpḫrt bn il*, see RS 1929: 2, line 4. Also cf. Johannes Friedrich, 'Kleine Bermerkungen zu Texten aus Ras Schamra und zu phönizischen Inscriften', *AfO* 10 (1935–6), 82.

[13] That *tzedeq* and *mishpaṭ* are divine elements in Israelite and Canaanite theology, see above, p. 54. Cf. also Roy Rosenberg, 'The God Sedeq', *HUCA* 36 (1965), 162 f.; the remainder must be read with caution.

[14] In Babylonian traditions, *kittu* ('justice') and *mešaru* ('right') were personifications of justice; and are separately and together described as *ašib maḫri Šamaš* ('seated before Shamash') and as *sukkulu ša imitti* ('minister of the right hand'). See Knut Tallqvist, *Akkadische Götter-epitheta* (Helsinki: Helsingforsiae, 1938), 342, 374, 455.

[15] The depiction of the doorposts shaking and the Temple being filled with smoke (Isa. 6: 4), echoes theophanies of the divine advent (Ps. 68: 8–9) and appearance upon Sinai (Exod. 19: 18–19).

which also had theriomorphic features), which served as a chariot; fire and lightning flashed from these 'beings (*ḥayyot*)' or cherubim; and the whole complex was itself a fiery sight, set within a cloud of incandescent radiance roundabout (Ezek. 1: 4–28).[16] The 'sound of the wings of the cherubim sounded... like the voice of El Shaddai when he spoke' (Ezek. 9: 5).

2. Heavenly Messengers. The divine beings of the chariot world were only in part the stays of the throne, or the courtiers reciting hymns of praise; others served as delegated agents of the divine will to human beings on earth, or acted as a military vanguard when the divine throne rode forth as a chariot to perform some mission on earth.[17] These agents were called God's 'messengers (*mal'akhav*)', 'stewards (*meshartav*)', 'hosts (*tzeba'av*)', or 'spirits (*ruḥot*)' (Pss. 103: 20–1; 104: 4); according to the book of Job, a divine power named 'the Satan' roamed the earth on behalf of YHWH, and was twice delegated to bring sufferings upon Job—but not to kill him (Job 1: 6–12; 2: 1–7). A particularly notable example of the way these powers were used to intervene and effect changes in human affairs is found in 1 Kings 22: 21–2. This passage brings to a climax an episode in which the prophet Micaiah ascends into the divine world and sees YHWH upon His throne, with the heavenly host in close attendance (vv. 19–20). He then reports that YHWH asked the assembly, 'Who will entice (King) Ahab, so that he will go up to battle (against Aram) and fall in Ramot Gilead?'; and 'one said thus and another said thus'—

> until a certain spirit (*ha-ruaḥ*) came forward and stood before YHWH and said: 'I will entice him'. And YHWH asked him, 'With what?' And he replied, 'I will go forth and become a lying spirit (*ruaḥ sheqer*) in the mouth of all the prophets. And (YHWH) answered, 'You will entice and you will prevail—be gone and do it!' (vv. 21–2)

The machinations and manipulations of human existence by YHWH and the divine assembly are depicted here as a matter of fact, and are grounded in the sense that divine spirits could be transformed into the agents of psychic states of people on earth—a sensibility or conception that must also lie behind such texts as 1 Sam. 9: 10, wherein a 'spirit of God (*ruaḥ 'elohim*)' is said to have seized Saul and caused him to prophesy; or 1 Sam. 16: 23, which reports that 'whenever a spirit of God (*ruaḥ 'elohim*) came upon Saul (causing depression),[18] David would take up the lyre and play it; and then Saul would be

[16] Striking parallels between Ezekiel's vision and old Babylonian sources have recently been proposed by Peter Kingsley, 'Ezekiel by the Grand Canal: Between Jewish and Babylonian Tradition', *JRAS* 3rd ser, 2 (1992), 339–46.

[17] On a hierarchical division between a high god (El), active gods (including Ba'al), and messenger gods at Ugarit, see Lowell K. Handy, *Among the Hosts of Heaven: The Syro-Palestinian Pantheon as Bureaucracy* (Winona Lake, Ind.: Eisenbrauns, 1994).

[18] Not 'the spirit of God', as commonly rendered, for this is tendentious and also not attested in this text.

inspired (*ve-ravaḥ*) and relieved, and the evil spirit (*ruaḥ ha-raʿah*) would leave him'.[19] No less significant is the account of the human movement in the opposite direction, whereby a prophet is able to audit and visualize the deliberations within the heavenly assembly. Certainly another trace of this phenomenon (in addition to the case of Micaiah's heavenly transport) is preserved in Jer. 23: 18, where the true prophet is described as 'he who has stood in the council (*sod*) of YHWH, and seen and heard His word'. As in Ps. 89: 8, the *sod* referred to here is the heavenly council of divine powers.

Even more instructive is the evidence preserved in Isaiah 6; for not only does the prophet see YHWH seated upon His throne, with seraphs in attendance, but he is also an active participant in the heavenly events. According to the report, upon seeing this holy spectacle Isaiah was struck with a sense of his own impurity, and is only purified when one of the seraphs takes a coal from the heavenly altar and touches his lips, telling him that his sin is now purged (vv. 6–7). Significantly, after this purification of his mouth, Isaiah heard the voice of the Lord saying, 'Whom shall I send? Who will go for us?'; and he responded: 'Here I am; send me'—much like the spirit in 1 Kings 22: 21, which also responded to a divine request for a messenger. Moreover, the fact that YHWH asks 'Who will go for us (*lanu*)?' gives further support to the claim that the query was posed to the divine council in which Isaiah participated,[20] and resulted in the fact that the messenger from the throne world is a human being, and not one of the heavenly hosts. A scene of heavenly purification is also found in Zech. 3: 1–7, where the high priest Joshua is given a divine investiture, and instructed how he may have future access to the heavenly hosts (called *ha-ʿomedim*, because they 'stand' before the King in His court; cf. Isa. 6: 2).[21]

A remarkable reflex of the whole mythic conception of divine agency and metamorphosis we have been considering is preserved in the old patriarchal legends about Abraham—all the more powerful and mythic because of the naturalness of the narrative account, and because it does not refer to any heavenly court or indicate that the messengers are in fact incarnations from the divine world. But just this is the interpretation that compels itself from a close and unapologetic attention to the narrative in Genesis 18–19, which begins with the visitation of a small party of individuals to Abraham, while he was sitting near his tent at the terebinths of Mamre (Gen. 18: 1). At the outset, it seems that 'three men' appear before the patriarch (v. 2), who

[19] Clearly the *ruaḥ ʾelohim* here is the same as the *ruaḥ ha-raʿah*; and is perhaps better rendered as 'divine spirit'.

[20] See also H. Wheeler Robinson, 'The Council of Yahweh', *JTS* 45 (1944), 154.

[21] The term *ʿomedim* is used of royal court functionaries, as in the idiom *ʿomedim ʾet penei Shelomoh*, '(the elders who were) standing before Solomon'; cf. Akkadian *emedu ina pani*. In Zech. 3: 7, the term for 'access' to the heavenly realm is *mahlekhim*; see already Herbert G. May, 'A Key to the Interpretation of Zechariah's Visions', *JBL* 57 (1938), 178 n. 27.

rushes to provide them with hospitality; but whereas they all ask after Sarah (v. 9), only one of them announces that she will soon become pregnant (v. 10)—and that one is clearly identified in the sequel with YHWH (vv. 13–15). Moreover, even though the 'men' all get up to go to Sodom (v. 16), it is YHWH alone who tells Abraham of the plan to destroy the city (v. 17); it is with YHWH alone that Abraham has his intercessory dialogue (vv. 18–32); and it is YHWH alone who leaves Abraham after the colloquy (v. 33), as the two other 'messengers (*mal'akhim*)' enter Sodom (19: 1) and subsequently announce to Lot that they will destroy the city for its evil ways—'for the outcry (of oppression) is great before YHWH, and YHWH has sent us to destroy it' (v. 11).[22]

One can hardly doubt that these narratives preserve a precious record of the ancient belief in divine agency, whereby YHWH and His messengers could materialize in human form upon earth in order to perform certain tasks—in the present case, YHWH announces Sarah's pregnancy and Sodom's doom to Abraham; whereas the two messengers pronounce the destruction of Sodom to Lot. The subsequent transfiguration of the men back into divine spirits is not recorded, though we can get a sense of one way that such a de-materialization was believed to occur from the report of the ascension of the messenger of YHWH who appeared before Manoaḥ and his wife in the sacrificial flame burning upon the altar (Judg. 13: 20).

Other cases of metamorphosis report myths of the punishment or descent of heavenly beings into earthly existence. The cause of the demotion is not always indicated. For example, in Isa. 14: 4–21 the king of Babylon is rebuked for his hubris and divine pretensions, and mockingly identified with Helel ben Shaḥar, a luminous day star who was cast out of heaven. It is not stated just what that astral deity did to be brought down; but one may perhaps reconstruct the underlying myth from the diatribe in which the king is ironically identified with the god. 'How have you fallen (*nafalta*) Helel ben Shaḥar'—you who 'thought (*'amarta*) in your heart, "I shall ascend (*'e'eleh*) heaven, raise my throne above the stars of El,[23] and sit in the mountain of (the divine) assembly in the recesses of Saphon;[24] I shall ascend upon a cloud

[22] See also M. L. West, *The East Face of Helicon: West Asiatic Elements in Greek Poetry and Myth* (Oxford: Clarendon Press, 1997), 124, who strikingly notes that the three 'immortals' bless those who give proper hospitality (Abraham's childless wife is promised a son; Lot and his family are given advance warning of the doom of Sodom. The two narratives thus form a diptych on the theme of hospitality and its rewards. West (p. 123) notes Greek myths in which wandering gods in disguise bless those who host them. The biblical passages have been compared with the Greek myths by Franz Dornsieff, *Antike und alter Orient: Interpretationen* (=*Kleine Schriften*, i; Leipzig, 1956), 232.

[23] Stars appear to be members of the divine pantheon at Ugarit; cf. *CTA* 10. 1. 3–4. Precisely the phrase 'stars of El' is found in a fairly late Phoenician inscription from Italy (6th c. BCE). See Mitchell Dahood, 'Punic *hkkbm 'l* and Is. 14, 13,' *Or.* 34 (1965), 170–2.

[24] MT *be-har mo'ed* ('in the mountain of meeting'). For the proposed emendation to *paḥar mo'ed* ('assembled gathering') see above, n. 12.

(and) be like Elyon"!' (vv. 12–14). From this rebuke it may be assumed that the god fell because of his pretension for high estate in the pantheon. That such a mythic structure existed is confirmed in Canaanite sources from a half-millennium earlier. Here too we read of an astral deity (named Athtar) who 'ascended (*yʿl*)' beyond his station to the recesses of Saphon; and when he sat upon the throne of Aliyan Baʿal he proved inadequate and descended to rule the underworld.[25] The theme of punishment is not found here, but enough of a resemblance exists to confirm that the political diatribe in Isa. 14: 4–21 has reworked a myth of a pretentious god who undergoes a change of status and leaves the heavenly hierarchy.

The scene depicted in Psalm 82 presents a different account of divine demotion. It opens with a report of Elohim standing in judgement over the 'gods' in the 'council of El', and rebuking them for evil and partiality in their rule over earthlings (vv. 1–2).[26] For such behaviour, God pronounces their fate, saying: 'I thought (*ʾamarti*) that you were gods, even the sons of Elyon—however, you shall die like mortals and fall (*tippolu*) like one of the (divine) princes (*sarim*)' (vv. 6–7). Explicitly in this case, the crime is injustice, and the punishment is death like the mortals and descent to their realm, as occurred to 'one of the princes' in an earlier time. These *sarim* were themselves part of the heavenly hosts, from which realm delegated agents could also descend in a human guise to help or instruct mortals (Josh. 5: 13–14).[27] In Dan. 8: 10–11 the seer hears a dream that describes a horn that 'waxed great even to the prince (*sar*) of the (heavenly) host' (v. 11), and 'caused to fall (*va-tappel*) to earth some of the host and some of the stars' (v. 10). The

[25] *CTA* 61. 55–67. For a recent analysis, see Hugh Page, Jr., *The Myth of Cosmic Rebellion* (SVT 65; Leiden; E. J. Brill, 1996), 90–4. On the god Athtar, see Page's reassessment (ch. 6); for earlier views, see Mark Smith, 'The God Athtar in the Ancient Near East and his Place in *KTU* 1.61.1', in Ziony Zevit *et al.* (edd.), *Solving Riddles and Untying Knots: Biblical, Epigraphic, and Semitic Studies in Honor of Jonas Greenfield* (Winona Lake, Ind.: Eisenbauns, 1995). And cf. P. C. Craigie, 'Helel, Athtar and Phaeton (Jes 14: 12–15)', *ZAW* 85 (1973), 223–5.

[26] There is no reason to presume that this judgement scene is a nomistic replacement of a ruder myth depicting sexual misdemeanours, as reconstructed by Julian Morgenstern, 'The Mythological Background of Psalm 82', *HUCA* 14 (1939), 29–126; nor to replace Elohim with YHWH, as is commonly done. If a change occurred, it may well have been expanding the high god El into Elohim, thereby nativizing the myth. Note that one of the mythic residues in this psalm is the reference to the divine assembly as 'the sons of Elyon'—an undoubted reference to the old high god of the Canaanite pantheon and his sirelings. This type of residue has been analysed by L. Clapham, 'Mythopoeic Antecedents of the Biblical World-View and their Transformation in Early Israelite Thought', in Frank M. Cross, Werner E. Lemke, and Patrick D. Miller, Jr. (edd.), *Magnalia Dei: The Mighty Acts of God: In Memory of G. E. Wright* (New York: Harper & Row, 1976), 112 f. The clear shift to a later perspective is the call for YHWH to arise and judge the earth (v. 8).

[27] The being appears like a 'man' (*ʾish*), but identifies himself as 'the prince (*sar*) of the (heavenly) hosts of YHWH'. Double terminology also occurs in Gen. 32: 24, 28–9; and one will note that the being must depart because of the rising of the morning (star?) (*shaḥar*). Cf. also Judg. 13: 9–10; and one may wonder in this regard whether the being called here (*ʾish ha-ʾelohim*) is best rendered 'a man of the gods' (a divine being in human form)—and not 'a man of God', which completely obscures the mythic metamorphosis involved. We noted above that two of the three 'men' who appear before Abraham in Gen. 18: 2 are designated 'angels' in 19: 1.

punishment for such pride and pretension to power will be divine doom (v. 25).[28] In another version of this theme, a king of Greece, 'waxed great over every god, and spoke fantastically against the God of gods (El of the *ʾelim*)' (Dan. 11: 36); but in the end he and his horde would be doomed on the day the archangel Michael, 'the great *sar*', would arise on behalf of the faithful who await divine salvation (12: 1).

Clearly, ancient mythic structures inform these diatribes and dreams, transposing old fabulations of divine pretensions or impropriety into political judgements against royal power.[29] Still other writers reduced this myth to an absolute cipher, as in the reference to 'fallen beings' (*nefilim*) who roamed the earth in primordial times (Gen. 6: 4). For the biblical tradent, this mythic trace was kept separate from the brief report of the miscegenation between the 'divinities' and the women (v. 2). As in Psalm 82, a crime by the gods is associated with a myth of a divine fall. The predominant Jewish, Christian, and Gnostic traditions of subsequent centuries also keep the myths of sexual mixture and divine descent distinct; but in one notable midrash, the two were strikingly blended—producing a promiscuous mega-myth from both themes.[30]

3. The Mobile Throne and God's Earthly Dwelling. Whereas YHWH's essential dwelling is in heaven, he is not limited to that realm, and descends to earth for various purposes. According to priestly traditions, YHWH instructed Moses and the people to build Him a sanctuary that He might dwell therein—on earth, upon the cherubim—which constitutes His throne-chariot for His *kabod* in the holy of holies of the Tent of Meeting (Exod. 25: 8, 11–22; 29: 43–5; 40: 34–8).[31] But God's visitations to the earthly realm were not restricted to fixed ritual moments, and they could be initiated by crises requiring his divine intervention. For example, a cluster of traditions form around the various complaints of the Israelites in the desert: after the distress, YHWH's *kabod* appears on earth in public view, within a cloud, and a divine judgement is then given to alleviate the situation (Exod. 16: 7–11; Num. 14: 2–25; 16: 1–30; 17: 6–25; 20: 2–12). This scenario is also reflected in Psalm 99, which opens in praise of YHWH who dwells upon the cherubim (vv. 1–5), and goes on to report His responsiveness to Moses, Aaron, and Samuel; when they call upon Him, He answers them in a cloud (vv. 6–9).

During the monarchic period, it is from His heavenly Temple that YHWH roars His judgement over His earthly territory (Jer. 25: 30), even as He also

[28] For an astral interpretation of the *sarim* in this passage, see George F. Moore, 'Daniel viii. 9–14', *JBL* 15 (1896), 193–7. In v. 25 the *sar ha-sarim*, or 'Prince of princes', is God.

[29] In Obad. 3–4 the topos is used in an entirely figurative way.

[30] See *Pirkei de Rabbi Eliezer* 22.

[31] For traditions regarding the Tent of Meeting, see Menahem Haran, 'The Nature of the ʾOhel Mo ʿedh in Pentateuchal Sources', *JSS* 5 (1960), 50–65.

roars His judgement from His earthly dwelling (Amos 1: 2; Joel 4: 14–17). It is from 'His place' in heaven that He may descend to battle (Micah 1: 3). In many psalms the appeal is for God to come to earth and manifest His judgement on behalf of His servants (cf. Pss. 94, 96–9)—and one may observe that this role of YHWH as a saviour and judge is a major feature of Yahwistic monotheism. In addition to such exhortations as 'appear (*hofi'a*)' and 'rise up (*hinnasei'*), judge of the earth' (Ps. 94: 1–2), we have also noted such dramatic expressions as 'arouse yourself (*'urah*)', 'wake up (*haqitzah*)' and 'arise (*qumah*)' (Pss. 44: 24; 74: 22; cf. 7: 7; 35: 23; 59: 5–6). All of these terms convey an intensity of expectation and dependence upon divine judgement.[32]

According to Deuteronomistic tradition, God was attentive to human prayer from His heavenly dwelling (1 Kings 8: 49); for though the Temple built by Solomon also had a throne in the shrine, and the ark was set within the holy of holies under the wingspan of giant cherubim (1 Kings 7: 23–7), Deuteronomic theology emphasized that the earthly Temple was for YHWH's name (Deut. 12: 5, 11). In part, this change was due to a radical shift of sensibility in these circles, dramatically put in Solomon's mouth: 'Will God truly dwell on earth? Truly, neither the heavens or the heavens of the heavens can contain you, how much less this House which I have built!' (1 Kings 8: 27).[33] Other instances of post-exilic theology confirmed this grand vision of a cosmic deity ('Thus says YHWH: "The heavens are My throne and the earth My footstool—what kind of House shall you build for Me, what place could serve as My abode?" '; Isa. 66: 1). Nevertheless, priestly circles envisioned a new Temple and spoke of the future return of the *kabod* to the holy of holies, where it would again take up residence (Ezek. 43: 1–5); indeed, the Lord explicitly states that this is 'the place of My throne and the place of the soles of My feet, where I shall dwell among the people of Israel' (v. 7). One can hardly miss the polemical tone of this assertion; clearly for Ezekiel there was no contradiction between God's spectacular appearance on a heavenly chariot (Ezekiel 1), and His dwelling upon the cherubim in the Temple. Both the transcendental and immanent poles were part of his mythic theology.

Between the appearance of the chariot above the Chebar canal in Babylon (in 593 BCE), and the return of YHWH to His earthly abode, the throne with

[32] Particularly striking is the case of Psalm 82, in which old images of the divine pantheon and the miscarriage of justice by the other divine beings are reported, and then the psalmist calls upon YHWH to 'arise' and 'judge the earth, for you will inherit all the nations'. This universalistic motif is striking, even as it puts the future divine dominion within a mythological context. For a penetrating analysis, see Samuel E. Loewenstamm, '*Naḥalat YHWH*', *From Babylon to Canaan: Studies in the Bible and its Oriental Background* (Jerusalem: Magnes Press, 1992), esp. 355–60.

[33] For an analysis of the theological and conceptual layers involved, see Marc Brettler, 'Interpretation and Prayer: Notes on the Composition of 1 Kings 8: 15–53', in Marc Brettler and Michael Fishbane (edd.), *Minḥah le-Naḥum: Biblical and Other Studies presented to Nahum M. Sarna in Honour of his 70th Birthday* (JSOTSS 154; Sheffield: JSOT Press, 1993), 17–35.

the divine *kabod* upon it descended to Jerusalem prior to its destruction (in 587/6 BCE). During this visitation, the abominations wrought in the Temple are shown to Ezekiel (Ezekiel 8); and he then sees six divine beings ('men') emerge in the city, each with his weapon (*keli mapatzo*), and among them a heavenly scribe (Ezek. 9: 1–2). The instructions of how to single out the righteous from the sinners are imparted to him by 'the *kabod* of the God of Israel' (v. 3; also called YHWH in v. 4), which then gets off the cherub it was riding upon and moves to the platform of the Temple. This mythic scene of God and His heavenly attendants draws to a dramatic climax as the divine scribe performs his task of marking selected people for salvation (9: 4), while the other messengers begin the work of punishment (vv. 6–7)—despite Ezekiel's attempt at intercession (v. 8). The scribe is then told by the Lord to 'step inside the wheelwork' of the chariot, 'under the cherubim', and fill his 'hands with glowing coals from among the cherubim, and scatter them over the city' (Ezek. 10: 2; cf. vv. 6–8). After that, the *kabod* returned from the platform and alighted upon the cherubim (10: 18)—moving first to the eastern gate of the Temple (v. 19), and then outward to 'the hill east of the city' (11: 23). With that, the *kabod* then left Jerusalem—thus paradoxically fulfilling the statement of the wicked citizens, 'YHWH has abandoned (*ʿazab*) the land, and YHWH does not see!' (9: 9).

This case of YHWH's abandonment of His shrine—resulting in a withdrawal of protective presence—is a theological topos widespread throughout the ancient Near East. In diverse texts and scenes, gods like Marduk, Ningal, and Sin, express anger and displeasure with their wards and leave their temple and city (sometimes ascending back to heaven, though in other cases going into exile).[34] The use of the verb *ʿazab* in Ezek. 9: 9 to express divine action reflects a sentiment found in other post-exilic literature (cf. Isa. 49: 14; 54: 7; 60: 15); it too has its Mesopotamian parallels which state that 'Sin left (*ezib*) Ur',[35] and that a person's protective 'gods abandoned him (*izibušu*)'.[36]

[34] Thus it is recorded in the Sumerian lament over Ur that Sin 'abandoned' her city and people; see Samuel N. Kramer, *Lamentation over the Destruction of Ur* (AS 12; Chicago: University of Chicago Press, 1940), 62 ff. (ll. 373–7); and cf. Adam Falkenstein, 'Fluch über Akkade', *ZA* 57 (1965), 53 ff. (ll. 60 ff.). In the Assyrian epic of Tukulti-Ninurta 'Marduk abandoned his lofty shrine' (of Esagila), 'Sin left Ur', and 'Annunitu does not approach Akkad'; see W. G. Lambert, 'Three Unpublished Fragments of the Tukulti-Ninurta Epic', *AfO* 18 (1957), 42–5 (ll. 30, 40, 44). In the inscriptions of Esarhaddon, because of the sacrilege of Sennacherib, 'Marduk was angry' and 'the gods and goddesses who dwell' (in Esagila) 'fled ... up to heaven'. See R. Borger, *Die Inschriften Asarhaddons Königs von Assyrien* (*AfO* Beiheft 9; Graz: E. Weidner, 1956), par. 11, ep 8, A + B; trans. from Morton Cogan, *Imperialism and Religion: Assyria, Judah and Israel in the Eighth and Seventh Centuries* B.C.D. (SBLMS 19; Missoula: Scholars Press, 1974), 12. And in the Harran inscription of Nabonides, Sin became angry with his city of Harran and 'went up to heaven'; see C. J. Gadd, 'The Harran Inscription of Nabonides', *AnSt* 8 (1958), 56–65.

[35] Cf. Lambert, 'Three Unpublished Fragments', 44 f. (l. 40).

[36] D. D. Luckenbill, *The Annals of Sennacherib* (OIP 2; Chicago: University of Chicago Press, 1924), 64.22–4; and trans. after Cogan, *Imperialism and Religion*, 11. It should also be noted that

The remarkable mythic character of the scenario in Ezekiel 9 is particularly instructive for allowing us to perceive the structure of the divine world and its engagement in human affairs. No less instructive is the employment of human agents to enact earthly punishment. The topic is already found in Isa. 10: 5 (a century and a half earlier) where Assyria is designated YHWH's agent of doom against Israel, the 'rod of my anger (*sheibeṭ ʾapi*)' and 'staff of my fury (*maṭeh* . . . *zaʿami*). The mythic dimension of this figure is somewhat obscured by the larger rhetorical thrust of the unit, where YHWH again uses the figure of a rod and staff in order to demonstrate the folly and arrogance of the king of Assyria in thinking that his victory against Jerusalem is due to its own might, and not realizing that he is merely an instrument of a divine plan (vv. 13–15); and also to give an oracle of comfort to the people of Zion, saying 'Have no fear of Assyria, who beats you with a rod (*ba-sheibeṭ*) and wields his staff (*maṭeihu*) over you as did the Egyptians' (v. 24). This notwithstanding, the full mythic character of the divine rod emerges clearly in Jeremiah 51, where YHWH prophesies doom against Babylon in vengeance for its role in the destruction of His Temple (v. 13). In this context God speaks of the Medes as His 'war club (*mapeitz*)' and 'weapons of war (*kelei milḥamah*)' (v. 20; and cf. Ezek. 9: 2, where the divine envoys each have a *keli mapatzo* in their hands).[37] The oracle goes on to chant to the *mapeitz* in hideous fury: 'With you I clubbed nations, with you I destroyed kingdoms, with you I clubbed horse and rider'—and on and on until the full wrath of divine anger against Babylon will be requited (vv. 20–4).

The mythic overtones of this battle are again sounded in an ironic allusion to the old combat myth of the dragon. In the course of one oracle of doom, YHWH cites an 'inhabitant of Zion' who cries: 'Nebuchadnezzar king of Babylon devoured me and discomforted me; he swallowed me (*bela ʿani*) like a dragon (*tannin*), he filled his belly with my dainties;[38] . . . O, let the violence done to me and my kin be upon Babylon!' (vv. 34–5). In response, YHWH promises that He will 'take vengeance' for his city by both drying up the sea of Babylon and having it flood her with 'roaring waves' (vv. 36, 42); and further, in fulfilment of Zion's cry, He adds that 'I shall requite Bel in Babylon (*bel be-babel*), and make him disgorge what he has swallowed (*bil ʿo*)' (v. 44). The rhythmic and alliterative quality of this statement gives it the force of an incantation, recited against the god of the evil city. The earthly

there are also biblical references to the exile of foreign gods into captivity. Note Isa. 46: 1–2 (with respect to Bel and Nebo of Babylon); and Jer. 48: 7 (with respect to Chemosh of Moab). Based on the rhetorical type and language involved, it is likely that the references in Amos 1: 15 and Jer. 49: 3 to the exile of *malkam* ('their king') actually indicates a national deity as well (Milkom of the Ammonites). On this latter, see E. Peuch, 'Milcom, le dieu Ammonite en Amos 1: 15', *VT* 27 (1979), 117–25.

[37] Cf. above.

[38] Reading with the *qeri*.

battle of vengeance is thus in the end a battle of the gods—YHWH against Bel—and a mighty vindication of the power of Israel's lord.[39]

4. The Netherworld. The lowest spatial realm in ancient Israelite mythical conceptions is the land of the dead, called Sheol or Abaddon (Job 26: 6).[40] In addition to being populated by former earthlings, whose former estate is evoked (cf. Job 3: 13–19), there are also 'shades' known as *repha'im* (Job 26: 5).[41] The return of the dead in a recognizable form to the world of the living (thus making a reverse traversal of zones), is most famously and brazenly depicted in the evocation of Samuel by a female wizard with powers over the netherworld (1 Sam. 28: 3–14). Significantly, the shade of Samuel is described as a 'divine being (*'elohim*)' arising from the beyond.[42] The personification of these *repha' im* is also found in Isa. 14: 9, where these beings (and Sheol itself) are said to quake in apprehension of the advent of the king of Babylon to their region—so terrifying is his nature in the land of the living.

It is also arguable (from several hints) that the old Canaanite deity of death, Mot, may even be mentioned in the Hebrew Bible. Particularly intriguing is the reference to a *mehumat mavet* that overtakes the people of Ekron (1 Sam. 5: 11). In light of the reference in Zech. 14: 13 to a *mehumat YHWH*, or '(war) panic of YHWH', brought against the peoples who attack Jerusalem, one may reasonably conclude that the *mehumat mavet* experienced by the Philistines is not simply a death panic, but the terrifying 'panic of Mot' himself.[43] Also intriguing and suggestive in this regard is the divine word spoken against those Judaeans who 'make a covenant with *mavet*, and a pact with Sheol' (Isa. 28: 15). But here we are at the borderland between myth and metaphor, and it is impossible to say just how these references are to be taken.[44]

[39] For other battles between the gods, in which YHWH triumphs, cf. Exod. 12: 12; 1 Sam. 5: 4; 1 Kings 18; and Isa. 46: 1. Also note Deut. 32, which states that YHWH has brought the nations to punish Israel lest they think that their gods have given them benefits. Significantly, whereas MT v. 43 reads 'nations', the LXX and Qumran read 'gods' and 'sons of the gods'. This reading is undoubtedly to be preferred.

[40] Abaddon may mean something like 'Forgetfulness' (cf. Lethe). The realm of Sheol is also described as *bor*, 'Pit', and *shaḥat*, 'Hole' (Ps. 30: 4, 10).

[41] These spirits are like those known as *rp'um* in Canaanite mythology. See Conrad L'Heureux, 'The Ugaritic and Biblical Rephaim', *HTR* 57 (1974), 265–74; and Johannes C. de Moor, 'Rapi'uma-Rephaim', *ZAW* 88 (1976), 323–45.

[42] The Hebrew term is *'elohim 'olim*, 'gods arising' (v. 13), though in v. 14 the visage is in the singular. It is nevertheless possible that more than one spirit was seen, but only Samuel was requested. The ancient rabbis sensed this issue, and inferred from the text that more than one spirit appeared (specifically Moses and Samuel); see *BT. Ḥag.* 4b and *Tanḥuma, 'Emor*, 2.

[43] See W. Hermann, 'Jahwes Triumph Über Mot', *UF* 11 (1979), 372. For the reconstruction of a battle against Mot in Hab. 3: 13, see my comments above, p. 000 n.

[44] It is also hard to assess the status of the image in Jer. 9: 20. For the suggestion that YHWH entered the netherworld, see Alan Cooper, 'PS 24: 7–10; Mythology and Exegesis', *JBL* 102 (1983), 37–55.

C. MYTH AND METAPHOR

One of the paradoxes of myths is the way they create the sense of a living or literal truth through an 'artful indirectness'—by the way they 'bear their contexts along with them, in their premises as stories. It is for this reason that myths appear to create or even to reflect the living contents of a world'.[45] Thus though myths are fictions, they are for all that real fictions which are embedded in their own presuppositions and cognitive claims. It is only where these claims are weakened, or where the fictional act is exposed, that myths may become metaphors which betray the constructed nature of the images or imagined worlds they sponsor. In the texts we have examined, biblical myth was seen to include the great acts of YHWH—in primordial times and on behalf of his people in the historical era; as well as modalities of His personality—being an angry or compassionate deity, who is variously engaged or withdrawn from His worshippers and their earthly condition.

The dramatic depiction of God's deeds and emotions in terms of a stark and concrete mythic realism raises the question of how the biblical authors themselves understood these accounts. The answer is not an easy one, but it is of very great importance, since whether certain images are to be construed on the actual or on the figurative plane has considerable bearing on the way we may now penetrate the living theology and mentality of ancient Israel.[46] By way of summation, we may advert here to several criteria introduced earlier, as we attempted to determine, in the various cases, whether the images are first-order descriptions—whereby the texts *immediately* and concretely convey their sense through the imagery used; or whether they are second-order descriptions—whereby the texts convey their sense more *indirectly*, by means of the literary figures used. In the first type, the language of the myths have a direct or primary semantic import; whereas in the second type, the images or accounts have a double semantic import, at once calling attention to the literal level as incongruous or nonsensical (e.g. that God has a hand), and then superimposing another meaning upon it that is deemed to be the real purport or intent of the figure.[47]

It was argued earlier that mythologems tend to convey a direct meaning when the figures used are similar to those found in related ancient Near Eastern texts, where they occur in an indisputably mythic context;[48] and

[45] Lenn Goodman, 'Mythic Discourse', in Shlomo Biderman and Ben-Ami Scharfstein (edd.), *Myths and Fictions* (Leiden: E. J. Brill, 1993), 108.

[46] See Wheeler Robinson, 'The Council of Yahweh', 151 and 157, who speaks in this vein regarding the divine council.

[47] I here adapt for present purposes, the discussion by Eva Feder Kittay, *Metaphor: Its Cognitive Force and Linguistic Structure* (Oxford: Clarendon Press, 1987), 89; however, in her view, at the first level the import of the metaphors are forgotten or dead.

[48] Cf. my use of the principles of parsimony and charity above, pp. 17–20. Also note the comments of Gary Lang, 'Dead or Alive? Literality and God-Metaphors in the Hebrew Bible', *JAAR* 62 (1994), 524f.

further, where the discourse is set within an arc of intentionality that gives the speakers' words a literal purpose. Thus in the various divine petitions where the combat motif occurs, the appeal to God to remember His past acts and save His servants from suffering makes it unlikely that the speaker would be depicting fictional or metaphorical elements. Similarly, from the other perspective, when God refers to His own saving actions, it is also unlikely that the import of His words is merely figurative. However, when the literary figure strikes one as impossible (e.g. that Pharaoh is a *tannin*), one immediately perceives a gap between the image (the dragon) and its vehicle (the king), and regards it as an ironic figure.

Another way that myth is portrayed is through a succession of dramatic actions and images. Within this setting, certain figures tend to be taken mythically and directly; whereas outside such a context they float loose as separate tropes or metaphors. For example, in many stark depictions of YHWH as a warrior coming to battle, His fury is depicted in terms of snorting fire from His nostrils. The fantastic realism of the imagery tends to have a more direct mythic impact in a context filled with other fantastic features, than it does when it occurs alone. In such cases, the isolated reference to God's anger as a fuming nose conveys a more metaphorical and hyperbolic sense. The same holds true for images of God's arm or face: in a dramatic or visionary context these figures function as the active anthropomorphic elements of living myth; whereas when they appear as isolated images, they seem to function more as metaphors for divine power or presence. Medieval allegorists (like Maimonides) do not make this distinction.

It should be added that the movement between myth and metaphor is labile—with old or dormant images coalescing in new ways, or losing their mythic vitality and dramatic quality. This is true both for the whole range of mythologems ancient Israel shared with its neighbours, and for the many new adaptations and variations found in the Hebrew Bible itself. Mythopoesis is thus a living process, with its own traditions and processes of development.

D. MYTH AND TRADITION

In examining features of myth and mythmaking in the Hebrew Bible, it is clear that myth is itself a feature of cultural tradition—not simply some archaic component of consciousness or creativity. Myths arise and develop within spheres of culture, and attest to this repeatedly, through what is received, revised, or rejected. The 'work' of myth, so-called, is thus as much a matter of deliberation as of spontaneous intuition; as much a product of fixed genres and phraseology as of innovative combinations or mixed forms (the so-called *Mischgattungen*).

The dynamic between a received *traditum* and a transmitted *traditio* unfolds along two axes: the overall stream of Near Eastern myths, of which ancient Israel was a component; and the internal stream of biblical traditions, in their various forms and formulations. The examples reviewed portrayed such actions as the divine combat against sea monsters, the advent of the deity to war or judgement upon a heavenly chariot (often a meteorological complex), the thunderous roar of the divine hero and its effect upon the earth, and the withdrawal from or rejection of His Temple by the deity because of ritual offences committed therein; they also presented interior divine states, and such moods as anger or mercy, and such mental faculties as memory or forgetting. These components are also found in ancient Canaanite and Mesopotamian sources of many kinds—including mythic, hymnic, and historical compositions. Their stylistic parallels or reflexes in Israelite literature show them to be part of a broad cultural continuum, specific theological or idiomatic differences notwithstanding. It thus serves little purpose to consider the biblical features as the borrowed or fragmentary elements of pagan civilizations, unless the purpose is to dismiss them as merely metaphoric or frozen figures—as stylistic conceits with no inherent validity or vitality. But the biblical evidence examined belies this characterization, insofar as its mythic imagery and language are dynamic and purposeful compositional features. Hence the use or adaptation in ancient Israel of common Near Eastern topics like primordial battles with sea monsters should no more stigmatize the inherent vitality of this mythic feature in its new setting than, say, the possibility that the battle between Marduk against Ti᾿amat in the Babylonian creation account reflects the (borrowed) atmospheric components of a West Asiatic milieu.[49] By the same token, the hymnic references to YHWH's advent on a storm cloud, with earth-shattering effects, is no less a dramatic mythic reality than comparable depictions of the manifestations of Adad or Ishtar.[50] Close attention to context and expression has repeatedly provided the measure for assaying and asserting the validity of mythic features in Hebrew Scripture—and this criterion should be the determinative one for any such evaluation.

It was repeatedly demonstrated that diverse circles of ancient Israelite tradition integrated mythic components throughout the course of Israelite literature, in different genres and for a host of different purposes. In this context, the following sequences are illustrative.

1. The theme of 'God's heavenly advent to battle or judgement' recurs repeatedly over the course of a millennium. Already in the oldest poetry, YHWH is celebrated as the one who fought for His people from on high, and routed the population of Canaan for His people: 'O Jeshurun, there is none

[49] See Thorkild Jacobsen, 'The Battle between Marduk and Ti᾿amat', *JAOS* 88 (1968), 104–8.
[50] For the evidence, see above, pp. 45–6, 55.

like God (El), who rides through the heavens (*rokheb ba-shamayim*) to help you, through the skies in his majesty . . . He drove out the enemy before you, by his command (*va-yo'mer*): "Destroy"' (Deut. 33: 26–7). Other old victory hymns similarly 'extol Him (Elohim) who rides the clouds (*rokheb ba-ʿarabot*)' when He goes forth 'at the head of (His) army', surrounded by 'myriads and myriads of chariots'; who caused the earth to tremble, and issued his 'decree' (*'omer*) against the kings of Canaan (Ps. 68: 5, 8–9, 12–18). Ancient military hymns also sing of God's victories in those days—of how He 'came forth from Seir' and 'the earth trembled; the heavens dripped . . . [and] the mountains quaked before YHWH' (Judg. 5: 4–5). Such a victory was wrought with the aid of the cosmic armies of God, as the singer acknowledges. 'The stars fought from heaven, from their courses they fought against Sisera. The torrent Kishon swept [the kings] away, the raging torrent, the torrent Kishon' (vv. 20–1). Ps. 18: 8–20 gives an even more epical version of such divine battles, and of God who not only rides on clouds and cherubs, but blasts with His breath, roars with His voice, and hurls His shafts of lightning to rout the foe.[51] The theme of God's roar also heralds divine action or judgement in many prophetic sources over the centuries (cf. Amos 1: 2; Jer. 25: 30–1; Joel 4: 14–17). Similarly, oracles of judgement against the nations or their gods include the mythic theme of a divine advent upon a 'swift cloud' (*ʿab qal*; Isa. 19: 1), or 'in a whirlwind' and striding upon a 'cloud' (*ʿanan*; Nah. 1: 3).

2. The 'appearance of the Lord (or His *kabod*) upon a heavenly chariot' also figures in events of judgement in different circles. In priestly (or related) sources, this could be to judge a local dispute (Num. 14: 2–25; 17: 6–25), or ritual abominations in the national Shrine (Ezekiel 10–11). In liturgical sources, this figure could celebrate YHWH's cosmic rule over Zion, and His support for a royal viceroy who receives divine aid on the day of battles. In one celebrated expression, an older oracle reported as 'YHWH said to my lord, "Sit at My right hand while I make your enemies your footstool"' (Ps. 110: 1), was invoked as a word of enduring promise to a king: 'YHWH will stretch forth from Zion your mighty sceptre; hold sway over your enemies! . . . YHWH is at your right hand. He crushes kings in His day of wrath. He works judgement upon the nations, piling up bodies, crushing heads far and wide' (vv. 2, 5–6). Other liturgies recall different oracles of divine protection and support of the king's hand. In Psalm 89 this feature assumes a mythic resonance through reference to the Lord's victories against sea monsters as a precedent of cosmic power (vv. 10–11), and the

[51] One may add that the mythic traditions were also carried and expressed in artwork. See, for example, in H. P. L'Orange, *Studies in the Iconography of Cosmic Kingship* (Oslo: H. Aschehoug & Co. (W. Nygaard), 1953); and also in 'The Smiting God: A Study of a Bronze in the Pomerance Collection in New York', *Levant*, 4 (1972), 111–34.

presentation of his promise of royal aid through the figure of God setting the king's 'hand upon the sea, his right hand upon the rivers' (v. 26).[52]

3. These mythic configurations recur without any significant gap down to the last stratum of biblical literature. A close look at the imagery found in Daniel 7 is most instructive in this regard, since it is permeated with the mythic terms and traditions that we have been considering.[53] This chapter begins with a vision of four winds 'stirring up the great sea' (v. 2), from which various beasts arise—the fourth being the most awesome, with ten horns and a 'new little horn' that emerges as the visionary gazes upon the spectacle (vv. 7–8). Thereafter, a figure called the 'Ancient of Days' (*ʿatiq yomin*) is seen sitting upon a heavenly throne, surrounded by flames and wheels flashing fire (v. 10); 'thousands upon thousands serve him, myriads upon myriads stand before him' (v. 11); and 'one like a human being came with the clouds of heaven (*ʿananei shemayaʾ*)', and 'reached the Ancient of Days and was presented to him' (v. 13). In the interpretation given to Daniel by one of the heavenly attendants, the fourth beast arising from the sea represents a particular political threat, and the final little horn a most arrogant affront against the 'Most High (*ʿilaʾah*)' (v. 25)—but in the end it will be 'destroyed' by the heavenly court forever, and 'dominion' given to 'the people of the holy ones of the Most High (*qadishei ʿelyonin*)' (v. 26), as 'an everlasting kingdom (*malkhut ʿalam*)' (v. 27).

Although portrayed as components of a vision symbolizing a succession of political empires down to the mid-second century BCE, interpreters have recognized in the foregoing images traces of earlier Canaanite and biblical mythologems. The roiling sea that sets the context for the offence, and the multiple beasts that arise from it, recall images of a multi-headed sea monster fought and vanquished by a divine hero;[54] the Ancient of Days upon his throne of judgement with divine attendants is an old portrait of the pantheon, and the divine epithet *ʿatiq yomin* has evoked El's epithet *ʾab šnm*, 'Father of Years', for many commentators;[55] the one like a human being who appears upon the 'clouds of heaven' recalls many similar portrayals of YHWH, most notably the designation *rokheb ba-ʿarabot* ('Rider of the

[52] For this psalm and its mythic dimensions, and a Mesopotamian parallel, see above, pp. 33, 42–3.

[53] For a comprehensive overview, see the presentation of John J. Collins, *Daniel* (Hermeneia; Minneapolis: Fortress Press, 1993), 286–91.

[54] See Collins, ibid. 287f.; and also in 'Stirring up the Great Sea: The Religio-Historical Background of Daniel 7', in A. S. van der Woode (ed.), *The Book of Daniel in the Light of New Findings* (Leuven: University Press, 1993), 121–36. For an early identification of the fourth beast with the sea-monster Ltn found in *CTA* 5. 1. 1–3 above, see Otto Eissfeldt, *Baʿal Zaphon, Zeus Cassius und der Durchzug der Israeliten durchs Meer* (Halle: Niemeyer, 1932), 25–30.

[55] Frank M. Cross, *Canaanite Myth and Hebrew Epic* (Cambridge, Mass.: Harvard University Press, 1973), 16; earlier, Leonhard Rost, 'Zur Deutung der menschensohnes in Daniel 7', in G. Dalling (ed.), *Gott und die Götter: Festgabe für Erich Fascher zum 60. Geburtstag* (Berlin: Evangelische Verlag, 1948), 42.

Clouds'), and of Baʿal, who bears the epithet of *rkb ʿrpt* ('Rider of the Clouds');[56] the heavenly 'holy ones' (*qedoshim*) with whom the Jewish people are aligned, are part of the divine pantheon known by that term in Canaanite and Israelite literature;[57] and finally, the 'everlasting kingdom' (*malkhut ʿalam*) to be given to the 'people' recalls a similar idiom used of the kingdom of Baʿal (*mlkt ʿlmk*) and of YHWH (*malkhut kol ʿolamim*).[58]

Such continuities and correlations are sufficient to show the ongoing vitality of these mythic themes for over a millennium, and their reuse in diverse settings and circles in ancient Israel.[59] To assume a mythic gap is clearly presumptuous, despite the widely scattered evidence; and any assumption that the biblical images are merely frozen figures, without meaning or vitality, ignores the function of the evidence in its received settings. If the imagery were dead, why use it? What would be the purpose of its use in purposeful contexts? One should thus rather suppose that the very diversity of forms and features is indicative of ongoing mythic creativity; and the fact that the genres carrying these mythic features are themselves not mythic should also not be determinative in deciding the contextual or stylistic validity of the individual cases. Take Exod. 24: 15–18, for example. Should the fact that Moses enters the divine chariot cloud at Sinai, there to encounter the *kabod* of God, be reduced to a stylistic figure, or be one that prefigures God's presence in the tabernacle and Moses' encounters with him there?[60] Why not rather assume that Moses is presented as a person able to cross between the natural and supernatural realms, and that the mythic imagery used to depict such an episode serves historical purposes even as it gives a mythic dimension to history? The stylistic decision to present Moses in this way was certainly not intended to neutralize its religious import. Any evaluation of the meaning of the passage must bear such considerations in mind.

4. The recognition that mythic traditions may be carried by non-mythic genres may lead to comparative evaluations or annotations. It was noted

[56] *CTA* 2. 1. 2. For the link to Dan. 7: 13, see J. A. Emerton, 'The Origin of the Son of Man Imagery', *JNES* 9 (1958), 225–40; earlier, Rost, 'Zur Deutung der menschenschnes', 41–3.

[57] Cf. Friedrich, 'Kleine Bermerkungen Zu Texten aus Ras Schamra', 82; and also F. M. Cross and R. J. Saley, 'Phoenician Incantations on a Plaque of the Seventh Century B. C. from Arslan Tash in Upper Syria', *BASOR* 197 (1970), 45 and n. 19; and Ps. 89: 6, 8; Job 15: 5.

[58] Cf. *CTA* 2. 1. 6; and Ps. 145: 13.

[59] This point is sufficient to my mind for pointing to an inner-biblical stream of mythic tradition (albeit grounded in common Near Eastern elements), rather than Canaanite channels of transmission. For the latter consideration, see Collins, *Daniel*, 291–4. The ongoing vitality of the cult of Baʿal Haddu into late times need not be determinative in this regard, and the reuse of the sea combat in Christian visionary texts like Revelation 12 could derive from inner-biblical and Jewish traditions (like Daniel 7). The evidence for the Baʿal cult is assembled by Rollin Kearns, *Vorfragen zur Christologie* (Tübingen: Mohr–Siebeck, 1982), iii. 46–57; the case for a mythic background in Revelation 12 has been made by Adela Yarbro Collins, *The Combat Myth in the Book of Revelation* (Harvard Dissertations in Religion, 9; Missoula: Scholars Press, 1976), esp. ch. 2.

[60] Cf. Exod. 40: 34–5; Num. 14: 10–11.

earlier that a myth of a fallen deity was used in the political diatribe found in Isa. 14: 4–23; and that this structure may be detected elsewhere in Scripture, albeit with variations of emphasis and terminology. The diatribe against the king of Tyre in Ezek. 28: 11–19 also lends itself to comparative analysis. For one thing, it is obvious that this text, like others of the same type, inveighs against a human king for his divine pretensions, and condemns him to death for this hubris. For another, the polemic is also a more mythic version of the rebuke for presumptions of godliness found in vv. 1–10. In the latter, the royal leader is castigated for fatuous vainglory, as evidenced by his boast: 'I am a god (*'el*); I dwell in the divine assembly (*moshab 'elohim*),[61] in the midst of the seas'—like El himself.[62] But God condemns the ruler to an ignominious death: nothing will remain of his pompous and false boasts. In this formulation the mythic dimension is used ironically, as part of the political polemic, with no implication that the king ever achieved divine wisdom (*leb 'elohim*, 'the heart of a god'; v. 6) or immortality. There is also no indication that the ruler's 'radiance' (*yif'atekha*) is a divine aura,[63] or that its desecration is done by any other than human beings (vv. 7–8).

By contrast, in the more mythic version of this rebuke the king of Tyre is portrayed as a beautiful and wise divine being, created by God and put in 'Eden, the garden of God', amid precious gems and fire-stones. Moreover, he is also called a 'cherub' whose place is on 'the sacred mountain of God'. From the outset, the king was also perfect in his character and demeanour. But this changed in due course, when 'wrongdoing' was committed in his 'trading' practices, and he 'grew haughty' because of his beauty and radiance. God then 'desecrated' and 'banished' this cherub from the holy mountain and 'threw him down' before kings, consuming him in fire for his desecration of this holy precinct.[64]

In this version, as well as in those above, political polemic is palpable, and it provides the basis for the crimes condemned (notably Tyre's trading ventures). Nevertheless, what predominates throughout is the portrayal of

[61] The idiom *moshab 'elohim* has been thought to mean the 'dwelling of a god' or the like; but it seems that the phrase wishes to mark the difference between the singular *'el* and the plural *'elohim* (understood as the divine assembly). The term *mtb* refers to the abode of a god in Ugaritic sources; see next note.

[62] According to *CTA* 4. 4. 21–2, El's abode (*mtb*) was 'in the midst of the headwaters of the two oceans'.

[63] This translation follows Moshe Greenberg, *Ezekiel 21–37* (Anchor Bible 22a; New York: Doubleday, 1997), 572, 575, who follows the rendering in the Syriac and Targum versions. Note also that in Deut. 33: 2 the *hif'il* form of the verb (*hofi'a*) is preceded by the phrase 'YHWH ... shone (*zarah*) upon them from Seir', suggesting that *hofi'a* also has the sense of 'radiated' (Rashbam glosses *he'ir*, 'shone'). The idea of a divine luminosity is established in Mesopotamia (as a *melammu*); and for scriptural examples, see also above, pp. 53–4.

[64] For the double structure of the piece, see Ilana Goldberg, 'Poetic Structure of the Lament over the King of Tyre', *Tarbiz*, 58 (1989), 277–81 (in Hebrew); and the adaptation and use of it in Greenberg, *Ezekiel 21–37*, 587–9.

the being's divine perfection in knowledge and beauty prior to his banishment and death. No doubt some of these mythic features replicate components found in other diatribes against pretentious kings, as noted; but the portrayal of a being who has divine-like knowledge and is banished from Eden because of sin also evokes the mythic tradition found in Genesis 3, and invites a comparison of common elements. From this perspective one will note that the myth of Adam's eviction from God's garden, and the punishment of mortality, mutes any reference to him as a divine-like or immortal being, and presents the acquisition of 'the knowledge of good and evil' to be a metamorphosis of sorts—a becoming 'like the gods' (v. 5), whose penalty is death.[65] Hence the myth in Genesis provides an aetiology for all human mortality (through a scene of deceit and misappropriation of divine knowledge), in contradistinction to Ezekiel's lament over one being's death (because of pride and misuse of his god-given knowledge). One may even wonder whether the appearance of a cherub outside the 'garden of God' in Gen. 3: 24 is a reflex or echo of the myth of that being's banishment found in Ezek. 28: 16.[66] Whatever the case, comparison of these versions shows how a common mythic tradition could be formulated for different cultural purposes.

5. These variations are also indicative of the ongoing mythic imagination in ancient Israel, and its diverse channels of expression. It furthermore underscores just how dependent we are upon the compressed or tendentious versions of myths preserved in a given *traditum*. The situation is exacerbated when a given formulation leaves unclear whether it represents a living tradition of myth, or a poetic conceit that reflects the transformation of myth into a cultural idiom.[67] The following examples illustrate aspects of this relationship between myth and tradition.

(*a*) In Job 25: 2 a comment on the awesome and exacting power of God's judgements opens with the statement, 'Dominion and fear are with Him, He makes peace in His heights (*bi-mromav*)'. Commentators have frequently pondered the relationship between these two phrases, and particularly the meaning of this act of peace. Is the expression some theological assertion of God's cosmic power, indicating his overall dominion; or is it a trace of some mythic tradition linked to an unstated theomachy at the beginning of creation or any time thereafter? Nothing in the context helps resolve this matter; and we would be almost completely at a loss were it not for references in

[65] I prefer to render 'like the gods (*kei-ʾlohim*)' rather than 'like God', because of Gen. 3: 22.

[66] For a hypothetical reconstruction of an Eden myth with a cherub as the original protector of the trees, see Moshe D. Cassuto and Richard D. Barnett, s. v. *kerub*, *Entziqlopedia Miqraʾit* (Jerusalem: Mosad Bialik, 1962), iv. 242.

[67] For a consideration of the shift from myth to metaphor, designated a 'cultural language', see Jurij M. Lotman and Boris Uspenskij, 'Mito, nombre, cultura', in Jurij Lotman *et al.* (edd.), *Semiotica de la cultura* (Madrid: Ediciones Cátedra, 1979), 124f., 133.

other genres to divine wars in heaven. Particularly valuable is the mythic tradition found in Isa. 24: 21, which forecasts a future time when 'YHWH will requite (or: punish) the hosts (*tzebaʾ*) of heaven (*ha-marom*) in the heights (*ba-marom*), and all the kings of the earth on earth'. Such battles are apparently simultaneous, with the Lord defeating the tutelary gods of the nations in heaven in conjunction with His defeat of their earthly viceroys. In another allusion to such matters, a prophecy is addressed to the nations in Isa. 34: 2, stating that 'YHWH is angry at all the nations, furious at all their hosts (*tzebaʾam*)'. One might infer that the hosts mentioned here simply refer to earthly armies, but the sequel suggests that a battle against heavenly troops is indicated. 'All the host of heaven (*tzebaʾ ha-shamayim*) shall moulder; the heavens shall be rolled up like a scroll and all their host shall wither... For my sword shall be drunk (*rivvetah*) in the sky; behold, it shall come down upon Edom... to wreak judgement' (vv. 4–5). In a notable variant, the large Isaiah scroll from Qumran states that God's 'sword shall be seen (*teiraʾeh*) in the sky' in connection with His acts of earthly vengeance. Possibly influenced by this reading, but certainly confirming the overall reality of heavenly wars, is the remark in the *Sibylline Oracles* that 'a clear sign' of 'the end of all things' shall be 'when swords are seen at night in starry heaven... this is the end of war which God, who inhabits heaven, is accomplishing';[68] and similarly, several centuries later, Flavius Josephus speaks of various signs foretelling a future desolation—one of which was 'when a star, resembling a sword, stood over the city'.[69]

Certainly this biblical and post-biblical tradition confirms the persistence of a mythic notion of a divine sword wielded in heavenly battle. Such portrayals have a sense of vividness and prophetic urgency, and may help confirm that some trace of divine battles is indicated in Job 25: 2. To be sure, the latter image affirms the making of peace, not war, and it may even indicate the settlement of strife or rebellions by members of the heavenly pantheon.[70] Either way, the correlation of this passage with a mythic tradition of heavenly battle has significant implications for its literary and cultural status.

(*b*) In the course of a promised blessing for obedience, Moses states that 'YHWH, your God... will bless the fruit of your womb and the fruit of your land, your grain and wine and oil, the calf (*shegar*) of your herd and the lambs (*ʿashterot*) of your flock' (Deut. 7: 12–13). The overall sense is clear,

[68] Book 3. 796–807, as rendered by John J. Collins, in *The Old Testament Pseudepigrapha*, ed. James H. Charlesworth (Garden City, NY: Doubleday & Company, 1983), i. 379 f.

[69] See *The Jewish War* VI. v. 3 (289–90), as rendered by H. St John Thackery, in *Josephus*, III: *The Jewish War. Books IV–VII* (Loeb Library; Cambridge, Mass.: Harvard University Press, 1928), 460 f.

[70] Because of the stern context, it has been supposed that MT *shalom* ('peace') should be vocalized *shillum* ('retribution'); see Naftali H. Tur-Sinai, *The Book of Job* (Jerusalem: Kiryat-Sefer, 1967), 374 f.

but not the precise force of the terms *shegar* (*nomen agentis*: *sheger*; Exod. 13: 10) and *ʿashterot* (*nomen agentis*: *ʿashtarot*; sing. *ʿashtoret*; Judg. 10: 6). The divine aspect of the first term is not indicated in the Hebrew Bible; but the second one (*ʿashtoret*) is the Phoenician goddess of Sidon (1 Kings 11: 5), also worshipped in Israel (1 Sam. 12: 10). How then should the divine blessing be construed? The answer is not made easier by the fact that the name Šagar/Sagar occurs as the divine name for the moon god responsible for cattle (especially the bull-calf) in Mesopotamian texts from the Old Babylonian period on.[71] And closer to home, the name Šgr appears in a Ugaritic god-list,[72] and the divine pair Šgr and ʿAštr is mentioned in the Deir ʿAllah inscription.[73]

Is, then, the phrase 'the *shegar* of your herd, the *ʿashterot* of your flock' in Deut. 7: 13 simply a neutral (or neutralized) 'cultural expression', without any particular mythic force, or does it still convey the power of these divinities responsible for the fertility of calves and lambs? Certainly we must recall in this regard that Hosea rebukes his people for believing that her 'lovers' (the *baʿalim*; Hos. 2: 15) 'provide' her sustenance (v. 7), and not knowing 'that it is I who provides for her the grain, the wine, and the oil' (v. 10). Moreover, the prophet accuses Ephraim of religious deceit, and Judah of 'still following El,[74] and being faithful to the holy ones (*qedoshim*)' (Hos. 12: 1) of the pantheon—presumably divinities like Šgr and ʿAštr who were among the powers (or *baʿalim*) of fertility. As in the previous assertion of superiority, YHWH again adds that when Israel shall repent and reject her idolatrous ways, 'I shall become like a verdant cypress—your fruit comes *from Me*' (14: 9).[75] One can hardly miss the polemical tone here, and conclude that this provides a clue for interpreting Deut. 7: 12–13, where it

[71] See Stephanie Dalley and Beatrice Teissier, 'Tablets for the Vicinity of Emar and Elsewhere', *Iraq*, 54 (1992), 90f.

[72] See Michael Astour, 'Some New Divine Names from Ugarit', *JAOS* 86 (1966), 284 (based on *Ugaritica* 5.3.9).

[73] Cf. Manfred Weippert, 'Die "Bileam" Inschrift von Tell der Alla', *ZDPV* 98 (1982), 100f.

[74] This renders *ʿod radʾim ʾel*, and follows W. Reines, 'Hos. 12:1', *JSS* 2 (1950–1), 156f.

[75] In the preceding clause YHWH says 'It is I who answer (*ʿaniti*) and will look after him (*ve-ʾashurennu*)'—a puzzling expression, that seems to remind the reader that God's power over the sources of life will 'answer (*ʾeʿneh*)' his people's needs, that 'the earth shall answer with grain and corn and oil' (Hos. 2: 23–4). Faced with the conundrum of Hos. 14: 9. Julius Wellhausen offered a remarkable emendation of *ʾani ʿaniti ve-ʾashurennu* to *ʾani ʿanato ve-ʾasherato*, 'I am his Anat and Asherah'; that is I, YHWH, am the power of fertility that Israel has falsely worshipped as Anat and Asherah. See his *Die kleinen Propheten übersetzen mit Notizen* (Skizzen und Vorarbeiten 5; Berlin: Töpelmann, 1893), ad loc. The force of this emendation is now indirectly confirmed by the expression 'YHWH and his Asherah' found in the Kuntillet ʿAjrud inscriptions (from the 8th c. BCE), as Moshe Weinfeld has astutely noted, in his 'Kuntillet ʿAjrud Inscriptions and their Significance', *SEL* 1 (1984), 122. In the inscription, Asherah is presented as the consort of YHWH, whereas Hosea denies this and regards the fertility powers ascribed to Asherah as an aspect of his comprehensive power. Deut. 16: 21 prohibits 'planting an Asherah—any tree—near an altar for YHWH, your God, which you make for yourself'. Such cultic representations presumably reflect a theology and worship of Asherah as YHWH's consort.

is stated that YHWH is the one who will bless His faithful ones with fertile seed and wombs 'on the land that He swore... to give you'. Hence it is likely that the passage does indeed refer to old deities of fertility, but that these have been incorporated into a theology of YHWH's singular power to provide and produce all the bounties of life.[76]

(*c*) The final example is of an entirely different sort, and shows an aspect of mythic tradition in the Hebrew Bible on the borderline of cultural language—where the mythic figures serve as literary tropes for psychological processes. The unexpected case comes from Songs 8: 6–7, where the beloved states that 'love is mighty (*ʿaz*) as death (*mavet*), passion as fierce as Sheol; its flames (*reshafeha*) are flames of fire, a mighty flame (*shalhebetyah*): mighty waters (*mayim rabbim*) cannot quench love, nor rivers (*neharot*) drown it'. This depiction presents the fury of love in terms of two similes and two metaphors, which arguably vibrate with mythic nuances: for the similes comparing love to *mavet* and Sheol may allude to the destructive powers of Mot, the god of death,[77] and to the realm of the underworld; whereas the identification of the heat of passion with mighty 'flames' (*rishpei ʾesh*; *shalhebetyah*) evokes both the divine powers of Reshef,[78] the agent of fever and delirium, and the fury of Yah or His heavenly force.[79] And if these allusions were not enough, the figures of the waters also have mythic nuances in Scripture, as we can see clearly in Hab. 3: 8, 15, where the *neharot* and the *mayim rabbim* both figure in a scene of theomachy against mythic waters.[80]

[76] This polemic against the old Canaanite divinities, and the assertion of YHWH's role as fertile provider, is one more link connecting Deuteronomy and Hosea, including polemics against idolatry. On this point, see Moshe Weinfeld, *Deuteronomy and the Deuteronomic School* (Oxford: Clarendon Press, 1972), appendix B, esp. pp. 366 f.

[77] Further reason to suppose a mythic allusion in the simile *ʿaz ke-mavet*, 'mighty as/like death', may be found in the occurrence of the personal name ʿAzmavet (2 Sam. 23: 31), among the heroic warriors of biblical antiquity; and the depiction in Ugaritic myth that *mt ʿz*, 'Mot was strong' (*KTU* 1. 6 vi: 17). Also suggestive is Ps. 49: 15, which may contain a trace that Mot (MT *mavet*) shepherds the dwellers of Sheol. Cf. already Kimḥi's construal, though he depersonifies 'death'. The MT cantillation seems an attempt to demythologize the older image.

[78] Cf. Deut. 32: 24, which refers to *reshef* as a plague sent by God (by his arrows of destructions, v. 23); and Hab. 3: 5, where *reshef* is part of the retinue of divinities surrounding the divine chariot as it goes into battle (for this feature, see above, pp. 000–0). Much mythological evidence in ancient Israelite and Near Eastern sources has been collected and discussed by D. Conrad, 'Der Gott Reschef', *ZAW* 83 (1971), 157–83; and by Samuel Loewenstamm, s.v. *reshef, Entziqlopedia Miqraʾit* (Jerusalem: Mosad Bialik, 1976), vii. 437–41. See also André Caquot, 'Sur quelques démons dans l'Ancien Testament (*Reshep, Qeteb, Deber*)', *Semitica*, 6 (1956), 53–68.

[79] For the fiery fury of God, cf. Deut. 32: 21–2; fiery agents appear in Pss. 97: 3 and 104: 4. Note also the mythic figure in Ps. 18: 9, where YHWH spits fire from his mouth against his enemies; and also in Amos 7: 4, where he uses fire and even consumes the 'Mighty Tehom'. For the passage in Amos, see also Delbert Hillers, 'Amos 7, 4 and Ancient Parallels', *CBQ* 26 (1964), 221–5. More broadly, see Patrick Miller, 'Fire in the Mythology of Canaan and Israel', *CBQ* 27 (1965), 256–61.

[80] For this battle, see above, pp. 55–6. The terms are also correlated in Ps. 93: 3–4. For an attempt to delineate the mythic features of *mayim rabbim*, see Herbert Mays, 'Some Cosmic

In our trope, these waters are powerless against love, whose might exceeds them both. And indeed, we may suspect that the love poet wishes to evoke this very point, as he seeks to convey the myth-like powers of passion. A tradition of myth thus serves the author with highly charged resonances, even as the divine powers remain subtly concealed within their stylistic tropes and never quite emerge as independent personifications.[81]

The relationship between myth and tradition is thus part of the living dynamics of *traditum* and *traditio*, as materials are received, revised, revivified, and reformulated. There is no one trajectory of development here, but many patterns are realized in diverse genres for different purposes. One feature, however, does not occur in the Hebrew Bible and must await the manifold processes of later Jewish mythmaking—and that is the use of the entirety of Scripture as a thesaurus for ongoing mythic creativity. Indeed, it is only when the *traditum* of ancient Israel becomes the canon of rabbinic Judaism that all of its features may be developed or combined to create new myths. This new orientation will help sponsor the remarkable developments our subject undergoes in classical Midrash over the next centuries. It is to this subject that we now turn.

Connections of *Mayim Rabbîm*', *JBL* 74 (1955), 9–21. Also note that Canaanite El's river is called *rbm* (*CTA* 3.3.35–6).

[81] Remarkably, in a Ugaritic myth it is stated that 'El's power is like the sea (*kym*); El's power is like the flood (*kmdb*)'; see *CTA* 23. 33–5 (Gordon, *UT* 52). The evocation of power here (*yd*) also alludes to sexual potency.

II
Rabbinic Myth and Mythmaking

5
Introduction

A. THE PHENOMENON: TOPICS AND TECHNIQUES

Rabbinic and other post-biblical Jewish literature is a vast fund of myths and mythic traditions—some surviving from ancient Near Eastern antiquity, and much more deriving from both Graeco-Roman Palestine and Sassanian Babylonia during the first five centuries of the common era. The spread and diffusion of this material is not always clearly marked or traceable; and the fragments of tradition that are known often appear in a diversity of sources (not all of which are Jewish). It is thus a matter of particular interest when it is possible to follow the permutations of one topic over a vast temporal and geographical expanse, as is the case, for example, with the mythic motif of heavenly giants and other beings who were punished because of their sexual contact with earthly women. In this particular case, the meagre and opaque evidence surviving from the biblical text and its Greek translation (Gen. 6: 1–4) is greatly supplemented by texts preserved in the Dead Sea Scrolls, as well as in pseudepigraphic, midrashic, and even Manichaean sources.[1] Undoubtedly, features of this mythic tradition are very early, and have been distorted by their ancient Israelite tradents; whereas other elements certainly reflect expansions of the theme in the course of its ongoing reception. In yet other instances we can observe how mythic traditions from one locale were reported centuries later in another—as when Rav Dimi (one of the peripatetic *neḥutei*) 'returned' (literally, went down) to Babylonia (in the fourth century CE), and reported to his colleagues there about old mythic traditions about the sea monster that he had learned in the academies of the Land of Israel.[2] Some of these features are of great antiquity and reflect features not reported in the Hebrew Bible, in any shape or fashion.[3]

Certainly, the issues of continuity and creativity must be evaluated in each specific instance. But what is particularly notable with respect to the rabbinic

[1] A substantial amount of material has been assembled and discussed by John C. Reeves, *Jewish Lore in Manichaean Cosmogony: Studies in the Book of Giants Traditions* (Cincinnati: Hebrew Union College Pres, 1992). And see also in Bernard Heller, 'La Chute des anges: Shemhazai, Ouzza et Azael', *RÉJ* 60 (1910), 202–12; and Josef T. Milik, *The Books of Enoch: Aramaic Fragments of Qumran Cave 4* (Oxford: Clarendon Press, 1976).

[2] See my *The Exegetical Imagination: On Jewish Thought and Theology* (Cambridge, Mass.: Harvard University Press, 1998), esp. pp. 47–8, 53–4.

[3] Various specific instances will be adduced in due course.

sources themselves, is that the mythic and related traditions survive in this literary setting through their transmission by a given sage or tradent—and this often accounts for the way a whole range of mythic creatures or events otherwise unknown are adduced and represented. That is to say, the topics are 'voiced' (by named or unnamed speakers) in brief statements, and reported apart from any larger narrative context; and they are introduced as data or elements bearing upon a specific rabbinic topic or theme, and are thus presented or expanded upon as mythic elements in their own right. For example, it is in the context of a halakhic query about the exact meaning of the biblical term *zevaʿot* (a determination bearing on the type of blessing to be recited upon experiencing this natural phenomenon) that the word is taken to indicate earth tremors and its aetiology is variously linked to the compassionate tears of God falling into the Great Sea.[4] Similarly, it is within the context of a halakhic classification of certain morphological types that the cosmic *ziz*-bird (a mythic creature whose wingspan can eclipse the sun's orb) is adduced,[5] or the *ʾadnei sadeh* (who 'is a man of the field, and lives from his umbilical cord') is cited and discussed.[6] By the same token, it is in the context of a cluster of traditions about the primordial gathering of waters on the third day of creation (Gen. 1: 6) that we are told that when the upper and lower waters were separated (on the preceding day) they cried[7]—an event undoubtedly reflecting some myth of personified powers deprived of their primordial commingling or syzygy.[8] The full account is not given.

In these and other examples, brief, allusive, or fragmentary mythic matters not found in the Hebrew Bible are preserved. No apology is made for their content; rather, they are treated as significant topics of mythic tradition that are duly recorded, annotated, and discussed. Indeed, the fact that they are adduced by rabbinic sages, and are variously incorporated into halakhic or

4 Cf. *BT Berakhot* 59a, and the discussion below.

5 *Leviticus Rabba* 22.10; in the edition of Mordecai Margulies (Jerusalem: Wahrmann Books, 1962), iii. 523. For the gigantic size of the bird, see the description in *BT Baba Batra* 73b.

6 *M. Kilʾayim* 8.5, where he is classed as a wild animal and a human being for different laws. The comment in *JT Kilʾayim* 8.4, 31c correctly renders the Hebrew *ʾadnei sadeh* as Aramaic *bar nash de-ṭur* ('a man of the field'), for *ʾaden* is a variant of *ʾadam* and *ṭur* is not 'mountain' but field (as proved by Saul Lieberman in *Tarbiz*, 8 (1937), 367). For other matters and the folklore issues involved, see the review by Daniel Sperber, *Magic and Folklore in Rabbinic Literature* (Tel Aviv: Bar-Ilan Press, 1994), 21–5.

7 *Genesis Rabba* 5.4; in the edition of Juda Theodor and Chanokh Albeck (Jerusalem: Wahrmann Books, 1965), i. 34f. (hereinafter, Theodor–Albeck).

8 See explicitly in *Siddur Rabba de-Bereiʾshit Rabba*, in *Batei Midrashot*, ed. Abraham Wertheimer (Jerusalem: Ketav Ve-Sefer, 1980), i. 368 (par. 10). The biblical text is, of course, quite restrained on the subject, merely stating that God himself first proclaimed a division between the upper and lower realms by fiat; and then 'made' the expanse that provided the separation (Gen. 1: 6–7). For myths of separation, cf. K. Marót, 'Die Trennung von Himmel und Erde', *Acta Antiqua Hungarica*, 1 (1951), 35ff.; see also W. Staudacher, *Die Trennung von Himmel und Erde: Ein vorgriechischer Schöpfundsmythus bei Hesiod und den Orphikern* (diss.; Tübingen: K. Bölzie, 1942).

exegetical works, gives them particular authority and validity within the broad expanse of the official oral tradition—investing them with a mode of 'curricular credibility' that exceeds mere folk dicta without any particular status or context. Chief among the means of authorizing and validating this diverse mythic material is Scripture itself.

With the closure of the scriptural canon, the entire content of the Hebrew Bible—the central and authoritative corpus of written teachings for Judaism—was the major source and resource for mythic traditions.[9] It served as a 'source' insofar as its content signalled the central topics of interest, both by virtue of what was said and what was not said. Thus the creation of the world, the exodus from Egypt, the revelation at Sinai, the destruction of the Temple, and the exile of the nation, were among the major issues whose details would be elaborated upon—both to amplify details and explain ambiguities or seeming contradictions in the biblical text, and to specify features of divine activity or feeling during these events. With the fixing of the language and orthography of Scripture, some of these mythologoumena might originate with the text itself. But it did not necessarily start or stop there; for alongside the Hebrew Bible a vast fund of oral tradition continued to exist on these and other topics, and many new myths developed around the biblical events themselves and God's role or reaction—not to mention those traditions received (from without) or generated (from within) about fantastic creatures or the sights and sounds of the natural world. It is just here that Scripture serves as a cultural 'resource', providing *post hoc* textual proof for the various myths already in circulation. This is particularly evident where the given exegetical support is blatantly forced or counter-intuitive, so that one must rather suppose that the biblical text now gives authority to a pre-existent mythic assertion. But either way, whether as originary source or as secondary resource, the 'hidden myths' of Scripture are revealed or justified. They appear as features integral to the composite oral tradition, and are not relegated to any special or secondary status.

Given the fundamental and pervasive correlation of the myths with scriptural citations in rabbinic literature and culture, we may profitably turn now briefly to a specification of some of the hermeneutical processes involved. These examples will thus provide an introduction to the exegetical character of rabbinic myths and mythmaking, as well as some of the stylistic features and spectrum of interests found within this cultural corpus. Hence the following cases may be deemed propaedeutic and typical, but hardly systematic or exhaustive. In fact, some of the topics discussed below shall be taken up in a fuller form or along a wider arc of examples in subsequent chapters.

[9] For the dynamic between a closed canon and open interpretation, see my discussion in *The Exegetical Imagination*, ch. 1 ('Midrash and the Nature of Scripture').

I. Aetiological Specification

The sounds and sensations of the natural world have been a primary source of mythic speculations since time immemorial. Among these we may count the rumbling of the earth during an earthquake. Rav Qaṭṭina once pondered its 'meaning', and he queried a necromancer by whose home he chanced to be during such a tremor.[10] The necromancer chastised the sage for his lack of knowledge and told him that 'Whenever the Holy One, blessed be He, remembers His children who are in distress among the nations of the world, two drops fall from His eyes into the Great Sea and His voice resounds from one end of the earth to the other'. Qaṭṭina, we are told, had a technical reason for judging the necromancer's explanation deceitful (if there were two drops one would have expected a double tremor, not one); but the narrator of the episode goes on to say that the 'real reason' the sage denied this aetiology of the tears 'was to prevent the people from being led astray after the necromancer'. Accordingly, we are told that Rav Qaṭṭina himself explained the phenomenon as 'God clapping His hands, as it states (in Scripture), "I too shall clap my hands together and abate My anger" (Ezek. 21:22)'. In an addendum we are further informed that a Rabbi Nathan explained the event as 'God groaning, as it states, "I shall abate My fury against them and be calm" (Ezek. 5: 13)'; while the sages, among other interpretations, say that the event is 'God stamping in the heavens, as it states, "A shout echoes throughout the earth like the sound of those who trample the vats" (Jer. 25: 30)'.[11]

This passage is instructive on several counts. First, it presents a rabbi asking a necromancer about the meaning of a natural event, and the latter responding in mythic terms, saying that the earth tremors are the result of God's tears, shed in compassion for His people's suffering. Significantly, this explanation is without any scriptural basis, and this absence sets it off from the several interpretations offered by Qaṭṭina and his associates, who not only identify the natural event with divine anger, but hook that reason to various verses in Scripture. Indeed, the proof-texts offered are taken out of their original context and have nothing to do with the issue at hand—serving rather to demonstrate the biblical basis for certain types of divine pathos. One will also be struck by the list of multiple explanations. The 'myth of earthquakes' thus has several variants, with no version deemed more authoritative than another. Each sage makes his own myth and (unlike the necromancer) leans on Scripture for support. The result is that the citation itself assumes a mythic dimension, an exegetical refraction of the mythic assertion cast upon its surface.

Many of these features recur in a cluster of speculations on the number of pillars that underpin the world.[12] In one Talmudic source we are told, in

[10] *BT Berakhot* 59a, noted above (n. 4). [11] Ibid. [12] In *BT Ḥagigah* 12b.

rapid succession, that the world stands on twelve, seven, and one support respectively, and verses from Scripture are adduced to enforce these claims (Deut. 32: 8; Prov. 9: 1; 10: 25). But as proofs these texts are quite forced, and it is quite unclear how all these verses were construed in terms of cosmic pillars. Certainly, one can readily see how the citation of Job 9: 7 ('Who shakes the earth from its place, till its pillars quake') could have elicited mythic explanations from Scripture, though the specifics are lacking; however, one is much more puzzled about the exegetical use in this connection of Deut. 32: 8, since it apparently refers to boundary markers on earth, and not pillars subtending it. Our report has not explicated the matter and we are left to our own imaginative devices. Equally suggestive, but directly contradicting these foregoing speculations, is the assertion that God actually supports the world on His arm. This statement is linked to Deut. 33: 27. To make this mythic remark work, the plain sense of the puzzling biblical passage, 'and underneath are the everlasting arms (*umi-taḥat, zeroʿot ʿolam*)', was presumably construed as stating 'and beneath (His; namely, God's) arms, is the world (*umi-taḥat zeroʿot, ʿolam*)'.[13] Hence we have moved from a textual phrase that seems to be part of an assertion of God's providential aid for His people to a mythic emblem of a cosmological nature.[14] One can hardly doubt that we have here a pre-existent myth in search of a proof-text—which it found by clever exegesis.[15] By contrast, no support is adduced for another myth of this aetiological type, which states that the world 'hangs' from the fins of the sea monster Leviathan.[16]

II. Value Attribution

The ancient rabbis read Scripture with their own theological values, and in accord with certain inherited traditions, so it is no wonder that their mythic perceptions of God's acts are in part freighted with a predetermined cultural load. Among these topics is the hermeneutical principle: 'Whenever (the Tetragram) YHWH is mentioned, (it indicates God's) Attribute of

[13] This proof also appears in *Siddur Rabba de-Bereishit Rabba*, ed. Wertheimer, i. 366 (par. 8), where it is said that both this world and the one to come are under God's arm, and appear like an amulet suspended from the arm. And see also the idiom in Peter Schäfer (ed.), *Geniza-Fragmente zur Hekhalot-Literatur* (Tübingen: J. C. B. Mohr, 1984), 100 (= T–S K 21.95 C 1a:14f.).

[14] For the understanding that the passage indicates that God carries Israel protectively in His arms, see R. David Kimḥi and Ibn Ezra, ad loc.

[15] This proof-text concludes a series which contends that the pillars rest on the mountains, which rest on the waters, which rest on the wind—which is supported by God's arm. There would thus seem to be an attempt to create a meta-myth from the various parts of the anthology.

[16] See *Zohar* II. 34b. This tradition is related to the earlier version in *Pirkei de-Rabbi Eliezer* 9 (end), where it is stated that the 'middle bar (*bariaḥ*)' upon which the world 'stands' lies between two fins of Leviathan. This statement is presumably based on a mythic extrapolation of Leviathan's cognomen *naḥash bariaḥ* ('slant serpent'; Isa. 27: 1). An explicit link between the bars and pillars of the earth is made in *Pirkei de-Rabbi Eliezer* 10 (regarding Jonah 2: 6). The mythic meaning of the foregoing Zoharic passage will be considered below, in Part III.

Mercy . . . (and) whenever (the divine Name) Elohim is mentioned (it indicates God's) Attribute of Judgement'.[17] Such a principle guided the reading of many passages, and suggests that God's particular pathos is marked in the Torah by the presence of a specific divine Name. Indeed, given the different occurrences of these names (separately or in combination) one is led to perceive a certain volatility in the divine nature—of a mythic and highly personalized sort. God is neither an impassive nor otiose deity, but, following the lead of Scripture itself, is one who cares for and responds to His creatures. It is notable, therefore, that in the two places where the above principle is cited, it occurs in the context of a biblical verse stating that 'Elohim remembered' a particular individual and accorded them their just due;[18] and that it is introduced by the midrashic comment: 'Woe to the wicked, who turn (God's) Attribute of Mercy into (His) Attribute of Judgement'. For not only will God give the righteous just deserts, because of their acts of mercy or piety or justice, but He will also impose a punishment in response to iniquity and disobedience. The human and divine realms are thus intertwined, such that human actions can effect divine pathos and reaction.

This powerful myth of the divine personality, and the role of names in marking the modalities of God's nature, comes to striking expression in an old comment on Gen. 2: 4 ('On the day that YHWH Elohim made heaven and earth').[19] The sages were puzzled why the 'full Name' (YHWH Elohim) only first appears at this point (for only the name Elohim occurs in Genesis 1); and thus some ancients reasonably suggested that the complete Name was used because the work of creation was now full or complete.[20] But other interpreters went further, and used this formulation (implying the conjunction of the Attributes of Mercy and Judgement) as a wedge to open a mythic space within the fixed narrative. A parable provides the means: Deftly, the lemma is compared to a king who had two cups, and pondered that if he poured hot liquid into them they would crack, whereas if he poured cold liquid into them they would contract. Neither solution was just right, and so he determined to mix the two fluids, 'and (the cups) stood (firm)'. The implication of this parable is then drawn for the case at hand, and a mythic narrative is presented whereby the Holy One ponders the problem of creation. 'If I create the world with the Attribute of Mercy, sins will multiply;

[17] This is the formulation of R. Samuel bar Naḥman in *Genesis Rabba* 33. 3 and 73. 3 (Theodor–Albeck 308, and 847), with textual examples. A fuller discussion of the principles and theology involved will be given below.

[18] Referring to Noah and Rachel, in Gen. 8: 1 and 30: 23. The commentators are particularly puzzled by the use of the name Elohim with acts of beneficence. A solution is that this marks the *status quo ante*, when God was in His mode of judgement. A full discussion will be taken up below.

[19] *Genesis Rabba* 12. 15 (Theodor–Albeck, 112–13).

[20] The comment is given anonymously in *Genesis Rabba* 13.3; it is presumably based on the fact that Gen. 2: 4 opens with the clause, 'These are the generations of the heavens and the earth'—a statement of totality.

(whereas if I do so) with the Attribute of Judgement, the world will not last. The only thing is for Me to create it with both attributes—and would that it might stand fast!'[21]

In this remarkable myth of origins we are made privy to a problematic divine ambivalence—for if only mercy were employed in the creation, injustice would run rampant; but if justice were to prevail, the world would be destroyed by punishment. Indeed, we may imagine that the ambivalence belongs to the mythmaker as well, who perceived a world with both goodness and evil and invented a mythic theodicy to account for it. But if this was his sense, it is also remarkable that he does not have God say in some superior way that He will administer the world with mercy and justice, as is needed and according to His sovereign judgement.[22] Rather, he presents a god who is neither sure how to proceed with the creation, nor completely sure of the result. The name YHWH Elohim thus allows the exegete to invent a myth of divine limitations—a somewhat tragic-comic trailer to the biblical account in Genesis 1. Basing himself on the semantic values traditionally attached to the divine Names in Scripture, and their conjunction at this point, the mythoplast inserts a counter-myth into the text wherein God creates by fiat, sovereignly asserting that all is 'good'. Our teaching thus provides a more ambiguous truth about creation, but a truth no less marked and authorized by the language of Torah—through exegesis.

III. Verbal Re-specification

In certain cases, the letters of Scripture provide the basis for a mythic invention designed to explain or otherwise account for some thing or event. For example, in the context of an explanation of why the 'dry land' (*yabashah*) is called *'eretz*) ('earth') in Gen. 1: 10, we are told that the primordial earth was an obedient creation of God's, and ceased to extend when He 'said' so. This compliance is strikingly formulated by an exegetical play on the noun itself, since we read that 'the dry land' was called *'eretz* because 'she wished to do His (God's) will' (*she-ratzta la-ʿasot retzono*).[23] One may suppose that our myth was one of several accounts telling how the land, sea, or sky acquired their limits[24]—narratives that were supported by a mythic etymology of the

[21] The image of two cups and the nature of God's attributes is old, and is already attested in the writings of Philo. See the valuable discussion of Shlomo Naeh, '*potērion encheiri kyriou*: Philo and the Rabbis on the Powers of God and the Mixture in the Cup', *Scripta Classica Israelica*, 16 (1997), 91–101.

[22] Also note the teaching in *Genesis Rabba* 14.1 (Theodor–Albeck, 126), where Prov. 29: 4 ('A king establishes (*yaʿamid*) the earth with justice') is construed to indicate that in Gen. 1: 1 Elohim created the world 'with (the Attribute of) Judgement'.

[23] *Genesis Rabba* 5. 8 (Theodor–Albeck, 37).

[24] Cf. the variant of the foregoing mythic type in *BT Ḥagigah* 12b, where the 'world' continued to expand until the creator 'roared' out His order for it to stop. In this account the emphasis is on divine power, not creaturely submission, and the reference to roaring suggests confrontation not compliance.

divine name *ʾEl Shaddai*, as meaning that God (El) is He who (*she-*) said *dai* ('enough') to His creations when they grew out of hand and threatened to overwhelm the world with their profusion.[25] In the context of such tales, the letters of *ʾeretz* in Gen. 1: 10 provided welcome proof from Scripture.[26] It seems less likely that the myth itself originated with creative exegesis.

More daring and of greater cultural significance is another myth of origins that uses Scripture to prove that God created the world with letters from His own Name—not by word or breath, as other texts would suggest.[27] To achieve this result R. Eleazar invoked the difficult verse in Isa. 26: 4 ('For in (*be-*) Yah (YH) the Lord (YHWH) you have an everlasting Rock (*tzur ʿolamim*))', and exegetically construed it to mean that 'with (*be-*) the letters Y–H, YHWH fashioned (*tziyyer*) His world (*ʿolam*)'. Going further, R. Abbahu noted that the noun *ʿolamim* is in fact plural ('worlds'), and thus understood the verse to mean that with each of the letters of the divine Name, Y and H, the Lord created a world—the present world with the letter *H*ey, and the world to come with the letter *Y*od. It is thus that the creation is inscribed with the powerful letters of the Tetragram, these being the substance of the world, not the Attribute of Mercy (or Judgement).

It is obvious that such mythic speculations are of an esoteric and even magical sort, and depend upon prior assumptions about the power of divine names.[28] Armed with this knowledge, mythmakers like R. Eleazar and R. Abbahu could make their remarkable claims and validate them through Scripture. As in the other cases, rabbinic mythopoesis matches a mythologoumenon with the letters of sacred writ, and thereby reveals its basis in that source. Indeed, in the foregoing case, an epithet of divine praise (namely, the metaphor that God is an everlasting Rock) is now interpreted as a mythic statement about the mysteries of origins. The duplication of versions of the creation story's details hardly undermines this myth's authority; in fact, it rather shows that it was the subject of lively speculation, given the complexity of decoding its scriptural trace.

IV. Textual Correlations

In certain striking instances, the exegetical mythmaking does not rest on individual proof-texts, but on the correlation of several passages from within the canonical whole. Most instructive is the teaching that Genesis 1 reveals

[25] This appears in the example from *Genesis Rabba* 8. 7, and elsewhere. The etymology of the divine Name is explicated in *Genesis Rabba* 46. 3 (Theodor–Albeck, 460), with many tradents. The etymon is also connected to the heavens in 8. 7; and cf. in *Pirkei de-Rabbi Eliezer* 3.

[26] Presumably, the noun *ʾeretz* was understood as an apocopated form of the verb *ʾertzah*, 'I wish'.

[27] For the text and variants, see *Genesis Rabba* 12. 10 (Theodor–Albeck, 107–9). I have considered other aspects of this text, and parallels, in *The Exegetical Imagination*, 14–18.

[28] See also this teaching in the magical corpus, *ʾOtiyot de-Rabbi Aqiba* (Version A), in *Batei Midrashot*, ed. Wertheimer, ii. 363.

some of the mysteries of origins, but formulated them in a neutral and laconic style. Full knowledge of these events, and their full mythic reality requires reading the opening narrative of Scripture in light of other passages. 'R. Judah son of R. Simon said, At the beginning of the creation of the world "He (God) revealed hidden things" (Dan. 2: 22); as it is written, "At the beginning Elohim created the heavens" (Gen. 1: 1)—but it does not explicate (this point). Where does it (in fact) explicate (this)? Subsequently, (in the verse) "He stretched out the heavens like gauze" (Isa. 40:22). (And further, it says) "and the earth" (Gen. 1: 1)—but does not explicate. Where does it explicate (it)? Subsequently, "And to the snow He said, 'Be earth'" (Job 37: 7). (And it also says,) "And Elohim said, 'Let there be light'" (Gen. 1: 3)—but does not explicate. Where does it explicate (it)? Subsequently, "He wrapped Himself in light as a garment" (Ps. 104: 2).'[29]

Quite dramatically, the formal account of Genesis 1 is given mythic depth through correlation with other passages in Scripture. Indeed, these latter are not read as so many independent metaphors and stylistic flourishes, but as dramatic mythic moments at the beginning of the creation when God stretched out the heavens, and transformed the moisture of snow into the matter of earth, and wrapped Himself in light as a primary element. Gone is the exalted and terse language; and in its stead come the plastic images of poetry. But these are not deemed mere fictions, but bold mythic elaborations of the initial narrative of Scripture. Perhaps there is even a glimmer of theory here, myth being a dramatic elaboration of hints in the formal narrative of origins. In any case, the exegete at once reveals a mythic core to Genesis 1 while at the same time re-valorizing the poetic images found elsewhere in the biblical text. For the sage, mythic accounts are in truth a more visible and tangible version of the secrets of beginnings—the former being a type of literary truth of precious specificity. Indeed, if Genesis 1 is presented as a divine revelation of hidden things, the myths are their bolder explication. At least according to R. Judah, myth is another language of God's primordial acts, even one that goes deeper into the unknown and portrays the living drama of creation. One is even tempted to regard his teaching as an assertion that myth is itself exegesis, a mode of inspired imagination. More need not be said.

V. Concretization

The preceding examples of mythmaking have focused primarily on originary events in primordial time and on extraordinary moments in the course of nature. To give an account of the events, the rabbinic sages used Scripture in diverse ways. To further exemplify their mythopoeic procedures, we turn here to an event in sacred history (the revelation at Sinai). Certainly anyone

[29] *Genesis Rabba* 1. 6 (Theodor–Albeck, 4).

reading the biblical account will be mostly impressed by its muted mythic tone—for whereas the moment is charged with thunder and tremors, one would not know from the narrative in Exodus 19 that these features are the regular components of a divine advent (often including a chariot and with full entourage) in both biblical and ancient Near Eastern sources;[30] and one would be even more struck by the explicit aniconic discourse that characterizes its recollection in Deuteronomy 4.[31] Indeed, the latter source repeatedly emphasizes that the people did not see any vision at that time, but only heard God's voice speaking from out of the fire that spewed from the mountain 'up to the heart of heaven' (Deut. 4: 11–12, 15, 33, 35). All the more remarkable therefore is the mythopoesis that turned the invisible into the visible, and declares that the assembled people saw nothing less than the divine word on that occasion.

But rabbinic opinions divided about what exactly took place: according to 'the rabbis' (namely, the majority opinion), the divine *dibbur* ('word') emerged from the mouth of God and went around to the entire assemblage—such that each and every 'word' of the Ten Commandments spoke directly to each and every one of the people, and asked them if they accepted that word and all the future laws that would be derived from it over the ages; however, according to R. Yoḥanan, each *dibbur* was taken from the mouth of God by an 'angel' (or 'messenger'), who brought it around to each and every person, asking them if they accepted this word and all that would be learned from it.[32] The reason the rabbis spoke as they did was because they understood the passage 'Lest you forget the things (*debarim*) which your eyes saw (*raʾu*)' (Deut. 4: 9) to refer to the way each *dibbur* appeared directly before the people, while R. Yoḥanan based his version on the strength of the phrase 'You were shown (*horʾeita*) to know' (Deut. 4: 35)—whose indirect locution meant for him that each *dibbur* of God was presented to the people by an agent, that they might know its teachings and implications.

The Midrash does not resolve this difference: both myths stand together, just as the two verses occur in the same chapter of Scripture. Moreover, neither myth resolves the contradiction between its teaching and the plain sense of the text. For the sages, the word of God was a living, hypostatic entity, and in their myth they further personified it. By concretizing the language of Scripture they made the text agree with their theology. Not just to the ears of the people, then, as Moses stressed, but before their very eyes did the word of God repeatedly appear at Sinai. Only a different theology with different purposes (such as that enunciated by Paul to the Galatians) would suggest that the revelation by means of a intermediary was

[30] For examples, see Part I above.

[31] The admonition in Deut. 4: 16–19 is itself based on the imagery of Genesis 1, as I have shown in *Biblical Interpretation in Ancient Israel* (Oxford: Clarendon Press, 1985), 321 f.

[32] See *Song of Songs Rabba* 1. 2. ii.

a lesser act, attesting to the inferiority of the Law itself—a counter-myth to end the myth.[33]

VI. Personification

Above we referred to the myth of the separation of the primordial waters, and suggested that behind this account is the notion of the sexual commingling of masculine and feminine waters. Such a bold personification of the natural world would seem so far from biblical theology as to make its appearance in rabbinic sources doubly unlikely. But here too the latter-day interpreter must proceed with caution, with full cognizance that Scripture does not contain the full tradition of ancient Israelite myth, any more than the textualization of rabbinic oral culture represents it entirely. An eye to both the inexplicit and explicit phrase will, however, correct this perception, and even show how verses from Scripture were reread to dramatize a myth of masculine and feminine waters.

We may start with the apparently puzzling reference to fields 'of Baʿal' in mishnaic and toseftan traditions dealing with tithings and sabbatical produce.[34] In context, the phrase *sedeh baʿal* refers to lands dependent upon rainfall (not irrigation),[35] and this suggests that the rabbinic term derives from old mythic notions of fields fructified by the ancient Canaanite god of the storm.[36] Now obviously the rabbinic interpretative rules just noted do not advocate any belated syncretism, and the hermeneutical issue before us is whether the foregoing designation is simply an empty legal phrase, or whether it retains some mythic resonance.[37] Evidence for the latter comes from the toseftan version itself, where the term for rainfall has strong sexual overtones.[38] A later amoraic query as to the meaning of this term (*marbaʿot/*

[33] See Gal. 3: 19. The statement that the Law was given *diʾangelon* ('by means of angels') and *en cheiri mesitou* ('by means of an intermediary') parallels the teaching attributed to 'the rabbis', for whom the word was taken to the people by a *malʾakh* ('angel') or *ʿal yedei shaliaḥ* ('by means of a messenger'). This feature suggests that our Midrash goes back to tannaitic times.

[34] *M. Shebiʿit* 2. 9 and *Tos. Shebiʿit* 2. 4.

[35] Cf. *Aruch Completum*, ed. Alexander Kohut (Vienna: Menorah, 1926), ii. 141 f., s.v. *baʿal*; and *Toseftaʾ Zeraʿim*, ed. Saul Lieberman (New York: The Jewish Theological Seminary of America, 1956), 170 n.

[36] Jacob N. Epstein, *ZAW* 33 (1911), 82 f., provides evidence for a mythic reading of the legal phrase, but refrains from any explicit formulation.

[37] For a related issue cf. the phrase *qeber tehom* in *M. Parah* 3. 2 and 6. The term is treated with full halakhic seriousness as pertains to 'corpse impurity' (see also Rashi on *BT Sukkah* 21a), even as it seems to relate to the old mythic notion of the Tehom, the watery abyss mentioned in Gen. 1: 2 and given dramatic mythic formulation in rabbinic literature, where it represents the primordial waters of chaos. See further below.

[38] The *editio princeps* reads *marbaʿot*; MS Vienna has *meriʿot*. On this, see Lieberman, *Toseftaʾ Zeraʿim*, who notes that the latter term is like *marbiʿot*, and compares it to mishnaic *ʿonot*. The sexual usage of the verb *rabaʿ* occurs in Lev. 18: 23; 19: 19; 20: 16. In his *Tosefta Ki-Feshutah, Zeraʿim* (New York: The Jewish Theological Seminary of America, 1956), ii. 500, Lieberman gives a sexual connotation to *ʿonot* as well, linking it to the marital *ʿonah* due a wife according to Exod. 21: 10. In this regard, note the mythic and sexual puns in Hos. 2: 23 f.

meriyot) reinforces this sense,[39] and the Talmud even adduces the corroborative teaching of Rav Judah, who said: 'Rain is the husband (*baʿalaʾ*) of the soil'.[40] Remarkably, the sage supports this mythic epitome with a citation from Isaiah 55: 10 ('For just as the rain or snow falls from heaven, and does not return there, but moistens the earth, and fertilizes it [*ve-holidah*; lit. sires it] and makes it yield vegetation, and gives seed [*zeraʿ*] for sowing and bread for eating'). Furthermore, he interprets the pro-generative aspects of rain (whose drops are engendering seeds) quite concretely, and with an active (and personalized) mythic force.[41] It is therefore reasonable to conclude that mythic ideas (with varying intensity) about the rain and earth as a conjugal pair were in circulation in ancient Jewish culture. And since such ideas are at least conceptually related to assertions about the sexuality of the upper and lower waters, one may also suppose that the notion of a 'field of Baʿal' is also part of a mythic complex that retained its vitality for a millennium and a half. Vestigial formulations are therefore no proof of vestigial notions.[42]

What is more, these vestigial myths do not always indicate how they were integrated into the monotheistic traditions of Scripture and Judaism. It is therefore wrong to assume that an individual mythic fragment is faded or pagan simply because the *traditum* reports it in a stark or condensed form. Arguably, the fact that divine powers with sexual characteristics are not depicted in Genesis 1 could lead one to suppose that their presence in later commentaries betrays a foreign element. But such reasoning limits the 'Judaizing' of mythic notions to their neutralization, and thus puts the classical rabbinic tradition at odds with myth.[43] A closer look at the exegetical forms of Midrash suggests more intriguing and positive processes. For as stressed earlier, the mythic elements of the sages are nearly always correlated with biblical verses and put into an exegetical setting. They are thus subordinated to Scripture as oral explications of written teachings. The textual grounding (scriptural) moreover, formally aligns the later writings with the monotheistic tradition and provides the canonical context within which the myths are Judaized.

39 In *BT Taʿanit* 6b, R. Abbahu asks: 'What is *rebiʿah*?', and goes on to say that it is 'that which fructifies the ground'. The query alludes to its earlier citation as a *beraitha* (ibid. 6a), but derives with the explanation from *Tos. Taʿanit* 1.4.

40 *BT Taʿanit* 6b.

41 Just this verse (emphasizing the verb *ve-holidah*) is noted by R. Ḥananel in his comment on *BT Moʿed Qaṭan* 2a; but he understands the term 'field of Baʿal' to be a metaphor based on human intercourse, 'like a husband (*baʿal*) and his wife'. However, there is no doubt of the mythic emphasis of the text; nor is there any doubt that the motif is ancient. Cf. J. Van Dijk, 'Le Motif cosmique dans la pensée Sumérienne', *AcOr* 28 (1964), 36f.

42 A variant vestige of this ancient theme is preserved in Isa. 62: 4–5, where the restored land of Israel is called 'espoused' (*beʿulah*) and its acquisition as 'espoused' (*tibbaʿel*). The prophet compares this relationship to when 'a youth espouses (*yibʿal*) a maid'. The verb has strong and explicit sexual connotations.

43 See the discussion with references in the Introduction.

This process of scriptural correlation is fundamental to the cultural hermeneutics of the rabbis. Hence far from evincing the depletion of assumed 'hurtful' or problematic elements, rabbinic Midrash rather 'scripturalizes' its myths with unapologetic energy and thereby gives them the seal of biblical authority. A more expansive version of our fragment about the male and female waters will exemplify this point and further corroborate its mythic validity. The account is found in Midrash *Genesis Rabba* 13.13, in the context of a verse dealing with the lower waters (Gen. 2: 6).[44] In a specific teaching bearing on the phrase 'deep called to deep' (Ps. 42: 8), we are told that

R. Levi taught: The upper waters are masculine and the lower ones are feminine, and these (upper waters) say to those (lower waters): 'Receive us, (for) you are the creation of the Holy One, blessed be He, and we are His agents'. Whereupon they (the lower waters) received them (the upper ones), as it is written (in Scripture): 'Let the earth open up, etc.' (Isa. 45: 8), like this female who opens for the male; 'that they (the heavenly rains)[45] produce the fruit of salvation' (ibid.), for they are fruitful and multiply; 'and let victory blossom as well' (ibid.), this (refers to the) rainfall; '(Yea) I the Lord have created it' (ibid.), for the establishment of the world and for its inhabitation.[46]

The rabbinizing of living myth is exemplified here in a typical and instructive manner. R. Levi's teaching opens with a query about the meaning of a biblical phrase about rushing waters, used in the Psalms as a trope for the speaker's anguish. This phrase is correlated by the sage with a non-scriptural myth of the upper and lower waters, whose content goes well beyond the earlier reference to them as masculine and feminine powers. In the present instance, the figurative calling of the 'deep' in Psalm 42 is transformed into a myth of rainfall built around a speech of the upper masculine waters to their lower female partners—two creatures of God. This mythic *and* monotheistic dimension is reinforced by the scriptural citation from Isaiah, which is boldly elucidated in terms of the sexual opening of the earth to the fructifying powers of the rain, and by a renewed emphasis on God as creator. Since the novel interpretation of the two biblical passages is counter-intuitive, and can hardly be imagined as their plain sense, we may conclude that the myth of upper and lower waters presented here long preceded its formal reception into Jewish tradition through scriptural exegesis. For his part, R. Levi is neither apologetic nor self-conscious about the elements of this fertility myth. To the contrary, he lends his authority to its citation and even provides the scriptural basis for its monotheistic reformulation. His

[44] In Theodor–Albeck, 122 f.

[45] See the beginning of the verse and the comment of R. Tzvi Wolf Einhorn (the Maharzu), ad loc. Most versions read *tippataḥ* for MT *tiftaḥ*. Septuagint MSS apparently read *vayefer*, and 1 QIsa (a) has *vayifraḥ*; the Midrash is based on our MT reading.

[46] In *Genesis Rabba* 32. 2 (Theodor–Albeck, 294) R. Levi's teaching is highly truncated and demythologized.

exegetical work provides proof that the evaluation of mythic features in the Midrash must take account of their full and diverse contexts and forms of expression.

B. MYTH AND SCRIPTURE

The foregoing review of typical uses of Scripture in rabbinic mythmaking suggests a double process. On the one hand, myths of various sorts were initially part of the oral tradition: in some cases they were sponsored by the thematics and episodes of Scripture (topics like the creation, or revelation at Sinai); whereas, in other cases, these topics were part of the overall cultural (or natural) environment (like the meaning of earth tremors and their rumble). As a secondary process, the myths were connected to Scripture through one exegetical technique or another—these connections being deft and daring transformations of the plain sense of the text. One is led to this 'supposition of (exegetical) secondariness' by the great disparity that often exists between a given mythologem and its scriptural proof, as well as the sense that meditation on the meaning of a given phrase would be unlikely to lead to the mythic tradition at hand. However, one must also presume the 'priority of exegesis' as a factor to be reckoned with: both because of the primacy of interpretation in rabbinic culture, and because the relationship between the text and the mythologem evokes such a possibility. This is particularly so given the fact that the rabbis do not interpret globally, but rather focus on the biblical text phrase by phrase (if not word by word). Such a technique of delimitation at once isolates these literary units from their larger context and permits the kind of speculative focus and emphasis that would concretize a metaphor, or otherwise produce those transformations of sense and syntax that are so characteristic of the midrashic imagination. It goes without saying that such hermeneutic orientations do not come to the biblical text *tabula rasa*, but are rather often guided in one exegetical direction or another by latent or active theological traditions (like the notion of divine attributes).

With these reflections we come to the hermeneutical circle of rabbinic mythmaking. Where does a pre-existent myth end and its scriptural support begin—such that we could say that a given myth is clearly independent of or primary to any subsequent shaping by or contact with the biblical text? And, conversely, Where does exegetical invention begin and a brand new myth result—such that we could assert that the myth is a hermeneutical event wholly independent of pre-existent themes or traditions that may precondition the choice of proof-texts? So formulated, there is no easy or single answer to this dilemma, not least because of the complex conjunction of Scripture and tradition in the rabbinic imagination. The possibility of a solution is made more elusive by the combination and coordination of the two in our received sources. Only in rare instances can the latter-day interpreter clearly isolate a mythic dictum, like R. Levi's remark about the genders of the upper and lower waters, from the biblical exegesis that follows—a matter aided in this case by their formal and linguistic differences; or show the impact of an underlying hermeneutical principle, like the meaning of certain divine names, upon a given mythic fabulation—a matter required in these cases by the otherwise groundless nature of the teachings proposed. In the absence of such instances, the best the interpreter can do is to enter the circle at the point where the lemma and its comment meet, and assess their stylistic and exegetical interrelationship. For whether the myth precedes the proof, in fact, or the text sponsors the mythologem, the mythic fabulation will always have a verbal or thematic link to Scripture, and this connection is a basic feature of rabbinic mythopoesis.

Moreover, this fundamental biblical connection establishes the double authority of rabbinic myth. First and foremost, it grounds the myths in the language of Scripture, and makes them part of its overall truth. Mythopoesis is thus not simply another feature of the constitutive or aesthetic imagination, but part of the meaning of Scripture and its rabbinic recovery. This meaning will include any number of narratives not mentioned explicitly, as well as theological teachings about divine action and feeling from primordial time to the end-time of redemption and heavenly reward. These mythic allusions are obscured by the plain sense of the text, and are found in numerous fragments and forms, only apparently discontinuous or unrelated. The numerous proof-texts that may be hunted down or used to flag a given point attest to the lively trust of the sages in the resources of Scripture on any of these points, and the belief that more than one verse may illumine any given subject. Thus in paradoxical ways to be explored at length, myth is one of the secrets of Scripture—both with and against its grain.

This leads to the second type of authority of the 'biblical connection', and that is the authority of tradition itself. For however obvious, it must nevertheless be emphasized again that the myths are mediated by the rabbis themselves (whatever their origin among the people), and often in chains of transmission. Thus the mythic teachings are elevated to the level of Midrash and the work of the academies, and kept alive by schools of tradents at the oral level, and by the written collections in which they are now found. Moreover, the very differences between the sages on any given point attest to their mythopoeic inventiveness and to the plasticity of myth at this time. It has both the fluidity of topic and variety of a living cultural element, realized in ever new forms of expression. Exegesis is thus not here a devolution of the mythic imagination, but, in rabbinic culture, its creative expression and revitalization—the means whereby Scripture was transcended and transformed, while being expanded in content and elevated in value.

C. DELIMITING THE FOCUS

Given the very broad range of topics available to rabbinic mythmaking, and in the interests of both comprehensiveness and typicality, we shall focus in the following chapters on two main topics: divine strife with the sea; and divine involvement in the destiny of Israel. Both represent important matrices of rabbinic myth, and offer a diversity of representations of its exegetical work and resources.

Under the category of 'sea strife' we shall observe the forms and variations of this mythologem in the primordial time of origins (*Urzeit*), at the exodus, in relation to the Temple and its foundation, and in the final or end-time of redemption (*Endzeit*). In certain cases the topics are treated as isolated themes, but there also evolved attempts to organize more comprehensive accounts of the traditions, thus coordinating a number of these themes into larger matrices. This creative development shows the creation of new mythic genres and the ongoing validity of the topics themselves. The overall thematic of confrontation and defeat focuses on aspects of divine power and cosmic order.

Under the category of 'divine involvement' we shall observe the mythic patterns and pathos of God's participation in ancient Israelite suffering during the Egyptian bondage and its aftermath, the destruction of the first Temple and the people's exile to Babylon, and the final redemption or restoration to the homeland. These topics serve as the primary prisms for rabbinic reflections on the destruction of the second Temple (by the Romans, 70 CE) and the ensuing diaspora, as well as God's own *imitatio hominis* and the contingency of the divine destiny with the fate of the nation. Here in remarkable ways new myths of divine suffering are invented, with bold representations of divine feelings and actions. The links to the biblical text reveal daring exegetical manoeuvres, some of which are marked by such terms as *kivyakhol* ('as it were') and such expressions as *ʾilmaleiʾ sheha-dabar katub ʾiy ʾefshar le-ʾomro* ('were the matter not written [in Scripture] it would not be possible to say it').[47] The first of these seems to open up a space between the myth and the text, and its usage raises questions as to the status or ontological validity of the particular mythologem at hand; the second would appear to close up such a space and to imply that the bold myth is itself inscribed in Scripture, but just how this is so will also require some explication. Both patterns involve a large number of the texts to be examined below, but not exclusively so. As with the preceding topic, the many sub-themes are often grouped into clusters of varying sizes. What is distinctive is

[47] The term *kivyakhol* and its functions in midrashic literature will be taken up in a comprehensive manner in Appendix 2, though texts using this term will be treated in the main body of the book and discussed as pertinent to the context; considerations of the expression *ʾilmaleiʾ sheha-dabar katub* will be taken up in the pertinent contexts of this book.

the attitudes they reflect about divine providence and the interrelationship between myth and history. Remarkably, this topic is marked by expressions of the limitations of divine power, and even the absence or withdrawal of control.

Both of the preceding topics will be studied according to a method that will combine typological analysis with concerns for comparison and context. This approach will allow us to focus on both smaller and larger common features (within the 'types': both strife and sympathy), and on their various differences in different literary settings. Only in certain cases will it be feasible or productive to show clear lines of historical development, or to indicate how a particular matrix moves from the simple to the complex or vice versa. The transmission and nature of the material often inhibit such conclusions, since a condensed or abbreviated version of a myth need not mean that its themes are either inchoate (and waiting to be developed) or truncated (and thus the reduction of its themes), but may only reflect the literary representation or reception of traditions in a given source. Such issues must remain subject to careful and unprejudiced analysis, just as one should not predetermine if an apparently apocopated version is a frozen or faded fragment of a myth. Nevertheless, when possible, attention will be given to tannaitic and amoraic levels of tradition, and to the enumeration of the tradents. The latter is an old and thorny matter, given the variations often evident in parallel traditions;[48] but we shall attempt to track the pattern of attributions, to see at least what the traditions about the traditions may indicate, and whether there were any notable schools and chains of transmission particularly interested in these various mythic matters. We shall see that this was indeed the case.

Finally, we shall also have occasion to turn to a topic that combines the two earlier issues of divine power and contingency—but from the human side. Here the subject of myth-and-ritual shall be considered from the perspective of the effect of human behaviour (proper ritual; proper legal action) upon the divine, and will show the power of such works to enhance or diminish divine might or mercy. The impact or role of human praxis upon cosmic and divine maintenance reconnects realms often thought to be utterly distinct in Jewish monotheism, and thus provides another avenue into ancient rabbinic myth. Rather than marking faded myths or halting mythic theologies, these texts reveal a realm of living mythic religiosity in the heart of rabbinic Judaism.

[48] Cf. the considered discussion of Sasha Stern, 'Attribution and Authorship in the Babylonian Talmud', *JJS* 45 (1994), 28–51, with literature cited.

6
God and the Primordial Waters

A. DIVINE COMBAT AND THE PRIMORDIAL WATERS

The old myths of Near Eastern antiquity had a long afterlife—and were variously filtered and reformulated by many tradents east and west. A particularly valuable resource is the 'Phoenician History' composed by Philo of Byblos in the late first or early second century CE, which preserves mythic traditions deriving from Sanchuniaton, a scholar of earlier antiquity, who, the pagan philosopher Porphyry claims, reworked the records of a Phoenician priest (named Hierombalos) for his king, Abibalos of Beirut. Portions of this material are preserved in fragments found in the *Praeparatio evangelica* of the fourth-century Church Father Eusebius of Caesarea.[1] It has even been suggested that Sanchuniaton (and someone called Mochos, whose work was preserved in Greek translation by one Laitos) incorporated versions of an old cosmogonic myth that may have influenced Thales and the oldest Orphic theogonies;[2] and there is no doubt that features of its god-lists reflect Canaanite traditions of the oldest known sort, whose biblical reflexes are already more muted.[3] Moving in the other direction, some old Israelite dragon myths known in the rabbinic academy of R. Yoḥanan in Tiberias (early third century CE) were conveyed to the Jews of Babylon by Rav Dimi in the early fourth century CE;[4] conversely, the remnant of a Babylonian theogony appears in the Neoplatonic treatise entitled *Difficulties and Solutions of First Principles* by Damascius (458–538 CE) from about a century later.[5]

[1] For these sources, see the materials collected and translated by Harold W. Attridge and Robert A. Oden, Jr., *Philo of Byblos: The Phoenician History* (CBQM 9; Washington, DC: Catholic Biblical Association of America, 1981), pp. 16–19, and p. 24 n. 19. The afore-noted point by Porphyry is in *Praeparatio evangelica* 1. 9. 21. The dating asserted here follows Attridge and Oden (p. 1).

[2] See M. L. West, *Early Greek Philosophy and the Orient* (Oxford: Clarendon Press, 1971), 28–36; idem, *The Orphic Poems* (Oxford: Clarendon Press, 1983), 103–5, 198–201; and in *Classical Quarterly*, 44 (1994), 289–307.

[3] See above in Part I, p. 54, with references.

[4] See *BT Baba Batra* 74a–75b. From this period or slightly later in Mesopotamia, we also have Jewish magic bowls in which the powers of evil are routed with reference to an earlier defeat of *yamā'* (Yam) and *livyatan teninā'* (Leviathan the dragon). See James A. Montgomery, *Aramaic Incantation Texts from Nippur* (Philadelphia: University Museum, 1913), text 2; and also Cyrus H. Gordon, in *Or.* 10 (1941), 273. Significantly, the language of these incantations use the same god names as those imported into Babylonia by Rav Dimi from Tiberias.

[5] See in Charles E. Ruelle, *Damasciou diadochou aporiai kai leseis peri tōn protōn archōn* (Paris: Klincksieck, 1889), i. 321 f. W. Robertson Smith, '*Thalatth* in Berosus', *ZA* 6 (1891), 339, has

I. Separation of the Waters

Among the congeries of Near Eastern myths in late antiquity, rabbinic sources provide an intriguing repository of old, reworked, and invented accounts of the primordial waters and divine encounters with them. Some appear in fragmentary form, as brief renditions of a myth followed by one or more scriptural proof-texts; others employ such standard midrashic genres as the parable, and use these to develop or enforce the mythic teaching at hand; while still others incorporate the mythic account into larger complexes of mythic themes and traditions.

In an earlier discussion, mention was made of a comment in *Genesis Rabba* 5. 4 by the Palestinian sage R. Berekhia, that 'the upper waters were not separated from the lower ones except with a cry (*bekhi*)', as it is written, 'He dams up the rivers at their source (*mibbekhi*)' (Job 28: 11). It provides a typically rabbinic fabulation of a mythological tradition: the mythologem itself (of a primordial event) is mentioned briefly, and is followed by a proof-text that serves to give that event scriptural support. In this case the key element (a cry) is verbally marked both by its emphatic place in the mythic report and by the linguistic tally between it and the biblical text (achieved through clever midrashic exegesis—a sure sign of its belated or secondary ascription).[6]

given a phonetic explanation for the pronunciation of *Tauthe* in Damascius as *Tāmtu* (*Tiāmtu*); he has also proposed an emendation resulting in the name of this god in a Babylonian theogony noted by Berossus (*c.*275 BCE). This account was transmitted via Alexander Polyhistor (1st c. CE) and Eusebius (*c.*340 CE); and it was preserved into the Middle Ages by Synkellos, an 8th-c. monk in Constantinople. Cf. the version of Eusebius in *Eusebi chronicorum libri duo*, ed. Alfred Schoene (Berlin, 1875), i, cols. 14–18. On Berossus and his tradition, see P. Schnabel, *Berossos und die babylonische-hellenistiche Literatur* (Leipzig & Berlin: B. G. Teubner, 1923). See now the study by Stanley M. Burstein, *The Babylonaica of Berossus* (Sources from the Ancient Near East, 1. 5; Malibu: Udena Publications, 1978). Note particularly the theogonic tradition adduced in a so-called 'doubtful Pragment' (p. 172). Here it is recorded that 'the Babylonians... make two first principles, Tauthe and Apson, making Apson the husband of Tauthe and calling her the mother of the gods'. Tauthe and Apson are Ti'amat and Apsu, respectively.

The possible evidence for some version of the Babylonian combat myth known as *Enuma elish* at Palmyra, centuries earlier than Damascius, is more indirect. An inscription from 24 CE indicates that Babylonian merchants were involved 'in the construction of the temple of Bel' (*bnyn' dy h[k]kl' dy bl*); and another from 45 CE records that the temple had been dedicated on 6 Nisan 32 CE—precisely the date when the Babylonian (New Year) Akitu festival was known to have been celebrated and the creation myth recited. For this inscription, see J. Cantineau, *et al.*, *Inventaire des inscriptions de Palmyre* (1930–), ix, no. 1. See also R. du Mesnil du Buisson, 'Le Bas-Relief du Combat de Bel contra Ti'amat dans le Temple de Bel à Palmyre', *Les Annales Archéologiques Arabes Syriennes*, 26 (1976), 83–100. For issues of dating, see H. J. W. Drijvers 'The Syrian Cult Relief', *Visible Religion*, 7 (1989), 69, on p. 7; and for an overall statement, see Fergus Millar, *The Roman Near East 31 BC–AD 337* (Cambridge, Mass.: Harvard University Press, 1993), 323. Pertinent considerations concerning the identity of Bel at Palmyra, and the continuity of the Akitu festival, are found in Stephanie Dalley, 'Bel at Palmyra and Elsewhere in the Parthian Period', *ARAM* 7 (1995), 137–51.

[6] The noun *bekhi* in the myth is linked to the scriptural phrase *mibbekhi neharot* (lit. 'from the sources of the rivers'), a variant of *nibkhei yam* in Job 38: 16, where it is parallel to the 'springs of *tehom*'. Remarkably, the key idiom is itself ancient, and a mythic toponym for the dwelling of El in Ugaritic sources; note *mbk nhrm // apq thmtm* in *CTA* 4. 4. 21–2. The final vowel /i/ of *mibbekhi*

Nevertheless, the account is thematically opaque.[7] What is the context of this rupture, and what act is assumed? Close attention to the editorial arrangement offers meagre help.

Looking at the larger group of teachings in which R. Berekhia's report of the 'separation' occurs, one will note that it follows another comment by the same sage concerning a primordial time when 'the whole world was water in water (*mayim be-mayim*)' (*Genesis Rabba* 5. 2). Since R. Berekhia's two remarks form a natural sequence (in which the first deals with the aboriginal commixture of waters and the second their separation into upper and lower zones), one would suppose that they rightfully belong together—among comments dealing with God's decision in Gen. 1: 6–7 to divide the original waters with a firmament. Their present dissociation (in *Genesis Rabba* 5. 2 and 4) is presumably due to the fact that R. Berekhia's comment on the world being 'water in water' (5. 2) has been used here to introduce a group of interpretations which understand this phrase as marking the confluence of all the earthly waters after the separation, and just prior to traditions that speak of their pooling into fixed areas as acts of obedience to God's command (in Genesis 1: 9). Following these acts of piety and subservience, R. Berekhia's mythologem (in 5. 4) about the waters crying stands out, and suggests a less compliant version of the waters' separation.[8] This is some gain; but one must still wonder why the commingled waters were separated in the first place, and why they cried. For possibilities, we must cast a glance at mythic traditions and exegesis found elsewhere in rabbinic literature.[9]

A comment found in the late midrash *Seder Rabba de-Berei'shit* provides a more complicated scenario of events *in illo tempore*. Pausing to provide an adequate setting for God's command in Genesis 1: 6, the text takes the form of an aetiological query plus mythic explanation. 'Why did the Holy One, blessed be He, separate (the upper and lower waters)? Because the upper waters are male and the lower waters are female, and when they sought to mate (*le-hishtammesh*) they sought to destroy the whole world. At that time the waters ascended the mountains and descended to the hills, (and) the male waters chased the female ones, until the Holy One, blessed be He, roared

is an old genetival ending in a bound form (cf. Deut. 33: 13); but our midrashist heard herein an echo of the 'cry' in his mythic tradition and thereby opened new depths in the mythic allusions in Job 28: 11.

[7] The notion of markedness, following its usage by linguists, refers to oppositions and their valuation, and focuses on the meaning of a specific case of non-equivalence. Moreover, 'the marked term of an opposition provides an additional, more specific piece of information in comparison with the unmarked term'; see Linda Waugh, *Roman Jacobson's Science of Language* (Risse: de Ridder, 1976), 89; and further, eadem, 'Marked and Unmarked: A Choice Between Unequals in Semiotic Structure', *Semiotica*, 38 (1982), 299–318.

[8] The sense of a strong physical act of rupture is underscored by the language; i.e. it did 'not' (*lo'*) occur 'except' (*'ela'*) through crying.

[9] For mythic traditions about the separation of the heaven and earth, see above, p. 96.

against them, as it says, "At your roar they fled" (Ps. 104: 7).'[10] According to this mythic account, the motivation for the separation was due to the unchecked sexuality of the waters and the threat of chaos before the creation could be completed. Moreover, this erotic feature dramatizes a danger inherent in the nature of the primordial waters—perhaps on the insight that 'the waters' of Gen. 1: 2 (like the Tehom and the darkness) are among the untamed elements that preceded God's acts of order.[11] Hence, immediately after separating the light from the darkness, the waters are also separated. The present myth thus provides the motivation for this act, and marks the triumph of divine might against this threat to the world. Certainly the separation was no benign event. Indeed, it transpired through a blast of divine anger; but the wail of the waters is not heard.

The relative lateness of the preceding myth does not mean that its theme of primordial promiscuity was equally late. In fact, just this element is emphasized in an earlier and more personified version of the matter found in the Talmud (*BT Baba Batra* 74b). Here we learn that:

> Rav Yehuda said in the name of Rab: All that the Holy One, blessed be He, created in His world He created male and female. Even Leviathan the slant serpent and Leviathan the twisting serpent He created male and female; and had they mated with one other they would have destroyed the whole world. (So) what did the Holy One, blessed be He, do? He castrated the male and killed the female, preserving her in salt for the righteous in the world to come, as it is said, 'And He will slay the dragon in the sea' (Isa. 27: 1)...(And the reason He killed her was because) fish are dissolute.

The general theme of the profusion of the primordial waters is now condensed around two sea creatures. Nevertheless, here again we have a myth in which a threat to the world due to sexual profligacy is aborted—this time by castration and killing. Indeed, the absence of the theme of the upper and lower waters shows that the topos of excess was not dependent upon some form of 'separation myth', and could easily attach itself to other biblical verses. One may even suspect that the prototype for such primordial proliferation goes back to ancient Mesopotamian mythology, where it is precisely the mating of the primordial sea-gods Apsu and Ti'amat, and later Laḫmu and Laḫamu, that produced a proliferation of gods and a noisy commotion—all of which resulted in the great battle between Marduk

[10] See in *'Otzar Midrashim*, ed. J. D. Eisenstein (New York: Eisenstein, 1915), ii. 314 (col. 2). One should probably read 'valleys' (*bqʿt*) for 'hills' (*gbʿt*), as in a version of this up hill and down dale theme of the water given by R. Joshua in *Genesis Rabba* 5. 4 (Theodor–Albeck, 34); and cf. *Pesikta Rabbati*, ed. Meir Ish Shalom (Vilna: J. Kaiser, 1880), addendum 1, 192b (hereinafter: Ish Shalom). In this case the movement dramatizes obedience to the divine word.

[11] Cf. the creation myth in *Pesikta Rabbati*, addendum 2 (Ish Shalom, 203a), that begins: 'When the Holy One, blessed be He, created the world he said to the Prince of Darkness, "Begone from me, for I wish to create light and planets" '.

and the sea monster Ti'amat, and Ti'amat's death (*Enuma elish* I. 1–10; IV. 20–120). This event does not occur in Rab's myth, but one is struck by the themes of violence and chaos that are featured in the rabbinic account. Certainly its sources lie in imaginative musings and models far removed from the order and calm registered in Genesis 1. Indeed, in a remarkable manner Rab's teaching provides a clear counterpoint to the biblical statement that 'Elohim saw' that the 'great sea monsters' were 'good', and that He 'blessed them, saying, "Be fruitful and multiply and fill the waters in the seas"' (Gen. 1: 21–2). Clearly, living myth has seeped into the seams of Scripture.

II. Suppression of the Sea

The sequence of mythic traditions found in *Genesis Rabba* 5. 2–4 marks a certain transformation of the relationship of God to the pooling of the waters mentioned in Scripture; for while the divine command in Genesis is uttered in impersonal and staid terms (as befits the impersonal nature of the elements in this imperious creation myth), the rabbinic revision introduces personal and dramatic elements. Thus after stating that 'Rabbi Berekhia (and Rabbi Yudan) said that the whole world (was) water in water', the anonymous editor of the midrash first asks: 'And Scripture says "to one place"?',[12] and then shows how this feat was done. A series of cases follow, which, as noted, present the sea as obedient to the divine will. Hints of more restive responses are sensed in the background, where they remain. In the first of these traditions we have a parable of leather bottles which were filled with air and piled up in the palace, and when the king needed this space he released the air and put them in a corner. This episode is then compared to God's acts at the time of origins: 'The Holy One, blessed be He, trampled (*darakh*) all the waters of creation and put them into the Ocean'. To prove the point, the verse 'And He (God) trod (*dorekh*) upon the back of the sea' (Job 9: 8) is adduced in support.

Presumably the waters are deemed impassive or inert here, and the divine command was assumed to initiate God's own action; though one need not strain too far to perceive in the proof-text chosen (dramatizing an act of trampling) something more than a mere act of deflating or pressing out the waters was presumed. The ensuing mythic traditions offer a related paradox, when it portrays more personal expressions of the waters' compliance to God's command. In the first of these, R. Levi uses the verse 'The rivers raised up, O YHWH, the rivers raised their voice, yea the rivers raised their cry (*dokhyam*)' (Ps. 93: 3) to indicate that the river waters exhorted themselves to comply with the command of God, with the result that He forthwith 'trod the

[12] Lit. 'And you say', this being a rabbinic formula used to query the meaning of Scripture when it appears to be nonsensical for one reason or another.

sea (*darakh ha-yam*)' and brought it under control.[13] This action and verb bring R. Levi's interpretation in line with the preceding uses of the verb *darakh*, and, like them, mark a certain suppression of the waters clearly at odds with their apparent obedience. Some 'rabbis' (cited here) even opined that the term *dokhyam* indicates what the rivers said to the seas: 'We are suppressed (*dakkim*), receive us; we are crushed (*dokhekhim*), receive us'—thereby reinforcing the theme of submission and obedience that dominates this mythic pericope.

Our suspicion that some suppressed *agon* lurks in the wings is confirmed by the very different presentation of this primordial event in other midrashic sources. In these, the old Near Eastern mythic theme of a divine battle against the waters resurfaces. Particularly notable is the version found in *Midrash Shoḥer Ṭov* to Ps. 93: 3, where the scriptural phrase 'the rivers raised up (*nase'u*)' is now used to indicate the upsurge of rebellious pride.

> When the word came forth from the mouth of God (lit. the Power): 'Let the waters be gathered' (Gen. 1: 9), the mountains and hills arose from the ends of the earth and dispersed themselves throughout, so that valleys formed in the midst of the earth, and the waters flowed and gathered therein, as is said, 'And He called the gathered waters "seas"' (ibid.). Immediately thereafter the waters became arrogant (*nitga'u*), and arose to cover the earth as before, until the Holy One, blessed be He, roared and squashed them (*kabshan*) under the soles of his feet... And where did the waters go?... [the matter may be compared to] water bottles (*nodot*) bloated with air and filling up the storeroom, but when the air departs from them they may be cleared away to one spot. Similarly, when the whole world was water within water, what did the Holy One, blessed be He, do? He squashed (*kabash*) them, and they were deflated; as it says, 'Behold, He (God) restrains the waters, and they dry up' (Job 12: 15). And it says: 'And he trod (*dorekh*) upon the back of the sea' (Job 9: 8); and also, 'He heaped up the waters of the sea like a mound (*ned*)' (Ps. 33: 7)...[14]

In this mythic episode, the components found in *Genesis Rabba* 5. 2–3 are reordered and transvalued.[15] The initial compliance of the mountains to God's command is disrupted by the pride of the waters, which threaten to flood the earth and restore their former dominance over the dry land; to prevent this, God intervenes in fury and squashes the rebellious waters underfoot; and finally (after some traditions about boundaries for the sea, among other matters), we have an account of the dispersal of the defeated

[13] The term used for 'command' here is *kilifsin*, deriving from Greek *keleusis* (also noted by Theodor–Albeck, 33), as it was pronounced; the term is undoubtedly a midrashic play on Hebrew *qolam*, 'their voice'. The midrashic reading takes *dokhyam* as implying *da[r]akh yam*.

[14] In the edition of *Midrash Psalms* by Solomon Buber (Vilna: Romm, 1891), 415. The introduction to the parable of the water bottles is opaque; I have translated according to my understanding of the text.

[15] For an approach to the issue of transvaluation and myth, see James Jakob Liszka, *The Semiotic of Myth: A Critical Study of the Symbol* (Bloomington: Indiana University Press, 1989), pt. 4.

waters into various oceanic pools, with another reference to the squashing of the water's pride, and the citation of various proof-texts to augment the point. Hierarchy once threatened is now restored.

Particularly striking in this version of the myth are the marked elements of overweening pride (vs. obedience), and the squashing of the waters (vs. simply stomping out their air). Presumably, the term *nitgaʾu* was chosen to indicate the act of arrogance in order to contrast the rebellion of the waters with the opening exaltation of God's sovereignty, 'YHWH is king, He is robed in grandeur (*geʾut*)' (Ps. 93: 1). It is also noteworthy that the verb *kabash* was employed to express the violent suppression of the waters; for although this term does not occur in Scripture to indicate a divine battle with the sea, it is a precise cognate of the term used in *Enuma elish* IV. 129 to mark Marduk's defeat of the sea dragon ('The lord [Marduk] trod (*ikbus*) on the legs of Ti'amat').[16] One may therefore suppose that this Babylonian myth (in one form or another) had earlier entered ancient Israelite or Jewish traditions and affected the present formulation. In this connection, we may also observe that when Marduk fought Ti'amat she was distended like a bloated bag by the evil wind which he unloosed into her body (IV. 97–100). The parable of the water bottles filled with air in our midrashic myth, and the stomping out of the sea's air by God himself, may possibly echo this old motif.[17] But it remains muted.

A significant intensification of the sea's rebellion marks the myth found in *Midrash Tanḥuma (Buber), Ḥuqqat* 1.[18] For in this case the primordial event of the pooling of the waters is personalized through a confrontation between God and the prince of the sea, who is killed for his refusal to obey the Lord of all creation. This topos incorporates an element known from an earlier report transmitted by Rav Yehuda in the name of Rab, preserved in the Babylonian Talmud.[19] In the present context, it provides a dramatic precedent of divine power and world ordering.

May the Supreme King of kings, the Holy One, blessed be He, be praised, for He created His world with wisdom and skill. His greatness is beyond inquiry, His wonders innumerable—as it is written, 'He gathered the waters of the sea like a mound, and put the deep in vaults' (Ps. 33: 7). And just what does this mean? When the Holy One, blessed be He, created the world, He said to the prince of the sea (*sar*

[16] This point is also made by Irving Jacobs, 'Elements of Near Eastern Mythology in Rabbinic Aggadah', *JJS* 28 (1977), 3; but he does not mention our Midrash (n. 12); and note the earlier remark by Samuel Daiches, 'Talmudische und midraschische Parallelen zum babylonischen Weltschöpfungsepos', *ZA* 17 (1903), 397.

[17] Presumably, just this old tradition of the sea monster as a distended wind-bag would explain the exegetical choice of Ps. 33: 7 as a proof-text (inspiring the mythmaker to perceive in the noun *ned* an allusion to the *nod(ot)*).

[18] See in the edition of Solomon Buber (Vilna: Romm, 1885), 49a/b (with MSS variants); and parallels in *Tanḥuma, Ḥuqqat*, 1 and *Numbers Rabba, Koraḥ* 18. 22.

[19] *BT Baba Batra* 74b.

shel yam): Open your mouth and swallow all the primeval waters (lit. the waters of creation).[20] He answered: Master of the World, I have enough (water) of my own—and began to wail (*libkot*).[21] (Thereupon, God) kicked him and killed him, as it is said, 'He stilled the sea with His might, and smashed Rahab with His skill' (Job 26: 12). (And thus you find that the prince of the sea is named Rahab.) What did the Holy One, blessed be He, do? He squashed them (*kabshan*; namely, the waters of creation) and trampled them (*darkhan*),[22] and thus it (the sea) received them (the waters), as it is said, 'And he trampled over the earth, YHWH the God of Hosts is His name' (Amos 4: 13).

A comparison of this myth with the one found in *Shoḥer Ṭov* shows the flexibility of the midrashic fabulations and a certain sharpening of the action. For one thing, the drama in the *Tanḥuma* version is introduced by a citation from Ps. 33: 7. This has the effect of privileging Scripture and presenting its formulation as a condensed feature of the myth—its core component, as it were.[23] Moreover, the simile 'gathered like a mound (*ka-ned*)' serves to highlight or anticipate the striking mythic event to come, when the trampled waters were poured into the sea. In this respect, the figure stands in marked contrast to its role in the midrash (*Shoḥer Ṭov*) to Ps. 93: 3, where it comes after the analogy of the water bottles and the divine action. Indeed, its function here serves to emphasize the simile itself—not as a fantastic deed, but as a scriptural proof of the preceding analogy which presented God's displacement of the waters in parabolic and comprehensible terms.

Mythic augmentation also occurs in the *Tanḥuma* text through its personification of the encounter between God and the prince. Here the divine command is not 'Let the waters be gathered', but a direct command to the sea creature, 'Open your mouth and swallow'. Given the magnitude of the request, and the emphasis on the event, one may suspect that the being called *sar shel yam* is not so much the viceroy of the sea (or its tutelary power) as an embodied trace of Sea (Yam) himself, the figure known as *zbl ym* ('Prince Yam') in Ugaritic myth.[24] Be this as it may, the rebellious refusal of this

[20] I believe the idiom *meymey berei'shit*, 'waters of creation' alludes to the water present before the acts of creation (Gen. 1: 2). The locution is tendentious, in any case, and uses the construct form of the noun *berei'shit* in the *status absolutus*.

[21] Following Buber, this last phrase is added; it occurs in the *Tanḥuma* and *Numbers Rabba* versions. It is hard to know if this motif of wailing is related to the motif of crying noted earlier; for here the cry precedes the suppression, while there the separation (of a conjoined pair?) apparently resulted in the crying.

[22] See in Buber, p. 49b nn. 4 and 5 for MSS variants.

[23] The citation functions as one of the 'elementary sequences' of the mythic narrative. For this expression and feature, see Claude Bremond, 'The Morphology of the French Fairy Tale: The Ethical Model', in H. Jason and D. Segal (edd.), *Patterns of Oral Literature* (The Hague: Mouton, 1976), 49. In the Conclusions to Part II, I shall speak of the proof-texts in rabbinic myth as units of action.

[24] This connection between the titles was already sensed by Cassuto, in 'The Israelite Epic' (*Biblical and Oriental Studies* (Jerusalem: Magnes Press, 1975), 83), although he softens the mythic valence of the Ugaritic title by translating it 'Prince of the Sea'. The title in *BT Baba Batra*

figure to absorb the primeval waters and allow the dry land to appear is dealt with without mercy: the culprit is kicked and killed by God Himself. The sin is thus not an expression of desire or arrogance, as in other rabbinic myths of this type, but an act of outright disobedience. Accordingly, the punishment serves as a central component of this fabulation; though its inclusion results in a certain stylistic disturbance. One will readily note that the squashing of the waters is not their active suppression, but an act of displacement that follows the death of the prince of the sea—and thus does not require such aggressive behaviour. Indeed, there is no hint in this myth that the waters of creation have either sexual passion or physical power. The glitch in the creation lay elsewhere—additional testimony to the mythmaking imagination of the rabbis and the lability of the process.

III. A Cycle of Strife and Suppression

Just above we observed that the proof-texts serve as scriptural summaries, condensations, or reflexes of elements of the myth—providing authoritative pivots for the fabulations; and that they also help determine its structure—piling up examples for dramatic effect (as in the conclusion to the myth in *Shoḥer Ṭov*), or establishing the sequence of the action (as in the *Tanḥuma* text, where it marks the prolepsis and dramatic action). An even more perspicuous example occurs in *BT Baba Batra* 74b–75a. We have made passing reference to portions of this unit, and shall now focus on the pericope as a whole.

Following a series of legends and tall tales of the sea told primarily in the name of Rabba bar Bar Ḥama, a shift in tone is introduced by a reference to the creation of the sea dragons (*tanninim*) in Gen. 1: 21, and the notice that whereas in Babylon this word was taken to mean 'sea gazelles', R. Yoḥanan (of Tiberias) said that this noun referred to both Leviathan the slant serpent and Leviathan the twisting serpent—presumably because of the plural form—whom God promises to punish in Isa. 27: 1. Whereas this promise is future-orientated for the serpents, it now serves to introduce a series of traditions that begin and end with a Leviathan episode. Talmudic tradition thus considered the order of presentation crucial, and marks this by mnemonics of key words introduced into the text. The following summary follows the sequence of elements.[25]

Topic I opens with the statement that 'All that the Holy One, blessed be He, created in His world He created male and female'. This is said to include

74b is *saro shel yam*. This terminology recurs elsewhere, in legal contexts, showing the ongoing vitality of the deity. Notable is the reinterpretation of *M. Ḥullin* 2. 9 ('One may not slaughter [in such a manner that the blood runs] into the sea (*le-tokh yamim*)') in *BT Ḥullin* 41b, 'Why is it taught that one may not slaughter into the sea?—It is, one may presume, because it might be said that he sacrifices to the daimon (or deity) of the Sea (*le-sara' de-yama'*)!'

[25] For the full pericope, see Appendix 1, Text A.

the two Leviathans mentioned in Isa. 27: 1; but because their mating threatened to destroy the world, God castrated the male and killed the female, preserving her with salt for the righteous in the world to come. A similar danger with respect to the earth monster Behemoth was also averted; and a comparative discussion of the two events follows.

Topic II also deals with the time of origins, 'When the Holy One, blessed be He, wished to create the world', and reports how He summoned the prince of the sea to swallow the primeval waters, and he refused and was killed. The proof-text adduced is Job 26: 12 ('He stilled the sea'). Another tradition refers to the stench of the dead monster, and says that 'if' it were not buried beneath the waters, no creature could endure the odour.

Topic III follows a geographical arc, describing the flow of the Jordan river from its source in 'the cave of Paneas' down to the outlet in 'the Great Sea'—being the 'mouth of Leviathan'. The proof-text is Job 40: 23. (A query on this point is raised and resolved.)

Topic IV deals with the verse 'For he has founded it upon the seas and established it upon the waters' (Ps. 24: 2), and explains 'it' in terms of 'the seven seas and four rivers that surround the Land of Israel' (presumably understanding the pronoun to refer to *ha-ʾaretz*, 'the land' in the previous verse).

Topic V depicts a 'hunt of Leviathan' in 'the future'. The prince Gabriel cannot catch him; only 'his Maker' can 'draw the sword' against him, as Job 40: 19 is adduced to prove. The event itself is not described.

Topic VI depicts traditions of the monster Leviathan, when he eats and drinks. (Proofs are given.) There is also a reference to the dragon's foul breath, which, 'if' it were not spiced, 'no creature could stand its odour'.

Topic VII refers to how 'In the future, the Holy One, blessed be He, will make a banquet for the righteous from the flesh of Leviathan'. Various texts are then adduced regarding this disbursement of food.

Topic VIII refers to how 'In the future, the Holy One, blessed be He, will make a tabernacle for the righteous from the skin of Leviathan'. Various proof-texts are adduced to deal with this point and the particular covering used for others.

This text has all the marks of an ordered anthology of rabbinic traditions, coordinated to construct a coherent and fluent mythic ensemble (or narrative). First, as already noted, there is a series of mnemonic terms that fixes the sequence of Topics I–VI. Hence the editor was not just recording or collecting mythic topics, but had a specific order in mind which he conveys precisely through the mnemonic. We can confirm by noting that this pattern establishes a succession of events from the primordial past, when the Holy One created all creatures in sexual pairs—but castrated the male Leviathan and killed his consort (to prevent the destruction of the earth), to the future to come, when God will catch this remaining dragon and slay him as well. The use of the flesh and skin of female Leviathan is described in Topics VII–VIII. The latter also form a fixed pair, as one can see from the stylistic parallel that introduces each one ('In the future, the Holy One, blessed be he, will make'); and the two of them are coordinated with the opening scene. The anthology opens with reference to the fact that the slain Leviathan will be salted away for the righteous in the future; and the banquet from her flesh, and other uses of her body, are described at the end. The whole pericope thus moves from the *Urzeit* of origins to the *Endzeit* of eschatology, with the deaths of the dragons serving as the leitmotiv.

This sense of a ring structure and theme is confirmed by the other topics. Note first that, within the frame of Topics I and VII–VIII, Topics II and V–VI also form an inner pair. Each is composed of a tradition about a dragon-slaying: in IIa this is the ancient rebellion of the sea and its capital punishment by God; in V this is a future hunt for big game fish and its victorious conclusion by God. Thus the inner frame parallels the outer one with a dragon sequence at the beginning and end of time. Moreover, in IIb and VI this pair is also linked by references to the stench of the dragon and the statement that 'were it not' (*'ilmalei'*) for a solution 'no creature could stand its odour (*reiḥo*)'. And finally, within these two units is a pair of traditions about the ancient waters, Topics III and IV. In the first case, the emphasis is on the flow of the Jordan throughout the Land of Israel and into the mouth of Leviathan, whose body is the Great Sea. In this formulation, one may see a variant of the myths of the displacement of the waters of creation into the sea following their suppression or its death. This topic is paired with another that reads the creation imagery in Ps. 24: 2 in concrete mythic terms, and enumerates the seas and rivers that surround the Land. With these two traditions of this-worldly waters set within two frames of sea traditions, each marking the beginning and end of time, the full chiastic pattern emerges—literary testimony to a comprehensive hyper-myth moulded out of older ones. Talmudic tradition is careful to mark the tradents by name, and even to voice some variant views and queries; but it is the anonymous anthologizer who is the mythmaker of note, taking assorted mythologems from east and west and creating a new narrative for his colleagues in Babylonia.[26]

[26] Among the tradents from the West, there is R. Yoḥanan bar Nappaḥa (d. 279 CE), a head of the academy of Tiberias; R. Isaac II, his student; and Rav Dimi, who visited the Land of Israel to get its traditions. On the other hand, it is notable that nearly all of the tradents in the East are associated with the academy of Pumbeditha. R. Judah (d. 299) who founded this school was a contemporary of R. Yoḥanan and consulted with him (*BT Qidd.* 39a); Rabba (d. 330) was a subsequent director (and tradent of R. Yoḥanan); and Rav. Dimi was associated with this academy and reported to Abayye (d. 339); and R. Aḥa b. Jacob lived in nearby Parfunya. It thus seems that our mythic ensemble was composed in Pumbeditha, and used many Tiberian traditions.

Given its scope and structure, this pericope permits an analysis that extends beyond the individual components. Certainly one point relates to the construction of rabbinic myth around biblical proof-texts. These not only provide scriptural authority for later fabulators, but also mark the compressed thematics of the piece. In the present case, the alignment of traditions forms the morphology of the myth—such that Scripture appears in a new light, refracted through these fragments as so many pieces of a canonical kaleidoscope now brought into focus and pattern.

The choice of the pieces always remains in the hands of the mythmaker, and thus more than morphology is involved. Motif and theme become defining features of the pattern. In *BT Baba Batra* 74b–75a this involves a balance between death and order, between *agon* and power. The Holy One of rabbinic culture is portrayed as supreme over His creation—resolving unexpected events and crises with punishments that will benefit humankind in this world (by the establishment of a habitable order of seas and dry land) and in the future (by rewards given the righteous from ancient events). In this regard, one will be especially struck by the recurrent motif of orality that marks all aspects of the myth. Thus we read that the female Leviathan is destined to be the food eaten by the just in the future (Topics I and VII); that the prince of the sea is asked to swallow the waters of creation, while the male Leviathan swallows great gobs of sea on a daily basis (Topics II and VI); and that the river Jordan flows throughout the Land of Israel and into the mouth of Leviathan, the Great Sea (Topic III).

Of these thematic components, particularly remarkable is the ingestion or incorporation of the Leviathan by the righteous at a heavenly banquet.[27] For this means that they are rewarded by the bodily flesh of an ancient monster, whose death the myth justifies by calling it 'dissolute'. From a structural point of view, this act of eating or incorporation provides a kind of (physical) synthesis that integrates without fully resolving the essential polarity of the myth: the hierarchy which exists between the Lord of creation and His creatures.[28] This order is disrupted by sexual excess and rebellion (symbolized by the personified waters), but is firmly restored through acts of castration and murder—both hoary mythic themes and solutions. For their part, the righteous are figures who mediate between the high divine order and low human condition through their godly behaviour and fulfilment of God's commands. Serving the Lord as model creatures, they are provided the dragon's flesh as a reward for their temperance and obedience. Generations

[27] The motif is old and preserved in pseudepigraphic sources; cf. 1 Enoch 70: 7–10 and Baruch 29: 4.

[28] For an effort to use structuralism to interpret an Egyptian myth of strife, see Robert A. Oden, Jr., '"The Contendings of Horus and Seth" (Chester Beatty Papyrus No. 1): A Structural Interpretation', *HR* 18 (1978–9), 352–69.

of synagogue poets have kept this mythic drama of punishment and reward in the mind of the faithful.[29]

B. THE WATERS OF TEHOM AND THE TEMPLE

I. Suppression of the Tehom

In unexpected ways, the topics of myth burst through the language of Scripture and transform the text in their image. The waters of Tehom are a case in point—for if nothing is said about these primordial waters in Gen. 1: 2, or their place in the process of creation, certainly more figurative accounts of the ancient deep hardly seem to fill in this gap. For example, in a hymn extolling divine justice and care, the psalmist proclaims, 'O YHWH . . . your righteousness is like the mighty mountains (*ke-harerei'el*), and your justice (like) the great deep (*tehom rabbah*)' (Ps. 36: 6). The parallelism here between righteousness and justice suggests that the spatial axis of the similes functions to indicate the heights and depths of God's actions, rather than the exaltation of the just and the demotion of the wicked.[30] Divine justice is deemed firm and far-reaching, extending even to the nethermost depths.

This notwithstanding, the similes of this passage and their resonance intrigued later commentators, who sought to penetrate the mysteries of divine providence hidden here. Drawing upon or developing a myth of origins, R. Simeon bar Yochai provides a remarkable transformation of the verse. The version of his teaching in *Midrash Aggadat Berei'shit* 4. 1 gives a full formulation.

> 'Your righteousness is like the mighty mountains'. Rabbi Simeon bar Yochai says: 'Invert (the words of) Scripture (and read thus), Your righteousness is over your justice as mighty mountains are upon the great deep (*tehom*)'. How then (should one interpret)?[31] Just so: The Holy One, blessed be He, measured the waters of the mighty Tehom, and wherever He saw a *tehom* whose waters surged strongly He took a high mountain and put it over that mighty deep; and thus He squashed (*kabash*) each and every *tehom* with a mountain, so that the waters could not rise and flood the entire world. And just as He affixed mountains upon them, so that they should not flood the world, so did He suppress (*kabash*) (His) judgement with (His) righteousness, that He might not destroy the world through judgement.[32]

[29] See the texts in Jefim Schirmann, *The Battle Between Behemoth and Leviathan According to an Ancient Hebrew Piyyut* (Proceedings of the Israel Academy of Sciences and Humanities; Jerusalem, 1970), IV, no. 13, pp. 24–43. On the subject of *piyyuṭ* and rabbinic myth, see my discussion in the Conclusions to this Part.

[30] My view follows Ibn Ezra, citing R. Moshe Chiquatilla; for the other view, cf. Rashi and Kimḥi.

[31] *ha'iykh* here is like *hey'akh*, used in hermeneutical contexts; cf. *M. Abodah Zarah* 2. 5.

[32] In the edition of Solomon Buber (Cracow: Joseph Fischer, 1903), 8 f.

In this explication, the simile 'Your righteousness is like mighty mountains' is understood as a mythologem compressing an old cosmogonic act. The scriptural formulation, moreover, accounts for the multiple mountains of the myth, as well as for the multiple waters of the deep. In his fabulation, R. Simeon establishes a congruence between the two: the Holy One affixed many mountains over the many waters. Moreover, something of an old combat theme may lurk behind the notion that the Lord squashed (*kabash*) each *tehom* when He saw that its waters increased in force (*mitgabbrim*); for, as we noted earlier, just this verb is used in other rabbinic myths to indicate the quelling of the sea, as well as in the Babylonian epic *Enuma elish* to depict Marduk's trampling of Ti'amat.[33]

The use of the verb *kabash* in the theological application of the myth is also notable and suggests that the 'judgement' which God suppresses is His own attribute of justice. For not only is this verb used in Scripture to indicate the eradication of sins (through the arousal of mercy; Micah 7: 19), but is used in just this sense in one of the most remarkable rabbinic texts of late antiquity. According to an old tradition, when the High Priest Ishmael ben Elisha once entered the Holy of Holies he was asked by God to bless Him, which he did in these words: 'May it be favourable before You, that Your mercy suppress (*yikhbeshu*) Your anger, and Your mercy dominate Your attributes (*middotekha*), so that You deal with Your children with mercy and not judge them by the strict letter of the law'.[34] Our perception that R. Simeon's homily is concerned with an inner divine dynamic is reinforced by the fact that his teaching was keyed to the very same Sabbath Torah reading (the *seder* of Noah) and linked to the very same verse ('Then Elohim remembered Noah'; Gen. 8: 1) used later by R. Samuel bar Naḥman, when he taught his hermeneutical principle that the divine names YHWH and Elohim refer respectively to the attributes of mercy and justice.[35] However, as compared with the use of this principle in *Genesis Rabba* 12. 15, where God's act of creation is portrayed as a tentative mixture of these attributes for the sake of ongoing human existence, the present teaching emphasizes the predominance of mercy in this combination.

R. Simeon's remarkable use of a myth about suppressing the primordial waters in a theological homily is also instructive for the way the stylistic figures of Scripture are mythologized. Upon examination we see that both the explicit and implicit similes of the text ('Your righteousness is like mighty mountains' and 'Your justice is (like) the great Tehom') have been read as the concrete components of a dramatic action by God. And further, by crossing

[33] See above, pp. 117–19.

[34] See *BT Berakhot* 7a. Just before, a tradition is given in the name of Rav that this was God's own prayer.

[35] See *Genesis Rabba* 33. 3, and the discussion above, pp. 99–101.

these components in the way the sage advises, a hyper-simile is constructed, so that the divine acts (affixing mountains upon the waters) are compared to the two divine attributes (with the result that the quality of righteousness is placed uppermost over justice). This hermeneutical achievement is spelled out in the sequel, with the myth coming first and the dynamic of the two attributes following, analogically. Other versions of R. Simeon's teaching are more compressed and delete the hermeneutical principle and the myth, so that the theme of suppressed waters is collapsed into the first part of the analogy.[36] The fact that the motif of flooding and the verb *kabash* remain in these cases shows their link to some fuller version of the homily. But withal, in these several instances the old myth has lost its vigour and figures merely as a dangling trope.[37]

II. Tehom and Temple

Other rabbinic traditions report that the Tehom was plugged or stopped up by other means. For example, one source gives us the brief but remarkable statement that the Leviathan drinks from the lower waters, and when he finishes, he 'returns his fins to their place and stops up the Tehom';[38] another states that, during the flood, 'the heroes (*ha-gibborim*) put their foot over the Tehom and stopped it up'.[39] But more diverse and pervasive by far are the mythic traditions about a stone called *ʾeben shetiyah* (whose slim outcropping appears within the Temple), which is the foundation stone of the world, cast into the ocean by God himself.[40] As told in the Targum Yerushalmi on Exod. 28: 30, it was with this stone, upon which 'the Great and Holy Name (*shemaʾ rabbaʾ ve-qadishaʾ*)' was incised, that 'the Lord of the world sealed up (*ḥatam*) the mouth of the mighty Tehom (*tehomaʾ rabbaʾ*) at the beginning' of the creation.[41] This image conveys the sense that the stone served as a plug

[36] Cf. *Genesis Rabba* 33. 1 (Theodor–Albeck, 300); *Tanḥuma (Buber), Noaḥ* 8 (17b–18a); *Shoḥer Ṭov* 36 (250). *Genesis Rabba* attributes the teaching to R. Yoḥanan in the name of R. Josiah, and mentions the principle of inversion; *Shoḥer Ṭov* transmits the homily anonymously.

[37] In the preceding examples (n. 34) there is also a trend to move from the divine attribute of righteousness to humans ('the righteous') or their actions ('[acts of] righteousness'); or from the divine quality of justice to human misdeeds.

[38] See *Pesikta Rabbati*, addendum 1 (Ish Shalom, 194b).

[39] *Genesis Rabba* 31. 12 (Theodor–Albeck, 285).

[40] See the anonymous *beraitha* in *BT Yoma* 54b, and the explication of R. Isaac the smith, based on Job 38: 6. The Temple tradition occurs in *M. Yoma* 5. 2; and cf. *Tanḥuma, Kedoshim*, 10.

[41] Also cf. the Targum to Eccles. 3: 11 (and references to the *shemaʾ rabbaʾ*). The tradition is also found in the Targum to Songs 4: 12, which used the trope of the garden and a 'sealed fountain' (*maʿyan ḥatum*) to refer to the maiden. In the Targum, the garden is linked to the garden of Eden, from which cosmic waters flow, and then the statement is made that if the fountain had not been sealed with the divine Name 'it would have gone out, and flowed, and flooded (*ve-shaṭif*) the entire world'. The mythic aspects of this identification of the waters of Eden with a cosmic flow are obvious. From the structure, this portion appears to be an addition to the Eden theme, and the use of the reference to the divine Name links it to other targumic traditions.

against its upsurge, much like the mountains in R. Simeon's myth. The tradition of such a sealing motif is attested earlier, however,[42] and in sources from the earliest centuries of the common era was connected with the power of the divine Name. Notably, in the apocryphal Prayer of Manasseh God is praised for having 'bound up the sea . . . by your word' and 'shut up (*kleisas*) the Tehom (*abysson*) and sealed it (*sphragisamenos autēn*) with your terrible and glorious name' (ll. 3–4).[43] This topic also underlies the apocalyptic vision of John in Rev. 20: 1–3, in which he saw an angel descend from heaven, seize the primordial dragon and cast it 'into the Deep (*abysson*)—which he then shut up (*ekleisen*) and sealed (*esphragisen*)'.

A striking and stylistically developed combination of the two motifs (a plug or seal for the deep and the divine Name) occurs in a Talmudic tradition (*BT Sukkah* 53a–b) which retains a residual awareness of the danger posed by the Tehom, lest it rise up and destroy the world. The event is dated to the time when King David dug trenches to test the suitability or worthiness of the site for the future Temple.

R. Yoḥanan said . . . that when David dug the pits (*shittin*), the Tehom (*tehomaʾ*) arose and threatened to submerge the world. 'Is there anyone', David asked, 'who knows whether it is permitted to write the (divine) Name upon a potsherd and throw it into the Tehom so that it should subside?' No one said a word, (so) David said: 'Whoever knows the answer but does not speak, May he be suffocated!' Thereupon Aḥitophel adduced an a fortiori argument to himself: If, for the sake of establishing peace between a man and his wife, the Torah said 'Let My Name which was written in sanctity be blotted out by the water',[44] how much the more so may it be done for the peace of the entire world. So he replied: 'It is permitted'. (David) then wrote the Name upon a potsherd and threw it into the Tehom and it subsided sixteen thousand cubits.

According to another version (*JT Sanhedrin* 10. 2, *ad fin.*), the potsherd was already in place when David dug down fifteen hundred cubits; and when David wished to raise it, the sherd balked and told the king 'that I am suppressing (*kabesh*) the Tehom'.[45] Nevertheless the king lifted it up and the Tehom gushed forth. But now Aḥitophel does not function as a wise counsellor, but thinks that David will be suffocated and he will rule in his

[42] Yehuda Liebes has suggested that the references to cosmic sealing in *Sefer Yetzirah* 1. 13 attest to some old version of this cosmogonic myth; see his *Torat ha-Yetzirah shel Sefer Yetzirah* (Tel Aviv: Schocken, 2000), ch. 23, esp. pp. 177–9.

[43] See the text in *Psalmicum Odis: Septuaginta: Societas Scientiarum Gottingensis*, ed. A. Rahlfs (Göttingen, 1931), x. 361–3. For a summary of views on its date, and a proposal for the 1st or 2nd c. CE, see James H. Charlesworth, in *The Old Testament Pseudepigrapha*, ed. Charlesworth (New York: Doubleday & Co., 1985), ii. 627 f.

[44] The reference is to the ordeal of the woman suspected of adultery, found in Num. 5: 11–31; specifically, 'be blotted out' (*yimmaḥeh*) alludes to *u-maḥah* in v. 23.

[45] The text has the impossible *rnʾ*; hence it makes sense to read *dnʾ* (i.e. *de-ʾanaʾ*, 'that I') here. The personal pronoun (*ʾnʾ*) also appears in a repetition of the sherd's words.

stead. The king, however, knew what to do, and 'said what he said and overcame' the Tehom.

In these two fabulations, David functions as a temple founder who is able to quell the upsurge of the primordial waters, and seal it shut with the power of God's Name or a magical incantation.[46] The use of the phrase 'and (it) threatened to submerge (*mishṭefaʾ*) the world' in both cases clearly harks back to old myths about the dangerous deep,[47] even as the occurrence of the verb *kabash* in the second version further attests to a suppression of these waters.[48] The victory now occurs in historical time, and the building of the Temple is set over this site.[49] In this way, rabbinic tradition imagines the establishment of the shrine of God on the axis of world origins.[50]

But this conjunction of the motif of the shrine with the creation has an earlier and important antecedent in a tannaitic teaching transmitted to later authorities. Specifically, one must mention the teaching which R. Joshua b. Levi credited to R. Simeon bar Yochai. Commenting on the verse 'And it was on the day that Moses completed (*vayyekhal*) building the tabernacle (*le-haqim ʾet ha-mishkan*)' (Num. 7: 1), we are told that on that day the creation of the world was complete and was no longer on shaky foundations. Now one may suspect that the use of *vayyekhal* in our passage (about Moses) called to mind the use of the very same verb in Gen. 2: 2, in the summary statement that 'Elohim completed His work' of creation on the seventh day. But this verbal association remains in the background, and instead a wholly mythic reading of Num. 7: 1 is given, which in fact undoes the literal sense of Gen. 2: 2, thus suggesting that the myth preceded the exegetical justification. The midrashic teaching goes as follows:

> Scripture does not say *le-haqim mishkan* but *le-haqim ʾet ha-mishkan*. And what was established with it? The world was established with it; for until the tabernacle was established, the world tottered (*rotet*), but after it was established the world was firmly founded (*nitbasses*). Hence Scripture says, 'And it was on the day that Moses completed building the tabernacle'.[51]

[46] The phrase 'he said what he said' suggests a recitation, and the variant of the tradition in *Midrash Samuel* 23. 2, ed. Solomon Buber (Cracow: Joseph Fischer, 1893), 63a uses the phrase 'he said a word (*miltaʾ*)'. The latter word means a magical 'spell'. In a case found in *Ecclesiastes Rabba* 3. 11, a Persian woman uttered a *milah* which used the ineffable Name.

[47] The Babylonian version has *le-mishṭefaʾ*; one should correct the Jerusalem Talmud *miṭpaʾ* accordingly.

[48] D. Sperber, *Magic and Folklore in Rabbinic Literature* (Tel Aviv: Bar-Ilan, 1994), 51 f., is thus wrong to suppose that this verb is a 'magic technical term', and this affects his reconstruction of ancient traditions about sealing the abyss.

[49] For a consideration of the Temple and primordial waters in relationship to the water ritual performed during Tabernacles, see D. Feuchtwang, 'Das Wasseropfer und die damit verbunden Zeremonien', *MGWJ* 54 (1910), 539–52, 713–29; and 55 (1911), 43–63.

[50] In Midrash *Shoḥer Ṭov* 91. 7, God presses the *ʾeben shetiyah* down into the abyss (*tehomot*) with his foot. The text adds that this place is the world navel, upon which the Temple was built.

[51] *Pesikta de-Rav Kahana* 1. 4 (Mandelbaum, 9).

Two features in the text conjoin in this remarkable teaching. The first is the temporal point, left implied in the comment as preserved, that *vayyehi* ('And it was') is not just a narrative ligature, but alludes to something ('it') that now had come into a new being—and that something was the world itself, established firmly when the tabernacle was itself erected. This second point is deftly made: since the phrase uses *ʾet* here, the teacher capitalizes on its potential, and reads it as the preposition 'with', and not (as syntax demands) as a particle introducing the accusative. We may thus reconstruct R. Simeon's parsing of the verse to have been something like this: 'And (the world) was (established also), on the day that Moses completed building with the tabernacle (the world)'; that is, the world was complete with the completion of the tabernacle. To be sure, the teacher (or tradition) leaves this reading altogether implicit; but something like it is demanded by the explicit mythic statement that the world was also established firmly on the day that the tabernacle was set up. And if no combat is noted and no containment of the primordial abyss is alluded to, nevertheless we have an important mythic teaching that presupposes that the world is not finally or firmly finished until the site of cultic habitation is established—a final act arresting the instability and chaotic potential of the creation.

III. Okeanos and Torah

A most remarkable transvaluation of the themes of sealing and suppressing the ancient waters occurs in *Midrash Tanḥuma, Bereiʾshit*, 1. Here, following an account of how God took counsel with the Torah at the time of creation, and an exaltation of its powers and properties, we are told that 'with it' or 'by its means' (*bah*) God 'sealed the sea Okeanos, so that it may not go forth and submerge (*yishṭof*) the world . . . and with it He suppressed (*kabash*) the Tehom, so that it would not flood the world . . .'. Such a version is a myth of myths—combining the topics and terms we have been considering in a new composite, and giving them the ultimate rabbinic pedigree: Torah.[52] God's primordial Torah is now the instrument that leads to the restraint and containment of the antagonistic sea—a striking triumph of *logos* over the watery waste.

[52] According to a striking fabulation adduced in the *Yalkut Shimoni*, i. 766 (on Num. 23: 9), in the name of the *Yelammedenu*, we are told that God sought a place upon which to create the world, until he found a fitting 'stone' (*piṭraʾ*), whose name is Abraham, called a 'rock' (*tzur*), as we learn from Isa. 51: 2, 'Look to the rock from which you were hewn'. This tradition is clearly related to the *ʾeben shetiyah* myth, since it speaks of God digging *temliom* (read: *temlios* or *temliosim*), or 'foundations', the very word (*temliosim* = Greek *themeliosis*) used in the Talmudic tradition about David (*JT Sanhedrin* 10. 2). I surmise that the use of *piṭraʾ* with respect to Abraham and origins may mean that this tradition is intended to counter the Gospel tradition about Peter, who is also characterized as a rock (*petra*) of foundations (Matt. 16:18). Possible links between the old *ʾeben shetiyah* traditions and certain New Testament passages has been fully explored by Joachim Jeremias, 'Golgotha und der heilige Felsen', in *Angelos: Archiv für neutestamentliche Zeitgeschichte und Kulturkunde* (Leipzig: Eduard Pfeiffer, 1925), esp. pp. 108–28.

This leads to a final example, which continues the theme of the world-establishing power of Torah and shows the unleashing of chaos when it (or what represents it) is denigrated or desecrated. Admittedly, this example comes from a very late source, but it occurs there solely as a midrashic component spliced into another context.[53] Through it we may see the continuity of our theme and its transformation.

After an initial statement that although the world was created by the Name of God, it was only completed by concrete actions (as Scripture explicitly indicates, by twice referring to the work that Elohim had 'done (*ʿasah*)' (Gen. 2: 3)), the passage continues.

For that reason it is (also) written, 'And the tablets were the work (*maʿaseh*) of God (Exod. 32: 16))... Come and hear: When Moses broke the tablets, as it is written "And he broke them beneath the mountain" (ibid., v. 19), Okeanos surged from its place and went forth to flood (*lishṭafaʾ*) the world. Moses saw that Okeanos came towards him and wanted to flood the world. Immediately, he took the calf that the people made and burnt it in fire... and scattered it upon the waters' (ibid., v. 20). (Whereupon) Moses stood over the waters of Okeanos and said: 'O waters, waters, what do you want?' (And) they replied: Isn't the world only sustained because of the Torah of the tablets and the Torah that Israel traduced? (And since they worshipped the golden calf, we want to flood the world.)[54] Immediately, Moses said to them: 'Surely whoever worshipped the golden calf is given over to you (for punishment),[55] and let the thousands of them who perish suffice'. Thereupon, 'He scattered (the idol grinds) upon the waters' (ibid.). But the waters did not subside until Moses took water from them and made the people drink it;[56] only then did Okeanos sink back to its place.

This mythic revision of the historical narrative draws lexical currency from the reference to God's work at the completion of the creation and the making of the tablets, thereby implying that the latter were also of world-building significance. And this hint is subsequently confirmed by the fact that the ancient waters erupt at Sinai when the Torah on the tablets is broken. Indeed, much as in the foregoing *Tanḥuma* passage Torah is a means and agent of cosmos, now here, the destruction of Torah (through sin and smashing) at the foot of Sinai (literally, 'under the mountain') threatens to return the world to watery chaos—endangering the creation itself, and requiring an encounter between Moses (at once culture-hero but now also mythic saviour) and Ocean (at once primordial chaos but also mythic judge).[57]

[53] The source is *Zohar* II. 113b. There is no mystical or esoteric dimension to the account.

[54] A supplementary variant.

[55] The text reads 'whatever' (*mah*); I have emended *mah* to *man* ('whoever').

[56] The author refers here to the last part of the biblical verse being treated, but does not cite the Hebrew as earlier.

[57] A standard epithet of the river god in old Canaanite texts is *špṭ nhr*, 'Judge River'. A transmutation here is the use of water as an ordeal, modelled on the ritual in Num. 5: 11–28, esp. vv. 21–4, 27. In Mesopotamia, the water ordeal could include immersion in the river (Codex

One must imagine that the mythopoeic symmetry that linked the creation (by Torah) and the site of Law-giving was aided at the textual level by the reference to the waters into which Moses threw the grinds of the idols; and also by the fact that the destroyed and scattered idols were then given the people to drink. For later mythmakers, these details would have served as narrative signs of a sequence to be embellished through dramatic dialogue. The result is an event that echoes ancient combat motifs and draws on their mythic allusions, without enacting such a scene in earnest. Indeed, legal negotiation and placation have replaced theomachy, and the punishment of those human sinners who endanger the creation replaces the destruction of rebellious gods. Thus if the unbridled and immediate upsurge of the waters from beneath Mount Sinai hint at ancient mythic energies, the forensic concern of the waters with justice betokens a taming of the old terrors. Nevertheless, one is thrust from the historical narrative into an archaic mythic scene, and with it the sense that Torah is a cosmic force and Sinai a renewal of creation—with destructive chaos surging just beneath the plane of worldly order.

Hammurapi, par. 2), or a draught. In a Middle Assyrian text, the sequence of the ordeal is 'They will draw (water), drink, swear and be pure'. See my discussion of this and related matters in 'Accusations of Adultery: A Study of Law and Scribal Practice in Num. 5: 11–31', *HUCA* 45 (1974), 25–45.

7
Myths of Participation and Pathos

We turn now from myths of divine *agon* and triumph against a primordial enemy (the primeval waters or sea dragon), at the time of world origins and later foundational moments, to divine acts performed in the course of Israel's sacred history—and beyond. Here, too, myth is present as the correlation between divine activity and events in the world and history. What is particularly striking is the dramatic symbiosis between them. According to one distinguished historian of ancient religions, the involvement or participation of gods in the events of origins or ends is one of the defining characteristics of myth—it being (in part) a type of narrative 'in which the gods themselves are set in a milieu which is vaster than themselves and which in various ways transcends them and in which they are not only the subjects but also the objects of events'.[1] Certainly YHWH's active involvement in the great events of Israelite redemption, or the various modes of His providential intervention (punishment, exile, and restoration), are major topics of the scriptural record; but as we shall now see, this involvement is radically transformed in rabbinic literature—resulting in diverse myths of divine self-limitation and/or participation in the events befalling the nation (especially servitude and suffering).

A transitional moment is marked in Hebrew Scripture itself, as we may observe from a certain textual difficulty found in Isa. 63: 8–9. Ostensibly, this passage is part of a prologue proclaiming the graciousness of YHWH (v. 7) and His glorious acts on behalf of Israel (vv. 8–9)—specified in subsequent lines (vv. 11–14). As part of this introit, particular mention is made of God's special relationship to Israel and His providential care and beneficence for them. 'And He said: "Surely they are My people"...; so He became their deliverer (v. 8). In all their troubles (*be-khol tzaratam*) He was troubled (*lo* (the *qere*) *tzar*), and the angel of His presence delivered them. In His love and pity He Himself redeemed them, raised them and exalted them all the days of yore' (v. 9). The recitation goes on to record YHWH's acts of redemption, in the hope of arousing His favour and deliverance from the present bonds of exile (vv. 15–19).

This seems clear enough; but how is one to understand the blatant contradiction between the emphasis on God's direct act of redemption (v. 8), and

[1] Ugo Bianchi, *The History of Religions* (Leiden: E. J. Brill, 1975), 141.

the statement that the 'angel (*mal'akh*) of His presence (*panav*)' (v. 9) did the deed? Perhaps, one might say, this statement echos the tradition found in Num. 20: 16, which says that God 'sent a *mal'akh* who freed us from Egypt'. But there is still no escaping the contradiction in Isa. 63: 8–9; and further, quite a different idea is recorded in Deut. 4: 37, where Moses tells the people that it was YHWH who 'took you out of Egypt with His presence (*panav*)—with His great power'. The Septuagint rightly emphasizes this singular divine act by translating 'His presence' with the pronoun *autos*, 'Himself'. An even more vigorous rejection of a divine mediator is found in an ancient midrash on Deut. 26: 8, in which the biblical words 'And YHWH brought us out of Egypt' are underscored by the litany: 'not by a *mal'akh*, and not by a *seraph*, and not by a messenger—but (solely) the Holy One, blessed be He, by Himself (*be-ʿatzmo*)'.[2]

Given these considerations and the explicit emphasis on divine deliverance in Isa. 63: 8, one will prefer the Septuagint reading at the beginning of v. 9—'neither a messenger nor an angel' took them out, only God alone. Significantly, the first part of this version (the negation 'not') is supported both by the Masoretic tradition as written (the *ketib*: *lo'*, 'not'), and by the large Isaiah scroll found at Qumran. In addition, one should note that the Greek reading 'messenger' (*presbus*) forms a synonymous parallel with the word 'angel', and was presumably derived from a construal of the Hebrew consonants *tz-r* as the noun *tzir* ('messenger') and not the verb *tzar* ('troubled').[3] But just where does this leave us? On the one hand, it reconciles one problem (the contradiction between a direct and indirect deliverance) while, on the other, it introduces another difficulty, since there is now a thematic and syntactic discontinuity between the opening clause of v. 8 ('in all their troubles') and its sequel regarding the mediating agents.[4]

Quite evidently, confusions and complexities have crept into the text as a result of theological concerns that construed the two opening clauses of v. 9 in terms of God's providential involvement in Israelite history ('In all the troubles'; 'He was troubled'). Taking into account the foregoing resolution of the second clause (as referring to a messenger) it becomes evident that the first clause (dealing with divine action) is best regarded as the conclusion to the preceding verse, which speaks of YHWH as Israel's saviour; namely, 'He became their deliverer (v. 8b) *in all their troubles* (v. 9a)'. The following reconstruction of Isa. 63: 7–9 results:

[2] See in *Midrasch Tannaim zum Deuteronomium*, ed. David Tzvi Hoffmann (Berlin: Itz-Kowski, 1908–9), 173. For other applications of the phrase, see Judah Goldin, 'Not by Means of an Angel and Not by Means of a Messenger', in *Religions in Antiquity: Essays in Memory of Erwin Ramsdell Goodenough* (suppl. to *Numen*, 14; Leiden: E. J. Brill, 1968), 412–24.

[3] Note the explicit parallelism of *mala'kh* and *tzir* in Prov. 13: 17.

[4] Targum Jonathan also reads 'not', and in the process creates a new theological issue (whenever the people sin and deserve trouble, God does not trouble them for it) and a new solution (the angel rescues them). Cf. Rashi's reformulation.

I will recite the gracious acts of YHWH . . . for the House of Israel . . . (v. 7). He (God) thought: 'Surely they are My people, children who do not play false'; so He became their deliverer (v. 8) in all their troubles. Neither by a messenger nor by an angel, but His (YHWH's) presence alone delivered them (v. 9).

But our solution of the textual problems should not erase or elide the creative processes that smuggled into the biblical text a theology of divine pathos and suffering at total odds with the remarks expressed by the ancient Israelite prophet. For indeed, though the precise process of this transformation eludes us, the result does not. Hebrew Scriptures are now marked by a striking mythic transvaluation, whereby the ancestral God of deliverance and might now also participates in the sorrows of the people. Many subsequent generations of readers have found theological warrant and comfort in its providential assurances.

Moreover, this intensified focus on the pathos of God, and His participation in the events of biblical Israel, marks a shift from the *historia sacra* of the people (the keynote of Scripture) to the *historia divina* of myth (a keynote of Midrash). More remarkably, the latter phenomenon is located within the former—in and through the language of Scripture. The result is that the mythic fabulations of the rabbis constitute a midrashic register only partly disclosed at the level of biblical plain sense; and also that the pattern of imagery or semantic structure of a given biblical verse (or phrase) often conditions the sequence of divine actions revealed in the midrashic myths. Such a parallelism or correlation of realms—of the divine with the national—marks the complex interrelationship of myth and history in these rabbinic sources. It is to this topic that we now turn.

A. MYTHS OF DIVINE PARTICIPATION: EGYPTIAN SERVITUDE AND OTHER EVENTS

I. A Cycle of Servitude and Salvation

The participation of the divine Presence (*Shekhinah*) in the events of Israel's historical servitude (both in Egypt and in exile), as well as its various redemptions (from Egypt and other exiles), is marked in an important early cycle of comments found in the *Mekhilta de-Rabbi Ishmael, Bo*ʾ 14. This tannaitic collection opens with an interpretation of Exod. 12: 41, which ostensibly states that the whole host of Israel were delivered from Egypt at the precise moment when the 430 years of their sojourn in that land was concluded (cf. v. 40). But the opening comment offers an unexpected twist: not only did the people themselves come forth, divine beings did so as well.

'And it came to pass on that selfsame day, that all the hosts of the Lord went out from the land of Egypt' (Exod. 12: 41). These are the ministering angels. And so you find that whenever Israel is enslaved the *Shekhinah*, as it were, is enslaved with them. As it is said, 'And they saw the God of Israel, and under His feet', etc. (Exod. 24: 10). But after they were redeemed what does it say? 'And like the very heaven for purity' (ibid.). And it also says, 'In all their troubles He was troubled' (Isa. 63: 9).—So far I learn (that God was with Israel) only during communal trouble. Whence might I deduce this for the trouble of the individual? (From) Scripture (which) says: 'Let him call upon me, and I shall answer him; I shall be with him in trouble' (Ps. 91: 15). And it also says, 'And Joseph's master took him', etc. (Gen. 39: 20). And what does it say next? 'But the Lord was with Joseph' (ibid., v. 21). And it also says, 'From before your people, whom You redeemed for Yourself from Egypt, the nation and its god' (2 Sam. 7: 23). R. Eliezer says: An idol crossed the sea with Israel, as it is said, 'A rival crossed the sea' (Zech. 10: 11).[5]—And which one was that? The idol of Micah. Rabbi Akiba says: Were it not written in Scripture, it would be impossible to say it. As it were, Israel said to God: You redeemed Yourself.

And so you find that wherever Israel went into exile, the *Shekhinah*, as it were, went into exile with them. They went into exile to Egypt, the *Shekhinah* went into exile with them, as it is said, I exiled myself to the house of your fathers when they were in Egypt (1 Sam. 2: 27). They went into exile to Babylon, the *Shekhinah* went into exile with them, as it is said, 'For your sake I sent myself to Babylon' (Isa. 43: 14). When they went into exile to Elam, the *Shekhinah* went into exile with them, as it is said, 'I shall set my throne in Elam' (Jer. 9: 38). They went into exile to Edom, the *Shekhinah* went into exile with them, as it is said, 'Who is this that comes from Edom?' (Isa. 63: 1).

And when they return in the future, the *Shekhinah*, as it were, will return with them, as it is said, 'Then the Lord your God will return with your captivity' (Deut. 30: 3).[6] Note that it does not say 'The Lord your God will bring back (*heshib*)', but rather '(he) will return (*ve-shab*)'. And it says, 'With me from Lebanon, my bride' (Songs 4: 8).—Was she actually coming from Lebanon? Was she not rather going up to Lebanon? What then does Scripture mean by 'with me from Lebanon'? This: You and I, as it were, went into exile from Lebanon; (and) you and I will go up to Lebanon.[7]

In this tannaitic collection, a variety of mythic fabulations are 'found' in Scripture—though this is not always self-evident to the latter-day reader, or even to the ancient circle of disciples who interject puzzled queries into the account ('Whence might I deduce'; 'And which one was that?'; 'Was she actually coming from Lebanon?'; and 'What does Scripture mean?'). Something of the give and take of the study hall may thus be replicated in this unit, and this only underscores the fact that the fabulations are created through exegetical readings and applications of the scriptural passages adduced. In

[5] 'Rival' translates *tzarah* (1 Sam. 1: 6), which is used by the sages to indicate a false god, rival to the Lord (*BT Yoma* 9b); here it ironically counterpoints the earlier reference to God being with individuals in their 'trouble (*tzarah*)'.

[6] Lit. 'the Lord will return your captivity'. I have translated with the midrashic sense presupposed, for the sake of the comprehensibility of the passage here. The exegete construes the word *'et* not as a nonce particle preceding the direct object, but as a preposition meaning 'with'; the fact that a simple *kal*-form of the verb is used, instead of the causative *hif'il*, serves to justify this exegesis. See the ensuing discourse; and below.

[7] See the text in the edition of Hayim Horovitz and Israel Rabin (2nd edn.; Jerusalem: Bamberger & Wahrmann, 1960), 51 f.

the process, new and old interpretations are presented; and as a result, we have a highly stylized and structured pericope depicting divine participation in events of the nation past and future. Note that the servitudes are balanced by redemptions—both realized and promised; and that considerations of time ('whenever', *kol zeman*) are balanced by those of space ('wherever', *be-khol maqom*).

II. The Brickwork on Earth and in Heaven

The scriptural lemma that precedes this entire series of teachings is the aforenoted phrase from Exod. 12: 41. Without clarification, the midrashic comment simply annotates the lemma 'all the hosts of the Lord went out' as referring to the angels. This seems puzzling, since the whole concern of the prior biblical narrative had been with the nation, and v. 40 even noted that the time of the sojourn of the 'people of Israel' was 430 years. But for rabbinic eyes it was more notable that the formulation in v. 41 made reference to the 'hosts of the Lord' (*tzebaʾot YHWH*), and that the verb 'went out' (*yatzeʾu*) indicates a process of departure and not God's act of deliverance. For both features are in marked contrast to the doublet of our formula found in v. 51, which states that 'It came to pass on that selfsame day that the Lord took out (*hotziʾ*) the people of Israel from Egypt by their hosts (*ʿal tzibʾo-tam*)'. Now since such variations could hardly be either fortuitous or stylistic, given rabbinic principles of scriptural economy, the first formulation was taken as textual evidence for the presence of God's own angelic host with the Israelites in Egypt and during their departure.[8] But what of God Himself, where was He all this while? Other passages would account for that.

Exod. 24: 10 is the first such text adduced in this connection. According to the sages' account of it above, the first half of verse 10, 'And they saw the God of Israel; and under His feet', etc., refers to an act of enslavement of the Lord Himself; whereas the second half of the verse, 'And like the very heaven for purity', refers to the time after the people's redemption. How so? What corroborates such an exegetical assertion? The present rendition is terse and opaque in the extreme (and possibly even deliberately truncated or suppressed); but based on contemporary and other variants, we are justified in isolating two textual markers in the passage. The first is found in the remainder of the phrase cited: under his feet was 'the likeness (*ke-maʿaseh*) of a pavement (*libnat*) of sapphire'. Given the proposed negative valence of this clause, interpreted to mean that God was enslaved 'with' Israel, one may

[8] In fact, the two verses are indeed stylistic variations, and serve to bracket off the legal insert found in vv. 43–50. Such a 'resumptive repetition' was an ancient scribal device for incorporating interpolations. See H. Wiener, *The Composition of Judges II,11 to I Kings II, 46* (London, 1929), 2; and C. Kuhl, 'Die "Wiederaufnahme"—Ein literar-kritisches Prinzip?', *ZAW* 65 (1952), 1–11. In the present case, the term *ʿetzem* ('selfsame') appears before and after the interpolation of a law enjoining one not to break an *ʿetzem* ('bone') of the paschal lamb.

suspect that the term *libnat* was understood to encode or allude to the term *libenim* ('bricks')—the object that most specifically marks the labour of the Israelites in Egypt (Exod. 1: 14; 5: 7–8, 16, 18–19). Accordingly, the midrash obliquely asserts that during Israel's servitude something 'like' (*ke*-) the 'work' (*maʿaseh*) of a brick (*libnat*), or of brickwork, was seen beneath God's feet in heaven. This mythic hint is taken up in other variants, preserved in the Jerusalem Talmud and elsewhere. For example, according to the view of Bar Qappara (T5), 'before Israel was redeemed from Egypt, its (i.e., the brick's) imprint was seen on high (in heaven)'; and his contemporary R. Levi b. Sisi was even more explicit when he precisely referred to the *libnat ha-sapir* as a *lebeinah* ('brick'). The later master R. Berekhia (A5) reported these teachings but added his own opinion that the reason Scripture specifically says *ke-maʿaseh libnat* is to indicate both the brickwork and 'and all the tools' associated with it.[9] In this way the sage concretizes the term *maʿaseh* to refer to the 'work' tools involved in the labour (both basket and hoe), and gives the myth a more tangible content. But even his detailed account pales in anthropomorphic concreteness before the fabulation found in the lost *Midrash Abkir*, as reported by R. Eleazar Ha-Darshan, many centuries later. In it, the scriptural reference to God's feet, under which is the brickwork, is also taken into consideration: '*kemaʿaseh libnat hasapir*—a *remez*: just as Israel trampled the mortar to make bricks, so is it also, as it were (*keʾilu*), on high, "in all their troubles He was troubled" '.[10]

The heavenly sign of God's participation in Israel's toil is thus marked by brickwork (and tools) set in the firmament under the throne. And it is precisely the occlusion of God which this labour effects that is removed with the exodus. For if the final phrase in Exod. 24: 10 ('and like the very (*ke-ʿetzem*) heaven for purity') is said (in the *Mekhilta* and elsewhere) to refer to the redemption of the people, this can only mean that during that event the brickwork was removed and the very core of heaven shone forth in clarity. Significantly, the word for 'very' is *ʿetzem*, and this is the same term used to indicate the 'selfsame' (*ʿetzem*) day of redemption. Thus a second verbal tally with the exodus event (the first being the allusion to *lebeinim*) aligns Exod. 24: 10 with the textual lemma that inaugurates the entire teaching

[9] These several teachings are collected in *JT Sukkah* 4. 3; *Leviticus Rabba* 23. 8, ed. Mordecai Margulies (Jerusalem: Wahrman, 1962), 537 f.; and *Songs Rabba* 4. 8. 1. The term for work instruments is variously *ʾir/egaliyaʾ*, this being Greek *ergaleia*, 'artisan tools'.

[10] Preserved in R. Eleazar's *Sefer Ha-Gemaṭriyot*, as cited by Abraham Epstein from his personal copy, in '*Yalkut Shimoni*', *Haeschkol*, 6 (1909), 207. I regard the word *remez* here as a hint or marker of the mythic correlation spelled out, and not a reference to some figurative sense. The mythic idea is certainly ancient and part of the tradition. Indeed, it occurs prominently in a liturgical poem by Yannai. After noting that God saw the Israelites 'labouring in bricks (*lebeinim*)' and let them see the 'brick (*lebeinah*)' under His feet, he states that 'the trouble of His people is His trouble'. See in *Maḥzor Piyyuṭei Rabbi Yannai la-Torah vela-Moʿadim*, ed. Zvi M. Rabinovitz (Jerusalem: Mosad Bialik, 1985), i. 266 (l. 37) and 268 (l. 50).

(Exod. 12: 41), and suggests that the mythologem of the shining of heaven at the conclusion of God's participatory labour is itself encoded in the reference to the end of the Egyptian sojourn. Hence all surface evidence to the contrary, a profound myth of divine involvement in the tribulations and triumph of Israel is disclosed by exegesis—a bold fabulation that finds its very basis and authority in the historical narratives of Scripture itself.

III. The Hermeneutics of Divine Redemption

The mythmaking of our pericope is marked five times by the term *kivyakhol*, which was translated above by the expression 'as it were'. Three of these occurrences structure the collection as a whole, and have a common stylistic pattern: 'whenever' Israel was 'enslaved' or 'sent into exile', and when Israel would 'return' to its homeland—'the *Shekhinah* was with them'. Of these subunits, it appears that the accounts of the *Shekhinah*'s exile and return comprise an independent and core cluster (since Egypt is included there as the first place of exile), to which the mythic drama of divine enslavement in Egypt has been added. The other two occurrences of the term are embedded within specific teachings (that by Rabbi Akiba, regarding divine redemption from Egypt, is included in the enslavement section; and that regarding the exile of God and Israel from Lebanon is included within the restoration portion). Given such a pattern of repetition and emphasis, and the boldness of the teachings themselves, one is naturally drawn to the word *kivyakhol* and its force and function in these rabbinic myths.

Since the Middle Ages it has been routine for commentators to regard the term as some kind of euphemistic qualification of the daring remark with which it is found.[11] The word is thus assumed to unsay what has just been said. But why would such putative piety not only leave the bold assertions intact but even add biblical proof-texts in every case? Indeed, what would be the force of the teaching if the assertions of divine involvement were qualified and reduced to a mere trope? Now to be sure, by such a rhetorical strategy the effect of the fabulation would be undone; and there is no doubt that, in the course of time and in the hands of various copyists, the use of the term *kivyakhol* would change and sometimes even reflect some pious qualification of the textual content. But this aside, one must still wonder about its role in ancient exegetical Midrash.

Such considerations suggest the possibility that the term originally (and in our example, particularly) functioned to qualify the *exegetical basis* of the mythic fabulations asserted about God. That is to say, the teachers exhibit a self-conscious awareness of the tenuous scriptural nature of their bold teachings. Simply to make a mythic statement without any scriptural warrant

[11] As noted, a thorough review of opinions and an extended analysis of textual occurrences will be discussed in Appendix 2.

would be, for the rabbis, an empty act of fabrication and without authority. At the same time, Scripture does not manifestly say what the sages so boldly assert. Hence, I suggest, the term *kivyakkhol* is used to indicate that these myths about God are in fact grounded in Scripture—but only midrashically so, as it were. Thus it will be observed that in each and every instance of our *Mekhilta* pericope, biblical language is reused in order to provide the basis for a mythic fabulation. Nowhere is this clearer than in the rereading of the brickwork in heaven, just studied. But this is the case in all the other units adduced in this anthology. For example, the citation of God's self-revelation in Egypt (*nigloh nigleyti*) in the context of the *Shekhinah*'s exiles presumes that the latter phrase was remarkably construed to indicate God's own self-exile there (1 Sam. 2: 27);[12] moreover, the citation of God's redemptive act of sending (*shillaḥti*) messengers or allies to Chaldaea only makes sense insofar as this act was understood to indicate His own self-exile (reading: *shullaḥti*) to that place (Isa. 43: 14); and finally, the formulation of Deut. 30: 3 (*ve-shab YHWH... ʾet shebutekha*) is read so as to indicate that God will return *with* the nation from exile. In this instance, the fact that the biblical passage does not use the causative verb *heishib* ('bring back') is decisive, and allows the interpreter to reinterpret the particle *ʾet*—not as a marker of an action done by God, but as a sign of God's involvement 'with' the nation.[13]

The peculiarities of midrashic mythmaking become evident in these cases. They consist of a series of actions undertaken by God in tandem with Israel's history—each encoded within Scripture, and each revealed through a strong act of exegesis. Indeed, this involves a series of mythicizations of the biblical text which boldly transform old Israelite history into a series of patterns enacted by God himself. Of these, perhaps the most remarkable is the mythologem asserted by Rabbi Akiba (early second century CE). Its place in the overall structure is complicated by the textual history and give and take of the pericope. In order to disentangle this, let us return to the topic about the enslavement of the *Shekhinah* whenever Israel is enslaved. We noted earlier that this assertion was demonstrated by a mythical reading of Exod. 24: 10, concerning the brickwork of heaven. A second proof-text is then adduced from Isa. 63: 9, and read to mean that 'in all *their* troubles' God was also troubled. This statement about God's share in the nation's fate leads to a (parenthetical) query about the possibility of God also being with individuals in their personal affliction. In support, two proofs are adduced: Ps. 91: 15 ('I shall be *with him*) and Gen. 39: 20–1 ('and YHWH was *with Joseph*'). For it appears that the ensuing proof, 'And it also says: From before your people, whom You redeemed from Egypt, the nation and its

[12] This is a striking case where the exegetical point turns on a non-homonymic homograph (linking revelation and exile).

[13] Another similar use of this particle in Exod. 3: 17 will be discussed below.

god (*ʾelohav*)' (2 Sam. 7: 23), actually returns us to the earlier topic of God Himself being with the nation in times of trouble and adds that He even came out of Egypt with them.[14]

At this point, two traditions are adduced regarding the meaning of the passage from 2 Samuel. The first is brought by R. Eliezer (Akiba's contemporary),[15] who ignores the implication that God and the nation came out of Egypt, and construes the word *ʾelohav* to mean 'its gods'; namely, the idols taken by the Israelites from Egypt. Clearly, such a reading of the verse goes against the whole thrust of the preceding (anonymous) interpretation, and was undoubtedly transmitted here as one in a series of interpretations on that passage.[16] More consonant with the citation of 2 Sam. 7: 23 to suggest God's involvement in Israelite history, but taking the point in an unexpected direction, is the teaching of R. Akiba. It is his contention that the very language of Scripture supports the even more extreme myth that God also liberated Himself (together with Israel) from the enslavement of Egypt. To make this claim, he seems to bring two contradictory qualifications. In the first one, he offers the justification that if Scripture did not make this point it would also be forbidden for him to give such an interpretation.[17] But how does Scripture say this, and what is the force of the added qualification 'as it were'?

In light of our proposal that the term *kivyakhol* introduces a bold exegetical reading of a biblical passage about God, we take R. Akiba's point to be that while Scripture does indeed support his claim—for his interpretation changes no letter or vowel of the biblical text—the words of the passage must be construed in a bold new way. Instead of reading the phrase *padita lakh* as

[14] The textual basis for R. Akiba's interpretation lies in the biblical citation 'nation (*goy*) and its God'; by contrast, the Masoretic text reads 'nations (*goyim*) and its God'—but such a reading would not have inspired this midrash of God being with Israel (*the* nation *par excellence*). The Vulgate reflects the version cited in the midrash, as basically also the Syriac, though with a theological revision; but 4QSam[a] *ve-ʾohalim* (and LXX *skēnōmata*) seems like a hyper-correction. 1 Chron. 17: 21 simply has *goyim*, thereby deleting the difficulty.

[15] This is presumably R. Eliezer ben Hyrkanos, who is often in dispute with both R. Akiba and his teacher, R. Yehoshua ben Ḥananiah.

[16] There is a more personal and reactive contestation of this position by R. Akiba in *JT Sukkah* IV. 3, and it apparently preserves the original clash.

[17] The technical expression, translated earlier as 'Were it not written (in Scripture)', is *ʾilmaleiʾ sheha-dabar katub*. The hermeneutical function or use of the formula 'were it not written' is mentioned briefly above (p. 110); it will be considered further below. In tannaitic literature the force of the term is negative. See Yoḥanan Breuer, '*ʿAl ha-Lashon ha-ʿIvrit shel ha-ʾAmoraʾim be-Talmud ha-Bavliʾ*', *Meḥqerei Lashon*, 2–3 (1987), 129–31; and cf. M. Z. Segal, *Leshonenu*, 4 (1942–3), 207 f. Some conceptual and analytic considerations of the term may be found in Moshe Halbertal, '*ʾIlmaleiʾ Miqraʾ Katub ʾIy ʾEfshar Le-ʾomro*', *Tarbiz*, 68 (1998–9), 39–59. In my view, the opinion that the resulting anthropomorphic teachings create a kind of theological 'intimacy' (p. 59) understates the strong mythic fabulations involved. Mythic exegesis based on the scriptural text as written (*miqraʾ katub*) recurs frequently. In these cases, the contrast is between the text in its written form (*ketib*) as against its traditional recitation (*qere*). Mythic exegesis based on the *ketib* often revocalizes the letters, which is not the case with the *ʾilmaleiʾ* pattern.

referring to the nation which 'You (God) redeemed for Yourself', the sage interpreted it in terms of God Himself, and thus gave it the unexpected sense that 'You Yourself were redeemed'.[18] Hence, while nothing is changed in the scriptural text, the original eulogy of divine redemption now yields a new and remarkable myth of God's own self-liberation. Such a teaching is not even anticipated by the dramatic myth of divine participation in Israel's slave labour, mentioned at the outset of the pericope. Indeed, through R. Akiba, the new event erupts as a testament to the vital mythic imagination of the sages, and to their belief that such fabulations are also marked in Scripture.[19]

Following in the path of his teacher, R. Meir continues R. Akiba's mythic insight.[20] In remarks based on the divine instruction in Exod. 12: 1, 'This month shall be for you (*lakhem*)', the sage precedes his teaching about the festival of Passover with the following interpretation of God's words: 'The redemption (from Egypt) is for Me (*li*) as well as for you (*lakhem*)—as it were (*kivyakhol*), I was redeemed with you (*niphdeiti ʿimmakhem*); as it is said, "From before your people, whom you redeemed for yourself (*padita lakh*) from Egypt, the nation and its god" (2 Sam. 7: 23)' (*Exodus Rabba* 15. 12). This mythic fabulation is noteworthy, for one will observe that there is nothing in the plain sense of the lemma that supports R. Meir's inclusion of God in the exodus event; and indeed, that assertion is made simply by invoking the proof-text adduced by R. Akiba in the aforementioned *Mekhilta* passage—and without the strong expressions of self-consciousness with which it was proposed. In the present instance, the qualification is somewhat toned down and its mythic sense not defended. It is merely presented as a part of the tradition, and not requiring any further elucidation.

Although R. Akiba's use of 2 Sam. 7: 23 appears to be original to him, it should be remarked that the notion of a divine descent into Egypt for the redemption of the nation appears to derive from his own teacher, R. Yehoshua b. Ḥananiah.[21] Thus in a manuscript fragment preserved at the beginning of the *Mekhilta de-Rabbi Simeon bar Yochai*, 'R. Yehoshua

[18] 1 Chron. 17: 21 deletes *lakh*, thus leaving the textual stress on God's redemption of nations.

[19] In another remarkable tradition, R. Akiba interpreted Hos. 7: 13 to mean that the people spoke falsely against God when 'They said: "Is He preoccupied with us?—(rather) He is preoccupied with Himself (*ʿatzmo*)"!, as it says, "Because of Your people, which *padita lakh* (2 Sam. 7: 23)"' (*Exod. R.* 42. 3). This passage only makes sense if the people are presumed to understand the last clause as saying, 'which You redeemed for Yourself', namely, God was primarily preoccupied with His own self-liberation. R. Akiba seems at odds here with his own interpretation, or its potential danger, and rejects the notion that God's act was so self-centred, on the assumption that David recited praise not contempt (on this point, see the comment of the Meharzu, R. Ze'ev Wolf Einhorn, ad loc.; he also cites the lemma correctly, which has been mangled in the Vilna edition).

[20] For R. Meir and others (R. Simeon bar Yochai; R. Yosi ben Ḥalafta; and R. Judah bar Ila'ʿi) as students of Akiba; see Abraham Goldberg, 'All Base Themselves upon the Teachings of Rabbi Akiba', *Tarbiz*, 38 (1968–9), 231–54 (in Hebrew).

[21] Also noted by Norman J. Cohen, 'Shekhinta Ba-Galuta: A Midrashic Response to Destruction and Persecution', *JSJ* 13 (1982), 152f.

said: Why did the Holy One, blessed be He, depart[22] from the exalted heavens and speak to Moses from the midst of the bush? To show that when Israel descended (*yardu*) to Egypt, the *Shekhinah* descended with them; as it is said, "I shall descend (*ʾeireid*) with you" (Gen. 46: 4)'.[23] The manuscript tradition continues with indications of the *Shekhinah*'s ascent with Israel. Even more promising and significant for the issue at hand, however, is a teaching delivered by Ḥananiah, 'the nephew of R. Yehoshua', who commented on the proclamation of God's deliverance of Israel in Exod. 20: 2, '(I am the Lord, your God,) who brought you out (*hotzeiʾtikha*) of the land of Egypt', with the new mythic teaching: 'It (Scripture) is written (orthographically) *hwtzʾtykh* (thus allowing one to read *hutzeiʾtikha*; namely, that God 'was brought out with you'), as it were (*kivyakhol*), I and you (*ʾani ve-ʾatem*) went out of Egypt'.[24] Ḥananiah's fabulation here tallies with Akiba's mythic theology, and together with the two exegeses of R. Meir (just above, and in the assertion that God 'was saved' from Egypt in *Tanḥuma, Aḥarei Mot*, 12), shows the variety of expressions given to this topic in tannaitic times—teachings which transform the biblical account of Israel's historical redemption by God into a mythic event that includes God as well. It is furthermore notable that the mythologem is preserved in a distinct chain of tradition, from R. Yehoshua to R. Akiba to R. Meir.

IV. Some Variants and Variations

We may appreciate the exegetical and mythic expansiveness presented in the *Mekhilta de-Rabbi Ishmael* by a comparison of it with the version found in the *Mekhilta de-Rabbi Simeon bar Yochai*. Commenting on the same lemma, 'On the selfsame day' (Exod. 12: 41), this latter source gives the following terse formulation: 'This teaches that even the hosts of the Omnipresent were with Israel in (their) affliction, as it says, "In all their troubles He was troubled" (Isa. 63: 9); and it says, "Let him call upon Me and I shall answer him, I am with him in (his) trouble" (Ps. 91: 15); and it says, "From before Your people, which You redeemed (for Yourself) from Egypt, the nation and its god" (2 Sam. 7: 23)'.[25] Missing from this version is the tripartite

[22] The Hebrew verb, *nigleh*, is striking, since it at once puns on the sense of divine revealment from heaven, but also conveys the sense of an 'exile' from there for the sake of appearing among the people on earth. This may be part of the tradition that led to the notion of a succession of divine exiles.

[23] As transcribed in the edition of Jacob N. Epstein and Ezra Zion Melamed (Jerusalem: Mekize Nirdamim, 1955), 2, from the MS of R. Abraham Ha-Laḥmi, published in *Batei Midrashot*, ed. A. Wertheimer, ii. 103 (with corrections added).

[24] *Pesikta Rabbati* 21 (Ish Shalom, 110a). The version in *JT Sukkah*, 4. 3, is briefer, and is without the *kivyakhol* clause and the ensuing explication. The *Pesikta* manuscript tradition is stable. Cf. *Pesiqta Rabbati: A Synoptic Edition of Pesiqta Rabbati Based upon All Extant Manuscripts and the Editio Princeps*, by Rivka Ulmer (SFSHJ 115; Atlanta: Scholars Press, 1997), i. 510f.

[25] See *Mekhilta de-Rabbi Simeon bar Yochai*, Epstein and Melamed edn., 34.

structure of divine enslavement, exile, and return with Israel; also missing here is the drama of divine brick-building and liberation; and finally, one will note that the school setting and its queries are also missing in this version. By contrast, this teaching simply indicates that the divine host were with Israel in Egypt in their affliction, and supports that assertion with three diverse proof-texts—the first two speaking of God being with the people (understood as a collective and singular entity), and the last referring to his redemption of the people from Egypt. This congeries of scriptural passages, which is inconsistent about who was with the people in affliction, and the aspect of the redemption, stands in contrast to the more expansive version produced by the school of Rabbi Ishmael. In the process, the myths of divine labour and liberation are included, along with a string of examples showing that God was with the people in their various dispersions, and will be with them upon their return to their homeland.

Midrashic variations on the number or nature of the exiles endured by the *Shekhinah* also occur, but without any diminishment of mythic ardour. In our Ishmaelian corpus, these included the four lands of Egypt, Babylon, Elam, and Edom, together with scriptural proof-texts. A variant in *Exodus Rabba* 15. 16 keeps this number stable, though it substitutes the kingdoms of Media and Greece for Elam and Edom, and supports this change with scriptural verses taken from Isa. 21: 2 and Zech. 9: 14, respectively. A more condensed version of the tradition is found in *Leviticus Rabba* 32. 8, which limits discussion of the exile to Babylon and a reference to God's return from there.[26] This homily is thus linked to the theological polarities evident in the Ishmaelian pericope, but is so through a deft pun on Zech. 4: 2, and its reference to the 'bowl' (*gulah*) envisioned by the prophet above the lamp-stand. One interpretation gives consolation by understanding the *gulah* to refer to the *golah* ('exile') which God will undertake together with Israel in Babylon (citing Isa. 43: 14); the other one offers the antipodal hope of *ge'ulah* ('redemption'), when God will return with His people from this place of exile (citing Isa. 47: 4).[27]

Such variations show that the mythic theology of divine exile and return was not reduced to a hackneyed formulation, but remained a vital element that was evoked and revitalized in new settings and by means of new proof-texts. Further evidence of this occurs in an extended homily on laws dealing with the restoration of lost lands in the Jubilee year (Leviticus 25).[28] In the course of his remarks R. Samuel b. Gedaliah cites the opening portion of v. 35, 'If your kinsman, being in straits, comes under your authority (*u-maṭah*

[26] See Margulies edn., 755 f.

[27] *Eccles. Rabba* 4. 1 adds a citation from Micah 2: 13 (the emphasis undoubtedly falling on the last clause, 'Their king marches before them, YHWH at their head (*be-ro'sham*)'; not only does this refer to a divine return, but also offers a tally with 'its head (*be-ro'sho*)' in Zech. 4: 2).

[28] See *Tanḥuma Buber, Behar*, 2, in S. Buber, *Midrash Tanḥuma* (Vilna: Romm, 1885), 104.

yado ʿimmakh)', and refers this to the fall of Jerusalem, when the hand of the people 'shall fail (*tamoṭ yadam*) before Nebuchadnezzar'. Such an application is not especially remarkable, until the sage goes on to add that, on this occasion, 'The Shekhinah will be with them (*ʿimmahem*), as it were; as it says, "For their sake I was sent to Babylon" (Isa. 43: 14)'. To achieve this new sense, R. Samuel separated the word *ʿimmakh* from its plain sense, and understood it to counterbalance the enemy's invasion with God's involvement 'with' His people. This reading is reinforced by the scriptural sequel, which goes on to admonish the Israelite who gains this advantage over his compatriot—saying that if 'you hold him as though (he were) a resident alien, (nevertheless) let him live by your side (as a kinsman)'. Boldly and systematically, the teacher transforms the act of holding into a promise of God's support of His people, 'so that they do not perish by the hand' of Nebuchadnezzar; and he goes on to state that even though the nation may be regarded as aliens in Babylon, and subject to the lordship of this monarch, the Lord God 'will live at your side' in exile. The homily then goes on to add a number of details; but it is this act of divine participation in the history of the nation that stands at the mythic centre of the piece. Once again, the bold exegesis of Scripture elicits an unexpected mythic teaching from the plain sense of the text. Radically transformed into a drama of God's providential care, ancient law has become new prophecy.

V. Leaving the Shrine

Variety and variability thus mark the recurrent motif of the *Shekhinah* which accompanies Israel into its many exiles. Its mythic dimensions echo older Near Eastern elements. Earlier, in our discussion of the withdrawal of the Glory of YHWH from the inner precincts of the Temple of Jerusalem (Ezek. 9: 24), because of the sacrileges performed there, ancient Mesopotamian parallels were adduced.[29] There too deities were wont to abandon their shrine, in anger and rejection. In some cases the protective gods returned to their heavenly abode, thus leaving their temple in jeopardy; in others, the gods left their homeland and took up residence in foreign lands.[30] Most notably, in a so-called 'Marduk prophecy' datable to the reign of Nebuchadnezzar I (1124–1103) BCE) we read of three self-determined exiles which the god Marduk underwent (to Hatti, Assyria, and Elam)—leaving Babylon in distress and benefiting the new lands of residence.[31] A reflex of this motif occurs centuries later in connection with Sennacherib's treatment of Babylon;[32] and similarly, the annals of Ashurbanipal report that in the final

[29] See in the Conclusions to Part I. [30] See the sources cited above, pp. 78f. (nn. 34–6).

[31] See the reconstruction and discussion of R. Borger, 'Gott Marduk und God-König Šulgi als Propheten: Zwei prophetische Texte', *BO* 28 (1971), 3–24.

[32] Stephen Langdon, *Die Neubabylonischen Königinschriften* (Vorderasiatische Bibliotek, 4; Leipzig: J. C. Hinrichs, 1912), Nabonides 8, 1, 18–25.

campaign against Elam the goddess Nana was brought back to Elam ('a place not fit for her'), after her angry exile from Uruk for 1,635 years.[33]

As mythic features, these cases of divine withdrawal from a shrine bear comparison with our rabbinic sources. On the one hand, we also find in these texts the motif of God's ascension to heaven after the defilement and destruction of the Temple.[34] Similarly, God's departure from Jerusalem is also portrayed—though not with anger or rejection, but with great longing and sorrow. In a striking account, the *Shekhinah* is said to have departed the shrine in 'ten stages', hesitating over each feature; 'kissing the walls and hugging the pillars'; and wailing a lament on the way out: 'O farewell, My House! O farewell, My palace'.[35]

These features are notable. So too are the teachings that extol God's special love for His people, by descending into impure lands in order to redeem His people (*Exodus Rabba* 15. 5).[36] Equally significant are the accounts of divine willingness to take on the burdens and sufferings of the exile with the people. In one particularly noteworthy case, the same R. Aḥa who portrayed the sorrowful withdrawal of the *Shekhinah*,[37] cites Jer. 40: 1 dealing with the deportation of the prophet Jeremiah to Babylon, 'and he (*ve-hu*ʾ) was bound in chains'. Without any warning, but arising from a deep theological sensibility, the sage comments: '*kivyakhol* (as it were) He (*hu*ʾ)'—taking the words 'and he' not being a resumptive reference to the prophet but a special and telling reference to God's own participation in the event.[38] Adducing this midrash in another context, the medieval Tosafists either gloss it or give an important variant when they quote *Eicha Rabbati* as saying: '*kivyakhol* He (*hu*ʾ) Himself (*be-*ʿ*atzmo*)'.[39]

[33] M. Streck, *Ashurbanipal und die letzen Assyrischen Könige bis zum Untergange Nineveh's* (Vorderasiatische Bibliotek, 7; Leipzig: J. C. Hinrichs, 1916), 175.

[34] e.g. *ʾAbot de-Rabbi Nathan*, A, 34 (in the Schechter edn., 102); *Pesikta de-Rav Kahana* 13. 11 (in the Mandelbaum edn., i. 234); and *BT Rosh Hashanah* 31a.

[35] See *Pesikta de-Rav Kahana* 13. 11 (Mandelbaum edn., i. 234f.). The event is portrayed with even more pathos and lamentation in *Midrash Eicha Rabba, petiḥta*ʾ 25 (Buber edn. 29). The motif of divine withdrawal is also indicated in 2 Baruch 6: 1–2, which records that, at the time of the destruction of the Temple, a voice (of an angel) called 'from the midst of the Temple': 'Enter, you enemies, and come, you adversaries, because He who guarded this House has left it'. 4 Baruch 4: 2–3 refers to the angel calling to the Babylonians to enter, but without mentioning a divine withdrawal. Josephus (in *Bellum Judaeorum* vi.300) has the angelic host say, 'we are departing hence (*metabainomen*)'.

[36] In the name of R. Simeon (bar Yochai); but according to the *novellae* of R. David Lurie (no. 8), based on a passage from R. Beḥayye, the teacher was R. Simeon b. Lakish.

[37] In the *Eicha Rabba* version noted above (n. 35).

[38] *Midrash Eicha Rabba, petiḥta*ʾ 34 (Buber edn. 38); also in *Pesikta de-Rav Kahana* 13. 9.

[39] See on *BT Sukkah* 45a, s.v. *ʾani*, where the teacher is R. Yehudah. In the midrash itself, R. Aḥa adds another example: 'And I (*ve-ʾani*) am in the midst of the exile' (Ezek. 1: 1) was 'similarly' understood to refer to God. As in other cases, this exegesis may have influenced Origen, who interpreted the words *kai egō* (Latin, *et ego*) as referring to Christ. See his *Ezekielem Homilia* 1. 5, in *Origenes Werke*, vol. viii; *Homilien zu Samuel I, zum Hohenlied und zu den Propheten; Kommentar zum Hohelied in Rufins und Hieronymus' Übersetzungen*, ed.

This topos of the participation of the *Shekhinah* in the nation's exiles emphasizes divine willingness to share the sorrow and affliction of His people. The focus is thus not on divine anger or isolation, but on commiseration and care. Significantly, even the language of divine power is muted and transformed. One may particularly note that biblical assertions stating that God will 'be with' his people in times of need are affirmations of divine might on behalf of the faithful (cf. Ps. 91: 15). However, in their new midrashic transformations, such words of confidence indicate God's shared suffering with His people—and counterpoint the assertions that God has rejected or abandoned the Jews. Exilic history thus becomes the mysterious site of divine presence. An anonymous midrash of the rebellion at Sinai has presumably become a prism to project this point, in an unequivocable way: 'Even though they (Israel) are rebellious (says God): Truly, I shall not abandon them, and with them I shall dwell (*ve-ʿimmahem ʾani dar*'; *Exodus Rabba* 33. 2).

B. EXILIC SERVITUDE AND DIVINE REDEMPTION

I. *The Divine Hand and the Dynamics of History*

As examined earlier, the mighty or outstretched arm of God is the central mythic figure used in Hebrew Scriptures to dramatize divine power, even as the image of His weak or withdrawn arm serves to concretize the sense of divine absence or rejection. Rabbinic texts reflect both poles—though often in more dramatic or paradoxical ways. Particularly striking is an apparently old tradition, traced back to Rabbi Ishmael and preserved in the *Midrash Ha-Gadol* to Genesis 6: 15. Here, in conjunction with the divine instruction to Noah 'This is how you are to make (the ark)', we are told, first, that this verse 'teaches that God pointed out to Noah with His finger' just how he should build it.[40] Immediately thereafter, R. Ishmael reveals that 'the five fingers in the right arm of God are all a great secret'. He then enumerates the fingers, one by one, and indicates the divine acts performed by four of them (showing Noah the construction of the ark (Gen. 6: 15); smiting the Egyptians (Exod. 8: 15); inscribing the tablets (Exod. 31: 18); and indicating to Moses what the Israelites should give in order to save their lives during the desert census (Exod. 30: 13)).[41] The climax is 'the whole hand—with which YHWH will ruin the children of Esau that are His enemies, as it is written, "Your hand

W. A. Baehrens (GCS 33; Leipzig: J. Hinrichs, 1925), 329. And see, similarly, Theodoret of Cyprus, on Ezek. 1: 1, in *Opera Omnia*, ed. Joan L. Schultze, *PG* 81 (1864), 820 f.

[40] The motif of the deictic *zeh*, understood to indicate the pointing of a finger for instruction, is ancient, occurring in *Mekhilta de-Rabbi Ishmael, Boʾ* 1 (Horovitz–Rabin, 6) also in the name of R. Ishmael. But in *Siphre D'Be Rab 61*, ed. H. Horovitz (Jerusalem: Wahrmann, 1966), 58 f., the attribution is to R. Akiba.

[41] The first and last cases use the deictic *zeh*, the second and third refer explicitly to the 'finger' (*ʿetzbaʿ*) of God.

shall be lifted up over your adversaries" (Micah 5: 9); and it is written, "On that day YHWH will extend His hand a second time" (Isa. 11: 11)'.[42]

This conclusion is greater than the sum of the parts, and embodies a prophecy of redemption over Esau-Edom, the rabbinic cognomen for Rome and its hated hegemony. Indeed, the esoteric myth is deemed nothing less than 'a great secret' (*sod gadol*)—not, to be sure, the ancient mystery of the body parts of God, according to which, in one account, 'the whole universe is (the size of) one small finger . . . of the Holy One, blessed be He', but a mystery nonetheless.[43] This point is considerably softened in the version of R. Ishmael's teaching found in *Pirkei de-Rabbi Eliezer* (48), where the phrase *sod gadol* appears as *yesod ge'ulot*, 'a foundation of redemptions'.[44] While it neutralizes the esoterism, this formulation nevertheless reinforces the myth of redemption by the fingers and hand of God that is fabulated. In its main thrust, this mythologem continues older biblical images.

More paradoxical is the treatment of the withdrawn arm. As noted, the biblical topos occurs together with laments over divine rejection, and appeals to God to remember the great deeds wrought by His mighty arm in ancient times (cf. Ps. 74: 1–2, 11–14). Just how fundamental this combination is can be appreciated from the midrash found in *Pesikta de-Rav Kahana* 17. 5, which opens with the biblical lament 'Zion says, "YHWH has abandoned us, indeed the Lord has forgotten us"' (Isa. 49: 14), and continues with the assertion 'If I forget you, O Jerusalem, let my right hand forget its cunning' (Ps. 137: 5). At first sight, this juxtaposition of verses links a citation of the nation's complaint of divine rejection with an asseveration of remembrance using the figure of the right hand. But what is the purpose of this rabbinic collocation of scriptural passages, since the latter one manifestly deals with the oath of the people in exile? The combination would thus appear to be at most contradictory, and at least paradoxical. But this rhetorical move is only the beginning of a remarkable midrash that transforms the biblical text and introduces an unexpected mythic fabulation about God's response to the servitude of Israel's exile. The following is the pertinent part of the homily.[45]

R. Azariah and R. Abbahu said in the name of Resh Lakish: You find that when Israel's sins brought it about that enemies invaded Jerusalem, the enemies seized

[42] *Midrash Hagadol to Genesis*, ed. Mordecai Margulies (Jerusalem: Mosad HaRav Kook, 1967), 159.

[43] Preserved in a letter in the Cairo Geniza; see S. H. Kook, *'Iyyunim u-Meḥqarim* (Jerusalem: Mosad HaRav Kook, 1959), i. 108–19. And see also the discussion, in a broader context, of Meir Bar-Ilan, 'The Hand of God', in Gabrielle Sed-Rajna (ed.), *Rashi 1040–1990: Hommage à Ephraim E. Urbach* (Paris: Éditions du Cerf, 1993), esp. 326–31.

[44] According to the citation in *Arukh Completum*, ed. Alexander Kohut (Vienna: Menorah, 1926), iii, s.v. *ḥamesh*, the phrase is *le-sod ha-ge'ulot*; in *Yalkut Shimoni*, *Va-'era'*, no. 182, we have *le-sod ge'ulah*.

[45] *Pesikta de-Rav Kahana* 17. 5, Mandelbaum edn. i. 286f.

Israel's warriors and bound their hands behind them (*'aḥoreihem*). The Holy One, blessed be He, (then) said: It is written in Scripture (of Me), 'I shall be with him in affliction' (Ps. 91: 15); (and now when) My children are in affliction, can I be at ease?[46] (With that), as it were, 'He put His right hand behind Him (*'aḥor*), because of the enemy' (Lam. 2: 3).

Later on, God revealed to Daniel (when the hand would be visible), when He said to him, 'But you (Daniel), go on to the end-time (*qetz*)' (Dan. 12: 12). Daniel asked: (For what purpose,) to give a (personal) accounting and reckoning? God answered: 'You shall rest' (ibid.). Daniel responded: For eternal rest (without resurrection) God replied: 'And you shall arise' (ibid.). Daniel then asked him: Master of the Universe, arise with whom—with the righteous or with the wicked? God answered: 'To your destiny' (ibid.), with righteous ones like yourself. Daniel asked: When? And God replied: 'At the end of days (*qetz ha-yamin*)' (ibid.). Then Daniel asked him: Master of the Universe, (Does *yamin* mean here) at the end of days (*yamim*) or at the end of (bondage of your) right hand (*yamin*)? God answered: At the end of the right hand, the very one that is in bondage. The Holy One (thus) said, I have set an end for My right hand, for as long as My children are in servitude, My right hand shall be in bondage; (and) when I redeem My children, I redeem My right hand.

This is what David (meant when he) said, 'For the sake of Your beloved ones, may they be delivered; save Your right hand—O answer me' (Ps. 60: 7). David (thus) said to the Holy One, Master of the Universe, when Israel have merit, save them for the sake of Your beloved ones, Abraham, Isaac, and Jacob; and if not, do it for Your right hand's sake—'Save Your right hand—O answer Me' (ibid.).

The foregoing midrashic myth is composed of two basic parts and an additional comment. The first part sets the tone of the entire discourse; for in response to the ancient outcry of divine rejection, recited annually as a lection in the synagogue,[47] the homilist fabulates a divine answer. At first the scene of destruction and enslavement is depicted; and then God recalls His old promise of sympathetic participation in the people's affliction (as enunciated in Ps. 91: 15),[48] and announces that He will imitate them in their sorrow. Proof of this divine action is found 'as it were' (*kivyakhol*) in the verse 'He put His right arm behind Him because of the enemy' (Lam. 2: 3). But since the action is positively portrayed, we once again see that the qualification *kivyakhol* does not serve to undermine the mythic drama, or even to reduce it to mere metaphor. Indeed, the midrashic point serves notice that the biblical verse is no mere figure of speech, but a dramatic mythic element—now inverted. For if the biblical phrase indicates a human lament over divine wrath, wailing that God withdrew His arm 'because of (*mipnei*)' the enemy, and thereby allowed their invasion and destruction, the verse is

46 The term for affliction, *tzarah*, can also mean straits, and this elicits the opposite mode to being at ease.

47 Isaiah 49: 14 ('Zion says') is the opening line of the second of seven *hafṭarot* of consolation recited after the fast of Tishaʿ be-'Ab.

48 Used here to mark sharing in the affliction of the nation as a whole; this notably contrasts with the discourse in the *Mekhilta de-Rabbi Ishmael, pisḥa* 14, examined above.

now understood to mark the onset of divine compassion *after* the siege, when God put His own arm in bondage 'because of' what the enemy did to His people. The adverb *mipnei* thus serves as the pivot of this midrashic transformation of the meaning and purpose of Scripture. For we now have a myth of divine participation and sympathy wrested (exegetically) from a lament of judgement. In this light, the function of the term *kivyakhol* serves to mark this bold mythic invention—and to give notice that it is based 'as it were' on the biblical text; that is, as midrashically construed.

This graphic mythologem recurs in midrashic literature as a sign that God was involved in the sufferings of Israel, and would *not* forget or abandon Zion.[49] By means of an even more dramatic link to Ps. 137: 5 (read as a divine oath), God is said to have put His arm behind Him in remembrance of the Levites' act of cutting off their fingertips when their hands were bound, so that they would remember Jerusalem and not rejoice in psalmody while in exile.[50] Obviously, such passages were intended as positive expressions of divine compassion. But others were less impressed. Struck by the bold anthropomorphic detail, the mythologem of divine bondage, some were scandalized and noted such texts negatively. One such author was the Karaite Al Qirqisani (in 937 CE), who adduces the synagogue poet R. Eleazar Kallir's reference to God's arm being bound, as well an 'expression . . . by the Jews' to the same effect. The latter is undoubtedly a citation from the Koran (*Sura* v. 69) which states that 'The Jews say: Allah's hand is chained up'.[51] Such a reference was not intended as a compliment.

The antipode to this situation of divine and Jewish bondage is the revealment of the divine hand at the end of days. This mystery is disclosed to Daniel at the conclusion of a dialogue based on the concluding words of the book—such that the phrase *qetz ha-yamin* encodes the secret of the eschaton.

[49] See *Pesikta Rabbati* 31 (Ish Shalom, 144b).

[50] See *Shoḥer Ṭov* 137. 7 (Buber, 525); also *Pesikta Rabbati* 31, 144a–b.

[51] See the rendition of this section in Leon Nemoy, 'Al Qirqisani's Account of the Jewish Sects and Christianity', *HUCA* 7 (1930), 355. But he does not identify the quote as from *Surah* v. 69; for which see Jacob Mann, 'An Early Theologico-Polemical Work', *HUCA* 12–13 (1937–8), 414 f., n. 8. For early Islamic citations of Jewish traditions, see Menahem Kister, 'Ḥaddithū ʿn banī isrāʾīla wa-lā ḥaraja: A Study of an Early Tradition', *IOS* 2 (1972), 215–39. The *piyyuṭ* of Kallir cited by Al Qirqisani, *Ha-Yad ha-Ramah ʾasher be-Rahaṭ ʾAsurah*, is apparently that referred to by B. Halper in his *Descriptive Catalogue of the Geniza Fragments in Philadelphia* (Philadelphia: The Dropsie College for Hebrew and Cognate Learning, 1924), 112 f., Dropsie College MS 241. The phrase occurs on fo. 3b of the MS (my thanks to the Annenberg Research Institute for the photocopy) and is based on an interpretation of Songs 7: 6. While this phrase is commented on in *Midrash Song of Songs* on Songs 7: 6, and *Leviticus Rabba* 31. 4, there is no reference there to Lam. 2: 3; and in any case, in these midrashim the passage serves to mark a divine oath that the *Shekhinah* would remain in the Temple. Significantly, the verse is cited in Kallir's name by the Karaite Judah Hadasi, *ʾEshkol Ha-Kopher*, Alph. 81, letter *qof*, and there the sense is that because God's hand is bound and tied, 'he cannot release it in order to save his people'. The Hadasi reference is already adduced by L. Zunz, *Literaturgeschichte der synagogalen Poesie* (Berlin: L. Gerschel, 1865), 63, no. 26.

Puzzled by the use of the Aramaic plural noun *yamin* to denote 'days' at the end of a Hebrew sentence, Daniel pushes the point: does *yamin* really mean 'days' here (like Hebrew *yamim*) or is it rather the Hebrew word for 'right hand'. The term is amphibolous to the human ear, and so God is asked to specify the precise oracular sense of the passage. The answer is that the 'end' is the end of the servitude of the divine arm that is bound while Israel is in exile—hence the end of the *yamin* is dramatically portrayed as the end which God has set for the bondage of His hand. Such an interpretation is not at all obvious, and only makes sense in the context of the entire homily, which began with an account of God's sympathetic withdrawal of his arm when the nation went into exile. Indeed, Dan. 12: 12 serves as the mythic correlative to Lam. 2: 3. In its light, the oath in Ps. 137: 5 (which occurs at the beginning of the pericope) can only be understood as God's assurance to Zion that He will not forget her—for to do so would be to forget His own hand. Just as the withdrawal of that hand dramatizes God's sympathetic participation in the nation's servitude, so will its revealment at the end of days activate their redemption. God's mythic action and Israel's historical fate are correlated: 'When I redeem My children, I redeem My right hand'—no more and no less. The two are intertwined.[52]

The sense of divine redemption is intensified in the sequel, which adduces another proof-text for this myth from Ps. 60: 7. Here David is made to revise the old assertion of divine power. In its plain sense, the psalmist appeals to God, saying, 'In order that Your beloved ones be rescued, let Your right hand save (them)'. This plea is transformed into a complex motivation for the redemption of the people: if they have accrued merit, then let God rescue them for the sake of the ancestor; but if they have not, then may He rescue them for the sake of His own right hand. This construal of the verse as saying 'Save Your right hand!' reinforces the myth of the hidden hand. If it is put in bondage, it must also be redeemed—for God's own sake, and thus for the benefit of the people as well. Such concrete appeals take us beyond metaphor, and partake of a mythic drama. God's free act of sympathy with the people's bondage has resulted in a transformation of His own destiny: He too must undergo a type of redemption—and historical redemption may even depend upon it.

II. *A Cycle of Salvations*

The mythic rereading of passages like Ps. 60: 7 show that the theme of the divine arm was a part of living religious imagination. Other verses were

[52] One may wonder whether the homilist noticed that his first proof-text, Ps. 91: 15, contains both parts of the homily: the first clause states that God will be with the people in its affliction; whereas the second section has God say 'I shall give him length of days (*'orekh yamim*) and show him my salvation'. This assertion hints at the drama and exegesis of the midrash.

employed, as well. Notable is the transformation of Ps. 80: 3, which appeals to God to 'Rouse Your might, and come (*lekhah*) for our salvation'. According to R. Ḥilkiyah, in the name of R. Abbahu (who reportedly transmitted the preceding teachings), it was notable that the appeal to God to 'come' to the people's rescue is written with a full orthography (*lekhah* instead of *lekha*), so as to mark the fact that the cohortative should also be read as 'and to You (for salvation for our sake)'—that is, God is called upon to enact His own salvation, and thus Israel's as well.[53] To be sure, this eulogy could be understood as meaning that God is the true agent of every act of salvation. But as the preceding translation suggests, and the midrashic context demands, the phrase could also mean that every event of salvation includes God Himself. Significantly, just this is the mythic reading of the passage found in *JT Sukkah* 4. 3 (in the name of R. Abbahu), in connection with God's enactment of the brickwork of Israel's Egyptian bondage.[54] This is also the sense the passage has in a remarkable collection of verses on the subject of divine salvation found in *Tanḥuma, Aḥarei Mot* 12.[55] This anthology reads as follows.

R. Abbahu said: Every salvation that happens for Israel, is (also) that of the Holy One, blessed be He; as it is said, 'I shall be with him in affliction . . . and show him my salvation' (Ps. 91: 15–16). Israel said: Master of the universe, since You said '(Let him call upon me and I shall answer him;) I shall be with him in affliction', (then) 'Save Your right hand and answer me' (Ps. 60: 7). For if you answer us, (then) the salvation is yours, as it is said, 'And to You for salvation' (Ps. 80: 3)—so that the right hand may not remain behind, as it is said, 'He put His right hand behind Him' (Lam. 2: 3). R. Berekhia be-Rabbi, the priest, said: See what is written, 'Rejoice greatly, O daughter of Zion, shout aloud, O daughter of Jerusalem; for behold your king is coming for you, He is righteous and saved (*noshaʿ*)' (Zech. 9: 9). Scripture does not say 'righteous and saving (*moshiʿa*)' but 'He is righteous and saved (*noshaʿ*)'. It also says, 'Say to the daughter of Zion, "Behold your saved one (*yishʿekh*)" is coming' (Isa. 62: 11). Scripture does not say here 'Your saviour (*moshiʿekh*)' but 'Your saved one (*yishʿekh*)'—as it were, He is saved. Rabbi Meir said: 'YHWH saved (*va-yoshaʿ*) Israel' (Exod. 14: 30). (Note that this verb) is written here (with the orthography) *vyvshʿ*, hence (one may read it as) *va-yivashaʿ*, '(YHWH) was saved'—(thus) as it were, He was redeemed with Israel; and whenever Israel is redeemed, it is as if He is redeemed (as well). R. Ammi said: Moses lauds the community of Israel, 'Happy are you O Israel, who is like you, a nation saved (*noshaʿ*) by YHWH' (Deut. 33: 29). Scripture does not say 'a nation whom YHWH saves (*moshiʿa*)', but 'a nation saved by YHWH (*noshaʿ*)'. (Understand this by) a parable of a person who had a *seʾah* of wheat for the second tithe. What does he do with it? He pays money and (thereby) redeems it. The analogy is to Israel—how are they redeemed? Through (i.e. by means of) the Holy One, blessed be He, as it were; as it is said, 'a nation saved (*noshaʿ*) by YHWH'. The Holy One, blessed be He, said: In this world you are saved by human beings: in Egypt,

[53] *Midrash Shoḥer Ṭov* 80. 4 (Buber, 362).
[54] See above, pp. 136–7.
[55] Also *Tanḥuma Buber, Aḥarei Mot*, 18.

by Moses and Aaron; in the days of Sisera, by Barak and Deborah; among the Midianites, by Shamgar ben Anat, as it says, 'He also saved Israel' (Judg. 3: 31); and also by (other) judges. Since they were but human, you were repeatedly enslaved; but in the future I shall Myself redeem you, and you shall not be enslaved again. As it is said, 'Israel is saved (*noshaʿ*) by YHWH—(this being) an everlasting salvation' (Isa. 45: 1).

This collection of mythic exegesis is grouped around four teachers—one tannaitic master (R. Meir) and three fairly late amoraic masters (R. Abbahu, R. Ammi, and R. Berekhia).[56] In the teachings of R. Meir and R. Abbahu, the reinterpretation turns on construing a key biblical word in a passive sense, so that God is not presented as the agent of redemption but as one who undergoes it. The exegesis of R. Berekhia starts with the passive sense of the verb *noshaʿ*, but takes the designation of the king to refer to God Himself—and not the royal messiah to come.[57] R. Ammi appears to go even further, for in applying the verb *noshaʿ* to God (in reverse of the plain sense of Deut. 33: 29) he teaches that Israel is redeemed *through* God's own redemption. This goes considerably beyond the myth of divine participation in the people's bondage and salvation. Through the parable adduced, we are given to understand that God's own self-redemption is the very agency through which Israel's redemption is achieved—in the manner of a substitution or monetary exchange.[58] This act of divine commutation is marked by the preposition *be-* ('by' with sense of 'through'), in contrast with the formula *ʿal yedei* ('by means of') used of human saviours. Here as in other cases in this collection, the term *kivyakhol* does not undermine R. Abbahu's principle that 'Every salvation that happens for Israel is that of the Holy One, blessed be He'. It rather marks the bold mythmaking educed from Scripture, where it is found 'as it were', when the text is so reinterpreted.[59]

[56] R. Ammi is not mentioned in *Tanḥuma (Buber)*, ad loc.; R. Meir is mentioned again, in his stead. All four teachers are Palestinian. R. Meir was a student of R. Akiba, who taught divine redemption from 2 Sam. 7: 23 (see above). R. Abbahu (A3) and R. Ammi (also Immi; A3) were students of R. Yoḥanan (A2); the later R. Berekhia (A5), was a student of R. Ḥelbo (A4) and close to R. Ammi. These sages flourished between the mid-3rd and mid-4th c. CE.

[57] The versions provide an active sense (LXX, *sodzon*; Vulgate, *salvator*; Peshitta, *peroqaʾ*), but this goes against biblical usage. Cf. Pss. 20: 10 and 33: 16–18, where God as the agent of salvation is contrasted with the king-messiah as its recipient. Moreover, the noun *tzaddiq* must also be construed as a passive participle, with the sense of 'saved' (cf. Isa. 46: 13). See already Yair Zakovitch, '"Ani ve-Rokheb ʿal Ḥamor (Zech. 9: 9–10)', *The Messianic Idea in Jewish Thought* (Jerusalem: Israel Academy of Sciences and Humanities, 1982), 9. The two terms function as a hendiadys.

[58] For the redemption of the second tithe, see *M. Maʿaser Sheni* 4. 1–7.

[59] Saul Lieberman, 'Raymundo Martini and the Alleged Forgeries', *Historia Judaica*, 5 (1943), 90, has noted that in his *Pugio Fidei* 644 Martini cites the phrase 'Scripture does not say "The salvation of Israel" but "The salvation of God"' from *Genesis Rabba*; and he observes that this formulation may be based on a variant of R. Meir's above exegesis found in Cod. Rome of the *Tanḥuma*. See the citation in *Tanḥuma Buber, Aḥarei Mot* 18 (71 n. 184). One should note, that the phrase 'I shall show him the salvation of God' (Ps. 50: 23) is also cited at the beginning of

R. Abbahu was clearly drawn to this type of mythic exegesis, and enunciated his principle in connection with other verses. For example, commenting on 'I shall show him My salvation' in Ps. 91: 15, the sage implies that Scripture does not teach us here about God's act of salvation for Israel so much as His own; for he says, 'This is one of the difficult passages (*qashot*) where the salvation of the Holy One, blessed be He, is the salvation of Israel'.[60] Notably, this formulation is even bolder than that given above, and comes closer to R. Ammi's mythic theology. The same principle is given a more summary statement in a comment on Ps. 9: 15 ('I shall rejoice in Your salvation'), when R. Abbahu says, 'This is one of the five difficult passages which teach that the salvation of Israel is the salvation of the Holy One, blessed be He; as it is said, "For I rejoice in Your salvation" (1 Sam. 2: 1)'.[61] However, for all the putative theological 'difficulty' of these texts, R. Abbahu does not shy away from making the myth explicit—nor do his tradents.

We may conclude with one more case of a 'difficult' verse, also taught by R. Abbahu, and dealing with divine salvation. Its focus is the exodus from Egypt, and thus brings our discussion full circle. Moreover, like the homily by R. Levi ben Sisi on God's co-involvement with the brickwork in Egypt, this midrash was also reportedly recited in a synagogue—a further indication that we are not solely dealing with traces of scholastic theology, but with teachings presented to the people in a popular and public religious setting.

R. Yudan said in the name of R. Jacob b. Abina', in the name of R. Abbahu, in the synagogue of the village of Tiberias: 'I shall bring you up (*'a'aleh 'etkhem*) from the travail of Egypt' (Exod. 3: 17). This is a difficult (*qasheh*) matter; (which) therefore (we should understand as meaning that) the Holy One, blessed be He said: Since I and my children are partners (or: *shutafin*) in trouble (*be-tzarah*), it is only right that I be avenged (*she-'ippara'*) of their enemies.[62]

In this striking case (which reflects another version of R. Abbahu's theology), the scriptural lemma (Exod. 3: 17) is impliedly transformed to

our *Tanḥuma* collection, and was presumably understood by the editor to indicate God's own salvation—since he appends our catena to it (though without any exegetical addition). For the authenticity of Martini's citation, see Lieberman, *passim*; and cf. the evaluation of Ursula Ragacs, 'The Forged Midrashim of Raymond Martini—Reconsidered', *Henoch*, 19 (1997), 59–68.

[60] *Shoḥer Ṭov* 91. 8 (Buber, 401). The use of the word *qasheh* ('difficult') to mark a theological reading of scripture appears to be tannaitic. Cf. R. Akiba's comment in *GenRab* 22. 2 (Theodor–Albeck, 206). Also note the expression in John 6: 60, as already observed by Adolf Schlatter, *Der Evangelist Johannes* (Stuttgart: Calwer, 1930), 180.

[61] Ibid. 9. 14 (89 f.); reading *yeshu'ato* for *yeshu'atan*, since this word is followed by *hi'*, '(it) is'. The five passages are: Pss. 9: 15; 13: 6; 80: 3; 91: 15; and 1 Sam. 2: 1.

[62] *Pesikta Rabbati*, addendum, 2 (Ish Shalom, 196b). This is a rare use of *shutaf*; cf. also *Exod. R.* 2. 4 (Shinan edn. 111), 'I am a partner (*shutaf*) with them in their sorrow (*be-tza'aran*)'. I have translated *'ippara'* as 'be avenged', to suit the context and theology. In the present redactional setting, it has the further nuance of 'settle accounts' or 'collect a debt', since it has been attached to a teaching that uses the analogy of settling a debt with this terminology.

mean 'I (God) shall go up *with* you' (reading *ʾeʿeleh ʾitkhem*). Only such a reading makes sense of the opaquely transmitted teaching, though one must assume a clearer and fuller explication in its original presentation. A similar reuse of the particle *ʾet* (as 'with') in Deut. 30: 3 was discussed earlier in connection with verses transformed to indicate God's presence with the nation during their return from exile.[63] As there, older biblical figures portraying God's redemptive power for Israel are transformed into mythic moments inscribing His co-involvement with the nation in their travail and triumph. God alone remains the active force of redemption; but a deeper mystery is deduced.

III. Divine Pathos and Human Profanation

The salvation history that is revealed through the foregoing cases of mythic exegesis is not just a human matter—but a divine one as well. This is its striking dimension, and the one that inverts the dominant biblical perspective in which divine intercessory power is either appealed to as something withdrawn or inactive, or is celebrated as a fait accompli. The Hebrew Bible gives little reason to suppose that the account of God's wrathful withdrawal of His protective arm in Lam. 2: 3 could conceal a myth of sympathetic compassion, or that the exile of the nation could be the occasion either for divine affliction among them or redemption with them and for their benefit. But just this is the mythic view that midrash makes possible, transforming Israelite *Heilsgeschichte* into a divine drama. In the process, a myth of God's providential care and participation finds expression through numerous texts. This makes the rare counterpoint all the more striking, as when the suspicion that divine exile may be less a sign of God's protection than of His weakened power is projected onto Scripture. Put into the mouth of infidel foreigners, such an inversion of the myth is presented as a profanation. But for all that, the homily is the product of rabbinic sages—and so their countervailing spirit must also be taken as noted.

A teaching in this vein by R. Simeon b. Lakish (third century CE) starts with the verse 'It is honourable for a man to hold back from strife' (Prov. 20: 3), and then puts the following words into God's mouth. 'The Holy One, blessed be He, said: It would have been honourable for Me had I never become entwined (*nizdavagti*) with this people.' The sage then comments: 'You find that when Israel was exiled among the peoples, the Holy One, blessed be He, went among them to hear what they were saying. And what was that?—"The god of this people saved them from Pharaoh, Sisera,

[63] See above, in connection with the *Mekhilta de-Rabbi Ishmael, Boʾ* 14. The same exegetical point is also marked in the concluding proof-text from Songs 4: 8, 'With me (*ʾitti*) from Lebanon'; but there the prepositional use of *ʾet* is plain enough, and the midrash turns on the speaker being God.

Sennacherib, and all their ilk"; and they added, "He has always been of youthful vigour, so if one may say so (*kivyakhol*), matters have declined (*hizqinu ha-debarim*)"; as it is said, "And when He came to the nations to which they (the Judaeans) came, they (the nations) caused My holy Name to be profaned" (Ezek. 36: 20). Scripture could simply have said, "And when they (the Judaeans) came (to the nations)"; but rather it says "He came"; perhaps, as it were (*kivyakhol*), He Himself came. And what (more) did they say?—"(If) these are the people of YHWH, (how is it that) they have departed from His land?" (ibid.)'.[64]

This counter-myth is built around the textual difficulty of the verb 'he came' (Ezek. 36: 20),[65] which the sage chooses to interpret as marking God's own exile and travel into the lands of exile. But whereas earlier teachings used this divine exile to indicate God's shared affliction with His people, R. Simeon ben Lakish now suggests that it specifies a loss of divine vigour and an inability to save.[66] For in times past, YHWH rescued His people from their foes, and now He wanders among them. Perhaps He has aged, the nations profanely suggest, and He is no longer the vigorous redeemer of times past. Hence the exile is interpreted by the nations as a sign of God's senescence, even as the people's own presence in exile is deemed proof that they have been stripped of their divine patrimony. On this harsh reading, the passage in Ezek. 36: 20 offers little comfort, and even less comports with the positive myth of divine exile found elsewhere. Indeed, as noted, the fact of exile is taken to mean that divine redemption is not possible—a teaching that surely sounds the counterpoint of hope. Even the divine lament voiced here expresses pessimism, since God Himself rues the fact of His involvement (cf. *nizdavagti*) with the people, since it binds Him to their sorry fate. Surely such a lament marks the dark theological antipode of a more triumphal theology, as exemplified in a case where God responds to Israel's wholehearted acceptance of Him in exile with the words: 'I shall be your companion (*zivugkha*),[67]

64 *Midrash Eicha Rabba, Petiḥta'* 15 (Buber edn. 13).

65 A plural verb is required after v. 19; hence many emend *va-yabo'* to *va-yabo'u*, explicitly or otherwise.

66 For other teachings by R. Simeon dealing with divine depletion, of an even more poignant kind, see below, pp. 169–70.

67 The term *zivug*, 'partner', is used here in a muted way; however, elsewhere the related term *ben zug* has the connotation of marriage partner or even consort (i.e. a syzygy; cf. Greek *zeugnymi*, 'to join in marriage'; cf. *BT Soṭah* 2a). Of particular interest is *Gen. Rab.* 11. 9 (Theodor–Albeck, 95 f.), where R. Simeon bar Yochai teaches that the first six days of creation are each paired off (that is, each has a *ben zug*), but the Sabbath does not; therefore, at Sinai, God says to her: 'The Congregation of Israel is your *ben zug*', and quotes Exod. 20: 8, 'Remember the Sabbath day to sanctify it (*le-qadsho*)'—where the latter verb has the contextual sense of 'to consecrate (in marriage)'. There is an undoubted echo here of older notions of cosmogonic pairs or even consorts. A trace of this mythic notion still echoes in the biblical phrase 'the generations of heaven and earth' (Gen. 2: 4), and quite explicitly and remarkably in *Deut. Rab.* 2. 31: 'Rabbis say, "The Holy One, blessed be He, said to Israel: 'My children, everything that I created I created in pairs (*zugot*); the heaven and earth are a pair, the sun and moon are a pair, Adam and

and I shall go up with you (*ʾeʿeleh ʾitkhem*), as it is said, "For your sake I sent Myself to Babylon" (Isa. 43: 14)'.[68] However, it is only when the foreigners' profane insinuation of divine impotence is expressed by God Himself that this myth is killed—at the nadir of divine pathos (see below).

IV. Dwellings of the Shekhinah

The topic of God's connection to Israel is rendered in quite different terms in a unique teaching attributed to Zabdi ben Levi (A1) preserved in *Midrash Lamentations Rabba, petiḥtaʾ* 29.

'God brings the solitary ones home' (Ps. 68: 7). You find that before Israel was redeemed from Egypt, they dwelt by themselves (*bifnei ʿatzman*) and the Shekhinah dwelt by itself (*bifnei ʿatzmah*); but once they were redeemed they all formed one communion (*homoniyaʾ*). But once they (Israel) were exiled, the Shekhinah returned to (being by) itself and Israel by themselves. As it is written, 'The rebellious ones live in a parched place' (ibid.).

In this teaching, the sage construes the first phrase of the psalm in a striking way, and then understands the second one as its counterpoint. At the outset God (Elohim) is said to have taken the two solitary ones (*yeḥidim*; i.e. the people Israel and the *Shekhinah*, who each dwelt apart from one another) and caused them to dwell in harmonious accord (the term *homoniyaʾ* rendering *baytah*, 'home').[69] This suggests that when Israel was in Egyptian bondage they were alone, without the *Shekhinah*, and only merited an accord with it as a result of the redemption. However, after Israel sinned and were exiled from their homeland, the divine and human parties were once again separated, when Israel was sent into the 'parched land' of exile. Hence,

Eve are a pair, this world and the world to come are a pair—but My glory is one and unique in the world!" "' Over a century ago, Manuel Joël, *Blicke in die Religionsgeschichte zu Anfang des zweiten christlichen Jahrhunderts* (Breslau: Schottländer, 1880), i. 161, understood the passage in *Gen. Rab.* 11. 9 as referring to the Sabbath as Israel's '*Syzygos*', and indicated that the 'Syzygienlehre' comes from the ancient Orient, where the Gnostics would have received it (p. 107). His speculations can now be documented from ancient Gnostic sources, which expressly refer to a heavenly consort as a *syzygos*; cf. in the Papyrus Berolinensis (8502), 36,16–39, 4 and 44,19–47,16, trans. in Kurt Rudolph, *Gnosis* (New York: Harper & Row, 1983), 78, 80; and cf. Irenaeus, *Adversus haereses*, ed. W. W. Harvey (Cambridge: Cambridge University Press, 1857), i. 21, 3.

68 *Pesikta Rabbati* 30 (Ish Shalom edn. 141a). It appears that the phrase 'I shall go up with you' is a midrashic reading of Exod. 3: 17, similar to the teaching attributed to R. Abbahu, quoted above. The quote from Isa. 43: 14 also encodes a midrashic reading; see above, p. 000.

69 According to the verse, 'home' refers to the Land of Israel, but it is taken here (also) as a metaphor for common dwelling and unity. The word *homoniyaʾ* represents Greek *homonoia* ('agreement' or 'common mind'), and undoubtedly indicates the accord of the covenant. In *Mekhilta de-Rabbi Ishmael, Yitro, Deba-Ḥodesh,* 1 (Horovitz–Rabin, 206), the harmonious dwelling of the people at Sinai is marked by the phrase 'they were all of one mind' (*hishvu kullam leb ʾeḥad*); in *Pirkei de-Rabbi Eliezer* 41 this covenantal accord is called 'one voice' (*peh ʾeḥad*). See Kohut, *Arukh Completum*, iii. 216a, s.v. *hmwnyʾ*.

corresponding to the first part of the teaching, where Israel dwelt in Egyptian bondage alone, after their expulsion Israel also went into exile alone, without the *Shekhinah*. Presumably, R. Zabdi shared the older view that asserted 'that the *Shekhinah* does not reveal itself outside the Land', where there could be idolatry or impurity,[70] and thus also rejected the view that the *Shekhinah* was 'with' Israel at all times—both in Egypt and in its foreign exile. For him, the *Shekhinah* embodies a quality of divine immanence that is restricted to Sinai and to the Land of Israel, and has no special attachment or commitment to the people Israel that transcends their harmonious covenantal life in the homeland. Also notable is the fact that this sage presents the *Shekhinah* as a distinct and non-personified entity, though (like Israel) subject to God's transcendent power.

Now it is striking that R. Zabdi's midrash says nothing about the *Shekhinah*'s whereabouts after the nation's exile. Other sages were more opinionated, and chose different passages for support, as we can see from the range of positions collected and ordered in *Midrash Psalms* 11. 3.

'YHWH is in His holy sanctuary; YHWH—His throne is in heaven' (Ps. 11: 4). As long as the Temple existed, the *Shekhinah* was present within it; but when, on account of sins, the Temple was destroyed, He (the Lord) withdrew His *Shekhinah* into heaven; as it is said, 'YHWH—His throne is in heaven'.[71] R. Eleazar ben Pedat said, Whether destroyed or not, the *Shekhinah* does not move (*zazah*) from its place; as it is said, 'YHWH is in His holy sanctuary'—even though His throne is in heaven, His *Shekhinah* is in the Temple; as it is said, 'My eyes and heart shall always be there' (1 Kings 9: 3); and it also says, 'And He answers me from His holy mountain, Selah' (Ps. 3: 5)—even though it is a mountain, its holiness remains.[72] R. Eleazar (ben Pedat) (also) said, Note how Cyrus speaks, 'Let him go up to Jerusalem, which is in Judah, and build the House of YHWH, the God of Israel—He is the God (Elohim) who is in Jerusalem' (Ezra 1: 3)—even though it (i.e. the Temple) is presently destroyed, 'He, the Elohim' does not move from there. R. Simon said, Behold what is written, 'For you shall now leave the city and dwell (*všknt*, *ve-shakhant*) in the field' (Micah 4: 10): [It is written *vškynty*, it is read *všknt*][73]—even though it is destroyed and made a field, My *Shekhinah* (*šekiynatiy*) is in the field; and 'field' means Temple, as it

[70] Cf. *Mekhilta de-Rabbi Ishmael, Bo'* 1 (Horovitz–Rabin, 3).

[71] A variant formulation occurs in *Tanḥuma Buber, Shemot* 10 (Buber, 5), where also the tradent is R. Samuel bar Naḥman (A 3).

[72] In *Tanḥuma Buber, Shemot* 10, 'even though it is a mountain, it (remains) in its holiness'. The point is that the place remains sacred even though it is destroyed, and God's Shekhinah continues to reside there. It is puzzling why R. Eleazar did not simply resort to Ps. 11: 4b for his proof-text.

[73] Buber, ad loc., inserts this variant into his *editio princeps*, but correctly notes that the inverse would be correct (i.e. 'it is written *všknt*; it is read *vškynty*). It seems that the original *ketib* was the form *všknty* (2nd-person sing. fem.). For confirmation, see the expression 'it is written *všknty*', preserved in other midrashic sources. see *Tanḥuma, Noaḥ* 3, *Vayishlaḥ* 9, and *Yalkut Ha-Mekhiri* (ed. A. W. Greenup; London, 1909–13), ii; Micah, 28. Cf. also *Minḥat Shai* on Micah 4: 10. Further on the orthographic basis for the midsrash, see n. 79 below.

is said, 'Behold, the smell of My son is like the smell of the field' (Gen. 27: 27).[74] R. Aḥa said, the *Shekhinah* never moves from the western wall; as it is said, 'Behold, "He" (lit. this one) stands behind our wall' (Songs 2: 9). R. Yannai said, When a king of flesh and blood enters the reception room he cannot see what is in an inner room, but the Holy One, blessed be He, is otherwise. Thus: (while) 'YHWH is in His holy sanctuary ... His throne is in heaven—"His glory is on earth and in heaven" (Ps. 148: 13). He looks and sees all creatures, but no eye has dominion over him.'[75]

Despite the apparent variety of views, this anthology really represents only three distinct positions, based on interpretations of the two clauses of the opening lemma (Ps. 11: 4) and their relationship: (*a*) 'YHWH is in His holy sanctuary'; (*b*) 'YHWH—His throne is in heaven'). The first (anonymous) position (also represented by R. Samuel bar Naḥman)[76] takes the (*a*) clause to refer to the earthly Temple during the pre-exilic period, and construes the (*b*) clause to refer to the time after its destruction, when YHWH withdrew His *Shekhinah* to the heavenly heights. This event of God's vertical removal because of sin has its parallels in ancient Near Eastern materials, as we have seen;[77] and is also represented in midrashic sources as a seven-step process.[78] The second position (variously represented by R. Eleazar, R. Simon, and R. Aḥa) makes its point that the *Shekhinah* never left its earthly indwelling by reading the (*b*) clause before the (*a*) clause. Thus: God's throne is in heaven, but He is nevertheless also found in His earthly sanctuary, and does not ever leave it, even after it falls to ruin. Different texts are adduced to make this point in different ways: R. Eleazar uses one verse (from Ps. 3: 5) that helps him maintain that the earthly sanctuary was never desecrated, and thus remained a fit dwelling for God, despite the destruction of the building; and he uses another one (from Ezra 1: 3) to suggest that even Cyrus knew that Elohim remained in Jerusalem after the debacle; by contrast, R. Simon employs a (putative) scribal variant (*šknt*/*šknty*) in order to invert the plain sense of the passage and have God Himself say that His *Shekhinah* never left the earthly shrine;[79] and R. Aḥa uses another passage (Songs 2: 9) to further stress that God remained by the walls of his Temple even 'after' (*ʾaḥar*) it was

74 Allegorically taking 'my son' to be Jacob/Israel (though in disguise), and linking his odour (*reaḥ*) with the incense-savour (*reaḥ*) of the Temple; a different version of this midrash, using Micah 3: 12 to make the point about the 'field', is found in *Gen.Rab.* 65. 23 (Theodor–Albeck, 744).

75 Buber, ad loc., misses the scriptural quote, presenting it as the sages' own words.

76 Cf. above, n. 71.

77 See the earlier discussion, p. 78.

78 *Gen.Rab.* 19. 7 (Theodor–Albeck, 176).

79 I render *šknty* without the medial *yod* because I think that later scribes simply read the orthography of *Shekhinah* back into the verb. At variance here is only the final *yod*; since in grammatical terms the form *šknty* is simply a dialectal variant of *šknt* (both are 2nd-person sing. feminine verbs in the perfect tense; cf. the two variants in Jer. 31: 20, and see the form alone in Jer. 2: 20). According to the plain sense, God speaks to Israel about her fate; but according to the midrash, God speaks personally about the fate of his *Shekhinah* (the verb being taken as a 1st-person sing. form). For R. Simon, the variants have a twofold significance.

ravaged.[80] And finally, the third position (represented by R. Yannai) takes up the apparent doubling of the (*a*) and (*b*) clauses, to underscore the point that YHWH is always fully in His heavenly sanctuary, on His throne, but emanates His refulgent splendour earthward, thus manifesting His providential attention to all earthly life. Of all the positions, this one most strongly stresses God's transcendence, and does not portray the *Shekhinah* as the embodiment of His earthly presence.

In the first two of these positions, the *Shekhinah* is certainly affected by historical events; but the main focus is on a sacred place (be that the heavenly sanctuary, to which the *Shekhinah* is taken after the desecration of the lower shrine through sin; or be that the earthly sanctuary where the *Shekhinah* remains, since that place has not been defiled and remains a fit dwelling place for God). In the third case, God is not presumed to be impassive concerning earthly life, but He is portrayed as wholly transcendent in His heavenly dwelling and providential rule. Moreover, none of the positions suggests any special bond between the *Shekhinah* and the people Israel, or any participation in its fate. Similarly, there is also no indication that God or His *Shekhinah* feels pathos over the destruction of the shrine or the exile of the nation, or expresses it through tears or lamentation. Such personal and poignant responses by God to Jewish destiny will figure prominently in the sources to be examined below.[81]

[80] Lit. the biblical adverb means 'behind'; but I am inclined to understand its midrashic usage in more temporal than spatial terms.

[81] For another remarkable midrashic text in this vein, see *Pesikta Rabbati* 29, translated and analysed below, pp. 367f.

8
Myths of Divinity

A. DIVINE PATHOS AND PERSONALITY

Preceding discussions have explored the mythic acts of God, performed in sympathetic participation with the history of Israel. These dramatic expressions are frequently linked in the midrashic homilies and teachings of late antiquity with the theme of divine affliction or travail. Notably, this is portrayed as God being 'with' Israel in its times of difficulty—both the labour of Egypt and the servitude of exile. Left out of these accounts are the expressions of sorrow or anguish experienced by God, whether in response to Israel's cry of suffering or as a matter of personal loss or anguish. It is to just this broad emotional spectrum that we now turn, formulated with bold mythopoeic force. In the process, the volatile personality of the God of Hebrew Scriptures is greatly augmented, even as its portrayal of a punishing and wrathful deity is radically transfigured or re-evaluated.

Certain mythic features of ancient Near Eastern literature may provide a helpful perspective. Two elements converge. The first of these is a variety of laments over the destruction of temples and cities preserved in Sumerian literature from the last centuries of the third millennium BCE and thereafter. Among these are texts referring to the ruin of the shrines of Lagash (by Lugalzagesi of Umma);[1] Ur;[2] Eridu;[3] Uruk;[4] Nippur;[5] Kesh;[6] and Agade.[7] Although it has been questioned whether such diverse sources constitute a literary tradition as such, given the variations in form and the gaps of evidence, the overall generic similarities seem to outweigh these issues and even allow for comparative perspectives.[8] From this perspective, the

[1] Hans E. Hirsch, 'Die "Sünde" Lugalzagesis', in *Festschrift für Wilhelm Eilers* (Wiesbaden: Otto Harrassowitz, 1967), 99–106.

[2] Piotr Michalowski, *The Lamentation over the Destruction of Sumer and Ur* (Winona Lake, Ind.: Eisenbrauns, 1989).

[3] Margaret W. Green, 'The Eridu Lament', *JCS* 30 (1978), 127–67.

[4] *Eadem*, 'The Uruk Lament', *JAOS* 104 (1984), 253–79.

[5] Samuel N. Kramer, 'The Lamentation over the Destruction of Nippur', *Acta Sumerologica*, 13 (1991), 1–26.

[6] Idem, 'Kesh and its Fate', in *Gratz College Anniversary Volume* (Philadelphia: Gratz College, 1971), 165–75.

[7] Jerrold S. Cooper, *The Curse of Agade* (Baltimore: Johns Hopkins University Press, 1983).

[8] For a valuable consideration of a generic and comparative approach to Mesopotamian sources, see Tremper Longman III, *Fictional Akkadian Autobiography: A Generic and Comparative Study* (Winona Lake, Ind.: Eisenbrauns, 1991), chs. 1–2.

variations within the genre of city and temple laments show the plasticity and survival of the form throughout Mesopotamian history, down to Seleucid times.[9] Such generic consistency and longevity, moreover, have supported contentions that the biblical book of Lamentations, which mourns the ruin of Zion and its temple, is part of this overall cultural spectrum;[10] and even if there are not ample grounds for showing any direct influence of the Mesopotamian materials upon this work,[11] there are sufficient similarities of theme and expression to support a broad comparative consideration.[12]

Like the biblical book, the Mesopotamian city laments involve a variety of perspectives, with speakers using the first-, second-, and third-person voice;[13] but unlike this work, the Sumerian laments often include references to the weeping of a god or goddess. Thus in the 'Eridu Lament', after the city 'was smothered with silence as by a sandstorm', 'Its lord stayed outside his city... (and) wept bitter tears. Father Enki stayed outside his city as (if it were) an alien city. He wept bitter tears. For the sake of his harmed city, he wept bitter tears.'[14] And seeing the lord of Eridu bowed low, with 'his neck down to the ground', 'Its lady, the faithful cow, the compassionate one, the pure one, Damgalnunna, claws at her breast, claws at her eyes. She utters a frenzied cry... a bitter lament: "You, my city, whose woman does not dwell (there)... where is a lament uttered bitterly for you?"'[15] Of comparable interest is the later Akkadian lament uttered by Marduk over the destruction of Babylon, found in the fourth tablet of the Erra Epic, from near the end of the second millennium BCE.[16]

Remarkably, rabbinic midrash overcomes all biblical restraint and silence on this theme, and repeatedly evokes the mythic image of a lamenting and tearful deity.[17] The diversity of exegetical settings in which this topic is found

[9] See William C. Gwaltney, Jr., 'The Biblical Book of Lamentations in the Context of Near Eastern Lament Literature', in William W. Hallo, James C. Moyer, and Leo G. Perdue (edd.), *Scripture in Context*, ii: *More Essays on the Comparative Method* (Winona Lake, Indi.: Eisenbrauns, 1983), 191–211.

[10] Ibid.

[11] See already Thorkild Jacobsen, in *JNES* 1 (1946), 147 n. 32; review of *The Sumerians* by Samuel N. Kramer; and esp. the trenchent evaluation of Thomas F. McDaniel, 'The Alleged Sumerian Influence upon Lamentations', *VT* 18 (1968), 198–209.

[12] See the evaluation and catalogue of materials by F. W. Dobbs-Allsopp, *Weep, O Daughter of Zion: A Study of the City-Lament Genre in the Hebrew Bible* (Biblica et Orientalia, 44; Rome: Pontifical Biblical Institute, 1993), ch. 2 and appendix 2.

[13] See Gwaltney, 'Lamentations', 209.

[14] See Green, 'The Eridu Lament', 132 f. (*kirugu 1*, ll. 10–14). On this genre of weeping, see further, Samuel N. Kramer, 'BM 98396: A Sumerian Prototype of the *Mater-Dolorosa*', *EI* 16 (1982), 141–6*; and idem, 'The Weeping Goddess: Sumerian Prototypes of the *Mater Dolorosa*', *BA* 46. 2 (1983), 69–80.

[15] Ibid. 136–9 (*kirugu 5*).

[16] See Alfred Pohl, 'Die Klage Marduks über Babylon im Erra-Epos', *HUCA* 23.1 (1950–1), 405–9. Also, Luigi Cagni, *The Erra Epic* (Malibu: Udena Publications, 1977), 108.

[17] A number of the sources on divine lamentation have been collected and reviewed by Peter Kuhn, in his *Gottes Trauer und Klage in der Rabbinischen Überlieferung* (Leiden: E. J. Brill, 1978), though with a different emphasis and concern from that undertaken here.

underscores the grip it held on Jewish religious consciousness of late antiquity—in Palestine and Babylonia, in both homiletical and scholastic contexts.[18] We may approach the subject under three headings, expressing three modes of divine response to the destruction of the Temple and suffering of the people: memory and mourning; sympathy and sorrow; desolation and despair. In each type, the rabbinic interfusion of myth and history is realized differently.

1. Memory and Mourning

In this mode, God appears alone and withdrawn in sorrow—primarily absorbed with the loss of His Temple and His own personal plight. God's lament for the Temple comes to early exegetical expression in a tannaitic discussion on whether the night is to be divided into three or four watches. According to R. Eliezer (ben Hyrkanos; T2), a Palestinian teacher of the late first and early second century CE, the question can be solved by mythical midrash.

The night is comprised of three watches, and at each and every one the Holy One, blessed be He, sits and roars like a lion; as it is said, 'YHWH roars (*yishʾag*) from on high, and gives voice from his holy dwelling, roaring greatly (*shaʾog yishʾag*) over (*ʿal*) his own land (*naveihu*)' (Jer. 25: 30). (*BT Berakhot* 3a)

Thoroughly inverted here is Jeremiah's ancient oracle of divine doom against God's 'city' and the 'inhabitants of the earth' (v. 29)—delivered with a rhythmic emphasis on God's roar of anger as he comes to avenge evil (cf. Amos 1: 2). For now the adverb *ʿal* does not mark the site of divine aggression (i.e. 'over' the earthly abode of the nation), but the fact and focus of divine compassion, this being understood as God's groaning in sorrow 'on behalf of (*ʿal*)' His destroyed shrine (*naveihu*)[19]—three times nightly, as suggested by the threefold use of the verb 'roar' (*shaʾag*) in the passage. R. Eliezer's exegesis is thus clearly tendentious, and hardly a proper proof of the technical question about the number of watches—which makes it all the more significant and striking that this sage projects a myth of repeated divine lamentations in heaven over the shrine and its service. Other sages mark this mourning with still other biblical passages, among whom R. Nathan (a student of R. Akiba) is specifically named (*BT Berakhot* 59b). But in these cases only the fact of divine mourning is proved from Scripture, not its regular or ritual expression. It is, moreover, notable that in the debate over the number of watches found in

[18] The themes recur in the liturgical poetry (or *piyyuṭ*) of the synagogue, notably in the laments for Tishaʿ Be-Ab of R. Eleazar Kallir. Much material can be found in *Seder Ha-Qinot Le-Tishʿa Be-ʾAb*, ed. Daniel Goldschmidt (Jerusalem: Mosad Ha-Rav Kook, 1968), *seriatim*. For details and a consideration of the importance of this material, see below in the Conclusions to Part II.

[19] Understanding the noun in an alternative biblical (Exod. 15: 13) and standard rabbinic way (cf. *Mekhilta de-Rabba Ishmael, Beshalaḥ* 9, on Exod. 15: 13; Horovitz–Rabin, p. 146). For this traditional view, see also Targ; Jon.; Pesh.; Jerome (*hoc est super templum*); and also Kimḥi.

Tosefta Berakhot 1. 1, this same R. Nathan is the one who argues for three—not R. Eliezer. This variation may put in doubt whether the myth of mourning based upon Jeremiah's oracle is Palestinian in origin, or a feature of later Babylonian tradition.[20]

Another version of the threefold lament is given by R. Isaac bar Jacob in the name of Rab (BA 1; early third century, Babylonia). He opens with the same teaching ascribed to R. Eliezer earlier; but instead of providing the biblical proof-text, R. Isaac reports the content of God's lament as follows: 'Woe to Me (*'oy li*), for I have destroyed My house, and burnt My shrine, and exiled My children among the nations of the world' (*BT Berakhot* 3a).[21] The loss bemoaned here is clearly God's personal loss of the Temple and its worshippers. According to another tradition, reported of a certain necromancer by R. Qaṭṭina (from the generation after Rab), 'Whenever the Holy One, blessed be He, remembers His children who are in distress among the nations of the world, two tears drop from His eyes into the Great Sea, and His voice resounds from one end of the earth to the other—and (these tears) cause earth tremors'.[22] On this view there is divine groaning or roaring over Israel (only, and not the Temple), though not on a fixed basis; but there are also tears shed in sorrow, a matter not found earlier. Given these variations, it is striking to note that R. Eleazar ben Pedat (a student of Rab) interpreted the threefold repetition of the word 'tears' in Jer. 13: 17 as an expression of divine sorrow—'One for the first Temple, and one for the second Temple, and one for Israel, who have been exiled from their place' (*BT Ḥagigah* 5b). In this midrash the tears are not related to the evening watches, thus showing the diversity and flexibility of the mythologoumenon.

Another variation on this theme even provides a rabbinic parallel to the retreat of the lamenting god to his inner chamber, such as is reported of Enlil in the 'Curse of Agade' (209).[23] What is more, this case is also based on an

[20] This is the position of Ephraim E. Urbach, *Ḥazal: Pirkei 'Emunot ve-De'ot* (Jerusalem: Magnes Press, 1969), 132 n. 65. The toseftan tradition is also found in *JT Berakhot* 1. 1. The lateness of the tradition (projected on an earlier sage) may also explain the puzzling fact that our R. Eliezer would not have known the number of watches only one generation after the destruction of the Temple.

[21] The phrase 'Woe to Me (*li*)' follows the uncorrected reading found in the MSS. Cf. R. N. Rabbinovicz, *Diqduqei Soferim: Varia Lectionis in Mischnam et in Talmud Babylonicum* (New York, 1976), *Berakhot*, p. 4 n. 5 (MS Munich). It is also preserved in the anti-rabbanite polemic of the Karaite Solomon ben Yeruḥam; see his *Sefer Milḥamot Ha-Shem*, ed. Israel Davidson (New York: The Jewish Theological Seminary of America, 1934), ch. 4, p. 108 (ll. 8–15). And also in the polemics of Petrus Alfonsi; see the *Dialogus Petri, cognomento Alfonso, ex iudeo christiani et Moysi iudaei*, Migne, *Patrologia Latina* (=*PL*) 107: 550–1 (trans. *heu mihi*). Petrus' version was taken over by Peter Venerabilis (*PL* 189: 622); cf. the comparison made by Saul Lieberman, *Sheqi'in* (2nd edn.; Jerusalem: Wahrmann, 1960), 28 f. The standard Talmudic reading is now, *'oy la-banim she-be'avonoteihem*, 'Woe to the sons, because of whose sins, etc.' This is an apparent revision in light of Karaite ridicule.

[22] *BT Berakhot* 59b; the whole complex of traditions was discussed earlier.

[23] See the discussion of Cooper, *Agade*, 22 f.

interpretation of the first half of the prophetic passage just mentioned: 'If you will not hear it, my soul shall weep in secret for the pride' (Jer. 13: 17). In this passage, Jeremiah cries out that if the people will not attend to God's call to them (v. 16), he will withdraw in sorrow (v. 17). However, like the previous example, here too the speaker of sorrow is taken to be God Himself. The second teaching is also reported in the name of Rab—though now by one R. Samuel b. Iniya, who commented: 'The Holy One, blessed be He, has a place and its name is "Secret"' (*BT Ḥagigah* 5b). This unexpected exegesis turns on a concretization of the place of sorrow—transforming the idiom 'in secret' or 'secretly' into a specific place within the heavenly Temple (called 'Secret'). But this reading leaves the final phrase 'because of the pride (*mipnei geivoh*)' unresolved. Two views are then adduced which understand the obscure noun *geivoh* in terms of the 'pride' (*gaʾavah*) or glory that has been downtrodden—the pride of Israel and the pride of God.[24] It is for such a loss that the Lord weeps alone.

This resolved, a further problem is posed. How can one even speak of divine sorrow in the shrine, in light of the verse 'Honour and glory are before Him, strength and beauty are in His sanctuary' (Ps. 96: 6)? In order to decide the matter, the word *geivoh* is further explained to mean the inner chamber where God's mourning is in fact permitted. With this scholastic distinction, Scripture is harmonized and the myth saved. Brazenly, one anonymous teacher even put the mythic burden on the Bible itself. 'The Holy One, blessed be He, said, "My eyes shed streams of water over the ruin of My people" (Lam. 3: 48). If Scripture did not speak thus, the tongue that says this should be cut to ribbons!'[25] By so disguising his own attribution of the verse to God, the commentator deftly makes the myth inevitable—and thus ineluctable.

II. Sympathy and Sorrow

In several remarkable cases of old rabbinic mythmaking the divine is not portrayed as a bereaving 'other', but as a being in physical partnership with the sorrows of Israel—indeed, the two are figured as a complementary pair or even as two parts of the same body. Thus beyond any participatory bond or correlation, these texts present a mythic symbiosis between God and His people.

We begin with the myth of complementarity. It repeatedly comes to expression around the phrase 'My dove, My pure one (*tamati*)' (Songs 5: 2), which in numerous homilies is part of God's response to the people's expression of love

[24] Possibly, *geivoh* (*gwh*) is a contraction of *gaʾavah* (*gʾwh*) and tendentiously vocalized as a noun + pronominal suffix. In doing so, the Masoretes, like the rabbis of our midrash, may even have assumed that the noun was related to the Aramaic noun *go* (*gw*), 'inside'. Relatedly, *gwh* should be connected to the Syriac noun *gwʾ*, 'inward part'; for this suggestion, cf. N. Doniach's remarks in *AJSL* 50 (1933–4), 177f.

[25] *Midrash Zuṭṭa*, ed. Solomon Buber (Vilna: Romm, 1925), 58 (on Lamentations); and in version B, p. 78.

and expectation in the first part of the verse. According to R. Yannai, when God calls the people *tamati* he intends *tomyati*, 'My twin', by which is meant equivalence: 'I am not greater (or older) than she, and she is not greater (or older) than I'.[26] By this assertion, the sage seems to have God acknowledge the covenantal complementarity of Israel and her Lord. But R. Yehoshua of Sikhnin went further, reporting in the name of R. Levi (early third century, Palestine): 'The matter may be compared to twins (*teʾomin*). Just as one of them will feel the head pain experienced by the other, so the Holy One, blessed be He, said, 'I shall be with him in affliction' (Ps. 91: 15).'[27] Thus the word *tamati* is taken to encode God's confirmation that He is 'paired' with Israel in suffering. This exegetical move is opaque and unexpected. One may therefore suspect that underlying this myth of shared suffering is an understanding of the word *yonati*, 'My dove', in terms of affliction. Notably, the image of *ḥaron ha-yonah*, 'the anger of the oppressor' can be found in Scripture (Jer. 25: 38); and the verb *monim* is used in various midrashic homilies to denote the 'oppression' of Israel.[28] Thus R. Levi apparently construed *yonati* in Songs 5: 2 to mean 'My afflicted one', or perhaps even '(The one) who causes My affliction'—like a twin.

Even bolder is another teaching attributed to R. Levi. He again takes up the theme of sympathetic pain (with the same terms), but now constructs a myth of divine embodiment without parallel in the old rabbinic corpus.

'My eye, My eye flows with tears' (Lam. 1: 16). R. Levi said: (This verse may be) compared to a doctor whose eye ailed him. He said, 'Let my (good) eye weep for my (bad) eye'. Similarly, Israel is called the eye of the Holy One, blessed be He, as it is said, 'For all men's eyes will turn to the Lord, along with (like) the tribes of Israel' (literally, 'For to the Lord is the eye of man, and all the tribes of Israel') (Zech. 9: 1). The Holy One, blessed be He, said, as it were (*kivyakhol*), 'Let My eye weep for My eye'.[29]

As in his teaching on Songs 5: 2, R. Levi again approaches his exegetical task analogically.[30] Starting with the doubled use of the word *ʿeini* ('my eye')

[26] *Pesikta de-Rav Kahana, Ha-Ḥodesh*, 5. 6 (Mandelbaum edn. i. 87; *teʾomati* in MS Casanatense 3324); in *Songs Rabba* 5. 2, the reading is *teʾomati*, and the word *kivyakhol* occurs. For the phonetic crasis that produced this midrashic perception, see already Exod. 26: 24 and 36: 29 (in both cases, in the same verse).

[27] *Pesikta de-Rav Kahana* 5. 6 (Mandelbaum, 87 f.); the word *kivyakhol* occurs in *Songs Rabba* 5. 2.

[28] e.g. *Genesis Rabba* 88. 1 (Theodor–Albeck, 1077). Note also J. Theodor, 'Drei unbekannte Parashas aus Bereshit rabba', *Festschrift zum siebzigsten Geburtstage Jakob Guttmanns* (Leipzig: Gustav Fock, 1915), 159. The infinitive *lonot* ('to oppress' [Israel]) occurs in *Genesis Rabba* 79. 7 (Theodor–Albeck, 945); the reading in *Midrash Ha-Gadol* (to Gen. 33: 19), is *le-honot* (in the edition of Mordecai Margulies (Jerusalem: Mosad Ha-Rav Kook, 1967), 585); and correct Theodor–Albeck, 946 n., accordingly.

[29] *Midrash Lamentations Rabba* (Buber, 88).

[30] This R. Levi is a 3rd-generation Amora, student of R. Yoḥanan; he is to be distinguished from R. Levi b. Sissi (see above, p. 137), a 5th-generation Tanna, student of Rabbi Judah Ha-Nasi (usually just R. Levi in the Babylonian Talmud).

in Lam. 1: 16, the sage appears concerned with the human expression of grief marked in this verse—a concern that is deepened by the fact that *ʿeini* resonates with the language of anguish (*ʿonyi*, 'my suffering') in v. 9.[31] But this is not the way his exegesis continues. Instead of emphasizing the repetition as a sign of intensity, R. Levi distinguishes the two eyes and by means of an analogy understands the expression periphrastically—namely, one eye mourns for the other. This would appear to weaken the human grief involved. However, this is not the point of the analogy, whose real focus is shown to be God Himself, who has two eyes: one eye being His own, the other being the people of Israel. This point is introduced through a radical reading of Zech. 9: 1; for instead of the idiom *la-YHWH ʿein ʾadam* being taken as the universal regard of all persons for God, *la-YHWH* is taken as a possessive (i.e. 'the Lord has') whose object is a human eye—which is the nation, comprised of its tribes (thus: 'For the Lord has a human eye, (namely) all the tribes of Israel').

With this mythopoeic reading of Zech. 9: 1 inserted into the analogy of the two eyes, the full force of the reinterpretation becomes clear: God is the speaker of the verse, and His lament is over one of His eyes which has been damaged—this being the people Israel. Indeed, instead of the biblical lament marking the absence of God from the nation, it now underscores His active presence, expressed through tears and lamentation. For R. Levi, therefore, the wound of the people is construed as a wound for God Himself, since Israel is mythically transformed into part of the *corpus dei*—'for the Lord has a human eye'. The qualification *kivyakhol* at the end does not undermine this point, but rather fixes attention on the fact that this mythopoeic teaching has been derived from Scripture. Through such theology, the borders between history and myth collapse.[32]

R. Levi's teaching of divine tears complements Resh Lakish's bold teaching of divine suffering—that wherein God puts His arm behind Him, in sympathetic affliction or identity with Israel's exilic bondage.[33] Both reflect a profound relationship between God and His people, that reflects new understandings of the mystery of history and divine providence. This tendency is taken to a further level in 3 Enoch, where R. Ishmael ascends into the heights of heaven in order to view God and the mysteries. Guided on this

[31] Verse 16 is part of a succession of 1st-person laments in ch. 1 (cf. vv. 9b, 11, 12, 18, 20). These personal laments are to be distinguished from the 3rd-person lamentations in 1: 1–9a, 10a–11a, 15b, and 17.

[32] It is possible that R. Levi's teaching is not unrelated to the older tannaitic exegesis that interpreted the divine words in Zech. 2: 12, 'Whoever hurts you, hurts his own eye (*bat ʿeino*)' as a 'Scribal Correction' for the more radical reading: *bat ʿeini*, '*My* eye'—God's own eye. In the list of corrections found in *Mekhilta de-Rabbi Ishmael* at Exod. 15: 7 (and elsewhere), this is the first in the list. In *Siphre D'Be Rab, Behaʿalotekha, piska* 84, in the edition of H. S. Horovitz (Jerusalem: Wahrmann Books, 1966), 81–3, it precedes the traditions about God being with Israel in exile and in redemption.

[33] See above, pp. 147–50.

tour by the angel Metatron, the ancient sage is shown the letters engraved upon the Throne of Glory, by which heaven and earth and all their hosts were created' (ch. 41); he learns the power of divine Names (ch. 42); and he views the souls of the righteous, the wicked, the intermediate beings, and also the holy souls of the patriarchs (chs. 43–4). Towards the end, Metatron also shows Ishmael 'the curtain of the Omnipresent, which is spread before the Holy One, blessed be He, and on which are printed all the generations of the world and all their deeds, whether done or to be done, until the last generation' (ch. 45). Clearly, the concern is to learn the secrets of history; and thus it is most striking that the most hidden reality is 'the right arm of the Omniscient One, which has been cast behind (*nishlaḥat le-ʾaḥor*) Him because (*mipnei*) of the destruction of the Temple. From it all kinds of brilliant lights shine, and by it the 955 heavens were created' (ch. 48a).[34]

As the scene unfolds, R. Ishmael is borne up and shown the arm, and he hears the souls of the righteous exulting in praise, and reciting such verses as 'Arise, arise, put on strength arm of the Lord' (Isa. 51: 9). Then—'At that moment the right arm of the Omnipresent would cry, and five rivers of tears flowed from its fingers into the Great Sea, making the whole earth quake; as it is written, "The foundations of the earth will shudder; the earth will be rent in ruin; the earth will split asunder; the earth will bend and buckle; the earth will totter and tilt" (Isa. 24: 18–20)—five times, corresponding to the five fingers of the great right arm'.[35]

This culmination of the vision coordinates the various themes explored in earlier rabbinic texts—producing a mega-myth made up of features found in *Pesikta de-Rav Kahana* 17. 5 (regarding the withdrawn arm) and *BT Berakhot* 59b (regarding the divine tears). In the process the image of the arm is also transfigured, now becoming a hypostatic reality in the heights of heaven and visible to the transfigured sage. It is at the same time transformed into the font of sorrow, the channel whereby the tears of God flow downward into the world. No roar accompanies this silent stream; and it is only the vision of compassion that provides consolation, until the end of days—when God will bring about redemption 'for My sake' and for the sake of 'My arm'. The end of exile ends the myth.

III. Desolation and Despair

Alongside the foregoing myths of divine sympathy, a number of teachings focus on the divine anger that was released during the destruction of the Temple and nation, and also consider God's response to this behaviour.

[34] For the concluding section of 3 Enoch, beginning with this scene, see Peter Schäfer (ed.), *Synopse zur Hekhalot-Literatur* (Tübingen: Mohr–Siebeck, 1981), 34f. (MSS Munich 40 and Vatican 228, respectively; paragraphs 68–70).

[35] I have quoted the MT with its sum total of five references; the passage in 3 Enoch rephrases the end of v. 18, omitting the word 'earth' there, thus giving only four references overall.

What appear are not only examples of divine self-judgement for improper use of force, but, no less remarkably, psychological evaluations of this excessive violence, resulting in the expression of divine senescence and the need for human consolation. God's pathos for Israel is here turned inward, leading to self-doubt and self-pity. Through such sombre theological images, the myths of divine power and sympathy implode.

Critiques of divine justice centre around an older biblical image, through which God promises the people after the exile that He will protect His people and city with 'a wall of fire round about' (Zech. 2: 9). In its original context, this is an altogether positive oracle, and from the second or first century BCE it was applied to celebrate God as a 'righteous judge' (*Sibylline Oracles* 3. 702–6).[36] Many midrashic sources reinforce this theme of divine consolation and protection.[37] All the more significant, therefore, that in the generation that R. Levi was teaching his myth of divine sympathy, R. Isaac Nappaḥa (third century CE) gave the following discourse. Responding to both R. Ammi and R. Assi, who came to him and (respectively) requested him to teach some halakha and some aggadah, he cleverly chose to teach theology through the law, and in the process indicates that God is liable for infractions of His own law and must make payment for damages.

He said to them: I shall instruct you something which will be valuable to you both. (Scripture says,) 'If a fire breaks out and spreads to thorns' (Exod. 22: 5). (Now the expression) 'breaks out' implies 'of itself'. (But the passage continues, adding) 'He that kindled the fire shall surely make restitution'. The Holy One, blessed be He, said: It is incumbent upon Me to make restitution for the fire which I kindled. I kindled a fire in Zion, as it is said, 'And He kindled a fire in Zion which consumed its foundations' (Lam. 4: 11); and in the future I shall build it with fire, as it is said, 'For I shall be for her (Zion) a wall of fire round about, and I shall be the Glory in the midst of her' (Zech. 2: 9). Scripture opens with (reference to) damage done by a chattel (by itself), and concludes with damage done by the person, to teach that fire also implies agency. (*BT Baba Qama* 60b)[38]

R. Isaac's teaching is trenchant, and uses a homily on the law to teach that God must recompense Zion for damages. This is far from the position of a sovereign God beyond the law; nor does it say that because the people 'sinned with fire' (Jer. 7: 18) 'they were struck with fire' (Lam. 1: 13)—and in the end 'they shall be comforted by fire' (Zech. 2: 9).[39] Rather, God acknowledges the act of destruction and incriminates Himself. Going even

[36] For the date, see John J. Collins, 'The Sybylline Oracles, Book 3', in *The Old Testament Pseudepigrapha*, ed. J. Charlesworth (New York: Doubleday, 1985), i. 356.

[37] For a review of the sources, see Ira Chernus, '"A Wall of Fire Round About": The Development of a Theme in Rabbinic Midrash', *JJS* 30 (1979), 68–84.

[38] I follow Rashi's understanding of the conclusion (lit. the issue of agency is 'his fire is because of his arrow'). However, Rashi blunts the theological point.

[39] *Midrash Lamentations Rabba* 1 (Buber, 95). Also in *Pesikta de-Rav Kahana* 16. 11 (Mandelbaum, i. 280).

further, another fabulation has Jerusalem refuse the consolation of the prophets for the fires of destruction, inducing God to go to her Himself. In the process other transgressions of the Torah are confessed,[40] to the end that one bold version goes on to have God say, 'It is only fitting that I Myself go to appease her (Jerusalem), since I have transgressed the law (*she-ʿabarti ʾet ha-din*)'! Perhaps with such extraordinary judgements in mind, recriminations could be made which take ancient rabbinic theology to the brink.[41] Thus the Palestinian Amora R. Reuben (a contemporary of R. Isaac Nappaḥa) transmitted a statement of R. Ḥanina bar Ḥama, with all due caution but with no doubt about the point: 'If Scripture did not say so, one could not say this—"For YHWH is judged through fire" (Isa. 66: 16); (note that) Scripture does not say "(YHWH) judges (*shopheṭ*)" but "is judged (*nishpaṭ*)" '—not more and not less.[42] A more complete inversion of the theme of God's salvific judgement than this portrayal of divine punishment and purgation is hard to find.

But alongside the foregoing reflections on divine consolation of Jerusalem, two other Palestinian sages gave a powerful mythic revision of God's capacity to console the people. Presenting a more standard line, 'the rabbis' taught that with the successive loss of the tribes of Israel God was consoled with those that remained, until all twelve tribes were lost and He was left to lament them alone. R. Yoḥanan (bar Nappaḥa) and (his brother-in-law) R. Simeon ben Lakish took Scripture in hand and offered a more unexpected exegesis.[43] According to R. Yoḥanan, God's punishment of Israel could be understood by analogy to a king with two sons: angry with the first, he beat him and drove him into exile, saying 'Woe to this one (*ʾoy la-zeh*)' who has lost rest and peace; and when he became angry with the second son, he smote him and banished him likewise, but now reacted with the self-judgement, 'My (system of)

[40] *Pesikta Rabbati* 30 (Ish Shalom, 141a–142b).

[41] This sequence of texts is also adduced by Meir Eyali, 'Ha-ʾEl Ha-Mitzta ʿer Be-Tza ʿaram shel Yisraʾ el', in Sarah Heller-Wilensky and Moshe Idel (edd.), *Meḥqarim Be-Hagut Yehudit* (Jerusalem: Magnes Press, 1989), 46 f.

[42] *Midrash Shoḥer Ṭov* 1 (Buber, 21); also in *Songs Rabba* 2.3 (only naming R. Reuben); and in later collections (*Yalkut Shimoni*, Micah, no. 552; and Psalms, no. 692). It appears in a somewhat diminished form in Louis Ginzberg (ed.), *Geniza Studies* (New York; The Jewish Theological Seminary of America, 1928), 87. This interpretation of Isa. 66: 16 is repeatedly supplemented by Ps. 23: 4, which serves to celebrate that God is 'with' the sufferer. However, this addition undermines the whole force of the judgement against God, and I consider it to be secondary. Abraham Epstein, 'Bereshit-rabbati', *Magazin für die Wissenschaft des Judenthums*, 15 (1888), 95 regards the midrash to have 'Christian coloring', based on the imagery of the psalm, and hence is a response to Christian theology. This view ignores the force of R. Ḥanina's incrimination in the main part of the teaching. Remarkably, Qumran Isa[a] reads *yby[w?]ʾ lshpṭ*; and cf. likewise the LXX. These seem tendentious.

[43] See *Pesikta de-Rav Kahana* 15. 4 (Mandelbaum edn. i. 251 f.); and *Midrash Eicha Rabba, Petiḥtaʾ* 2 (Buber edn. 4). Both sages lived in Tiberias in the 3rd c. CE. According to the *ʾIggeret Rab Sherira Gaon*, ed. B. M. Lewin (Frankfurt, 1920), 83 f., R. Yoḥanan died in 279 CE, and had been head (*malakh*) of the academy for 80 years. R. Simeon died earlier.

training is bad'.[44] This, says, the sage, is like the two national exiles: when the ten northern tribes were exiled, 'The Holy One, blessed be He, began to recite over them this verse, "Woe to them (*ʾoy la-hem*) for they have wandered away from Me" (Hosea 7: 13)'; 'but when Judah and Benjamin were exiled, the Holy One, blessed be He, said, as it were, "Woe is Me (*ʾoy li*) for My loss" (Jer. 10: 19)'. The sequence of exiles is thus portrayed as a progressive personalization of laments—beginning with 'them' and concluding with 'Me'. The qualification *kivyakhol* ('as it were') does not mute the mourning, but rather calls attention to the attribution of the verse to God Himself.

R. Simeon went further. He too offers the analogy of a king with two sons, but his fabulation exacerbates the portrayal of parental violence and its result—again, in two stages. Angry with the first son, the king beats him to death, and then laments him; and then angry with the other one, he likewise beats him to death, but now says, 'I have no power to lament them' and requests that the female keeners come and do the job. This, we are again told, is like the national exiles: when the ten tribes went into exile, God mourned them, saying 'Hear now this word, for I raise (*noseʾ*) a lament over you, O house of Israel' (Amos 5: 1); 'but when Judah and Benjamin went into exile, the Holy One, blessed be He, said, as it were, "Henceforth I have no more strength to lament over you, therefore 'Call the keeners and have them come... and let them speedily raise (*tisʾenah*) a wail over us (Jer. 9: 16)"'. (Note that) Scripture does not say here 'over them (*ʿaleihem*)' but "over us (*ʿaleinu*)"—for Me and for you (*didi ve-didhon*); nor does it say "you shall raise their eyes with tears", but "our eyes"—for Me and for you; and it does not say, "their eyelids shall flow with water" but "our eyelids"—for Me and for you (Jer. 9: 16–17)'.

With this teaching, Amos's doom prophecy becomes a divine lament, just as God's evocation of a dirge to come is construed as a lament for God as well as the people. Here the move is from a word of self-sufficiency to one of dependence, from 'I' to 'us' and 'our'. In the process, with a combination of mythic daring and exegetical concreteness, R. Simeon evokes the image of a violent and spent deity, in need of human care and consolation—at once broken by His fury and by His loss. Such a divine figure takes us far from any theology of an omnipotent and independent judge, and projects a myth of divine limitation and need onto Scripture. Other sages intimate likewise, as when a homily on God's words of solace 'Comfort ye, comfort ye (*naḥamu naḥamu*), O my people (*ʿammi*)' (Isa. 40: 1) takes an unexpected hermeneutical turn at the conclusion: *naḥamuni naḥamuni ʿimmi*, 'Comfort Me, comfort Me—with Me'![45]

The representation of divine weakness here recalls the earlier noted aspersion of the nations, who saw Israel dispersed throughout their lands, and,

44 Aram. *ʾana huʾ de-tarbuti bishaʾ*.

45 *Pesikta de-Rav Kahana* 16. 9 (Mandelbaum, i. 276).

recalling earlier acts of redemption, now wondered about its God, 'He has always been of youthful vigour (*naʿar*), thus if one may say so, matters have declined (*hizqinu*)'.[46] With this bold remark a certain polymorphy in the perception and the portrayal of Israel's ancient God—who was seen as a youthful warrior (*gibbor*) at the Sea and a greybeard (*zaqen*) teaching Torah at Sinai[47]—has been hardened into a polarity of might: He was once a God of power and victory, but He has become senescent and weak. This near blasphemy could be held in check by being represented as the words of heathen peoples. Very different, therefore, is the extensive fabulation found in *petiḥtaʾ* 24 of *Midrash Lamentations Rabba.*[48] Here, after God puts His arm behind Him at the time of the fall of Jerusalem, averring that He would not have need of it until the end to come, a different reaction sets in after the flames consumed the Temple and He decided to return to His heavenly home. 'At that time, the Holy One, blessed be He, began to cry and said, "Woe is Me (*ʾoy li*), what have I done"?!'—for now His shrine is lost and He fears ridicule among the nations.

In response to this, the great angel Metatron came to give solace, and offered to cry on God's behalf—but this was rejected and God threatened to retreat to the privacy of His inner chamber. Immediately thereafter, God then goes to His ministering angels and invites them to see what has become of the Temple; but this sight only exacerbates His sorrow. 'At that time, the Holy One, blessed be He, began to cry and said, "Woe is Me for My house (*ʾoy li ʿal beiti*)—where are My children, where are My priests, where are those who love Me . . . ?"' God then requested of Jeremiah that an embassy of patriarchs come to console Him, 'for they know how to cry'. Soon a procession of lamentation and mourning moved towards the Temple—a cortege involving Abraham, Isaac, Jacob, and Moses. 'And when the Holy One, blessed be He, saw them (approach), at once, "On that day, YHWH, God of hosts, summoned to crying and lamenting, to tonsuring and girding with sackcloth" (Isa. 22: 12);[49]—and if Scripture did not say so, it would be forbidden to say it. And they went crying from one gate to another, like a person "whose dead (relative) lies before him";[50] and the Holy One,

[46] See *above*, p. 155.

[47] See *Mekhilta de-Rabbi Ishmael, Shirta* 4 (Horovitz–Rabin, 129; *Pesikta Rabbati* 33 (Ish Shalom, 155b); and ibid. 21 (100b–101). The latter passage closes with an anti-Christian polemic; see Ish Shalom, 101a, n. 31; and also Arthur Green, 'The Children in Egypt and the Theophany at the Sea', *Judaism*, 2 (1974), 455 f. The variation young–old recurs in Gnostic sources. On this matter, see the discussion of Gedaliahu Stroumsa, 'Polymorphie divine et transformations d'un mythologeme', *VC* 35 (1981), 412–34. See also the consideration of this theme in the context of the theophanic forms of God, by Elliot Wolfson, *Through a Speculum that Shines: Vision and Imagination in Medieval Jewish Mysticism* (Princeton: Princeton University Press, 1994), 33–41.

[48] *Midrash Eicha Rabba* (Buber edn. 25 f).

[49] The citation silently and strategically changes the MT, 'My Lord God of hosts summoned'. For another possibility, and a fuller consideration of this verse, see below, Conclusions to Part II (p. 228–9).

[50] Citing the beginning of *M. Berakhot* 3. 1.

blessed be He, was lamenting and saying, "Woe to the king who was successful in his youth (*shebe-qaṭnuto hitzliaḥ*), but who, in his old age (*be-ziqnuto*), was not successful" '.

In this unique fabulation, the assertion of the weakness and failure of God is transformed from a heathen blasphemy into a personal lament. It brings the myth of effective divine power to a close, and replaces it with a myth of tears—not shed by God in sympathy for the sorrows of Israel, but in self-commiseration for the twilight of His fame. This is in part elicited by the fear of mockery of the nations; and one may presume that in saying so our rabbinic mythmaker had his ear to historical reality.[51]

One final tradition may be added here, which retrojects God's limited control over human action and His struggle with wrath back to the beginning of the creation. It is here that we first find God in self-reflexive prayer—without benefit of human prayer or exhortation (as in *BT Berakhot* 7a); the second time is after the destruction of the Temple, when God prays for human repentance so that He can bring about its speedy building—an event not to be done before that, and which may only be hoped for by Him. Such psychological lucubrations take us deep into the divine personality as presented in rabbinic myth.

R. Berekhia said: At the beginning of the creation of the world, the Holy One, blessed be He, made a *sukkah* in Jerusalem, so to speak, wherein he used to pray: May it be acceptable (*yehi ratzon*) that My children do My will (*retzoni*), so that I shall not destroy My house and My temple. When sin caused [the destruction], what does it say: 'He stripped His *sukkah* like a garden; He destroyed His tabernacle (*moʿado*)' (Lam. 2: 6)—the place where He used to make Himself known (to Himself; *mitvadaʿ*)[52] in prayer. And since it has been destroyed, He prays: May it be My will (*yehi ratzon milefanay*), that My children repent so that I may bring about the building of My house and Temple. This is (the purport of), 'In Salem (*shalem*) will be His *sukkah*' (Ps. 76: 3).[53]

The dynamics of the divine will are poignantly presented here, particularly the contrast between God's *ratzon* and that of humans who may do His will, and also God's concluding evocation to Himself that His people repent so

[51] Among the pagan blasphemies against the God of Israel, those of the Roman general Titus, when he entered the Holy of Holies in Jerusalem, were most repeated in different variations. According to the *Genesis Rabba* MS used in the edition of Theodor–Albeck (BM Add. 27169, at 10. 7; i. 82 f.), Titus 'defied and blasphemed' God; in *Sifre Deuteronomy* 328, ed. Louis Finkelstein (New York: The Jewish Theological Seminary of America, 1969), 378 f., he says, 'If he is a god, let him come and prevent (the rending of the ark cover)'; and in the *editio princeps* (Venice, 1545) there is an elaborate statement that divine might is limited to the sea and water.

[52] The verb *mitvadaʿ* (*mtwdʿ*) puns on *moʿed* (*mwʿd*).

[53] *Midrash Shoḥer Ṭov* 76.3 (Buber, 171a). The final citation conceals a midrashic pun, understanding it to say, 'His *sukkah* (i.e. Temple) shall be (rebuilt) when (the people's heart) is whole (*be-shalem*)'. For futher analysis, see below, pp. 375 f. In a different version of the first prayer (also based on Ps. 76: 3), God prays that He may behold the building of His Temple. See *Genesis Rabba* 56.10 (Theodor–Albeck, 608).

that He may effect the rebuilding of His shrine. From this, it would seem that God cannot elicit His mercy against anger or punishment—so as to contain it or bring about different human behaviour. Indeed, God only seems able to pray for the proper action of His (future and present) children. Only this behaviour can stem the outbreak or continuation of divine doom, even against His own desire and will. Other teachings take the efficacy of human action as its main subject matter, and consider its impact upon God Himself. It is to this topic that we now turn.

B. HUMAN ACTS AND DIVINE ACTIVATION

In the preceding discussions, we have observed how the ancient rabbinic myths reveal traces of a cultural mentality about divine power and personality in response to the fate or history of Israel. Complex symbiotic relations are portrayed, which range from God's sympathetic imitation of Israel's suffering to the enactment of a divine redemption—involving the nation and God Himself. Such mercy is portrayed as an expression of divine compassion. What we have yet to explore is how these mythic notions may be related to ritual or halakhic actions. Several sources afford a glimpse into this aspect of rabbinic thought, and how it was imagined that the divine personality was affected or changed by human behaviour. By way of a prologue, certain temple traditions and their mythic interpretation shall be explored first.

1. The Ark and the Cherubim

We begin with an old ritual from tannaitic times, depicting the ritual process during the period of penitence and fasting undertaken in the time of a declared drought. According to *M. Taʿanit* 2. 1, the following actions are required: 'What is the order (of procedure) for the (last seven) fast days (for rain)? The ark (*teivah*) is carried out into the open area of the town and wood ashes are put on the ark, on the head of the Nasi and the head of the Ab Beit Din.[54] Everyone (else) takes some and puts it on his own head. The elder among them (then) addresses them with words of admonition (to repentance).' Both Jonah 3: 10 and Joel 2: 11 are then adduced to exhort penitent behaviour among the people. Further prayers and practices are then specified to induce divine mercy.

Subsequent rabbinic teachers pondered these procedures and offered various explanations. Among these, there is the following. 'Why do they put wood ashes on the Torah scroll?[55] R. Judah ben Pazzi said, This means to say

[54] These two officials were the head and vice-president of the Great Sanhedrin in Jerusalem, respectively.

[55] This substitution of 'Torah scroll' for 'ark' in the Mishnah is the preferred reading (found in all MSS; references in early works; and also the ruling of Maimonides in *Hilkhot Taʿanit* 4.1); see

(*ke-lomar*), "I will be with him in affliction" (Ps. 91: 15); (and) Resh (R. Simeon ben) Lakish said, (It means to say,) "In all their afflictions he was afflicted" (Isa. 63: 9)' (*BT Taʿanit* 16a). These comments are remarkable, for they not only shift attention away from the acts of human penitence found in the first part of the Mishnah, but ignore the litany of supplications for divine compassion that follows. With bold assurance, these two Palestinian sages of the middle and late third century teach that the Torah shrouded in ash is like the *Shekhinah* in sympathetic affliction for her people. Such a notion of the Torah as a symbolic embodiment of God on earth is virtually unique, though some near parallel to this idea can be found in homilies attributed to R. Nathan and R. Levi, two contemporary Palestinian sages whose teachings about divine pathos have been noted earlier.[56] According to R. Nathan, the special nature of the ark was that the *Shekhinah* spoke from above it, between the cherubim, and from there 'they empower Israel' (*megaddelin le-Yisrael*); moreover 'all the miracles that were done for Israel were because of the ark, since the *Shekhinah* was within it'.[57] For R. Levi, the specialness of the ark among all the vessels of the sanctuary was because 'the Torah was there(in), and the *Shekhinah* was there with it'.[58] Such conceptions derive from old teachings about the self-contraction of God between the staves of the ark, and even add a measure of dramatic intensity.[59] But they are a far cry from the notion that the Torah in the ark is an embodiment of the *Shekhinah*,[60] who is with the people in all of their afflictions—including rituals for the end of drought. And just this is the mythologoumenon that arguably informs the ritual commentaries of R. Simeon and R. Judah.

R. Nathan's idea of the empowerment effected by the cherubim may be connected with several other texts which attest to mythic conceptions relating to the Temple. Particularly striking is the tradition preserved by Rav Qaṭṭina, who said: 'When Israel would come up (to the Temple) for the Festival, the curtain (of the ark) would be removed for them and they would be shown the cherubim whose bodies were intertwisted (*meʿurim*) with one another, and they would be addressed as follows: Behold! You are beloved before God as the love between a man and woman' (*BT Yoma* 54a).[61] This

the critical edition of *Massekhet Taʿanit*, ed. Henry Malter (New York: The American Academy for Jewish Research, 1930), 57 (note to l. 15). *JT Taʿanit* 2.1 reads 'ark'.

[56] See pp. 98 and 165–6. [57] *Tanḥuma, Va-yaqhel* 7. [58] Ibid.

[59] For the traditions about such self-limitation, see the texts collected and annotated by Peter Kuhn, *Gottes Selbsterniedrigung in der Theologie der Rabbinen* (Munich: Kössel, 1968), esp. 47–60.

[60] For other mystical notions of the Torah, see Moshe Idel, 'The Concept of Torah in the Heikhalot Literature and its Metamorphosis in the Kabbalah', *JSJT* 1 (1981), 23–84 (in Hebrew).

[61] In the sequel (54b) Resh Lakish gives another version of the coupling and the contempt of the pagans who see it. There is no doubt but that the verb *meʿurim* has sexual overtones and is related to *ʿervah*, 'nakedness', as can be seen already in the proof-text found in the Talmud in connection with Resh Lakish's tradition (Lam. 1: 8; 'they saw her nakedness (*ʿervatah*)'). The

depiction of the relationship between the cherubim conveys strong erotic overtones connected with the inner sanctum of the shrine, and may be an iconic trace of some esoteric doctrine. R. Qaṭṭina's teaching may thus reflect a more exoteric variant of a deeper mystery.[62] More dynamic is another one that seeks to resolve a scriptural contradiction in the portrayal of the figures. According to the account in Exod. 25: 19–20 the two cherubim in the tabernacle were affixed on either side of the ark, and faced one another with their wings spread out above; whereas according to the account in 1 Kings 6: 23–7 the figures 'inside the inner chamber' were set up with their wings extended, with the outer wings of each touching the walls on each side 'and the wings in the centre of the chamber touched each other'. This difference of orientation is resolved by the comment that 'the former case (with the faces turned to each other) obtains when Israel does the will of God, whereas in the latter case (with the faces turned outward) Israel does not do the will of God' (*BT Baba Batra* 89a). The mythical import of this exegetical harmonization is that these intertwisted love-figures—expressions of divine love—are the result of Jewish obedience to the Law;[63] that is, ritual performance activates a type of erotic relationship within the Temple.

Among these fragmentary confluences of myth and ritual are others that are even more suggestive, and convey the notion of the Temple as a font of fertility because it is here that God has His 'bed' and lies in holy matrimony. That such stark mythic notions of a divine *hieros gamos* or sacred marriage—notions of great and persistent force—are imposed upon Scripture does much to attest to their vitality in Jewish circles of late antiquity. Especially bold and forthright is the following unit from an anonymous homily found in *Midrash Tanḥuma (Buber), Naso*ʾ 16.[64]

noun *maʿor* used with respect to the 'open space' in the figuration of the cherubim, is also cited in the Talmud (54a) with sexual implications; and it is to be compared to such a use of *maʿor* in Nahum 3: 5, as noted by Moshe Weinfeld, 'Yesodot Niqbiyim be-Teʾurei ha-ʾElohut ha-Yisraʾelit', *Beth Miqra*, 40 (1995), 352. Rashi also understood *meʿurim* as 'cleaving' in the sexual sense.

[62] Remarkably, R. Menahem Kasher, in '*Ha-Zohar*', *Sinai: Sefer Yovel* (Jerusalem: Mosad Ha-Rav Kook, 1957), 56, went so far as to suggest that this episode clarifies the conjunction in *M. Ḥagigah* 2. 1 of the prohibition to explicate the laws of *ʿarayot* (prohibited sexual relations) with prohibitions dealing with such esoteric subjects as the creation and the heavenly chariot. In Kasher's view, the subject of the prohibition deals with the mystery of God's love for Israel (i.e. the prohibition *ʿervat ʾabikha ve-ʿervat ʾimmekha loʾ tigalleih* in Lev. 18: 7 was taken to mean: 'Do not reveal the syzygy of your Father (God) and your Mother (Knesset Israel)). Cf. *BT Niddah* 31b. For Knesset Israel as a heavenly hypostasis of the Jewish people, see *BT Berakhot* 35b. This whole matter would be a profound esoteric transformation of the ancient prophetic motif of the 'love' of Israel's 'espousals' with God (Jer. 2: 2), and the depiction of 'entering' the covenant in the bold erotic terms of God covering Israel's *ʿervah* (Ezek. 16: 8); it would also be a trace of the great antiquity of Jewish mythic and mystic notions of a *hieros gamos*. See further below. For notions of divine participation in human sexuality, see in Appendix 2 (pp. 343 f).

[63] This is also the opinion of Moshe Idel, 'Sexual Metaphors and Praxis in the Kabbalah', in David Kraemer (ed.), *The Jewish Family: Metaphor and Memory* (New York: Oxford University Press, 1989), 202.

[64] Buber edn. 32 f.

'Behold the bed of Solomon, sixty warriors surround it' (Songs 3: 7). And what was Solomon's reason for being occupied with a bed, since it is written 'Behold the bed'? But the fact is that he (Solomon, *shelomoh*) was actually occupied with the King of Peace (*sheha-shalom shelo*). 'Behold the bed'—this is the Temple. And why was the Temple compared to a bed? Because just as this bed is for the purpose of fertility and increase, so the Temple caused everything within it to be fertile and increase. As it is said, 'and the staves (of the ark) lengthened' (1 Kings 8: 8); and it also says, 'and the gold (of the Temple) was fertile' (2 Chron. 3: 7),[65] since it sprouted fruit; and it also says, 'And he (Solomon) built the Lebanon Forest House' (1 Kings 7: 2). And why was it (the House, or Temple) compared to a forest? Because just as a forest is fertile and increases, so the Temple causes everything within it to be fertile and increase. Hence Scripture says, 'His bed'.

Just as remarkably, in another noteworthy fragment, the verse 'Our couch is in a bower' (Songs 1: 16)—spoken by the maiden to her beloved—is interpreted as the fertile bed of the Shrine ('Just as a bed is for fertility and increase, so the Temple is for fertility and increase').[66] And finally, pushing the myth to the limit of propriety with bold physical explicitness, the question of how the lengthened staves of the ark could be 'seen' as protruding from the curtain within the sanctuary, but 'not be seen without', was answered by one R. Judah, who said that 'They pressed forth and protruded as the two breasts of a woman; as it is said, "My beloved is to me as a bag of myrrh, that lies between my breasts" (Songs 1: 13)'.[67] According to this remarkable statement, the ark with its staves is a female figure—the 'bed' of her lover for the sake of fertility and increase.[68]

This mythic notion of God's presence in the Temple as a type of sacred bonding or syzygy, also comes to expression in a teaching that was variously connected with the completion of the Tabernacle and the future restoration of the Temple. According to the view of R. Simeon ben Yosni, as transmitted by R. Tanḥum, the statement of the beloved to his bride, 'I have come to my garden, my sister, my bride' (Songs 8: 5) means God's advent to marriage—for '*le-gani*, to my garden' is understood as meaning '*le-genuni*, to My bridal chamber', by a play on the Greek word *geneē* ('birth-place'; thus: a place of conception).[69] The renewal of the Temple and God's presence in it will therefore betoken the renewal of fertility on earth. In the words of one ancient dictum, 'When the service of the Temple exists, the world is blessed

[65] Reading *prvym* as *peruyim*, instead of *parvayim*, i.e. 'from Parvaim'.

[66] *Yalkut Shimoni* (Songs), ii, no. 985.

[67] *BT Yoma* 54a.

[68] Thus explicitly in *Midrash Shir Ha-Shirim*, ed. Eliezer Grünhut (Jerusalem: Hatzvi, 1907), 15b.

[69] See *Pesikta de-Rav Kahana* 1. 1 (Mandelbaum, i. 1). For the meaning 'birth', see A. Kohut, *Arukh Ha-Shalem* (Vienna: Menorah, 1926), ii. 321. The tradent is presumably R. Tanḥum bar Abba, a Palestinian aggadist of the mid-4th c. On the rabbinic terminology, cf. Richard Steiner, 'The Aramaic Text in Demotic Script', *JAOS* 111 (1991), 362; in the sacred marriage ceremony portrayed, the king calls to Nana and says 'In thy bridal chamber (*bk.n.nky (m)* = *bgnnky*) a priest sings'.

for its inhabitants and the rains fall in their season'; but when it does not exist, this great bounty fails.[70]

II. The Arousal of Mercy and Power

Among the most elusive mythic images in the biblical corpus is the exhortation that seeks to arouse God from His slumber in order to redeem Israel from her foes. 'Arouse Yourself (*ʿurah*)! Why do You sleep, O Lord? Awaken (*haqitzah*)! Do not abandon us forever. Why do You hide Your face, (and) forget our distress and oppression?... Arise, to our aid! Redeem us, for the sake of Your faithfulness!' (Ps. 44: 24–5, 27). Each of the verbs in this supplication beseech divine action; and in the first part, the supplicant counterpoints his appeals with accusations of abandonment. The interpreter is thus faced with understanding the nature of the images—particularly the two opening references to divine sleep. Are these mere metaphors for divine inaction, or even an ironic innuendo like Elijah's sarcastic appeal to the prophets of Baʿal to shout louder, for 'perhaps he is asleep and he will awake (*va-yiqatz*)!' (1 Kings 18: 27). But it is hard to imagine that the psalmist would seek to induce divine intervention through derogatory aspersions. We must thus suppose that the supplication speaks metaphorically, but draws its striking imagery from old mythic notions—notions that are also echoed in the following cultic response to a worshipper, 'Your protector will not slumber; Behold, the protector of Israel will neither slumber nor sleep!' (Ps. 121: 3–4). As a liturgical assertion it resembles (in form and mythic concreteness) the statement of Samuel, when he rent the kingship from Saul and said: 'Surely the victor of Israel will neither deceive nor relent' (1 Sam. 15: 29).

The puzzling nature of the evocation 'Arouse (*ʿurah*) Yourself! Why do You sleep, O Lord' is compounded by the fact that in the Mishnah we learn of a group of people called *meʿorerim* ('Arousers' or 'Awakeners') whose practice was abolished by Yoḥanan the High Priest (*M. Maʿaser Sheni* 5.15).[71] According to the explanation of the Tosefta (*Tos. Soṭa* 13.9), 'The *meʿorerim* are the Levites, who recite from the dais, "Arouse yourself! Why do You sleep, O Lord?"'. But when and to what purpose they did this is not stated, although the practice appears to bear a striking resemblance to the morning rituals in Egyptian temples when the gods were awakened ('Awake happily in peace'), as has been observed.[72] Nevertheless, the Tosefta immediately quali-

[70] See ʾ*Abot de-Rabbi Natan*, A, 4, Schechter edn. 19 f.

[71] See the discussion of Saul Lieberman, *Hellenism in Jewish Palestine* (New York: The Jewish Theological Seminary of America, 1962), 140–3.

[72] See Lieberman, ibid. He adduces the work of Alexandre Moret, *Le Ritual du culte divin journalier en Egypt* (Annales du Musée Gurmet, Bibliothèque d'études, 1; Paris: E. Leroux, 1902), 122 ff. I have followed the translation of the Berlin papyrus (3055) produced by Robert Ritner, in W. Hallo *et al.* (edd.), *The Context of Scripture* (Leiden: E. J. Brill, 1997), i. 55–7. The

fies its report with an explanation of the verse given by R. Yoḥanan ben Zakkai to his students,[73] 'And does God in fact sleep?! Does not Scripture already say, "Behold, He neither slumbers nor sleeps" (Ps. 121: 4)? Hence (we should take the reference to divine arousal as meaning that) whenever Israel is mired in sorrow and the nations of the world enjoy tranquillity, (one supplicates) so to speak, "Arouse! Why do You sleep?"'

Thus we have an early qualification of the mythical practice which also makes no mention of God being with Israel in its sorrow. Indeed, R. Yoḥanan's explanation of the view (applied to his own time, after the destruction), presumes divine withdrawal and disengagement from Israel; and it was thus taken over (anonymously) by later tradition.[74] In the same vein is the punning comment by R. Berekhia in the name of R. Eliezer, who said: 'Until the end (*qetz*) comes, the Holy One, blessed be He, made Himself, so to speak, like one who has slept (*ke-yashen*)—"And He awakens (*va-yaqatz*) like one who has slept" (Ps. 78: 65)'.[75] Here too we find a metaphorically muted myth, with no indication of divine sympathy for or participation in the historical afflictions of Israel. The sense of arousing divine action is absent.

A more activist strand of mythical thought deserves note. We have observed the use of the phrase 'When Israel does the will of God' in connection with the conjunction of the cherubim, and the reference to the benefits which accrue thereby for the people.[76] This phrase (in positive and negative valences) also recurs in a variety of other contexts, attesting to the role of human behaviour in the balance of divine power and emotions. Scriptural exegesis serves as the vehicle whereby this myth of divine–human symbiosis comes to expression. We may begin with an apparently early pair of comments found in the *Mekhilta de-Rabbi Ishmael* (*Beshalaḥ* 5),[77] which gives an instructive twist to images discussed earlier.

'Your right hand, O Lord, is glorious in strength' (Exod. 15: 6). When Israel does (*ʿosin*) the will of God, they make (*ʿosin*) the left hand the right; as it is said, 'Your right hand, O Lord', 'Your right hand, O Lord'—twice. But when Israel does not do the will of God, so to speak, they make the right hand the left; as it is said, 'He put

morning liturgy was recited from the New Kingdom until Roman times. For a late reference to this practice in Greek, reported from the temple of Serapis, cf. Lieberman, p. 142 n. 25 (the priest 'awakens the god', *egeirei ton theon*). One may add that in Babylonia there were also morning rituals, including one telling the priest to 'Open the eye of that god'; see Sidney Smith, 'The Babylonian Ritual for the Consecration and Induction of a Divine Statue', *JRAS*, pt. 1 (Jan. 1925), 46 (BM 45729, rev. l. 53), and the comment on p. 59.

73 This is also the view of Saul Lieberman, *Tosefta Ki-Fshuta* (New York: The Jewish Theological Seminary of America, 1973), pt. VIII, Order Nashim, 746. He adds that when Yoḥanan the High Priest officiated, Yoḥanan ben Zakkai was not yet born.

74 See *Shoḥer Ṭov* 121.3 (Buber, 505 f.). 75 Ibid. 78. 18 (Buber, 356).

76 See above, p. 174; and note the phrase *megaddelin lahem*.

77 Horovitz–Rabin edn. 134.

His right hand behind Him' (Lam. 2: 3). When Israel does the will of God, He does not sleep; as it is said, 'Behold, He neither slumbers nor sleeps' (Ps. 121: 4). But when Israel does not do the will of God, so to speak, He does sleep; as it is said, 'And He awakens like one who has slept, like a warrior enthused by wine' (Ps. 78: 65).

According to this homiletic anthology, human actions have an effect upon God. The first teaching focuses on the figure of the hand of the Lord, and construes the doubled use of *yeminkha* ('Your right hand') in Moses' song to mark the mythologoumenon that when Israel performs the divine will the left hand of judgement and wrath is converted to the side of mercy and redemption—thus producing a kind of double bounty for Israel; but that when they do not fulfil the will of God, then God's right hand of victory is withdrawn, resulting in the people's doom and destruction. By this juxtaposition, not only are two specific moments in Israelite history highlighted (the victory at the Sea and the destruction of the Temple), but the hand of God also marks the recurrent nature of divine providence in response to covenant behaviour. The mythologem thereby achieves a durative force. The same holds for the figure of sleep. Presented as God's ongoing response to human action, the notion of wakefulness gives dramatic concreteness to the nature of divine involvement in the history of Israel.

Israel's effect on divine action and personality has other notable resonances. In particular, there is a kind of empowerment or disempowerment that human prayer and behaviour may have upon God. Earlier, we had occasion to note the remarkable prayer which the High Priest Elisha was asked by God to recite on His behalf, so that divine mercy might dominate judgement.[78] In a variation on this theme, we have the mythic fabulation of R. Yehoshua ben Levi as found in *BT Shabbat* 89a. The sage narrates a scene that occurred when Moses ascended to heaven, where he finds God affixing coronets to the letters of the Torah and remains in respectful silence, until he is rebuked with the words: 'Moses, is there no (greeting of) peace in your city?' Moses indicates that it is not proper for one to initiate a greeting to one's master. But God replies: 'Nevertheless, you should have helped Me (*le-ʿazreini*)'; whereupon Moses 'immediately cried out, "And now, may the power (*koaḥ*) of YHWH be increased, as You have said" (Num. 14: 17)'. Although the context is not stated, the implication is clear. God wants and needs Moses' help in His response to humans, and Moses utters the words he recites to God (repeating God's own statement of His attributes of mercy in Exod. 3: 6–7) after the sin of the spies had evoked divine wrath. As in that biblical episode, so also here, in this rabbinic myth, Moses tries to induce God's power to overcome wrath—in rabbinic terms, it is even an attempt to elicit or increase power in the Name YHWH, which stands for the attribute

[78] See above, p. 172, regarding *BT Ber.* 7a.

of mercy.[79] The old words of solicitation and supplication now have the force of an incantation.[80]

The personal quality of this mythic dialogue is reduced to more formal expressions elsewhere. Particularly instructive is the cluster of teachings in *Pesikta de-Rav Kahana* 25. 1.[81] In one case, the meaning of the phrase 'And a person of pure hands will increase strength' (Job 17: 9) is applied to Moses, 'who increased the power of the Almighty (called here *Geburah*);[82] as it is said, "And now, may the power of YHWH be increased" '. On this view, the nature and locus of the empowerment is not specified. An ensuing rabbinic tradition fills this lack by an Aramaic translation of the biblical citation, 'May the power of your mercy be strengthened'; and by the Hebrew paraphrase, 'Strengthen (*hagber*) the attribute of mercy over the attribute of judgement'. Such renditions make clear that the biblical prayer was understood to refer to the power of the divine Name YHWH, the appellation marking God's attribute of mercy.[83] Just how this was to have an effect on divine efforts is specified by R. Yudan, who suggested that the cohortative expression used by Moses bolstered heavenly might on analogy with 'a strong man (*gibbor*) who was trying to lift a boulder cut away by a stone mason', and who was encouraged in his athletic feat by a passer-by who said, 'Your power is wondrous; keep up your strength like a strong man'. In both instances, the human speaker vitalizes his addressee through verbal exhortation. Hence for the teachers of this myth, Moses' prayer is not presented as a petition—but as an act of effective power.

The midrashic pericope now shifts from the special character of the words of Moses, to the broader situation of those who enact the will of God—both the 'righteous' (*tzaddiqim*) and 'Israel'.

[79] See above, pp. 99–101, and further below.

[80] I agree with Y. Liebes's characterization of this narrative as intimate and psychological, but disagree that the biblical citation makes it less mythic than the encounter between God and the priest. For Liebes's views, see his 'De Natura Dei', in *Studies in Jewish Myth and Jewish Messianism* (Albany: State University of New York Press, 1993), 15–17.

[81] In the Mandelbaum edn. ii. 379 f. The teachings of this text have been discussed in terms of theurgic augmentation by Moshe Idel, *Kabbalah: New Perspectives* (New Haven: Yale University Press, 1988), 157 f., and also in terms of affecting the divine attributes by Y. Liebes, 'De Natura Dei', 17 f. I follow this approach, though in what follows I shall try to nuance the strata of the anthology.

[82] Overall, see the discussion of the term *Geburah* and divine power by E. Urbach, *The Sages*, ch. 5. A full analytic typology has been undertaken by Michael Zank, 'The Rabbinic Epithet *Gevurah*', in *Approaches to Ancient Judaism, xiv*, ed Jacob Neusner (1998), 83–168.

[83] For the meaning of the divine names YHWH and Elohim in terms of the attributes of mercy and justice, respectively, see above pp. 99–101; this matter will be treated further below. Note that the MT of Num. 14: 17 reads Adonai, not YHWH, but YHWH is required by sense and by the way Exod. 34: 6–7 is understood in v. 18 (i.e. 'YHWH is a gracious and compassionate God', etc.). But many MSS have YHWH in v. 18; this is also the way the lemma is cited (three times) in the midrashic passage; and this is the Name behind YY in Onqelos. Based on his comment, ad loc., this reading appears to have been known to R. Saadia Gaon; but Ḥezquni had 'AD(onai)'.

R. Azariah (said) in the name of R. Judah bar R. Simon: Whenever the righteous do the will of the Holy One, blessed be He, they add (*mosifin*) power in the Almighty (*ba-Geburah*);[84] as is said, 'Let the power of the Lord increase, etc.'; and if (they do) not, so to speak, 'You weaken the Rock that bore you' (Deut. 32: 18). R. Judah bar R. Simon said in the name of R. Levi ben Parṭa: Whenever Israel does the will of the Holy One, they add power in the Almighty; as is said, 'Let us make might in God' (Ps. 60: 14). And if (they do) not, so to speak, 'They went without power before the pursuer' (Lam. 1: 6).

It is here succinctly stated that the divine structure may be empowered or impoverished by the nature of human obedience. Indeed nothing is stated about ritual intention; rather, there appears to be some sort of inherent correlation of effect between the action below and reaction above.[85] Moreover, nothing is specified in these mythologoumena about the increase of divine power to quell wrath and activate mercy; rather, the various sources (including the use of Num. 14: 17) seem to refer to a general augmentation of divine might or its depletion. The midrashic tradition appears to take the sense of divine increase in stride in both cases, and only adds the qualifier 'so to speak (*kivyakhol*)' when the issue of decrease is asserted—though this qualifier may be used here also to mark the fact that the first citation reinterprets the biblical reproach that the people 'forget (*teshi*)' God (Deut. 32: 18) into one of making him weak;[86] and the second one transforms the phrase about the people's lack of 'power' during the exilic flight (Lam. 1: 6) into a statement about the absence of God (denoted by the cognomen 'Power') at that time—although it is unclear whether this means that God has withdrawn from the people or that this is a reference to divine depletion and incapacity to help (comparable to the assertions about divine senescence and lack of 'power' discussed earlier).[87] But either way, and in conjunction with the positive use of power, the upshot is that the divine nature or personality is not a static entity, but is rather in constant dynamic symbiosis with the behaviour of Israel (note the phrase 'whenever').

[84] The version in *Lamentations Rabba* 1.6, is 'increase power in the *Geburah* on high'. This specification presumably serves to differentiate this *geburah* from the idea of certain lower creatures who 'increase in strength (*mosifin koaḥ*) with age' (*BT Shabbat* 77b). This usage corresponds to the Greek sense of *dynamis*, which means the natural power to cause an effect. Cf. E. Fascher, s.v. 'Dynamis', in *Reallexicon für Antike und Christentum*, ed. Theodor Klauser (Stuttgart: Hiersemann, 1959), iv, col. 15–426.

[85] The lack of intention in having a divine effect is what Moshe Idel calls the sensory pole of the Jewish performance of the commandment. See his observations in 'Some Remarks on Ritual and Mysticism in Geronese Kabbalah', in *JJTP* 3 (1993), 115, 122. As I shall show below, there are also cases where the effect is produced by a type of intention accompanying the act.

[86] Construing the verb from the stem *t-sh-sh* (not *t-sh-y*).

[87] See above, pp. 170–1. Some reference to the depletion of divine power must be assumed, in accordance with the structure of these and other teachings. The version of this section found in *Lamentations Rabba* is: 'so to speak, they weaken the great Power on high, and they also go without power before the pursuer'.

The preceding mythologoumena about divine power and the volatility of the attributes are attached to teachers from the mid-third century in Palestine. But the overall notion is certainly earlier, and already found in an anonymous tannaitic teaching on Deut. 32: 18, where it appears as a divine admonition: 'Whenever I (God) wish to do you good, you weaken the power (*koaḥ*) above'.[88] No further qualification delimits this reproach, which appears in connection with specific instances of Israel's rebellion and ingratitude. It remained for other sages to extend the mythic potential of this phrase into an assertion of the effects of human righteousness or obedience to the commandments upon God and His Names.[89]

III. Transformations in God and the Divine Names

As we saw just above, a tradition stemming from both R. Yoḥanan and R. Yose b. Ḥanina (both second-generation Amoras) interpreted Moses' prayer 'Let the power of the Lord increase' (Num. 14: 17) to be an exhortation to God that He empower His attribute of mercy so that it might dominate His attribute of judgement. Specifically, it would appear that the precise purport of the exhortation is that God augment the power of the Name YHWH, this being the cognomen of His attribute of mercy. According to biblical tradition, Moses learned that 'YHWH is God gracious and compassionate' (Exod. 34: 6) from God Himself, after the apostasy of the calf, and he now applies that knowledge to appeal for God's merciful intercession after the infidelity of the spies. By tannaitic times the notion that the occurrence of the Name YHWH in Scripture signalled the manifestation or ascendency of the attribute of divine mercy was a theological principle, formulated in abstract terms and with proof-texts. Commenting on Moses' own reference to his act of divine intercession after the calf episode, when he said 'I supplicated YHWH (at that time)', an anonymous homilist picks up on the Name YHWH, and remarks: 'Wherever "YHWH" occurs (in Scripture) this is (*zoh*) the attribute of mercy, as is said "YHWH, YHWH, God gracious and compassionate" (Exod. 34: 6); (and) wherever "Elohim" occurs this is the attribute of judgement, as is said "The case of both parties shall come before the Elohim" (Exod. 23: 8), and "Do not curse Elohim" (Exod. 22: 27)'.[90] One can hardly miss the explicit identification of each Name with an attribute of God's nature, such that each one marks a distinct power within God.[91]

[88] *Sifre Deut.* 319 (Finkelstein, 365).

[89] For the use of this mythologem in connection with a specific commandment, see the long homily transmitted by R. Judah ben Simon in the name of R. Levi ben Parṭa in *Leviticus Rabba* 23.12; it has been commented upon as a case of augmentation by M. Idel, *Kabbalah*, 159. I shall consider another aspect in the discussion below. There are many other uses of the formula 'If Israel does', etc. and that deal with aspects of divine aid or withdrawal; cf. *Sifre Deuteronomy* 355. See further in Appendix 2, pp. 377–83.

[90] *Sifre Deuteronomy* 27 (Finkelstein edn. 41).

[91] The teacher apparently identifies God's self-revelation in Exod. 34: 6 as meaning that YHWH is God in His gracious and compassionate mode; and note also that in choosing the

1. Dynamism of the Names. It is just this theology of divine Names that underlies R. Yoḥanan's teaching, as also that of his student R. Yose b. Ḥanina. Another of his students, R. Samuel b. Naḥman, a generation later, quotes the older tannaitic tradition (using similar but also additional proofs) as he struggles to makes sense of some apparent scriptural contradictions. In the process he also gives another aspect of the role of the righteous in affecting the divine being.

'And Elohim remembered Noah' (Gen. 8: 1). R. Samuel b. Naḥman said: Woe to the wicked, who turn (*hofkhin*) the attribute of mercy into the attribute of judgement. Wherever YHWH is mentioned (this is) the attribute of mercy, (as is said) 'YHWH, YHWH, God gracious and compassionate' (Exod. 34: 6), and it is (also) written "And YHWH saw that the evil of mankind was great... and YHWH regretted that He made mankind... and YHWH said "I shall blot out mankind"' (Gen. 6: 5–7). (But) Happy be the righteous, who turn (*hofkhin*) the attribute of judgement into the attribute of mercy. Wherever Elohim is mentioned (this is) the attribute of judgement, (as is said) 'Do not curse Elohim' (Exod. 22: 27), (and) 'the case of both parties shall come before the Elohim' (Exod. 22: 8), and it is (also) written 'Elohim heard their groan and Elohim remembered His covenant' (Exod. 2: 24), (as well as) 'And Elohim remembered Rachel' (Gen. 30: 22)—(thus too) 'And Elohim remembered Noah'.[92]

In this compact and opaque formulation, R. Samuel deals with the apparent contradiction between the older principle of the meaning of the Names YHWH and Elohim, and the fact that some verses, like the very one that inaugurates the teaching ('And Elohim remembered Noah') do not bear this out, and even use a given Name with verbs denoting an opposite divine attribute (e.g. Elohim is used in conjunction with a person 'remembered' for good; while YHWH is used in conjunction with negative judgements). The sage resolves these contradictions by his teaching of the power of the wicked or the righteous to 'turn' one attribute into another—that is, to cause a change in the balance of attributes and thereby effect a reversal of their relative dominance. Hence on this understanding, when Scripture records an apparent contradiction of the principle of divine powers, we are to understand that the Name given represents God's providential mode *ante quem*, prior to the human actions that change it. Thus the evil of the generation of the people before the flood overturned God's mercy (as evidenced by His Name), and the result was a decision to destroy them; and, similarly, the righteousness of Noah was able to turn God's wrathful judgement during the flood (as evidenced by His Name) into a positive regard for him. Accordingly, Scripture does not contradict the main principle, but rather reveals a

proof-text from Exod. 22: 7 he finds a reference for divinity as *ha-ʾelohim*, which he takes to mean the distinct attribute of Elohim.

[92] *Genesis Rabba* 33. 3 (Theodor–Albeck, 308).

deeper one—namely, the capacity of human action to influence and change the divine mode of action. But one must still wonder, on this view, about the status of these modalities and the relationship between the two revealed Names and the God who incorporates them or rules over them. One could certainly understand how some sages could draw the implication that this view implies the existence of 'two domains' or 'sovereignties' (*reshuyot*) in heaven pertaining to the divine governance of the world[93]—and for all we know they may have correctly perceived an esoteric doctrine about Divinity itself or the divine pleroma under God's sovereignty.[94] Presumably the key issue turned on the nature and status of the hidden (providential) powers revealed by Scripture.

2. Sacrificial Intentions. Another striking trace of these matters may be detected in an old mishnah dealing with sacrifices, and in comments preserved in contemporary works of halakhic exegesis. First, the mishnah:

> An offering (*zebaḥ*) must be slaughtered while mindful of (*le-shem*) six things: of the offering, of the offerer, of the Name (*ha-Shem*), of the altar fires, of the odour, (and) of the sweet savour; and if it is a sin-offering or a guilt-offering, of the sin.[95] R. Yose said: Even if one was not mindful in his heart of one of these things, it (the offering) is valid; for it is a condition enjoined by the court that the (validity of) intention (is ascertained) only with respect to the one who performs (the offering). (*M. Zebaḥim* 4. 6)

The mishnah is divided in two parts: the first specifies what an offerer must be mindful of when performing an offering; the second accepts the topics of valid intention, but sets the condition that it is only the mind set of the one who actually performs the offering that determines its validity or invalidity, and no one else.[96] This argument actually extends a feature found in the initial statement of the mishnah, which enjoins that someone who is not the officiant (and presumably the owner) focus on the offering being performed *and* on the (priestly) person who is actually doing the offering. R. Yose's important caveat is that even if the owner did not have valid thoughts concerning the nature of the sacrifice or its purpose (among other matters), this was not a determinative consideration, and the governing condition was dependent solely upon the priest actually invested with the authority to

[93] For the aspersion based on scriptural features, and types of rebuttal, see *Mekhilta de-Rabbi Ishmael, Beshalaḥ* 4 (Horovitz–Rabin, 130).

[94] We shall consider in the Conclusions to Part II the striking fact that sages involved in such (and related teachings), like R. Samuel b. Naḥman and R. Jacob b. Aḥa (who transmitted R. Yose b. Ḥanina's teaching), were demonstratively involved with well-known esoteric topics.

[95] In fact, each item in the list is preceded by the phrase *le-shem*; thus *le-shem zebaḥ* (the offering) or *le shem ha-Shem* (the Name).

[96] Thus the proper intention of the cult functionary who performs an offering would override the faulty intention of its owner. In this mishnah, R. Yose's position is based on a rule of law; in *M. Ḥullin* 2.7 this ruling serves as a premiss for legal reasoning.

perform the offering on the owner's behalf. Thus would the validity of sacrifices in the shrine be safeguarded.[97]

But what may be said of the final four topics stipulated in the initial statement of the mishnah? At the very outset it must be noted that the sages derived their list from Scripture, which states explicitly that an offering shall be burnt on the altar and turned into smoke: 'a fire-offering of sweet-savour(y) odour to YHWH' (cf. Lev. 1: 9, 17; 3: 5). Thus each element of the phrase has been designated as a distinct matter of intention. But what does this really mean, and what could be involved in distinguishing between the odour (*reaḥ*) and the sweet savour (*niḥoaḥ*)? The formulation is opaque and puzzling, as is the reference to 'the Name' (i.e. the ineffable Name YHWH), rather than some other cognomen of the Tetragram that would leave no doubt that the focus of intention was the Lord God.

In all these matters the mishnah conceals more that it reveals—and perhaps for good reason. For when the formulation can be pressed to disclose a bit more, the reader will note that the formula *le-shem* does not simply or only denote that the offering must be made 'while mindful' of certain things.[98] The formula can also be taken to mean that an offering is to be performed 'for the sake of' these matters. Granted, this understanding contradicts R. Yose's comment on the mishnaic formulation and his concern to indicate the locus of proper intention. But this imputation of agential purpose and effect here is supported by contemporary commentators. Indeed, their comments suggest that our mishnah has profound esoteric matters in mind, and bring us closer to the framer's mind than does R. Yose's reference to a construction of the court whose import is to guarantee that the transfer of authority to perform an act includes (in this case) the transfer of intentionality as well.

Let us examine *Sifre Numbers* 143 in this regard, and note the remarks attached to the phrase 'A fire-offering of sweet-savoury odour (*reaḥ niḥoaḥ*) to YHWH' (Num. 28: 8):

(Anonymous:) A gratified (or comforted) spirit (*naḥat ruaḥ*) is before Me, for I have spoken and My will is done. R. Simeon b. Azzai said: Come and see! Whenever

[97] Of course this is the purpose; in actuality, alertness and attention were not to be presumed, as we can deduce from the comment by R. Eliezer ben Jacob on the injunction 'To serve Him (*le-ʿobdo*) with all your heart' (Deut. 7: 8): 'This is a warning to the priests that their heart should not be divided (*ḥoleq*) while performing the sacrificial service (*ha-ʿabodah*)' (*Sifre Deut.* 41; Finkelstein, 88). This apparently refers to their lack of focus or split attention during sacrifices, which would mean that they perform a given offering but do not focus on the specific sacrifice involved. Note that the need to be mindful of the specific 'offering' being performed is an explicit issue of our mishnah; and note as well that R. Yose also uses the term 'heart' in the context of ritual intention.

[98] Cf. *Sifre Deut.* 128 (Finkelstein, 186): '"And you shall perform the *pesaḥ*-offering" (Deut. 16: 1), that its performance be for the sake of (*le-shem*) the *pesaḥ*-offering'; and cf. ibid. on v. 2. See also *Mekhilta de-Rabbi Simeon ad* Exod. 12: 11 (Epstein–Melamed, 14); but cf. *Mekhilta de-Rabbi Ishmael*, ad loc. (Horovitz–Rabin, 23, ll. 2–3)

sacrifices are mentioned in the Torah, (the divine Names and epithets) Elohim, your Elohim, Shaddai, and Tzeba᾽ ot are never mentioned; but rather (only the divine) Name YH(WH), the unique Name (*Shem ha-meyuhad*)—so as not to give the *minim* (heretics) a pretext to lord it up (or: rebel; *lirdot*).[99]

The explications given in this passage are opaque; no concession helps the reader. Each formulation is cloaked in a stenographic shorthand, leaving the interpreter to ponder their sense. The first mask conceals the phrase *reaḥ niḥoaḥ*, which the (anonymous) interpreter takes (by way of verbal puns) to indicate divine comfort when the people do God's will. Taken in a weak sense, the force of this remark would be to indicate divine satisfaction or emotional repose when the commandments are rightly performed; but in a stronger sense, it would appear to indicate that when the people do the divine will a state of graciousness is effected in God's own emotional constitution—so that this first-person formulation of the impact of actions upon divinity here is similar to the oblique formulary found elsewhere, which states that when individuals 'do God's will' they add strength to the attribute of mercy (named YHWH). And when interpreted in this manner, one could also understand the preceding mishnaic statement that one must have both the *reaḥ* and the *niḥoaḥ* in mind when performing an offering in the same way; that is, the proper intention of an offerer was to focus on the ascending odour of the oblation, whose purpose was to effect (was 'for the sake of') divine mercy. As a normative legal formulation, the mishnah adroitly conceals its esoteric dimension, but no other interpretation seems reasonable in light of the mishnah's terminology (*le-shem*), its separation of the terms *reaḥ* and *niḥoaḥ* for special intention, and the wording of the anonymous commentator in *Sifre Numbers* 143.

These considerations have further bearing on the mishnah's requirement that one perform the sacrificial offering *le-shem ha-Shem*, 'for the sake of (or with mindfulness of) the ineffable Name' YHWH. According to the comment of R. Simeon, the purpose of the scriptural use of YHWH in conjunction with sacrifices (and no other Name or cognomen) is to prevent any false or heretical conclusions as to the focus of the offering. Now this is difficult to understand, and may even imply that some people believed that there were a hierarchy of divine powers represented by the different names and that these were the recipients or beneficiaries of the oblation (whether the spilt blood or the smoke of the consumed flesh). Against such a position, R. Simeon ben

[99] See *Siphre D'Be Rab*, ed. H. S. Horovitz (Jerusalem; Wahrmann Books, 1966), 191. A variant in *Siphra D'Be Rab*, ed. Louis Finkelstein (New York: The Jewish Theological Seminary of America, 1983), ii. 22 (*Nidaba* 2.5), attributes the second comment to Rabbi Yoseh, and omits the list of the divine names not used. The phrase *la-minim... lirdot* has the sense of giving the heretics the opportunity to lord it up by having justification for their heresy (regarding which, in this instance, see below). See also *BT Yoma* 40b (MS Munich, Cod. Hebr. 95).

Azzai (in *Sifre Numbers* 143) apparently says that the offerings are to be given exclusively 'to YHWH'—to the Lord supreme. But there is another (and not mutually exclusive) possibility, and that is that the offerings are not directed to the powers of might or judgement symbolized by the names Elohim or Shaddai, but to the attribute of mercy nominalized by the Name YHWH. This interpretation would align the offerer's required intention upon the ineffable Tetragram with particular focus upon the *reaḥ niḥoaḥ*, and mean that the real esoteric purport of the rite was to influence and enhance divine mercy—for the ultimate benefit of the individual or community.

For the worshipper who wanted to bring the transcendent God into an attentive regard for His creature(s), and especially to assuage His wrath by inducing His mercy, the proper intentions of a properly performed sacrifice were just the thing.[100] For the sages, this was even communicated by the language of Scripture itself (both in the several words of the phrase 'a fire-offering of sweet-savoury odour to YHWH', and especially in its specification of the Tetragram)—for those who knew how to read and interpret such hints. No wonder that when the Temple was destroyed some rabbis enjoined the study of the scriptural rules of sacrifice, for which the student could reap a beneficial effect (see *BT Menaḥot* 110b).[101]

3. Depletion of the Name. A quite different dimension of the interrelation between human acts and the divine Name occurs at the end of a long homily found in *Leviticus Rabba* 23. 12.[102] The homily is attributed to the amora R. Simeon ben Lakish, and deals with the effect of adultery upon the shape and visage of an embryo already in the mother's womb. In his view, God will transform the *khalaqṭirin* (facial characteristics) of the foetus into the image

[100] The power of sacrifices and its sweet odour is clearly and boldly found in biblical sources. Note especially Moses' blessing of the tribe of Levi who 'shall place incense (*qeṭorah*) in Your nostril, and the whole-offering upon Your altar' (Deut. 33: 10). The assuagement of the sweet savour 'smelled' by YHWH is concretely expressed in Gen. 8: 20 f., after the flood. While this formulation is in priestly terminology, the motif is ancient; indeed, according to the epic of Gilgamesh, Utnapishtim tells Gilgamesh how, after the flood, he left the ship and offered sacrifices, whose 'sweet fragrance' the gods 'smelled' and gathered about (IX. 155 ff.). The role of the odour of sacrifices to influence the gods in Israel and Mesopotamia has been treated by Victor Hurowitz, in *Biblical Archeology Today* (1990), 262–6.

[101] The importance of the incense offering in rabbinic debates has been often discussed, but the matter has now been put on a new footing in the study by Israel Knohl and Shlomoh Naeh, 'Milu'im ve-Kippurim', *Tarbiz*, 62 (1993), 17–44. Among other considerations, the authors conclude that the smoke of the incense invoked God and made him manifest (pp. 30–3). This can be seen in halakhic sources such as *Sifra, Aḥarei Mot*, ch. 3, halakhah 11, according to MS Vatican 66, in *Torat Kohanim*, ed. Louis Finkelstein (New York: The Jewish Theological Seminary of America, 1957), 353, where the smoke of the Glory and the smoke of the incense are conflated, with the result that God appears by means of this incense. A related notion is explicitly formulated in non-halakhic sources, such as *Tanḥuma, Tetzavveh* 15, which cites Songs 1: 12 as a proof-text (linking the wafting spice and the coming of the divine Beloved).

[102] Margulies, 548.

(*demut*) of the adulterer, so that the crime will be visible and publicly known.[103] In the amoraic stratum appended to the conclusion, R. Judah bar Simon reported a tradition that invoked Deut. 32: 18 in this regard; a verse that rebuked Israel for 'forgetting the Rock who bore you' (*tzur yeladekha teshi*), which is interpreted to mean 'You have weakened (*hitashtem*) the power of the creator (*yotzer*)'—since God is portrayed as indecisive concerning which face to form in the foetus.[104] The final section is even bolder. After the anonymous observation that '(The letter) *yod* (of the word *teshi* (*tšy*) is written in) minuscule, and there is nothing like it (elsewhere) in Scripture', the following teaching occurs.[105]

R. Isaac said: 'We (commonly) find that in the case of transgressors, the thief benefits but the person stolen from is deprived; the robber benefits but the person robbed is deprived. But here (in this case), both (apparently) benefit. Who (then) is deprived? The Holy One, as it were; since He destroys signs (*samemanin*).'

Now this version of the teaching (based on MS British Museum 340)[106] appears to allude to the facial features lost when God changes the appearance of the foetus, and thus links back to the initial homily about the 'characteristics'. The implication would be that the erasure is a loss for God, although this is not an unqualified loss since a new image of God appears on the embryo. Hence, the teaching is puzzling; and this puzzlement only grows if we take into account the comment about the small letter *yod* found in the Masoretic text. For while it certainly refers to the word *teshi* in Deut. 32: 18, the comment has no bearing on the teaching (of R. Judah) just concluded, and no apparent bearing on the teaching of R. Isaac.

A solution to these complications may be deduced from other versions of this teaching, which do not read *samemanin* but *samemanav* (found in MSS Oxford Neubauer 147 and 2335; Paris 147; Vatican 32). For although one could read this reference to 'His signs' as also referring to the facial features of the child created by God in His image, this is an odd way to refer to this matter and is even less free of contradiction than the preceding instance.[107] Hence, it is more likely that the teaching refers to one of God's own signs—a matter left obscure were it not for the editorial scholion about the minuscule letter *yod*, which leads one to suppose that what has been adversely affected is

[103] Ibid. 546f. The key word apparently derives from Greek *charactērion*; see S. Krauss, *Griechische und lateinische Lehnwörter im Talmud, Midrasch und Targum* (Berlin, 1898, 1899), 291, with the sense of facial lines or characteristics.

[104] For uses of this verse to indicate that human sins weaken God or His power of mercy, see above, pp. 181–2.

[105] The comment is in Aramaic, and all levels of the text are in Hebrew. I regard it as a late insertion; see the ensuing discussion.

[106] This is the London MS, the *editio princeps* of the Margulies edn.

[107] Margulies, ibid. 548, note to l. 5, prefers the reading *samemanav*, but then adds more difficulties when he says that God 'removes His signs at the creation of a *mamzer*-foetus' (i.e. conceived through adultery). Just what signs are permanently removed at that time?

one of the letters of the divine Name—either the *Y(od)* of YaH or of YHWH. Indeed, there would be no other purpose to the scribal comment were it not supposed to be pertinent to R. Isaac's teaching in some way, and the only real pertinent link between the reference to the minuscule letter and God's own sign or component is a letter in God's Name.[108]

We are thus faced with a multifaceted morphology of divine Names at different points in the scriptural text, marking God's providential attitude toward Israel (in justice or mercy), or signalling Israel's changed or (as here) sinful behaviour. Human action thus has an effect upon the divine nature, and this is reflected by a bimorphism of divine Names (Elohim and YHWH); and even further, the weakening of God (or His powers of mercy) due to acts of human sin is inscribed as a principle in Deut. 32: 18, and exemplified by such acts as adultery, as we see in R. Isaac's comments on an older homily. All this leads to a somewhat mystic theology of the divine Names found in the biblical text, which is assumed to encode exoteric signs of changes in God's very nature or personality.

4. Completion of the Name and Throne. Another notable hint in this direction is a comment on Exod. 17: 16, where Moses proclaims: 'For (*ki*) the hand is upon (*ʿal*) the throne (*kes*) of YaH; YHWH will war with Amalek from generation to generation'. Even as a separate statement, this verse has long been confusing: the force of the *ki* clause is obscure; the placement of the hand on the throne is puzzling, and the identity of the hand not stated; and one will wonder about the relationship between the two clauses, and the variation of the Names YH and YHWH. R. Levi in the name of R. Ḥuna b. R. Ḥanina resolved the issues in the following way:

As long as the seed of Amalek exist in the world, the Name (*ha-Shem*) is not complete (*shalem*) and the throne (*kese*ʾ) is not complete; (but) when the seed of Amalek will be destroyed from the world, the Name will be complete and the throne will be complete. What is the (scriptural) proof? 'The enemy is no more, (leaving) everlasting ruins; You have brought down their cities, their memory is destroyed' (Ps. 9: 7). And what follows this? 'But YHWH will sit forever, He has set up His throne for judgement' (ibid., v. 8).[109]

In this interpretation, the *ki* clause has been understood temporally (as 'when'; or 'for as long as'), and the hand assumed to be that of Amalek, which reigns over (*ʿal*) other nations, resulting in the diminution of God's dominion, symbolized here by the abbreviated divine Name YaH and the defective spelling of the word for throne (*kes* not *kese*ʾ). This situation stands

[108] For this minuscule letter in the Masoretic tradition, see *Massekhet Soferim* 9.6, ed. Michael Higger (New York: D'Vei Rabbanan Press, 1937), 203; and for references in manuscript lists from the Cairo Geniza, see Jose Fauer in *PAAJR* 36 (1967), 6.

[109] See *Pesikta de-Rav Kahana* 3. 16 (Mandelbaum, 53), and parallels in *Pes. Rab.* 12 (Ish Shalom, 51), and *Tanḥuma Ki Teitzei*ʾ, 11 (end).

over against the second clause, which is parsed to mean that when there will be war against Amalek, and victory, YHWH (the full form of the Name) will abide forever. And all this is proved by a passage in Psalms which speaks of the obliteration of the memory (*zikhram*) of the enemy and the reign of YHWH upon His judgement seat (*kis'o*) forever. The terms of this passage correlate with the homily; and most particularly, the reference to the lost or destroyed memory alludes back to the homily and also to Deut. 25: 10, in which the obliteration of the 'memory' (*zekher*) of Amalek is issued as a command to the Israelites upon their triumphant dispossession of their enemies during the conquest and settlement of the Land of Canaan. Recollection of this command on the Sabbath before the feast of Purim is the liturgical context of the homily.

For present purposes, the striking point is that a brief form of the divine Name is interpreted as a sign of the historical domination of the grave enemy of Israel, and only its destruction will result in the true divine dominion, symbolized by the full divine Name. Transferred from an ancient commandment to an eschatological hope, the homilist implies the diminishment of God during the present historical era, a diminishment caused by the triumph of arrogant powers and the oppression of Israel. The homily thus gives hope for a divine battle to come, after which the Lord alone will reign supreme upon His heavenly throne. Only a subtle and daring parsing of the passage permits this reading; and only an underlying assumption that the morphology of divine Names in Scripture denotes divine states would have induced such a comment and such a hope. For the seeker of signs, traces of God's providence are found in the biblical text: He who is incomplete now, when divine dominion is overrun by evil powers, will yet be complete in the future time. Midrash thus inflects a word of assurance with the promise of things to come; but for the present, before that time, a decoding of the divine Names may foretell the nature and myth of the completion of God's purpose.

9

Conclusions and Other Considerations

Ancient rabbinic myth and mythmaking develop along two thematic tracks. One is marked by a *thematic continuity* with mythic topics, images, and scenarios found in earlier ancient Near Eastern and biblical sources or traditions. Particularly notable were the diverse accounts of a divine combat with a primordial sea monster, the figure of a divine arm of power, and the abandonment by a divine being of their city or temple due to displeasure at human behaviour. The second track is marked by *thematic innovation*, whereby new mythic themes, figures, and topics are developed. These include the participation of God in the various afflictions of Israel, in its exiles, and in the redemptions to come; and they are also represented by dramatic divine labours and mourning, as well as by accounts of divine impoverishment and weakness. Both tracks focus on features of God's actions and personality. These mythic modalities are of an extrovert and introvert character, respectively. That is, they focus on external divine behaviours and actions, as well as internal emotions and passions.

But whether the various topics of rabbinic myth are continuous with their predecessors, or discontinuous with these cases, the mythic teachings or instructions are themselves not self-standing. That is to say, the myths do not appear as an independent genre, independently presented. They are rather variously linked to Scripture and presented alongside it. Hence the scriptural verse and its mythic content are two languages presented in tandem: the first being solely biblical in content and character, the other being wholly rabbinic in its formulation and form. Put differently, we may observe that the mythic content is doubled—being both the encrypted, fragmentary, or obscured myths of Scripture, and the explicit, elaborated, and detailed myths of the rabbis. Accordingly, Scripture serves both as the proof-text for any given myth and its core form, apart from the exegetical explication. Granted, in numerous cases the scriptural proof-text is arguably a secondary juxtaposition or justification of the mythmaker; nevertheless, even this addition indirectly proves the point at hand. Rabbinic myth does not appear by itself, but as a function or feature of Scripture.

Scripture serves rabbinic myth in two further respects. The first is as its thematic source, the second as its hermeneutical resource. By 'thematic' is meant the fact that the topics of rabbinic myth are the topics of world origins and Israelite sacred history (creation, exodus, temple, and exile) as found in Scripture, and just this has determined the catalogue of elements taken up in the previous discussions. Tracking the topics of rabbinic myth in this way highlights the biblical basis or point of departure for the rabbinic enterprise; at the same time, it also provides a perspective on the relationship and degree of difference between the two cultural levels. This matter pertains to the 'hermeneutical' factor at hand, insofar as the rabbinic myth is correlated to its scriptural source through various modes of midrashic ingenuity. In the simplest cases, the proof-text parallels the rabbinic fabulation in a direct and uncomplicated way; and then by increasing degrees of exegetical activity the biblical content is reinterpreted (explicitly and otherwise) by new emphases on the syntax or words of Scripture, or even by bold adjustments of its letters and vowels. This phenomenon is of great significance for our subject. For if midrashic exegesis is the tap root of the rabbinic imagination in general, in our specific case it is a trigger and technique for the very invention and vitality of myth. Put differently, ancient myth and its traditions do not decline in the rabbinic period, or somehow fade from view, but rather undergo a remarkable development or recrudescence, and through the tools of Midrash display some of the very operations of its creativity no less than their often remarkable content. Hence exegesis is not the pruning hook set against the fertile bough of myth and its language by later recipients or readers, but rather the tool for the justification of myth and even for its bountiful creation, acculturation, or elaboration.

In presenting the content of rabbinic myth in the foregoing Part (II), I have, as just noted, picked up on numerous themes found in Scripture. In doing so, I have grouped them according to their narrative elements and morphological features; and in some cases simple and complex forms have also been distinguished. In this way I show how the given components of a text or theme have been recontextualized by different tradents or put into different combinations. The basic and recurrent features thus constitute what may be called the 'deep structure' of a particular mythic fabulation—this structure being an ahistorical construct for analytic purposes; whereas the concrete ways that these features are found in our sources constitute their 'particular modes' of historical actuality. Hence the common structures serve as a kind of synchronic abstraction, for the primary purpose of analytic classification or typologization; whereas the variants themselves indicate the diachronic specificity of the structures and themes, in their multiple forms of expression. In this way I have tried to avoid the danger of constructing a series of abstract composites of mythic themes of narratives, in comparison with which the actual cases of myth are considered the partial or incomplete realizations of 'the (given) myth', or merely substitutes for each other in some hypothetical system (à la Lévi-Strauss). By contrast, my concern throughout has been to highlight that which is stable or changing in a series of cases, but with the full understanding and emphasis that each particular case is simultaneously both structure and variant. Rabbinic mythmaking is thus always found in its *specific* cases, and the many diverse realizations of any topic show its vitality and creativity over many centuries.[1] In short, multivocalness marks a primary characteristic of rabbinic myth, and is a distinctive feature of its forms of creation.[2]

It is also characteristic of these forms of mythic fabulation that they appear as the sayings of specific sages, and as part of a chain of tradition. The myths are thus received through a succession of voices: redactor *x* says that rabbi *y* said (the given *traditum*) in the name of rabbi *z*; and these sages also cite Scripture as proof. There is thus not only a diachrony of voices but a hierarchy of them as well; for the myths are asserted in terms of the earliest known teacher, and these stand altogether under the authority of the Torah of Moses or other books of sacred Scripture. Hence like Midrash generally, rabbinic mythmaking is part of the oral tradition, which records the stages of transmission to the degree possible. This also means that the myths under discussion are ultimately not the products of the untutored folk, but of the scholars and authorities of classical Judaism. Such an assertion does not mean that the myths are not popular creations in any respect, or were not received by the people at large (in sermons, for example); it only means that the formulations found in our sources preserve the stylistic idiom of the sages, and are produced in the condensed and elliptical idiom characteristic of this class and its collections of traditions. Both points are important, for they firmly situate the mythic sayings in the mouth of the authoritative teachers of rabbinic monotheism, and within the major anthologies of its schools. All this serves to locate the variety of rabbinic myths as elements of 'tradition'—itself to be learned and transmitted. To further explore these matters, we turn to the subjects of myth and tradition; myth and language; and myth and history.

A. MYTH AND TRADITION

The two components of *traditum* and *traditio* are essential to the mythmaking process, and to midrashic exegesis generally.[3] Together, they direct attention

[1] This analytic focus follows the lines of the critique of Lévi-Strauss offered earlier; see above, p. 22. In fact, it comes closer to the concerns of Vladimir Propp, as he rearticulated them (also in debate with Lévi-Strauss) in his *Theory and History of Folklore*, trans. Ariadna Y. Martin and Richard P. Martin, and ed. with introd. and notes, by Anatoly Liberman (Minneapolis: University of Minnesota Press, 1984). See also the considerations of William O. Hendricks, 'Structure and History in the Semiotics of Myth', *Semiotica*, 39 (1982), 131–65. My sense of 'seriality' has been sharpened by Peter Munz, *When the Golden Bough Breaks: Structuralism or Typology?* (London: Routledge & Kegan Paul, 1973), esp. ch. 2.

[2] These comments reflect musings based on P. Bogatyrev and R. Jakobson, 'Die Folklore als eine besondere Form des Schaffens', in *Donum Natalicium Schrijnen* (Nijmegen–Utrecht: N. V. Dekker & Van de Vegt, 1929), 900–13. My thanks to Prof. Galit Hazan-Rokem for bringing this article to my attention.

[3] See the earlier reference to this pair, above, pp. 23–5.

to the fact that every articulation of myth arrests a stream of tradition transmitted from the past (the *traditio*) into some fixed form (the *traditum*), even as, more broadly, the phenomenon of rabbinic mythopoesis is part of a process of oral tradition (the exegetical *traditio*) that is based on written Scripture (the canonical *traditum*). Hence the forms and formulations of midrashic mythmaking are constitutive of tradition-building generally, even as the meanings of the biblical text are transvalued, due to changing circumstances and sensibilities. Rabbinic myths thus emerge at a certain point in time, projecting fabulations onto the ancient Scriptures of Judaism that in many cases could hardly have been expected or anticipated. The sages are thus not merely the tradents of mythologoumena revealed in the past,[4] but innovators who reveal divine behaviours *in illo tempore*—projecting their own latter-day versions of events upon an ancient mythic horizon.

I. Tradents and Transmission

What then was the nature of the transmission and articulation of the mythic teachings? The spotty specimens of evidence allow us to point out two life-settings for this process: the study hall of the sages and the synagogue of the people. The evidence for teaching myths and evaluating them is embedded within the sources. For example, we noted earlier that in *Mekhilta de-Rabbi Ishmael, Bo*ʾ 14 the statement that God is with Israel in all its afflictions provokes the comment: 'So far I learn only of communal trouble. Whence might I deduce this for individual affliction?'—And a citation is provided in proof. Similar scholastic interventions are found in *BT Baba Batra* 74b, as the different treatments of the male and female Leviathan are compared, or as R. Aḥa bar ʿUlla voices objections to the use of specific passages. Also notable in that source are the various references to Rav Dimi reporting in Babylon (presumably the academy of Pumbeditha) teachings on sea dragons which he learned from Rabbi Yoḥanan (head of the academy of Tiberias). Such reports indicate how mythologoumena travelled among the schools and became known to different rabbinic communities over the centuries.

Of a quite different sort were the teachings of mythic theology to the people in synagogue discourses. Here, too, the evidence is meagre but of precious value. Two examples are notable. In one case, we have the statement that R. Berekhia and R. Jeremiah (late fourth-century sages in Palestine) said in the name of R. Ḥiyya bar Abba (about one century earlier) that R. Levi bar Sisi (perhaps a half-century earlier, *c.*200 CE) 'preached' (*darash*) the myth about God's heavenly brickwork in the Babylonian city of Nehardea;[5] and the transmitter of this report does not fail to add a twist by R. Berekhia and Bar Qappara (*Leviticus Rabba* 23. 8). This account adds to the previous

[4] Cf. the formulation of Hubert Canick, *Mythische und historische Wahrheit* (Stuttgarter Bibelstudien, 48; Stuttgart: Verlag Katholisches Bibelwerk, 1970), 20f.

[5] See the myth above, pp. 136–8.

evidence about the diffusion of mythologems from west to east; and it also underscores the homiletic setting of the *traditio*.

A later example is that reported by R. Yudan (late fourth century, Palestine) and Jacob bar Abina that R. Abbahu (about a century earlier) 'preached in the synagogue of Kefar Tiberias' on the biblical verse 'I shall bring you up (*ʾa ʿaleh ʾetkhem*) from the affliction of Egypt' (Exod. 3: 17), and said: 'A difficult teaching; (but on its basis, one may) conclude that the Holy One, blessed be He, said, "Since I and my children share (conjointly) in the suffering (*shutafin ba-tzarah*), it stands to reason that I shall punish their enemies (*ʾippara' mi-soneihem*)" '.[6] This is the same R. Abbahu who variously taught that 'The salvation of Israel is the salvation of the Holy One, blessed be He', and who also repeatedly noted that such teachings are 'difficult'.[7] We may therefore construe his opaque homily as a reinterpretation of the scriptural passage, taken to teach *ʾe ʿeleh ʾitkhem*, 'I shall go up *with* you'.[8] One can only imagine the fuller version of the sage's words in his address to the people. But even from this brief résumé we may infer that his mythic assertion was not deemed to be beyond the pale of acceptable monotheistic theology.

The chains of transmission are particularly notable in these cases, since they exhibit links over many generations—down to and including the anonymous redactors. Now it has become something of a critical commonplace to regard the rabbinic representations of their traditions with a sceptical eye, particularly because of the tendentious purposes that may be detected in various sources.[9] But this notwithstanding, an examination of the tradents of the mythic teachings shows remarkably stable patterns of transmission and even striking correlations between certain teachings and certain schools or sages. At the very least, we have consistent traditions about tradents and transmission; but we may also have valuable indicators of the circles within which rabbinic mythopoesis was cultivated and carried on. Some of the more arresting patterns may be summarized as follows.[10]

1. Chains of Tradition. Teachings about the *Shekhinah* being with Israel in bondage and exile originate in tannaitic times, with R. Yehoshua ben Ḥananiah and his student R. Akiba;[11] and these continued to be transmitted in Palestine in the name of R. Simeon ben Lakish throughout the amoraic period, by R. Abbahu and also R. Azariah (early fifth century CE).[12] The

[6] See addendum II to *Pesikta Rabbati* (Ish Shalom, 196b). [7] Above, p. 153.

[8] For a similar use of the particle *ʾet* in Deut. 30: 4, see *Mekhilta de-Rabbi Ishmael, Boʾ* 14 (Horovitz–Rabin, 52).

[9] See for example, Richard Kalmin, *Sages, Stories, Authors, and Editors in Rabbinic Babylonia* (BJS 300; Atlanta: Scholars Press, 1994), ch. 1.

[10] Documentation in the following will be brief and selective.

[11] Cf. *Mekhilta de Rabbi Simeon* (Epstein–Melamed, 2), and *Mekhilta de-Rabbi Ishmael, Boʾ* 14, respectively; discussed above, pp. 138–42.

[12] See *Pesikta de-Rav Kahana* 16.

related mythologoumenon that the *Shekhinah* or God was redeemed with Israel also follows this stream of tradition: it is taught by such tannaim as Ḥananiah, the nephew of R. Yehoshua ben Ḥananiah;[13] by R. Akiba;[14] by his student R. Meir;[15] and by such later amoraic sages in Palestine as R. Ammi, R. Abbahu, and R. Berekhia.[16] These teachings do not seem to have had any great resonance in Babylonia; although a version of the account of the *Shekhinah* in exile was incorporated into the Babylonian Talmud (*BT Megillah* 12b) in the name of R. Simeon bar Yochai, another student of R. Akiba. Also, the tanna R. Levi bar Sisi preached about God's participation in the bondage of Egypt in Nehardea, but this myth was transmitted within Palestine through the established channels of R. Abbahu and R. Berekhia.[17] And, finally, the account of God binding his arm in sympathy with Israel's suffering was also Palestinian, beginning with R. Simeon ben Lakish and including teachings by R. Abbahu.[18] R. Aḥa, who taught that God was in sympathetic bondage during Israel's suffering, and went into exile with Israel bound in chains,[19] was a Palestinian Amora in the generation between R. Abbahu and R. Berekhia.

In sum, it is evident that all of the academies of amoraic Palestine transmitted versions of these several interrelated myths: the academy of Sepphoris (by R. Levi bar Sisi, R. Berekhia, and R. Azariah); the academy of Tiberias (by R. Simeon ben Lakish, R. Ammi, and R. Jeremiah); the academy of Caesarea (by R. Abbahu); and the academy of Lydda (by R. Aḥa). The various interconnections between the sages and schools are also part of this traditionary process, for over four centuries.

2. Centres of Study in Palestine. Among these centres of tradition, the great academy in Tiberias, through its founder R. Yoḥanan (around the beginning of the third century), played a major role in the making and diffusion of myths and mythic theology. Let us first note that R. Yoḥanan is credited with at least five traditions about the Leviathan, in the materials arranged in *BT Baba Batra* 74b–75a; and among these, four were reported in Pumbeditha—two by Rabbah (its dean in the early fourth century), and two others by Rav Dimi, when he returned there after going to Palestine to learn its teachings. Moreover, it is also R. Yoḥanan who taught the myth of the foundation stone found in *BT Sukkah* 53a–b.[20] In another vein, Rabbah

13 *Pesikta Rabbati* 21.

14 See *Mekhilta de-Rabbi Ishmael, Bo'* 14.

15 *Exodus Rabba* 15. 2 and *Tanḥuma (Buber), Aḥarei Mot* 12.

16 See in *Tanḥuma (Buber), Aḥarei Mot* 12, collectively.

17 See above, regarding *Leviticus Rabba* 23. 8.

18 See *Pesikta de-Rav Kahana* 17. 5.

19 See *Shoḥer Ṭov ad* Ps. 98: 1 (Buber, 422), for the image of the servitude of God's arm; *Lamentations Rabba, Petiḥta'* 34, for the image of chains.

20 However, according to *BT Makkot* 11a, this tradition is reported 'in the name of R. Yehudah in the name of Rab', who was R. Yoḥanan's contemporary in Babylonia. See further on Rab below.

taught that God created the world with the letters Y and H of the tetragram—in the name of R. Yoḥanan.[21]

We are also told that both R. Yoḥanan and his brother-in-law R. Simeon ben Lakish gave teachings about divine lamentations after the punishment of the people.[22] This is notable, for one student of R. Yoḥanan, R. Eleazar ben Pedat, also taught about divine laments and tears;[23] whereas another one, R. Isaac Nappaḥa, gave a homily at the request of two other colleagues in Tiberias, R. Assi and R. Ammi, and spoke of God's confession of responsibility for igniting the flames that destroyed the Temple, and his promise of recompense measure for measure, by becoming a protective wall of fire for the people on their future return to Zion.[24] This same R. Isaac also taught about the *Shekhinah* in exile;[25] and his other teacher, R. Levi, not only did likewise,[26] but also gave various dramatic teachings about the symbiotic suffering of God for the sorrows of Israel.[27]

3. Babylonian Evidence. Palestine was thus the source and continuous site of this mythopoesis. But as we have also noted, a number of these traditions were preached or reported in Babylon, and others were anonymously redacted in the Babylonian Talmud, thereby ensuring their place in the developing rabbinic curriculum. On the other hand, we can also point to what may be native Babylonian mythologoumena. Among these we have two cases where Rav Judah ben Ezekiel (founder of the academy of Pumbeditha, mid-third century) reported Leviathan traditions from Rab (founder of the academy of Sura, a generation earlier);[28] and a tradition that he also formulated an account of the foundation stone.[29] Moreover, it is reported in the name of R. Samuel ben Iniya that Rab also said that God roars three times each night, as he laments for the Temple and his exiled people.[30] In this regard, we may also recall the *traditum* of his student, R. Qaṭṭina, who reported the explanation that earth tremors were caused by divine tears shed for Israel in exile. And although he did not doubt God's sorrow, he disagreed with the details of his informant's view; and, according to the redactor, offered the alternative myth that the earthquakes result from God clapping his hands in grief.[31] The same Rav Qaṭṭina further reveals his mythic proclivities in an account about the coupling cherubs in the

[21] Cf. *Genesis Rabba* 12. 10 and *JT Ḥagigah* 1. 2.

[22] See *Midrash Eicha Rabba, Petiḥta*ʾ 2 (Buber edn. 4).

[23] *BT Ḥagigah* 5b.

[24] *BT Baba Qama* 60b.

[25] See *Exodus Rabba* 15. 16.

[26] Ibid. 23. 5.

[27] Cf. *Pesikta de-Rav Kahana* 5. 3; and *Lamentations Rabba* (Buber, edn. 88).

[28] *BT Baba Batra* 74b. According to the *ʾIggeret R. Sherira Gaon* (Lewin edn. 78–81), Rab (or Abba b. Abba) founded the academy of Sura in 219 and presided over it as its head until his death in 247 CE.

[29] *BT Makkot* 11a.

[30] *BT Berakhot* 3a; and see above (pp. 162–3) for the possibility that the similar tradition linked to R. Eliezer ben Hyrkanos is really of Babylonian origin.

[31] *BT Berakhot* 59b.

Shrine—a detail that scandalized the pagans, but not this rabbi or his tradents, since this teaching about the relationship between eros and observance is reported without any rabbinic approbation.[32]

While the overall Babylonian evidence is limited, we also find here certain chains of tradents and patterns of thematic concern. Such material thus tallies with the Palestinian sources, and lends credence to the possibility that the streams of mythopoeic thought and exegesis in rabbinic Judaism flowed in channels cut by masters and disciples, and by their mythmaking heirs over the centuries.

II. Literary Creations and Composites

As we have repeatedly observed, one aspect of rabbinic mythmaking was the individual or isolated invention that elaborates upon a specific theme or verse usually for a specific occasion or in the context of a specific discussion. If these teachings were deemed worthy of cultural preservation and transmission by particular sages or schools, many of them could eventually appear in one or another collection of midrashic traditions (and that is just how we know of them, in fact). Such diversity is of historical interest, for it highlights both the variety of formats (or contexts) in which a tradition might be embedded and the different formulations (or emphases) of a given teaching. Two broad types are instructive. One may be called the 'static' type, and is exemplified by the occurrence of isolated teachings, or by the stringing together of similar teachings in a list; the other is more 'dynamic' in nature, and is characterized by the combination of a series of different teachings into a conceptual sequence. Both types are forms of tradition-building or gathering, but the difference between them is the difference between topics of mythic tradition and the development of new mythic compositions and narratives.

1. Topical Anthopogies. We begin with the 'static' type of tradition-building, whereby a scriptural verse and its mythic meaning is presented as a distinct instruction by one sage or chain of sages, and is collected into a series of instructions on the same or related topic. Characteristic of this type is the listing of different opinions and proof-texts in *BT Berakhot* 59b concerning the specific expression of divine sorrow that causes earth tremors; or the collection of speculations in *Midrash Psalms* 11. 3 regarding the particular place that the *Shekhinah* resides after the destruction of the Temple. Both instances are anthological lists only, and provide no narrative ligatures that would serve to connect the separate elements into a more unified (conceptual or temporal) series. In these cases, tradition merely gathers teachings on related topics into a thematic cluster.

[32] See *BT Yoma* 54a, and the discussion above.

Different therefore is the collection of teachings found in the *Mekhilta de-Rabbi Ishmael, Bo'* 14, for in this instance two temporal series are conjoined; one series of instances in the past (beginning with the sojourn in Egypt), when the *Shekhinah* repeatedly went into exile with the people of Israel; and another series of cases in the future to come, when the *Shekhinah* will return to the homeland with the exiles. The two lists thus comprise a virtual proto-narrative; for although the episodes are part of a coherent temporal and theological sequence, they remain schematic in both form and substance. There is thus a discernible tension between the static quality of the different examples and their dynamic correlation as witnesses to God's involvement in Israel's sacred history. Hence if the episodes provide evidence for the coherence of God's providential care, they are presented as a series of distinct historical cases. In the end, this prismatic quality predominates and the midrashic passage remains an instructive catalogue—but not a coherent narrative.

2. Textual Correlations. We may attain another perspective on the relationship between the two types of tradition-building (the 'static' and the 'dynamic') by attending to an assortment of interpretations of Job 37: 6 ('[God] commands the snow, "Become earth!" '). An old tannaitic teaching preserved in *BT Yoma* 54b is a good place to begin. This pericope is organized around speculations about the *axis mundi*, the foundation point of origins. In that context, R. Yehoshua's teaching is recalled. Different from other sages who variously taught that the creation of the world began from its centre, R. Yehoshua taught that 'The world was created from the margins, as it says "He said to the snow, 'Be earth!' ", etc.' But what does this mean? The apodictic assertion is without context or explanation, and we are left puzzled as to why creation of the earth from snow is from the margins or borders of primordial matter. The instruction simply stands as transmitted, without further comment or justification.

The gaps in R. Yehoshua's teaching are somewhat filled by the remarks of R. Judah b. Pazzi, preserved in *JT Ḥagigah* 2. 5. Here we are told that 'At the beginning the world was water within water. What is the proof? "And the spirit of Elohim hovered over the water*s*" (Gen. 1: 2). He then turned this into snow, (as it says) "He casts down hail like flakes" (Ps. 147: 17); and He further turned this into earth, (as it says) "He said to the snow, 'Be earth!' " ' What this mythic teaching adds is both context and sequence: the context of the speculation is the primary creation narrative of Genesis 1, and the sequence of transformations is water, snow, and then earth. In this way, R. Judah coordinates a series of figurative phrases found in diverse parts of Scripture, dealing with certain meteorological or other divine acts, and gives them authority by virtue of their connection with Genesis 1. The result is that the two texts take on new coherence and importance, and become components of the biblical myth of origins whose elements are scattered throughout Scripture.

The latter point is taken up in *Genesis Rabba* 1. 6, where R. Judah bar Simon teaches: 'At the beginning of the creation of the world He (God) "revealed hidden things and concealed them" (Dan. 2: 22),[33] as it is said, "At the beginning Elohim created the heavens" (Gen. 1: 1)—but did not explicate. Where did He explicate? Later on (in Scripture, where it says) "He spread out the heavens as a thin cloth" (Isa. 40: 22). (And it further states in Gen. 1: 1) "And the earth"—but did not explicate. And where did He explicate? Later on (where it says) 'He commands the snow, 'Become earth!' " '. As one can readily observe, Genesis 1: 1–2 again provides the context for the verses adduced from the prophets and Job, so that these verses are not isolated phrases dealing with the creation, but a series of specific dramatic elements that attain coherence and dynamic focus through their incorporation into the opening text of Scripture.

The opening verses of the book of Genesis are also the scriptural frame for a series of speculations found in *Pirkei de-Rabbi Eliezer* 3. In the context of 'eight things' that 'were created on the first day' (including the heavens, light, darkness, 'tohu', and 'bohu') we are informed as follows: 'Where is the earth created from?—(God) took snow from under the Throne of Glory and threw it upon the waters, and the waters congealed and became the dust of the earth, as it says, "He said to the snow, 'Be earth!' " ' Here also narrative coherence predominates over mere lists and phrases,[34] even as the text includes some new speculations concerning the origin of snow and the creation of the earth. Linked to these mythic matters, but considerably more opaque and retrograde in terms of narrative style and format, is the reflex of this teaching found in *Sefer Yetzirah* 1. 11. Here we cryptically read as follows: 'Three—water from air. He engraved in it "tohu", "bohu", mud, and clay. He made them like garden beds; He set them like a wall; He covered them with a type of thatch, and poured snow upon them and the dust (of the earth) was made, as it says "He said to the snow, 'Be earth!' " '[35]

The foregoing cases attest to the widespread nature of the myth about snow within rabbinic speculations about the creation, despite the fact that the theme is unattested in the scriptural account found in Genesis 1. By correlating the laconic reference to the creation of the earth in that passage

[33] I translate the phrase according to its midrashic usage here; in its biblical context the passage apparently means 'He revealed hidden and concealed things'.

[34] This is particularly clear when this teaching is compared with the list of 'ten things' created on the first day in *BT Ḥag.* 12a. *Pirkei de Rabbi Eliezer* 3 integrates the style and content of *BT Ḥag.* 12a and *Gen. Rab* 1. 6.

[35] I have followed the critical reading established by Ithamar Gruenwald, 'Preliminary Critical Edition of *Sefer Yezira*', *IOS* 1 (1971), 145. In that edition the text reference is 1. 13. The reference to 'three' refers to one of the primordial esoteric gradations mentioned in this work.

with the events depicted in Job 37: 6 and Ps. 147: 17, sages like R. Judah b. Pazzi and R. Judah bar Simon presented the element of snow as a feature of world origins. The result is not only a more detailed version of the primordial acts of creation, but an integration of them all into the context of Genesis 1. This imaginative embedding gives the particular event recorded in Job 37: 6 new authority, even as it reveals an unexpected mythic depth to the formulations of origins found at the beginning of Scripture.

3. Dynamics of Plot. Another perspective on the development of narrative coherence between one or several mythic texts does not focus on their correlation with a common or base narrative, like Genesis 1. It rather highlights the plot dynamics that obtain within one verse or between several different or successive passages.

i. The simplest example of this type is the single sentence whose components are restructured into a dramatic sequence. The statement 'And they saw the God of Israel, and under His feet there was the likeness of a pavement of sapphire, and like the very heaven for purity' (Exod. 24: 10) is a case in point. In its original narrative setting, it reports a vision of God in heaven, on His heavenly throne, with a double depiction of the luminescence of the firmament beneath. Indeed one could justifiably render the twofold description of the shining as a synonymous parallelism, stating that the illumination below the divine seat appeared 'like the splendour of a sapphire, like the very essence of the heavens in radiance'. However, as we noted, the midrashic explication in *Mekhilta de-Rabbi Ishmael, Bo*ʾ 14 transformed this passage utterly, and rendered the two phrases as antipodes of a dramatic process: the first clause was understood to refer to the brickwork seen in heaven during the servitude of Egypt; the second to the spectacle of glory after the exodus itself.[36] That is, the single verse was explicated as a mini-myth, and the redundant depiction rendered as two distinct moments in the movement from slavery to freedom and God's participation in that process. The original parallelism is thus reconfigured as two poles of a coherent narrative, with human and divine aspects to each part.

ii. A more complex way to render the same structure is by the use of two different verses. The teaching in *Pesikta de-Rav Kahana* 17. 5 is a case in point. In it, a rereading of Lam. 2: 3 and Dan. 12: 12 provides the antipodes of a myth of (divine) servitude and redemption. At the outset, God is portrayed as binding His right arm behind His back, in sympathy with the historical servitude of Israel; subsequently, He promises Daniel (to whom eschatological esoterica are revealed) that He will free His arm at the end of days (the 'right arm' of God and the 'days' of bondage being exegetically

[36] See above, pp. 136–8.

correlated). Separately, each passage is thus one part of a larger myth embracing exile and salvation; combined, the two provide the structure for the overall midrashic myth.[37]

iii. The conjoining of separate biblical verses may also serve a specific sequence of actions in a new rabbinic narrative. Simple and complex subtypes may be discerned. Among the former is *Tanḥuma (Buber) Ḥuqqat* 1, which portrays a primordial rebellion of the sea dragon and the ensuing divine response. The mythic narrative is generated by the phrase 'He (God) heaps up the ocean waters like a mound (*ned*)' (Ps. 33: 7). The teacher wonders just what this might refer to, and then presents an account of God's request of the Prince of the Sea to swallow up the primordial waters (presumably so that the dry land may appear). However, the Sea refuses this divine word—claiming that it is already filled with its own waters—and starts to whine. Thereupon God kicks this being and kills it, as Scripture says, 'With His strength He quelled the Sea, and with His wisdom He smashed Rahab' (Job 26: 12).[38] The result is the mound mentioned by the psalmist. One will note that both biblical verses (Ps. 33: 7 and Job 26: 12) reflect the end of the process, and do not explicitly indicate the initial events that led to the Sea's rebellion and destruction at the beginning of creation.

The lack is filled in a version of this myth found in the Midrash *Shoḥer Ṭov* (to Ps. 93: 3). Here the original context of the Sea's rebellion is presented as resistence to God's command 'Let the waters be gathered in one place', so that the dry land might appear (Gen. 1: 9). Notable in this instance is that the waters first comply, though they subsequently became arrogant and 'arose to cover the earth as before'. It was at this turn of events that they were squashed and defeated by God. It will also be recalled that, in this version of the myth, the theme of the waters being piled up in a 'mound (*ned*)' (Ps. 33: 7) is also transformed, and exegetically revised to mean that the primordial waters were pooled together into a 'water skin (*nod*)'. Only in a variant added to this example is there any reference to the defeat and drying up of the waters of creation.[39] Hence a mythic narrative of pooling is kept distinct from one portraying the destruction of the sea.

In an even more elaborate instance of this theme recounted in *Exodus Rabba* 15. 22, the divine command to the waters (Gen. 1: 9) precedes a series of divine responses to the rebellion of the sea: the quelling of the waters and the smashing of Rahab (quoting Job 26: 12); the killing of the waters and their crying 'until this very day' (quoting Job 38: 16); and the roar against the sea and its flight (quoting Ps. 104: 7). Thus, in this case, a number of diverse scriptural citations are arranged sequentially as so many episodes of one narrative whole. The strategy of composition holds this series together by

[37] See the detailed analysis, pp. 146–50.

[38] See above, pp. 118–19.

[39] Citing Job 9: 8 and 12: 15. On this version, see pp. 117–18.

means of narrative ligatures ('after', *keshe-*; 'when', *keyvan she-*). The move from episodic composites to a true composition is not fully achieved, however, since the separate episodes are often contradictory in their new collocation (e.g. the killing is followed by the crying which is followed by the fleeing of the waters—a most improbable order), and since the several actions are each self-sufficient and centre around the limited topic of rebellion and punishment.

iv. Two more successful attempts to create a sustained mythic narrative through the combination of separate episodes deserve special note. One is the combination of traditions found in *BT Baba Batra* 74b–75b. As demonstrated earlier, this pericope preserves a collection of eight distinct topics (with proof-texts) that deal with primordial sea monsters: beginning with their creation at the creation of the world; continuing through their profligate propagation that lead to the divine decision to limit or kill the primal pair; and on through assorted commands, rebellions, and battles until the final destruction of the male Leviathan by God (after the failure of the angelic prince Gabriel); the use of the flesh and skin of the monster to benefit the righteous at the end of days.[40] Each of these episodes or topics is exegetically linked to scriptural texts, and they have been arranged in a deliberate and artful manner—as is evident both by the coherent sequence of actions, and by the mnemonics placed at the beginning of each of several subunits. The origins of the overall plot is rather more puzzling, and one may wonder whether the sequence of separate battles at the beginning and end of time was already known to the various Palestinian sages now mentioned as the sources of the mythic traditions; or whether these scholars merely had a series of separate traditions at hand, and the present sequence and drama is the products of their latter-day Babylonian transmitters or redactors. Either way, the received series of events and their stylistic patterning demonstrate artfulness and coherence of a singular sort—a precious exemplar of large-scale rabbinic mythmaking from late antiquity.[41]

A second example is taken from *Pirkei de-Rabbi Eliezer*, and is part and parcel of a tendency of this relatively late work to integrate earlier traditions

[40] See the discussion at pp. 120–4; and the full translation in Appendix 1.A.

[41] Much deserving of separate note in this context is the mythic fabulation found in *Pesikta de-Rav Kahana, Parashah ʾAḥeret*, Mandelbaum edn. 456 (with parallels in *Tanḥuma, Nitzavim* 4 and *Yalkut Shimoni*, ii, par. 927), which presents a great battle against the Leviathan. We have already observed that this episode is an important component of the traditions in *BT Baba Batra* 74b–75b. The fact that this entire episode is extended through a rereading of the verse sequence in Job 41 (mostly in order; only the reference to Behemoth in v. 8 is deferred to the end), and does not involve a theomachy involving God directly, suggests that the version in the *Pesikta* is a derivative and more moderate version of the topos known from the Talmud. It has the distinct merit of showing how one episode could be developed into a more extensive mythic form; and also for demonstrating another model for how a rabbinic myth could be compiled from units of Scripture.

by deleting the names of rabbinic tradents and adding ligatures to bind separate episodes into a coherent sequence.[42] When it comes to mythic matters, we may thus observe the invention of fabulations that utilize a wide range of older traditions for the construction of comprehensive accounts of primordial or other events. For example, chapter five of the *Pirkei de-Rabbi Eliezer* narrates the events of the third day of creation. It begins with a statement of the *status quo ante* ('On the third (day) the earth was level as a plain, and the waters covered the face of the earth'); and then turns to the divine command that changed matters ('And when the word went forth from the mouth of the Almighty, "Let the waters be gathered" [Gen. 1: 9], . . . then'). The narrator goes on to describe the new situation, when the mountains arose and caused the waters to pool in the valleys formed by this upheaval. These events were, however, disrupted by an act of rebellion:

> Forthwith (*mi-yad*) the waters became arrogant and rose up to cover the earth as before, until the Holy One, blessed be He, roared against them, squashed them (*kibashan*), and put them under the soles of His feet, and measured them in the hollow of His hand, that they neither increase nor decrease.

In this brief segment, we can see features of an older myth of combat, similar in terminology and description to those discussed earlier[43]—but without reference to any sage, or to any verse that could serve as its scriptural anchor (like the divine command in Gen. 1: 9; or the reference to the waters' uprising in Ps. 93: 3).[44] Moreover, in this reuse of it, the narrator has added the ligature *mi-yad*, which serves to integrate the *traditum* of rebellion into the précis of the biblical creation account. The result is that the mythic episode becomes part of the fabulation of origins presented in the midrash, and the divine acts of suppressing the waters are no more nor less mythic than the divine command that the waters be gathered in one place, or the subsequent measurement of them in the hollow of God's hand. Thus each divine act (by speech, foot, and hand) is a dramatic mythic event conveyed by one of the verbs that appear in rapid succession in the narrative. The result is a unified (or coherent) chain of images of divine actions *in illo tempore*—events conveying a concrete sense of mythic actuality, with no palpable sense of metaphor.[45]

[42] For a consideration of some of the editorial features of this work, see Yaakov Elman, 'Rhetoric, Motif, and Subject-Matter—Toward an Analysis of Narrative Technique in Pirke de-Rabbi Eliezer', *Jerusalem Studies in Jewish Folklore*, 13/14 (1991–2), 99–126 (in Hebrew). See also his comments in 'On the Character of the Late Midrashic Literature', *Proceedings of the Ninth World Congress of Jewish Studies* (Jerusalem: World Congress of Jewish Studies, 1986), iii. 57–62 (in Hebrew).

[43] See above, pp. 117–20.

[44] See *Gen. Rabba* 5. 2–4 and esp. *Shoḥer Ṭov ad* Ps. 93: 3, discussed above. These sources are not mentioned by Jeffrey Rubenstein, 'From Mythic Motifs to Sustained Myth: The Revision of Rabbinic Traditions in Medieval Midrashim', *HTR* 89 (1996), 146–58, where he treats this chapter along lines taken up here.

[45] This is particularly clear in the image of measuring, which transforms the rhetorical features of Isa. 40: 12 into a feature of mythic actuality.

The composite nature of this chapter is also clear from the sequel to this episode, where we are first told that 'the deeps' were in fact created before the divine command to the waters, and then receive teachings about these depths as sources of sustenance for the earth. A series of dicta from the sages add specificity. According to R. Yehoshua, one of these depths is near Gehenna, and bubbles forth water for human delight; whereas R. Judah taught that once each month ducts rise from these depths in order to irrigate the earth. The account then turns to the relationship between the depths below and the clouds above, and how one depth calls to the other to bring up water for the clouds. At this point, the narrative becomes more mythically charged. For once the clouds are watered from below, they send forth rain to the earth, an event that is personified in terms of a male–female syzygy: the rain inseminates the earth with its fluids, and their absorption by the earth is an impregnation—described both in terms of a whore-mongering widow, and of a blessed virgin bride.[46] In the latter case, biblical proof-texts are added; but these do not diminish the mythic tone of this account. Indeed, all told, the literary effect is actually quite striking, since the mythic fabulation is first presented in its own right, and not as an explication of Scripture. The biblical passage thus functions dramatically as a scriptural confirmation of the mythic teaching. Put differently: the biblical proof-texts are presented as part of the overall mythic fabulation, rather than as dicta in need of mythopoeic elucidation. In such settings, the myth achieves a modicum of narrative independence and authority. Comparable literary compilations of primordial mythic materials are also found in the later *Midrash Konen*.[47]

In the foregoing types, the rabbinic fabulation is composed of separate dramatic episodes that have been combined into new composites or compositions. In this form, they provide an instructive perspective on the double process of 'tradition-building' and 'the making of mythic narratives'. Hereby, all the texts from Scripture on a given subject, plus all the rabbinic elaborations of these themes (with their proof-texts), are potential building blocks for the process. Altogether, they show the ongoing mythic impulse in rabbinic sources and the construction of new literary genres and forms. Before continuing with other aspects of this literary creativity, we may take advantage of the diverse examples of rabbinic myths dealing with primordial waters to offer some observations about structure and composition.

v. In the most minimalist sense, a structural analysis of mythic narratives will involve (1) the determination of core thematic elements or components (their themes or plot types) and (2) a consideration of how these features occur (their order and conditions) and are expressed (their style and

[46] The word *miyad* occurs twice more in this sequence, with dramatic affect.

[47] See in *Bet Ha-Midrasch*, ed. Adolf Jellinek (reprint, 3rd edn.; Jerusalem: Wahrmann Books, 1967), ii. 25, for the mythic separation of the waters on the second day of creation.

motifs).[48] Since the rabbinic exemplars regularly refer to biblical proof-texts, or are based upon them, a brief restatement of the biblical evidence about 'sea battles' will prove instructive.

Limiting ourselves to the major components, we may sum up as follows. A number of prismatic or summary frames treating mythic episodes occur in Scripture, and refer to events either (*a*) at the beginning of time (*Urzeit*), during the creation: (i) Isa. 51: 9; (ii) Ps. 74: 13–14; (iii) Ps. 89: 11; (iv) Ps. 104: 7; (v) Job 9: 8; (vi) Job 26: 12; (*b*) in historical time (*Heilsgeschichte*), during acts of divine deliverance: (i) Isa. 51: 10; (ii) Ps. 18: 14, 16; or (*c*) at an eschatological end-time (*Endzeit*), during events of divine victory or salvation: (i) Isa. 27: 1; (ii) 50: 2. These occurrences typically involve God as a cosmic agent and victor, and the 'sea' (variously named or personified) as the element defeated or destroyed. A variety of verbs indicate violent acts of God smashing ((*a*) i, ii, vi), piercing ((*a*) i, iii), or trampling ((*a*) iv) the sea dragon; drying or shrivelling the sea ((*a*) i; (*c*) ii); or giving a thunderous blast of fury that routs the foe ((*a*) iv; (*b*) ii). In a few instances reference is made to a positive attribute of God's action (power and cleverness; (*a*) vi), and His weapon (a sword; (*c*) i); or to a negative attribute of the sea (pride; (*a*) iii), and its physical character (twisted or slant; (*c*) i). To the extent that more than one action-verb occurs in any given frame, this is due to the stylistics of 'poetic parallelism' and one should not regard it as marking any sequence of dramatic actions. Moreover, as noted earlier, this phenomenon of episodic doubling also means that the sea is referred to by different epithets or names. Thus even though the passages draw upon a great fund of mythic traditions in their portrayal of divine battle, the differences between the lines lead to contradictions that make any reading of the 'parallel phrases' in terms of a larger or coherent narrative difficult if not impossible. Only rarely, and due to a deliberate attempt by the author or speaker to create or invoke a pattern of 'types', are separate mythic events conjoined or correlated in the same literary unit or passage ((*a*) i; and cf. Psalms 74 and 77, overall).

We now return to the rabbinic material, and note that here also the myths involving strife with or control of the sea fall into three temporal periods. These are, first, events occurring at (*x*) the beginning of time (*Urzeit*), in the course of the creation: (i) *Genesis Rabba* 5. 2–4 (*GR* 5. 2–4); (ii) *BT Baba Batra* 74b–75a (*BB* 1); (iii) *Tanḥuma (Buber) Ḥuqqat* 1; (iv) *Shoḥer Ṭov* 93. 5; (v) *Pirkei de-Rabbi Eliezer* 5; (vi) *Exodus Rabba* 15. 22; (vii) *Aggadat Bereishit* 4. 1; (viii) *Seder Rabba de-Berei'shit*; (ix) *Tanḥuma Genesis* 1; second, events occurring at (*y*) in historical time (*Heilsgeschichte*), sometimes because of human sin: (i) *Mekhilta de-Rabbi Ishmael, Baḥodesh* 6; (ii) *Sifre Deut.* 43; (iii) *Genesis Rabba* 23. 7; (iv) *JT Sheqalim* 6. 3; but also during the foundation

[48] Cf. the comments of E.-K. Köngäs and P. Maranda, 'Structural Models in Folklore', *Midwest Folklore*, 12 (1962), 135, 153.

of a shrine: (v) *BT Sukkah* 53a–b; (vi) *JT Sanhedrin* 10. 2; and third, events occurring at (*z*) the end-time (*Endzeit*): (i) *BB* 2; (ii) *Pesikta de-Rav Kahana, Parashah 'Aḥeret*; (iii) *Tanḥuma, Nitzavim* 4. In each of these periods, diverse components can be isolated; and these are found in a variety of combinations or action-sequences, and with diverse terminology.

An examination of the events at the *Urzeit* shows that these involve several situations, and are mostly set within the context of Genesis 1 or presuppose its terminology or conditions. In some sources, the initial *status quo ante* may be called (1) the 'commingling of the waters'. According to the opinions of R. Yudan and R. Berekhia in (*x*) i (*GR* 5. 2), this primary state is called 'waters within waters' (*mayyim be-mayyim*). However, neither this terminology nor this situation is specifically found in Scripture, and at most we may suppose that they are based upon the *post quem* situation, when God put the firmament into the waters and therewith made a separation 'between the waters' (*mayyim la-mayyim*) (Gen. 1: 6). Notably, this situation is not presented in sexual terms, or as an episode fraught with any danger. However, by contrast, the excesses of the sexually cohabiting waters is spoken of in (*x*) viii as a situation that endangered the world; whereas in (*x*) ii this great prolixity is focused on the sea monsters, referred to generally in Gen. 1: 21 as 'the great *tanninim*', but deemed in our rabbinic myth to be both male and female and named 'the slant serpent' and 'the twisted serpent' (Isa. 27: 1).

The first situation is linked to a second one, which may be called (2) 'the separation of the waters'. According to a teaching of R. Berekhia in (*x*) i (*GR* 5. 4), the upper waters were separated from the lower waters 'with a cry' (interpreting Job 28: 11)—though without any indication of the divine motivation or the cause of the crying. According to (*x*) viii, the divine response to the danger was to 'roar' at the waters and cause them to flee apart (based on Ps. 104: 7); the action in (*x*) ii was more fateful, since God 'killed' (*harag*) the female and castrated the male. In neither of these last two cases was there any act of rebellion or resistance of the waters; rather, the divine intervention comes to correct a natural excess of a created element.

A third situation involves the lower waters, and may be called (3) 'the restriction or limitation of the waters' so that the dry land might appear. A conditioning moment is God's fiat, 'Let the waters be gathered into one place' (Gen. 1: 9). In several separate instances, the waters willingly obeyed the divine command and pooled themselves aside ((*x*) i; *GR* 5. 3); though this cluster is preceded by a case of compliance in which the biblical proof-texts refer to God as trampling upon the waters, in order to press them into the ocean (Job 9: 8; 12: 15)—thereby hinting at some myth of the waters' resistence or impassivity to God's word, and requiring His more active or aggressive intervention (*GR*, 5. 2). In other texts, the waters' rebellion against this divine command at or near the beginning of creation is stated explicitly, and called an act of pride ((*x*) iv; interpreting Ps. 93: 3; see also (*x*) v); and in other instances, God's command to the Prince of the Sea (identified as Rahab) is to swallow the primordial waters, but that divine entity refused and was kicked (*baʿaṭ*) and killed (*harag*) by God in response ((*x*) ii, iii, and vi, citing Job 26: 12), or trampled (*darakh*) and quashed (*kabash*) by Him ((*x*) iii, citing Amos 7: 13; but only squashed in (*x*) iv, citing Job 12: 15). In the latter cases, the specific verbs of aggression used in the mythic episodes are not matched by the language in the biblical proof-texts, thus suggesting that these 'battle narratives' were originally told or formulated independently of Scripture.

A fourth group of sources seems unrelated to the foregoing mythic dramas, even though they also deal with what we shall call (4) the 'containment of the surging Deep', or use some of the key terms of the above-noted episodes of suppression. Among those cases where God is the active power against the primordial waters during the creation, are such episodes as God repeatedly quashing the upsurging deep with mountains ((*x*) vii); or God once and for all sealing the mighty Tehom with a stone (Targum Yerushalmi on Exod. 28: 30), or quashing it with the Torah ((*x*) ix). Altogether unique is the mythic variant that says, 'If (Leviathan) were not crouching (or squatting; *rabutz*) upon the Tehom and quashing it (*kobesh ʿalav*), the (waters of) Tehom would rise up and flood the world'. But despite this grave possibility, 'When Leviathan wishes to drink', but is not able to do so because the waters of Okeanos are salty [49]—he 'raises one of his fins, and the Tehom rises up and he drinks; and when he finishes drinking, he returns his fin to its place and stops up (*sotem*) the Tehom' (*Pesikta Rabbati*, suppl. 1).[50] The serpent Leviathan thus serves here as a plug over the primordial waters, preventing a world-threatening flood from arising from the netherworld. But such an overflow of the Tehom is no mere hypothetical danger, and recurs as a historical event on several distinct occasions (see below).

We may thus turn attention from mythic events at the *Urzeit* to (*y*) episodes involving the upsurge of the primordial waters in historical time. As noted (above), two primary types occur. One puts the cause in terms of acts of idolatry or impudence, as when people in 'the generation of Enosh' began to call their idols by the name YHWH, and the Lord punished them so that 'Okeanos rose and flooded a third of the world' ((*y*) i,[51] ii; (*y*) iii gives later speculations on the actual geographical extent of the flooding); or when 'the generation of the Separation' built their Tower to heaven ((*y*) iv), and the Great Sea 'went forth' and flooded the earth.[52] It will be noted that these

[49] On this mythic topic, see *Tanḥuma (Buber), Ḥuqqat* 1.

[50] Ish Shalom, 194b. The verb *satam* (stopped up) is also found in *Tanḥuma, Bereishit* 1, in connection with blocking the waters of Okeanos (*per* MS Cambridge 1212); whereas *Ḥatam* (sealed) is used in the *editio princeps* and MSS Oxford 153 and 2337.

[51] Horovitz–Rabin, 223.

[52] The point is made through a clever reinterpretation of the phrase 'sea of foul waters (*ha-mutzaʾim*)' in Ezek. 47: 8—the plural *mutzaʾim* taken to refer to 'two occasions' that the Great Sea 'went forth' (*yatzaʾ*) in a flood. In *Genesis Rabba* 26. 7 'the generation of the Flood' is a third

waters are not rebellious or fractious, but the instruments of divine justice; indeed in such passages as (*y*) i and ii the punishment is linked to a verse from Amos 5: 8, referring to God as He 'Who calls to the waters of the sea and pours them over the earth'. And in another striking variation, taught by R. Abba b. Kahana in the name of R. Levi, the flood waters during the generations of Enosh and the Separation were set aside at the beginning of creation; for they interpreted God's ancient command: 'Let the waters be gathered (*yiqqavu*)' (Gen. 1: 9) as meaning, 'Let the waters await (*yeqavvu*) what I shall do with them in the future'—at which time He said, 'Let those very same waters turn, rise, and proceed forward' (*Genesis Rabba* 5. 1).[53]

A less providential account of the waters occurs in a later source (*Exodus Rabba* 15. 7). In it, God 'sought to establish the world in the beginning', but had initial difficulties in finding a secure 'foundation' for it until the patriarchs arose. For at the outset the world was comprised 'only of water', and when God wished to fix it at various points, different wicked generations (that of Enosh and the Separation) sinned so that 'the waters rose up and drowned them' and 'did not permit Him to establish upon them a foundation'—until the patriarchs came and 'were found worthy', so that God said 'On these I shall establish the world'. This image of divine difficulty at the beginning is not entirely offset by the punishing waters, since in the account it also appears that the waters act on their own (without any divine summons), and are only securely put in place and prevented from surging upwards by the advent of the truly righteous patriarchs. Indeed, the mythic tension latent in this account (and signalled from the very outset by the remark that the world was originally only water) is even more explicitly indicated by the parable that precedes the account. In it, God's attempt to establish a firm foundation for the world is likened to a human king who wished to found a state, but every time he chose a site the 'waters arose from the depths and did not permit it' or 'overturned it', until a rock was found upon which the world could rest secure.[54]

In the foregoing accounts, more of the restive or fractious power of the subterranean waters comes to the surface, and bears traces of an older myth of the primordial Tehom only partly concealed in the 'creation myth' of world foundations formulated in this midrash about God and the waters of destruction. It is also notable that, in the foregoing fabulation of origins, the capstone securing the creation is embodied by the patriarchs, whose rectitude

occasion of world destruction through water. This tradition is more fully elaborated upon in *Tanḥuma (Buber), Noaḥ* 24, and also in *Exodus Rabba* 15. 7 (see further, below). Another tradition, preserved in *Zohar* II. 113b, indicates another potential flood at the incident of the Golden Calf.

[53] Theodor–Albeck, 32. See also *Genesis Rabba* 28. 2.

[54] Cf. the tradition noted above, p. 129 n. 52.

or worthiness blocks the primordial waters—not the monster Leviathan and not the stone that seals over the roiling abyss.

In other versions, the waters of Tehom are held in check by a stone or sherd with the divine Name written on it, and this is the foundation upon which the Temple itself was established. In two separate cases ((*y*) v and vi), the latent danger of these old waters is still evident; for when David lowers shafts into the watery depths he courts a cosmic disaster. By contrast, in a distinct midrashic tradition about the founding of the sanctuary of Beth-El by God, no such threat is evident as He dramatically secures its foundation by taking the headstone that Jacob used for a pillow and thrust it down to the 'nethermost depths' (*ʿomeq tehomot*) with his foot (*Shoḥer Ṭov* 91. 7). Thus both sanctuary and Temple serve as an *axis mundi*, or point of connection and intermediation between the divine realms above and the chaotic waters below. There is also a palpable trace in these accounts of the ancient mythic theme of the establishment of the world and the heavenly shrine upon the defeated waters of chaos. This topic is most famously known from the great battle and building scenes found in *Enuma elish* IV–V; but one will also recall the striking link between the divine combat against the sea and the references to the building of a temple recorded in Exod. 15: 6–8,17. Perhaps here we can locate the historical reflex of a matter preserved in more concrete mythic terms in rabbinic memory and imagination. In this regard, it bears mention that an outcropping of stone was reportedly situated within the ancient Temple (*M. Yoma* 5. 2); and that a contemporary tradition even linked this to the foundation stone of the world cast into the waters by God Himself (*BT Yoma* 54b).

Now if the primordial Tehom continued to surge beneath the inhabited world, though plugged or sealed for safe-keeping by God or some culture hero; and if the dangerous serpents of the deep were killed, castrated, or suppressed by God at the time of the creation, one relic of this mythic past continued to frolic about in the world—and that is Leviathan, whom YHWH had 'created to sport with' (Ps. 104: 26). Biblical tradition says no more; but according to (*z*) i (*BB* 2), a special sporting event would occur in the *Endzeit*, when this dragon would be killed and its flesh served to the righteous as a reward. The master of the hunt was to be the heavenly prince Gabriel; but we are not privy to the battle, and only told that without God's help he could not succeed. A more elaborate account of this battle occurs in (*z*) ii (with variations in (*z*) iii). Here God instructs various divine helpers to do the job; but these beings fail ignominiously, until the earth-monster Behemoth is summoned by God to engage Leviathan in a violent combat that leaves both beings dead in a dramatic stalemate of might. Notably, the account in (*z*) i merely draws on two verses from Job 40, whereas (*z*) ii produces a fabulously wrought 'biblical' myth, by culling and reinterpreting ten verses from Job 41, and even reworking the sequence for dramatic effect. Given this textual core, there is little link to the older fights with dragons found in other midrashic myths—save for the motif of 'overweening pride' (*ga'avah shel ma'alah*) ascribed to the Leviathan (based on Job 41: 7).[55] But this attribute is presented not so much as the rebellious trait of a creature who refuses or disregards a divine command, as a quality of its massive nature or pomposity. Nevertheless, it is just this base impudence that rabbinic tradition singles out for mention, and that impels the Holy One to plan the sea monster's death and destruction.

vi. Three more inclusive considerations may be added to the preceding analysis of structural components of 'myths of the sea' in rabbinic midrash. The first of these bears on the *scriptural context* of the myths, and in particular the primary setting of Genesis 1. For example, the explicit separation of the waters is the setting for discussions of a prior condition of the world as 'water within water', and this provides the framework for various treatments of these waters (as gendered or not; as separated by force or not; and as longing for or achieving reunion or not). Similarly, the divine command to the waters to 'gather' in one place leads to various accounts of the response of these waters (as obedient or not; as initially obedient but then rebellious; as rebellious and then obedient; as prideful or impudent; and so on); and corresponding to the negative responses of the waters there are assorted divine reactions against them (like roaring; stomping; pooling; upturning mountains; sealing; stopping up; kicking; and killing). From other texts we see other ways that the primordial waters were contained or stabilized (with a stone or a shard or a seal—with or without the divine Name; with the Torah; with the body of Leviathan; and with the appearance of the patriarchs); but we also can see that the initial situation of creation or containment of the waters was not necessarily final, and that the world could be endangered by various means (like the natural spawning of the sea monsters; or Leviathan's desire to drink fresh water; or human sin; or breaking the divine seal over the abyss), and these lead to a necessary repair of the situation (by God or a hero).

Significantly, most of these derivative situations or acts are linked to other verses in Scripture that deal with the sea or the monsters in one way or another; and the stringing together of these verses or the situations associated with them results in the expansion of simple scenarios into collections of mythic actions. These vary greatly depending upon the anthologist, but all together reflect an assumption that the fragmentary and diverse mythic episodes scattered throughout Scripture (as well as the different terms connected with them) have a certain coherence or order that may be reconstructed. Given this recurrent situation, it is quite striking how few citations

[55] This rabbinic phrase seems to indicate some 'extraordinary hubris', though possibly a pride best reserved for a divinity 'on high'.

from (*a*) and (*c*) were reused in (*x*) and (*z*); how often new biblical texts are employed by the sages or similes are reread in mythic terms; and how often divine actions against the monster use terms unknown to the biblical tradition (but in some cases attested in Near Eastern mythology). Clearly the mythic sources available to rabbinic teachers were far more pervasive and varied than what might be supposed from Scripture alone. This makes the sages' concern to recreate or manifest a rabbinic 'biblical mythology' all the more significant.

The second consideration follows upon these observations, and bears on the *multiformity* of these myths. Numerous settings are used; with numerous terms, agents, and means; and these occur in numerous combinations. Accordingly, it is precisely in its episodic variety that the suppleness of rabbinic myth is evident, together with its protean capacity to be renewed in different genres for different purposes. No reconstruction of a hyper-myth would therefore do justice to the phenomena, or permit one to say that an exegete actively selected certain elements or rejected others from some set authoritative schema or mythic thesaurus. To be sure, our investigations show that mythic narratives like the combat with the sea are comprised of an assortment of basic components, and that certain thematic schemata were evidently instrumental in producing the resulting narratives. But these patterns never appear altogether formulaic, rigid, or otherwise determined; and the great marvel must be at the variety of forms and genres, and not the similarity of features and the recurrence of sequences. Each myth must therefore be taken as witness to itself alone, and not as a partial instance of a larger species or some subset of an abstract model. To proceed otherwise is to obscure the uniqueness of the phenomena at hand, or overlook the concrete actuality of rabbinic myths and the creative combination of components over the centuries.

The final consideration bears on the issue of *hierarchy*, and allows us to emphasize that God is the 'victor' of all battles—despite the great diversity of myths of combat that are found and despite the multiplicity of means and agents that are used. Seen in this way, the following qualification of myth is in order: the rabbinic myths of combat against the sea remain monotheistic and limited throughout. For though there is an evident drama in the combats, and even a striking personification of the antagonistic serpents and of God Himself, these battles are no true theomachy against divine powers prior to acts of creation, but ultimately punishments enacted against rebellious, resistant, or impudent creatures *after* the creation. This is the case even though a comparative analysis shows traces of older mythic themes in the Midrash, in which the primordial waters are dangerous foes, and in various places God appears to be hesitant if not even somewhat compromised (if only temporarily) in His acts of punitive power. Hence the almighty supremacy of YHWH over His creatures accounts for the often droll dramas that result—

as when the sea dragon whines or flees or stinks and is destroyed; or when God punishes it by castration or kicking or stuffing it into some water-bag. Thus the myth has its limits: creatures remain creatures, and are ultimately subservient to the supremacy of their Creator. For if there is an archetypal sin enacted by the sea monster, it lies in its pride or disobedience of God—these being acts of rebellion that constitute the negative pole of Judaism and its values. It is thus hardly surprising that the body of Leviathan provides food for the righteous, since they are exemplary creatures on the earth—at once obedient, humble, and submissive to God and His word. In this sense, the myth of the rebellion and punishment of the monster reinforces the religious virtues of Judaism, and for all its drollery also serves such high-minded ends.

III. Liturgical Tradition and New Creations

The liturgical poetry (*piyyuṭ*) of late classical Judaism complements and extends our earlier discussions of mythic themes and traditions, drawing upon earlier or contemporary midrashic topics and representing them in new forms and combinations.[56] In the following summation of evidence, most examples will be taken from the major poets of the later Roman and early Byzantine period in the Land of Israel (roughly from about the fourth to seventh centuries CE)[57]—Yose ben Yose; R. Yannai; and R. Eleazar bi Rabbi Kallir, though several other known authors or anonymous compositions shall be noted.[58]

The importance of this corpus of poetic materials cannot be sufficiently stressed for the present discussion—not only because it attests to the recitation of mythic topics at regular stations during the synagogue liturgy, but because the various citations or allusions are presented as thematic features in their own right—without the addition of biblical proof-texts or exegetical qualifiers (like *ʾilmaleiʾ* or *kivyakhol*) that might appear to mediate or soften the content. At most, one will note the occasional use of phrases that annotate some of the more opaque statements; but the evident intent of the poet here is to transmit meaning, not explain it away (and he actually

56 The midrashic presuppositions and allusions are fully evident in the notes to the editions listed in n. 58. In some instances, the liturgical form gives precious evidence of the early order of some midrashic collections; see Menahem Zulai, 'Piyyuṭ Qadmon veha-Petiḥot de-ʾEicha Rabbati', *Tarbiz*, 16 (1945), 190–5. The relationship between the literary forms of Midrash and Piyyuṭ were presented and analysed in the pioneering study of Aharon Mirsky, *Maḥtzavtan shel Tzurot ha-Piyyuṭ* (Tel Aviv: Schocken, 1968). But see already Zeev Jabetz, 'Ha-Piyyuṭim ha-Rishonim', in Simon Eppenstein *et al.* (edd.), *Sefer Le-David Tzvi* (*Festschrift zum siebigsten Geburtstage David Hoffmanns*) (Berlin: Lamm, 1914), 69–71.

57 For a reconsideration of the social, historical, and literary evidence, see Yosef Yahalom, *Piyyuṭ U-Metziʾut Be-Shalḥei Ha-Zeman He-ʿAtiq* (Tel Aviv: Hakibbutz Hameuchad, 1999).

58 Note the following editions: *Piyyuṭei Yosi ben Yosi*, ed. Aharon Mirsky (2nd edn.; Jerusalem: Mosad Bialik, 1991) (=*Yosi*); *Maḥazor Piyyuṭei Rabbi Yannai La-Torah Vela-Moʿadim*, ed. Zvi M. Rabinovitz (Jerusalem: Mosad Bialik, 1985), i–ii (=*Yannai*).

provides a precious and unexpected source of cultural commentary on these midrashic units).[59] Accordingly, just as there is a demonstrable continuity and creativity in the transmission of midrashic myths over the centuries, there is also an ongoing creativity and diffusion of the mythic material in the liturgical poems. The notable differences are as follows: the mythic material occurs in greater depth and diversity in the Midrash; but their occurrence in Piyyuṭ reflects a more popular base and life-setting. Hence, if some of the mythic topics found in the Midrash reflect actual sermons in the ancient synagogues,[60] and not just scholarly ideas or speculations in the academy, the liturgical poetry was sung by precentors during public prayer and intimately integrated into it.[61] This notwithstanding, it remains a question just how much of the arcane content or allusive references of these prayers the average congregant could grasp.

Following the format used earlier, three time periods shall be specified: (*a*) *Urzeit*; (*b*) *Heilsgeschichte*; and (*c*) *Endzeit*. We first note mythic components found in (1) 'fragmentary citations or references'; and after that (2) 'more extensive patterns or poetic creations' shall be presented.

1. Fragmentary Uses. (*a*) *Urzeit*: In liturgical cycles on the events of creation, Yose speaks of God's banishment (*geirash*) of the sea into pools,[62] thus alluding to the rebuke of the swarming waters; and he also indicates their containment by the word *bariaḥ*,[63] which suggests that the 'slant serpent' (*naḥash bariaḥ*) of Isa. 27: 1 was interpreted as a lock or bolt (*bariaḥ*) that kept the waters in check.[64] In a similar (but anonymous) cycle, the waters 'flee' at the roar of God;[65] but the subsequent phrase *ʿad loʾ yabriaḥ ʿal beriḥei metzulah* ('until he (Leviathan) was set over the bolts of the deep') suggests that the serpent was the lock or barrier over the nether waters,[66] as stated elsewhere in midrashic tradition.[67] Another poem complements this role of the serpent, when it parallels the term *bariaḥ* with the phrase *sagur beʿad tehom* ('closed around Tehom').[68] But considerably more complex is the rendition of Yannai, who says that on the fifth day God created *naḥash*

[59] Cf. below, in connection with the redemption of the *Shekhinah*.

[60] See above, pp. 153 f., 194 f.

[61] On various considerations, see Ezra Fleisher, "Iyyunim be-Vaʿayat Tafqidam ha-Liturgi shel Sugei ha-Piyyuṭ ha-Qadum', *Tarbiz*, 40 (1970–1), 41–63; and also Shulamit Elitzur, 'Qahal Ha-Mitpallelim Veha-Qedushtaʾ Ha-Qedumah', in Sh. Elitzur *et al.* (edd.), *Keneset ʿEzra: Sifrut Ve-Ḥayyim Be-Vait Ha-Keneset; Meḥqarim Muqdashim Le-ʿEzra Fleisher* (Jerusalem: Magnes Press, 1996), 171–90. The poets apparently learned from one another, and thus transmitted certain literary figures and content into different settings; cf. the intriguing evidence collected by eadem, 'Midrash u-Fesuqo be-Reʾi ha-Payṭanut', *Sinai*, 89 (1986–7), 99–109.

[62] *Yose*, p. 130, l. 21. The banishment is usually indicating by the language of flight, referring to Ps. 104: 7 (*Genesis Rabba* 5. 1; also *Tanḥuma, Ḥayyei Sarah* 3).

[63] Ibid. [64] For this usage, cf. Deut. 3: 5.

[65] See *ʾAz Be-ʾEin Kol*, ed. Yosef Yahalom (Jerusalem: Magnes Press, 1997), p. 70, l. 52 (for the midrashic parallels, see n. 62). [66] Ibid. 71, l. 64. [67] *Pirkei de-Rabbi Eliezer* 9.

[68] See *ʾAz Be-ʾEin Kol*, appendix, p. 164, ll. 115 f.; cf. p. 80, l. 161.

bariaḥ lebabo / ʿal mei tehomot [hi]rkibo sebibo;[69] for here the first clause seems to indicate that 'the serpent's heart was wily (or misleading)', thereby suggesting that this creature was the deceitful snake (*naḥash*) in the Garden of Eden, whereas the second clause states that 'it was set over the deep waters roundabout'. The notion that the serpent was like a plug over the deep is also found in midrashic sources.[70]

(*b*) *Heilsgeschichte*: (i) In a clear allusion to the theme of God's participation in Israelite history, Yannai first refers to divine suffering, when he says 'In all our sufferings You also suffered' (*bekhol tzaroteinu lekha tzarah*);[71] and then goes on to spell out clearly how God participated in the travail in Egypt: '(When we were) overworked with bricks You saw us (in) time / and showed us a brick underneath Your feet' (*perukhim bi-lebeinim lanu ʿeit raʾita / taḥat ragleykha lebeinah horʾeita*).[72] Clearly these lines refer to the midrashic traditions based on Exod. 24: 10,[73] which reinterpret the *libnat ha-sapir* (or 'pavement of sapphire') under the divine throne as a sign in heaven that God was participating in Israel's travail of brickwork. And further, the bi-colon here makes explicit what the rabbis often kept implicit or allusive; and it also presents the act of divine sympathy as a historical fact, not as mythic exegesis. One will further observe that the poet has omitted the recurrent particle *ke-* (like; as) in the biblical lemma, thereby eliminating any sense of similitude or qualification from the scriptural source and its rabbinic reformulations.

(ii) In other instances, Yannai refers to the mythic motif of God abandoning His Temple and accompanying Israel into its Babylonian exile: 'I sent (*shillaḥti*)' the people 'from before Me / and it was because of them I was sent (*shullaḥti*) to Babylon and accompanied (*livviti*) their exile'.[74] The pointed verbal reciprocity that opens the line dramatizes the interconnectedness between God's act of punishment and His ongoing presence; a comparable instance is found in another place, which says: 'He banished you (*ʾetkhem yigaresh*) and was banished with you (*ve-ʾitkhem yi[tga]resh*)'.[75] In the latter citation, the key verb *garash* (banish) is otherwise unattested with this theme;[76] whereas the verb *shillaḥ* (send) is commonly used with regard to the *Shekhinah* accompanying Israel into the Babylonian exile.[77] On the other hand, Yannai's use of the verb *livvah* (accompany) may actually derive from

[69] *Yannai*, i. 86, ll. 26 f.

[70] See *Pesikta Rabbati* 194b, cited above (p. 126).

[71] *Yannai*, i. 266, l. 32.

[72] Ibid. 267, l. 37.

[73] See *Mekhilta de-Rabbi Ishmael, Boʾ* 14, and the other sources discussed above, pp. 136–8.

[74] *Yannai*, ii. 324, ll. 22 f. The ten-staged exit of the Shekhinah from the Temple is elaborately portrayed by Kallir in a poems for the fast day of Tishaʿ be-ʾAb; see in Ezra Fleisher, 'Qompozitziyot Qaliriyot le-Tishaʿ be-ʾAv', *HUCA* 45 (1974), 19–21 (Hebrew pagination).

[75] This new fragment of Yannai's poem on *seder* 52 (Exod. 11: 10) was published by Shalom Spiegel, *ʾAbot Ha-Piyyuṭ*, ed. Menahem Schmelzer (new York: The Jewish Theological Seminary of America, 1997), 67 (v. 2).

[76] Ibid. 308. However, the phrase *yigaresh ʾetkhem* is used for Pharaoh's banishment of the Israelites in Exod. 11: 1.

[77] See above, p. 139.

Yose, who has his speaker say that God 'accompanied me (*ve-nilvah li*) into exile'.[78] His use of this term for this theme is innovative, and without any known biblical or midrashic precedent. A more ornate strategy is used by Kallir when he offers a successive chain of verbs for the various exiles of the nation—complementing the standard verb *galu* ('they were exiled') of the *Mekhilta de-Rabbi Ishmael, Boʾ* 14 (upon which the poem is based) with *hubeʾu* ('they were brought'), *naʿu* ('they wandered'), and *nadu* ('they wandered'); but retaining the verbs for the *Shekhinah's* banishment found in his rabbinic source, undoubtedly because these terms derived from proof-texts.[79]

(iii) The old mythic topic of God's mighty arm in history also recurs in Yannai's work; and what is particularly striking is the way it intensifies ancient biblical phraseology. For example, the prophetic statement in Isa. 63: 9, which says that God 'made His glorious arm march at the right hand of Moses' (*ha-molikh liymin Moshe zeroʿa tifʾarto*), hovers between metaphor and myth, though it leaves the impression that this divine hand is a hypostatic reality and not a mere figure of speech.[80] Withal, any ambiguity on this score is removed by the liturgical line which says that God gave his religious ordinances 'to the one (Moses) who leads on (his) right (*ʾel molikh liymin*);[81] (and) You joined Your right arm to his right arm (*yeminakh liymino ḥibbarta*)'.[82] The mythic concreteness of this passage is notably sharpened by the epexegetical addition, which boldly aligns and even joins the arm of God to the arm of Moses.[83] Through such an image, myth and history dramatically fuse.

(iv) This bold fusion is also felt in presentations of God's presence in His Shrine. For as in several striking midrashic statements,[84] we also have liturgical depictions of the inner sanctum as a place of erotic and physical intimacy. Thus, by joining the imagery of royal throne to that of the nuptial tryst and bower (in Songs 1: 13, 16), Yannai has God indicate His advent to His sanctuary with the following words to Israel: 'I Have come to My garden, O My sister . . . here I shall s[it upon] My throne / and here I shall lie upon My bed (*u-foh ʾalin ʿal ʿarsi*)'.[85] The deft exegetical manoeuvres of earlier rabbinic

[78] *Yose*, p. 112, l. 19.

[79] The poem is the extensive *Be-ʿEser Makkot* recited on Passover; the pertinent section may be found in *Maḥazor le-Regalim: Pesaḥ*, ed. Jonah Fraenkel (Jerusalem: Koren, 1993), 123; the compositional variety was noted by Menahem Schmelzer, 'Some Examples of Poetic Reformulations of Biblical and Midrashic Passages in Liturgy and Piyyut', in Bezalel Safran and Eliyahu Safran (edd.), *Porat Yosef: Studies Presented to Rabbi Dr. Joseph Safran* (Hoboken, NJ: Ktav: 1992), 222.

[80] See above, p. 48.

[81] Presumably as God's right-hand man; the reworking is opaque.

[82] *Yannai*, i. 353, l. 7.

[83] The poem is an early attestation of this mythic reworking; for the topic is otherwise only attested in the late *Exod. Rabba* 21. 6. Here the teacher glosses Isa. 63: 12 with the remark that God 'placed his right hand on Moses'.

[84] See above, pp. 174–7.

[85] *Yannai*, ii. 55–6, ll. 44–5.

tradition are bypassed here, and one is left with a concrete mythic statement by God. Indeed, the listener would now have to make a new effort to transform this remark into a metaphor. Yannai offers no apology, and does not give even the slightest qualification for his words.

(*c*) *Endzeit*: As noted, one of the great events in the end-time was to be a battle against Leviathan; and this topic is mentioned by Yose,[86] and others.[87] In these snippets the references are brief and allusive, such that the drama of battle and the awesome nature of the dramatis personae lose much of their mythic force. This feature is restored in the longer versions presented below.

2. Extensive Units. (*a*) *Urzeit*: The larger cycles of the days of creation that appear as part of the epic prologues to the priestly *ʿAbodah* (or sacrifice-) service recited in the Yom Kippur liturgy, do not develop the mythic themes of strife with the sea or related matters, and merely mention them as brief topics and traditions.[88] By contrast, certain themes in sacred history and in the end-time are more fully developed from midrashic sources.

(*b*) *Heilsgeschichte*: Particularly noteworthy is R. Eleazar bi Rabbi Kallir's use of the series of examples dealing with the participation of the Shekhinah in the redemptions of Israel found in *Mekhilta de-Rabbi Ishmael, Boʾ* 14 and *Tanḥuma, Aḥarei Mot* 12, among other places.[89] The poetic rendition is striking both for its inclusiveness, but also for the various epexegetical comments that clarify the opaque teachings and transmit them as historical events. Thus, the mythic content is not justified—but simply recited in recollection of God's past acts of salvation, and in the hope that this great beneficence will again be repeated. The liturgical occasion for the prayer-poem is the sixth day of the festival of Tabernacles, called Hoshana Rabba (The Great Hosanna or Salvation), when the worshippers circumambulate the synagogue six times. In the processional, the precentor exclaims:[90]

As You saved the mighty (Israel) from Lud (Egypt) with Yourself (*ʿimmakh*) / when You went for to save Your people (*ʿammakh*) So save now!
As You saved a nation and (its) God / (terms) explicated as (*derushim*) God's salvation So save now!
As You saved the great hosts (of Israel) / and with them (*ʿimmam*) the angelic hosts So save now!
As You saved the innocents from the house of bondage / O Gracious One, as You saved those enslaved with manual labour So save now!
As You saved the drowning by splitting the depths / (and) made Your Glory passed through with them (*ʿimmam*) So save now!

[86] *Yose*, pp. 131–2, ll. 27, 32 (*ʾAzkir Geburot*).
[87] *ʾAz Be-ʾEin Kol*, p. 80, ll. 158–64, and appendix, pp. 164–5, ll. 115–20.
[88] See the texts referred to above, nn. 62–3, 65–6, 68.
[89] See the translations and detailed discussions, pp. 134–6, 138–42, 151–4.
[90] See the text printed in *Maḥazor Sukkot, Shemini ʿAtzeret, ve-Simḥat Torah*, ed. Daniel Goldschmidt and completed by Jonah Fraenkel (Jerusalem: Koren, 1981), 181.

As You saved the plant (Israel) which sang 'And He saved' (*va-yoshaʿ*) /[91] (and) her deliverer (God) is marked (in Scripture by the reading) 'And He was saved' (*va-yivvashaʿ*)[92] So save now!
As You saved (Israel) proclaiming 'I took you out' (*ve-hotzeʾti ʾetkhem*) / (but) pronounced 'I was taken out with you' (*ve-hutzeiʾti ʾitkhem*)[93] So save now!
As You saved those circling the altar /[94] laden with willows to surround the altar So save now!
As You saved the Ark with wonders when wrongly taken /[95] causing grief to Philistia with (God's) Wrath,[96] and it was saved So save now!
As You saved the congregation whom You sent (*shillaḥta*) to Babylon / (and) for their sake O Merciful One You were sent (*shullaḥta*) there[97] So save now!
As You saved the captive (*shebut*) tribes of Jacob / Return You (with them) and restore the captive (*tashub ve-tashib shebut*) tents of Jacob And save now!
ʾanaʾ veho, Save now (*hoshiʿah naʾ*)!

This remarkable composition is replete with many midrashic allusions an references, embedded within the poem and presented as part of God's historical acts of salvation (beginning in Egypt and ending with a future restoration from exile). Particularly striking is the theological ballast between the first and second lines of each couplet: the first being a citation of or reference to a scriptural passage, the second providing its midrashic transformation (often with a clarifying comment) and focusing on God's participation in the salvations of Israel. The repetition of the phrase 'with You' (*ʿimmakh*; *ʾitkhem*),[98] underscores the correlation between the divine and human realms. Indeed, for R. Eleazar Kallir, history is a manifestation of divine salvation in a twofold sense; and it is just this fact that gives him solace and hope.

The essence of this mythic theology is climactically stated at the end of the prayer, with the poet's allusion to a teaching of R. Judah found in the Mishnah (*M. Sukkah* IV. 5). According to this source, the following practice was performed in the Temple during the festival of Tabernacles: 'Each day (the people) would go around the altar once, saying, "Please, O Lord (*ʾanaʾ YHWH*), save us! Please, O Lord, let us prosper!"[99] (But) Rabbi Judah said, "I and Ho (*ʾani va-ho*), save us!"' That is, the sage pronounced the petition *ʾanaʾ* plus the divine Name YHWH (or some abbreviation thereof) in such a

[91] Citing Exod. 14: 30, but referring to the Song of the Sea.

[92] This reading is made possible by the orthography *vywšʿ*. The reference to God's own salvation as marked (*metzuyenet*), has a second allusion to Israel being special to, or distinguished by, God.

[93] Citing Exod. 20: 1; the teaching repoints the orthography *vhwtzʾty ʾtkm*.

[94] Referring to Temple times (see *M. Sukkah* 5. 5).

[95] The reference is apparently to the taking of the Ark by the Philistine (1 Sam. 4: 11 ff.); the sinful misappropriation is rendered by *ke-hufshaʿ* (referring to the transgression); the word plays on 'As You saved', *ke-hoshaʿta*.

[96] The punishment of *ḥaron* (wrath) is retribution for taking the *ʾaron* (Ark)—measure for measure.

[97] i.e. the *Shekhinah* (called Merciful One) was sent by God.

[98] Note also *ʿimmam*, 'with them', in the fifth stanza.

[99] Ps. 118: 25.

way as to sound like a petition to God to save the human speaker (the Hebrew petition being a calque of the Aramaic pronoun 'I') and Himself (*ho* sounding like the Hebrew pronoun *hu*ʾ, 'He')[100]—a bold notion in itself, but one that supports and confirms R. Eleazar's venerable midrashic theology. Just as the salvation of God and Israel were conjoined in the past, so he now (following his understanding of R. Judah's words) invokes this conjunction as a warrant for future hope. Divine myth and Israelite history thus comprise one interfused reality, and are remembered and invoked together.

(*c*) *Endzeit*: We conclude this review of mythic elements in ancient Jewish liturgy poetry with the final part of a long epic poem on the battle between Leviathan and Behemoth composed by R. Eleazar Kallir.[101] The *mise en scène* is the Garden of Eden, where groups of the righteous are gathered under the tree of life, to partake of the flesh of Leviathan.[102] The great combat itself is framed by praises of God that play midrashically on the letters *ʿ-l-m-w-t* (ll. 12–15) and *ʿ-l-m-y-m* (ll. 147–56)—thereby ascribing to Him the power to lead the righteous 'beyond death', and give them 'two worlds' and 'vigour'; as well as such epithets as 'Eternal One', 'Rock of Ages', and Creator of the 'Two Worlds' with the letters of His Name. The description of the monster and the battle draws principally from Job 41, with a dozen and a half allusions or references to its terminology,[103] incorporated into extended rhyming units. All the details known from rabbinic sources, and many others, are drawn out and embellished, bringing to the ear of the worshipper an account of the fabulous fight and slaughter. In the end, all glory goes to God, whose faithful fulfilment of this event betokens trust and hope in the messianic era to come.

What impresses the reader is the biblicism of the language, as it creatively weaves midrashic topics into a self-sustaining myth of the final days. No scriptural verses are directly cited, such that one might perceive a gap between this rabbinic epic and its ancient source; and there is no simile or suggestion that the images portrayed are in any sense fictions or figments of the imagination. Rather, the whole account is replete with the concrete verisimilitude of mythic discourse. The suggestion that one must suspend

[100] This is also the view of Rabbeinu Hai Gaon (see *ʾOtzar Ha-Geʾonim*, ed. B. M. Lewin (Jerusalem, 1934), vi. 2, p. 66); *Tosafot* to *BT Sukkah* 45a, s.v. *ʾani vaho*); and cf. also *Ṭur, ʾOraḥ Ḥayyim, Hilkhot Lulav*, no. 660.

[101] For a critical edition and annotation, see Jefim Schirmann, *The Battle Between Behemoth and Leviathan According to an Ancient Hebrew Piyyuṭ* (The Israel Academy of Sciences and Humanities; Jerusalem: Sivan Press, 1970), iv. 327–69 (text: pp. 350–9; 156 lines). The unit is part of the *silluq* called *Va-Yikhon ʿOlam*.

[102] As noted earlier, this topic frames *BT Baba Batra* 74b–75a; cf. also *Songs Rabba* on Songs 6: 8.

[103] The skein of verses is redeployed for dramatic effect (thus: Job 41: 22, 23, 7, 12, 24, 10, 6, 19, 20, 17, 14, 8, 7, 12).

belief or engage in it does not arise. As with all powerful myths, this great battle has the quality of a 'real presence' conveying narrative truth. The liturgical setting adds to this aura, even as the celebration of God's power confirms its authority as a religious teaching for the people, who shall bless 'the Faithful One (*ha-ne'eman*) / for all that He planned (*zimman*) / is fixed for the end of time (*heqitzo le-qeitz u-zeman*)'.

B. MYTH AND LANGUAGE[104]

The diverse phenomena of rabbinic myth typically occur on two tiers of language: Scripture (meaning the Hebrew Bible) and Exegesis (meaning Midrash). These tiers are generically distinct but culturally bound, resulting in modes of scriptural citation and midrashic comment. The citation is rarely more than a phrase; or, if more is given, this serves to set up or isolate certain operative words of mythic significance. Correspondingly, the comment may be long or short, depending upon circumstances and need; and it may precede the citation or follow it with varying effect. Whether named or anonymous, the comment presents itself as an event of rabbinic culture, and part of its reception or revision of the meaning of Hebrew Scripture—the canonical writings of ancient Israel.

The boundedness of these tiers of language are pertinent for a consideration of the relationship of Scripture to Myth or Myth to Scripture. By virtue of their typical collocation, one is led to perceive Scripture (specifically, the pertinent parts cited) as containing the myths in various condensed or opaque forms, and to perceive the myths as restating or reformulating meanings of Scripture so that it will be directly and dramatically understood. Hence, each myth occurs twice: once in Scripture, and then again in the commentary. Such a doubling of the myth in its implicit and explicit forms presents the various myths as located within Scripture. Thus, like Midrash generally, the sage revoices the language of Scripture; and like the midrashic collections overall, the mythic statement is not diminished by being included among other comments.

This said, it is also commonly the case that these two tiers of language are so dramatically different, and the content of the commentaries so completely distinct from the apparent plain sense of their scriptural source, that one may conclude that the rabbinic myths are quite independent feats of the imagination and only secondarily attached to Scripture. Indeed, the content of the myths and mythic theology is often so counter-intuitive from what one might suppose a given passage to say as to dispel any claim that these myths

[104] In using this rubric, I deliberately allude to Ernst Cassirer's seminal study, *Sprache und Mythos* (Studien der Bibliothek Warburg, 6; 1925); trans. Susanne Langer as *Language and Myth* (New York: Harper & Brothers, 1946). I would like to regard my considerations as a continuation of Cassirer's great project, hereby adding the exegetical factor to the discussion.

are 'scriptural' or made from Scripture in the first place. Rather, these myths are remade with Scripture and from its linguistic resources, and mould the imagination into new authoritative forms—although once these new attachments are made and prove compelling, similar myths are then often found and made from similar scriptural sources. The mythic process is thus both dialectical and composite; and thanks to the complex exegetical attachments of the myths to the language of Scripture, diverse oral traditions and theological intuitions surface as rabbinic teachings and texts. In the fractured interstices of the two tiers, one can thus sometimes sense living myth before its momentous exegetical rebirth and subordination to Scripture.

I. Myth and Scriptural Exegesis

Since interpretation is a crucial and critical feature of the creation and justification of myth in ancient rabbinic culture, and since Scripture is given as its authoritative source, it behoves us to provide a review of typical ways that this linguistic attachment is marked.

1. 'Written' Scripture; New Emphasis. On certain occasions where the written tradition is retained and pronounced, but a new emphasis results in new mythic content, the teaching appears with the statement: 'Were not (*'ilmalei'*) Scripture (variant: the Word or Matter) written (*katub*) thus, it would not be possible to say it'. In once such instance, adduced earlier, the scriptural phrase 'The nation that You Yourself redeemed (*padita lakh*)' (2 Sam. 7: 23) was read to say 'that You redeemed Yourself'; that is, the original objective genitive was construed as a subjective genitive, thereby radically transforming the sense but nothing else in Scripture.[105] Another notable usage also pivots on a genitival construction, but now boldly transforms the designation of Moses as 'a man of God (*'ish ha-'elohim*)' (Deut. 33: 1) into a re-presentation of him into nothing less than the 'husband (man) of God (bride)'.[106] As earlier, not a jot or tittle in Scripture is touched; however, nothing remains the same. The hint of the divinity of Moses latent in this attribute of divine servitude provides the prism for a connubial myth whose origins and meaning for ancient Judaism are largely lost; and one can only wonder how much more lies beneath the surface of Scripture, unremarked by the sages.[107]

The same exegetical phenomenon without a marked phrase also occurs. Examples of this range from novel parsings of a phrase[108] to new emphases

[105] *Mekhilta de-Rabbi Ishmael, Bo'* 14; see above, pp. 140–1.

[106] *BT Megillah* 31a.

[107] For the traditions that Moses' investiture in garments of light designates him as a god and king, see Wayne Meeks, 'Moses as God and King', in J. Neusner (ed.), *Religions in Antiquity: Essays in Honor of E. R. Goodenough* (Leiden: E. J. Brill, 1968), 354–71.

[108] Cf. the transformation of Deut. 33: 27 in *BT Ḥagigah* 12b, discussed above, p. 99.

on single words or elements.[109] These are tips of myths, whose topics extend far beyond the Scriptures they cite.

2. 'Written' Scripture; Nothing Else. On certain occasions when the teacher (or editor) wishes to highlight the particular character of the language of Scripture that makes for the myth, and to emphasize that precisely this construction occurs, and no other, so that the new meaning based upon it (which now includes or indicates God) cannot lightly be dismissed as an egregious or tendentious rewriting of the biblical text, the comment is preceded by some version of the formula: '*x* (a hypothetical variant of Scripture) is not written (*ketib*) here;[110] (but) rather *y* (Scripture as received)'. Typical is the teacher's emphasis that in Jer. 9: 17 God does not bid the prophet to call the keeners to wail 'over them' (Israel) and 'their eyes' to shed tears; but rather explicitly refers to 'us' and 'our eyes' and 'our eyelids', such that the exegetical conclusion to be drawn is that these women are in no wise merely asked to wail over the nation alone, but over God as well: 'Me and them (*didi ve-didhon*)'—for He is in great sorrow and aggrieved by the people's recurrent sins, and by the time of the exile of Judah without any 'strength' to mourn, and in need of consolation Himself.[111] The unexpected or received formulation of Scripture is thus converted into inescapable myth, presented as the primary intention and plain sense of the divine directive. Only the elaboration belongs to the sage.

The same exegetical phenomenon without a marked phrase also occurs. Examples also involve myths of divine involvement, and derive from the perception that apparently peculiar grammatical features (like prepositions) encode mythic meanings of a quite different sort (like genitives or direct objects).[112]

3. 'Written' Scripture; New Vocalization. On certain occasions when the written orthography may yield a new mythic meaning, and the teacher wants to stress that he has not departed from written Scripture but revealed a deeper sense, the phrase 'it is written (*ketib*)' precedes the letters that are then reread (against the plain sense). Typical is the transformation of the the letters *v-y-w-š-ʿ* in Exod. 14: 30; for though traditionally pronounced *va-yoshaʿ* ('He (God) saved' Israel), they serve to support the midrashic

[109] In diverse instances, the preposition *ʿal* in Jer. 25: 30 shifts from 'against' to 'on behalf of' in *BT Ber.* 3b (see above, p. 162); the particle *ʾet* in Deut. 30: 3 shifts from a nonce element marking the accusative to the proposition 'with' in *Mekhilta de-Rabbi Ishmael, Boʾ* 14 (above, p. 139).

[110] A variant of *kaʾn* ('here') is *ken* ('truly').

[111] *Pesikta de-Rav Kahana* 15. 4; the teacher is Resh Lakish.

[112] For example, the preposition *le-* ('to') in Zech. 9: 1 ('For the eye of every man turns to YHWH (*le-YHWH*)') was construed in a genetival sense ('For YHWH has a human eye') in *Lam. Rabba* (Buber edn., p. 88) probably because just this formulation was written, and not the more expected form *ʾel* (which would have removed all ambiguity).

recitation of them as *va-yivvasha*ʿ ('He (God) was saved' with Israel). Clearly here the myth precedes the exegetical reworking.[113] Similarly, the pre-existence of the myth of the exile of the *Shekhinah* conditions the exegetical preference for the Masoretic written text (*ketib*) in Micah 4: 10 over the one as read (*qerė*); for then the letters *v-š-k-n-t-y* could be used instead of *v-š-k-n-t*, and the traditional vocalization and meaning ('For you (Israel) shall now leave the city and dwell (*ve-shakhant*) in the field') could be midrashically read as speaking of a double exile of Israel with the divine presence ('For you (Israel) shall now leave the city and My *Shekhinah* (*ve-Shekhinati*; shall be) in the field').[114]

The same exegetical phenomenon without a marked phrase also occurs. Typical cases involve the explicit use of the Masoretic *qere* (often written into the citation of the passage), and the implicit revocalization of the *ketib* (that must be presumed for the citation to make midrashic sense).[115]

4. Scripture Remains; Amphiboly Revises. In certain cases the exegesis exploits a perceived paronomasia or ambiguity; and this is most striking and dramatic when the word-play comes to light through the midrashic process, and reveals a striking homograph where the term(s) involved serves different semantic registers or even linguistic domains. A striking and instructive instance occurs in 1 Sam. 2: 27, where the scriptural phrase *galoh galiti* clearly means 'I (God) revealed (Myself to your ancestors)' in Egypt, but the midrashic correlate construes these very words to say that 'I (God) exiled Myself' with you in the land of Egypt—a transformation that turns an act of divine self-revelation into a phenomenon of exilic presence and immanence.[116] One may agree that this reading is counter-intuitive, and shows that certain theological ideas or presentiments may precondition the exegetical imagination, and embolden it to discover a radical or paradoxical encoding of divine reality within the consonants of Scripture.

Just as bold is the perception that the Aramaic word *yamin* ('days') in Dan. 12: 13 is exegetically linked to the Hebrew word *yamin* ('right hand') in Lam. 2: 3, such that the reference to the fulfilment of the days of human exile is correlated with the arm that the Lord bound behind him on the occasion of the doom and destruction of Jerusalem (Lam. 2: 3). At that time, according

[113] *Tanḥuma, Aḥarei*, 12.

[114] *Midrash Psalms* 11. 3 (see above, pp. 157–9). In actuality, there is no grammatical difference between the *qere* and *ketib*; for the later is an archaic or Aramaicizing (2nd-person fem. sing.) form of the verb.

[115] For the first case, the traditional reading of Isa. 63: 9 (*lo*; 'He has' sorrow) serves the sage's purpose; for the second, the reading of Isa. 43: 14 as 'For your sake I (God) was sent (*shullaḥti*) to Babylon' (and not MT 'I sent (*shillaḥti*)') must be presumed, since the explicit context of the citation deals with the exile of the *Shekhinah* together with the people.

[116] Ibid. For the issue of revelation and the Holy Spirit outside the Land of Israel, see W. D. Davies, *Jewish and Pauline Studies* (Philadelphia: Fortress Press, 1984), 72–83 ('Reflections on the Spirit in the Mekilta: A Suggestion').

to the Midrash, God swore not to forget His arm; and the people Israel made a similar oath after it went into exile.[117] Hence the suffering of Israel and of God are mythically joined. A similar correlation is proclaimed regarding the redemption to come, since the end of days will be the end of the bondage of God's own arm. Manifestly, this myth is as mysterious as it is bold; but it is striking that neither the mystery nor the boldness is qualified or compromised. Rather, the two linguistic registers starkly link God and Israel in servitude, and connect their relationship in the final days to come.[118] God's redemption of His own arm is bound to the redemption of the nation in history, but is also its active force. Theological relation is figured as a correlation, and the divine myth as a historical phenomenon.

The two tiers of Scripture and Midrash thus intertwine in a variety of ways, and are marked by reciprocal loops of authority and authorization. For the sages, the presence of Scripture both assures and asserts the presence of myth.

II. Myth and Metaphor

In an earlier discussion it was proposed that one way to assess whether a given figure was a myth or a metaphor was to consider whether related elements occurred in the same context and whether they were in any way sequentially related or gave any other signs of being features of a concrete action.[119] Thus if a prophet proclaims that God will come in a fury, and refers to His advent upon a cloud or with blazing nostrils, the images could simply be metaphoric figures or frozen conventions when depicted separately. However, if the prophet adds to the portrayal of the nostrils something about God's eyes and hands and feet, and presents them as part of a manifestation that strikes terror in those who behold it, then there is at least the presumption of myth if not its concrete actuality. For myths draw no trailers that flag their existence, beyond what may be adduced by pointing to cultural conventions (both external and internal) and the evidence itself. Myths and metaphors oscillate in the eye of the beholder and over time, emerging or receding according to intellectual temperament and sensibility. Persons, periods, and cultures are all marked by these shifts. The following comments attempt to catch this type of movement in the exegetical act, as it were, and will propose several criteria as an analytic tool. In this way it may be possible to draw some inchoate aspects of rabbinic myth and mythmaking into the open, and to provide a heuristic model for their consideration.

The criteria may be formulated as follows: the language of biblical metaphor is transformed into rabbinic myth through the specification or spotlighting of a specific textual element (especially a noun or verb); that element is treated in terms of a real and concrete action or feeling involving God

[117] *Pesikta de-Rav Kahana* 17. 5.

[118] Ibid., also the preceding teachings in the Midrash.

[119] Above, pp. 81 f.

(primarily, directly or indirectly); and that deed or quality is portrayed as a feature of a dramatic event or narrative. The manner of specification, transformation, and dramatization varies in relation to the text and exegetical technique involved. Typically, the metaphor is a phrase isolated from a larger whole; and the mythic rereading of it is one feature of a larger drama. Among the topics considered above, the following examples are exemplary.

1. A Word: Over-determined. In Jer. 25: 30, the prophet delivers a divine proclamation of imminent doom: 'YHWH will roar (*yishʾag*) from on high, He gives voice from His holy dwelling; He shall surely roar (*shaʾog yishʾag*) against (*ʿal*) His land . . .'. The oracle is dominated by the verb *shaʾag* (roar), and its threefold repetition intensifies the projected advent of wrath. The image conveys a tumultuous uproar to come, through a verbal figure of ferocity and rapine. A similar trope occurs at the outset of Amos's prophecies and with the very same terms (Amos 1: 2), though without the repetition of *shaʾag* and thus without the climactic intensity of Jeremiah's usage. To be sure, the mythic overtones of a storm-god's atmospheric advent rumble in the background;[120] but the figure conveys an ominous scene through the rhetoric of redundant synonyms, not a series of separate actions.

However, in the reuse of this verse in *BT Berakhot* 3b it is precisely the verbal repetitions that underlie the interpretation that God groans in sorrow over His destroyed Temple during each of the three watches of the night.[121] The actions are specific and sequential, and thus convey a divine drama enacted nightly; a recollection of sorrow that mourns from on high the ravaged site of sacrifices below. In the transformation of the older metaphoric image into a dramatic myth, the verb *shaʾag* now uncharacteristically conveys a lament and the preposition *ʿal* binds it to the object of elegy 'for' which God mourns. The thematic inversion of the metaphor by the myth is no less remarkable.

2. A Phrase: Redetermined. In Lam. 2: 3, the elegist speaks of God's wrath against Israel and how 'He withdrew His right hand from before (*mipnei*) the enemy' and consumed the nation with His fiery fury. These words portray God's use of the enemy as the rod of His anger, when He simultaneously withdrew His protection from the people and allowed the invaders to perform His work of doom and destruction. Clearly, the arm of the Lord functions here as a figure of God's protective providence—now removed; and is no more a literal statement than the first clause, which says that God 'cut down' the 'horn of Israel', or the subsequent images of God stringing a

[120] For this imagery, see above, pp. 19 f., 45 f. One may suppose that the final clause, which states that God's roar will 'echo (*yaʿaneh*) like the grape-treaders' (cry of) "*heidad*"' continues this theme through deft allusions to the reverberation of thunder claps (Exod. 19: 19) and the Syro-Mesopotamian storm-god (H)Adad.

[121] See above, pp. 162 f.

bow or swallowing Israel and all her ramparts (vv. 4–5). The fantastical quality of these images, and the fact that they occur among a series of tableaux delineating disaster, leave the strong sense that these images are merely metaphorical tropes and not a specific sequence of actions.

The reuse of the image in *Pesikta de-Rav Kahana* 17. 5 totally transforms the trope from a figure of wrath to a specific divine act of mercy and compassion.[122] In a teaching attributed to Resh Lakish, the verse is cited to confirm the statement that when God saw the heroes sent into exile with their hands bound behind, he recalled His promise to be with Israel in their 'affliction (*tzarah*)' (Ps. 91: 15). Taking that oath literally, God then says that He cannot now remain 'at ease' if His people are afflicted and 'in straits (*tzarah*)', and thus 'puts His right hand behind Him on account of (*mipnei*) the enemy' and what they have done to His people. Hence, because a specific sequence of actions is presented as a concrete divine imitation of human bondage, we now have the depiction of a mythic event paralleling a historical one with singular specificity. In the process, the preposition *mipnei* shifts from being a spatial indicator to an explanatory term marking the reason for God's act of compassionate suffering. And like the preceding example of God's roar, a metaphor of wrath is replaced by a myth of imitation.

In this case, the syntax of the passage remains intact. In other instances, this is not so. Exemplary is Deut. 33: 27, noted above, which says that 'The ancient God is a refuge' on high 'and below (His) everlasting arms' are extended. It would seem that this imagery conveys divine providence and protection,[123] giving two complementary metaphors of help and support. However, when this poetic parallelism was read as a continuous narrative in *BT Ḥagigah* 12b, the figure of the divine arms below was radically reconfigured and the syntax of the passage redivided. Now the ancient God is portrayed on high, in His heavenly abode, and 'beneath His arms—the world'. The older topic of protection is here a mythic image of the cosmos; and the metaphor of God's arms supporting His creatures is reread as a compressed drama of the creation hanging below the creator. The new sequence of the two images shifts attention from the older complementary metaphors to a more concrete myth of the structure of the universe and its dependence upon God.

3. A Phrase: Recontextualized. In Psalm 114 the scene is set: 'When Israel came out of Egypt' (v. 1), 'the sea saw and fled / the Jordan turned tail' (v. 3) and the mountains and hills skipped like rams and lambs (v. 4). Each of these elements is then asked why they acted in such a manner (v. 6), and the answer given is: 'because (*mipnei*) of the Lord ... (and) God of Jacob' (v. 7), of awesome and shattering power (v. 8). Hence we are given a depiction of the

[122] See the full discussion and variants above, pp. 147–50. [123] So, Kimḥi and Ibn Ezra.

terror of the natural world before the might of God. But there are puzzles. The historical setting of the exodus first leads one to suppose that the sea is the Reed Sea, and the reference is to its splitting; and that the Jordan's flight refers to its miraculous division at the entrance of the tribes into the land. But what then of the mountains and hills, and what about the answer that specifically says that the earth reels before the Lord? How does this relate to the sea and what it saw? The psalmist does not say, and nothing in Exodus 14–15 provides explicit help. Moreover, the shift from the apparently historical events to more general references tends to undermine the specific reference to the sea seeing, and this neutralization of the act seems reinforced by the chorus's subsequent query, 'What is it, O Sea?' (or, 'What has happened to you?'), which is the introit to the answer that all the earth shudders before the Lord. The personification of the sea, and the animal-like behaviour of the mountains, thus serve to intensify the metaphors, but without any further specification that would make them more concrete embodiments of emotions. The metaphors thus charge the hymn with a numinous dimension, without demanding any special credulity from the listener.

But the use of this passage in *Mekhilta de-Rabbi Ishmael Beshallaḥ* 4 changes matters considerably;[124] for the passage is adduced to support an unexpected event arising from an ambiguity in Exod. 14: 21. The puzzlement is the phrase 'And Moses extended his hand over the sea, and YHWH drove (back) the sea with an easterly wind the whole night'. For if Moses extended his hand, how do we understand God's subsequent action? Does the passage imply that the man Moses is the visible historical agent of God's invisible supernatural action? Or is it rather a case of double causality, doubly described?[125]

For the midrash at hand, neither explanation is the case, and it is rather presumed that the two actions conceal a gap, to be filled by a mythic narrative. Hence in this account, Moses tried to command the sea, and did what he could to get the sea to retreat; but the sea resisted his charge unafraid, until the Lord Himself appeared and struck terror into it and it fled in fear. Proof of this dramatic episode is found in Ps. 114: 3, in the statement 'The sea saw and fled'—that is, the sea saw the Lord manifest, and could not stand the sight. Accordingly, the phrase in the psalm was deemed a mythic fragment, an image to be activated by exegesis and cited in support of the narrative. But one could just as weli imagine that the figure of the fleeing sea was in fact an old mythic fragment marooned in this psalm as a metaphoric trope. In any event, the key issue is to observe that the literary figure of the sea in the psalm has been fleshed out in the midrash and its personality

[124] In Horovitz–Rabin, 102 f.

[125] For the topic of double causation in biblical literature, see the important considerations adduced by I. L. Seeligmann, 'Menschliches Heldentum und Gottliche Hilfe—Die doppelte Kausalität im alttestamentlichen Geschichtsdenken' *TZ* 19 (1963), 385–411.

developed—thus giving a mythic resonance to the trope and making it part of a larger episode that dramatizes divine might at the sea and against it.[126] Indeed, it is most remarkably the mythic sensibility of the sages, quite entirely against the plain sense of the Pentateuchal narrative, that perceived in this psalm the mute echo of an old conflict with the sea, and gave that literary resonance its full mythic tone.

4. A Sentence: Respecified. This final example brings us to the borders of metaphor and its transformation into myth. The passage is the pronouncement in Isa. 22: 12, 'On that day the Lord YHWH of hosts summoned (*vayiqra'*) to (*le-*) weeping and lamenting, to tearing hair (tonsuring) and girding with sackcloth'—but unheeding the call to mourn, the people did the opposite, saying 'Eat and drink, for tomorrow we shall die' (v. 13). Clearly, the prophet's word proclaims the advent of doom and the need to mourn the terror to come, piling up a series of acts to be done. Indeed, the list hammers out a tattoo of terror that gives each one of the separate acts a somewhat figurative quality, marking them off as so many metaphors of the doomsday at hand.

This dramatically changes in the reuse of the passage in the *Pesikta de-Rav Kahana* 15. 3, since in Bar Qappara's bold teaching, God calls out (*vayiqra'*) to the angels 'concerning' (*le-*) the rites of mourning, asking their instruction about behaviour based on what human kings do.[127] And this the heavenly 'host' proceeds to enumerate, mentioning first the act of hanging a sackcloth upon a door, which God purports to imitate by saying that 'I shall clothe the heavens with darkness' (Isa. 50: 3), as well as several other human acts and divine conformity to them. These acts of empathy with Israel's sorrow are thus specific ritual behaviours, which are taught one by one, so that their concrete nature cannot be doubted. The borders of metaphor thus meld into myth, as God becomes the agent of pathos. The overall effect is cumulative in a dramatic way, through a series of detailed acts of mourning known to all hearers of the teaching.[128] The exegetical shift of the preposition *le-* from the marker of a list to a particle that introduces God's query 'concerning' such acts of mourning on earth, directs the listener to a myth

[126] Daniel Boyarin, *Intertextuality and the Reading of Midrash* (Bloomington: Indiana University Press, 1990), ch. 6, has also deliberated upon this passage, and has also perceived the movement from metaphor to myth (p. 98), though in different terms; but his perception that there is now a 'revivification' of 'repressed elements' (pp. 100, 102), runs counter to the evidence and discussions throughout the present book.

[127] The word 'Lord (*Adonai*)' in the Masoretic text cited above may have been a scribal marker for proper pronunciation of the tetragram that follows (*i.e.* as *Adonai*, 'Lord'), and not a separate appellation or title, for it is notable that the midrash cites a biblical version that reads 'YHWH God of hosts'.

[128] For the phenomenon of extinguishing lamps (one of these acts), see Saul Lieberman, *Greek in Jewish Palestine* (New York: Feldheim, 1965), 103–5, adducing *Gen. Rabba* 70. 19 (Theodor–Albeck, 818).

about divine care coupled with a portrait of a less than omniscient deity in need of counsel from His heavenly ministers. Nor should it go unnoticed that this mythic episode was created by splitting off the epithet 'hosts' from the name YHWH, and treating it as a separate angelic entity. The result is that this epithet is no mere neutral apposition of divine dominion over the powers above, some demythologized appellation ('YHWH of hosts'); but instead, in this exegesis, the epithet is vivified as a collectivity of personified forces, which advise and instruct their overlord on high.[129]

With this we conclude an accounting of the morphologies of language in rabbinic myth and mythmaking, and turn to the God who is so variously depicted and so marvellously manifest.

C. MYTH AND THE MORPHOLOGIES OF GOD

Throughout the course of the inquiry into rabbinic myths, we find God portrayed in various guises and passions—in both visual and emotional modalities, consonant with His role as a mighty and merciful Lord, involved in the historical life of the people Israel, with whom He is bound by covenantal obligations and promises of protection. The question now at hand is to consider the status of these diverse portrayals from reflections found in the midrashic texts themselves, taking into account comments within midrashic sources on how and why the images are produced. In part, we are dealing with the images of God 'in manifestation and essence'; that is, with the multiple modes of divine appearance or designation and the theological principle of monotheistic unity. The topic exceeds the present framework, and shall be considered here from the more limited perspective of the mythic modes considered in Part II. This broader scope shall be suggested through examples that include, but also extend, features treated earlier.

Two types of coordinates may be formally discerned, and are distinguished by special terminology, though in some cases these types overlap or intersect and thus provide some perspective on internal developments or flexibility within the tradition. One axis involves the external and internal modalities of divine activity. Thus at the external pole of manifestation, we have to do with the appearances of God in power and might and sympathetic participation in Israelite history; whereas at the internal pole of divine activity we have to do with the arousals of God to justice and judgement or mercy and compassion. These latter cases have in large part to do with interior states or actions wholly or partly hidden from human view. However, as remarked, there are cases where these ideal types converge. Particularly notable are the instances (see presently) where the divine manifestation is said to reveal a specific

[129] The midrashic formulation 'YHWH God of hosts' (see n. 127) more adequately supports the exegesis than the MT.

pathos of God. In this way, images of divine appearance and qualities of divine sensibility are correlated.

The second axis involves the divine or human source of the appearance. Thus where God is deemed the initiating or even sole agent of the manifestation, we have statements that He appeared or revealed Himself in certain ways, without any corresponding remark concerning the human role in this process. On the other hand, there are also instances in the Midrash where the active imagination of certain persons is praised for its role in producing images or portrayals of God. This pole does not exclude situations where both types are involved, such that God's revelation to humans beings elicits a mode of attentive reception that formulates and transfigures this apperception in a variety of anthropomorphic or anthropopathic terms. The result is a correlation between divine presence or pathos and its human representations. To be sure, none of this even remotely yields a deliberate phenomenology of religious experience and expression, or provides anything like an intentional deliberation of the interrelationships between divine revelation and human imagination. Still, we must deal with what we have; and this is itself of considerable value for the outline of rabbinic attitudes that it traces.

I. Divine Manifestations and Their Meanings

Scripture is replete with the varieties of God's manifestations to Israel and the nations, and these are variously summarized and evaluated in early and late sources. These sources are of considerable value for the present discussion.

1. Images of the Divine Warrior. A cluster of tannaitic traditions bearing on our topic is preserved in *Mekhilta de-Rabbi Ishmael, Massekhta᾽ de-Shirah, Beshalaḥ* 4,[130] occasioned by the verse 'YHWH is a man of war; YHWH is His Name' (Exod. 15: 3). In group (i) R. Judah began by saying 'Truly this is a rich passage, (corroborated in detail) in many places (throughout Scripture)'.[131] He thus interprets the figure of God as a man of war as a generalized or paradigmatic formulation, that can be illustrated by numerous examples. These cases are then delineated under the heading that '(Scripture) tells that He was revealed (*nigleh*) to them with all the implements of war'.

[130] Horovitz–Rabin, 130–1.

[131] The teacher is R. Judah bar Ila῾᾽i (T 3), a student of R. Akiba; repeatedly referred to as R. Judah in the Mishnah. He was a major figure of his generation (*BT Sanh.* 20a). The principle of a 'rich' scriptural unit, that is illustrated or corroborated by numerous other passages, contrasts with a 'poor' unit that needs other passages for explication or clearer expression (this last is formally preserved as the 17th of the 32 hermeneutical rules attributed to R. Eliezer b. Yosi Ha-Gelili, of Bar Kokhba's generation; but the formulation arguably derives from rules of the Gaon R. Samuel bar Hofni and his sources, as shown by M. Zucker, 'Le-Pitron Ba῾ayat 32 Middot u-Mishnat Rabbi Eliezer', *PAAJR* 23 (1954), 1–39). For another instance of R. Judah's use of this principle, also in the *Mekhilta*, see Horovitz–Rabin, 101 (on Exod. 14: 19).

Eight examples with proof-texts are noted: the divine 'hero' appeared with a sword, as a charioteer, with coat of mail and a helmet, with a spear and battle-axe, with bow and arrows, and with shield and buckler—a veritable 'man of war'.

Now in this list, there is no justification or qualification of these polymorphic images of God's appearance in battle *per se*. Nevertheless, an issue is raised that ponders the possibility that these mythic images reveal something about God's own nature as a lord of battles. 'I might understand (from this evidence) that He has need[132] of any of these measures (*middot*).[133] (But this inference is not possible, since) Scripture (forthwith) states "YHWH is His Name"—(to teach you that) He (really) fights with His Name and has no need of any of these measures'. While it is stylistically arguable that both this problem and its resolution come from R. Judah, as his rhetorical attempt to save both the images and divine honour, another point is added that questions this answer and thus seems to belong to another interlocutor in the academy. He says, 'If so, why does Scripture have need to specify each one separately?' And the new answer counters: 'So that if (these expressions of divine might) were needed by Israel, (they might know that) the Holy One, blessed be He, fights their battles for them. And woe for the nations of the world! For what do they hear with their ears (by these pronouncements)?—that truly the One who spoke and the world was created will fight against them.'

R. Judah's teaching is instructive at several levels. At the outset, at the level of plain sense, it conveys the fact that the scriptural statement that YHWH is a man of war cannot be read away, for it is confirmed by many other detailed accounts of divine appearance in battle-gear. But the concrete realism of the imagery might lead one to suppose that God has some 'need' of these mythic measures; hence the subsequent phrase is adduced and midrashically construed to teach that God really fights with His Name. However, this shift to the second clause makes the first one more puzzling, and the question is then asked why Scripture has 'need' of such imagery if it is not theologically accurate. The final point conveyed is doubly pedagogical: God appears in all these many measures in order to assure Israel that if they shall have 'need' of any of them, at any historical time, they shall be used on their behalf; and in order to warn the nations to heed the prophetical warnings that they hear, and know that the Lord of creation will fight against them. Thus are the

132 The printed editions have *velo'*, which appears to be a theological addition to offset the point (namely, he does not have a need); but this contradicts the point and the subsequent statement, as well as this common tannaitic query. Hence it is best to delete the word, as also in Lauterbach's edition (i. 30, and n. to l. 12); Horovitz–Rabin retain it; but then one must read the phrase (oddly) as a query.

133 For an analysis of this word in terms of forms of divine appearance, see the textual and comparative evidence I adduced in *The Exegetical Imagination* (Cambridge, Mass.: Harvard University Press, 1998), esp. 64–72.

mythic images saved as pedagogical truths, without either undermining their concrete validity or limiting God to their use. According to R. Judah, the many shapes of divine appearance are merely figural modalities, but altogether necessary for all that.

Group (ii) of the ensemble returns us to the lemma and offers a new interpretation. At the outset the query is posed: 'Why is (this verse) said?', suggesting that another theological or pedagogical explanation may be expected. However, at first the hermeneutical process seems puzzling and the answer does not make sense. According to the text, it is said that the phrase 'YHWH is a man of war' occurs because God 'was revealed (*nigleh*) at the sea as a warrior doing battle'; and then, also without further clarification, the passage adds that 'He was revealed at Sinai as an old man full of compassion' (the proof-text adduced is from the beginning of Exod. 24: 10, 'And they saw the God of Israel'). Only after references regarding the redemption are added, is an answer to the initial question provided: 'So as not to provide a pretext for the nations of the world to say that there are two (divine) powers; but rather "YHWH is a man of war, YHWH is His Name"—He, it is, who was in Egypt, and He, it was, at the sea; He, it is, who was in the past, and He, it is, who shall be in the future; etc.'

It would appear from the form of the initial question and its answer that the original issue concerned the apparent redundancy of the Name YHWH, and that this repetition was adduced to rebut any notion that YHWH is or was other than the one and only God of Israel, the only power in heaven at all times. Later midrashic tradition fleshed out this terse formulation in the light of the notion that the manifestations of the Lord as a young warrior and an old man at different points in the biblical narrative indicate that two different divine powers were involved—especially since two different divine Names are also used (YHWH at the sea; Elohim at Sinai), and since these names seem to reflect different qualities of Divinity (military power in the first case; judicial compassion in the second). The answer provided by this text in its final form is that YHWH is the one true Name of the Lord, who Himself integrates all the qualities of might and mercy, and is the one and only power in heaven.[134]

[134] The *Mekhilta de-Rabbi Simeon* (Epstein–Melamed, 81) reflects a more compressed version of this overall tradition. The structural complexity noted above is minimized here, since the opening query 'Why is this said?' is absent, and the answer that treats the Name in different periods is presented as part of a separate interpretation. It was long since noted by I. Lewy, 'Ein Wort über die Mechilta des R. Simon', *Jahresbericht des jüdisch-theologischen Seminars* (Breslau, 1889), 9 n. 1, that the tradition about seeing the God of Israel (Exod. 24: 10) is absent and presumably secondary in the *Mekhilta de-Rabbi Ishmael* (a view that is apparently cited with approval by Horovitz–Rabin, note to l. 15, pp. 129 f.). However, this is a problematic presumption, since in the *Mekhilta de-Rabbi Ishmael* version Exod. 24: 10 supports the appearance of God at Sinai, and Dan. 7: 9 supports his appearance in the future; hence, to remove the reference

The complexity of the final form notwithstanding, this unit clearly complements the first one. The purpose of the repetition of the Name YHWH in Exod. 15: 3 is now purportedly to prevent any false conclusions to be drawn from the polymorphous appearances of God in Scripture: for God is one and only one, even though He is manifest in many different ways and for many different ends in the course of history.[135] The mythic images are thus presumed to be real and potentially misleading guises, so that an appropriate theological intervention is deemed necessary in order to prevent any religious error or heresy. R. Judah showed no such concern.

2. Divine Metamorphoses. The tradition on the subject of divine appearances preserved in *Songs Rabba* 1. 9 provides further instruction. It is transmitted in the name of R. Akiba, R. Judah's teacher.[136] The verse commented upon is Songs 1: 9, 'I have compared you (*dimmitikha*) to a mare among Pharaoh's chariots, my fairest'. And the midrashic comment continues: 'Now Pharaoh road upon a male horse, and as it were (*kivyakhol*) the Holy One, blessed be He, was revealed (*niglah*) on a male horse, as it is written, "He rode on a cherub and flew" (Ps. 18: 11). Pharaoh reasoned, "Since this male horse kills its owners in battle, I shall ride a mare", as it is written, "As a mare, etc." Then Pharaoh rode on a red ... a white ... (and) a black horse; (and) as it were the Holy One, blessed be He, was revealed on a red ... a white ... (and) a black horse, as it is written "You lead horses through the sea" (Hab. 3: 15)—many horses.'[137] The explanation then goes

is to remove the temporal sense and sequence of the unit, which I contend came into this passage as a coherent unit.

It will be noted that our text correlates the divine Names and their qualities differently from usual rabbinic usage (with YHWH marking mercy, Elohim marking judgement; see above, pp. 99–101, 183 f.).

This variation, however, tallies with standard Philonic usage; for a review of earlier evaluations and new considerations, see N. A. Dahl and Alan F. Segal, 'Philo and the Rabbis on the Names of God', *JJS* 9 (1978), 1–28. In this context, it bears note that Philo, *Deus Imm.* 60 and 68, considers the anthropomorphism of God as 'man of war' in Exod. 15: 3, and also adduces a host of military weapons. Our *Mekhilta* passage would thus be an 'independent' Palestinian witness to Philo's notion (so Dahl and Segal, ibid. 18). Philo's suggests a similar pedagogy for the imagery, as well; for in addition to indicating that God accommodates His figure to the masses (60), he also notes that such military images are designed to evoke fear in their beholders (68).

135 The earliest tradition may have been more spare; for in addition to units (i) and (ii), there is another that considers the paradox of God as omnipresent yet in specific forms (iii), and a final one that returns to the theme that God really only fights with His Name, adducing a new prooftext (iv). This editorial structure suggests that (i) and (iv) comprised the original unit, before subsequent interpolations.

136 I have given this version second, and R. Judah's first, since the Akiban teaching provides new terms and issues that lead into successive examples.

137 This phrase (*susvan pagiyan*) is clearly an Aramaic gloss of the Hebrew content and the word *suseykha*; though the exact meaning is more obscure. The Matnot Kehunah interprets *pagiyan* as 'alternating' (*mitḥalfin*); but with no basis. Better would be to correct to *sagiyan*,

on to say that Pharaoh went forth with various weapons or tools of war, and that the Holy One did likewise.[138] Twelve items are mentioned, and each one is matched by a biblical proof-text, providing a grand display of polymorphic appearances by God.[139]

Two points are puzzling: the first is the absence of any reference to God's appearance as a mare after Pharaoh's change of horse; and the second takes us back to the opening verse, and its meaning for R. Akiba. Certainly, the subject (I) is God for the sage, and the female beloved (you) is Israel, in accordance with the standard allegorical substitution of the male and female figures found throughout this Midrash. But God comparing Israel to a mare hardly fits the mythic drama of the teaching, and thus one is led to perceive the new intent implied here: that God is understood to say to Israel, 'I seemed like (or, took on the form of) a mare for your sake!' On this view, the term of comparison refers to a mode or image of divine appearance, assumed by God on behalf of the beloved. And it is this meaning that is anticipated from the outset, in the quoted lemma, and only ironically alluded to after Pharaoh takes a mare and the opening words of the verse are cited with reference to him and his chariot horses.[140]

R. Akiba's remarkable use of Songs 1: 9 to teach about the figural manifestations of God at the sea transforms a version in which revealed appearances are stressed,[141] and puts the accent squarely on deliberate divine guises—including animals. The core element of this mythic tradition is presumably simply the manifestation of God as a mare at the sea, as we may infer from its isolated use in the sharp exchange between R. Akiba and R. Pappius.[142] Either way, the new myth depends on the historicizing allegory of the Song then current, and the sense that such divine appearances were phenomenological events and not the very nature of God. In this way, the myths have a new transparency while yet presuming the ontic reality of

'many'. This fits the sense, presumes a simple scribal error, and uses a word that actually translates 'many' in TJ Hab. 3: 15.

[138] The list begins with 'Pharaoh went out', and five items follow. There then comes a teaching of R. Levi (two items; the first repeats the last of the preceding list, 'arrows'), and this is followed by the phrase 'Pharaoh went out' and seven items. Clearly, the R. Levi material is an interpolation, requiring a redactional resumption of the incipit.

[139] The term *kivyakhol* recurs throughout, though it was absent in the *Mekhilta* passage where similar items of war are mentioned. See further in Appendix 2, p. 350.

[140] In this citation, the old genitive ending of *le-susati* ('to a mare') is impliedly construed as a personal pronoun suffix marking the king himself ('my mare').

[141] This is a further reason for regarding this version as based on earlier prototypes. See above, n. 134.

[142] This is the brief version found elsewhere in *Songs Rabba* 1. 9, also reported in the name of R. Akiba. However, in the *Mekhilta de-Rabbi Ishmael* (Horovitz–Rabin, p. 112) the mare image is presented as the myth of Pappius; this attribution is also found in the Geniza texts published by Zvi M. Rabinovitz, *Ginzei Midrash* (Tel Aviv: Tel Aviv University Press, 1977), 6, and in the *Mekhilta de-Rabbi Simeon*, 68. The term *kivyakhol* is used in these cases. See Appendix 2.

the experience.[143] Nothing more is said of the modes of divine actualization or vitalization.[144]

II. Human Imagination and the Image of God

In addition to the divine generation of images, several other sources focus on the human production of the anthropomorphic and anthropopathic imagery. The former are represented by external appearances and depictions, the latter by internal states and qualities.

1. Image and Imagination. Of singular importance is the following amoraic teaching found in *Pesikta de-Rav Kahana* 4. 4.[145]

'A man's wisdom illumines his face' (Eccles. 8: 1). R. Yudan said: Great is the power of the prophets who imagine (*medammin*) the image (*demut*) of the Power (*Geburah*) on high as a human image (*demut ʾadam*). (As is said,) 'I heard a human voice (*qol ʾadam*) from the middle of Ulai calling out' (Dan. 8: 16). R. Judah b. R. Simon said: And there is another verse clearer than this; (namely,) 'and on the semblance (*demut*) of the throne, (there was) an image (*demut*) similar to the appearance of a human (*ʾadam*)' (Ezek. 1: 26). 'And the strength (*ʿoz*) of his face will change (*yeshunneʾ*)' (Eccles. 8: 1). For He changes (*mishtanneh*) from the attribute (*middah*) of judgement to the attribute of mercy with respect to Israel.

[143] Elliot Wolfson, in *Through a Speculum that Shines* (Princeton: Princeton University Press, 1994), 38 f., articulates similar conclusions, though he is inclined to speak of '[t]he inherent docetism of the aggadic tradition', and also asserts that the 'forms of appearance . . . reflect the inherent nature of that which is visualized'.

[144] Possibly more may be gleaned more circuitously. Thus, a comment on Songs 2: 9 ('My beloved is like (*domeh*) a gazelle') in *Songs Rabba* 2. 9 takes the beloved as an allegory for God and goes on to say that just as a gazelle jumps from one place to another, so God appeared in different places (like Egypt, the Sea, and Sinai), and these manifestations are correlated with various physical appearances. But such proofs go beyond the analogy, and this may have led Yannai to comment on this verse: 'He *tzalaḥ* and succeeded (*hitzliaḥ*) in various forms (*dimuyot*)'; see in *Maḥazor Yannai*, Rabinovitz edn., ii. 227 (also adduced by Wolfson, *Through a Speculum*, 35). Now it is clear that a play of words extends *domeh* to *demuyot*, this being a clever midrashic reading of the passage that brings out the implied sense of the old comment. But what of the play between *tzalaḥ* and *hitzliaḥ*? Perhaps all that is involved in the first term is that God brought about the 'speedy' realization of the images—a point that has some philological justification, noted by Hanokh Yalon, *Pirkei Lashon* (Jerusalem: Mosad Bialik, 1971), 239 f. Now Yalon also notes that the phrase *qafatz ʿalav ha-dabar* found in the Midrash (used to convey the occurrence of prophecy; see Lieberman, *Greek in Jewish Palestine*, 165–7) is similar to biblical uses of *tzalaḥ* in connection with prophecy (1 Sam. 10: 6, 10), and sees this as confirming a sense of 'haste'. But perhaps Yannai's usage is more precise and cunning; for insofar as *qafatz* is used in our midrash with respect to the leaps of a gazelle, and thus God's many appearances, the poet may use *tzalaḥ* in the same sense and even allude to the biblical sense of divine 'infusion'. If so, the word *tzalaḥ* in the poem would (also?) convey the nuance of 'actualization'. Such a sense would fill in our knowledge of the rabbinic notion of God 'alighting' or 'descending' into the world of earthly forms, in one or another mode or manifestation.

[145] Mandelbaum edn. i. 65 f.

The passage deals with the external appearances of God, and their relation to human imagination and behaviour. It is divided into two parts, based on two phrases from Eccles. 8: 1. The first part focuses on anthropomorphism, and the power of the prophets to imagine the supernal image of God in human shape; the second part focuses on anthropopathism, and the qualities of God's ongoing relationships with the people. Both parts are in Hebrew and taught by R. Yudan; they now frame a supplementary comment in Aramaic by R. Judah b. Simon, which was interpolated to provide another (better) proof-text for R. Yudan's statement about the prophets' anthropomorphic imagination.[146]

The first teaching focuses on the issue of external image and human imagination through the noun *demut* and the verb *meddamin*; however, there is no verbal link to the lemma, which apparently serves to say that the wisdom of a person illumines his face with inspiration. On the other hand, the second teaching picks up on the verb *yeshunne*ʾ in the lemma and interprets it with respect to God's changing modalities to humans; and thus it must understand *ʿoz panav* as indicating the 'anger of His (God's) face' which will change from judgement to mercy.[147] Oddly, then, the word *panav* ('his face') would seem to have two different references in each of the hemistichs: in the first instance, it would refer to the wise person; in the second, to God himself. Alternatively, in the initial lemma, it may be human wisdom that causes God to shine His face upon the person with beneficent inspiration; there would then be a conjunction between the two half-verses. This reading would provide a notion of divine inspiration for the bold acts of human imagination performed by the prophets; that is, their power to imagine God in human terms is itself a God-given power, and no mere human act or capacity.[148]

2. The Sources of Imagination. A more complex notion of the interaction of divine and human dimensions in the production of images of God is suggested by a striking comment on the phrase *dimmitikh raʿayati* (Songs 1: 9) found in *Songs Zuṭa*. The interpretation says: 'The word *dimmitikh* means images (*demuyot*). This teaches that God was revealed to Israel through an image (or figural form; *dimyon*); (for) just as a person sees his friend and says

[146] It may well be that two understandings of *meddamin* are involved: R. Yudan construing it as referring to an act of the imagination, but R. Judah taking it as an act of comparison. This would explain the different texts used. At any rate, the issue is not to add an auditory example to a visionary one (as Wolfson, *Through a Speculum*, 37), but to replace it. The issue in both cases is anthropomorphic constructions. The two sages are contemporaries (3rd c. the Land of Israel).

[147] *ʿoz panim* is usually the negative human trait of impudence or bold-facedness in rabbinic texts (*M. ʾAbot* 5. 20; *BT Ber.* 16b); here, *ʿoz* evokes the usage *ʿoz ʾapekha*, 'the fury of Your anger', said of God in Ps. 90: 11.

[148] For the formulation of the dictum of prophetic powers as the projection of a human 'form' (*tzuraḥ*) upon the divine creator (*yotzrah*) in *Gen. Rab.* 27. 1 (Theodor–Albeck, 255 f.), see the discussion above (Chapter 1), and in my extended study (noted Ch. 1, n. 33).

"This is so-and-so", similarly Israel looked upon the Holy One, blessed be He, and imagined (*meddamim*) Him'.[149]

Based on the comment, it is clear that the lemma is not read as God saying to Israel 'I have compared you', but rather 'I have seemed to you' or even 'I was imagined to you' in figural forms. Indeed, in this instance, the sage sets forth a notion of divine revelation that is dependent upon human imagination and some prior epistemological apperception. For in saying that it was through an image or figural form that God was revealed to all Israel, the author is not so much suggesting that humans reveal God through their imaginative powers as that in their focusing upon God (the text uses the verb *mistaklim*, suggesting a more meditative or intense looking) they imagined Him in a manner that He gave Himself to be revealed to them. Thus the interpreter has achieved a striking conceptual breakthrough: at once preserving God's singular authority and initiative in the act of revelation, while emphasizing the human imaginal component and capacity that shapes the divine Presence into forms recognizable to it in human terms. The morphologies of God are thus truly divine, but just as certainly human.

3. Multiple Forms Divine. Among the morphologies of divine appearance, one final aspect remains to be noted. It concerns the forms of heavenly beings that are created to do God's will on earth. A passage in *Genesis Rabba* 21. 9[150] provides a unique mythic aetiology of these entities, linking them to 'the flashing, revolving sword' (Gen. 3: 24) that is placed outside the Garden of Eden to guard against human encroachment. The various terms used are explained in the following way: 'the flashing sword (*lahaṭ ha-ḥereb*)' (is so called,) since His attendants are (beings of) 'flashing fire (*ʾesh loheṭ*)', (and) 'revolving (*mithappekhet*)' (indicates) that alternating (*mithappekhim*) (forms emerge from it:) sometimes men, sometimes women, sometimes spirits, sometimes angels'. The poet Yannai knows a variant of this midrash, based on Ps. 104: 4 ('He makes His angels "spirits"; His attendants "flashing fire" '), and even includes another striking detail when he says that God has myriads of messengers—some 'are made men, (some) made women, (some) made spirits, (some) made fiery bolts, (beings) made of every semblance (*demut*), who do (His) every bidding'.[151] That is, God creates a host of forms to do His will, including beings in the image of men and woman. These entities are all vitalizations or materializations of His creative power: not morphologies of God Himself, but of divine powers actualized to perform tasks for their Lord.[152] A late expression of this myth in *Exodus Rabba* 25. 2 elaborates on

[149] *Midrash Zuṭa ʿal Shir Ha-Shirim, Rut; Eicha; ve-Kohelet*, ed. Solomon Buber (Berlin: Itzkowski, 1894), 15.

[150] Theodor–Albeck, 203. [151] *Piyyuṭei Yannai* (Rabinovitz edn.), i. 120f.

[152] It appears that an interesting ancient variant of this theology, specifically of 'forms' emerging from God and returning to Him, is the 'Jewish' position polemicized against in Justin

these details, and even fills in notable supporting proof-texts from Scripture.[153]

III. Morphologies of God and the Modalities of Monotheism

On the basis of the texts adduced and analysed, the following conclusions may be noted. YHWH is the one and only and supreme power in heaven, despite visionary appearances to the contrary or implying contrariety; and further, He is one in overall purpose, which is variously to show or reveal to Israel and to the nations His protective providence and guidance for His people—through images of a heroic youth fitted out for war or of a compassionate elder seated in judgement. Anthropomorphic and anthropopathic images thus serve an earthly design and human needs, but are emphatically not needed by God in any essential way, who is more mystically connected with his Name as a 'man of war'. Hence God permits or inspires these and other depictions in His spokesmen the prophets, or otherwise produces such impressions upon the imagination of the nation itself. These matters were not always clear or accepted by all Jews, who could be led astray by such textual evidence of apparent divine diversity; hence such errors and confusions are rebutted with incisive vigour by the sages, on the basis of Scripture itself and through the striking strategy of drawing the proper theological conclusions from similar texts[154] or from the very context that induced the misreadings.[155]

The oneness of God, then, does not therefore mean that God is not subject to diverse manifestations, or that He is impassive in nature. To the contrary, God is portrayed in the sources as actively engaged in earthly existence and as reactive to Israel's covenantal deportment. Thus according to some views, these human actions affect God directly and His powers of mercy and judgement, and this is even stated (in diverse terms) as empowering or even diminishing the divine being. This makes God variously subject to human action and prayer to help strengthen certain modalities affecting His nature and decisions (be these modalities within or without God's own self). The effect of such divine reactivity due to human sin (personal and collective) may result in God's withdrawal or disengagement from the people, or (in the best of possibilities) some sympathetic participation or alignment with

Martyr's *Dialogue with Trypho* (ch. 28); see the analysis of Shlomo Pines, 'Ha-ʾEl ha-Kabod veha-Malʾakhim lefi Shiṭah Teʾologit shel ha-Meʾah ha-Sheniyah la-Sefirah', *JSJT* 6. 3–4 (1987), 1–14 (in Hebrew).

[153] A notable point is that this catalogue of forms is linked to the phrase *ʾelohei ha-tzebaʾot* (Hos. 12: 6), taken with precise literalism as 'God of *the* hosts', which is then interpreted (via an Aramaic stem) to refer to the angels that God 'makes according to His desire (*tzibyono*)'—beings that include the 'semblance' or 'image' (*demut*) of men and women.

[154] *Mekhilta de-Rabbi Ishmael* (Horovitz–Rabin, 130).

[155] See *BT Sanh.* 38b (R. Yoḥanan).

Israel's fate. Correspondingly, proper actions have the capacity to strengthen God's mercy or even to draw His presence (by stages) down to earth.[156] There is thus an interactive bond between God and Israel, whereby the diminishment of proper human life below has a correspondence on high, and similarly as regards right action. From these and related matters we say that divine omnipotence is not on the theological agenda here, so much as modalities of divine potency and presence; and God's supernal transcendence is also not on the theological agenda here, so much as modalities of divine immanence and care. God is not in a sense complete or fully empowered when sin, exile, or Amalek exist, and this incompleteness was variously figured in terms of types of God's self-bondage or limitation, or more mystically in terms of the incompleteness of the divine dominion (throne) or Name.[157] Our sources do not indicate how widespread these mythic notions were or how (or if) they were integrated. The theologies themselves are merely topical comments, linked to verses, though it is also apparent (especially so in the existing anthologies of related teachings) that these teachings have shared coordinates and characteristics that link them together at the level of theme and structure.

Thus the divine being or personality was not static, but was rather dynamically engaged or correlated with Israel in ways that affected the balance of inner states or determinations. God's own nature is thus mythically portrayed as affected by Israel's life, and never abstract or abstracted from human personalities; in fact, to the contrary, he is boldly imagined in their image and mirrors their strengths and weaknesses on high. The extent and character of these and other depictions depend on the vigour of the exegetes themselves, and only rarely is this curtailed or modified by the sense that certain suggestions go over the line of what is appropriate to say or imply (the paradigm case is the interchange between R. Akiba and R. Pappius on several topics).[158] But even these cases are preserved in public texts, presumably to demonstrate or suggest just where the line might be drawn—for a

[156] A strong, though concealed, teaching of this matter is found in *Pesikta de-Rav Kahana* 1. 1 (Mandelbaum, 2), where the reward of the righteous is first adduced on the basis of Ps. 37: 29a; and then their capacity to 'cause the Shekhinah to settle on earth (*yashkinu Shekhinah ba-ʾaretz*)' is proved by means of v. 29b, *yishkenu la-ʿad ʿaleyha*—which literally simply means that 'they (the righteous) shall dwell forever upon it (the earth)', but which, in light of the theologoumenon just noted, was undoubtedly understood to mean that the righteous 'shall cause (the Shekhinah) to dwell (*yeshakkenu*) forever upon it'. The power of the righteous is more than a capacity to strengthen divine qualities; it even effects the descent of the divine to earth.

[157] See above, pp. 189–90.

[158] See in *Mekhilta de-Rabbi Ishmael* (Horovitz–Rabin, 112 f.), and variants in *Songs Rab.* 1. 9. The positions and the language of the various topics have undergone considerable editorial tampering (to soften the positions) at various times during the transmission of these interlocutions. An analysis and use of important MSS and Geniza fragments has been undertaken by Menahem Kahana, 'Mahadurot Ha-Mekhilta de-Rabbi Ishmaʾ el le-Shemot bi-Reʾ i Qeṭa ʿei ha-Genizah', *Tarbiz*, 55 (1987), 499–515; he also considers the underlying theological difficulties of the different positions taken (particularly Pappius' gnostic or gnosticizing notions).

rabbinic culture rife with vigorous exegetical achievements but without official means for censoring theological ideas that were broadly within the monotheistic pale and did not lead one to false worship or practice. Only at certain mental borderlands and at certain times would it be suspected or sensed that some theologies were too close to views espoused by some 'others' for comfort. In such circumstances, the only viable option would be responsible restraint, governed by personal self-regulation or collegial criticism.[159]

It must finally be stressed that ancient rabbinic culture as it was preserved attests to a great range of theological options on any number of topics. Its monotheistic theologies were not monolithic, and the very nature of the great midrashic anthologies attests to the valorization of multiple exegetical examples for virtually every verse or phrase of the central texts read liturgically on Sabbaths and the Festivals or Fasts (the Torah and the five Scrolls), as well as key phrases from other texts read on these same occasions (the Prophets)—examples that range from the bold to the banal, be the topic theological or behavioural, and be the subject God or the people of Israel.

The movement of certain topics from collection to collection shows how they were revalorized by disciples or tradents in different settings and times. Naturally, certain schools had certain proclivities and preferences, even as the channels of transmission were cut by sages with similar proclivities and interests.[160] This meant that within different circles different exegetical emphases were stressed and different topics valorized. These subgroups shared similar theological sensibilities and styles within the larger textual community of ancient rabbinic Judaism and its ritual norms and practices. Later groups would similarly privilege and revalorize those scriptural sources and their earlier interpretations, insofar as that rang true to their theological imagination; and when certain teachings touched on esoteric subjects, they might even be restricted to smaller circles of disciples and passed on as secrets of a special nature. There are some indications that this was the case on several fronts, and one notable instance is preserved regarding R. Samuel bar Naḥman, who was approached by R. Simeon ben Yehotzadak with a query.

R. Simeon ben R. Yehotzadak asked R. Samuel bar Naḥman, Since I have heard that you are a master of Aggadah, (tell me) whence the light was created? R. Samuel said, The Holy One, blessed be He, wrapped Himself in a garment and the splendour of His Glory radiated from one end of the world to the other. He spoke to him in a whisper. R. Simeon was astonished at this and said, This (matter) is stated explicitly in Scripture, 'He wrapped Himself in light as with a garment' (Ps. 104: 2), and you say

[159] On such matters, see Judah Goldin, 'The Freedom and Restraint of Haggadah', in his *Studies in Midrash and Related Literature*, ed. Barry Eichler and Jeffrey Tigay (Philadelphia: The Jewish Publication Society, 1988), 253–69; and also Fishbane, *The Exegetical Imagination*, 20f.

[160] See the earlier discussion on tradents and transmission above, pp. 194–8.

it in a whisper?! R. Naḥman answered, Just as I have heard it in a whisper, I told it to you in a whisper.[161]

We have in this remarkable report a tradition of secret transmission made public, a breaking of the seals of ritual instruction by someone who undoubtedly felt like R. Simeon about the explicit and exoteric nature of the scriptural passage. But this betrayal would hardly be the norm in circles where the information involved esoteric wisdom about divine mysteries, where access to a master's secrets were more hierarchically controlled, and where the circles were limited to tried and true elites.[162] In some groups these secrets were originally independent of Scripture, and were only belatedly linked to its textual hints; in others, the myths and mysteries were variously discovered or confirmed or extended by modes of pneumatic interpretation in select circles of disciples, whose scriptural discourses even had a ritual character or ambiance. Either way, the citations of importance would be preserved and revalorized with every new instruction, forming a mythic lexicon of special esoteric significance. Later, through the influence of powerful and often new mythic energies current in twelfth- and thirteenth-century Provence and Castile, respectively, the older themes of ancient rabbinic myth were galvanized and transformed, resulting in theological images of hitherto unimagined range and detail; and if these images often remained, by nature, concealed in the garments of esoteric mystery, they were now brought to the light of day and made available to ever new circles of disciples. This great new moment of mythic vitality shall be taken up below.

IV. The Powers and the Pleroma

In the mythic theosophy of the ancient rabbinic sources, the divine world is comprised of a complex of elements: a series of seven heavens, at whose peak is a chariot-throne borne by polymorphic beings, and upon which sits God in the appearance of a human form; at His service is a vast retinue of angelic beings, which number in the myriads of myriads downward toward the earth—the other pole of God's royal realm and rule. This upper complex of elements may be designated as the divine pleroma; and this pleroma is particularly marked by various qualities or entities that help constitute God's nature and rule. Also included in this realm are forms or entities that are regarded as heavenly hypostases by different teachers or groups.

[161] *Gen. Rab.* 3. 4 (Theodor–Albeck, 19 f., with parallels). The world's light thus derives from a primordial divine light, mediated through a cloak donned by God. This is some old mystic image, portraying the act of creation by a world Magus. See further, Viktor Aptowitzer, 'Licht als Urstoff', *MGWJ* 72 (1928), 363–70. See also Robert Eisler, *Weltmantel und Himmelszelt* (Munich: C. H. Beck, 1910), i. 224–7; and Alexander Altmann, 'A Note on the Rabbinic Doctrine of Creation', *JJS* 7 (1956), 195–206.

[162] On this broader topic, see Nicholas Séd, 'Les Traditions secrètes et les disciples de Rabban Yohanan ben Zakkaï', *RdHR* 184 (1973), 49–66.

The midrashic sources rarely provide an account of the whole pleroma, and usually one must be content with selected pieces of it—in all their diversity and partiality. Moreover, even the diverse fragments hardly constitute any common knowledge that one can speak of with assurance prior to their appearance in the assorted midrashic anthologies. But for all that, some reference to these elements is in order here, at the conclusion of our account of ancient rabbinic myth. For in a striking manner, they variously attest to a mythic realm above and beyond human history, and anticipate theosophical aspects of the metastatic structure of Divinity found in a host of medieval Jewish texts and tracts.

1. Primordial Elements. An ancient comment in *M. ʾAbot* 5. 1 has it that 'The world was created by ten words (*maʾamarot*)', thereby imposing a decadic structure of divine *logoi* upon the seven days of creation, but without any further elaboration.[163] Later explications were more forthcoming, as in the homiletic formulation that links the value of human life to the world 'created by ten words'—a connection that may indeed point to old speculations of a primordial, divine *anthropos* from whose heavenly body or bodily structure the world was formed.[164] More theosophical by far is the explication of a similar dictum transmitted in the name of Rab (BA 1): 'By ten things (*debarim*) the world was created: By Wisdom (*ḥokhmah*), by Understanding (*tebunah*), by Reason (*daʿat*), by Strength, by Roar, by Might, by Righteousness, by Judgement, by Loving kindness, and by Compassion' (*BT Ḥagigah* 12a). Significantly, there is no mention in this teaching of primordial *logoi*, but only of certain qualities—and these of a vastly different nature and status in the divine economy. Thus there is no indication here that these 'things' are created entities (as is Wisdom, in Prov. 8: 22), and exterior modalities through which God created the world; rather, indeed, they appear to be qualities of God's own being or nature: some (the first three) are qualities of intellection; some (the next three) are qualities of power; and others deal with qualities of justice (two) and mercy (two). Altogether, then, there are two triads and two pairs of elements; and these deal with mind, might, and heart respectively. Hence we may suppose that the 'things' represent something of the inner-divine powers, manifest at the creation and in the ongoing governance of the world.

[163] This came to be understood as marked by the ten times that the word *vayyomer* ('and (God) said') occurs in connection with the creation (nine times in Genesis 1, and once in Gen. 2: 18); this overlapping of narrative shows it to be a secondary speculation.

[164] The homiletical point is made in *ʾAbot de-Rabbi Natan* A, 31; Schechter edn. (3rd edn.; New York: Feldheim, 1967), 90f. M. Idel, *Kabbalah: New Perspectives* (New Haven: Yale University Press, 1988), 114–122, has proposed a reconstruction of the older theosophical speculations, based on Gnostic fragments preserved in patristic sources, and hints in ancient and medieval rabbinic texts.

The biblical citations that are appended to Rab's list are also of some interest, as they attempt to add scriptural proofs. Some of these clearly show that they have roots in older mythic speculations or interpretations of biblical verses, as in the support drawn for the first triad from Prov. 3: 19–20a ('YHWH founded earth with wisdom, established heaven with understanding, and with His reason cleaved the deep'). But others show a more forced or obscured link to Scripture—as in the use of the verse 'The pillars of heaven tremble, terrified at His roar' (Job 26: 11) to indicate God's creation; for the passage quoted seems to undo the point at hand, and indicate the undoing of creation and not its establishment. It is only when the wider context is considered that one notes that the previous verse (v. 10) refers to establishing a 'boundary' for the 'waters', and thus dimly hints at a mythic battle against the primordial waters at the time of the creation. As noted earlier, the verb 'roar' often marks this strife in biblical and midrashic sources;[165] and so it seems that if Rab's list retains some vestige of God's bellicose blast which once drove back the sea and gave it limits, later tradents make a more tenuous point, certainly more obscure and on the surface somewhat misleading.

The triad of *ḥokhmah*, *tebunah*, and *daʿat* recur in a later text, with evident links to these old theosophical speculations. Indeed, the formulation in *Pirkei de-Rabbi Eliezer* 3 (end) gives a notable blending of traditions, stating that 'The world was created with ten words (*maʾamarot*), and (these) were comprised (*kullelu*) in three (qualities); as is said, "YHWH created earth with wisdom, etc." (Prov. 3: 19–20)'.[166] Notable is the correlation between the creative words and the modalities of intellection, without any justification; and notable as well is the unification of the decad into a comprehensive triad. This feature would seem to indicate that the first three qualities in Rab's list were deemed to be the higher or more abstract of the ten, and thus comprised the others *in nuce*.[167] If this be the case, there may have been a theosophical distinction made between the three upper qualities of divine intellection and the other seven attributes. Alternatively, the point here may be that the ten creative *logoi* are activated by, and are the realization of, God's mental qualities. The world is thus not the haphazard result of diverse divine attributes (like justice and mercy),[168] but rather the product of reason and deliberation. Presumably, some philosophical myth lurks in the background.

165 See above, pp. 55, 61 n.10, 115, and 117.

166 Thus according to the *editio princeps* (Constantinople, 1514), and also in the three Casanatense MSS used by M. Higger in his edition, *Ḥoreb*, 15–16 (1944–5), 90; but the second edition (Venice, 1544) adds 'And they are wisdom, understanding, and reason' before the proof.

167 This theosophical use of the verb *k-l-l* would lend support to the contention of M. Idel, *Kabbalah: New Perspectives*, 117f. and 330 (n. 37) that the 'golem'-tradition in *Midrash Abkir* (preserved in *Yalkut Shimoni*, Genesis, no. 34) should be interpreted to mean that 'the whole world was concentrated' or comprised in the primeval *anthrōpos*.

168 See above, pp. 99–101.

Even more remarkable is the variation of these traditions in *Midrash Shoḥer Ṭov* (50. 1).[169] It bears citation in full.

'A Psalm of Asaph. God (El), God (Elohim) the Lord (YHWH) spoke and called the earth' (Ps. 50: 1). Some heretics asked R. Simlai, What does 'El, Elohim, YHWH, spoke' mean? He said to them, It is not written 'They spoke and called' but 'He spoke and called'. His students (later) said, Our master, you repulsed those with a (broken) reed,[170] but what will you answer us? He said to them, the three Names are one, as when a person says artisan (*'umnon*), builder (*banyan*), (or) architect (*'architeqtinon*). And why does (Scripture) mention the Name of the Holy One, blessed be He, here, three times? This teaches that the Holy One, blessed be He, created His world with three Names, (which) correspond to (the) three good qualities (*middot*) with which the world was created—with wisdom, with understanding, and with reason; as it says, 'YHWH founded earth with wisdom, established heaven with understanding, and with His reason cleaved the deeps' (Prov. 3: 19–20).

The query posed by 'heretics' to R. Simlai (A 2) ponders the meaning of the multiple divine Names in Ps. 50: 1, and indirectly suggests that more than one god is indicated thereby. But this possibility is rejected by the sage, who uses the singular verb found in this context to suggest otherwise. But this does not satisfy his disciples, who go on to dismiss the rebuttal as being insubstantial ('with a reed'), and they press for a more serious answer for those in his inner circle. The first answer seems to be equally rhetorical, and suggests that these divine Names are simply synonymous epithets and mean the same thing. Certainly, this is a puzzling response, and raises more questions than it answers. Hence it is not surprising that a further query follows directly upon it, and asks why all three Names are necessary, if they are in fact 'one'. A more esoteric answer is now given, and says that these were the three Names with which God created the world, and that these Names correspond to three qualities of intellection involved in this act (citing Prov. 3: 19–20). This correlation is most extraordinary and reveals a theosophical view of the creation supported by midrashic mythmaking—one in which the Names found in Scripture tally with mental qualities. One may assume that the link to the creation was suggested by the phrase '(He) spoke and called earth', which, is transferred from its original context (in which the 'earth' is summoned to deliver God's people to judgement) to a more protological scene.[171] Hence, God's creative *logoi* actualize modes of intellection (here called *middot*), and these are encoded in divine Names. In this way, the strands of earlier traditions are integrated into a more extended expression of mythic theosophy.

[169] S. Buber edn. 278 f.

[170] One should delete 'broken'; it does not occur in the earlier version of *JT Berakhot* 9. 1, or in the other expressions of this debate form found there.

[171] The eschatological setting is appreciated by R. David Kimḥi (*Peirush*, A. Darom edn. 116) and R. Menaḥem Ha-Meiri (*Peirush*, S. Cohn edn. 102).

Just when and where this striking speculation arose cannot be determined, though one may suppose that it is related to teachings similar to those found in the *Pirkei de-Rabbi Eliezer*, in which the words of creation are clearly linked to three mental qualities utilized by God in His acts of creation.[172] But this particular theosophy of Names is also dependent upon an older polemical form found in *JT Berakhot* 9. 1, where it is included among a series of six heretical queries addressed to R. Simlai, where the common denominator concerns texts that could be supposed to indicate a multiplicity of gods.[173] The structure of (1) heretical query (based on a scriptural phrase) plus (2) sage response (based on the same context) is sometimes supplemented by (3) a query by the disciples (for a more substantive answer) plus (4) a special sage response (based on some rabbinic theology). Just this core occurs with respect to the problem of Ps. 50: 1, and thus the further query and response in *Shoḥer Ṭov* (regarding the meaning of the threefold use of divine Names) is certainly a supplement, giving the piece a deeper theosophical turn. The antiquity of this debate form and the special instruction to the disciples is suggested by its use in connection with the riposte given by R. Yoḥanan ben Zakkai (T 1) to the query of a 'gentile' regarding the apparently magical features found in the Red Heifer ritual—though in this case the presenting situation is a rite (not a text), and the answer deflects the protagonist with an argument using comparative evidence. Only in the subsequent, private response to the students does the sage cite Scripture; but his explanation of it inhibits further discussion by labelling the rite a divine 'decree'. As a result, any deeper speculation of meaning or purpose is categorically foreclosed.[174]

2. Divine Qualities and the Throne. The placement and structure of divine qualities is also the topic of another fragment of ancient Jewish theosophy found in *ʾAbot de-Rabbi Natan* A, 37.[175] In this teaching, the focus is on a heptad of elements (not a triad or a decad), and their place in the pleromatic configuration is noted:

[172] Dependence of the *Shoḥer Ṭov* on this source is also suggested by the common extension of the three qualities to the building of the Tabernacle and Temple.

[173] See the MSS variations set forth in *Synopse zum Talmud Yerushalmi*, i/1–2, ed. Peter Schäfer and Hans-Jürgen Becker (Tübingen: J. C. B. Mohr, 1991), 220–3. The string of cases is connected by the phrase *ḥazru ve-šaʾalu* ('[the heretics] again asked'); but the units are not all of a piece (the 5th has an answer by R. Yitzḥak; and only the 2nd–5th have a special answer for the disciples).

[174] See the passage in *Pesikta de-Rab Kahana, Parah* 4. 7 (Mandelbaum edn. 74). It might be suspected that this tannaitic tradition was remoulded by amoraic convention, and is thus no evidence for the antiquity of this debate form. However, David Daube, *The New Testament and Rabbinic Judaism* (London: School of Oriental and African Studies, University of London, 1956), 141–50, has given good reason to suppose that the feature of 'public retort and private explanation', found in the Gospels of Matthew (15: 1 ff.) and Mark (7: 1 ff.) in connection with the ritual of hand-washing, depends on just such a 'specific Rabbinic form'.

[175] Schechter, 110.

Seven qualities (*middot*) serve before the throne of the (divine) Glory (*kabod*), and they are these: Wisdom, Righteousness, Justice, Mercy, Compassion, Truth, and Peace; as it is said, 'I shall betroth you to Me forever; I shall betroth you to Me with Justice and Judgement, (and) with Grace and Compassion; and I shall betroth you to Me with truth, and you shall know (*ve-yadaʿat*) YHWH' (Hos. 2: 21–2). R. Meir says: For what reason does Scripture say 'and you shall know YHWH'?—To teach that any person who has in himself (*she-yesh bo*) all these qualities (*middot*) knows the Knowledge of God (*yodeaʿ daʿato shel maqom*).

It is clear from this presentation that these *middot* are heavenly forms or qualities in the pleroma, that serve God's dominion and rule (nothing is said here about the creation). It is likely that they are primordial entities brought into being by God (as is Wisdom, according to Prov. 8: 22), or are some other embodiment of divine attributes that 'serve' God as agents of His cosmic command. Indeed, we noted earlier that similar forms or powers appear in ancient Israelite speculations of the heavenly world (for example, in Ps. 89: 15 'Righteousness and Justice' were supports of God's throne, and 'Mercy and Truth' served before Him), even as 'Righteousness and Equity' were already divinities mentioned in the old Canaanite and Phoenician pantheon.[176] Hence our rabbinic speculation is part and parcel of mythic theosophies or great antiquity;[177] what singles it out is the enumeration of a heptad of qualities, and the positing of their localization and function. Notable, too, is that they are not called 'ministering angels' (*malʾakhei ha-sharet*) but 'qualities that serve' (*middot ha-meshammeshot*) before the throne.

The connection between heavenly *middot* and the proof-text from Hos. 2: 21–2 must be ancient, for a link between the two is already presupposed by R. Meir (T 3) in his explanation.[178] This teaching stresses the component of knowledge, and states that if a person has incorporated or otherwise interiorized the supernal qualities something akin to having the 'Knowledge of God' will result. Surely a mode of theosophical gnosis is alluded to here, as the capstone of religious achievement; but what that knowledge is, and just how it might be attained through the realization of righteousness, mercy, and truth by an individual is not stated. Only as a possibility might one suppose that R. Meir sets as a spiritual ideal the realization on earth of the divine qualities; so that, through their full embodiment in action, the human self may intuit or apprehend the way and being of God, whose dominion or governance of the world is itself guided by these same *middot*.

[176] See above, p. 54.

[177] Peace also appears as a hypostatic element in Ps. 85: 15, along with Righteousness, Justice, and Truth.

[178] It is idle to speculate on the original number; but one can at least detect the possibility that these lists reflect conceptual considerations. Note that the rabbinic heptad breaks down into three pairs of elements (justice; mercy; and truth/harmony) plus superordinate wisdom; whereas the biblical pentad has two pairs of elements (justice; mercy) plus the mediating quality of truth.

Less hopeful is an assertion found just after this text, in which it is stated that 'because of sin, it is not given for man to know (*leydaʿ*) the (divine) likeness (*demut*) on high; for were it not for this (namely, sin), all the keys would be given to him and he would know (*yodeaʿ*) with what (*be-mah*) heaven and earth were created' (*ʾAbot de-Rabbi Natan* A, 39).[179] But here, again, the precise nature of the divine knowledge is left obscure, and one can only infer that this heavenly figure is the manifest Lord of creation (like the Demiurge known from Gnostic sources),[180] enthroned on high, and that knowledge of His being gives access, in some way, to the secrets and means of creation. Clearly, this is a theosophical apprehension different from the one previously noted, which advocates some human actualization of the hypostatic qualities found in the pleroma on high. And yet, for all that, a common denominator between them may be perceived in the nomistic precondition of the divine knowledge to be attained; for in both cases the realization of transcendental gnosis depends upon the proper human activation or performance of certain divine demands or qualities, and cannot be achieved otherwise.

3. The Patriarchs and the Throne. There is another fragment of mythic theosophy in the old midrashic sources worthy of note here, for it too deals with the divine pleroma and its elements. The example involves the well-known dictum of R. Simeon ben Lakish, that 'The patriarchs are in fact the (divine) Chariot' (*ha-ʾabot hen hen ha-merkabah*)—an opaque phrase that seems to allude to some esoteric secret, but that leaves one little to build on. The only cues are the three proof-texts cited.[181] Read idiomatically, the expressions *va-yaʿal ʾelohim me-ʿal Abraham* (Gen. 17: 22) and *va-yaʿal me-ʿalav ʾelohim* (ibid. 35: 13) must be construed to mean that 'Elohim departed from' Abraham and Jacob, respectively; and the phrase *(ve-hinneh) YHWH nitzav ʿalav* (Gen. 28: 13), must similarly mean that 'YHWH stood over' Jacob—while he slept at Bethel. But if we read the proofs in this way, the texts retain their strong anthropomorphic aspect, but leave the dictum empty of any clear or apparent sense. For this reason we are constrained to attempt a more concrete reading, which yields the more mythic image that 'Elohim ascended upon' Abraham and Jacob, in the first passage, and that 'YHWH stood upon' Jacob in the second. But we are still left bereft of sense. Just what could R. Simeon have meant?

179 Schechter 116. The knowledge is thus one of means; and this links it to the other speculations, noted earlier, which say that the world was creation 'with' (*be-*) ten *logoi* or things.

180 This is the suggestion of Saul Lieberman, in 'How Much Greek in Jewish Palestine?', in Alexander Altmann (ed.), *Biblical and Other Studies*, (Brandeis Texts and Studies, 1; Cambridge, Mass.; Harvard University Press, 1963), 141.

181 See the passages in *Genesis Rabba* 47. 6; 69. 3; and 82. 13 (Theodor–Albeck, 474 f.; 793; and 983), and parallels.

Granted, the immediate context leaves us empty-handed; but a vast number of speculative snippets indicate that the patriarchs were deemed in some circles to be elements of the divine Chariot, upon which the Lord God was enthroned and manifest.[182] Hence, when Scripture speaks of God ascending upon Abraham or Jacob, we have to understand that He was mounted upon their mythic form on high. Nothing clear, in this regard, is stated about Abraham; but the patriarchal figure of Jacob evoked a rich mythology—sometimes portraying his supernal visage as a heavenly prototype of his earthly one (engraved upon the Chariot),[183] and sometimes referring to him as an angelic or even divine power.[184] Even more remarkable is the midrashic tradition that interprets the verse 'He (Jacob) set up an altar there and called it El-Elohei-Israel' (Gen. 33: 20) as the patriarch saying to the Lord: 'You are God (Eloah) for the beings above (*ba-ʿelyonim*), and I am god (Eloah) for the beings below (*ba-taḥtonim*)'—no more and no less. Just as striking in this regard (though with a diminution of Jacob's authority), is the explication of this verse in a tannaitic tradition found in *BT Megillah* 18a, which presents God Himself as the speaker.

R. Aḥa said in the name of R. Eleazar: From where do we know that the Holy One, blessed be He, calls Jacob 'god'? (From the passage where) it is written, 'He called him El, the God of Israel (Elohei Israel)' (Gen. 33: 20). For if you suppose that Jacob called the altar by the name 'god', it would have been necessary to read 'Jacob called it'. However, it says 'He called him' (namely, Jacob). And who called him? El, the God of Israel.

Clearly, in these passages (and others) Jacob is a divine being or element on high—a part of the heavenly pleroma, and in some cases even a feature on the Chariot itself.[185] Hence when R. Simeon says that 'The patriarchs are in fact the Chariot', he speaks of the personified image or being of the patriarchs on the throne. But this mythic reality does not allow us to determine the ontological relation between these figures and the historical personalities known as the patriarchs. Perhaps they were assumed to be docetic manifestations of their heavenly form; or perhaps they were more concrete embodiments of divine elements on high: there is no way to know.[186]

[182] Cf. such passages as Targum Yerushalmi (M. Klein, *The Fragment-Targums of the Pentateuch* (Rome, 1980), 57) and Targum Ps.-Jon. on Gen. 28: 12; *Genesis Rabba* 68. 12 (Theodor–Albeck, 788); and *Midrash Yelammedenu* (in *Batei Midrashot*, ed. S. Wertheimer (Jerusalem: Makhon Ketav Ve-Sefer, 1980), i. 156).

[183] See previous note. [184] See *Genesis Rabbah* 78. 3 (Theodor–Albeck, 921).

[185] In a *piyyuṭ* of Yannai to Gen. 28: 12, the angelic host surrounds the Chariot and, upon seeing the image of Jacob there, sanctify God as the 'God of Israel'. See *Piyyuṭei Yannai*, ed. Z. M. Rabinovitz, i. 168 f. This mythic representation stands between the 'divinizations' of Jacob expressed by Jacob and God, noted just above.

[186] According to Philo, *De confusione linguarum* 146, Jacob was an angelic manifestation of the Logos. For a comparison of this passage with the Prayer of Joseph, see already Edmund

For latter tradition, the figure of Jacob, especially, was the focus of meditative or mystical regard.[187] But at least one midrashic source gives direct proof that the dictum of R. Simeon could be radically spiritualized, and thus an indirect indication that the patriarchs served as models of more inward meditations and mystical experiences. According to *Midrash Ha-Gadol* (on Gen. 28: 13),[188] the phrase 'The patriarchs are in fact the Chariot' was explicated as follows: 'Because the form of the Chariot (*tzurat ha-merkabah*) was chiselled in their hearts (i.e. the hearts of the patriarchs), and (the phenomenon of) the Chariot requires it to have a Rider, they were called a Chariot' of God.

Such a passage does not deny the myth of the pleroma, any more than the earlier one regarding the qualities that serve before the throne of Glory. But each in its own way instructs us how the components of the divine world could be personalized or interiorized in the heart or mind of a seeker after the concrete reality of God—be that a matter of knowledge or presence. In fact, in both cases, mythic ontologies in the supernal realm have been actualized as an inner truth for the individual. They thus anticipate the profound mystical transformation of myth which is a subject in its own right.[189]

Stein, 'Zur apokryphen Schrift "Gebet Josephs"', *MGWJ* 81 (1937), 283. By contrast, some midrashic comments on Isa. 49: 3 portray the 'glorification' of the man Jacob onto the throne; see the cases discussed in Appendix 2, pp. 340 f.

[187] See the rich and nuanced studies of Micheline Chaze, 'De l'identification des patriarches au char divin: Recherche du sens d'un enseignement rabbinique dans le Midrash et dans la Kabbale prézoharique et ses sources', *RÉJ* 149 (1990), 5–75; and of Elliot Wolfson, 'The Image of Jacob Engraved Upon the Throne: Further Reflections on the Esoteric Doctrine of the German Pietists', in his *Along the Path: Studies in Kabbalistic Myth, Symbolism, and Hermeneutics* (Albany: State University of New York, 1995), ch. 1.

[188] Edition of Mordecai Margulies (Jerusalem: Mosad ha-Rav Kook, 1968), 504 f.

[189] It is not certain if the *Midrash Ha-Gadol* passage here is ancient or the product of the later compiler, so at the least one would have to say that this passage provides a conceptual or phenomenological anticipation of later developments. It may be observed that the spiritualizing of R. Simeon's dictum is also reflected in the comment on Gen. 17: 22 (p. 409), where we are told that God ascended upon Abraham and Jacob 'because they were sanctified for the presence of the *Shekhinah*; whereas (God) was revealed to the other prophets in the Glory (*ba-kabod*), each one according to his strength (or capacity)'.

III
Jewish Myth and Mythmaking in the Middle Ages

10
Introduction

A. SOME RECEPTION-HISTORIES OF MYTH

The streams carrying the contents of rabbinic myths into the Middle Ages were many and diverse, as we have seen, and included not only late anthologies of Midrash (as *Pirkei de-Rabbi Eliezer*, *Berei'shit Rabbati*, and *Midrash Tanḥuma*),[1] but also much liturgical poetry (by such influential composers as Yose ben Yose, Yannai, and R. Eleazar Kallir), and the tractates of the Palestinian and Babylonian Talmuds then in circulation. The diversity of these sources suggests not only a diversity of settings in which these traditions were learned, recited, and preached; it also indicates the variety of audiences that could have been addressed by this material, in the study halls and synagogues. Comments on certain Talmudic passages by various rabbis, furthermore, show how Jews in different parts of the Diaspora dealt with some of the bolder or more perplexing passages in this literature; and the reactions of a number of hostile or contentious readers show that this material entered still other circles (through conversions and other means) and led to still other responses. All this comprises the ongoing life of Jewish myth, and the direct impact it had on its readers.

Sorting out the patterns is instructive. Three types may be noted: (1) a defence of the straightforward sense of Scripture and the Midrash, where they speak in bold imagery about God; (2) a denunciation or denial of the apparent, straightforward sense of these and other passages; and (3) an affirmation of the religious language and depictions in these corpora as a sacred code of the higher mysteries.

Characteristic of the first position, which takes a literal approach to the anthropomorphisms and anthropopathisms found in both the Hebrew Bible and rabbinic literature, is that formulated in *Ketab Tamim*, by R. Moses Taku, a thirteenth-century German talmudist.[2] The author takes a strong, uncompromising position on these matters—citing numerous sources verbatim, in versions known to him. Among these we may particularly cite the

[1] As an example, one can note the influence of *Pirkei de-Rabbi Eliezer* on medieval works like *Sefer Ha-Zikhronot, Hu' Dibrei Ha-Yamim Le-Yeraḥmiel* (critical edition by Eli Yassif (Tel Aviv: Tel Aviv University Press, 2001); cf. the midrashic allusions and citations dealing with the opening week of creation (adduced by Yassif, *passim*), and particularly the annotation 'ke-meforash be-Firkei de-R. Eliezer' (p. 79).

[2] Ed. Raphael Kirchheim, in *'Otzar Neḥmad*, 3 (1860), 54–99.

reference discussed earlier, from *BT Berakhot* 3a, where it is reported that God periodically mourns over His destroyed Temple, 'roaring like a lion, . . . "Woe, for I have destroyed My House" '.[3] Throughout, the polemical thrust of the work is obvious; for what is at stake is nothing less than the veracity of 'the *'aggadot* of our Talmud, upon which we rely'.[4] The most commonly named interlocutor and object of R. Moses' ire is R. Saadia Gaon, who systematically defanged the straightforward sense of Scripture and Midrash, and substituted allegorical meanings instead.[5] This effort is deemed nothing else than 'idle chatter' by our author, for to him the sages were inspired by 'the holy spirit'.[6]

Saadia's denial of the offending sources, takes us to the second type of response. In part, his evasions of the surface sense of these texts is fuelled by virulent Karaite denunciations of the bold midrashic formulations, as we can clearly see from the specification of rabbinic 'abominations' formulated by such nearly contemporary authors as Jacob al-Qirqisani, in his *Kitab 'al-'Anwar* (The Book of Lights), and Salomon ben Yeruḥim, in his *Sefer Milḥamot Ha-Shem* (The Book of the Wars of the Lord). Significantly, both polemicists highlight the reference to divine wailing in *BT Berakhot* 3a in their lists of aggadic outrages;[7] and it is quite notable for the inner history of these polemics that the Muslim theologian Ibn Ḥazm (eleventh century, Spain) also gives special emphasis and rebuke to this very motif of divine mourning (although in his citation the archangel Metatron, known in his words as 'the small God', is the speaker),[8] and the Jewish convert Petrus Alfonsi (twelfth century, Spain) also vents his anger against this passage, calling it a 'blasphemy' against God.[9] Even more scornful are the

[3] See ch. 8 above, n. 21, for the received version and variants.

[4] *Ketab Tamim*, 63. *'Aggadot* is used here in a comprehensive sense, to designate all the narratives, teachings, and legends of rabbinic literature.

[5] Cf. Simon Rawidowicz, 'Saadya's Purification of the Idea of God', (see Ch. 1, n. 15). See also Harry A. Wolfson, 'Maimonides on Negative Attributes', in *The Louis Ginzberg Jubilee Volume* (New York: Jewish Theological Seminary of America, 1945), 411–46.

[6] *Ketab Tamim*, 70.

[7] See in Israel Davidson, *Sefer Milḥamot Ha-Shem* (New York: The Jewish Theological Seminary of America, 1934), 108 (ch. 14, esp. ll. 15–16), and Leon Nemoy, 'Al-Qirqisani's Account of the Jewish Sects', *HUCA* 7 (1930), 352.

[8] Cf. Ignacz Goldziher, 'Proben muhammedänischer Polemik gegen den Talmud', *Jeschurun* (ed. Koback), 8 (1872), 102–4. The reference to Metatron as 'Y"Y Qaṭan' (Lesser YHWH) is also given by Qirqisani, apparently quoting *BT Sanh. 38b* (where R. 'Idit says that the name of Metatron is 'like the name of his master'). See the Arabic citation in G. Scholem, *Major Trends in Jewish Mysticism* (New York: Schocken Books, 1941), 366 n. 107. The received rabbinic formulation seems like a pious circumlocution or correction. For early references to the 'lesser Yaho' in pseudepigraphic and gnostic sources, see Scholem, ibid. 68 f.; and for the notion of a 'small god' in late antiquity, as attested in Greek, Latin, and even Jewish sources (*JT Abodah Zarah* 2. 3), see S. Lieberman, appendix 1, in Ithamar Gruenwald, *Apocalyptic and Merkabah Mysticism* (Leiden, E. J. Brill, 1980), 236 f., in the context of discussing the meaning of 'Metatron'.

[9] See *Diologus Petri, cognomento Alphonsi*, in *Patrologia Latina*, ed. J.-P. Migne (Paris, 1854), 157: 550–1.

fulminations on this and related passages voiced by his French contemporary, Petrus Venerabilis of Cluny.[10]

The mythic proclivities of certain midrashic texts perplexed more sympathetic readers as well, across the Jewish world, as we can see from questions addressed to Rabbeinu Ḥai Gaon, the head of the 'Babylonian' academy of Pumbeditha in the eleventh century, and annotations to the Talmud by Rabbeinu Ḥananel of Kairouan at the same time. In the first case, the Gaon responded to queries about the statement in *BT Berakhot* 59b reporting God's tears and acts of distress on account of the destroyed Temple,[11] explaining that the depiction had no substance whatever and was merely 'a figure of speech (*be-torat mashal*)'.[12] Commenting on the same passage, R. Ḥananel first observed that its rhetorical function was 'to demonstrate to Israel that the Holy One, blessed be He, has not abandoned them'; and then proceeded to unhinge the very actuality of the trope, saying that the image does not refer to real 'tears from the eye, but rather (to) drops (that seemed) like tears'.[13] To this docetic rationalization he added that God does not kick or clap or groan in despair either, but rather 'the Holy One, blessed be He, commands an angel' to do this. Some two centuries later, this position was transmitted in a commentary on liturgical poetry, *ʿArugat Ha-Bosem*; and in it the whole matter was summed up with the remark, 'Everything (was done) by an angel'.[14]

Clearly, these types of reaction do not denounce this mythic *ʾaggadah* in the manner of the traducers of Jewish traditions; but they do deny it any straightforward sense. Hence if there is any affirmation expressed here, it draws upon the conviction that these rabbinic comments could not offend religious sensibilities and erroneously ascribe physical qualities to God.[15] Rightly regarded, these comments are metaphorical formulations analogous to the anthropomorphic figures used by the prophets in Scripture, who 'spoke in the language of men'.[16] Maimonides was rather more guarded about the veracity of all the teachings of the sages in rabbinic literature,

[10] See *Tractatus adversus Judaeorum*, in *Patrologia Latina*, ed. J.-P. Migne (Paris, 1854), 189: 622. A comparison between this text and Petrus Alfonsi's is made in S. Lieberman, *Sheqiʿin* (2nd edn.; Jerusalem: Wahrmann, 1960), 28 f. See my earlier discussion in *The Exegetical Imagination* (Cambridge, Mass.: Harvard University Press, 1998), 30–2, where some conclusions are offered regarding continuities between Karaite and Christian polemics.

[11] See above, p. 98, and the detailed analysis in *The Exegetical Imagination*, 24–6.

[12] In *ʾOtzar Ha-Geʾonim: Thesaurus of the Geonic Responsa and Commentaries*, ed. Benjamin M. Lewin (Haifa and Jerusalem, 1928–43), *Berakhot*, 'Teshubat', 2. R. David Kimḥi likewise apologized for the expression 'roar' in Jer. 25: 30, saying that 'He roars from on high' is *ʿal derekh mashal*, 'a figurative expression'.

[13] Lewin (ed.), in appendices to *ʾOtzar Ha-Geʾonim, Berakhot*, 62 f. See now in *Peirushei Rabbeinu Ḥananel bar Ḥushiel le-Massekhet Berakhot* (Jerusalem: Lev Sameḥ Institute, 1990), 130.

[14] See *Sefer ʿArugat Ha-Bosem*, ed, Ephraim E. Urbach. (Jerusalem: Mekize Nirdamim, 1962), iii. 108 f.

[15] See *ʾOtzar Ha-Geʾonim, Berakhot*, 'Teshubot', 131. [16] Ibid.

and noted that through ignorance they could sometimes be in error of scientific truth.[17] On the other hand, those formulations that appear to contradict theological or other principles of Judaism, required study to penetrate their true and proper purpose.[18] The mythic imagery of these texts is thus not what it seems to be, and the prism of philosophical allegory is often the necessary corrective to such misprision.[19]

A proper reading of Scripture and the rabbinic Aggadah in the Talmud and Midrash marks our third type, as well; however, it is characterized by a new spirit of affirmation that regards the images and language of these texts as encoding profound mysteries of a supernal nature. The works dealing with these matters in the twelfth and thirteenth centuries show different treatments of this topic, and we shall note several examples here as a prologue to our consideration of some myths in the book of *Zohar*, which shall be the central subject of this Part. The ensuing examples take up mythologoumena and themes considered earlier.

I. The Mythic Discourse of the Bahir

The first work of this type that is known is the book of *Bahir*, which appeared in Provence in the twelfth century. It was the subject of many researches by Gershom Scholem over his entire academic career, and these are summed up in a penetrating manner in his masterwork *Origins of the Kabbalah*.[20] Indeed, this book is a foundational moment in the history of the Kabbalah, although its own origins and antecedents are often in doubt.[21] A whole host of topics are taken up (including matters of the alphabet, cantillation notes, and the Divine Throne); but the overarching concern is to discuss the ten gradations or *logoi* that comprise the supernal realm of Divinity, and to adduce both

[17] See Alexander Marx, 'The Correspondence Between the Rabbis of Southern France and Maimonides about Astrology', *HUCA* 3 (1926), 356.

[18] In his commentary on the Mishnah, Maimonides referred to a plan to write a systematic work on the teachings in the Midrash Aggadah, 'demonstrating which must be understood literally and which metaphorically'; see *Peirush Ha-Mishnayot*, ed. Joseph Kafiḥ (Jerusalem, 1958), *M. Sanhedrin, Pereq Ḥeleq*, 209. Note also the principle he enunciated in *Teshubot Ha-Rambam*, ed. Joseph Blau (Jerusalem, 1958), ii. 715f.

[19] See Marc Saperstein, *Decoding the Rabbis: A Thirteenth-Century Commentary on the Aggadot* (Cambridge, Mass.: Harvard University Press, 1980), for his comprehensive introduction to the problems posed by the Aggadah for medieval interpreters, and his study of the allegorical commentaries of R. Isaac b. Yedaiah. See also, in this vein, Yitzhak Twersky, 'R. Yedaiyah Ha-Penini u-Feirusho la-ʾAggadah', in Siegfried Stein and Raphael Loewe (edd.), *Studies in Jewish Religious and Intellectual History presented to Alexander Altmann* (Alabama: The University of Alabama Press, 1979), 63–82 (Hebrew pagination).

[20] Ed. R. J. Zwi Werblowsky and trans. from the German by Allan Arkush (Philadelphia and Princeton: The Jewish Publication Society and Princeton University Press, 1987), 49–198.

[21] Scholem, *Origins of the Kabbalah*, repeatedly sought to find parallel with ancient mythic materials of a Gnostic sort. Moshe Idel has added to this discussion, with new examples and an emphasis on the Jewish background for the material; see 'Le-Baʿayat Ḥeqer Ha-Meqorot shel *Sefer Ha-Bahir*', *JSJT* 6 (1987), 55–72.

the words of Scripture and the teachings of the sages as textual supports for such speculations. In the process, mythic imagery appears and mythic discourses unfold—characteristically as units in their own right, with no evident attempt to gather certain topics under one heading or smooth over contradictions.

While the work purports to be an ancient Midrash taught by R. Reḥuma'i and R. Amora, among others, the frequent opening query *ma'i dikhtib* ('what is the meaning of the passage?') belies this midrashic presumption insofar as the formula does not introduce a homily on the cited unit, as is common in old rabbinic sources,[22] but rather gives a specific answer (marked by the term *'ela'*) that relates the opening passage to a particular gradation or process within the divine realm. The *Bahir* thus abounds in esoteric annotations and clarifications of diverse citations, and not in open-ended exegetical inquiries. Nevertheless, these various explications of the mysteries are often formulated in a highly mythic manner. The following cases are typical.[23]

1. The Source of All. Section 14 opens with an extended quote from a teaching found in a variant form in *Genesis Rabba* 3. 8, which presents the view of R. Yoḥanan that the angels were not created until the second day of creation, 'So that no one could say that Michael stretched out (the universe) at the south side of the firmament, and Gabriel (was) at the north, and the Holy One, blessed be He, arranged it in the middle; but rather, (in Scripture God says) "I, YHWH, Who made everything (*kol*), Who alone stretched forth the heavens and unaided (*me-'itti*, lit. 'from Me') spread out (*roqa'*) the earth" (Isa. 44: 24)'. The midrashic source goes on to specify that the phrase is actually written *mi 'itti* ('who was with Me') in order to make the point that God had no 'partner' in the work of creation. This specification is not given at this stage in the *Bahir*, but it was adduced at the end of the comment on this midrash, which taught:

It is I who have planted this 'tree' so that the whole (*kol*) world may delight in it and with it I have spread out the All (*kol*), and called its name 'All'—for on it depends the All and from it emanates the All; all things need it and gaze upon it and long for it; and from it souls fly forth. I was alone when I made it and no angel can raise himself above it and say: I preceded You; for when I spread out My earth and planted and rooted this tree and had them delight in each other and Myself delighted in them, who was with Me (*mi 'itti*) to whom I could have revealed this mystery (*sod*)?

What we have in this section is a remarkable myth of origins formulated through a midrash denying any angels a share in the work of creation, on the basis of a biblical proof-text. However, this verse is now taken to another

[22] Cf. the teachings of Rava in *BT 'Erub.* 21b.

[23] The citations follow the critical edition and paragraphs in Daniel Abrams, *Sefer Ha-Bahir 'al pi Kitbei Ha-Yad Ha-Qedumim* (Los Angeles: Cherub Press, 1994).

level, and used to specify a primordial process and structure in the supernal realms. Close analysis shows the skilfulness of this exegetical specification. The 'I' of the lemma is also the speaking voice of the new myth; so that God Himself narrates this account of origins. Then, the biblical reference to God making 'everything' is transformed into God establishing the 'whole' world through a cosmic tree which He planted in His earth, and which spans the 'All' upon which 'All' depends. Apparently, a pun on the word 'stretched forth' (*noṭeh*) in the lemma stimulated the sense that God 'planted' (*naṭaʿti*) something in the upper realms; and presumably the word *me-ʾitti* not only suggested to the author that the formation of the earth was 'from' God alone, but that this earth emerged 'from' God Himself (that is, 'from Me') and was itself a supernal dimension or gradation in which the structure of All-Being is rooted and from which all else is emanated. Since this tree is at the very source of all created Being, the truth of the midrash is proved: God is the Source of all sources, and no one was 'with' Him at all—let alone any one who could be told the 'mystery' now being revealed in this text.[24]

The myth is thus told three times: first, in the midrashic narrative taught by R. Yoḥanan, which denies the role of angels; second, in the biblical proof that he adduces, which emphasizes the sole existence of God at the time of His creation; and third, in the teaching of the *Bahir*, which utilizes both texts to reveal that God is Other than the All but that it is rooted in Him (in the symbolic domain called 'earth'). Accordingly, there are also three creation myths told: the first being a narrative about the stretching forth of the vault of heaven by angels at the corners and God in the centre (it is denied); second, by a statement that God is the supreme and only Lord of creation of the 'world' (it is affirmed); and third, by a theosophic myth that transforms the language of Scripture (and the hints of the midrash) into an account of the monistic structure of the 'world' of All-Being (it is revealed). With deft ambiguity aided by the variants *me-ʾitti* and *mi ʾitti*, the *Bahir* straddles between a myth of a God who is distinct and totally other than the source of all Being, and one that affirms Him as being the Source of that very source.

2. The Cosmic Column. The truncated nature of the tree symbolism in section 14, which lacks an account of such matters as its sustenance by divine

[24] Scholem, *Origins of the Kabbalah*, 71, adduces section 14, but pays no attention to the exegetical nature of this teaching, and only remarks that the word earth 'perhaps' symbolizes a higher sphere. In his dissertation, *Das Buch Bahir* (Leipzig, 1923; repr. Darmstadt: Wissenschaftliche Buchgesellschaft, 1970), 17, Scholem already understands the 'tree' as a symbol for 'die Gesamtheit aller Sephiroth'—and not the specific gradation of *Yesod* ('Foundation'), that also bears the cognomen 'All' (cf. Ramban on Gen. 24: 1, where he also cites this passage from the *Bahir*). For a consideration of some of the sources that bear on the tree symbolism discussed in this myth, see Elliot Wolfson, *Along the Path* (Albany: State University of New York Press, 1995), chap. 2. For the wider scope of the imagery, and of inverse trees, see the discussion of Adolph Jacoby, 'Der Baum mit den Wurzeln nach oben und den Zweigen nach unten', *Zeitschrift für Missionskunde und Religionswissenschaft*, 43 (1928), 78–85.

powers from above and human actions from below, not to mention the very integration of its organic elements, suggests that we have but a fragment of a mythic topos known to the author and his circle.[25] Some of these missing matters are taken up by another myth of origins reported in the Babylonian Talmud (*BT Ḥagigah* 12b) and transformed in the *Bahir* (section 71).

The old rabbinic teaching states, 'The world rests on one pillar, and its name is "righteous"; for it states that "The righteous is the foundation of the world" (Prov. 10: 25)'.[26] It is clearly a teaching in two parts: a rabbinic *logion* and a biblical proof-text. The first of these is a piece of mythic lore similar to the words of the psalmist, 'Righteousness and justice are the support of His throne' (Ps. 97: 2)—though now there is one base with one name, and this base supports the world itself and not the divine throne.[27] The ethical import of this mythic assertion is hardly in doubt, and it is reinforced by a scriptural passage that speaks in a hyperbolic fashion, valorizing the role of the human righteous in the maintenance of the world. Indeed, the rabbinic teaching establishes a concordance between the two parts and thus gives the first assertion a human component it did not originally have.

When the *Bahir* takes up this matter, it only apparently has any similarity with the earlier version, since in this theosophic work the focus of attention is on the supernal realm.

He taught: A single column spans from the earth to heaven, and its name is 'righteous'—after the (human) righteous. When there are righteous (persons) upon earth, it (the column) is strengthened, and when there are not, it is weakened; and it bears the entire world, for it is said, 'The righteous is the foundation of the world' (Prov. 10: 25). But if it is weak, it cannot sustain the world?! Hence (we learn),[28] Even if there were only one righteous person on earth, he would maintain the world.

In this mythologoumenon, expounded by R. Berekhia, there is a double perspective. Taking its point of departure from the teaching in *BT Ḥagigah* 12b, it appears, first, that the column in question ascends from the earth below to the heavenly realm of God, and that this column supports this cosmic 'world' insofar as it is a configuration of righteous persons (or even just one of them, according to the qualification).[29] Hence proper action has a direct effect on the entire divine sphere, which is dependent upon such human behaviour (namely, performance of the commandments). However, from another perspective, the column in question may also be said to span from the divine sphere called 'earth' (that is, the lowest gradation in it) to

[25] Cf. Scholem, *Origins of the Kabbalah*, 72 f.

[26] This is a striking transformation of the biblical verse, whose teaching about the fates of the wicked and the righteous resembles Ps. 1: 3–4.

[27] For the mythic features of Ps. 97: 2, see above, p. 54.

[28] *BT Yoma* 38b.

[29] Scholem, *Origins of the Kabbalah*, 153, reads the problem added as a positive assertion, not a query; but this complicates matters. In light of the earlier statement that the world can be supported by a weak column.

the one called 'heaven'—which is apparently the highest gradation, so that the righteous on earth would establish a bond that sustains the entire cosmic structure. This realm is now symbolically the 'world' mentioned in the rabbinic and biblical passages; and given the focus on the 'entire' (*kol*) sphere of Divinity, it is unlikely that the pole in question only joins two lower gradations (i.e. the earth and heaven), although some allusion to this conjunction cannot be excluded, with the import that the righteous constitute a channel linking two parts of the whole.

It is instructive to follow the exegetical character of the mythmaking here, for the explication of the elements is the very substance of the mythic narration. It is also significant that it is the midrashic exposition and elaboration that is explicit, whereas the theosophical aspect is allusive and unspecified. In this way the new myth is revealed and concealed simultaneously; and only those in the know would understand the true significance of the teaching. For the true adept, the cosmic nature of human action means that righteous behaviour below has a divine dimension on high and that these two realms are mysteriously one. The act of mythmaking thus serves as a mode of theosophical instruction, and a means of initiation into the supernal mysteries.

II. Some Mysteries of the Aggadah According to R. Azriel

1. The Divine Voice. The relationship between rabbinic Midrash and the higher mysteries is taken up in other works of the period, although in more esoteric or allusive ways. One of these texts is a series of comments on Talmudic Aggadot penned by R. Azriel (thirteenth century, Gerona), who adapted an earlier work of this type by his close compatriot R. Ezra.[30] In it a whole host of passages are cited that range across the wide spectrum of rabbinic subjects (laws, rituals, and assorted theological and other dicta), and there are extensive quotes from many pertinent midrashic sources. However, as suggested above, the author seems concerned to guard the secret character of his teachings and often hedges his terse comments with phrases like 'you should know', or 'all this is explained to the adept', or even 'I am not even able to hint to you this secret here'.[31] This factor often gives the comments of Azriel a dense and barely decipherable quality. For example, in referring to the report in *BT Berakhot* 3a about a divine voice overheard by R. Yose moaning like a dove over the destruction of the Temple ('I heard a *bat qol* cooing like a dove, and saying "Woe"', etc., there occurs only the briefest annotation. 'We already know what the *bat qol* is.'[32]

[30] See *Peirush Ha-ʾAggadot Le-Rabbi ʾAzriel*, ed. Isaiah Tishby (2nd ed.; Jerusalem, Magnes Press, 1983).

[31] Ibid. 42 f.

[32] Tishby, ibid. 63(1a). The statement refers to the mystical sense of the term *bat qol*. For usages in classical rabbinic sources, see Lieberman, *Hellenism in Jewish Palestine*, appendix I (pp. 194–9).

R. Azriel does not break the seal on this secret; but since the simple meaning of *bat qol* would not have perplexed any versed rabbinic reader, who regularly encountered it as a 'happenstance communication' by God, we may perforce assume that he gave a more esoteric sense to R. Yose's audition. And since a quite literal translation of this term is 'daughter (*bat*) of a voice', it is likely that the mystic conceives of the communication as from a feminine divine potency, which is in a subordinate relation to a masculine (or paternal) Voice.[33] The cry would thus be that of the supernal *Shekhinah* (the daughter); and by this transference, the old myth is extended upward into a cosmic sorrow.

2. The Recesses of Divinity. In another rabbinic passage dealing with divine mourning for His Temple, a different exegetical strategy occurs after citing the midrash in *BT Ḥagigah* 5b.[34] In that passage, Jer. 13: 17 is interpreted as describing God's entering His heavenly sanctum and crying for the loss of His earthly shrine. The two terms used in the verse, *mistarim* (hidden section) and *geivoh* (inner unit), are explained as referring to outer chambers (*batei bara'ei*) and inner ones (*batei gava'ei*) respectively—the first being a place where, under these special circumstances, mourning takes place among the heavenly hosts, whereas the second area is more inward and only a place for divine glory and joy. The lamentation by the angels in the outer area is then proved by a scriptural citation, in which they are said to 'cry outside' and 'weep bitterly' (Isa. 33: 7). Such sorrow is explained as meaning that the divine judgement was not levied in full, as planned. A second-order myth follows.

The 'inner chambers' (*batei gava'ei*) are the crowns, which are spiritual and extend upwards; the ones of which it is written, 'Glory and splendour are before Him' (Ps. 96: 6). These (chambers) are called 'dwelling' (*ma'on*), (as it says,) 'A dwelling (*me'onah*) of the primordial God, and beneath (it) are the eternal arms' (Deut. 33: 27);[35] meaning: beneath the dwelling are the arms, which are like what is written, 'He (God) leads forth at the right hand of Moses, the arm of His splendour' (Isa. 63: 12). And the 'outer chambers' (*batei bara'ei*) are[36] 'the disciples of YHWH' (Isa. 54: 13) with the shining light, which is the speculum that shines. And concerning this, it is said (that) 'darkness envelops the light', since it (the darkness) is its source; and that is (the meaning of) 'He puts darkness as His hiding place, His tent roundabout Him' (Ps. 18: 12); and (also) 'His locks are curled and black as a raven' (Songs 5: 11)—and they have said, '"His locks": upon His form';[37] and it is (also the meaning of) 'the waters

[33] This pattern is actually spelled out in MS Vatican 441, 42a, and is cited to this effect by Tishby, ibid. 63 n. 3.

[34] See above, p. 164, for an analysis.

[35] I translate according to the ensuing explanation; for the plain sense and earlier rabbinic reinterpretations, see p. 99.

[36] Reading *hem*, with MS Vatican 185, in parallelism with the opening explanation. The *editio princeps* reads *ba-hem*, 'in them', which makes sense but somewhat complicates the syntax.

[37] Reading *be-qomato*, with MSS Vatican 185 and Parma 1390. The 'curls' on the Divine Anthropos are mentioned in mystical texts speculating on the dimensions of the divine Form; cf. *The Shi'ur Qomah: Texts and Recensions*, ed. Martin S. Cohen (Tübingen: J. C. B. Mohr, 1985),

conceived and gave birth to darkness' (*Exodus Rabba* 15. 22)—which is even proved by the passage 'darkness of water, thick clouds of the sky' (Ps. 18: 12).[38]

This commentary takes us deep into the theosophical myth of R. Azriel—indeed, as a commentary on a rabbinic midrash, it is a revision of this older myth of God's heavenly chambers and a transumption of its exoteric content onto a transcendental plane. The explanation is structured into two parts, which divide this supernal arena into two realms: the realm of *gava'ei*, the highest and most interior dimension, and the realm of *bara'ei*, the lower and more outward sphere of the divine hierarchy. The first realm is the most exalted and spiritual of the two, in the sense that it is the locus of the more conceptual or abstract essences, and is not depicted in anthropomorphic imagery, as are the subsequent and lower potencies. Indeed, according to the scriptural gloss, the upper 'crowns' are called 'glory and splendour', and are found 'before' the primordial God(head), which is not named but is only indicated obliquely. Our passage does not otherwise specify the meaning or names of these two supreme divine gradations, although from the fact that they constitute a 'dwelling' above, we may say that they are an upper Temple, which contains the highest Crown (the primordial God; the Ancient of Days), and His two attributes of Wisdom and Understanding. Below this supreme triad of the divine hierarchy of powers extend the two potencies called 'arms' in the same biblical passage. By virtue of this imagery, these lateral extensions assume an anthropomorphic aspect.

The passage from Isa. 63: 12 develops this theme, indicating that one of these divine arms or potencies (the right one) goes forth to the side of Moses and is called the 'arm of His splendour (*tif'eret*)'. Hence, the middle gradation between the two arms has the cognomen 'Moses' (by virtue of the verse used) as well as the attribute Splendour. Altogether they seem to constitute a second triad below the upper dwelling. Presumably, the 'outer chambers' which are mentioned next are lower in the structure, and related to the master teacher Moses as 'the disciples of YHWH'. The choice of this epithet is not specified, but one may speculate that the term 'disciples' was chosen because of a paronomastic association between the Aramaic word for these 'outer' chambers (*bara'ei*) and the one for 'sons' or disciples (*bera'ei*). However this may be, it would also seem that a word-play on *bara'ei* accounts for the designation of the sphere of 'Moses' as 'the shining (*bahir*) light'—quite apart from the fact that the 'speculum that shines' is associated with Moses alone in rabbinic literature, as the most pure grade of prophecy which he merits as the most superior of all the prophets (*BT Yebamot* 49b). The lower 'sons' are

46 (*Siddur Rabbah*, ll. 73 f.), and 97 (*Sefer Raziel*, l. 186, *per* MS BM Or. 6577). In these texts the curls are part of the description; hence an annotation like the one cited by R. Azriel is unnecessary.

[38] Tishby, *Peirush Ha-'Aggadot Le-Rabbi 'Azriel*, 139–40 (39b).

thus refractions of this 'shining light', the 'disciples' of 'Moses' and the 'outer' or more revealed chambers of the divine hierarchy. The overlapping symbolisms are legion.

The 'shining' is then portrayed as an illumination from the darkness (this being the more inward and recondite aspects of the divine Being). Three distinct passages are then homologized: the first utilizes Ps. 18: 12 to convey the sense that the light is enveloped in a dark cover; the second uses Songs 5: 11 to add a more anthropomorphic modality to the depiction of the superiority of darkness in the divine structure; and the third one returns to Ps. 18: 12 by way of a proof given to a midrash portraying a kind of 'theogony of potencies', in which the darkness is itself preceded by 'waters'. To make that work exegetically, the phrase *ḥeshkat mayyim* in the psalm would have to be understood not as a description of the waters ('the darkness of the waters'; that is, 'the dark thunderheads'), but of the darkness ('the darkness *of* the waters'; that is, 'the darkness that comes *from* the waters').

It is clear from the preceding that R. Azriel's articulation of a theosophical myth occurs as a series of annotative fragments that invoke Scripture and Midrash as proof. Indeed, the esoteric teaching is nowhere articulated, but must be reconstructed from the passages. Paradoxically, these passages are read concretely and symbolically at the same time—since it is precisely the concrete drama of details that animates the successive statements of portions of the 'myth' and gives the spiritual realities in the supernal spheres their tangible and figurative aspects. Through the images, in fact, these realities are imaginable; and although one might consider the chain of annotations somewhat sterile and lacking in narrative coherence, both the variety of imagery and the homologies projected attest to the speculative energy that underlies the commentary. The overlapping structures include the Temple, the divine Anthropos, Moses and his disciples, darkness and light, and sexual progeneration. No one of these structures or images says it all, but rather gives selective aspects of the subject; and this very lack of one consistent pattern of imagery is all the more striking in view of the fact that the biblical and the midrashic proofs are asserted dogmatically—and not as exegetical speculations. Hence, I would judge it too harsh to assert that the dogmatic correlation of fragments (by the word *ve-zehu*, 'and this is') is altogether mechanical and scholastic. Rather, it would seem that just these correlations are the mark of a mythic creativity that attempts to give coherence to the traditions that came to hand.

From this point of view, one of the notable features of R. Azriel's mythic labours is the way he integrates teachings that were circulating around Gerona in his day, and presents them in a new annotative pattern. Two examples may be adduced. The first brings us back to the image of a 'dwelling' at the beginning of the commentary. A version of this is reported in the name of R. Ezra by R. Jacob ben Sheshet.[39] According to the citation, there are 'thrones' with attributes on high; but these are different from 'the crowns, which (are) called a manner of "dwelling"; and that is a "Dwelling of the primordial God",' etc. One will note that the vocabulary is similar; however, R. Azriel extends the annotation, and by setting forth the issue of 'arms' extends his discussion to another dimension of the divine structure, which is then correlated and extended by the quotation from Isa. 63: 12. Thus one of the characteristics of R. Azriel's mythmaking was to combine passages into a chain of comments, that could be read coherently as an encryption of the divine emanation by one in the know.[40]

The second example takes us to the end of R. Azriel's use of esoteric tradition, and his citation of the black curls upon the head of the divine Anthropos as symbolic of the darkness that envelops the potencies in the upper realms of the Godhead. It is a notion that is followed by a statement of this process in terms of a progeneration. The two images are presented as dealing with the same situation. A similar position is taken by R. Jacob ben Sheshet in another of his treatises,[41] though he presents the two teachings in a different sequence: 'The meaning of "The waters conceived and gave birth to darkness": this is the hair on the head; as it says, "His locks are curled and black as a raven's" '. It is evident that in this explanation the two passages are more fully conflated than in R. Azriel's, where a sense of the process of emanation is more clearly indicated.

Another parallel is even more instructive with respect to the patterns of esoteric mythmaking being considered, and that is the commentary of R. Ezra on Songs 5: 11.[42] Here, each of the two clauses are dealt with separately:

> 'His head is finest gold': all-inclusive, crowned, and enwreathed. 'His locks are curled and black': this is what is written, 'He puts darkness as His hiding place, His tent round about Him; the darkness of waters'—because they were the beginning of the generation of the waters. And this is what our sages, of blessed memory, said in *Exodus Rabbah*, 'The waters conceived and gave birth to darkness'.

Here we have two notable phenomena: the division of the verse into two parts, and an exegetical sequence on the second clause that unfolds in a careful pedagogical manner. Nowhere is it said that the reference to this

[39] In his treatise *Ha-ʾEmunah Veha-Biṭaḥon*, printed in *Kitbei Rabbeinu Moshe ben Naḥman*, ed. Ḥayyim Chavel (Jerusalem: Mossad Ha-Rav Kook, 1964), ii. 399.

[40] Since R. Jacob's citation of Deut. 33: 27 breaks off before the reference to 'arms', it cannot be stated for sure that R. Ezra did not deal with it. However, as R. Jacob does cite the latter's reference to the 'dwelling', and disagrees with it, one would have expected him also to have given R. Ezra's view of the 'arms' if there was one, since he also gives his position on this topic (for him, the words of the verse refer to names of souls).

[41] *Sefer Meishib Debarim Nekhoḥim Le-R. Yaʿaqob ben Sheshet*, ed. Georges Vajda (Jerusalem: Israel Academy of Sciences and the Humanities, 1968), ch. 9 (B 75b), p. 124, ll. 308 f.

[42] In *Kitbei Rabbeinu Moshe ben Naḥman*, ii. 502.

imagery is the supernal divine realm; but in light of R. Azriel's commentary it is evident that this one also moves from the upper Crown on the divine Anthropos downward—beginning with the black curls of His head, which are linked to the darkness that is engendered by the waters. At the same time, although the sequence of explanations is more logical here than in R. Azriel's version, one is left with the impression of a disjointed series of images that do not quite constitute an integral mythic sequence. It is perhaps the overall structuring of R. Azriel's commentary into two related chambers that gives it a measure of coherence, or the fact that the Anthropos is also more dominant throughout. Whatever the case, the comments there give the impression of a dynamic interrelationship—despite the diversity of topics; whereas R. Ezra's more coherent commentary seems to remain a static series of images that do not quite come together as a unified mythic gestalt.

3. Divine Exile and Return. A very different intellectual strategy is to be found in a fairly long unit dealing with the rabbinic myth of the exile and restoration of the *Shekhinah*.[43] Here R. Azriel simply cites a series of old midrashic passages, beginning with the cluster of materials on the subject found in the Talmud at *BT Megillah* 29a. No comment is added; there is only a catena of other passages on the same theme (*Mekhilta de-Rabbi Ishmael, Bo*ʾ 14; *JT Sukkah* 4. 3; *Tanḥuma, Noaḥ*, 3; *ʾAggadat Shir ha-Shirim* (Buber, edn., p. 36); *Lamentations Rabba* 1. 54 and *petiḥta*ʾ 15; *Shoḥer Ṭov* 9. 14; *Tanḥuma, Aḥarei*, end). Inherently, this unique collection is of much interest, and even gives proof-texts otherwise unknown. But this is all; there is no further explanation or even hint of any symbolic reading. One can only assume that the mere citation of such texts was deemed sufficient for the theosophist to know that he was dealing with the topic of the exile and the wandering of the Shekhinah in impure realms, as well as the promise of her ultimate restoration and return to her pure realm in heaven. But this dimension of the myth is concealed from view; and it is only suggested by the lack of annotation or commentary. Indeed, it is in this silence that the pathos of some secret myth is suggested.

In reviewing the foregoing examples and patterns of exegesis and annotation, several points stand out. First and foremost is the fact that biblical and midrashic passages are given esoteric interpretations by means of types of exegesis whose techniques are left obscure and must be reconstructed from the given units. These fixed meanings do not carry with them any alternative exegetical speculations, but have the character of theosophical secrets disclosed by a master. The teacher's voice is dogmatic and authoritative,

[43] Tishby, *Peirush Ha-ʾAggadot Le-Rabbi ʾAzriel*, 121 f. (27a–28a).

whether this be by saying that 'this is' the meaning of a given verse, or by the assertion that one passage correlates with another. To the extent that we are able to reconstruct the exegetical elements that are involved, we can see both a concretization and dramatization of discrete biblical and midrashic phrases—which are presumed to take place on a higher spiritual plane. The diversity of the passages that are invoked show a creative energy and mythic imagination; though the unity and coherence of the imagery is not always evident or spelled out. But just this allusiveness bears witness to the recondite nature of the subject matter, and the constraints on its explicit articulation—though a bit less so in the various polemical and pedagogical treatises produced by such theosophists as R. Jacob ben Sheshet or R. Todros ben Joseph Abulafia.

In this material (the *Bahir* and the commentary of R. Azriel) we may also observe the tendency for one voice and one comment to occur; and to the degree that several passages are simultaneously given, these are variously correlated by the teacher. There is thus an impulse towards coherence among the teachings used in the tradition; but there is no systematic exploration of new verses, or the tendering of diverse exegetical possibilities by different sages or disciples. All of which stands in a marked contrast to the book of *Zohar*, which bursts upon the scene of the thirteenth century (Spain) with no real precedent—offering bountiful and multiple interpretations of many verses of Scripture (especially from the Torah) and the teachings of the sages (in the Talmud and Midrash)—and giving expression to the different voices of a particular spiritual fellowship, including diverse alternatives to some specific passages.[44] The result is a vast tapestry of the Jewish spiritual imagination, revealing a mythic passion to narrate every nuance of the divine dynamism found in Scripture, and a desire to reveal this Scripture as the living myth of God's own Being—both hidden and revealed.[45]

[44] For considerations of this medieval dating, see the classic discussion of Gershom Scholem, *Major Trends in Jewish Mysticism*, lecture 5, in which a case for individual authorship by R. Moses de Leon is made; and the compelling analysis of Yehuda Liebes, 'Keitzad Nitḥabberah Sefer Ha-Zohar', *JSJT* 8 (1989), 1–71, where the case for a circle of authors is advanced. An English rendition, 'How the Zohar was Written', appears in Liebes's *Studies in the Zohar* (Albany, NY: SUNY Press, 1993), 85–138, 194–227.

[45] The passion and quest of this creativity have been ably captured by Yehuda Liebes in his 'Zohar ve-ʾEros', *ʾAlpayyim*, 9 (1994), 67–119. For some specifics concerning Zoharic hermeneutics, see Idel, *Kabbalah: New Perspectives*, ch. 9; Wolfson, *Through a Speculum that Shines*, ch. 7 (and his earlier studies, noted there); and Fishbane, *The Exegetical Imagination*, ch. 7. Two recent attempts to consider Kabbalistic hermeneutics within the framework of a theory of language and interpretation, are Moshe Idel, *Absorbing Perfections: Kabbalah and Interpretation* (New Haven and London: Yale University Press, 2002); and Elliot R. Wolfson, *Sprache, Eros, Dasein: Kabbalistische Hermeneutik und poetische Einbildungskraft* (Berlin and Vienna: Philo Verlagsgesellschaft, 2002).

B. THE MANIFESTATION AND MYSTERY OF THE *ZOHAR*

The book of *Zohar* appeared in Castile sometime in the mid-thirteenth century, the product of a prodigious mythic energy and filled with a vast inventory of mythic themes and topics. There is virtually nothing in the extensive corpus of earlier Jewish literature that signalled its coming; and even where one can, in retrospect, identify some similar interests and expressions, the volume and vitality of their new realizations in this collection of commentaries and confabulations mark a quantum leap of the Jewish mythical and mystical imagination—unequalled or at least unparalleled ever since. No word of Scripture or phrase from the Midrash left the wheelhouse of its creative energy untouched and untransformed, and often many times over.

The *Zohar* purports to unlock the secrets of divine Being encoded in Scripture, spelling out, in numerous locutions, the emanation of Divinity from the sources of its own hiddenness in the primordial All—called *ʾEin Sof*, or 'Boundless Infinite'. This mysterious process unfolds, first and fundamentally, in a totally spiritual and preternatural sphere, wherein the most recondite truths are gradually exteriorized and differentiated; it then extends outward and beyond this sphere into the temporal universe as we know it. There is no break or gap between these successive domains: the 'divine reality' is one in all its parts, in both its esoteric and exoteric expressions. In truth, then, one cannot know or speak of anything other than this one reality—though an unenlightened mind, and even Scripture itself, might lead one to think otherwise; namely, that there is a world both distinct and other than God, its creator.

The emanations of divine Being occur in successive stages, even hierarchical gradations. Commonly, this series of powers is known by the names *Keter*, 'Crown'; *Hokhmah*, 'Wisdom'; *Binah*, 'Understanding'; *Ḥesed*, 'Mercy'; *Geburah*, 'Might'; *Tifʾeret*, 'Splendour'; *Netzaḥ*, 'Eternity'; *Hod*, 'Glory'; *Yesod*, 'Foundation'; and *Malkhut*, 'Kingdom'. Separately and together, they symbolize the ten principle modalities and attributes of the divine Being; and in their dynamic expressions dispose into diverse gestalts or configurations. For example, the entire process may be imagined as a series of concentric exteriorizations, as in the successive excretions of a silk-worm (*Zohar*, I. 15a); or as a straight line that is protracted from an infinitely compact and recessive point (I. 18a); or as a flame that rises from a glowing coal or burning lamp, and appears in different hues or colours (I. 50b); as well as many other patterns that are inspired by such natural images as a river and its tributaries, or a tree trunk and its many branches. Undoubtedly one of the most powerful of these images is that of the human being, transforming the disposition of the grades into an Anthropos with a full array of physical features. Such a form effects the arrangement of a series of triadic gestalts (mental features in the head above; emotional features in the body below; and generative features in the lower torso);[46] or of binary units (often in gender pairs like father-mother; husband-wife; or king-queen); or even of singular forms (like the spinal column). But the most important gestalt, which overlaps all the others, is the quaternary structure of the divine Tetragram. Arrayed from top to bottom, this configuration of letters (Y-H-V-H) approximates an anthropomorphic image—a hieroglyph in the truest sense of the *deus revelatus*. From this point of view, the unity of the sacred Name symbolizes the unity of the Godhead and all reality. Scripture encodes this mystery in the innumerable microforms of its letters, words, and sentences, as the teachings of the *Zohar* try to show again and again.

These 'showings' of the inner dimensions of God's Being, produced through exegetical initiative, are the final and public stage of a complex process of revealment and concealment. This process is said to originate in the hidden recesses of the *'Ein Sof*, and unfold in a manner whereby each gradation simultaneously manifests a modality of Divinity, while concealing those yet to emerge. The lowest divine gradation, the 'Kingdom', is thus the most fully manifest of the ten potencies, although it too has a complex character: concealing the utterly spiritual levels of Divinity within, while being the beginning of its revealment and access to the mystic. It is also the womb in which the physical world is formed, and the place through which it emerges as God's own creation. In this latter sphere, all of the forms of worldly existence are themselves embodiments which conceal the spiritual structures that animate them from within. This is particularly so for the human being, who replicates the divine Anthropos most completely; for the peoplehood of Israel, which is the corporate manifestation of the 'Kingdom' of God on earth; and for the Holy Scriptures, which are replete with numerous encryptions of the divine Hierarchy (in its parts; in their interrelationships; and in their integral unity). Hence the words of Scripture are like vessels, containing and concealing the great theosophical Myth of God's Self-Revelation; and the process of their interpretation is the disclosure of this myth as a multiform spiritual drama. The outward language of Scripture thus conceals the inner reality of divine Being in all its dynamic vitality; and the hermeneutical elaboration of that language restates the Myth in numerous forms, all of which express the many nuances of that drama when its cast of characters (the potencies) are recast in different roles and relationships. Scriptural exegesis is thus, itself, a spiritual act, and a way to realize the deep mysteries of God's own Being.

[46] The phenomenon of triads has a deep mythic resonance; see Hermann Usener, *Dreiheit: Ein Versuch Mythologischer Zahlenlehre* (Bonn: Carl Georgi, Universitätsbuchdruckerei, 1903).

It bears comment at this point that the myths of the divine Myth encoded in Hebrew Scriptures are structured by the events or circumstances, as well as the language and imagery, of any given passage. And since this text covers the acts of creation; the biographies of personalities; and diverse national occurrences and institutions, the forms by which the ongoing divine processes are represented are by turns natural, human, and historical. All of these take on archetypal significance in the text, and focus strong attention on elemental features of experience (like light and dark; sun and moon; male and female) and emotions (like anger and mercy; desire and restraint; activity and passivity), without these becoming independent powers or forces. Rather, they are always viewed as earthly expressions of spiritual processes which are variously abetted or frustrated. The particular contexts of the biblical narrations further delimit the meaning of the forms represented, so that the acts of Abraham or Moses show the action of the divine potencies under specific conditions; or the meaning of such natural archetypes as springs or wells is affected by the account of Isaac, for example, who dug wells and repaired them so that people could be nurtured from these sources. This becomes a specific instance of how the patriarchs laboured to open channels in the supernal mysteries, so that their spiritual benefits might flow into earthly existence (*Zohar* I. 141a/b).

In the main, the divine processes concealed in the *Zohar* are from a 'time' before creation, when these higher potencies became manifest in physical forms. However, there are instances where the time before this time is discussed and the beginnings of the process portrayed. One notable case of such myths of ultimate origins builds on a fragment of old rabbinic *ʾaggadah* and reworks it in a remarkable way. It may serve as an instructive instance of the esoteric transformation of midrashic elements in the *Zohar* and a first example of its modes of mythic discourse.

According to the report in *Genesis Rabba* 3. 7,[47] R. Judah bar Simon was struck by the formulation *va-yehi ʿereb* ('and there was evening') after the first day of creation, and not *yehi ʿereb* ('let there be evening')—as one might have expected, insofar as there had not yet been any evening or morning prior to this. He thus reasoned, from the formulation of Scripture, that 'there was an order of time prior to this'. R. Abbahu drew a more striking conclusion, and said that 'The Holy One, blessed be He, used to create worlds and destroy them, until He created this; (and said) "This one is pleasing to Me; those are not pleasing to Me" '. The source or basis of this myth is not certain; and one can be sure that it was not itself derived from Scripture, but only linked to it by the verb *va-yehi*, which R. Abbahu presumably understood to mean that *now* evening came to be, but before this no fixed order of reality had been established. His position is thus different from that of R. Judah's, and a most

[47] Theodor–Albeck, 23.

remarkable case of cosmogonic speculation. For this sage Genesis 1 is not the absolutely first creation—and even preserves the verbal trace of prior acts of world-making. However, the reason for the destruction of these former worlds is not indicated. Just this stimulates the *Zohar*'s mythic imagination.

It is taught in the *Sifraʾ de-Tzeniʿutaʾ*: Before the *ʿAtiqaʾ de-ʿAtiqin* ('Most Primordial One') prepared His attributes (*tiqqunoi*),[48] He constructed kings, inscribed kings, and estimated (the measure of) kings; but they did not survive, so that after a time He set them aside and concealed them. This is what is meant by 'And these are the kings that ruled in the land of Edom' (Gen. 36: 31). 'In the land of Edom'—(meaning) in the place where all the 'judgements' exist; and none of (these kings) could survive until the 'white head', *ʿAtiqaʾ de-ʿAtiqin*, was prepared (*ʾitetaqin*).[49] When He was prepared, He prepared all the attributes below; He prepared all the attributes of the upper and lower worlds. From this we learn 'Unless the leader of the nation is prepared first, his people are not prepared; but if he is prepared, they are all prepared; and if He is not prepared, the people cannot be prepared'.[50] How do we know this? From the 'Ancient of Days' (*ʿAtiq Yomin*), because so long as He was not prepared in His attributes, all these that had to be prepared remained unprepared, and 'all the worlds were destroyed'.[51] This is what is meant by 'And Bela the son of Beor ruled in Edom' (ibid. 32). '(He) ruled in Edom'—this is a [precious] mystery, [meaning] the place where all the judgements are bound and suspended. 'Bela son of Beor'—it is taught: he is the harsh verdict,[52] most powerful, because of whom a thousand thousands of yelling and wailing ones are bound together. 'And the name of his city was Dinhavah' (ibid.). What is Dinhavah? It indicates 'give judgement (*din havah*)'; as it says 'The leech has two daughters: Give, Give (*hav hav*)' (Prov. 30: 15). When (Bela) went to dwell there, he did not survive, and was not able to survive, and 'all the worlds were destroyed'. What is the reason? Because Man (the supernal Anthropos) had not yet been prepared; for the preparation of Man in his image comprises (the) All, and all (the potencies) can live in him. And since this preparation of Man did not exist, they were not able to survive and live and were annulled. Do you really think that they were annulled—for indeed they are all comprised within (the) Man?! Rather (say that) they were annulled and removed from that preparation, until the preparation (of the image) of Man came into being. When that image came they were all comprised (in it) and took on another existence: some of them were sweet; (some of them were both sweet and not sweet); and some of them were not sweet at all. (*Zohar* III. 135a/b; from *Idra Rabba*)[53]

[48] Lit. 'enactments', but used here to indicate the 'qualities' of the divine Nature or Being.

[49] Punning on *tiqqunoi* primarily; also on the name *ʿAtiqaʾ*.

[50] The idiom as a whole, and especially the opening words, *kol reishaʾ* ('every head') allude to the phrase 'everyone/thing (*ha-kol*) follows the head' (or leader; *ha-rosh*), found in Midrash *Pirkei de-Rabbi Eliezer*, ch. 42.

[51] Alluding to *Gen. Rabba* 3. 7.

[52] This phrase means literally 'render' or 'cut a judgement', and thus refers to Bela, whose name suggests 'Destroyer' (*b-l-ʿ*).

[53] The nature and function of this *Idra* (or Assembly) has been considered at length by Yehudah Liebes, in 'The Messiah of the Zohar', in his *Studies in the Zohar*, 4–48, 68–71, 74–82, and notes. For his treatment of other aspects of the kings of Edom elsewhere in the *Zohar*, see pp. 65–9.

This is a mythic account of prior constructions of potencies in the supernal realm; reasons for the failure of these potencies to survive; and the emergence of a comprehensive form that allows these potencies to endure, in dyads and triads of counterpoint and balance. The temporal sequence is therefore threefold: a time 'before', of disaster and death; a new time, in which order and structure emerge; and a subsequent period, of coexistence and endurance among the elements. The old *ʾaggadah* of many destroyed worlds clearly played a catalytic role for the later mythmakers.

Close examination shows that our myth is comprised of three levels, which may be stylistically distinguished. One level is that of the narrative discourse, which speaks about the initial time before the Primordial One prepared His attributes, and goes on to relate how He later prepared the upper and lower worlds in the image of Man which comprised all the supernal elements. The second level interrupts this discourse with commentaries on Gen. 36: 31–2, and even affects the language of that discourse, as in the designation of the early creations as 'kings', and probably also the reference to the Primordial One as 'white hair'—since this quality (of pure mercy) is the antidote to 'Edom', which alludes to the colour red (*ʾadom*) and the attribute (of strict judgement) associated with it in Kabbalistic lore. More important for the myth overall is the fact that these exegeses of Scripture are said to confirm the narrative, thereby showing that its words are preceded by Pentateuchal authority. The myth is thus stated twice, in two different forms.

The third level variously interrupts both the narrative and the commentary with scholastic interventions, all couched in the language of Talmudic dialectics ('Hence we learn'; 'How do we know this?'; 'Do you really think?... Rather'). Significantly, after these queries, there often follows some allusion to or use of rabbinic traditions (the allusion to the tradition of starting from the 'head', in *Pirkei de-Rabbi Eliezer* 42; the reference to the tradition of destroyed worlds, in *Genesis Rabba* 3. 7; and the reuse of a rabbinic tradition about the city of Dinhavah in *BT ʿAbodah Zarah* 17a, which seeks to apply the doom of strict judgement upon the world). And, finally, the qualifications interposed into the discourse show the myth in a setting of reception and ongoing revision.

The issue of stylistic levels and changes in the myth also allows us to recognize contradictions in the terminology. Thus, for example, the narrative refers to the fact that the Primordial One 'concealed' the kings; the exegetical unit says that they could not 'survive'; and the scholastic traditions refer to the fact that they were 'destroyed'. In addition, the narrative part refers to the divine Creator as the *ʿAtiqaʾ ʿAtiqin*; whereas the scholastic portion connects this to a tradition about the *ʿAtiq Yomin*. All of which shows us a vital mythic process of inclusion and correlation of elements, as the core myth developed and was expanded and changed in the telling. The putative citation of the final form of the myth from a book of secret wisdom, gives it the seal of hidden wisdom, which is surely one of the meanings of the book title *Tzeniʿutaʾ* ('Concealment').

The foregoing example of reworked biblical and midrashic passages in the *Zohar* provides an initial view of its creative spirit and bold mythic imagination. In the ensuing chapters, we shall return to two themes discussed earlier in this book—the battle with the primordial dragon at the beginning of creation, and the exile and suffering of the Shekhinah over the destroyed Temple—and follow them into two remarkable Zoharic narratives. Nothing quite like them exists; they take the mind of Jewish myth to unique heights.

11
The Primordial Serpent and the Secrets of Creation

Introduction

Over the centuries, different passages from the stock of biblical references to an ancient combat between God and a great sea dragon gained special prominence in Jewish texts; and these recur as the topics of commentaries or midrashic teachings—new and old. The old images thus migrate across time and space, simultaneously regenerated and reapplied in ever new ways, and testifying to a range of imaginative possibilities. For example, referring to the mystical meaning of 'the great sea serpents' in Gen. 1: 21, R. Baḥye b. Asher (thirteenth century, Spain) states that these creatures refer to the 'four camps (of angels) that are exterior to the *Shekhinah* (or: supernal Matron) of the Holy One, blessed be He—to glorify and exalt Him with songs and praises'.[1] This view is, significantly, a virtual citation of a remark found in a special section dealing with 'The Secrets of the Creation' included in the commentary on the Song of Songs by R. Baḥye's contemporary, R. Ezra of Gerona. At the beginning of the comment on 'the great sea serpents', we find a close parallel to the previous comment, when it states that the serpents 'are four camps, which are exterior to the *Shekhinah*'.[2]

There then occurs this striking variation in R. Ezra's text: 'And corresponding to them (the serpents), it says (in Scripture) "Leviathan, whom You have created to sport with" (Ps. 104: 26)—and the Holy One, blessed be He, created it to extol Him and to exalt Him with words of songs and praises'.

[1] In *Rabbeinu Baḥye. Bei'ur 'al Ha-Torah*, ed. Ḥayyim D. Chavel (Jerusalem: Mosad Ha-Rav Kook, 1982), i. 41. On pp. 40–1, R. Solomon ibn Adret is cited with an allegorical view of the matter (*'al derekh ha-sekhel*). This view is criticized in a more realistic reading of the monsters by R. David ben Judah He-Ḥasid, as found in the *Shiṭah Mequbetzet* of R. Bezalel Ashkenazi (IV 75, *ad BT Baba Batra* 75a); however, ibn Adret himself gives a decidedly realistic interpretation in his commentary on this Talmudic passage (printed with the *'Ein Ya'aqov*). This position cannot be reconciled with the allegorical view attributed to him, and it is not in line with his orientation. A strong allegorical interpretation is given by R. Abraham ben ha-Rambam, in *Milḥamot Ha-Shem*, ed. Reuven Margoliot (Jerusalem: Mosad Ha-Rav Kook, 1963), 66, where the *naḥash* is taken as the 'evil urge' and the slaying of the dragon to mark the suppression of 'physical desires'. The *naḥash* is likened to the 'evil urge' also in *Zohar* I. 35b and 80a.

[2] See *Kol Kitbei Rabbeinu Moshe ben Naḥman*, ii. 510. The fact that R. Baḥye uses the same word as does R. Ezra (*miḥutz*; 'exterior to'), to refer to the placement of the angelic troops, obviates Chavel's suggested emendation of it in Baḥye's comment. In Recanati's Torah commentary, ad loc. (Jerusalem reprint, 1961; 7a), the phrase given is simply 'these are the four camps of the *Shekhinah*'. Recanati probably knew R. Baḥye's commentary here; and cf. further, below.

Nothing more of this mystery is indicated here; and we are left to speculate whether the serpent Leviathan somehow circumscribes this encampment (like some Ouroboros), or is rather a mythic representation of the male consort of the female principle *Shekhinah*—hence related to the masculine gradation of *Tif'eret* within the Godhead, and thus a positive force.[3] As regards the secret of the troop of angels, R. Baḥye goes on to say that he has 'seen' a passage from 'The Midrash of R. Simeon ben Yochai' regarding four archangels on high (namely, Michael, Gabriel, Raphael, and 'Uriel);[4] and he then concludes with this cryptic comment: 'And this is the secret (or mystical sense) of "His chariot is purple" (Songs 3: 10)—and the enlightened person will understand'.[5] R. Menaḥem Recanati is much more forthcoming; for after noting the identification of the serpents with the four camps of the *Shekhinah*, he goes on to refer to the phrase 'His chariot is purple (*'argaman*)', saying that the first four consonants of that word (*'-R-G-M*) constitute 'an acronym for 'Uriel, *R*aphael, *G*abriel, and *M*ichael—(these comprising) the chariot of the *Shekhinah*'.[6] Once again, these 'great serpents' are a positive power in the divine realm and not a chaotic or rebellious force. But one must also conclude that their mythic dimension has been considerably camouflaged and even neutralized by the bare presentation of theosophical identities.

A quite different interpretation of the primordial serpents is found in the teachings of R. Yitzḥaq Ha-Kohen, a contemporary of R. Ezra and R. Baḥye. His view takes us to a new level, in which the serpents of Scripture conceal secrets of the origin and even persistence of evil in the deep dimensions of the Godhead itself. In one striking formulation, we are told of a 'wondrous' mystery regarding the supernal existence of 'a pure Leviathan . . . called "serpent" (*tannin*)'—corresponding to which there is 'a great impure serpent (*tannin gadol ṭame'*)' who is analogized to Pharaoh 'who is sprawled in all his rivers', and will be defeated in due time by the powers of good.[7] This analogy, of course, refers to Ezek. 29: 3 even as the reference to a final battle

[3] Just this is the opinion of R. Yose in *Zohar* I. 34b; and it is cited by Recanati (see above, n. 2). R. Yose emphasizes that the word 'Leviathan' can be construed to mean 'coupling' or 'joining'; and he has in mind the sexual syzygy of this pair (the phallic aspect of the serpent imagery is also obvious).

[4] This work apparently indicates our *Zohar*, and the comment cited is similar to the one found there at I. 46b. Chavel notes (*Rabbeinu Baḥye: Bei'ur*, i. 42) that this is one of the ways that R. Baḥye refers to this work; and he adduces his comment on Exod. 21: 22 at v. 23 (in ibid., ii. 223), where also 'I have seen' and a reference to R. Simeon's Midrash are mentioned together. This is indeed similar to the comment found in *Zohar* ii. 114a. However, Ephraim Gottlieb has noted G. Scholem's lecture comment that this teaching 'is not found in the first printings of the *Zohar* and has been restored to the *Zohar* from R. Baḥye'. See Ephraim Gottlieb, *Ha-Qabbalah be-Kitbei R. Baḥye ben 'Asher* (Jerusalem: Qiryat Sefer, 1970), 172.

[5] *Rabbeinu Baḥye: Bei'ur*, 42. [6] *Rabbeinu Baḥye: Bei'ur*, (in the same paragraph).

[7] Gershom Scholem, 'Qabbalot R. Ya'aqob ve-R. Yitzḥaq', in *Mada'ei Ha-Yahadut*, 2 (1927), 100 f. (text of Yitzḥaq's treatise).

with a serpent explicitly alludes to the midrashic event found in *BT Baba Batra* 74b.[8] Significantly, both topics are featured prominently in one of the most remarkable and extensive mythic episodes preserved in the *Zohar*; and there is every reason to suspect that the mystical secrets of R. Yitzḥaq were known to the author of this myth, who in his own way expands upon received traditions about a structure of evil and chaos that parallels the powers of good and even derives its sustenance from this higher source.[9]

A. SERPENT MYTHS AND THE MYSTERY OF EVIL

1. 'The Great Serpent' in Zohar II. 34*a*–35*b*

The entirety of this remarkable myth is translated in Appendix 1 (B), and will only be summarized here according to its sequence of topics; but some pertinent citations will be included in the subsequent analysis.[10]

The presentation of the myth of 'the great serpent' is given in three parts: (1) the prologue, in which a secret instruction by R. Simeon is broached, along with various passages (biblical and midrashic) that mark some of its textual contours; (2) a narrative myth of origins, in which the extrusion of the powers of evil out of the divine structure is portrayed, though without recourse to Scripture or any other traditional sources; and (3) an exegetical account of the same origins, in which we now learn of a series of battles with various sea monsters, with imagery and texts drawn from a rich stock of scriptural sources, and which give the reader a sense of the patterns of recurrence or recrudescence of these mythic events in ongoing historical time.

Part 1. R. Simeon determines that the time is now right to 'reveal' some esoteric 'mysteries', and he begins by directing his disciples' attention to the precise wording of the opening phrase of the liturgical unit, in which the Lord commands Moses to 'Enter (*bo*ʾ) into Pharaoh' (Exod. 7: 1)—and not just 'Go to' that ruler, since by this language He directed Moses to enter the deeper mysteries of 'Pharaoh', who is allegorized as the 'great serpent' upon whose fins the world hangs. Moses, however, backed away in fear; and after God unsuccessfully tried sending in other messengers in his stead, announced

[8] The passage is cited according to its rabbinic title, as '(The) Chapter (called) "One Who Sells a Boat" '.

[9] Scholem, 'Qabbalot', 33, draws attention to the fact that both in the teachings of R. Yitzḥaq and in our Zoharic myth (*Zohar* II. 34b) there are two structures of emanation (of good and evil), and that both refer to the *ʾaggadah* of 'destroyed worlds' and mean by it the negative powers that were not able to subsist (in R. Yitzḥaq's treatise, 'Qabbalot', 88). Yehuda Liebes, in 'The Messiah of the Zohar', *Studies in the Zohar* (Albany, NY: SUNY Press, 1993), 16, has suggested another link between the two traditions, noting that the reference in the *Zohar* (II. 34a) to the fact that only a special few have the secret knowledge (of evil) that is here taught has a striking parallel with a similar formulation by R. Moses of Burgos (the chief student and tradent of R. Yitzḥaq) concerning those who know the mystery of 'the left column' (negative emanations).

[10] As many of the textual references are annotated in the Appendix, they are not given here.

to 'Pharaoh ... "the great serpent" ' that He would Himself rise 'against him' (Ezek. 29: 3). R. Simeon then adds that the true mystery of this will be told to his disciples, who already 'know' some divine secrets.

The second part of the prologue constitutes a second opening of the unit. Hereby R. Simeon begins with the passage in Genesis (1: 21) where it is said that 'Elohim created the great sea serpents'; and after giving the established midrashic meaning of this phrase, tells another myth.

Part 2. R. Simeon now recites a complex myth about 'the great serpent' and his troop. It is a myth of origin and ongoing occurrence. Out of the left side of the divine hierarchy, coming from the gradation of *Geburah*, or Harsh Judgement, there emerges a certain channel which produces three drops, and from each of these three more drops emerge and swell into streams—becoming a total of nine rivers, alongside the initial great stream. These rivers are embodied as sea monsters of various types, and are the negative shells or dross leeched by the supreme hierarchy itself, in its own process of spiritual purification. All these negative forms depend upon their spiritual archetypes—and the very great serpent most of all, who periodically swims up to the great basin on high, which gathers all the streams of Divinity into one abundant pool. There are thus nine upper rivers in the spiritual realm, and these flow into the lower divine Sea, which is further tempered and 'flows peacefully' because of special drops emerging from the right side of Divinity, the gradation of Mercy known as *Ḥesed*. This myth stands on its own terms, and is not otherwise clarified or explained.

Part 3. In this section, R. Simeon at first builds on the preceding part when he observes that the phrase 'God created' is found in connection with the Creation itself as well as the great serpents (Gen. 1: 1 and 21). From this he concludes that each act of the ten divine sayings at the beginning of the book of Genesis is paralleled by the ten rivers of the divine hierarchy.[11] Which is to say, the ten *logoi* found in Scripture are in truth esoteric sayings that encode the formation of the ten supernal gradations or 'rivers' mentioned in the preceding myth. This secret matter, however, is deemed by R. Simeon to be known to his disciples, who have studied it. Less well known are the allusions to the secret of the negative hierarchy—of the 'great serpent' and his troop—in the account of creation. This mystery is then articulated.

The explication takes the form of interpretations of several passages in Genesis 1; and what is particularly striking is the fact that sea monsters are contained or killed by divine acts of one sort or another—based on biblical

[11] This refers to the famous rabbinic dictum, 'The world was created with ten sayings (*ma'amarot*)' (*M. 'Abot* 5. 1)—that is, the ten verbal commands where Scripture states *va-yo'mer*, 'And [God] said'. Cf. the lists found in *'Abot de-Rabbi Natan* B, ch. 45. 2 and *BT Megillah* 21b.

passages and on rabbinic teachings, known and unknown. At least five such acts of control can be detected here. (i) The statement that 'the earth *was* waste' (Gen. 1: 2) is understood to refer to an earlier time, when the female consort of the great serpent existed beside him; and since their conjoint existence threatened to flood the world, she was slain by God, and thus the world became a habitable place.[12] (ii) The following statement, that 'darkness *was* over the face of the abyss' (ibid.), also refers to a prior situation, when the monster had covered over the lights in the deep abyss; hence God breathed upon this evil spirit and quenched it, with the result that 'the spirit of God' now ruled 'over ... the waters' (ibid.). (iii) After God created the lights, their luminescence tempted the great sea monster and he provoked the river Giḥon (one of the rivers that flowed from Eden) to join his troop on the 'other side', since Giḥon had some share in the 'light' which the great monster wanted; in response, God concealed the light and also 'divided the light from the darkness' (ibid. 4)—an act which further 'divided the (upper) waters from the (lower) waters (of the other side)' (ibid. 6). (iv) In yet another act of combat, God again breathed against the spirit of the sea monster, whose deadly breath had desiccated the grasses in the upper realm; and once God so acted, He commanded 'the earth' to 'put forth grass' (ibid. 11)—an order that conceals the secret of the earlier, bad situation. And finally, (v) the reference to the setting up of 'lights (*me'orot*) in the firmament' (ibid. 14) marks the creation of the 'slant serpent' (Isa. 27: 1); for the spelling of *me'orot* alludes to the word *me'eirat*, which means 'malediction', and thus indicates a name of this serpent which goes forth into the world every fifty years and confronts the sea monster[13]—although it is not he that slays it, but God alone, who punishes this 'river' for its pride in thinking that 'My river belongs to me, (and I have made it for myself)' (Ezek. 29: 3). This fixed confrontation between the two serpents (the 'slant one', of the earth, who is also called the 'wily' one (Isa. 27: 1) and is identical with the devious snake in the Garden; and the 'great serpent', of the sea) suggests some division or antagonism within the negative spheres, which is overcome by God's superior might. The discourse ends here.

How are we to understand this myth, as a whole and in its component parts? What makes it work?

The instructional component of the myth is its dominant and most inclusive characteristic, and one that must be emphasized at the outset. The decision by R. Simeon to teach cosmic mysteries to his disciples is mentioned at the very beginning of Part 1 (in the initial reference to the serpent and its

[12] This alludes to the event depicted in *BT Baba Batra* 74b.

[13] The interpretation is made possible by the fact that the word *me' orot* is spelled without the letter *vav* after the *'alef*.

fins); and this same theme is taken up again at the beginning of Part 3 (along with another reference to the serpent and its fins). Moreover, this pedagogical element bears on the initial question concerning the reason Scripture uses the word 'enter', in connection with God's order to Moses to confront the Pharaoh; and the decision to delve into the esoteric layers of prior rabbinic teachings is repeated throughout the narrative. Particularly noteworthy is the strong exegetical character of these teachings, especially the esoteric interpretations of phrases in Genesis 1 regarding divine battles or confrontations with sea monsters. Throughout, the overarching voice of instruction is that of R. Simeon (the mystical master of these myths), as reported by an omniscient narrator of his words.

The salient feature of 'the dragon myth' is thus the secret wisdom which it makes known—not just to the companions alone, who are presented as ones 'who know the secrets of their Lord', but to everyone who is now privy to these reported mysteries (that is, to every reader of the text). This mode of indirect communication to non-initiates is not the least of the ironies of the book of *Zohar*, here as elsewhere. However, the teachings are far from straightforward and several layers can be distinguished.

At the outset, we are told that God Himself instructed Moses into the mysteries of the sea monster, leading him by stages into its depths. Rabbinic readers would readily respond to the nuance of this language, since this report of divine pedagogy, in which Moses (master of exoteric knowledge) is led 'domain after domain (*ʾidrin betar ʾidrin*) towards the serpent', would recall an older rabbinic interpretation of Songs 1: 4, 'The King brought me to His chambers (*ḥadarav*)', according to which Elihu son of Barachel the Buzite 'will reveal (*viygalleh*) to Israel the domains (*ḥadrei*) of Behemoth and Leviathan'.[14] We are not informed just what this disclosure consists of; but it undoubtedly involves the esoteric nature of these monsters as part of the work of creation,[15] since this instruction is mentioned together with the fact that Ezekiel 'will reveal (*viygalleh*) to them the domains (*ḥadrei*) of the Chariot (*merkabah*)'.[16] Other teachers were more explicit, and construed the

[14] *Songs Rabba* 1. 4. A remarkable ancient parallel occurs in the Coptic gnostic treatise 'Pistis Sophia', where Jesus explains to Maria about the places of punishment in the 'outer darkness', and says that 'The outer darkness is a great dragon' that 'surrounds the whole world', and that 'it has twelve chambers of severe punishments' within it. See *Pistis Sophia*, text ed. Carl Schmidt, trans. and notes Violet Macdermot (Nag Hammadi Studies, IX; Leiden: E. J. Brill, 1978), Book III, ch. 126, pp. 634f. For other parallels, see the Excursus below.

[15] Presumably, rabbinic teachers assumed that Elihu (who speaks in Job 32–37) clarified the divine hints about these two monsters in Job 40: 15–24 and Job 40: 25–41: 26, respectively.

[16] This refers to the esoteric content of Ezekiel 1. The secrets of the creation and of the throne are the two principle aspects of ancient Jewish esoteric knowledge (cf. *M. Ḥag.* 2. 1). It is notable, in this regard, that the context of this midrashic comment includes reference to the creation (in the names of R. Yannai and R. Berekhia); and the preceding paragraph adduces the mystical matters in *Tos. Ḥag.* 2. 2 (regarding entering the domain of heavenly mysteries) in connection with Songs 1: 4. See also in *Leviticus Rabba* 16. 4 (Margulies, 354f.).

reference to entry into the king's chambers in Songs 1: 4 as indicating that 'The matters that were hidden (*mesutarin*) from humankind from the six days of Creation the Holy One, blessed be He, revealed to Israel'.[17]

An older rabbinic tradition thus lies behind the language of the *Zohar*, and the fact that the matter involves supernal secrets is further confirmed by R. Simeon's stated intention 'to reveal mysteries (*le-gala'ah razin*)' to the worthy adepts. But what are they? What was it that so frightened Moses when he was inducted into hidden knowledge of this monster and saw that it was 'rooted in the supernal roots (*mishtaresh be-sharshin 'ila'in*)', and that 'several gradations are deposed (*mishtalleshin*)' from its body? Here too there is certainly an esoteric reworking of the midrash about the 'slant serpent (*naḥash bariaḥ*) "between" whose "fins" rests the middle bar (*bariaḥ*) of the world'.[18] But wherein lies the *mysterium tremendum*, the great fear that terrified such a one as Moses? R. Simeon does not explicate directly, either here or elsewhere. Just what secrets are the disciples given to 'know' (and the reader as well) which caused Moses himself to falter?

Most certainly they learn of the negative gradations, symbolized by the serpent and its offspring, which are rooted in the supernal hierarchy, and which descend or emanate in their own interconnected series. Hence, they are taught that the powers of evil emerge from spiritual sources and that they are fundamentally linked to them. All this is communicated through the narrative 'myth of the drops', in the first instance, which makes a special point of the fact that the lower powers actually continue to draw sustenance from the waters of holiness above. It is notable that this myth of divine Unity simply portrays the emergence and differentiation of the powers of the left side in straightforward narrative terms—without any hint of crisis or danger. Indeed, it is presented as an impersonal process; and no divine Being or supreme personality intervenes to oversee the development or to enforce the hierarchy of powers.

It is in the second myth of these matters that we learn of a very different situation. Here the account is very much centred around acts of combat or containment of sea monsters by a supreme Personality, the Holy One, blessed be He, who is the Lord of the creation and the maker and enforcer of its order. But to be more precise, and properly penetrate this account, it is necessary to present the teaching of R. Simeon on its own terms.

According to the master, many know that the work of Creation is indicated by the ten *logoi* in that account; but 'there are few who know to find allusions (*le-rimza'*) in the work of Creation to the secret (*raza'*) of the great serpent'.

[17] *Midrash Shir Ha-Shirim*, ed. Lazar Grünhut (Jerusalem: Hatzvi Press, 1907), 8a.

[18] *Pirkei de-Rabbi Eliezer*, ch. 9; first editions read 'its two fins'. In *Zohar* 1. 108a, we are told that 'the whole world depends on one fin of Leviathan'. The ambiguity here is due to the fact that the phrase 'depends on' (or 'rests on') translates *qa'im*, and this is a literal translation of the verb *'omed* used in the midrash. The term can imply a support but also a base.

And these are found by presenting various acts of creation in Genesis 1 as events which follow the defeat (in one way or another) of a monster. That is to say, the myth of God's acts of creation through expressions of His supreme *logos* conceals and follows prior events of an *agon* or strife against sea serpents. It will be recalled that in the old Israelite Scriptures the acts of creation by *logos* were separate from all the many snippets of divine combat against a primordial monster found in the prophets or psalms, and wisdom literatures. Moreover, in the many rabbinic revisions of this theme, the *agon* against the sea was some act of divine power against a rebellious or prideful monster, which refused to comply with God's creative will, and was not itself a primordial process or primary feature of God's acts of world-ordering. By fundamental contrast, in ancient Babylonian myths like *Enuma elish*, it was precisely the slaying of a monster that was the beginning of the acts of world-building—in fact, it was one of its constitutive features.

Remarkably, in R. Simeon's present teaching just this mythic feature recurs in conjunction with God's verbal acts of creation. Indeed, there is a quite remarkable conjunction of *agon* and *logos* here, one that retains both the power of the physical combats and the power of the spiritual word. Repeatedly, Scripture cites the creative *logos* of God; and alongside these references occur numerous terms for strife (note the use of *qaṭal*, to indicate the killing of the she-monster; of *maḥatz*, to mark the smiting of the serpent's head; of *baṭash*, to dramatize the smashing of the spirit of evil; and of verbs such as *shakhikh*, *kafif*, and *darakh*, to refer to the acts of suppressing, overcoming, and trampling the monster). Altogether, they introduce and underscore a more turbulent process: it is not simply that a stream emerged from the left side of Divinity, and produced a new order of elements; but rather somehow, in a manner not stated, the streams of monsters emerged alongside the upper spiritual grades in some simultaneous fashion, and only as each threatening act of dissolution or disaster was averted was the creation ordered and stabilized. It is hard to reconcile this series of battles with the myth of the drops, and it is possible that Parts 1 and 3 had an independent or prior cohesion. In any case, it is only the 'myth of the slaying of the monster' in preternatural time that gives meaning to the mystery of the world hanging on or linked to the fins of the serpent; and indeed, the slain monster underlies the account of the Creation (the supernal gradations) *and* the world of human habitation as well (since the latter encodes the former). Hence the powers of strict judgement and evil underpin the realm of order, and even constitute part of its *prima materia*. There is therefore no separation between the good and evil realms, which are interlinked and intricately bound to one another. Moses saw this and withdrew in fear; and now the companions are instructed into the mystery of origins and reality by R. Simeon.

But is this merely an initiation into secret knowledge, and no more? One might initially presume so, on the basis of remarks made by R. Simeon regarding teaching the mysteries and the notice that the disciples 'know the secrets of their Lord'—or some of them, at least. We are told that it is for such persons that the myth is revealed. But why?

Some clue to this query may be found in the prologue to the myth, when R. Simeon says that after Moses withdrew from entering the gradations of the monster, and other messengers were not able to 'approach (*li-qrabah*) it', God Himself took over and had 'to wage a battle (*le-ʾagḥaʾ qerabaʾ*) against it'. By this verb the narrator alludes to the conclusion of the mythic battles in *BT Baba Batra* 75a, when God takes over from His angelic host and defeats the mighty serpent of the sea—an ultimate act, at the end of time. The importance of this same verb for our myth is furthermore indicated by the fact that we are informed at its end that it is 'only the Holy One, blessed be He, who wages (*ʾagaḥ*)' the victorious battle against the sea dragon—and no other one. Hence these references to divine battles frame the entire myth, and give it the overall stamp of an *agon.*[19]

It may therefore be supposed that the knowledge of the myth is not unrelated to the acts of strife. On the one hand, what is known is that God's battles and combats against primordial water-monsters stabilized the creation itself (in both its supernal and earthly dimensions), and that therefore the 'World' itself hangs on the fins of this element. To know this is to know that it is only through strife with chaos (often in the disguise of the good powers) that the divine order is formed and maintained, over and over again. Indeed, the cycles of strife are even built into the cosmic order, as we learn from R. Simeon himself, who tells us of upsurges within the watery waste every seventy years and a clash between the serpents of the sea and the earth every fifty years. These calibrations according to human time units (ten sabbaticals and one jubilee period) do more than mark a myth of recurrences; they also brings this myth into the realm of human history. The fact that the serpent of the earth is also the 'Tempter' in the Garden, adds to the implication that the human struggle with 'the Other Side' is part of an ongoing need for world maintenance. R. Simeon states that neither Moses nor many other divine messengers could fully 'enter' this mystery—to combat evil and defeat it. Only God Himself will bring about the periodic victories and the final redemption; but in the meantime, this great task falls upon the disciples, who are now informed about the interrelationships between the gradations of holiness and evil, and also upon those who hear this secret indirectly, through its formulation here in the *Zohar*. One may even assume that this great task

[19] An interesting variant of this point occurs in I. 35a, where we are told that the great serpent tried to 'provoke' the primordial waters of 'Giḥon' (verbal stem *g-w-ḥ*, 'burst forth') to join 'the other side', and this caused a division within these waters—one part going to the other kingdom, another remaining in Eden and serving as an 'oil' for the seeds of light there. It is notable that David had his son Solomon anointed king from the substance of this spring (1 Kings 1: 33); for it is comprised of the waters of the true Kingdom, that will be victorious overall.

was one of the purposes of such a public disclosure of the secrets, and that 'now' was truly a time for all to act on God's behalf.[20]

In speaking of Moses' failure to enter the whole mystery of the 'great serpent', and then teaching the secret to the hilt, R. Simeon is revealed as the greater master of secret wisdom.[21] And one may presume that he was believed to be the greater in action, as well. In one notable case, we even find R. Simeon reciting a conjuration against the supernal serpent, and overpowering it for the good of the world. This episode occurred while he was on a journey with his son, R. Eleazar, and a snake moved toward them. At once R. Simeon grabbed the reptile by the head and stilled it; but as its tongue continued to move, 'He said: Snake, snake, go and tell the supernal serpent that R. Simeon exists in the world. He then put its head into a crevice in the ground and said: I decree that just as the lower one has returned to the crevice in the ground, so the upper one will return to the crevice in the great Abyss (*tehoma*ʾ)' (*Zohar* III. 15a). Thereupon the sage heard a voice that praised him as one who issues decrees which the Holy One Himself obeys; whereas Moses' words are less potent, for his prayer of entreaty on behalf of the nation (Exod. 32: 11) was full of fear, and not as pleasing or effective before God (ibid.).[22]

To live within the myth, one must first know it; and to know the origin of the supernal serpent, and its domain, allows one to do battle against it in all its spheres of influence. The common-sense distinctions between myth and history thus break down. All earthly actions have a supernal effect, and all are correlated or connected with events on high. For all those whose consciousness partakes of such mythic realities, no action is wasted.

II. Other Cosmogonies and Myths of the Serpent

1. The Cunning Serpent. The myth of the left side just presented (*Zohar* II. 34a–35b) gives us a vision of evil that is leeched from the divine structure like some alloy or waste.[23] A kind of external and inverse pattern of gradations

[20] This important point is repeatedly and variously stressed by Y. Liebes, in his essay 'The Messiah of the Zohar', *passim*.

[21] For this theme in the *Zohar*, see Boaz Hus, 'Ḥakham ʿAdif Mi-Nabiʾ—R. Shimʿon ve-Moshe Rabbeinu ba-*Zohar*', *Kabbalah*, 4 (1999), 103–39; he adduces this passage on pp. 117 f.

[22] In this assertion, the biblical statement that 'Moses entreated (*va-yeḥal*)' God (Exod. 32: 11) is taken to mean that 'he trembled' or 'grew ill'. The idiom used is *ʾaḥid leih pargoda*ʾ, a scribal error obviously based on *ʾaḥazato podgara*ʾ; in *BT Soṭah* 10a this is given as the explanation for one who is 'sick (*ḥalah*) in his legs' (R. Judah thus uses a medical term correctly, since *podgara* refers to some foot 'gout' in Greek and Latin). In the *Zohar*, this expression has been cleverly linked to the midrash in *BT Berakhot* 32a, where the statement about Moses' entreaty (*va-yeḥal*) is taken to mean that 'Moses stood in prayer . . . until *ʾaḥazato ʾaḥilu*ʾ—which R. Eleazar takes to mean a 'fire in the bones'. The same sage also interpreted Exod. 32: 11 to mean that Moses remained in his entreaty until 'he wearied Him (*heḥelahu*)'. This sense also underlies the thematics of our Zoharic passage, and together with the previous explanation, exemplifies the traditional knowledge and midrashic skill to be found in the *Zohar*.

[23] For a specific image of this type, see below (and n. 27).

thus results, one dominated exclusively by the left side and thus different from the spiritual hierarchy which is based on balance and the influence of the right side of mercy and grace. However, as is typical of the *Zohar*, this myth is not the exclusive type; and thus one may find alternative patterns, which show other mythic variations. One of these treats the relationship of evil to the divine hierarchy in a distinctive way—not presenting it solely as an exterior formation, but as a feature that actually invades and affects the spiritual gradation itself. This is the myth of origins found in *Zohar* I. 52a.

There are seven other lights,[24] which divide into seven seas, and one sea contains them. This one sea is the supernal sea in which all the seven seas are contained. These seven lights enter the sea and smite the sea on seven sides; and each side divides into seven rivers, as is written, 'And He will smite it into seven rivers' (Isa. 11: 15); and each river divides into seven streams and each stream divides into seven roads, and each road divides into seven paths, and all the water of the sea enter them. The seven supernal lights enter the sea—they are really six, emerging from the topmost one; and as the sea receives them, so it divides the waters to all the seas, (and) to all the rivers.

A sea monster below, on the left side, swims in all those rivers. He comes with his mighty scales, all as strong as iron and arrives [at the upper sea] in order to draw water (from it) and to defile the place. All the lights are darkened before him. His mouth and his tongue flare with fire; [and] his tongue is as sharp as a mighty sword until he comes to enter the sanctuary in the sea and the lights are darkened—and then he defiles the sanctuary, and the lights are darkened, and the supernal lights depart from the sea. Then the waters of the sea divide on the left side; and the sea is congealed and its waters do not flow.

And regarding the mystery of this matter it is written, 'And the serpent was more cunning than every beast of the field that the Lord God had made' (Gen. 3: 1)—(this being) the mystery of the evil snake that descends from above, and swims across bitter waters and descends in order to deceive (those) below, so that they (humankind) might fall into his nets. This snake is (the essence of) Death,[25] and it enters man's innermost secret parts,[26] and is on the left side. And there is another snake, of Life, (located) on the right side—(and) both of them accompany man, as they have established. (And it is written, that snake was more cunning) 'than any beast in the field', because no other beast of the field is as skilful in doing evil; for it is the dross of the gold. Woe to him who is drawn towards it; for (that beast) brings death to all who follow it—as indeed they have established.

This myth is presented as an 'established' truth about the holy gradations and the origin and role of the evil serpent. The theme of water dominates the first portion of the myth about the positive divine hierarchy—so much so that the older biblical mythologem about God smiting the sea into seven streams (Isa. 11: 15; a myth of combat used in a prophecy of redemption) is

[24] These are the seven gradations from *Binah* to *Yesod*, and flow into 'the sea' (*Malkhut*); this discussion follows another discussion of seven lights.

[25] The idiom is *mota' de-'alma'*, indicating that it brings death to the world; lit. it means 'the Death of the world'.

[26] *setim* connotes both a 'secret' and a 'sealed' realm.

now the basis for a primordial event in which God strikes the upper sea (itself the sum of seven superior streams) so that it divides into seven streams, and these further subdivide into multiples of seven. These streams extend beyond the sea—outside the upper hierarchy but at the same time part of its continuity. The origin of the 'left side', and the sea serpent that dominates it, is not stated here; although this origin of evil is alluded to at the end of the myth, when it refers to the dross of 'the gold'—this latter symbolizing the pure hierarchy from which the other powers are extruded.[27] As also in *Zohar* I. 34a–35b, the monster swims in the streams and even enters the supernal sea; but here the defilement of that realm is emphasized, and the monster does not retreat. Indeed, its invasion is said to cause a division in the supernal sea, shunting off a portion of it to the left side.

The splitting of the sea into a left and right side is most significant, for now there is a fixed presence of the evil sea monster within the upper hierarchy. This invasion and presence corresponds to the place of the cunning serpent in the Garden of Eden. And not only this, but the division of the sea into a left and a right side is repeated in the soul of each person, who has two inclinations (good and evil), thus indicating that the cosmic duality has become part of the human nature of things. Indeed, the cunning invasion of the serpent into the Godhead is mirrored in the presence of the evil urge in the heart of man. The evil side is thus not outside the hierarchy of Divinity, but very much within it; and just as there is a division between the upper evil serpent and the stream of the right side on high, so there is in the heart of man two serpents that vie for dominance and control.

In this radical myth of evil, the cunning serpent is a part of God—and thus a part of all beings created from His Being. One might even conclude that this is a radical Jewish myth of an aboriginal rupture or transgression, affecting the ensuing nature of all Being—the human condition most particularly, insofar as the primordial invasion of the cunning serpent into the spiritual hierarchy becomes the archetype for a psychological and spiritual condition that is fateful and ineluctable for every person. Only a disciplined will and constant vigilance may contain or control this situation in the heart of man, but cannot eradicate it. As something produced from God, the husks in which the evil serpent is coiled contain a power and wiliness that leaves God embattled within each person, created in His image.

[27] The image of 'dross of gold', like others referring to gold's filth or waste, recall topics of refinement and refuse found in medieval alchemy; cf. Gerhard Scholem, 'Alchemie und Kabbala. Ein Kapitel aus der Geschichte der Mystic', *MGWJ* 69 (1925), 26–7, 371–2. The notion of a refining fire that emerges from the gradation of *Geburah* ('Judgement') is given a powerful formulation by R. Moses of Burgos; see in Gershom Scholem, 'Le-Ḥeqer Qabbalot R. Yitzḥaq Ha-Kohen', *Tarbiz*, 4 (1932–3), 210. Related images also occur in the *Zohar*; for example, the 'filth of Judgement' (I. 74b) and the 'lees of wine' (I. 148a).

2. The Head of the Snake. Equally radical and stunning is another medieval myth about God and the mystery of evil. Here, again, the myth dramatizes an event in the supernal spheres; but the terms of its encoding make clear that its most visible reverberation and concrete expression take place in the realm of human history. The account speaks of a supernal snake whose head is bent down, like Israel in exile; whereas its tail is ascendant and dominant, like the nations of the world who lord it over Israel. The head of this snake thus corresponds to the *Shekhinah*, who shares Israel's fate and exile; and its tail corresponds to the evil powers of the Other Side—the two joined together in one body. The narration of this myth develops in an exegetical manner.

R. Eleazar began and said: 'Her voice goes forth like a snake' (Jer. 46: 22). Now that Israel is in exile, She (the *Shekhinah*) indeed goes 'like a snake'. When the snake bends its head in the dust, it raises its tail and dominates and strikes all those before it. So is it now in exile: its head is bent in the dust and its tail dominates. What causes the tail to rise up, and to dominate and strike?—The head, which is bent low. But this notwithstanding, what directs the tail and takes it on its journeyings?—This same head; for even though it is bent in the dust, it still directs it on its journeyings. Therefore, 'her voice is like that of a snake'. And at present the other nations who are joined to the tail rise up, and dominate and strike, while the head is bent in the dust. (*Zohar* III. 119b)

This mythic fragment takes us to a new level, with its theme of one snake that is both the power of holiness and the forces of domination. The head of the snake does not therefore invade the divine spheres of sanctity, and pollute its shrine; but it is the principle of Divinity itself, whose lower gradations are in fact the principalities of evil. Not even the slightest suggestion of duality is articulated in this myth of one Being, whose poles act in tandem—dramatically counterbalanced between aggression and suppression, and yet always directed by the head. Hence, however downtrodden the head (of Israel or its divine archetype), it thus remains the superior part of the entire entity, the counterweight to the rise of its hinder part.

The divine Being thus encodes a historical dimension; and so when the people Israel suffer in exile, at the hands of the other nations of the earth, their fate is shared by God Himself—even as another aspect of the Godhead is simultaneously strengthened. Myth and history are therefore interdependent, two aspects of one reality. They cannot be separated either in sorrow or salvation. This observation brings us to the next topic.

B. EXCURSUS ON COMPARATIVE TYPES

Our study of Jewish mythic traditions has revealed striking analogues in more ancient sources—leading one to reflect upon conceptual relationships and continuities between the topics. In earlier discussions, mention was made of terminological and thematic links between rabbinic myths of origins (dealing with a battle with a sea monster) and materials in Canaanite and in Mesopotamian literature; and earlier in this chapter, thematic and structural similarities between Zoharic traditions and *Enuma elish* were noted.[28] The recurrence of words or themes in sources separated by one or two thousand years raises intriguing issues about the movement of mythic traditions between cultural spheres of various types, and about how these materials were integrated into different literatures and intellectual settings. On the one hand (in the absence of evidence for direct influence), it is of human and cultural interest simply to observe similar mythic archetypes or forms within different literary complexes, despite differences in the nature of the account or its emphasis. On the other hand (whether or not there is any discernible or putative influences between the cases), it is of further intellectual and cultural interest to notice the different structural features that comprise the analogues which are correlated. By taking such a perspective, one can attend to the comparative morphologies of myth in the sources and consider the role of related materials in different cultures (or cultural strata)—without rushing to any judgement regarding influences or origins. Indeed, the occurrence of similar features may, in some cases, compel us to consider the possibility that similar myths may appear in dissimilar cultures when they share certain textual sources or mental predispositions (or both). It is just this latter point that bears some scrutiny when we observe some remarkable parallels between certain of the serpent traditions found in the medieval Zoharic corpus and some Gnostic myths from late antiquity preserved by the Church Fathers in their attempt to spurn or rebut views they deemed heretical or dangerous to nascent Christianity.

1. In our treatment of *Zohar* I. 52 and II. 34b–35a, we had the occasion to view myths of divine emanation in which a sea monster emerged from the 'left side' of this structure—a side that was correlated with impure evil powers which drew sustenance from the holy gradations. The result was a modified dualism: the negative powers emerged from the positive ones and formed a mirror image of them; but they were not altogether independent of them. In I. 52 the evil serpent crossed over from these supernal gradations and was transformed into the cunning snake in the Garden of Eden, which is the source of Death and which enters the 'secret parts' of all humans to tempt and seduce them away from God; it stands over against another serpent—of Life. An element of this tradition of a land serpent in the Garden also occurs in II. 35b; and at the beginning of this mythic narrative we are also informed that the sea monster grew from drops in multiples of three (II. 34b). A quite independent myth regarding the serpent in III. 119b does not speculate on the origins of the monster, but does link it to the *Shekhinah* and speaks about

28 See above, pp. 39 f., 115–19, and 280.

one serpent whose head was a positive power (Israel, now downtrodden in exile) and whose tail was a negative power (the foreign nations, now ascendant over Israel). This myth says nothing about a separate emanation of evil aeons or powers and conjoins the dual forces of good and evil in the *Shekhinah*. Hints of the conjunction of drops from the left and right sides (of evil and grace) in the lowest gradation of Eden-*Shekhinah* do occur in II. 34b, but this sphere is not personified as a serpent. It is rather a Shrine polluted by the sea monster.

Corollaries to these mythic features and structures can be noted in antiheresiological writings of the early Church. Two may be noted here. The first is adduced in the *Panarion* of Epiphanius of Salamis (*c*.375 CE), against a Christian sect referred to as the Nicolatians. In his version, Epiphanius notes a theogonic myth of procreation that utilizes the elements found in Gen. 1: 2, and then goes on to speak of the emergence of aeons from some supernal 'womb'. He summarizes thus:

(5. 1) Others of them make up some new names, saying that there was 'darkness' and 'depth' and 'water', and the 'spirit' separated them from each other. But the 'darkness' was resentful and vengeful toward the 'spirit', and hurrying upward it twined around the 'spirit' and produced, they say, something called 'Womb', which, when produced, conceived from the same 'spirit'. (5. 2) From 'Womb' were emitted four aeons, and from the four aeons another fourteen; and there came to be right and left, light and darkness. (5. 3) Later after all these was emitted a foul aeon which copulated with the 'Womb' mentioned above, and from this foul aeon and 'Womb' were produced gods, angels, demons, and seven spirits.[29]

Quite clearly we have here a dramatic mythic theogony based on a personification of the elements at the beginning of the book of Genesis, with the terms for darkness, water, and spirit given in the same Greek forms as found in the Septuagint. Remarkably, the water depth (biblical *tehom*) given is not called *abyssos* but *bythos*. Initially, the wind kept these elements separate until the power of darkness produced a womb upon spirit, who then conceived four aeons and their derivatives. Significantly, this copulation between darkness and spirit produced both darkness and light and the left and right sides. A subsequent foul aeon then copulated with the mother womb and produced a host of mixed progeny (gods, but also demons). Manifestly, this Womb (*Mētra*) is some cosmic mother who produces all types of beings from her matrix.

It is striking to note how a mythic mentality has generated a theogony out of the primordial elements that are found Gen. 1: 2, and produced a dualistic structure of qualities of darkness-light and left-right from it. Also notable is the new negative factor, which presents the various aeons as having been

[29] Epiphanius, *Ancoratus und Panarion*, ed. K. Holl (GCS 25; Leipzig: J. C. Hinrichs, 1915), i. 272–3 (*Panarion* 25. 5. 1–3).

produced from an antagonistic act of resentment by the darkness; and this would presumably have been a key notion in the mind of the mythmaker, who injected it as a dramatic element into the narrative of Genesis. Quite likely, some members of this sect had been Jewish and knew Hebrew; for in an immediately earlier section of the presentation the puzzling prophecy of Isa. 28: 10 is referred to, and the opaque Hebrew words *tzav la-tzav tzav la-tzav qav la-qav qav la-qav* are reproduced (as *saulasau saulasau* and *kaulakauk kaulakauk*), and they are given the explanation of 'tribulation upon tribulation' and 'hope upon hope'.[30] But there is no reason to conclude that the present myth of the origin of the evil, left side was transmitted within Jewish-Christian or Jewish gnostic circles into the Middle Ages, though it does attest to the great antiquity of the notion (and see below). This notwithstanding, we can still learn from this case about how mythic sensibilities could activate a dramatic reading from the Genesis passage. Of particular interest, in this regard, is the fact that Epiphanius gives his summary as a narrative myth—even though it clearly has an exegetical basis; and this type of formulation provides an interesting point of comparison with the narrative version of the production of the negative powers found in *Zohar* II. 34b, which occurs alongside the exegetical myth presented in II. 34b–35a.

In the myth just reviewed, nothing is said about any primary or superior God, and nothing further about the dualistic structures that emerged and their function in universal and human destiny. But just these features are of central concern in the mythic theogony and narrative found in the book of 'Baruch' by Justinos, according to the polemical summary give by Hippolytus of Rome (*c*.225–35). In this old treatise, a complex mythic theology begins with the following matters.[31] There are three 'unbegotten' or primal 'principles of the universe—two male (and) one female'. Of the male principles, the highest deity is called 'Good'.[32] He 'alone is called after this manner' and he alone possesses a power of 'prescience' concerning the universe. Beneath him, on the one side, is the other male principle, known as 'Elohim'—the creator or 'father of all begotten things'. Corresponding to him, on the other side, is the female principle called 'Edem' (or 'earth')[33]—a bimorphic being, both

[30] Clearly *tzav* is construed as 'command' or 'judgement', and *qav* as meaning 'hope' or 'expectation'.

[31] Hippolytus, *Refutatio omnium haeresium*, ed. P. Wendland (GCS 26; Leipzig: J. C. Hinrichs, 1916), iii; v. 26–7. For a penetrating investigation, overall, see Ernst Haenchen, 'Das Buch Baruch: Ein Beitrag zum problem der christlichen Gnosis', *ZTK* 50 (1953), 123–58.

[32] See Haenchen, 'Das Buch Baruch', 142–5, for a consideration of the philosophical concept; but he has difficulties with its identity with Priapus. By contrast, see Robert Grant, 'Gnosis Revisited', *CH* 23 (1953), 44; but he subsequently disavows the place of this being in Justin's account, in 'Les Êtres intermédiares dans le judaisme tardif', in Ugo Bianchi (ed.), *Le Origini dello Gnosticismo* (Lieden: E. J. Brill, 1967), 151. Decidedly positive is Maurice Olender, 'Le Système gnostique de Justin', *Tel Quel*, 82 (1979), 71–88; see esp. 71–2, 86.

[33] Possibly, simply, the Septuagint rendition of Eden; but Hans Jonas, *Gnosis und spätantiker Geist* (pt. I, Die mythologische Gnosis; Göttingen: Vandenhoeck & Ruprecht, 1934), 336 n. 4,

virginal and snake-like (in her upper and lower portions, respectively). These two principles are the prime genitors of Being, and their syzygy produces twelve paternal and twelve maternal angels, which comprise the good and evil sides of the cosmos, respectively. The third angel down on either side plays a special role. On the male side, the being is called 'Baruch' (or 'blessed'), whereas on the female side, she is called 'Naas' (being Hebrew *naḥash*, or 'serpent'). These two angels also represent the two trees in the Garden of Eden (the good tree of Life, and the baleful one of the Knowledge of good and evil); and both play a role in the creation of Man by the angels. Of particular interest is the statement that this human is formed from the upper part of Edem, which is of human form, whereas the beasts are created from her serpentine lower body—she therefore being the primal Mother of *all* life. After the creation, however, Elohim ascends in heaven to the good God, and decides to remain there; and this evokes the vile ire of Edem, who sets her angels against the spirit of Man, and in particular, the third angel Naas receives a 'great power to torment the spirit of Elohim which is in Man'. In response, her counterpart Elohim sends Baruch, the counterpart of Naas, down to earth to counsel Man in Eden. But he is not successful, and the serpent seduces both Adam and Eve. There are further attempts at saving intervention by Baruch and his successors in the course of history—a process that culminates with Christ, who is able to resist Naas and her wiles.

In this theogonic myth, dualistic antagonisms arise from within the primordial structure and continue in any number of human forms. But what is especially striking, given the mythic imagery found in *Zohar* II. 119b, where the arch-female principle (the *Shekhinah*) is presented in the form of a serpent comprised of a positive top half and negative lower one, is the portrayal of the primordial being Edem in the bimodal form of a female who is comprised of higher and lower forms. This presentation of the archetypal mother as snake-like and composed of two dimensions is a most remarkable instance of similar mythic structures in two apparently unrelated cultures and ideological systems. One must wonder whether these parallels are far too particular to indicate similar but unrelated mythic mentalities, or similar expressions of an archetype of divine unity. Alternatively, one would have to imagine that these features moved through unknown channels into medieval Jewish circles; or that they had roots in far older Jewish mythic speculations regarding serpents, presently unknown.

2. In *Zohar Ḥadash, Shir Ha-Shirim* 62c–63a,[34] we find what is an apparently unique Jewish case of mythic speculation about the primordial serpent.

suggests a blending of Hebrew *ʿeden* and *ʾadamah* (land). So already, Richard A. Lipsius, *Der Gnostizismus, sein Wesen, Ursprung and Entwicklungsgang* (Leipzig: Brockhaus, 1860), 60.

[34] In the edition of Reuven Margoliot (Jerusalem: Mosad Ha-Rav Kook, 1953). The collection called *Zohar Ḥadash* contains teachings not included in the first editions of the *Zohar*

The discussion takes its creative point of departure from the opening word of Scripture *berei'shit* ('In the beginning'), and, by means of a typical midrashic procedure, divides the word and repoints its vowels. The result is that we are now to read the line as if God, in the beginning, *bara' shit*, 'created channels' or crevices.[35] In older rabbinic myths, as we have seen, the waters of the primordial deep were stopped up in such channels; and in one image, the primordial sea monster is affixed to the top and so prevents the upsurge of waters that might endanger the world.[36] In the present theosophical setting, these channels represent primordial sources through which the waters of universal sustenance could flow, including the rains that would sustain and irrigate human existence. But these supernal founts, we are told, 'were sealed (*setimin*) from the beginning of the creation of the world until the building of the Temple', despite the heroic efforts of the patriarchs and many others—in whose days there was a 'drought' upon the earth (such physical woes symbolizing a concurrent spiritual crisis). It was only in the time of King Solomon that this dire situation changed; for when he built the Temple a new alignment and balance between the upper and lower spheres of reality was effected, and he was able to release the primordial sustenance. Notably, this act was achieved only when 'he removed' from these channels the serpentine 'twisted one (*'aqima'*) that lay around them'—an act that made possible the creative flow of 'song' (*shir*).[37]

Within this compact narrative is concealed a remarkable bit of mythic exegesis; for the entire speculation on the release of primordial bounty rests upon Solomon's theomachic act of removing the twisted serpent (*'aqima'* certainly alludes to the 'twisted snake' (Isa. 27: 1),[38] which is now assimilated to the primordial monster that blocks the flow of waters and the completion of the creation). How this liberation is achieved is not specified; but this act is here symbolized by transforming the *shit* (channel) into *shir* (song)—itself a symbolic event, since the letter *tav* (the 't' of *shit*) is imagined as being formed

(Cremona and Mantua, 1558–60), and was published in Saloniki in 1597. It is thought to be by the authors of the *Zohar*.

[35] A similar pun underlies the statement in *BT Soṭah* 49a, that 'the channels (*shitin*) were from the (first) six days of the creation', for here *berei'shit* is taken as referring to both the 'six' (*shit*; in Aramaic) days and the 'channels' (*shitin*). For a similar 'etymology' applied to a different myth, see *Gen. Rabba* 1. 4 (Theodor–Albeck, 6).

[36] See above, p. 126.

[37] Y. Liebes, in his *Torat Ha-Yetzirah* (Tel Aviv: Schocken, 2000), 123f., also adduces this passage in connection with a discussion of song in *Sefer Yetzirah* and in *Zohar Ḥadash* 5d–6a (the citation given on p. 310 n. 24 needs to be corrected).

[38] Note that in *Zohar* 1. 35a it is said that the primordial snake called *'aqalaṭon* ('twisted') is so called because it is *be-'aqimu tadir* ('always twisted' or 'wily'). Earlier midrashic traditions referring to the wiliness of the serpent (*naḥash*) are found in *Tanḥuma Va'era'* 4 (where the serpent is described as *me'uqam*) and *Tanḥuma (Buber) Va'era'* 11 (where it is called *mit'aqqeim*). The context pertains to a divine prophecy to Moses regarding Pharaoh, given in conjunction with the staff that becomes a serpent (the lemma is Exod. 7: 8–9).

orthographically by conjoining the letter *reish* (the 'r' of *shir*) with the letter *nun* (standing for the first letter of *naḥash*, 'serpent'). Hence, at the first, when God created the structures of existence, the twisted snake was conjoined to the bounty of song (or unlimited creativity), and this resulted in the blockages and limitations of existence. And it was only when the hero Solomon completed the creation, and established a right alignment within Being, by removing the snake or impediment from it, that the primordial bounty could flow into all the spiritual and material realms. In an arcane way, this process is represented orthographically; but, at the same time, we see that a profound insight motivates this myth. The teacher reveals here that the perfected state is one of song and bounty; and that the ancient sea monster symbolizes the inner and outer impediments that block the realization of God's cosmogonic ends and purposes—an achievement that is fulfilled only by a human being with wisdom and creative power.

The orthographic specifics of this myth would seem to set it off as a unique species of midrashic theosophy. How great is the wonder, therefore, when we turn to the Church Father Irenaeus' work against gnostical heresies (from about 180 CE). In it, we not only find mythic references to a primordial syzygy, and the emergence from the female called Sophia of a 'secretion of light' which is also called ' "Left" and "Vulgar Element" (*Sinistram et Prunicon*)'; but we also have an account of the progeny of this mother, and especially her first descendant, called Ialdabaoth.[39] Particularly notable is the statement that this creature despised its mother, and so focused upon the dregs below and produced an 'offspring'. This 'is the letter *nun*, which is twisted in the form of a snake (*hunc autem ipsum esse Nun in figura serpentis contortum*)'; and from it were generated various things, including envy and death.[40] We are also informed that 'this serpent-like, twisted *nun* (*Hunc autem serpentiformem et contortum Nun*)' was the source of further subversion against its parent.[41]

Quite remarkably, we have here a fragment of an orthographic midrash based on the Hebrew letter *nun*, which clearly stands for the 'twisted serpent' of Isa. 27: 1, now understood mythically as the logogram of perversity and subversion. Such a midrashic myth could only arise in Jewish circles which

[39] The text was originally written in Greek, the paraphrase only exists in Latin. For the critical edition, see A. Rousseau and L. Doutreleau (edd.), *Irénée de Lyon, Contre les hérésies: Livre I* (Sources chrétiennes, no. 264; Paris: Le Cerf, 1979), ii. (1. 30. 3 and 5). The name Ialdabaoth may be of Semitic (Aramaic) origin, and mean something like 'begetter of Sabaoth'; regarding this proposal, see Gershom Scholem, 'Jaldabaoth Reconsidered', in *Mélanges d'histoire des religions, offerts à Henri-Charles Peuch* (Paris, 1974), 405–21.

[40] Irenaeus 1. 30. 5. This phrase is missing in the text edition of W. W. Harvey, *Sancti irenari episcopi Lugdunensis libros quinque adversos haereses* (Cambridge, 1857), i, ad loc. However, the topos recurs several lines later, in nearly the same terms; see below, and n. 41.

[41] Ibid. The explanation focuses on the form or shape of the letter; but one should not forget that *nun* means 'fish' in rabbinic Hebrew and Aramaic (*nunā*; and cf. *nûnnu* in Akkadian).

had speculated upon the meaning of the shape of this letter and linked it to formulations found in Scripture. But once this notion has invaded a gnostic mentality (along with the notion of a left side, and of a demonic septet over against a holy one),[42] it was transmitted as a frozen element in other groups (like the Christian Gnostics that Irenaeus speaks about). Perhaps through these channels older speculations of the role of the snake and the left side influenced like-minded Jews in medieval Spain; though it is not impossible that ancient Jewish myths of this type were preserved within native cultural strata. Be this as it may, and in the absence of proof, it seems best to focus on comparative structures and types, and to observe how different cultures have employed such an orthographic feature in order to articulate a negative dimension in their mythologies. In the writings of Irenaeus, the Hebrew letter provides an emblem or sign of perversity; whereas, in the medieval Jewish exemplar, it partakes of more cosmogonic symbolism and serves as an antagonist of God. Only a mythic mentality focused upon the powers of the serpent as an agent of chaos could generate either image, though the different expressions depend upon the ideologies and cultures involved. As regards the notion of the left side, our Jewish sources (like *Zohar* III. 34b) express themselves in more dramatic mythic language than that evidenced in Irenaeus' topical summary.

[42] In I. 30. 9 we are told how humans were seduced into 'all kinds of evil by the lower septet (*ab inferiori hebdomade*) from the upper, holy septet (*sanctae hebdomadae*)'.

12
Divine Sorrow and the Rupture of Exile

The themes of destruction and sorrow and exile, which recur throughout midrashic literature, are not absent from the pages of the Zoharic corpus; and one will similarly observe the recurrence there of such older rabbinic themes as divine tears and mourning. What distinguishes their reuse is another matter: the drama and crisis in the supernal realms caused by the loss of the Temple in Jerusalem and the banishment of the nation from its homeland into foreign exile. In the new myth, the effect is not simply on the divine personality, which sorrows for its own loss and also that of the people, resulting variously in a withdrawal into the depth of heaven or a sympathetic sharing of Israel's woes in the exile. It is this and more, since these historical events cause doom and disaster in the divine structure itself—splitting off parts of Divinity, so to speak, and effecting a rent in the very fabric of its Being. Indeed, the new myth does speak this way; for Israel is not just an earthly embodiment of its supernal archetype, and the supernal Israel is not some idealized or spiritual prototype of the mundane reality. Rather, in the bold terms of the Zoharic myth, the two are mysteriously one—two different modalities of one and the same Reality. Myth is history and history is myth, for those who see with the eyes of R. Simeon and his disciples.

Of the numerous and varied expressions of this myth, three examples shall be considered. They are chosen as much for their content as for the exegetical character of their articulation. The first two cases provide terse teachings of two dimensions of the myth of divine rupture. The third one provides an extensive account of divine loss and longing, and shows how numerous older traditions could be assembled and transformed into one long narrative of lament.

A. DESTRUCTION OF THE TEMPLE

I. Rupture on High

In this first text, we find a passage dealing with the destruction of the Temple and its precedent in the supernal realm above. Remarkably, on the basis of one old mythic fragment found in Scripture, and a midrashic transformation of another one, this involves an initial act of rupture within the Godhead; only then (as a simultaneous corollary) is there a corresponding disaster in the material world of human habitation.

It is taught: 'Happy are you, O earth, when your king is of noble birth' (Eccles. 10: 17). What is 'earth'?—Earth without qualification; for it is taught: 'He cast down from heaven (to) earth the splendour of Israel' (Lam. 2: 1). This 'earth' is a mystery among the crowns of the holy King; and it is written about (in the verse) 'on the day that the Lord God made heaven and earth' (Gen. 2: 4). Whatever nourishment or food that this 'earth' received was from the place called 'heaven'; and the 'earth' was sustained from no other place except from the holy perfection called 'heaven'. When the Holy One, blessed be He, wished to destroy His home below, and the holy land below, He first put aside the holy land above and brought it down from the gradations where it was nourished from the holy 'heaven'; and afterwards He destroyed the one below. This is what Scripture (means when it) says, 'He cast down from heaven (to) earth the splendour of Israel'—at the outset; and afterwards (it says), 'He did not remember His footstool' (Lam. 2: 1). For it is taught: These are the ways of the Holy One, blessed be He. When He wishes to judge the world, He first renders judgement above; and afterwards it comes to be (in the world) below; as it is written, 'The Lord will punish the host of the high heaven on high', and afterwards 'the kings of the earth upon the earth' (Isa. 24: 21). (*Zohar* II. 175a)

This teaching begins with a rereading of Eccles. 10: 17. At the level of its plain sense, the verse praises 'a land' (*'eretz*) whose king is nobly born, 'the son of nobles' (*ben-ḥorim*)—and thus neither an upstart nor one born a slave.[1] However, the new reading focuses on the fact that the word used is 'earth' without any qualification (no definite article or attribute), and sees it as a sign that the supernal Earth is indicated hereby (this being the lowest of the divine gradations, the female dimension who is also referred to as the *Shekhinah*). This would further mean that the ruler is the divine King on high, who is also referred to in mystical lore as Heaven. But by way of confirmation, Lam. 2: 1 is adduced, and this is initially puzzling. For to what purpose is this cited? How is the statement 'He cast down from heaven (to) earth the splendour of Israel' a proof of the first passage? One might say that the primary benefit of the passage is that it also uses 'earth' without qualification; but the negative cast of the verse over against the praise of Ecclesiastes is not thereby dispelled. What could be the meaning and purpose of the metaphor here?

In the old rabbinical literature there is a striking midrash on this verse from Lamentations, and in it the terms of the image are concretized and we are told of a mythic drama that occurred at the time of the destruction of the Temple. In His displeasure at the people, God took the crown (or *tif'eret*, 'splendour') that was affixed to the image of Jacob's head upon the heavenly throne and cast it down to the earth below—thus symbolizing the fall and

[1] For this meaning of *ḥorim*, cf. Jer. 27: 20 and Neh. 2: 16. As the counterpoint to Ecclesiastes' praise, the psalmist states that 'the earth' cannot bear 'a slave who becomes a king'.

subjugation of the nation called by His name, 'Israel'.[2] In more mythic terms, this debasement of the tutelary presence of Israel on high marks the divine doom brought upon the nation.

The new myth may have this in mind, but proceeds in another direction. Here, the casting down to 'earth' refers to an act in the supernal heights, when God detached this gradation from its source of sustenance above (this being the holy 'heaven'), when He determined to punish Israel and its land below. The supernal spheres of 'heaven' and 'earth', arranged in their holy hierarchy from the beginning of the divine emanation of His Being, are now cut asunder and result in the fragmentation of all reality above and below. The destruction of the earthly temple is the dramatic consequence of this; and just this is marked by the second clause of the very same verse in Lamentations: 'He did not remember His footstool'. Hence when Scripture states that God 'cast down from heaven (to) earth the splendour of Israel', it must mean, when it is read concretely and in light of this mythic mystery, that 'He cast down earth from heaven'. The 'splendour of Israel' (*tif'eret Yisra'el*) must at least indicate the beauty and glory of Israel, that is now cast down. But for any mystic of R. Simeon's school, for whom *Tif'eret* also designated the divine gradation otherwise known as Heaven (and also King and Holy One), the casting out of the 'splendour' of Israel would surely connote the loss for Israel above (Earth) and below (the people and its land) of that source of supernal sustenance.

The myth of 'heaven' and 'earth' thus appears under three of its aspects. The scriptural phrase 'heaven and earth' symbolizes the connection and harmony of the two gradations, bound together by the ligature 'and'. This is the primordial state of unity and interconnection within the Godhead. The sins of Israel below, on its land, drastically affect the *Shekhinah* (also called: Assembly of Israel) and its Land (Earth) on high; and when God disconnects this earth from its heavenly source, and casts it off, a rupture occurs that affects both the supernal and mundane planes. This double process is twice marked in Scripture. First, as a matter of intention, when God announces that He will first punish the powers on high, and then turn to the principalities below. This dual process is articulated in Isa. 24: 21, at the conclusion of our passage. However, it is also marked as a fait accompli, when Lam. 2: 1 states that God both cast out 'earth' from 'heaven' and forgot His footstool. The event is thus completed both above and below—the rupture and disconnection on high being expressed in and through the exile of Israel. History thus enacts the myth in the supernal spheres, even as its traces are encoded in Scripture and await their exegetical disclosure.

[2] *Midrash Eicha* (Buber, 96). Other aspects of the theme of Jacob's 'visage' on the throne are discussed below, in Appendix 2 (pp. 340–1).

B. LONGING FOR REUNION

I. Two Myths of Divine Pathos

1. A different dimension of the myth of divine rupture and loss can be found in texts that take this situation as its main theme, and dramatize the great pathos that swells within the holy hierarchy of the Godhead for the restoration of its desecrated or fragmented unity. The pathos is emboldened by the personal voice of these gradations, particularly that of the *Shekhinah*, longing for reunion with her beloved Lord.

R. Eleazar began (with the verse), 'By night on my bed I sought (him whom my soul loves; I sought him but did not find him)' (Songs 3: 1). 'On (*ʿal*) my bed'; it should have said 'in my bed'. What is (the meaning of) *ʿal mishkabi* ('on my bed')?—The Assembly of Israel (*Shekhinah*) spoke to the Holy One, blessed be He, and petitioned Him concerning the exile, since she dwells among the other nations with her children, and lies in the dust. And since (*ʿal*) she lies (*shekhibat*) in an alien and unclean land, she said 'concerning (*ʿal*) my dwelling (*mishkabi*)' I petition, since I am dwelling (*shekhibnaʾ*) in exile. And 'concerning' that 'I sought him whom my soul loves', to deliver me from (exile). 'I sought him but did not find him', for it is not His way to cohabit with me elsewhere than in His palace. '(I sought him but did not find him;) I called him but he did not answer me' (Songs 5: 6)—for I dwell among alien nations, and only His children hear His voice; as it says, 'Did ever a people hear the voice of God'? (Deut. 4: 33).

R. Isaac said, 'By night on my bed'. The Assembly of Israel said: 'Concerning my bed' I pleaded with Him, that He might cohabit with Me and give Me pleasure, and give Me complete joy; for we have learned that through the King's cohabitation with the Assembly of Israel, numerous righteous come into their sacred inheritance, and numerous blessings are brought upon the world. (*Zohar* III. 42 a/b)

Two aspects of the myth are found here: the first focuses on exile, the second on eros. According to R. Eleazar, the mythic significance of Songs 3: 1 is that it expresses the longing of the *Shekhinah* while in foreign exile, downtrodden and dwelling in the impurity of alien lands. Her lament 'concerning' her debased and sorrowful 'dwelling' is the primary intent and accent of the unit of exegesis. To be sure, there is a secondary erotic overtone as well; for the Assembly of Israel, who endures the tribulations of the nation, beseeches Her Lord above to cohabit with Her, knowing full well that this union can only take place in His 'dwelling', not in any impure space. This ironic echo of the Temple in a cry of loss and petition of hope from the dust of banishment, inserts the longing of the Queen for union with her King into an account of her lowly and impure estate. It thus expresses a powerful and painful pathos, which is nothing other than the sorrow and pain of the people of Israel in its endless ages of exile. R. Eleazar gives voice to this historical sorrow, through the language of myth; and in articulating the lament of the supernal *Shekhinah*, gives a mythic charge and significance to the sorrow of an abased and abused nation.

R. Isaac's remarks are, by contrast, altogether erotic; and call to mind old rabbinic comments about a sacred cohabitation of God and His people in the Temple.[3] For him, the verse in Songs 3: 1 is a solicitation by the Queen for pleasure, partially offset by the sublimation of this desire in the promise of the righteous progeny that will result. The 'bed' is the conjugal dwelling of the holy Temple, where all beneficence is stored; and this being so, one suspects that R. Isaac's teaching was first and foremost a statement based on the verse at hand, and not a remonstration from the depths of exile. It would thus seem that this teaching of the sage was independent of a context of loss; but that now it complements the teaching of R. Eleazar, and expresses the desire of the people for their reunion with God, and for the spiritual beneficence that will result. The cry of the *Shekhinah* is thus the mythic lament of Israel; and the hope for cohabitation with the Lord is Israel's hope for redemption from the shards and the sorrows of history. Where myth ends and history begins is just as mysterious as where history ends and the myth begins. For the teachers who speak here, neither the one nor the other is truly the truth. In fact the two are really one, under the two aspects of time and eternity. It remains for the reader to ponder and to wonder at this mystery, so boldly expressed in these teachings of the book of *Zohar*.

2. The mythic themes of loss and longing were also realized in more extensive literary forms, and of particular note are the proems composed for the Midrash on the book of Lamentations found in the collection known as *Zohar Ḥadash*.[4] By way of example, we shall consider the last of these homiletical introductions, which picks up and develops themes and interpretations found in Part II and earlier in this Part. The full version is found in Appendix 1 (C), and only a summary shall be provided here, prior to the ensuing analysis.[5]

The dramatic narrative opens with the statement that the cry of Zion is heard 'every night', throughout the heights and depths of the world; and this lamentation is linked to the verse in Jer. 25: 30 where the prophet announces that the Lord 'roars from the heights' over the destroyed Temple. As the ensuing discourse makes clear, 'Zion' is the personified divine figure known as the *Shekhinah* (and called Matrona here); and Her lamentation echoes the

[3] See above, pp. 173–7.

[4] Regarding this collection, see above, ch. 11 n. 34. The texts and traditions on Lamentations have been connected to the early stratum of *Midrash ha-Neʿelam*; but it should be noted that this material is written in Aramaic and in a more expansive midrashic style than that early stratum.

[5] *Zohar Ḥadash* (Margoliot, 1953), 92b–d. Several readings are difficult and the result of scribal errors or intrusions (to offset some of the blunt erotic imagery). I have annotated where necessary or appropriate.

voice of 'the city' in the biblical book that 'sits solitary' and bemoans Her loss and lack of consolation. The cry of Zion in this proem unfolds in three parts.

In the first part, which is the first watch of the night, a cry reverberates above and below. The locus of concern here is the outer altar, upon which libations and offerings were made to sustain the *Shekhinah*. She thus wails, repeatedly, 'O My altar, My altar'; and she is joined in this sorrow by a chorus of angels called ᾿Er᾿eilim. These heavenly beings have been depleted through the tragedy of the destruction of a divine dimension (a letter of the Tetragram), and in this state of weakness wail like a woman, thus corresponding to the female *Shekhinah* and Her sorrows. But what is particularly poignant is the fact that the Matrona not only laments the loss of sacrifices, but emphasizes the blood of her children slain upon the altars. She is therefore deprived of their gifts of nourishment, and the possibility to nurture them.

The second part of the drama occurs 'in the middle of the night', at the second watch. The scene now shifts inward to the Holy of Holies, the '(inner) point of Zion'. This is the locus of the sacred Ark, depicted here as 'the place of Her dwelling and couch'. She therefore now wails, repeatedly, 'O My couch, My couch'; and in this lamentation recalls this couch as the place of Her cohabitation with Her Lord and King. Various verses from the Song of Songs are adduced here with a powerful erotic charge; for this couch is the place of a sacred marriage, where the Holy One gathered Her in His arms, took delight in Her body, and lay between her breasts. No qualifications soften the directness of the imagery, or the loss: 'O My husband, My husband', she cries, 'Where have You gone?'

This groaning and wailing continues into the final part, the third watch of the night. But now the content of the lamentation turns from the sacred objects of the shrine to the events of past history. God had sworn that He would not forget Zion, but He has apparently done so; and thus He is called upon to remember the faithfulness of the *Shekhinah* and the nation at Sinai, and the faithful of many generations. God has apparently only chosen to remember guilt and not acts of goodness, thus inverting His own attributes. Because of the loss and the absence of comfort, the Temple remains defiled, and this desecration is embodied in the howling of 'dogs' in the night.

But the third watch is not just a time of terrors, but also a time of transition from the dark of night to the light of dawn. And thus amid all the groaning, the *Shekhinah* takes the remaining Cherub to Her breast and suckles it there, even while it too sobs and cries. It is only then, like a ray of hope, that Her Lord appears and descends to Her from above, giving comfort with the ancient words once spoken through the prophet Jeremiah: 'Restrain Your voice from crying and Your eyes from tears . . . for there is hope for Your end' (Jer. 31: 16–17). This scene is like what has been taught by tradition, the narrator says, when it states that the last watch, near the dawn's early light, is when a babe sucks at its mother's breast and a woman converses with her husband. The allegorical meaning of this rabbinic dictum is clear, and not lost on the reader of this teaching.

The intense drama of divine pathos presented here derives its initial scene from the Babylonian Talmud, at *BT Berakhot* 3a, where it is taught that there are three watches to the night and the point is proved from Jer. 25: 30—where the world 'earth' is repeated three times in a passage depicting God's roar of sorrow over His destroyed shrine.[6] It is during each one of the three watches that God laments the fate of the Temple. Other rabbinic sources have been used, as well, as in the references to the wail of the angelic beings and also the allusions to the inner sanctum of the Temple as a place where God cohabits with His people.[7] But the main source is *BT Berakhot* 3a, which establishes the tripartite structure of lamentation in the teaching, and even provides the stylistic frame. Notably, the reference to the dictum about the babe in arms and the conversation between husband and wife near the dawn is taken from the same page of tradition.

The hint of myth in *BT Berakhot* 3a becomes a full-fledged drama of loss in our text. Quite notably, the divine subject who speaks in Jer. 25: 30 is now taken to be the female Shekhinah, the consort of the King of Heaven, who only appears in the very last scene. Otherwise He is withdrawn above, while She sorrows alone below. This inner splitting of the Godhead starkly personalizes the difference between the abandoned wife and caring mother down below, and the removed husband and unresponsive father on high. This difference may owe its spatial polarities in the first instance to alternative rabbinic images of God's response to the destruction of the Temple. In some cases, the Holy One withdraws to heaven, ascending its several gradations in increasing absence from the sins of the people; whereas, in other cases, the presence of the Shekhinah on earth, in or near the Temple, expresses the nearness of God and His ongoing commitment to the people and its future restoration.[8] Hence the divine is both transcendent and aloof, and immanent and engaged. This dual theology provides the seeds of our dialogue. Ultimately, the King responds to the entreaties of His Queen; and His words of hope give an eschatological ending to the piece.

Thus, whereas our author inherits a vast rabbinic inventory of mythic topics, he has transformed them into a three-act drama of sustained pathos.

[6] See above, pp. 162–3, for the exegetical transformation. For the correlation of three nightly watches and three divine tears in the *Zohar*, based on this biblical passage, see I. 189a.

[7] See the sources and discussions above, pp. 174–6 and 228 f., respectively. The echoes and transformations of these topics in the *Zohar* are considered just above, on pp. 196–8.

[8] For a discussion of these texts, see above pp. 156–9. The midrashic theme that the Shekhinah 'does not move' (*lo' zazah*) from the Temple after its destruction (cf. *Tanḥuma, Shemot* 10), specifically informs the teaching in *Zohar* I. 28a.

Each act has its own emphases—whether it is the first scene which stresses the altar and its sacrifices, and also the slain nation in the shrine; or the second scene and its stress on the couch and connubial union between the pair; or finally, the third scene which stresses the divine husband and the faithfulness of the nation in the past. And throughout, the pathos varies in intensity and focus, as the lament of the mother moves from topic to topic and from appeal to appeal—all in her effort to gain the attention of the Lord above. As readers, we are caught in this mythic web. From the time that the narrator sets the scene and tells us that he is bringing a teaching from the tradition, and moves from its opening statement to the drama and its several stages of development, the literary frame holds and the reader is absorbed in the immediacy and real presence of the myth. Indeed, there is also never a point where one is tempted to think theosophically, outside the frame of the mythic narrative. Nor is there any need to: the myth sets its terms and terminology, and the reader is conjured by the magic of its claims. The narrative presents the truth of this myth as self-evident. Even the introductory nod to tradition does not spoil this. Rather, the initial comment that the events to come occur 'every night' marks a transition for the reader—the point where he leaves the punctual and the episodic character of history and enters the durative and recurrent domain of myth.

We are thus readers of a great myth of a Mater Dolorosa, of a mother of sorrows who is abandoned by her Lord and entreats Him on behalf of her absent children. Even the scenes of eros and intimacy do not altogether obscure this maternal dimension; for if these seek to evoke a rapturous and loving past of union, such love-making is not the secret tryst of two adolescents (as found in the Song of Songs) but the connubial union of the Lord and His Lady in a sacred place, whose product are the 'children' of whom she speaks as a loving advocate. Only in one place does it seem that history breaks into the frame of the myth in a palpably raw and barely assimilated manner; and that is the references to the 'children' slain upon the altars in the first scene. One has the strong impression that this image is drawn from the memories of persecutions. And it therefore seems likely that the use of the word 'holy' (*qedoshim*) to describe these people is a deliberate evocation of the Jewish term for martyrs in the Middle Ages (namely, 'saints' or 'sanctified ones'). It is for this sorrow, too, that the *Shekhinah* weeps and gives these historical events some mythic permanence in her long-suffering memory, and that of her people.

13
Conclusions

In this Part we have considered aspects of a third level or dimension of myth in Judaism: the first being the inheritance of the Hebrew Bible, a product of ancient Israel and its wider Near Eastern context; the second being the inheritance of the Midrash and the Talmud, the product of rabbinic Judaism and its diverse historical conditions; and the third being the inheritance of any number of mystical tracts, and particularly the book of *Zohar*, an heir of these prior layers of tradition and their transformation. In every sense is the *Zohar* a kind of 'renaissance': at once an ingathering of earlier sources and their bold revivification.[1] There are no breaks in this chain, but rather continuities and innovation: different orientations to reception, renovation, and reformation. The old biblical fragments of myth were repeatedly reused and recontextualized, as were the midrashic teachings that took them over and revised them. In these cases, myth was found in Scripture (both directly and through exegesis); but Scripture itself was not myth.

This underscores what is truly new about myth and the *Zohar*. As a commentary on Scripture, the book of *Zohar* attempts to read and disclose the hidden myth formulated in the words of the Torah and other passages from the sacred canon. That is to say, the myth itself, as an inward and spiritual reality of divine Being, is unsayable and unknowable on its own terms; and only becomes knowable and sayable in the terminology of Scripture—when this is properly understood. One might thus fear that this refraction is a double distortion: first, because of its distillation through human language; and, second, because of its dependence on the human imagination and the vagaries of exegetical insight. But the fact that the Torah is deemed to be an aspect of Divinity itself; and that Moses is a perfect 'man of God', who has received the divine Wisdom in the mirror of his pure consciousness, betokens trust that the supernal truths have been transmitted through his wisdom and may be known by his true disciples.[2] The core of this truth is the myth of God's manifestation of His Being in a series of gradations and forms; and just this is encoded in the language of Scripture.

[1] This happy designation of the *Zohar* as a renaissance is made by Yehuda Liebes, 'Ha-Zohar ke-Renesans', *Daat*, 46 (2001), 5–11.

[2] See *Zohar* III. 149a/b and 152a. Also note the formulation in *Zohar Ḥadash, Midrash Shir ha-Shirim*, 70d, 'Blessed are those who study the Torah in order to know the wisdom of their Master, and who know and understand the supernal mysteries'—of which a brief synopsis follows.

Scripture is thus the myth of divine Being—formulated in the language and imagery of the everyday world. That is to say, Scripture is both the core myth *and* the many manifestations or expressions of it. For the core myth is embedded in the order of the creation and the structure of its created elements (trees, persons, streams); in the phases of nature (lunar cycles, or sunrise and sunset), and in its elemental power (sun, clouds, rain, and eclipse). Its modalities also find expression in and through the personal acts and historical relationships found in Scripture (of the patriarchs and matriarchs, fathers and sons, Israel and the nations), and its sacred institutions and rituals (the Temple sacrifices, Sabbath and festival observances, and circumcision). This means that the myth is encoded in many images and dynamics, both personal and natural; and in different types of relationship or disturbance. It also means that because the core myth and its structure can be replicated throughout the sensate and spiritual orders of being, all that can be experienced and known is both a reflection and refraction of the myth. Hence to 'read' the world according to its truth is to understand how it manifests the many configurations of the myth, which constitute the inner reality of God. And to read Scripture is to do the same, and more, because one can only 'read' the natural world correctly to the degree and extent that one knows (through Kabbalah, or 'Tradition') that the inner truth of Scripture is the reality of God's Being, and that it is present in all things.[3]

In a certain sense, then, the myth is a total one, embracing all orders of reality, spiritual and material; but to understand the myth requires a double seeing. It requires a reading of the images and persons of the world, and the texts of Scripture, in their concrete modes of manifestation or representation. It also requires a deeper seeing, that perceives in these physical forms the embodiments of the spiritual or transcendental divine order. Thus the figures of the world and the configurations of Scripture are not allegories for more intellectual truths. They are rather actual and concrete expressions of the higher worlds, manifesting the truths and realities of those worlds through the specific and sensate forms of physicality and literary representation.

There is no reading of this myth in ignorance. In ignorance there is only the world of nature and the narratives of the text. Only through the template of the hidden myth (as received through Tradition) can its external expressions be perceived and perused; and then, on this basis, might one reciprocally perceive through the phenomena of nature and the language of Scripture something more about this core myth and the complexity and interrelation of its structures. This at least is the hidden promise of informed observation and study. The goal is to know God.

[3] See especially the passage in *Tikkunei Ha-Zohar*, second preface, 17a/b. Here we are told how the gradations can be seen in the configuration of a person and in the realms of nature ('You created heaven and earth' and all its elements 'so that through them the upper realms might be known').

Two further considerations may be noted.

The many depictions of nature and history in Scripture thus encode, in polymorphic variety, the spiritual morphologies of the Divine Being, in its hierarchical structure and perfected order or balance (like the 'Primordial Man' in God's image); in its own inner crises or pre-formations prior to the establishment of a hierarchical order (like the death of the kings of Edom), or in the purgations that produced a negative series of archetypes, and the traces of their limitations (the emergence of the Serpent out of the 'left side' and the battles that preceded the order of the creation); and in the many modalities which occur outside of this spiritual structure and constitute the events of personal or national history (these, as extensions of this divine order in the mundane sphere, inevitably influence the totality of Divinity and its harmonics through their various activities).

Thus the hidden myth of Divine Being is encoded in the words and sentences of Scripture, and it is precisely in the exegetical pyrotechnics applied to these words and sentences that the great mystery is articulated. Repeatedly, the companions in the *Zohar* apply themselves to this task—sometimes using a tried and true midrashic technique (like the treatments of the preposition *'al*, giving it the sense of 'on', 'for', and 'concerning'; or in the way ambiguities are exploited for *mishkabi*, giving it variously the sense of 'throne', 'connubial bed', and 'land of exile'); and on other occasions building upon earlier midrashic conclusions (like the depiction of God throwing down the splendour of Israel), or the use of certain scholastic modes of investigation (like the way of opening a discussion with the suggestion, 'One would have expected *x*'). Many different possibilities of interpretation are offered on every page of the text, and these are not listed as so many 'different matters' (as in the static lists of our midrashic compilations) but as many different voices in a collective and common enterprise. In this process, the 'measure of coherence' or 'efficacy' is guided by the structure of the sentence and the pattern of its words; and the differences among the interpreters often revolve around different emphases or evaluations concerning that structure or pattern. Successful readings usually show a capacity to take the individual words and their order in a most concrete manner, and then through direct or indirect suggestion indicate how this sequence of words encodes a certain dynamic of the myth—consonant with the case at hand.

We thus get the myth at several levels of representation: first and foremost, there is the core myth, the hidden template received from Tradition and beyond all human representation; second, around this core myth, and the inspired creations of the ancient masters and *perfecti* (like Moses and Solomon and David), is the language of Scripture—which weaves its texture through numerous situations, in all of their necessary concreteness and imagery—thus reflecting or refracting the core myth in a human idiom; and finally, these representations of the myth would be unknowable were it not for the heirs of this Tradition, who seek to read Scripture in the light of this repository of wisdom, and who do so with an imaginative daring.

Hence, the core myth is one; its scriptural formulations are many; and the exegetical approximations are legion, even for any specific word and phrase. Exegesis thus reveals Scripture as the manifestation of the modalities of the core myth in human speech, even as these acts of human interpretation construct new myths that seek to express the unsayable archetype. Throughout, there is the conviction that Scripture manifests the Divine Being, and that in the works of earlier tradition (the Midrash) hints of the esoteric mysteries were often concealed. The medieval disciples of these old initiates collect these hints and try to articulate the core myth, for themselves and for those whom they would draw into their mystical circle. As this bold mythic imagination remoulds the face of Scripture, it beholds a new Judaism within its words. Zoharic tradition is a trace of that vision.

We thus conclude in confirmation of two topics raised in the Introduction to this book: the relationship of monotheism to myth and the notion of exegetical mythmaking. In the *Zohar*, the old mythic components found in the Hebrew Bible, and variously gathered and expanded in the midrashic corpus, together with the generation of new themes concerning God's personality and actions are the basis of a comprehensive 'Myth of the Divine Being', that extends beyond anything found in this earlier literature. Hereby, the powers of Divinity extend into everything and even produce or are congenitally linked to the whole complex of negative forces. The full diversity of existence is correlated with this Godhead, and a major goal of exegetical activity is to see and affirm this bond of all Being, labouring to enforce its positive energies and simultaneously weaken the negative ones. Monotheism is consonant with this comprehensive view of the Godhead, and it is variously expressed through myth (the representations of Scripture, and the exegetical approximations of the core myth that are produced by the companions). The two repeatedly intertwine and are mutually reinforcing. The Myth thus supports the theological assertion of monotheism: that God is one (albeit a complex and dynamic and even polymorphic unity); and the claim of monotheism is confirmed by those who know the core myth, and are able to understand from it just how the diverse manifold of reality is really One—the many modalities of the one and only God, in all the orders and realms of existence.[4]

[4] To be sure, the way the one God is related to, linked to, or comprises the totality of reality is neither a simple matter, in a work as complex as the *Zohar*, nor is it subject to a single characterization. A particularly radical formulation occurs in II. 85b, but thematic variants abound. Traces of ancient rabbinic speculations about the way the divine is present in the world but transcendent as well, is found in the well-known dictum of R. Yose (ben Ḥalafta; T 3), who deduces from God's statement 'Behold there is a place (*maqom*) with Me' (Gen. 32: 21), that 'The

Exegesis is the motor that makes the many myths of Scripture manifest; it extends and transforms older motifs like the serpent or the sympathy of God, and it reveals mythic episodes in images and metaphors—like the forlorn maiden looking for her beloved, or God casting out the splendour of Israel. In ever artful ways, new myths and narratives are produced; and in ever creative ways, the resources of tradition (Scripture, Midrash, and Kabbalah) are integrated and projected into transcendental domains. For anyone who might think that myths die with the death of comprehensive mythic cultures, and that exegesis is a post-mortem activity that takes over the shards of old images and at best patches together old vessels for a more potable content, the phenomenon of Jewish myth and mythmaking is instructive. Repeatedly, older myths and mythic episodes are gathered in the Midrash and energized through the power of exegesis, giving them new life and ongoing purpose. The climax of this process in the medieval world must be the book of *Zohar*. Not only are these older mythic topics taken over and further transformed, but it is through the magic of exegesis that a new and comprehensive mythic culture is articulated. Hence one may readily assume that many of the theological intuitions found in this work were spawned and developed independent of Scripture, without denying the power of exegesis to guide the new reader of Scripture to these ideas, and also to support them through the authority of Scripture.

Exegesis must therefore be vaunted as a distinct mode of the cultural imagination, and its capacity to generate and justify a vast amount of myths in Judaism is testimony to the fact that the phenomenon of myth is not simply a product of naive creativity—but rather a phenomenon that is moulded under many circumstances, and that can be revived by sophisticated techniques of literary interpretation.[5] It is no less significant that many of these mythic products of ancient and medieval Judaism bear the stamp of exegetical discourses and narratives—and that these forms give pleasure and delight and instruction. Precisely this has been the bounty of myth from time immemorial; and it has been one of the purposes of this book to present aspects of its multiform Jewish dimensions—long overdue.

Holy One, blessed be He, is the place of His world, but His world is not His place' (*Gen. Rabba* 68. 9; Theodor–Albeck, pp. 777 f.). R. Isaac makes a similar point, using the term 'habitation' (*maʿon*); and a striking parable by R. Abba bar Yudan concludes the series, and adds a different theological nuance. But none of the latter comments reflects any mystical sensibility. At the beginning of the *Genesis Rabba* unit, the later R. Ammi (A 3), ponders why God is called *Maqom*, and answers that 'He is the place of His world'. It appears that R. Ammi does not know R. Yose's teaching; but it is also striking that the editor of this pericope appears to side with the earlier position, because he places it *after* the one by R. Ammi, such that it now appears to be a response and rebuttal.

[5] This is, of course, a point that also applies to ancient Near Eastern and biblical mythopoesis, as I have noted, pp. 20–2.

14
Final Conclusions

The diverse and detailed subject matter treated in this work must be evaluated on its own terms, and no summary could do it fair justice; neither should one expect any new arguments at this point, to supplement or support any of the discussions already undertaken. Nevertheless, in a study such as this one, which covers nearly two thousand years of religious and literary history, various patterns and features have been emphasized in the different parts. It may therefore be of value to conclude here with attention to the overall patterns of this study, and to some dominant aspects of the landscape that has been traversed. Three considerations deserve particular emphasis.

1. First and foremost, this book has been an exploration of the *morphologies of myth and mythmaking* found in three distinct bodies of literature, from three distinct historical periods: the Hebrew Bible, from ancient Israel; the clusters or anthologies of Midrash, from ancient and early medieval Judaism; and the book of *Zohar*, from thirteenth-century Spain (or from related collections such as *Zohar Ḥadash*). Each of these corpora was taken up in turn, with a concerted attempt to delineate the distinct features and techniques of myth to be found therein; but the fact that these three collections of tradition are culturally linked and interrelated also allowed us to discern patterns and variations as materials moved from one locus to another. Specific attention was given to content dealing with divine actions and personality, both as a way to limit the vastness of the subject, but also to isolate a sphere of inquiry that could productively be compared with myths found in ancient Near Eastern texts and in the history of religions more generally. Given contentions that have denied the compatibility of myth with the monotheistic tradition overall, and with the Hebrew Bible in particular, such a strategy was deemed a sound starting point. The developments of myth in subsequent layers of Jewish tradition built upon this foundation.

Looked at from a *synchronic* perspective, the mythic contents of the different corpora can be seen in all their variety and all their specificity. This holds both for the range of expressions on any one theme (like the combat with the dragon; or the nature and drama of the creation) and for the diversity of subjects as a whole. The multiplicity stands as witness to the many occasions of mythmaking, and the importance of treating each expression as a mythic event in its own right. Differences testify to diverse contexts and concerns, and to different applications and literary opportunities. Naturally, the interpreter may choose to perceive types and patterns in the diversity. But this perception merely adds an analytical and comparative dimension, allowing one to see sameness and difference. It does not cancel the variety or even reduce the significance of individual cases.

Viewed from a *diachronic* perspective, it is clear that there was an ongoing reception, production, and transformation of myths and mythic themes over the course of two millennia, even though we cannot always be sure of the channels through which the streams of tradition flowed in any given case—and when the myths are native versions of common regional topics, or when they are naturalized adaptations of foreign elements. Such obscurities have reinforced the view that some mythic species in the Hebrew Bible are the dried pickings of a fertile pagan bough, rather than a home-grown bounty; but there is no proof for such a presumption. It is also unclear how certain myths move from one tradent to another among the network of rabbinic sages, seeming to disappear and reappear at odd intervals with undiminished poignancy. But this is hardly proof that these myths are simply fragments (faded or fictional) of some older religious order. The vitality of the evidence stares one in the face, if read with open eyes.

What is particularly striking are those cases where certain topics or terms found in one mythic tradition recur in another one more than a thousand years later and in altogether different literary and cultural settings. For example, we had occasion to observe that singular elements of ancient Near Eastern creation myths (dealing with the gender and separation of the heaven and earth; or specific terms for divine combat) appear in midrashic texts without there being any trace of these topics and language within the Hebrew Bible or in subsequent pseudepigraphic sources. And similarly, the theme of divine battles against the primordial dragon, and the function of its death as a key component in the creation of the ordered world, appears in the book of *Zohar* with full mythic power without any prior trace of just such a thematic feature in biblical or midrashic texts. A diachronic perspective on this issue does not compel one to imagine some secret or long-delayed influence of Mesopotamian mythology (like *Enuma elish*) on medieval Europe, but rather provides an opportunity to ponder the creative continuities of mythic themes in Israelite and Jewish culture—beneath the textual surface. Indeed, our literary sources are merely the outcroppings of ongoing mentalities.

On the other hand, viewing the similarities of mythic themes and structures in far-flung and often apparently unrelated sources, invites reflection on their typological relationships, and their different modalities and functions. Such typological comparisons may thus underscore similarities between late Jewish myths of the evil serpent and those found in earlier Gnostic sources, without the need to assert or presume hidden influences in the absence of evidence. It is conceivable that similar textual conditions and religious mentalities may produce similar mythic images, also without any actual historical connection. At the same time, and to re-emphasize, the flow of traditions are not always upon the textual surface; and the study of mythic themes in the sources we have treated must duly caution latter-day interpreters from overlooking the vitality and ongoing importance of cultural life that does not appear in our canonical texts. Our myths are known only insofar as they have been spoken and preserved, and only in the way that they have been formulated and transmitted by certain scholars and sages.

2. The myths that we have studied are thus *cultural forms* and the *concrete expressions* of a vital mythic imagination, found in classical texts of the Jewish monotheistic tradition. They do not occur either as private or inchoate musings, but as processed and particular statements made at specific times and passed on as part of a vast cultural enterprise. We may say that the myths do not occur in the abstract, but always as bound forms—bound to a given genre or occasion or citation from Scripture.

In the Hebrew Bible, as we have seen, the myths only appear as specific topics and in specific settings, and only in brief or condensed allusions to the divine action deemed pertinent to the need or purpose of the speaker. We thus have neither independent nor expanded mythic narratives in this corpus, but rather the application or adaptation of particular mythic topics to specific literary or rhetorical moments. The expressions are thus always partial and independent of one another, as so many separate or distinct *logia* about divine activity or emotions. Indeed, these mythic units do not occur as extensive literary events on their own terms, but as specific invocations and uses of the myth by a given person; and it is precisely this boundedness of the myths to specific human purposes that gives them rhetorical intensity, and attests to the ontological validity of these formulations for their speakers.

The myths of Midrash are different. For one thing, and most fundamentally, these myths are bound to Scripture itself—being related to it by exegetical innuendo or a detailed explication of specific phrases and verses. This is done with much ingenuity or insight; and often, to achieve a maximal impact, the speaker may utilize and transform any number of related verses from the total breadth of the scriptural canon, or may cull or collate them in a variety of patterns and lists. The validity of any given myth is thus dependent upon the validity of sacred Scripture, even if the myth is conceptually independent of it and only subsequently or tenuously linked to its language. While there is no telling just how the myth was heard, or the validity of its claims assessed, I would suggest that the very survival and transmission of certain mythic teachings over time and in diverse corpora is some further measure of its truth value—for some sages, at the least.

The exegetical bond between Scripture and myth implies that this canonical source conceals a deeper dimension about the acts and nature of God, and thus the language of the readable text is but the surface of another narrative about divine deeds or divine feelings hidden from immediate view. To know how to read rightly is thus to know that the historical character of Scripture is but the verbal outcropping of another narrative—not an account of Israel but of God, and not of the events of the earth but of the hidden acts of the Lord in heaven. One must be astounded by the daring of the sages, who searched the Scriptures and found there exegetical proof or warrant for God's sorrows and sympathies, and for His decision to share in the fate of Israel. Scripture is thus a measure of myth, for those who would know or listen to the testimony of the sages. But it is not myth itself.

In the book of *Zohar*, however, Scripture is itself the myth of God—no more and no less; and just this is its revolutionary addition to our subject. For the disciples of Rabbi Simeon, and for this master himself, the Hebrew Bible manifests the reality of divine Being under numerous historical conditions, and the secret nature of God under the conditions of His existential transformation from ultimate hiddenness to a mediated, refracted realization of transcendental truth—a transition from 'His naught' to 'His being', as the old book of *Yetzirah* would say it, and as many latter mystics (like R. Azriel of Gerona) would also assert in confirmation. For those in the know, the entirety of Scripture conceals the manifestation of divine Being. This ultimate morphology is the core 'Myth of Reality', but it is only known through proximate allomorphs—these being the events and narratives of Scripture. The fellowship of initiates leads us into this truth, as they live their life of ceaseless scriptural exegesis and interpretation of its mysteries. This mode of life is a mode of mythical living, for there is no separation between living the truth of Scripture and living within the truth of God. The two are one. Scripture suffuses all; for it is the real myth of God, insofar as this is ever or at all sayable in human speech or accessible to the human imagination. God's truth is refracted in fragments of myth bound by the syntax of Scripture. Learning to read is thus, in reality, a learning of the truth of Torah and its teaching of the myth of God, the ultimate One and Only. This myth cannot be known directly, but solely as a truth of tradition at the intuitive edge of the cultural forms of Scripture.

3. The three literary corpora that have been investigated provide different accounts or perceptions of what we may call the theosphere and its relation to the biosphere. The *correlations between these divine and earthly dimensions of reality* provide an index to the nature of myth recorded in these cultural strata.

In the Hebrew Bible, the divine Lord of creation rules both in heaven and earth—enthroned supreme in the heights among His cosmic retinue, and extending His dominion over the entire world. The theosphere and the biosphere are all subject to the one God's judgements and beneficence and might. As we have observed, these two realms are not altogether impermeable and the dimensions may be crossed in both directions, with appropriate metamorphoses of the beings involved. Nevertheless, there is a fixed hierarchy in the realms of reality, and a fundamental chasm that distinguishes God above from all the life forms below. For humankind, and this means particularly the people of Israel, there are two key points where divine power and care are correlated with earthly affairs. The first is the domain of the covenant, established between God and Israel. Hereby, there is a revelation of divine will and the promise of benefits or doom for humans who alternatively fulfil or disobey the conditions of agreement. A juridical order binds the two realms, with God alone as the judge and purveyor of deeds performed below. Correlations are repeatedly invoked that leave no doubt about Who is the source of life and peace and health, or how these boons may be activated and sustained by the nation; and, correspondingly, it is also clear that the terrors of death and strife and illness are the manifestations of God's punishments—through direct action, or the removal of Himself or of His favour (Leviticus 26 and Deuteronomy 27–8).

Accordingly, the civil and ritual commandments are variously correlated with divine rule or providence, so that human acts of obedience or disobedience can affect God's dominion in the world. Divine wrath and kindness are thus in some measure conditions not entirely out of human control—even though their expressions on earth are not always direct or discernible. For the supreme Lord and judge also reveals to the nation that He is a God of mercy; and thus, though judgement will ultimately come, He may forgive or relent or defer punishment at will (Exodus 34: 6–7). Israel is therefore dependent upon God's personality, and His deliberations of judgement and mercy; but they also have His covenant and its duties to give them hope and assurance. At the same time, it was believed that God's favour could be coddled with pleas and that His personal pride was not beyond appeal. As a last resort, past promises by God as well as merits performed by people might even be invoked to tip the divine scales towards mercy—or so a host of psalmists and prophets believed and hoped.

Decisively linked to this portrayal of God as both supreme judge and ruler, are other images of Him as the mighty Lord of battles who may rescue the needy from the grip of their foes. In this regard, the divine enforcer of covenant responsibility is also responsive to human prayer and petition. Thus, in the words of the psalmist, God promised that He would 'be with' His people (one and all) in their times of 'trouble', this being understood to mean that He would come to save and deliver them in times of woe (Ps. 91: 15). For this reason, psalmists would call upon the Lord in their distress and remind Him of His greats acts of power against the primordial dragon at the beginning of time, or His saving power against the roiling sea at the time of the Exodus, and request Him to come again in His might and save them from the new manifestations of distress and danger (Psalms 74; 77; 89). Ancient acts of divine power, portrayed in mythical terms, are thus invoked and correlated with personal situations in need of new acts of God's victory. In a quite similar way, prophets correlate the divine defeat of the dragon at the beginning of the world and the slaying of the sea serpent at the deliverance from Egypt with the nations's need for renewed gests of deliverance—whether from exilic bondage or the oppression of national enemies (Isa. 51: 9–11; Habakkuk 3). Thus older mythic acts are recalled here, too, in an effort to affect God and have Him manifest His might again, as in former times. The evocation of these ancient models shows the ongoing vitality of the myths in the present.

In the midrashic and related rabbinic literature, there is a continuation and intensification of earlier biblical features, by citation and elaboration. But there are also notable shifts and transformations, and these reveal some of the mythic dimensions and emphases that were described at length in Part II. Thus, if anything, there is a magnification of the dominion of the Lord in the highest heaven, with His Glory manifest upon a chariot-throne (to be perceived by mystics and celebrated by laity), and His royal realm extending throughout the cosmos, filled with myriads upon myriads of divine beings, and comprising a kind of spiritual omnipresence that suffuses the vast theosphere with a panoply of heavenly powers. However, at the same time, among the teachers and mythic teachings that we examined, strong emphasis was given to divine needs for help and assistance; and the effects of human actions upon the balance of God's mercy and judgement have a more volatile and determinative character than anything found in the Hebrew Scriptures. Observance of the commandments thus assumes a new mythic dimension in these midrashic sources, and indicates a correlation affecting both God and man.

The divine commandments are variously presented as agencies of influence, capable of increasing God's powers (for salvation, and mercy, and beneficence) when performed, or diminishing them (for doom, and judgement, and woe) when not properly performed. A host of terms emphasize this 'increase' or 'decrease' of powers; and a host of terms document their diverse effects upon God and upon Israel. Nor are such matters simply a matter of influencing the course of national destiny; but as various sources indicate, proper human actions and petitions may also result in beneficial divine effects upon the life of individuals (see *Pesikta de-Rav Kahana, Seliḥah*, 25). In several poignant passages, the complex correlation of covenant actions and divine dominion is formulated in the boldest terms—even speaking of God's needs and desires in ways that thoroughly transform the juridical austerity of the covenant, as well as the sense pervading the Hebrew Bible that the laws are conditions for human weal and not matters affecting God's own capacity or nature.

Precisely such a shift of emphasis is indicated by several striking cases of exegesis. In one instance, the passage 'If (*'im*) you follow My laws'

(Lev. 26: 3) is boldly transformed; for if the plain sense of the phrase emphasizes the conditionality of the covenant for humans, an early rereading turned the focus upon God, and took the words to mean 'that the Holy One, blessed be He, desires that Israel labour in the Torah' (*Sifra, Beḥuqqotai*). This transformation was achieved by a deft but decisive construal of the very term originally used to articulate the condition for divine beneficence (*ʾim*), as the one that indicates God's request or desire for proper behaviour (as if God said: 'would that' you follow My laws). And lest this appeal not fully suggest that a divine need is indicated, another teacher came and said: 'I (God) am happy and you (Israel) are happy (*ʾashrai ve-ʾashreikhem*)! And when is this so? When you observe My Torah—(as Scripture says,) "If (*ʾim*, interpreted as 'when') you follow My laws"' (*Leviticus Rabba* 35.3).

Two other teachers drop any rhetorical pretence from such a mythic theology of the covenant when they invoke the language of needs. Thus Rabbi Eleazar ha-Qappar (T 4) once had God Himself assert: 'My Torah is in your hands and the End (of Days) is in Mine—and the two of us need (*tzerikhim*) one another. You need Me to bring about the End; yet I need you too, that you observe My commandments, in order to speed the (re-)building of My House and Jerusalem' (*Pesikta Rabbati*, 31). And in a later generation, and even more starkly, Rabbi Aḥa b. Ada (BA 3) interpreted the distinction between 'one who worships God and one who does not worship Him' (in Mal. 3: 18) as referring to one who worships 'for the need (*tzorekh*) of God', as against one who worships 'not for the need of God', but rather for his own personal aggrandizement or fortune (*Midrash Psalms* 31. 9).

These ritual and legal correlations between the divine realm and human acts are complemented by the host of passages that were examined dealing with God's sympathy for Israel's sorrow and His participation in their destiny. Now the passage once invoked to assert that God would be 'with' Israel to deliver them from their troubles is the watchword for mythic theologies of God sharing in one way or another in the bondage, and sorrow, and exile of the nation (a participation that includes acts of imitative labour and constriction and bereavement). These divine identifications show a new range of correlations between human actions and those taken on by God—giving a bold mythic dimension to Israel's fate, and also to its realized and future redemptions. Significantly, as compared with features in the Hebrew Bible, these correlations in the midrashic texts do not express examples of divine power and victory over supernatural and historical forces occurring in the past, but refer to God's simultaneous and sympathetic enactment of the sorrows of Israel (often using passages that in Scripture evoke wrath or doom). And the portrayals of salvation not only indicate that God will also participate in these events; but they repeatedly speak of the fact that, in the times of redemption, He will also personally undergo a liberation from the constrictions and denigrations that He has endured during the exile (notably, this new sense is often achieved by radically inverting the verse in question, speaking of God's own salvation precisely through the terms which in the plain sense actually asserted His power to save humans). There is thus a bold shift from a Lord of battles who is called upon to intervene in history to a God of sympathy who identifies with the fate of Israel. Myths of consolation and sorrow are the supports found in Scripture in times of disaster, at least in some circles.

In the book of *Zohar*, the bond and interrelationship between the theosphere and the biosphere that we have suggested for the Hebrew Bible and the midrashic corpora are radically transformed. In this text, the theosphere embraces the biosphere, so that for the mystic the biosphere is really a modality or an actualization of the all-embracing theosphere. Hence the truths of the divine realm (as regards both its structure and the relationships among its parts) are replicated in every aspect of reality. Reality is one, and its truth, howsoever diverse, is also one. God, world, and mankind, and also the Torah, template of all, are correlated. This is the mythic and also the mystic truth of this work ('as is above, so below'); and the task of study and worship is to attain this deeper consciousness (*Zohar* III. 152a).

At the level of covenantal actions and behaviours, this means that the commandments are complexly correlated with the entirety of divine Being. Thus 'the commandments of the entire Torah are joints and limbs in the supernal mystery; and when all of them are joined together, they constitute one single mystery'. And in an even more radical formulation, we are told: 'every commandment comprises all the supernal gradations, even though each one has a level of its own' (see *Zohar* II. 162b; and *Zohar Ḥadash, Tiqqunim* 119c). The totality is thus inseparable; all is one whole. The actions that one performs in one sphere of Being are thus linked to all others: for there is no simple influence of one act or one behaviour, but rather all acts and behaviours are components of one interrelated whole, such that what any person does or does not do affects the entire skein of Being. It would not, therefore, be sufficient for a worshipper simply to call upon the Divine, as if this were some separate or distinct force. The possibilities for all rectifications are given through all of the commandments; and the balance of powers are given into the hands of humans, whose every action is deemed a crucial component of the divine whole.

We need not elaborate. But a final question imposes itself. It may be formulated as follows: Where, in this system, does myth end and mysticism begin? Or: Where in this world-view can we say that we have moved from a mythical reality into a mystical one?

There is no one or simple solution; and I would only suggest the following consideration. The move from myth to mysticism may be effected at the point where the component features of myth are not elements of an external narrative or divine drama, but rather spiritual components of a divine reality which the individual has internalized. Through this interiorization of the mythic dramas, the person assimilates the modalities of the divine reality and strives to actualize its truths in every thought and action. The language of myth thus gives shape to spiritual consciousness, and provides the armature and forms of imagination through which one may conceptualize 'the Whole' and bear it in mind at all times. Myth may therefore comprise and condition a mystical mentality—not by being transcended so much as by being fully subjectivized and lived. For the companions of the *Zohar*, the images of myth constitute an interior landscape of the soul by which they may, in truth, conform to the reality of God (II. 137a).

APPENDIX 1
Translations from Talmudic and Zoharic Sources

A. SEA MONSTERS AND BATTLES (*BT BABA BATRA* 74B–75A)

'And God created the great sea-monsters (*tanninim*)' (Gen. 1: 21). Here (in Babylon) they translated: sea gazelles. Rabbi Yoḥanan said: This refers to Leviathan the slant serpent and Leviathan the twisting serpent, as it says: 'On that day YHWH will punish with His harsh (and great and strong) sword (Leviathan the slant serpent and Leviathan the twisting serpent)' (Isa. 27: 1). (Mnemonic:) 'All', 'Time', 'Jordan'.

I. Rav Yehudah said in the name of Rab: All that the Holy One, blessed be He, created in His world He created male and female. Even Leviathan the slant serpent and Leviathan the twisting serpent He created male and female; and had they mated with one another they would have destroyed the whole world. (So) what did the Holy One, blessed be He, do? He castrated the male and killed the female, preserving her in salt for the righteous in the world to come; as it is said: 'And he will slay the dragon (*tannin*) in the sea' (Isa. 27: 1). And also 'Behemoth on a thousand hills' (Ps. 50: 10) He created male and female; and had they mated with one another they would have destroyed the whole world. (So) what did the Holy One, blessed be He, do? He castrated the male and cooled the female and preserved her for the righteous in the world to come; as it is said: 'Behold, his strength is in his loins' (Job 40: 16)—this refers to the male, 'and his force is in the muscles of his belly' (ibid.)—this refers to the female.

—There also (in the case of Leviathan), He should have castrated the male and cooled the female; (so why did he kill her)?—Fish are dissolute. Why then did He not do the opposite (and kill the male and preserve the female)?—If you want, say: Because it is written: 'There is Leviathan whom You have created to sport with' (Ps. 104: 26); and with a female this is not proper. Then here also (regarding Behemoth) He should have preserved the female in salt.—Salted fish is tasty; salted meat is not.[1]

II. And R. Yehudah said (further) in the name of Rab: When the Holy One, blessed be He, wished to create the world, He said to the Prince of (the) Sea (*Yam*):[2] 'Open your mouth and swallow all the waters in the world'. He (Sea) said to Him (God): 'It is enough that I stay with my own. Thereupon, He kicked him with His foot and killed him; as it is said: 'with His power He stilled Sea (*Yam*), and with His skill He smote Rahab' (Job 26: 12).

—R. Yitzḥaq said: From this we infer that the name of the Prince of (the) Sea is Rahab, and had the waters not covered him no creature could have stood his (foul) odour; as it is said: 'They shall do neither harm nor hurt on all My holy mountain, etc., as the waters cover the sea' (Isa. 11: 9). Do not read 'cover the sea (*la-yam*)' but 'cover the Prince of (the) Sea' (*Saro shel Yam*).

[1] This paragraph consists of scholastic discussions based on the previous mythic teachings.
[2] The title probably represents a softening of an address to Sea personified.

III. And R. Yehudah said (further) in the name of Rab: the Jordan issues from the cave of Paneas. It has also been taught: The Jordan issues from the cave of Paneas and passes through the sea of Sibkhay and the sea of Tiberias and rolls down to the Great Sea, and on until it reaches the mouth of Leviathan; as it says: 'He is confident because the Jordan rushes into his mouth' (Job 40: 23).—Raba bar ʿUlla objected: This (verse) is written of 'Behemoth on a thousand hills'! But, said R. Abba b. ʿUlla: When is Behemoth on a thousand hills confident? When the Jordan rushes into the mouth of Leviathan.[3] (Mnemonic:) 'Seas', 'Gabriel', 'Hungry'.

IV. When Rav Dimi came (back to Babylon, from the land of Israel), he said in the name of Rabbi Yoḥanan: What (means) that which is written: 'For He has founded it upon the seas and established it upon the rivers' (Ps. 24: 2)?—These are the seven seas and four rivers which surround the land of Israel. And these are the seven seas: The sea of Tiberias, the sea of Sodom, the sea of *Ḥelat*, the sea of *Ḥilta'*, the sea of *Sibkhay*, the sea of Aspamia, and the Great Sea. And these are the four rivers: the Jordan, the Jarmuk, the Keramyon, and Pigah.

V. When Rav Dimi came (back), he said in the name of Rabbi Yoḥanan. In the future, Gabriel will arrange a hunt of Leviathan; as it is said: 'Can you draw out Leviathan with a fish-hook, or suppress his tongue with a rope?' (Job 40: 25). And if the Holy One, blessed be He, does not help him (Gabriel), he will be unable to prevail against him (Leviathan); as it is said: 'Only his Maker can draw the sword against him' (ibid., v. 19).

VI. When Rav Dimi came (back), he said in the name of Rabbi Yoḥanan: When Leviathan is hungry he emits (fiery) breath from his mouth and causes all the waters of the deep to boil; as it is said: 'He makes the deep boil like a cauldron' (Job 41: 23). And if he did not put his head into the Garden of Eden, no creature could stand his (foul) odour; as it is said: 'He makes the sea like a spice-jar' (ibid.). And when he (Leviathan) is thirsty, he makes many furrows in the sea; as it says: 'He makes a path shine after him' (Job 41: 24).

—R. Aḥa bar Jacob said: The deep does not return to its strength until (after) seventy years; as it is said: 'One thinks the deep to be hoary' (ibid.); and hoary age is not (attained at) less than seventy years.

VII. Rabba said in the name of Rabbi Yoḥanan: In the future, the Holy One, blessed be He, will make a banquet for the righteous from the flesh of Leviathan; as it is said: 'The associates (*ḥabarim*) will make a banquet (*yikhru*) of it' (Job 40: 30). *Keirah* must mean banquet; as it is said: 'And he prepared (*va-yikhreh*) for them a great banquet (*keirah*), and they ate and drank' (2 Kings 6: 23). Associates (*ḥabarim*) must mean scholars; as it is said: 'You who dwell in the gardens, the companions (*ḥabeirim*) hearken to your voice, cause me to hear it' (Songs 8: 13).[4] The remainder (of Leviathan) will be distributed and sold out in the markets of Jerusalem; as it is

[3] This resolution may be by Raba bar ʿUlla himself, whose name was mistaken as R. Abba in the course of transmission.

[4] *Ḥabeirim* is a designation for members of the rabbinic fellowship.

said: 'They will divide it among the *kena'anim*' (Job 40: 30). And *kena'anim* must mean traders; as it is said: 'As for *kena'an*, the scales of deceit are in his hand, he loves to oppress' (Hos. 12: 8).—And if you wish, learn it from the following: 'Whose merchants are princes, (and) whose traders (*kena'aneha*) are the honourable of the earth' (Isa. 23: 8).

VIII. Rabbah said in the name of Rabbi Yoḥanan: In the future, the Holy One, blessed be he, will make a tabernacle (*sukkah*) for the righteous from the skin of Leviathan; as it is said: 'Can you fill his skin with *sukkot* (tabernacles; literally, darts)' (Job 40: 31). If one is worthy, a tabernacle is made for him; if he is not worthy (of this), a (mere) covering (*tziltzel*) is made for him; as it is said: 'And his head with a *tziltzel* (fish covering)' (ibid.). If one is (sufficiently) worthy, a covering is made for him; if he is not worthy (of this), a necklace is made for him; as it is said: 'And necklaces around your neck' (Prov. 1: 9). If he is worthy (of it) a necklace is made for him; if he is not worthy (even of this), an amulet is made for him; as it is said: 'And you will bind them for your maidens' (Job 40: 29). The remainder of (the skin of) Leviathan the Holy One, blessed be He, will spread upon the walls of Jerusalem, and its splendour will radiate from one end of the world to the other; as it is said: 'And nations shall walk by your light, and kings in the splendour of your shining' (Isa. 60: 3).

B. SEA MONSTERS AND THE MYSTERY OF EVIL (ZOHAR II. 34A–35B)

Rabbi Simeon began quoting: 'And God created the great sea monsters, and every living creature that creeps, with which the waters swarmed, according to their species' (Gen. 1: 21). This verse has already been explained. But 'And God created the great sea monsters' is a mystery. It is Leviathan and his mate.[5] 'Monsters' (*tanninim*) is written defectively,[6] because the Holy One, blessed be He, slew the female and served her to the righteous; and they have already explained it.[7]

'(Behold I am against you, Pharaoh, King of Egypt,) the great monster ((*tannin*) that lies in the midst of his rivers)' (Ezek. 29: 3). There are nine rivers,[8] and he lies among them. And there is one river[9] whose waters are peaceful, and into which the water pools of the Garden fall three times a year,[10] and when (they fall) twice the river is blessed, though not to a large extent, and when (they fall) once, (it is blessed) even less. This monster enters the river; it gathers strength, swimming

[5] The issue is that the monsters are not only a pair (see *BT Baba Batra* 74b above, Sect. A), but that they represent the principalities of evil in the system of the 'other side'. In the *Zohar*, the male power is Samael and Lilith is his mate.

[6] Written without the usual second *yod* to indicate that the male was without the female.

[7] *BT Baba Batra* 74b. This text would have been given a figurative or symbolic interpretation to suit the ensuing myth.

[8] This indicates the parallel sefirotic structure of the 'other side': nine plus one (for the tenth, see immediately).

[9] Tenth river, the particular abode of the great monster.

[10] The negative realm is sustained by the upper gradations.

as it goes, entering the 'Sea',[11] and swallowing fish of many kinds, and it rules and returns to the river.

These nine rivers rise continually, and there are trees and grasses of different kinds around them. The first river emerges from the left side[12] by a certain channel,[13] which goes on to produce three drops. Each drop splits up into three other drops, and from each drop a river is formed. These are the nine rivers, which gain strength as they go and flow around the firmaments.[14] From what is left of these drops, after they have completely emerged, a single drop remains, and it comes out slowly, falling among them, and a river is formed from it. This is the river that we spoke of, the one that flows peacefully. The stream continues to emerge and produces other large drops from the right side,[15] and from what is left of them a single drop remains (and emerges) slowly from the pools, and falls into the river that is peaceful. And this is the most abundant river of all.

When the four rivers that come out from the Garden of Eden flow out and separate, the one called Pishon falls into this river, and is included in it, and therefore the Kingdom of Babylon is comprised in it, Pishon being the Kingdom of Babylon. All the other rivers are replenished and nourished by this river.

In each river there moves and swims a monster, and there are nine of them, and each one has a hole in his head, as it is said, 'You shattered the heads of the sea monsters ...' (Ps. 74: 13). Even the great monster is like this, for they all draw in their breath from the realms above,[16] and not from the realms below.

It is written 'In the beginning God created' (Gen. 1: 1), and it is written 'And God created the sea monsters.' Every act of the ten sayings[17] is paralleled by the ten rivers. And there is a monster that moves for each one. Hence every seventy years the world trembles,[18] because when the great monster raises its fins they all tremble in those rivers, and the whole world trembles, and the earth shakes, and they are all comprised in the great monster.

'And the earth was waste' (ibid., v. 2). Rabbi Simeon said: The companions have studied the Creation and know it, but few are those who can see the allusion in Creation to the mystery of the great monster. Therefore we have taught that the whole world is dependent solely on its fins.

Come and see. 'And the earth was waste and void.' We have taught: 'Was'—and have explained, on the basis of the first interpretation that we gave, that when the great monster entered (the river) it immediately became full and overflowed, and (thus) extinguished the sparks that had been gathered together in the worlds that had been destroyed earlier.[19] The other monsters of which we have spoken existed and

[11] This symbolizes the *Shekhinah*, the gradation in which the holy forces are pooled, and which the monster penetrates.

[12] The rivers emerge from *Geburah*, the divine attribute of strict Judgement.

[13] Descending through the gradation of *Yesod*, also called 'stream' below.

[14] Presumably, the domain of the 'other side'; but possibly the actual firmaments.

[15] The sustenance emerges from *Ḥesed*, the divine attribute of Mercy.

[16] They receive influence through their blowhole.

[17] By which the world was *created*; namely, the ten *sefirot*.

[18] Some seismic event, based on a heptad.

[19] Before the present worlds were established, God created other worlds; but they could not survive and so were destroyed. Sparks fell from these worlds among the shards of the 'other side',

did not exist. Why? Because their strength was weakened so that they should not confuse the world more than once every seventy years. They gain their might from the power of the great monster. It is he alone that (gives them power) to prevail. And were his female to stand by him the world could not endure them; and so before the Holy One, blessed be He, slew the female—'the earth was *tohu* (waste)'. It was *tohu*; but after he had slain her it was *bohu* (void), and began to establish itself.

'And darkness (was upon the face of the abyss)' (ibid.)—before the act that He performed shone.[20] What did the Holy One, blessed be He, do? He smote the head of the male above, and he was subdued, for the abyss below did not shine. Why did it not shine? Because the great monster breathed a spirit upon the abyss and covered it with darkness, and he did not move below;[21] but another spirit passed from the realms above, and breathed and struck this spirit and quenched it. This is the meaning of 'And the spirit of God hovered over the face of the waters' (ibid.). And this is what we have taught, that the Holy One, blessed be He, struck the spirit with a spirit and created the world.

'And God said; Let there be light. And there was light' (ibid., v. 3). He kindled an illumination above, and it alighted upon the spirit that breathed, and (the monster) departed from the abyss and did not cover it. Once the abyss was illumined and he had departed, this illumination immediately shone upon his head and water came out from his nose; and a spirit breathed above. And (the monster) shone so much with this light that his light descended, sparkling into the seventy-two lights of the sun. When these lights took shape within the sun below, the wicked in the world took note of them and worshipped the sun. When the Holy One, blessed be He, looked upon these wicked people He removed His light and concealed it. Why did He conceal it? Because the monster would go up and down, smiting the rivers, so that He had to conceal it, and it was not revealed. And He sowed it as seed in the Righteous One, the gardener in the Garden,[22] and the seed that He sowed in the garden, secretly and invisibly, is derived from this light. When the great monster saw that the seed of this light was growing in the Garden, he provoked the river Giḥon (to join) 'the other side', and Giḥon's waters were divided, one path going into the seed that grew in the Garden, and shining there in the anointing oil of the seed, and it is called 'Giḥon'. And some of the anointing oil of this seed was removed for the anointing of King Solomon when he ascended the throne; as it is written: 'bring him down to Giḥon' (1 Kings 1: 33); and it is written: 'anoint him there' (ibid., v. 34)—there, and in no other place, because King David knew about this. Its other waters were removed to another kingdom,[23] and this is the kingdom that is strong. This great monster arouses it,[24] and the fins of this monster go up into this river in order to gather strength there. And all the other rivers

and their light continued to shine. But when the river started to grow through the strength of the great monster, these sparks were extinguished by the waters overflowing onto them.

[20] The act of Creation illumined the darkness (the realm of negative powers).

[21] Obscure; presumably the monster did not focus onto the realm below, but sought to prevent the light from penetrating the abyss.

[22] The concealed light becomes the seed of *Yesod*, called 'the Righteous', and he uses it to water the Garden, *Malkhut*, through the mystery of intercourse. The author reinterprets Ps. 97: 11.

[23] The 'other side'; it is dubbed 'strong' (cf. Dan. 2: 40).

[24] Giḥon.

rise and fall through the power of the great monster, and he returns and enters the peaceful river and rests there.

Then, when this light was concealed, so that the gardener whom we have mentioned might enter (the Garden), the primordial darkness emerged, and spread over his head through the hole that was pierced in it. And a single line was stretched out between the illumination of the light that was concealed and the obscurity of the darkness; as it is written: 'And God divided the light from the darkness' (Gen. 1: 4). The monster returned within the dividing line, and dispersed the rivers within the darkness, and in this dispersion the fish were separated from one another according to their species. When the upper, holy waters were divided, all the rivers were divided and they flowed into the peaceful river, which is the choicest of them all, and they flow in and out of it three times a day. And the fish that breed in these rivers are all separated from one another and are called '*Lilot*'.[25] They are the leaders of all the fish that go out; they rule over all of them, and are called 'the firstborn of Egypt' (Ps. 135: 8). From here the firstborn are scattered abroad, and they are all nourished by drinking from these rivers, and the great monster rules over them all. All this (occurs) because of the division of the upper waters; as it is written: 'Let it divide the waters' (Gen. 1: 6). The upper, holy waters were formed, and were divided above; and all of the lower waters were divided from one another, the holy from the unholy. Therefore the celestial angels are called 'separated',[26] because they are separated from one another into their different kinds.

'And God said: Let the earth put forth grass, herb yielding seed' (ibid., v. 11). The mystery of this is that when the great monster breathed spirit through the hole and moved against the upper world, he dried out all the grasses until another spirit breathed against this spirit and subdued it in the realms below. Then the grasses grew as they had grown at the beginning, and they ruled, and praised, and thanked the Holy One, blessed be He. Beasts, in their various species, emerge from the left side and enter the peaceful river, and try to reach the grasses, but they cannot and they return to their places. All these rivers swim along with the monster who rules over them, and they surround the grasses, but they cannot (reach them). At times, however, when the upper spirit does not breathe, and (the monster) exhales spirit through the hole toward the higher realm, as we have explained, this spirit rules over the grasses, and the peaceful river returns to its place, rising and falling. And because its waters are peaceful, it flows quietly. And the great monster goes up into the river, and all the grasses grow around the peaceful river. They grow on every side. Then the monster ascends and spreads himself among them, and returns to all the rivers.

'And God said: Let there be lights in the firmament of the heaven' (ibid., v. 14). This is the 'slanting snake' (Isa. 27: 1). Why 'slanting' (*bariaḥ*)? Because he is enclosed on two sides and goes out into the world only once every fifty years.[27] And (it is written) in the ancient books: This is the tortuous snake who is always involved in crookedness, and who brings curses upon the world. When this one rises the strength of the monster is broken and he cannot stand and his body perishes, because the Holy One, bless be He, subdues him in the midst of the sea when He enters it; and He tramples

[25] Plural of Lilith, the monster Samael's consort.
[26] The angels are 'separated intelligences'; the author draws upon philosophical terminology.
[27] The word *bariaḥ* also means 'bolt'.

upon the strength of the sea, the strength of the sea being the monster, as it is said: 'He treads upon the high places of the sea' (Job 9: 8). When this snake arises, what is written? 'He will slay the monster that is in the sea' (Isa. 27: 1); that is, the great monster, hence it is written: 'Behold, I am against you' (Ezek. 29: 3). This snake is 'malediction',[28] with curses for all, because he conquers him with the power of the great river called Ḥidekel, and we have already explained it.

This snake is on the dry land. When they go out to confront one another, the one on the dry land always triumphs, because all his paths and his powers are on the dry land, and he eats earth and dust all the time, as it is said 'dust shall you eat all the years of your life' (Gen. 3: 14). One grew up in the dust, and the other grew up in the water. The snake that grew up in the water is not so strong as the one that grew up in the dust. Therefore it is written *me'orot*, without (a *vav*).[29] (The snake of the dry land) confronts (the monster) of the sea; but even though he confronts him he does not fight against him. It is the Holy One, blessed be He, alone who slays him in the midst of the sea, as we have explained, because of his great pride; as it is said: 'He has said: My river belongs to me (and I made it for myself)' (Ezek. 29: 3).

C. DIVINE SORROW AND CONSOLATION: ZOHAR ḤADASH, EICHA[30]

We have learned: Every night a bitter cry for the pain of Zion is heard (from) the heights of the firmament (to the earth) below, and from below to the heights (above); as it is said: 'YHWH roars from the heights, and sends forth His voice from His holy sanctuary; surely does He roar over (*'al*) His Temple' (Jer. 25: 30).[31]

At the beginning of the night (at the first watch), She (the *Shekhinah*) begins to cry, and roars (from) the heights of the firmament downward to the place of the outer altar, and sees Her place destroyed and defiled, and that no (pure) place is found in it.[32] She groans and wails and cries out bitterly, saying: 'O My altar, My altar, My (place of) sustenance, that sated Me with various libations (and) various pure (and) holy offerings! All (manner of angelic) holy beings,[33] princely ones and designates, were sated and rejoiced in you, ate (the) sweet savours and distributed their portions in the highest firmament. Now are the corpses of holy saints sacrificed (lit. given) upon you;[34] My children are slaughtered upon you. Woe is Me, for their blood! And

[28] *Me'eirat*, written in Hebrew exactly like *Me'orot* (lights) in Gen. 1: 14, quoted earlier.

[29] So that it could be read *me'eirat* (malediction). See above.

[30] In the edition of Reuven Margoliot (Jerusalem: Mosad Ha-Rav Kook, (1953), *Midrash Ha-Ne'elam 'al 'Eichah*, 92b–d.

[31] The tradition occurs in *BT Ber.* 3a, discussed above; it is given an extended treatment in this midrash, taking up various traditions referred to above and in Appendix 2. The word *'al* in the proof-text is construed as 'concerning', as discussed above; and see later in this text, regarding Songs 3: 1.

[32] The scriptural source is understood, on the basis of the Talmudic explanation in *BT Ber.* 3a to refer to three watches; God is interpreted as the *Shekhinah*, the female gradation on high. The destruction and exile represents Her separation from Her beloved.

[33] Lit. 'holy men (*gabrin*)'; this undoubtedly translates the Hebrew term *'ishim*, used of 'angels' in medieval Jewish philosophy.

[34] This reference to martyrs (*ḥasidim qedoshim*) counters the preceding reference to the holy beings (*gabrin qadishin*).

all the beings, mighty princes and designates, fall from their places at the sound of their cry. (And) the (angels) sitting outside (the divine sanctuary) cry out and weep—these are the holy ʾErʾeliym, who are crowned by a letter of His holy Name (the letter *y*[*od*]), in which they rejoice and are sustained. At the sound of their weeping, this letter flew from them and ascended the highest heights, and they remained as a woman who cries and wails; as it is said: 'Behold, the ʾErʾelim cry outside' (Isa. 29: 1)—ʾErʾelim without a *yod* shout outside (the sanctuary).

'O My altar, My altar! Now that you have sated Me with the corpses of holy, saintly children, who have devoted their bodies and souls upon you—you are hidden away. Where shall I find you? Where is the fire (that was) upon you?' So did She groan and wail and cry in a mournful voice.

Six thousand holy beings from the four corners of the world, who ate the offering(s) daily, descended with Her and (they also) groan and wail over the altar of holocaust offerings. And there were (once) more (angels in the pleroma), but they were reduced. And even those who exist outside (the holy pleroma), (being) of 'another spirit', who were sated with the limbs and innards of the sacrifices (left over from the day and eaten during night), at the beginning of the night (they too) cry out and groan and wail for this altar, (saying:) 'Woe for the ass that has lost its trough, the place from which it was sated'. Who(ever) saw such a shout (as) the holy beings for the Matrona (*Shekhinah*)—from down below to above, from above to below?!

In the middle of the night (namely, the second watch), (God) enters the (inner-) point of Zion,[35] the place of the Holy of Holies, and sees that Her habitation (*motbah*) and couch (*ʿarsah*) are destroyed and defiled—She groans and wails, and (this cry) ascends from below to above and from above down below. And when (God) beholds the place of the cherubim—She groans a bitter cry, and lifts Her voice and says: 'O My couch (*ʿarsi*), My couch, the place of My habitation (*motabi*)!' Concerning that place it is written: 'On (*ʿal*) My bed (*mishkabi*) at night (I sought the one My soul loves)' (Songs 3: 1).[36] 'My bed', (this is) the couch of the Matrona. She groans and cries and says: 'O My couch, the place of My sanctuary, the place of precious jewels, the house of the curtain and mercy-seat, upon which were put sixty thousand myriads of precious stones, in orderly rows, column by column, in view of each other; (and also) rows of pomegranates spread out upon you in all four directions. The (entire) world exists on your account! (And) the Master of the world, My husband (Lord), would lie between My arms. And everything I desired and wished for, from Him, He granted at that time—when he came to Me, and placed His tabernacle in Me and took pleasure between My breasts.

'O My couch, My couch! Do you not remember when I came to you in joy and gladness of heart, and these eternal youths would go out to greet Me, striking their wings in joy before Me. The soil has gone up from its place, and see!—how it is forgotten. (And) the ark of the Torah that was here, whence sustenance went out to the entire world, and light and blessing for all. I seek out My husband; He is not here.

[35] The verb 'enters' (*ʿaʾil*) and later 'looks' (*ʾistakkel*) are masculine forms; but the Shekhinah is the subject throughout.

[36] This is undoubtedly to be construed midrashically, as 'Concerning (*ʿal*) My bed at night (i.e. during the watches) I sought the one My soul loves'.

I seek everywhere. At this time when My Lord would come to Me, many saintly sons (namely, souls) surrounded Him, and all these maidens prepared to greet Him. And we would hear from afar the sound of pairs of bells ringing between His feet, that I might hear His sound before he arrived. (And) all my maidens (would) praise and acknowledge the Holy One, blessed be He. And thereafter each would go home; and we were left alone, embracing with the kisses of love.

'O My husband, My husband! Where have You gone? This is the time I would seek You and see You everywhere; but You are not (here). Where may I seek You, that I not beseech You?! This is Your place, at this time, to come to Me. Truly, I am ready here; (but) truly You have forgotten Me. Do You not remember the days of love, when I lay in Your ardour, and was impressed by Your form just as You were impressed by Mine—like a seal that leaves its impress when set on the page, so did I leave My form upon You, so that You might take pleasure with My form while I was still in a strong passion'.

She groaned, in tears, and cried out: 'O My husband, My husband! The light of My eyes is darkened. Do You not remember how You placed Your left hand beneath My head and Your right hand embraced Me, in friendship and kisses? And You swore to Me that You would not forget Your love for Me ever; and You swore to Me: 'If I forget You, O Jerusalem, I would forget My right hand'.[37] But (now indeed) I am forgotten by You! And do You not remember how I stood before You at Mount Sinai,[38] (when) sixty myriad perfected ones accepted You upon them, and I was 'crowned' to You through them, more that all other nations, and we followed after You, accepting Your will?

'O My husband! Remember with how many holy children I stood before You in every generation, in the days of David, and Solomon his son? Do You not remember all the good they did before You. Is it meet for You to remember (only) sins and not merits? How have matters so reversed themselves with You (that You remember only iniquity)?! I beseech You; but You are not! I beseech You for My children, who are no longer! I beseach You concerning the holiness of this place, now defiled! The entire world was secure (lit. whole; *bishlam*) because of this place. Dogs did not bark at that time; all was whole.' She (continued thus) groaning and wailing, along with the entire (angelic) population above. And all the dogs were howling below, at the beginning of the third watch.[39]

She (then) went out and came and stood at the place of the altar of sweet incense. And She was groaning and wailing, and ascended above, and found one of the two cherubs that were (once) with Her—for since that time (after the destruction) she only had one; and that young lad (cherub) who remained, sucked from Her, crying and wailing.

[37] Taking the passage as a divine oath, as in the midrash in *Pesikta de-Rav Kahana* 17.5 (*Va-To'mer Tzion*), which is used here but given a mystical reference. The gradation *Shekhinah* is also known by the designations 'Zion' and 'Jerusalem'.

[38] Hereby, *Shekhinah* symbolizes the historical and supernal Israel.

[39] With this reference, the author returns to *BT Ber.* 3a, with which he began; the final citation, beginning with 'we have learned' is also from this passage—thus giving the entire sermon an *inclusio* form.

Then the Holy One, blessed be He, became present to Her,[40] and descended to Her, speaking to Her. And concerning this, it is written: 'Thus says YHWH, Restrain Your voice from crying and Your eyes from tears, for there is hope for Your end' (Jer. 31: 16–17). And concerning this we have learned, 'A suckling sucking from its mother's breast, and a woman speaking to her husband'.[41]

Up to here is the (homiletical) proem; from here onward is the beginning of the Scroll of Lamentations.[42]

[40] That is, became 'manifest (*'izdamen*)'; this verb alludes to the earlier remark of the *Shekhinah*, when She says 'I am ready (*zemina'*) for You'. There may be a messianic overtone, as well (cf. Dan. 7: 25).

[41] The Talmudic tradition in *BT Ber.* 3a is given messianic and supernal significance.

[42] The teaching thus functioned as a theological prologue to the ritual recitation of the elegy on Tisha' Be-'Ab.

APPENDIX 2
The Term *kivyakhol* and its Uses

This appendix[1] on the term *kivyakhol* (= *kibyakhol*)[2] draws upon my collection over many years of the available examples to be found in classical and related rabbinic sources: in published and critical editions; in published and manuscript variants; published and manuscript fragments from the Cairo Geniza and other library resources; and in data-base files in electronic form and data collected for historical research, such as the word files of the Israel Academy of Language. Several photocopies of unpublished manuscript fragments were made available to me through the courtesy of Prof. M. Bregman.

I have utilized all this material (as pertinent) in the categorization, analysis, and evaluation of ancient rabbinic and early medieval texts in which the term *kivyakhol* occurs. Almost universally, the term is found in the context of theological and homiletical teachings, and evincing a strong anthropomorphic and anthropopathic character in the framework of midrashic exegesis found in the great midrashic and Talmudic compendia (or extracts derived therefrom). Several examples are found in old legal sources (like the Mishnah and Tosefta), but the issues remain of a theological or homiletical sort and are exegetical in character. The organization and interpretation of the data is intended to bring some conceptual and thematic clarity to a sea of citations, and to elucidate opaque or otherwise elusive examples. Overall, this material supplements the examples of rabbinic mythic theology discussed in Part II. Hence, cases considered at length in the body of this book are only treated to brief annotations in this appendix. On the other hand, topics and texts that either extend or elaborate the categories and themes taken up earlier, are dealt with more fully here. In all instances, close attention has been given to the placement and apparent function(s) of the term *kivyakhol*. Considerable attention will be given to the techniques and character of the exegetical theology involved.

Because of inconsistencies in parallel versions, and the ongoing impact of scribal practices and pieties into the Middle Ages (long after the primary production of the exegeses themselves), it is not always possible to determine the authentic exempla of the term *kivyakhol* or estimate the precise stratification of the evidence. Hence, I have attempted to register all pertinent variations, and to highlight the function(s) of the term in the context of the hermeneutical and literary aspects of the passages. Similarly, the various difficulties and ambiguities involved in evaluating these midrashic teachings have been acknowledged and spelled out, to the extent that this is feasible or instructive. Thus I have sought to make the complexity of analysis and evalution as transparent as possible. Nevertheless, a number of practical determinations had to be made. For example, there are a large number of examples in the late midrashic collections (like *Midrash Tanḥuma*, *Midrash Shoḥer Ṭov*, and *Aggadat Bereishit*),

[1] Special abbreviations listed at end, pp. 402–4.

[2] The more conventional spelling *kivyakhol* is used throughout; variant vocalizations are given below.

where the term *kivyakhol* is often used in ways inconsistent with the patterns isolated and evaluated below. I have judged many of these instances to be the result of later scribal whims, introducing new euphemistic attitudes into the data, and have collected the majority of them at the end with no detailed analysis. Only when these cases preserve arguably authentic or characteristic usages (no matter how weak), or provide instructive examples (no matter how tenuous), some analysis or reference has been provided in the main body of this appendix. Similarly, parallels from the late compendium *Yalkut Shimʿoni* are not given—save for those special cases where notable variations or unique (or uniquely formulated) traditions have been preserved.

The following appendix is composed of three main parts: (1) an overview of the main interpretations of the term *kivyakhol*, and a statement of the considerations that will guide this inquiry; (2) a presentation and analysis of the textual evidence where the term *kivyakhol* occurs, with particular attention to its perceived functions; and (3) a final evaluation of the material assembled, with brief conclusions.

The Term

The following is a conspectus of explanations of the term *kivyakhol*, formulated by influential medieval and modern authorities.

1. Rashi (1040–1105) gives four distinct comments on the term. In *BT Yoma* 3b, he says that 'it is said against our wishes, as if it were possible to say so; and similarly every (case of) *kivyakhol* in the Talmud'. Thus in his view, the term serves as a euphemistic or apologetic qualification of certain remarks about divinity. More specifically, in *BT Meg.* 21a Rashi notes that 'it is said of the Holy One, blessed be He (when one speaks of Him) as like (*ke-*) a person, of whom it is possible (*yakhol*) to speak thus'. This comment is similar to his point in *BT Sanh.* 97a. In *BT Ḥag.* 13b Rashi also notes the use of the term with regard to the angelic host.

2. R. Judah Halevi (*c.*1075–1141) in the *Kuzari*, Book III (73), treats the term *kivyakhol* as marking a figure of speech about God, employed to strengthen or enjoin a theological point. Indeed, in his understanding, the term highlights a putative assertion that means: 'if it were possible for the matter to be thus and so, it would then be so'.[3] Thus Halevi regards the term *kivyakhol* as underscoring certain anthropomorphic features of midrashic rhetoric.[4]

3. R. Yom Ṭov b. Abraham Ishbili (Riṭba; *c.*1250–1330), in his annotations to *BT Yoma* 3b, adduces Rashi's above-cited opinion, and adds: 'But because it is written in Scripture (namely, the words that justify R. Jonathan's midrashic inference regarding divine preference for an individual offering) it is possible (*yakhol*) to say it.'[5] This

[3] See *Sefer ha-Kuzari*, trans. into Hebrew and annotated by Judah Even Shmuel (Tel Aviv: Dvir, 1963), 149. Isaak Heinemann has rendered Halevi's gloss on the term by 'if it could be so, it would be so'; see in *Three Jewish Philosophers*, edd. H. Lewy, A. Altmann, and I. Heinemann (New York and Philadelphia: Meridian Books and Jewish Publication Society, 1960), 105.

[4] The example he gives is, 'The sages said: When the Lord of the world descended to Egypt'. As Halevi notes, this teaching is not found in the Talmud, but in 'certain Passover prayerbooks (*siddurin*)'. The full version (of which this is the incipit) is preserved in the *Maḥzor Vitry* (see *Machsor Vitry*, ed. S. Hurwitz (Nuremberg: I. Bulka, 1923), i. 293). Recitation of this midrash was customary in Provence, according to R. Simḥah of Vitri.

[5] *Ḥiddushei ha-Riṭba*, ed. E. Lichtenstein (Jerusalem: Mosad Ha-Rav Kook, 1976), ad loc.

statement appears to be more than a gloss that justifies the comment, and may also be construed as an explanation of the term *kivyakhol*, taken to mean something like 'it is possible (to state the midrash)' since it has scriptural warrant or support. The term is thus a hermeneutical marker, not a euphemistic apology (Rashi).

R. Yeshuʿa b. Joseph of Tlemcen (15th c.) in his *Halikhot ʿOlam* (2.1) follows this tack, but adopts a more constrained position in his gloss on the term.[6] Basing himself on a Tosafist comment on *BT Meg.* 21a not found in our printed editions, which states that 'it (the term *kivyakhol*) is often used with regard to theological teachings (*haggadot debarim*) that are not respectful (*derekh kabod*) of God (lit. *maʿalah*),' R. Yeshuʿa drew the conclusion that the initial letters (*kv;* i.e. *kaf* + *bet*) of the term (which are numerically '22') are to be distinguished from the verb *yakhol* ('it is possible'). The result in his view is a hybrid or compound form, with *kv* functioning as a 'notarikon' (or abbreviation) that denotes the number of letters in the alphabet.[7] Accordingly, *k(i)v* + *yakhol* is taken to be a composite construction that paraphrastically indicates that 'it is possible for the Torah which was given through the twenty-two letters (of the alphabet) to speak so, but it is impossible for us to say it'. This explanation thus interprets the term *kivyakhol* as cautioning human exegetical restraint, while simultaneously acknowledging the scriptural basis for the comment.[8] However, R. Elijah Levitas (1469–1549) in his rabbinic dictionary *Sefer Ha-Tishbi* rebutted this explanation, and suggested that the term indicates that Scripture speaks about God 'as by (*kemo*) a possibility (*be-yakhol*), specifically "as for one who is able (*yakhol*) to accept this teaching." '[9] This explanation treats the term as marking a rhetorical possibility for the individual—and not a feature of the comment *per se*.

4. Similar euphemistic and rhetorical explanations of the term are highlighted by many modern interpreters.

N. Brüll understood *kivyakhol* as a term used to mark theological teachings in which something common or worldly is used ('was gewöhnlich geschieht, in dem was in der Welt gebräuchlich ist'). In his view, the meaning of the term is literally 'as in the possibility' ('wie in der Möglichkeit'), which he further explains as 'als ob es möglich wäre'.[10] This view basically follows the older opinion of A. Geiger, who apparently understood the term as marking a rhetorical construction, since he paraphrases

[6] *Halikhot ʿOlam* was written in 1467 and first published in Venice, 1634. I have used the third printing with additions and corrections (repr.; Jerusalem: Talpiyot, 1960–1), 9b.

[7] For 'notarikon', see simply H. L. Strack and G. Stemberger, *Introduction to the Talmud and Midrash* (London: T. & T. Clark, 1991), 33.

[8] In his super-commentary to *Halikhot ʿOlam*, R. Joseph Karo (*Kelalei Ha-Gemara*) adverts to Rashi's comment on *BT Yoma* 3b, thus construing the letters *kiv-* as a prefix marking 'as if' such a reading were possible.

[9] See in the reprint edition (Bene Brak: A. Kaufman & Sons, 1976), s.v. *kavyakhol* (so, as justified by the author), 38 f. The Tosafist comment found in *Halikhot ʿOlam* is cited with a minor variant ad loc. *Ha-Tishby* was first published in Isny, 1541. The opinion of *Ha-Tishbi* is also adduced by R. Yom Ṭov Lipmann Heller (1579–1654), in his glosses 'Tosafot Yom Tov' *ad M. Sanh.* 5.4. In his edition of *Pesikta de-Rav Kahana* (Mekize Nirdamim: Lyck, 1868), 120 a–b, n. 24 (s.v. *kbykl*), S. Buber adduces these foregoing opinions, without evalution. For the formula *veha-kol mimmekha loʾmar*, 'you are able to say all this', see the comment of R. Jacob of Kfar Ḥanin in *PesR 33*, and the comment of MIS in the note ad loc. *Kivyakhol* is there understood as indicating a teaching which one is able to give.

[10] See overall '*kvykl*' in *Jeschurun* (ed. Kobak), 7 (1871), 1–6. For his vocalization, see below, n. 18.

kivyakhol with the words 'als spräche man von Einem, bei dem so etwas möglich wäre'[11] (though the phrase 'von Einem' may hint at a euphemistic component, insofar as the dominant subject of these interpretations is God and His anthropomorphic and anthropopathic nature).

W. Bacher gives an explicit euphemistic explanation of the term, when he refers to it as 'a fixed expression used where there is a daring teaching about God, functioning to beg forgiveness (for the formulation)'.[12] He reinforces this view by a construal of *kivyakhol* as a 'notarikon' for *k(e'ilu ne'emar) b(e-mi she-) yakhol ('attah lomar zeh)*, 'as if it were said concerning one of whom you could say this'[13] (cf. Geiger). This rendition provides a corollary explanation, and is essentially taken over by A. Kohut.[14] Bacher's initial characterization (following Rashi) is reaffirmed by E. E. Urbach.[15]

5. Finally, A. Marmorstein parts company from the tradition that interprets *kivyakhol* as some kind of terminological disclaimer, and gives a new emphasis to the scriptural basis or legitimacy of the reading at hand. In his view, the term *kivyakhol* 'does not stress the idea or weaken the grossness of the conception, but indicates the scriptural basis of the exegetical teaching or homiletical truth'—since 'the term is either preceded or followed by a scriptural reference'.[16] He reinforces this positive view of the word by the proposal of another 'notarikon' of *k-b-y-kh-v-l*: *k(a-yotzei) b(a-dabar) y(esh) k(oaḥ) v(e-'efshar) l(omar)*.[17] This proposal is a compound solecism which, at best, can be rendered '(and) similarly, there is foundation (for the view) and one can adduce (Scripture in support)'. Despite the oddity of this explanation, Marmorstein's observation that the term *kivyakhol* is regularly found with a scriptural citation, and that Scripture has a positive function in such cases, is an important addition to the discussion and deserves further investigation.

From the foregoing explanations of the term *kivyakhol*, two considerations stand out. (1) The term is understood as qualifying the bold *content* of certain rabbinic teachings. This content characteristically deals with strong mythic portrayals of divine actions or emotions. In these cases, the term is said to inject a qualification or a hesitation before such material. (2) The term is understood as indexing the *scriptural basis* of the teaching. Such references appear as direct citations. In these cases, the term is said to indicate that the content may be condoned because it is grounded in Scripture itself. The first consideration thus refers to the theology itself; the second to its textual authority.

In effect, the two types of explanation highlight the two typical literary features of teachings where the term *kivyakhol* is found. In some cases, it occurs with the theological teaching (leaving the scriptural proof-text unqualified); whereas in others

[11] See his 'Recensionen', *Wissenschaftliche Zeitschrift für Jüdische Theologie*, 5 (1844), 271 n. 3.

[12] See s.v. *kivyakhol*, in his *'Erkhei Midrash*, trans. A. Z. Rabinovitz (Tel Aviv, 1923), 50 (in Hebrew) (orig. *Die exegetische Terminologie der jüdischen Traditionsliteratur* (Leipzig, 1899), i. 72).

[13] Ibid.

[14] In *Aruch Completum* (Vienna: Hebraïscher Verlag Menorah, 1926), iv. 130 (col. 2); and cf. the gloss s.v. *'ikuniyon*, ibid. i. 257 (MS Halberstamm).

[15] *The Sages* (Cambridge, Mass.: Harvard University Press, 1987), 709 n. 1.

[16] *The Old Rabbinic Doctrine of God*, ii: *Essays in Anthropomorphism* (1937; repr. New York: Ktav Publishing House, 1968), 131.

[17] Ibid.

it occurs with the scriptural proof-text (leaving the theological teaching unqualified). The reason for the preference for the one slot or the other is not always evident or certain, and often appears to be totally arbitrary. Presumably, such single qualifications were deemed sufficient for the teachers or tradents (including copyists) involved, *even though* the pertinent materials have the double feature of a theological teaching *plus* a proof-text.

One is contrained to ask: What does it mean to qualify the teaching, but not the scriptural support; and, conversely, to qualify the citation, but not the teaching itself? The matter is exacerbated by the fact that the qualification of the content often appears to undermine the rhetorical effect of the teaching from the outset, or even qualify a normative feature of rabbinic theology (like divine mercy or dominion). Similarly, the qualification of a scriptural citation must also be explained, especially as that affects the divine authority involved.

The complexity of the evidence does not always or easily allow us to get back to the original formulations of the teachings involved or to determine the meaning of the term *kivyakhol* for the teachers or tradents themselves. Undoubtedly, the term served various functions for various persons at various times; and some of these could even be totally disruptive additions to received materials, and devoid of any consideration as to the effect these interventions must have upon the meaning of the passages involved. Where stylistic or text-critical or manuscript evidence permits evaluations and judgements, such have been proposed. But overall it has seemed beneficial to focus primarily on the hermeneutical function of the term *kivyakhol* in its two contexts—a decision that yields the following additional perspective on the qualifications involved. Where the term occurs with the theological content, it qualifies the latter by marking the presumptive character of the teaching derived from Scripture (duly reinterpreted); and where the term occurs with the proof-text, it qualifies the latter by marking the presumptive reuse of the citation for the construction of the theology just proclaimed.

Examples for these assertions shall be found below. At this point it may suffice to add that on this perspective both the theological content and the proof-text are qualified in ways that help us attend to the positive constructions involved, as against negative constrictions placed upon the teachings and texts *per se*. Moreover, the chief value of this perspective lies in its heuristic potential for elucidating the dynamics and dimensions of the passages themselves—not its capacity to construct original intent. Withal, in some cases this viewpoint may also provide the primary intent of a given usage (particularly when the term qualifies the scriptural citation). But such determinations are not crucial, and remain secondary to the main purpose of this appendix—which is to elucidate the remarkable mythic content and exegetical theologies of rabbinic passages where the term *kivyakhol* is found.

Lexicographically, the term *kivyakhol* may be considered a counterpart to the word *yakhol*, regularly used in old midrashic discourse (especially legal) to propose an inference or possibility derived from Scripture—but one that is peremptorily rejected on the basis of another construal of the words of the text. In these cases, one exegesis trumps another. For its part, the term *kivyakhol* presents a certain theological teaching in aggadic or homiletical discourse 'as a possibility' (or 'as by a possibility'), which then proceeds to support that proposal by a scriptural citation—whose relevance must be midrashically construed.[18] As we have suggested, none of this requires that the term *kivyakhol* is original in any given case. It only stresses that the term serves as a way of marking the hermeneutical and constitutive character of the midrashic discourses involved, as well as their presumptive boldness.

With these considerations in mind we turn to the midrashic evidence itself, arranged by subject and theme.

The Texts

I. GOD AND THE UNIVERSE

A. Divine Supremacy

1. Dominion

(i) *MidPs 114.3* (B, 471).[19] A comment on *be-YaH shemo* (literally, a call to extol the Lord 'whose name is YaH', or 'by His name, YaH').

> R. Judah the Prince asked R. Samuel bar Naḥman: What does *be-YaH shemo* mean? R. Samuel bar Naḥman answered: Every place has a superior designated over its *biyya'* (dominion);[20] and who is designated *biyya'* of the world?—*kivyakhol* the Holy One, blessed be He; as it says, *be-YaH shemo*! Do not read *be-YaH* but *biyya' shemo* (i.e. 'His Name is Dominion'; that is, 'Lord' or 'Master').

The chronological sequence of Judah the Prince (*ha-nasi'*) (T4) asking a query of R. Samuel (A3) is impossible; hence one must prefer the version of this teaching found in *GenR* 12.10 (T–A, 108), where R. Yudan Nesiy'ah III (A3) poses the query. R. Samuel's comment presupposes knowledge of Greek *bia* (dominion); and in it the term *kiv.* does not qualify the reference to the Holy One as the Lord of the world, but rather marks the reference to Him through the ensuing interpretative gloss on the divine Name. Notably, the term *kiv.* does not occur in either *GenR* 12.10 or *JT Ḥag.* 2.1, 7c, where the reference is to the *biyah* of the world. The bold transformation of the divine Name through the use of the *'al tiqre* (do not read) exegetical form may account for the occurrence of *kiv.* in *MidPs 114.3*.[21]

2. Duration

(i) *Tan Tazri'a 2*. On the verse 'There is no holy one like YHWH, truly, there is no one beside You' (1 Sam. 2: 2), the query is asked:

[18] The element *yakhol* in the compound thus has a substantive quality, as already noted by Brüll (above, n. 10); but I do not think it necessary to follow his vocalization *kivayakhol*, 'as by the possibility'.

[19] Note that passages employing the term *kivyakhol* are cited by italicizing the text *and* the subsection; but in cases without the term, only the text is emphasized (note the citation *GenR* 12.10, later in the paragraph).

[20] See T–A, 108, n. 3, and the reference to the gloss *memshalah* (dominion) in MS *Liqquṭim*. W. Braude, *The Midrash on Psalms* (New Haven: Yale University Press, 1959), ii. 520 (n. 7) renders 'power'; he adduces the observation of S. Lieberman that Greek *bia* is equivalent to Latin *defensor civitatis* or *defensor loci*. For other official titles in *GenR* 12.10, see my comments in *The Exegetical Imagination: On Jewish Thought and Theology* (Cambridge, Mass.: Harvard University Press, 1998), 14; and p. 188 nn. 14–15.

[21] For this exegetical form, cf. A. Rosensweig, 'Die Al-tikri-Deutung', in M. Brann and I. Elbogen (edd.), *Festschrift zu I. Lewy's siebzigsten Geburtstag* (Berlin, 1911), 204–58.

> What does 'Truly, there is no one beside you (*biltekha*)' mean?—A king of flesh and blood builds palaces (and) they outlast (*meballim*) him, but the Holy One, blessed be He, outlasts (*meballeh*) His world—*kivyakhol*, 'Truly, there is none beside You (*biltekha*).'

This is a highly condensed teaching, utilizing the common trope which juxtaposes a human king to God in order to make a theological point. But what is it? The theology of supremacy or exclusivity is plain enough (though it is unclear whether this verse from Hannah's prayer is giving hyperbolic praise but not denying other divinities, or is making a categorical assertion of uniqueness). The comparison refers to duration (royal and divine), using a verb that alludes to *biltekha* in the lemma—thus indicating where the point of emphasis lies. But after the comparison, what is the force of the term *kiv.*, followed by the lemma? Surely, the purpose of *kiv.* is neither to deny the previous *theologoumenon* (about God's everlastingness) nor the ensuing proof-text. However, the sense of this proof in relation to the opening query and the explanation is obscure.

The solution lies in perceiving that the midrashist presumes a construal of *biltekha* as meaning *ballotekha*, so that the final phrase asserts of God that 'there is nothing that outlasts You'. That this is the intended hermeneutic is clear from the parallel version in *TanB Tazriʿa 3* (B, 33). After the assertion of *kiv.* and the proof-text, there follows the epexegetical comment: 'Truly, there is nothing that outlasts You (*ballotekha*).' Similarly, in a variant formulation in *BT Meg.* 14a, the exegetical technique is explicit: 'Do not read *biltekha* but *ballotekha*'—and then goes on to compare God to humans, the work of His hands. In this case, *kiv.* is unnecessary and not used; in *Tan Tazriʿa* (and Ca), the term marks the presumptive and implied rereading of the lemma.

In *BT Meg.* 14a, the teacher is given as R. Judah b. Menashia. This is probably a copyist's error for R. Judah Nesia (A1 or A3—assuming an original reading like R. Judah mi-Nishia; namely, 'from N.').

B. Divine Combat

1. Against Sea

(i) *PesR Addendum 1.1* (MIS, 183a). A tradition about the vanquishing of (the) Sea (Yam) at the time of creation. The rabbis give a brief allusion to this event through an interpretation of Ps. 93: 3, 'The seas arose, O YHWH ... the seas arose *dokhyam*.' They explained:

> 'The seas arose' ... What is *dokhyam*? *darakh yam* (i.e. 'He (God) trod over Yam'). (At the beginning) the waters of creation filled the entire world. What did the Holy One, blessed be He, do? He pressed (*kabash*) upon them—*kivyakhol*, and caused them to be gathered into 'Ocean'.

This is a mythic account of events presumed to have occurred at the gathering of the waters at the beginning of the world (stated neutrally and without mythic drama in Gen. 1: 9). It depicts a scene of upswelling and flowing waters, but notably no rebellion is indicated. In order to contain Sea, God pressed the waters into fixed domains. Scriptural support is found in the word *dokhyam*, which is presumed to be a contraction of the verbal element *dokh* plus the noun *yam*. By this means, the word *dokhyam* was midrashically interpreted to yield the mythic event narrated briefly.

Presumably, the verbal element *dokh* was construed as if from the verbal stem *d-kh-kh*, with the sense of suppression, and this meaning was explicated and rendered by the verb *darakh* (tread upon). Choice of this latter verb indicates the influence of mythic motifs in Scripture (cf. Job 9: 8), as well as other midrashic traditions concerning this mythic event which employ it (see above, pp. 116–17). For its part, the verb *kabash* also retains a trace of an old mythic battle or theomachy (see above, pp. 117–18). However, in this setting, the term *kiv.* signals it as an explication of the terse midrashic exegesis at the outset. But this second account is weaker, mythically speaking; the initial aggression against Yam being rendered here more impersonally.

II. GOD AND THE PANTHEON

A. Human Creation

1. Angelic Involvement

(i) *GenR 12.1* (T–A, 97–9; Lo). In the context of Gen. 2: 4, R. Ḥuna explicates Job 26: 14 to indicate the limited nature of human knowledge of God's ways. In the rhetorical crescendo he says that even the nature of the thunder is beyond man, 'how much the more so the nature (or order) of the world itself (*seder ʿolam*)!' To support this point, Eccles. 2: 12b is adduced as double proof ('for what can the man do who comes after the king?—even that which has already been done'). The first phrase was glossed by the comment, 'the King of the world; the Supreme King of kings, the Holy One, blessed be He', which suggests that the lemma was construed to mean something like, 'for what is man, since he comes (into existence) after God?'; or, 'that he might come to know (the ways of) God?' Several parables follow; and then the second phrase is cited, with the following comment:

> 'Even that which has already been done (*ʿasuhu*).' It is not written here *ʿshw* (namely, *ʿasahu*, 'he made him') but *ʿswhw* (namely, *ʿasuhu*, 'they made him')—*kivyakhol*, the Supreme King of kings, (the Holy One),[22] blessed be He, and His court (*beit dino*), who are appointed[23] over every one of your limbs, and set you upon your created form (*tikkunkha*); 'He made you and established you (*huʾ ʿasekha va-yekhonenekha*)' (Deut. 32: 6).

(ii) *EccR 2.12*. A variant of the preceding teaching. The final part reads:

> 'and set you upon your completed form (*tiqqunkha*)'. And if you should say that there are two powers, Scripture already says, 'He made you (*ʿasekha*) and established you' (Deut. 32: 6).

The comment on Eccles. 2: 12 emphasizes the orthography of the verb *ʿswhw*, whose plural form leads to the conclusion of a conjoint creation of man (namely, by God and His court). This is the primary and original purpose of the comment. The subsequent use of a verb in the singular form, in the statement about the establishment of man in the proof-text (Deut. 32: 6), ostensibly contradicts the initial exegetical point. This new emphasis may have entered in the course of the text's reception history, and the need to promote another theological sensibility. The version found in *EccR*

[22] Lo; in Pa, Ox, M, and ArCom (s.v. *ʿs*, b).

[23] rd. *niymanim* with *EccR 2.12*; so also T–A, MinY, ad loc. In Lo, *memunim*.

exemplifies this process, by raising the new possibility that the plural verb *ʿasuhu* indicates two divine powers involved in man's creation—this being a dualistic danger or heresy.[24] Such a reading is immediately countered by citing Deut. 32: 6, with its clear use of the verb 'to make' in the singular. The technique of rebuttal employed here was one of several means of countering problematic passages of this sort;[25] but this whole matter is clearly secondary to the original midrash, whose whole point is to prove a conjoint creation in valid theological terms.[26]

The term *kivyakhol* marks this theological teaching of man created by God and the angels—whose proof rests on the orthography used ('it is not written *x* but *y*'); and since the whole point of the midrash is to demonstrate this fact from Scripture, it seems that a principle function of the term is to highlight the relationship between the proof-text and the *mythologoumenon*—indicating that this teaching is only imputed, but not directly stated in Scripture.

In *GenR*, the tradent is R. Ḥuna (T5); in *EccR*, it is R. Simeon (ben Pazzi; A3)—a frequent carrier of *kiv.* traditions.

B. Other Involvements

1. The Heavenly Court

(i) *ExodR 4.3* (*ShR*, 148). Citing Jer. 10: 10, '*Va-YHWH* is a God of truth.'

> R. Eleazar says: Wherever *Va-YHWH* is said—(this means) *kivyakhol* He and His court. And the paradigm case (*binyan ʾab*) for all others is '*Ve-YHWH* spoke evil against you' (1 Kings 22: 23).[27]

An exegetical norm is given by R. Eleazar (ben Pedat; A3). The term *kiv.* connects the scriptural term to its meaning, and marks the presumptive nature of the exegetical claim. It does not qualify the existence of a divine court, which is presupposed by the plain sense of the paradigm case (1 Kings 22: 23). That instance contextualizes the use of the letter *vav* with the divine Name, understood to portray God in a court session. The letter *vav* is thus not only a lexical sign indicating a conjunctive particle but, when followed by a divine Name, is also a midrashic sign implying the co-involvement of the heavenly court with God.

[24] For aspects of this topic, see above pp. 232 f.

[25] Cf. *GenR* 8.9. From this perspective, the deletion of the exegetical hypothetical in *GenR* 12.1, and the retention of Deut. 32: 6 with the singular verb could be a tendentious redaction, based on this principle. A different proof occurs in *MdRI Beshalaḥ*, 4 (H–R, 130).

[26] This is one reason to regard the version in *EccR 2.12* as secondary to and derivative of *GenR 12.1*. More significant is the fact that the creation context is valid for *GenR*, but not so for *EccR*, which truncates the entire proemial introduction. Moreover, *EccR* carries over all the subsequent interpretations of creation found in the *GenR* pericope—matters irrelevant to the *EccR* context. J. Theodor, 'Recensionen', *MGWJ* 29 (1880), 186, noted that the present instance exemplifies the fact that *EccR* draws and assembles materials from proems in Midrash Rabba. He does not elaborate. The present analysis confirms his insight (at least in this case). By contrast, the form *tiqqunkha* in *EccR* may be original, as the noun *tiqqun* occurs earlier in the proem found in *GenR*. If so, the formulation *tikkunkha* in the latter was 'corrected' to conform to the proof-text from Deut. 32: 6.

[27] *binyan ʾab* indicates a scriptural genus by which a species of topically related passages may be adduced. The exegetical norm here is like Hillel's third hermeneutical principle, 'A *binyan ʾab* from one scriptural text' (see *Tos. Sanh.* 7.11).

For this type of exegesis by the same sage (called R. Lazar), see *GenR* 55.4 (T–A, 587), citing Gen. 22: 1, '*Ve-ha-ʾElohim* (And Elohim) tested Abraham.' The hermeneutical principle thus includes the DN 'Elohim'. T–A ad loc. follows most manuscripts against Lo, which gives '*Ve-YHWH*' as the principle. For the latter, see also *GenR* 51.2 (T–A, 533) regarding Gen. 19: 24, which deals with the punishment of Sodom. These two cases are without *kiv*.

(ii) *LevR 24.2 ʾEmor* (MM, 552). This brings R. Lazar's principle with the term *kiv.* to explain Job 1: 21 ('*Ve-YHWH* took').

(iii) *NumR 3.4 Bemidbar*. Citing Num. 3: 11, 'And I (*ve-ʾani*) indeed have taken the Levites,' extends the use of R. Eleazar's principle:

> Our sages say: Wherever it is said of Him, *ve-ʾani*—(this means:) *kivyakhol* the Holy One, blessed be He, and His court. And the paradigm case for all others is '*Ve-YHWH* spoke evil against you' (1 Kings 22: 23).

As above, *kiv.* marks the presumptive nature of the exegetical assertion. The principle of *vav* plus DN is extended to a personal pronoun.

For the cases in *ME Pet 34* (B, 38) and *PdRK 13.9 Dibrei Yirmiyahu* (BM, 232), where *vav* plus the pronoun *ʾani* (I) and *huʾ* (he) refers to God alone, see discussion below, IV.D.4(i). This is also the way R. Eleazar is reported to have understood '*Ve-hu'* is one' in Job 23: 12 (cf. *ExodR* 3.2).

C. *Size and Characteristics*

1. Size

(i). *SifNum 42 Nasoʾ* (H, 47). In an apparent addition to earlier versions,[28] we read at the beginning of a collection of contradictions and their resolutions:

> One verse (*katub ʾeḥad*) says, 'He makes peace in His heights' (Job 25: 2); and one verse says, 'Is there any number to His troops?' (ibid, v. 3); and one verse says, 'Thousands upon thousands serve Him; myriads upon myriads attend Him' (Dan. 7: 10). How can these passages (all) be maintained (*yitqayyemu*)? Before they (the Israelites) were exiled from their land, 'Is there any number to His troops?' (applies); after they were exiled from their land, 'Thousands upon thousands served him' (applies)—*kivyakhol*, the (size of the) heavenly retinue was reduced (*nitmaʿaṭah*).

An anon. teaching in a tannaitic corpus. The central contradiction is between Job. 25: 3 and Dan. 7: 10, as is clear from the resolution. The contradiction between two passages is in the standard format of establishing a distinction—here, the *ante quem* and *post quem* of the exilic event.[29] The term *kiv.* marks this exegetical explanation and the mythic solution. To assume otherwise is to regard the resolution as rhetorical and without any mythic validity (see also b, below).[30] A second resolution attributed

[28] See the stylistic argument put forward by H, ad loc. This passage > *YalShim, MH*.

[29] Job 25: 2b is adduced pleonastically, either because it was used in an immediately prior teaching, or also because v. 2a refers to 'Dominion and Dread', and these may have been understood as indicating (just) two angels. Cf. *PdRK* 1.2 (BM, 5), where these powers are named Michael and Gabriel by R. Jacob of Kfar Ḥanan.

[30] An even bolder mythic version of this type occurs in *ShQ* 46, ll. 73–6 (Siddur Rabba), where Song 5: 11 is interpreted to speak of the awesome size of the divine brow, and indicates that 'after

to Rabbi (Judah the Prince) (T4) in the name of Yose ben Dosta'i (T3) is more practical and less bold: each troop has 'thousands upon thousands', but there is 'no number to His troops'.

(ii). *BT Ḥag. 13b*. A variant of *SifNum 42*, also anon., using the formula 'one verse'.[31] However, in this case the Hebrew resolution formula, 'How can the passages be maintained,' is not used; rather, the Aramaic phrase *la' qashia'* ('no problem') appears—thus indicating the Babylonian redaction of the EI tradition. The resolution given is:

> One (namely, the first case) refers to when the Temple was standing; the other, to when the Temple was not standing[32]—*kivyakhol* the (size of the) heavenly retinue was reduced.

The resolution here refers to the Temple; the one above, to the exile. The term *kiv.* is used as above. Rashi's comment, '*Kivyakhol*: even with regard to the host of the *Shekhinah* (!) we must speak thus, just as one (*yakhol*) may speak about diminishment with respect to humans', presumes that we are dealing with a euphemistic qualification. But the issue is manifestly related to the contradiction in Scripture, which is hereby resolved. The solution is hermeneutical, and the term *kiv.* marks this point and the mythic assertion adduced. Otherwise, the solution would be mere rhetorical play (also above). A second resolution follows this one, as in *SifNum* (above), but now 'in the name of Abba Yose ben Dos[t]a'i'.[33]

(iii). *PesR 21 ʿAseret Ha-Dibrot (A)* (MIS, 103a). In this version, the second resolution comes first, attributed to 'Rabbi in the name of Abba ben Yosef' (a corruption of Abba Yose (T3)?). The second tradition is reported in the name of 'Rabbis'. The resolution formula used is *'ela'*, 'however'—

> Before the Temple was destroyed, the praise (*shibḥo*) of the Holy One, blessed be He, was complete (*mushlam*); (but) after the Temple was destroyed—*kivyakhol* the Holy One, blessed be He, reduced its nature. How so? He said, 'My House is (now) destroyed, so (should) My praise (*qillusi*) amount to a complete sum (*ʿoleh mushlam*)?!'

The form of resolution in *BT Ḥag.* 13b is apocopated and narrativized, obscuring the explanatory force of *kiv.* Thus the need for a second explanation using a different word for praise. It is introduced by *minalan* (here = 'how so?'),[34] a Talmudic formula that normally requests the scriptural source of an assertion—rather than serving as a neutral query, as in this teaching. The change in the number of the heavenly retinue was due to God's decision to reduce their chorus of praise 'after the Temple was destroyed'.

(iv). *LevR 31.6 'Emor* (MM, 723 f.). This version is apparently derived from a tradition like that found in *PesR 21*.[35] This is evident from continuities, changes,

the Temple was destroyed—*kivyakhol*, the expanse of this brow was reduced (*nitmeʿu*; rd. *nitmaʿeṭ*)'.

[31] The sequence of citations is inverted.

[32] This resolution implies the sequence as in *SifNum*.

[33] It is introduced as a *beraitha*; this designation may belong earlier.

[34] Lit. 'From where to us?'; namely, 'From where in Scripture may we derive this?' (Or, colloquially, 'How do we know this?')

[35] The textual relation is stated more strongly in MM 723 n. ('influenced by'), and even more so in MIS 103a, n. ('copied from').

and abbreviations. The first resolution, attributed to 'Rabbi' (pleonastically) cites Job 25: 3, Dan. 7: 10, and Ps. 68: 18. The second resolution, attributed to 'Rabbis', begins with *'ela'*. The first part is like 1c, above.[36] The divine justification here reads:

> He said: It is not right that My praise[37] should amount to its former sum (*ʿoleh kemo she-hayah ʿoleh*).

This final phrase somewhat implies the comment found in *PesR 21*. Both *LevR 31.6* and *PesR 21* explain the reduction of the divine retinue as due to God's decision to reduce His praise.[38] The tone of the decision is more judgemental in *LevR 31.6*. A different explanation for the diminution of praise is in 2b, below.

2. Characteristics

(i) *BT Ḥag. 13b*. An anon. tradition prior to that cited above in C. 1 (ii) presents another instance of two contradictory texts about the cherubim. In Isa. 6: 2, 'Each one had six wings'; whereas in Ezek. 1: 6, 'Each one had four wings.' This difference is resolved:

> The one (Isa. 6: 2) refers to when the Temple was standing; the other (Ezek. 1: 6) to when the Temple was not standing—*kivyakhol*, the wings of the cherubim were reduced.

As in 1b, the term *kiv.* introduces and characterizes the exegetical solution. Rashi's comment applies to this case, as well. The Talmudic tradition adds a query, 'Which (wings) were taken away?' Two opinions are given. R. Ḥananel reported in the name of Rab (BA, 1) that they were 'those with which they utter song'; whereas 'our rabbis' said they were the ones that covered their feet. Proof-texts are provided. This elaboration suggests that the tannaitic resolution had mythic validity, and was not deemed mere rhetoric by the above-noted Babylonian Amoras.

(ii) *LevR 31.6 'Emor* (MM, 723 f.; M2). In this MS version, a striking synthesis of teachings is found. First, the contradiction regarding the number of angels (here in the name of R. Isi b. Dusta'i) is given and resolved with references to the exile, and explained (with *kiv.*) as due to the reduction of the heavenly retinue. Then a tradition about the wings is given, which presupposes but does not give the contradictory verses.

> Our rabbis say: Before the Temple was destroyed, the ministering angels would utter praise (*meqallesin*) before the Holy One, blessed be He, with two wings; after the Temple was destroyed, the Holy One, blessed be He, said: My House is (now) destroyed, so (should) my Glory be praised?—*kivyakhol* the praise was reduced; as it is written, 'The pastures of peace (*shalom*) are destroyed' (Jer. 25: 37),[39] (viz. reduced) from the two wings of the complete (*shillum*) praise.

Components of this version are influenced by a tradition like *PesR 21*, especially the reference to a complete (*mushlam*) praise and the divine query—though now the reduction of song is based on Jer. 25: 37, where the phrase 'pastures of peace' (*na'ot ha-shalom*) is taken as a reference to the Temple of Jerusalem, whose name midra-

[36] But with *qilluso*, not *shibḥo*, and 'diminished *from* His retinue'.

[37] Rd. *qillusi* with Ox, Pa.; also in *PesR* 21.

[38] The verb used here is *miʿeṭ*.

[39] See the explanation of this verse below.

shically encodes the 'complete' praise (*shillum*);[40] and the verb *ve-nadammu*, 'destroyed', was midrashically construed as if it was *ve-niddamu*, 'became silent'. This tradition is apparently influenced by *BT Ḥag 13b*, where the issue of divine praise is linked to the wings of the cherubim. However, the presentation of the subject is different; and the contradictory verses about the wings are not given. The term *kiv.* now pertains to a deft reinterpretation of Jer. 25:37.

D. Agency

1. The Power of Peace

(i) *SifNum 42 Naso'* (H, 46). In a collection of teachings on peace, each introduced with the formula 'great is peace', we read:

> R. Eleazar son of R. Eleazar ha-Qappar, says: Great is peace, for even if Israel worships idols but there is peace among them—*kivyakhol* the Omnipresent said, Satan does not harm them; as it is said, 'Ephraim is bound to idols; leave him alone' (*ḥabur ʿatzabim ʾEphraim hanaḥ lo*; Hos. 4: 17). But when they are divided, what is said of them? 'Their heart is divided, let them now be punished' (Hos. 10: 2).[41]

The initial assertion and proof-text appear as a bound unit, with no reference to peace in the latter. R. Eleazar presumably parsed Hos. 4: 17 thus: '(If) he is connected (in fellowship), (then, even though) Ephraim has idols—leave him alone'; and he presumably also construed the imperative ('leave him alone') as God's command to a heavenly being. The term *kiv.* precedes this presumptive exegesis of the imperative and marks it as a special exhortation. Given the structure of the teaching, the statement 'Let them now be punished' is similarly a directive to the divine agent. So also in *NumR 11.7*. In both cases, the tradent is R. Eleazar b. R. Eleazar ha-Qappar (T5).

In *Derekh ʾEretz Zuṭa* 9.2 (DS, 53 f.), the divine instruction is obscured, as God says to himself, 'It is not my will to harm them.' Cf. similarly in *GenR* 38.6 (T–A 355 f.; Lo), 'I shall not have power over them.'[42] Finally, there is no divine word in *TanB Tzav* 10; *ḥabur* is glossed as 'make a fellowship (*ḥaburah*)'; the agent is the attribute of justice. The term *kiv.* does not occur in these cases.

III. GOD AND THE LEADERS

A. Abraham

1. Circumcision

(i) *TanB Lekh 24* (B, 80). When Abraham began to circumcise himself, he started to shake and said, 'I am old.'

> What did the Holy One, blessed be He, do?—*kivyakhol* He sent forth His hand and held (it) with him (*ʾaḥaz ʿimmo*), and Abraham cut until he was circumcised. Thus did Ezra give praise, saying: 'You alone are the Lord... You chose Abram... and made a covenant with him (*ve-karat ʿimmo berit*)...' (Neh. 9: 6–8). It is not written, 'made a covenant for him (*lo*)', but '... with him (*ʿimmo*)'.

[40] Jer. 25: 37 was understood as the Temple in *BT Ber*. 3b. Cf. Ps. 79: 7.

[41] *yeʾshamu*; the stem *ʾsm* is a by-form of *šmm* (cf. Ezek. 6: 6).

[42] Cf. *Tan Tzav* 7.

Remarkably, God is portrayed here as participating in Abraham's circumcision. The term *kiv.* precedes this *mythologoumenon*, which is exegetically established by a hyper-specification of the preposition used in Neh. 9: 8. The technical formula, 'It is not written *x* but *y*', underscores the hermeneutical character of the teaching. A variant occurs in *AgBer* 16 (B, 34 f.), also with *kiv.*[43]

Variants of the formulation in (i) occur in *ed. prin.* (Venice, 1545) and MSS of *GenR* 49.2—but without the term *kiv.* Note *inter alia* MH1, Ox, Ox4, St and Y (> Lo; see T–A, 498). The *ʿArugat ha-Bosem* cites a similar *GenR* tradition;[44] and Hadassi in *ʾEshkol ha-Kopher* 36 adduces this exegesis in the name of *GenR* and *Tan*, with the variant that God 'seized (*tafas*) his hand and sustained him (*heḥeziqo*), and the two of them' performed the rite. Cf. also *TanB Vayeraʾ* 4 B, 86), where Abraham says, '"Your right hand sustained me" (Ps. 18: 36)—when You held (it) with me (*ʾaḥazta ʿimmi*) the foreskin, and I cut' (cf. *AgBer* 16 (B, 35)). Unique is the citation of *GenR* regarding 'This is My covenant' (Gen. 17: 10) brought by *Sefer Milḥamot ha-Shem*: 'This teaches that the Holy One, blessed be He, showed our blessed ancestor Abraham his circumcision with His finger.'[45] This tradition is not found in *GenR* 47.9 (T–A, 476). Given that the pedagogical topos of divine demonstrations using a demonstrative pronoun ('this') uses heavenly prototypes,[46] it cannot be excluded that the first pronoun (his) may not refer to Abraham.

Overall, the tradition of God's participation in the circumcision rite is ancient. It was also known to the early synagogue poet Yannai (5th–6th c.), whose language may reflect an unknown variant: 'You held him (*tamakhta*) by his right hand.'[47]

2. God's Attributes Affected

(i) *SifDeut 311* (F, 351). Citing Deut. 32: 8.

> Before (*ʿad shelo' ba'*) our father Abraham came—*kivyakhol* the Holy One, blessed be He, judged the world with the attribute of severity (*ʾakhzariyut*)[48] ... But after our father Abraham came into the world, it (the world) merited to receive sufferings; and they (the sufferings) began to manifest themselves, as it is said, 'And there was famine in the land and Abram went down to Egypt' (Gen. 12: 10).

The occurrence of the term *kiv.* seems without any exegetical basis here. Possibly, the verb *be-hanḥel* in the lemma ('When (the Most High) gave inheritence (to the nations)') was interpreted as 'cause a flood' (R. David Pardo);[49] cf. Ps. 124: 4. The flood is, in fact, mentioned in the midrash as such a cruel punishment of extinction. Hence, with the advent of Abraham and 'the number of the children of Israel' (Deut. 32: 8) that were his descendants, God fixed the number of the other nations, and thus their continued

[43] The account is preceded by a midrashic play on Isa. 41: 2, which is applied to Abraham. The use of *kiv.* appears to be out of place.

[44] See *ʿArugat ha-Bosem*, ed. E. E. Urbach (Jerusalem: Mekize Nirdamim, 1963), iii. 154.

[45] See in the edition of I. Davidson (New York: JTSA, 1934), 75.

[46] Cf. *SifNum* 61 (H, 58 ff.).

[47] *Piyyuṭei Yannay* (Berlin: Schocken, 1939), 33; and cf. S. Lieberman in 'Ḥazanut Yannai', *Sinai*, 4 (1939), 238.

[48] *PRE* 7 understands 'came' as 'was born'. Instead of 'with ... cruelty', there is also the reading 'as a cruel person (*ke-ʾakhzari*)'; cf. see D (Venice, 1545), and Ox1. The reading is also cited by R. David Pardo in his commentary *Peirush Sifre de-Bei Rav* (Jerusalem: Lev Sameaḥ, 1990), iv. 234.

[49] Cited ibid. (n. 47).

existence. Alternatively, *kiv.* simply qualifies the strong statement about the cruelty of divine judgements in the pre-patriarchal past.

3. Divine Rule Affected

(i) *SifDeut. 313* (F, 354 f.). Deut. 32: 10 is applied to Abraham. The verb *yeboneneihu* is construed to mean, 'He (God) caused him (Abraham) to know Him.' The point is further elaborated.

> Before our father Abraham came into the world—*kivyakhol* the Holy One, blessed be He, was only king over the heavens; as is said, 'YHWH, the God of the Heavens, who took me' (Gen. 24: 7). But after Abraham came into the world, he made Him King over the heavens and the earth; as is said, 'I will make you swear by YHWH—the God of the heavens and the God of the earth' (v. 3).

The term *kiv.* emphasizes a presumptive interpretation of the difference between the divine epithets in Gen. 24: 3 and 7.[50] Were its function merely euphemistic, the force of the midrashic teaching would be lost. The phrase 'until ... came' is formulaic, as in 2(i) above. The anon. unit is condensed in a version in *GenR* 59.8 (T–A, 636): 'Before I made Him known to His creatures, (He was) "the God of the heavens"; since I made Him known ot His creatures, (He is also) "the God of the earth".'[51] This instance is without *kiv.*, and less bold than *SifDeut 311* (which has *himlikho*, 'made Him king', or 'caused Him to be king').[52]

4. God's Reward

(i) *SER 13* (MIS, 60).

> As a reward for our father Abraham, who accompanied the ministering angels, the Holy One, blessed be He, accompanied his descendants for 40 years in the desert; as is said, 'And YHWH went before them by day' (Exod. 13: 21). Were the matter not written, one could not say it—*kivyakhol*, as a father before his son, (or) as a master who carries a lantern before his servant ...

This tradition presupposes the rabbinic understanding of 'sending' as 'accompaniment' (in general and specifically regarding Gen. 18: 16; cf. *MdRI Beshalaḥ, Pet.* (H–R, 81); but the reward is different). Though the matter is written in Scripture, *kiv.* marks an exegetical extension with an emphasis on the hierarchical reversal. A variant occurs in *TanB Shelaḥ 11* addendum (B, 80), but *kiv.* is used oddly and euphemistically with the analogy; cf. the formulation in *ExodR* 25.6.

5. Messianic Age

(i) *MidPs 18.29* (B, 157).

> R. Yudan said in the name of R. Ḥama: In the future, the Holy One, blessed be He, will have the King Messiah sit at His right hand; (as is said,) 'YHWH said to my lord, sit at My right hand' (Ps. 110: 2), and Abraham at His left. Abraham's face fell and he said: The son of my descendants sits at the right side, and I at the left?! The

[50] *Kiv.* > *MidTan* (DH, 189 f.). [51] Attributed to R. Pinḥas (A5).

[52] *GenR* 59.8 may also have originally been linked to Deut. 32: 10, otherwise it is difficult to explain the theme 'I made Him known' (*hodaʿtiv*) in a verse dealing with swearing. Presumably, this verb interprets *yeboneneihu* ('He (Abraham) made Him known').

> Holy One, blessed be He, appeased him, and said to him: Your descendant is at My right, and I am at your right—*kivyakhol* 'The Lord at your right' (v. 5)...[53]

A bold reading of the sequence of verses (vv. 2 and 5) as a dramatic dialogue between God and Abraham resolves the apparent contradiction (if the 'lord' is at YHWH's right, how is 'the Lord' at your right?). The term *kiv.* bridges the resolution and the scriptural proof (v. 5), which is contrued in terms of Abraham.[54] Given these factors, and the messiology involved, it is unlikely that this forceful teaching would be undermined by a euphemistic qualification. It seems more probable that *kiv.* marks the presumptive reinterpretation of v. 5 as an expression of divine humility before Abraham.

As this divine exaltation of Abraham qualifies the Messiah's status, it may even have a polemical force. Cf. Matt 26: 64, where Jesus announces: 'Hereafter you shall see the son of man sitting at the right hand of the (divine) Power (*dynamis*).'

R. Yudan (A 4) transmits the teaching of R. Ḥama (b. Ḥanina?; A 2).

B. Jacob

1. Image on the Throne

(i) *TanB Num Bemidbar 22* (B, 19). Following the lemma (Num. 3: 40) are two teachings.

> (1) This is what Scripture says: 'Because you are precious to me, you are honoured (*nikhbadeta*) and I love you' (Isa. 43: 4). How so?—*kivyakhol* I have set your image (*'ikoniyan*) on My throne of Glory (*kabod*);[55] and by your name the angels praise Me, and say: 'Blessed is YHWH, the God of Israel' (Ps. 41: 14). Truly, 'Because you are precious to Me, you are honoured' (ibid.).

The verbal link between Num. 3: 40 and Isa. 43: 4 is submerged (both deal with substitutions; cf. the occurrence of *taḥat* in Num. 3: 41 and Isa. 43: 4b). The explicit teaching cites God's love for Jacob in Isa. 43: 4 and its cosmic consequence. The fixing of Jacob's image on the heavenly throne is an established topos (*GenR* 68.12; 78.3). The term *kiv.* does not render this in doubt or hypothetical ('as it were'). It rather indicates a striking use of Isa. 43: 4 in exegetical support of the teaching; namely, because God loves Jacob, He makes him part of the throne of Glory (*nikhbadeta* meaning here, 'you have become glorified'; namely, become an aspect of the throne of Glory). The repetition of Isa. 43: 4a at the conclusion underscores this point. Presumably v. 4b, 'I have put a man in your stead', also refers to this iconic substitute for Jacob upon the throne.

[53] The passage concludes with the midrashic lemma, Ps. 18: 36, *hoy ʿanvatekha tarbeni*, which is presumably understood as Abraham's response: 'Surely, Your humility makes me great.' In his disputation, Abrabanel had accused Hieronymus de Santa Fide of forgeries with respect to various *'aggadot*; however, with respect to a mythical reading of Ps. 110: 5, confirmation of authenticity may be found in Oxford MS Opp. 22 fo. 66 (Neubauer Cat. 167), as adduced by A. Neubauer in *The Book of Tobit* (Oxford: Clarendon Press, 1883), xxii–xxiv.

[54] In *MidPs* 110: 1 (B, 465), Ps. 110: 1 is midrashically applied to Abraham; and cf. the comments in *AgBer 18* (B, 37).

[55] The versions in *NumR* 4.1 and *Yelammedenu Bemidbar* (cited in *ArCom*, i. 257; s.v. *'kwnyn*) read 'on' and 'under' respectively. The vocalization may be *'ikoniyn*. It renders Greek *eikonion*.

The angelic praise noted here emphasizes that YHWH is the God of Jacob. Elsewhere, there are references to Jacob himself in godly terms. In one instance, Gen. 33: 20 ('And he (Jacob) built an altar and called it "El, God of Israel"') was interpreted to mean that the Holy One, blessed be He, called him (Jacob): 'El (God), the God of Israel' (*BT Meg.* 18a). Even more remarkable is the passage in *GenR* 79.8 (T–A, 949 f.) where this verse was construed to say that Jacob called 'himself' God, and said to the Lord: 'You are God on high and I am God below.' According to the citation of this midrash by R. Baḥye ben Asher (ad loc.), God Himself said this to Jacob! R. Baḥye took this to mean that Jacob's heavenly image is the counterpart to God's *Shekhinah* on earth.[56]

The second teaching follows:

> (2) Another interpretation. 'Because you are precious to Me.' The Holy One, blessed be He, said to Jacob: You are precious in My sight—*kivyakhol*, because I and My angels stood over you when you left Padan-Aram, and when you returned; as is said, 'Jacob left . . . and behold YHWH stood over him, etc.' (Gen. 28: 10–13).

It is unlikely that the term *kiv.* serves as a euphemistic qualifier here, since Scripture itself explicitly speaks about God standing (*nitzab*) over Jacob. More probable, therefore, is that *kiv.* marks the exegetical extension of the verse, whereby the angels who were on the ladder 'set' (*mutzab*) upon earth and ascending to heaven were also understood as standing watch over Jacob. A var. occurs in *NumR 4.1*.

This double teaching (with *kiv.*) also occurs in *Tan Bemidbar 19*; similarly in Ca.

2. Future Fate

(i) *PdRK 23.2 Rosh Hashanah* (BM, 334 f.). R. Samuel b. Naḥman (A3) interpreted the divine assurance to the nation in Jer. 30: 11, 'Do not fear, My servant Jacob, be not dismayed, O Israel', with respect to the patriarch Jacob who, in his dream, saw divine beings ascending and descending the ladder to heaven (Gen. 28: 12). The sage explained these beings as 'the tutelary powers of the nations', and said that God allotted fixed terms for their ascension or dominion over Israel—after which they would wane or descend in power. However, in the dream, the power of Edom (i.e. Rome) kept ascending and Jacob did not know how long this nation would rule.

> At that moment, Jacob was afraid and said: Will you say perchance that this nation will not decline? The Holy One, blessed be He, answered: 'Be not dismayed (*'al teiḥat*), O Israel' (Jer. 30: 11)—*kivyakhol*, even if you see it (Edom) sitting by Me, I shall bring it down; as is written, 'Should you ascend like an eagle, or set your eyrie among the stars, even from there I shall bring you down' (Obad. 4).

The preacher deftly uses Jer. 30: 11 as a divine response to Jacob's fear, for the words *'al teiḥat* (be not dismayed) were presumably construed to suggest (or imply) the sense *'el taḥat* ('beneath')—and thus convey the divine assurance that Edom would ultimately be brought 'beneath Israel' (i.e. be subservient to then). The term *kiv.* mediates between this citation and the ensuing explanation by God, thereby alerting the reader to a downfall exegetically encoded in Jer. 30: 11. It is less likely that *kiv.* introduces the second citation (from Obad. 4), since this is an explicit divine promise

[56] See *Rabbeinu Baḥye, Bei'ur 'al ha-Torah*; ed. Ḥ. Chavel (Jerusalem: Mosad Ha-Rav Kook, 1982), i. 288 f. And similarly, Recanati, ad loc.

addressed to Edom, and there would be no reason to qualify it. In fact, it would appear that this explicit quote reinforces the implicit promise marked by the word *kiv*.

Similarly, the same formula with *kiv.* occurs in *Tan Vayeitzei' 2* in Col2.

3. God's Promise

(i) *TanB Vayishlaḥ 10* (B, 168).

> 'And Jacob returned safe' (Gen. 33: 18). This confirms what Scripture says: 'YHWH will guard your departure and return' (Ps. 121: 8)—'your departure': 'and Jacob departed' (Gen. 18: 10); 'and return': 'And Jacob returned'. 'And you decree a matter, and it is fulfilled for you' (Job 22: 28). The Holy One, blessed be He, says to the righteous one (*tzaddiq*): If you have done My will, I shall do yours more than Mine—and 'You decree a matter, and it is fulfilled for you.' R. Berekhia the Priest said: What does 'and it is fulfilled for you' mean? The Holy One, blessed be He, said to the righteous one: I say something and you say something—*kivyakhol*, I annul Mine and fulfil yours; indeed, 'He fulfils yours' (*ve-yaqam lakh*).

The opening context sets up a pious confirmation of divine aid for Jacob through a correlation of scriptural passages. Nothing, however, anticipates the shift to a righteous person's decree. Moreover, the first explanation skirts the matter and only deals with God fulfilling the will of His obedient one. R. Berekhia's teaching explicates the verse, with the term *kiv.* marking that God is construed as the subject of *ve-yaqam lakh*. However, any link to Jacob or the *incipit* of the verse is missing. As rendered here, the unit is a sequence of non-sequiturs and utterly opaque.

R. Berekhia is A5.

Traces of the foregoing midrashic tradition occur in *YalShim*, Job §908, which is an otherwise unknown homily on Job 22: 28, interpreted in terms of Jacob and Gen. 33: 18. S. Buber suggests that this unit is the missing opening portion of the *TanB*, cited above.[57] It reads:

> 'And you decree a matter, and it is fulfilled for you' (Job 22: 28)—this refers to Jacob; 'and on your paths a light shines' (ibid.). Two paths (are implied), since it is written 'If Elohim be with me and guard me on this path' (Gen. 28: 20)—(and correspondingly God said) 'And surely I shall be with you' (ibid. v. 15); (and Jacob also said) 'And I shall return in peace' (*be-shalom*; v. 20)—(and correspondingly it says) 'and Jacob returned safely (*shalem*)'.

In this midrash there are verbal tallies between Gen. 28: 20 and Job 22: 28, as well as Ps. 121: 8 (guard); and it also clarifies Jacob (the righteous one's) decrees, reading the two subjunctive clauses as asseveratives.[58] R. Berekhia's foregoing explication may also have Jacob's words in mind, and understand God as suppressing His general promise in favour of Jacob's specifications. The concluding phrase of his teaching emphasizes that 'indeed, "God will fulfill"' the patriarch's decree. The term *kiv.* arguably marks this exegetical reading, and not merely a pious qualification of God's suppression of His own word.

[57] *Tan B Vayishlaḥ* 10, p. 168 note *ad loc.*

[58] In the firse case, *'im* (if) is read as an oath clause; in the second, *ve-shabti* (and (if) I return) is cut off from the subsequent apodosis, and possibly construed as an imperative (and (You) return me!).

4. Jacob, Leah, and God

(i) *JT Soṭah 3.4, 15a.* After Rachel makes a deal with Leah, giving her permission to lie with Jacob that night in exchange for Leah's mandrakes (Gen. 30: 15), the episode continues with Leah informing Jacob of her conjugal rights that evening (having 'hired' him with the plants). The narrator concludes, 'And he lay with her *ba-laylah hu*'' (v. 16). What does this mean? Proper grammar should have yielded *ba-layha ha-hu*', 'on that night'. Ever intent to find deep layers in Scripture, this odd formulation evoked a striking exegesis.

> R. Abbahu said:—*kivyakhol*, he (Jacob) had Him (*hu*') alone in mind; (for) he knew that this (plan) did not enter her mind save for the purpose of establishing the tribes (of Israel).[59]

In this bold exegesis, R. Abbahu construes the pronoun *hu*' as indicating God Himself—upon whom Jacob focused his mind while lying with Leah. The term *kiv.* precedes this striking exegetical presumption. The sage further justifies her act by stating that Jacob knew her noble purpose, and thus acceded to the deed. Another version of R. Abbahu's teaching only deals with this latter point, and gives it a theological justification in saying that 'the Holy One, blessed be He, foresaw that her sole intent was to establish the tribes—therefore Scripture had to say "come in to me" (v. 16)' (*GenR* 72.5 (T–A, 841)). In this version, the first part of the teaching is omitted.

The particular point made by R. Abbahu (A3) can be appreciated in comparison with the exegesis of this passage given by his teacher R. Yoḥanan in the preceding generation (A2). His teaching is preserved in *BT Niddah* 31a.

> What does Scripture mean by 'He lay with her *ba-laylah hu*'?'—It teaches that the Holy One, blessed be He, helped him in that act, since He foresaw that her sole intent was for the sake of Heaven, in order to establish tribes in Israel. As it says, 'Issachar is a strong-boned ass (*ḥamor garem*)' (Gen. 49: 14)—The ass of Issachar caused (*garam*) him 'to Issachar' (*li Yssakar*).

Two components comprise this teaching. The first is the bold inference that the phrase *va-yishkab ʿimmah ba-laylah hu*' means that 'he (Jacob) lay with her in the night (with) Him (God)'. This would be the only way to understand the reference to divine help in relation to the words of the verse; and there is no doubt that the *maʿaseh* involved is the sexual act itself. Confirmation of this perspective is found in a comment on this passage by R. Abraham Sabaʿ, who quotes the otherwise unknown *Midrash Hagalui* to the effect that Gen. 30: 16 means: 'That the Holy One, blessed be He, helped in her impregnation—for He is called *hu*'.'[60] Hence we may say that R. Yoḥanan (in the above passage) is far bolder than R. Abbahu (who only speaks of Jacob's divine intention); and note also that the inference given is without the term *kiv*.

[59] This is also the version preserved in the Geniza, published by L. Ginzberg in *Seridei Ha-Yerushalmi* (New York: JTSA, 1909), i. 210 (ll. 1–2), though the word *daʿatah* ('her mind') was accidentally dropped.

[60] See in his *Tzeror Ha-Mor*, ed. J. Alnaqawa (Tzeror Ha-Mor Institute; Jerusalem: Tzur ʾOt, 1985), 141.

It appears that later tradition found the formulation in *BT Niddah* 31a too bold and compromised it by adding a proof-text and dense explanation which is required neither by the opening form nor content. Indeed, the second part of the comment is confusing, and presumably suggests that the ass of Issachar caused Jacob 'to be hired' (construing the preposition + personal name as the verbal form *liyssakher*—not '(to go) to Issachar'). According to Rashi (ad loc.), who had this full version before him, the braying ass of Issachar caused Jacob to swerve by the tent of Leah on his way in from the field, and thus be engaged by her.[61] Such a midrash is clearly based on the first part of v. 16, but transforms and dislocates the opening teaching. It transforms it by requiring the sexual *maʿaseh* to be understood as the 'event' of encounter aided by God. But it distorts it, as well, since the clear intent of *va-yishkav* is the act in which God partook. The pious result leaves the meaning of the whole unit in shambles. R. Abbahu, who softened the divine involvement, does not use the final proof, nor is it found elsewhere. This is also true of the version found in *Bereishit Zuṭa* (ad loc.),[62] in which the first part of R. Yoḥanan's teaching found in *BT Niddah* 31a is joined to the second part of R. Abbahu's teaching, as reported in *GenR* 72.5. One may speculate whether this was an original reading or a conflation.

C. Joseph

1. Divine Promise

(i) *MidPs 80.2* (B, 362). The lemma, 'O Shepherd (*roʿeh*) of Israel, give ear; who leads (*noheg*) Joseph like a flock' (Ps. 80: 2) is variously interpreted as a plea for God to deal mercifully with Israel, just as Joseph requited his brothers with favour. A named teaching concludes the series.

> R. Menaḥama taught in the name of R. Abin: Just as Joseph's brothers requited him with evil deeds (*raʿot*), but he requited them with good ones, so we (Israel) have requited You (God) with evil deeds (*raʿot*), and You have requited us with good ones—*kivyakhol*, for (though) we have transgressed Your commandments, truly You (are He) 'who leads Joseph like a flock'.

The exegesis is compact and the function of *kiv.* obscure. The analogy to Joseph's acts of kindness, and their application to God, suggests, first, that the noun *roʿeh* in the first clause is a double entendre. It explicitly calls upon God, the superior Shepherd of Israel, to heed the psalmist's plea, and implicitly calls upon God (implied) to give (favourable) 'ear to the evil (*raʿah*) of Israel'. In the same vein, the verb *noheg* in the second clause not only refers to God 'leading' His flock, but also to His 'treating' them in the kind manner Joseph requited his brothers. Viewed thus, the term *kiv.* marks the exegetical reading of *roʿeh* with respect to the evil deeds (*raʿot*) of the people Israel, and the praise of God's providential treatment of them. Remarkably, in this homily Joseph is presented as the precedent for favourable divine behaviour, and thus the appeal for its continuity (this being the force of the final clause).[63]

[61] Also in *ArCom* iii. 433a (s.v. *ḥamor*), and the epexegetical comment reported.

[62] A midrashic compilation of R. Samuel b. Nissim Masnut, ed. M. Hacohen (Jerusalem: Mosad Ha-Rav Kook, 1962), 239.

[63] Buber, *Shoḥer Ṭov*, 362 n. 14, indicates the absence of the clauses marking Joseph's and God's favour in various MSS and the *ed. prin.*; such readings weaken the homily.

The tradent given here is R. Menaḥema, an obscure figure. To be preferred is the name R. Tanḥuma (A 5), found in the *ed. prin.* His source is R. Abin I (A4) or his son, R. Abin II (A5). The latter is frequently mentioned in Tanḥuma midrashim.

D. Moses

1. Intercession with God

(i) *SifNum 84, Be-haʿalotekha* (H, 83). This passage presents a striking interaction between Moses and God read into Num. 10: 34.

> When it (the ark) rested (*ube-nuḥo*), he (Moses) would say (*yoʾmar*): 'Dwell (*shubah*), O YHWH, among the myriads (*rebabot*) of the tribes (*ʾalfei*) of Israel' (Num. 10: 34). Scripture hereby indicates (*maggid*) that when Israel was travelling, they were thousands (*ʾalafim*), and when camping they were myriads—*kivyakhol* Moses said before the Omnipresent: I shall not allow (*meiniaḥ*) the *Shekhinah* to dwell[64] until You make Israel's thousands, myriads; since from the answer (*teshubah*) given you can comprehend (*teidaʿ*)[65] that He (God) said to them: 'YHWH, God of Israel, will increase you a thousandfold' (Deut. 1: 11).

This passage is exceptionally dense and elusive. In it, the term *kiv.* is apparently used to soften the bold condition set by Moses before God.[66] However, on the basis of the implication derived from the lemma, and its subsequent elaboration (with terms like *meiniaḥ* and *teshubah* alluding to *ube-nuḥo* and *shubah* in the lemma), it would seem that *kiv.* also serves to mark the exegetical innovation regarding Moses' statement to God—and God's putative reply. On the basis of the tally of terms in the lemma and interpretation, as well as the development of the homily, the following explication may be proposed.

The lemma was read atomistically, and its exegesis builds on such linguistic features as (1) the archaic orthography of *ube-nuḥoh* (where the final *heh* marks the third person masculine singular suffix, and refers to the ark); (2) the occurrence of the imperfect form *yoʾmar* (used to mark a future conditional); (3) the cohortative form *shubah*; and (4) the sequence of *rebabot* before *ʾalfei* (the latter means 'tribes'; but it is construed here to be the numerical 'thousands'). These features are homiletically exploited to yield a statement by Moses to God to the effect that he (Moses) would permit the *Shekhinah* to alight (taking *ube-nuḥoh* as if it refers to Moses' relation to the *Shekhinah*, which is putatively marked by the final letter *heh*, now taken as a third-person feminine singular suffix (namely, when Moses let the *Shekhinah* alight)) only if God 'would say' something about the increase of the people of Israel. Since the terms of this request are not explicitly given, the homilist infers the details from the trace of a divine 'answer' (the verb *shubah* is apparently construed as a bi-form of the noun *teshubah*) that is presumed to be the reference to 'myriads' and 'thousands' in the

64 Reading with *lishrot*, 'to dwell', as in the MSS; however, if one reads without *lishrot*, as in the *ed. prin.* (Venice, 1545), one must point *mnḥ* as *maniaḥ* ('I shall not give the Shekhinah rest', or 'have it settle').

65 The verb is used hermeneutically, to introduce a scriptural conclusion.

66 Only in Ro and *RH*.

lemma. Support for the latter interpretation derives from Deut. 1: 11, understood here as the words that Moses tells God to say (*yoʾmar* is now construed as a cohortative, 'let Him say').

If this reconstruction of the midrash is accurate, the term *kiv.* serves a hermeneutical function and marks the exegetical construction of events purported to occur in the lemma—regarding a coercive condition set upon God by Moses, and God's compliance. The concluding phrase, *rebabot ʾalfei yisraʾel*, is thus taken as evidence of God's blessing; namely, that the 'thousands of Israel' will become 'myriads' (that is, the *rebabot* will become *ʾalfei yisraʾel*).

A version of the homily occurs in *Sif Num Zuṭa* (H, 267) in the name of R. Judah (bar Ilaʾʿi; T3). But in this instance there is no initial statement of inference; the explication is presented as a statement by Moses,[67] without the term *kiv.* and without a condition put to God; and there is no presumed divine answer. Hence the exegetical link to the lemma is utterly opaque.

In other midrashic sources, a righteous person (*tzaddik*) can effect the descent of the *Shekhinah* because of his pious behaviour (*PdRK* 1.1 (BM, 2)). However, the present case is particularly notable since a person sets a condition for this divine descent, and even coerces blessings for the nation. Overall, this phenomenon is a variation of the theme of a *tzaddiq* whose decrees are obeyed by God, or who otherwise interferes with or overrules divine actions (see in (ii), 2(i), and E, below).

(ii) *Tan Vayeraʾ 19.*[68] This teaching presents an explication of the power of the *tzaddiq*, who may countermand a divine decree.[69] Eccles. 8: 4 is cited ('A king's command is authoritative, and none can say, "What are you doing?"'). The special case of Moses is adduced.

> Know that when (Israel) did that (mis)deed (with the Golden Calf), the Holy One, blessed be He, wanted to destroy them. Moses arose (and), *kivyakhol*, seized the Holy One, blessed be He, like a person seizes his fellow[70]—for Scripture states, 'And now, leave Me be . . . (that I may destroy them)' (Exod. 32: 10); and you may also learn this from another verse . . . (Deut. 9: 14).

Scripture does not indicate an act of physical restraint by Moses. But just this interpretation is the result of the concrete construal of the verb *haniḥah li* ('leave Me be') in this midrash. Hence, the term *kiv.* does not so much undermine the new bold assertion (which would weaken the rhetoric) as underscore the exegetical presumption at play, whereby God putatively begs Moses to 'let go of Me'. In this account, Moses appears to have acted boldly and aggressively as an intercessor—trying to stay the divine wrath. Notably, Moses' prior act is presumed, but not indicated. For a different rendition of the divine–human psychodynamics of this episode, see V. B.2(i) below.

[67] Here, Moses says, 'I shall not (*ʾeini*) permit the Shekhinah to descend (*tered*)'. The variant 'he shall not (*ʾeino*)' softens the statement but garbles the syntax; see in S. Horovitz, *Der Sifre Sutta nach dem Jalkut und andere Quellen* (Breslau: Alkalay & Son, 1910), 79.

[68] Following *ed. prin.* (Mantua, 1563), where par. 16–18 are addenda.

[69] On this power of the *tzaddiq* to influence God, see R. Mach, *Der Zaddik in Talmud und Midrasch* (Leiden: E. J. Brill, 1957), 112 f. See further below, p. 348.

[70] Similarly in Coll.

(iii) *MidPs 90.5* (B, 388 f.). Another teaching dealing with Moses' influence upon God, is based on an interpretation of the reference to Moses as an *'ish ha-'elohim* ('man of God', Deut. 33: 1) in terms of his being the husband (*'ish*) of God.[71]

R. Judah b. R. Simon said in the name of R. Simeon b. Lakish. Why is he (Moses) named *'ish ha-'elohim*?—Just as when a man (*'ish*) wishes to annul his wife's vow he may do so, or if he wishes to uphold it (*le-qayyem*) he may do so; as it says (in Scripture:) 'her husband (*'ishah*) may uphold it (*yeqimennu*) or her husband may annul it' (Num. 30: 14)—*kivyakhol*, (with respect to) the Holy One, blessed be He; (for) Moses said to Him: 'Arise (*qumah*), YHWH' (Num. 10: 35), and 'Return, YHWH' (v. 36).

The imperatives used by Moses to activate God's arousal to lead the nation, or His repose (Num. 10: 35 ff.), are interpreted in terms of the efficacy of a husband's word to uphold or annul his wife's vow. A series of verbal tallies are involved: (1) the word *'ish* links Moses to a husband; and (2) the verb *qum* ('get up') links Moses' divine exhortation (*qumah*) to a husband's ability to sustain his wife's vow (*yeqimennu*). The bold application of the marital analogy to Moses' relationship to God is thus an exegetical *tour de force*, hermeneutically marked by the term *kiv*. The discretion used by the tradents in formulating this teaching underscores its daring presumptions.

R. Simeon b. Lakish (A 2) and R. Judah b. Simon (A 4) are often linked in *kiv.* traditions, and constitute a chain of transmission.

2. Issues Decreed before God

(i) *ExodR 21.2.* A recurrent proof-text used to mark a *tzaddiq*'s powers to command God is Job 22: 25, 'You decree a word and it is fulfilled for you.' This is also the text used here (regarding God's word to Moses in Exod. 14: 15).

R. Levi said: Just as the Holy One, blessed be He, commands Moses and speaks to him, so did Moses issue commands *kivyakhol* before the Holy One . . . for indeed the Josephites say to him, 'YHWH commanded my lord (*'et 'adoni tzivvah YHWH*) . . . and my lord was commanded by YHWH' (Num. 36: 2).

As formulated, the text adduced from Num. 36: 2 does not appear to prove the point, and is apparently redundant. This leaves the homily confusing, since the lemma only deals with God's command to Moses. Hence one must assume that the first clause of the verse was construed to indicate that 'my lord (Moses) commanded YHWH'. This exegetical presupposition, which treats *'adoni* as both the subject and object of the verse,[72] provides the right symmetry to the opening analogy. The term *kiv.* thus marks the hermeneutical turn that links Job 22: 25 to Num. 36: 2, and anticipates the bold rereading of the latter verse.

The teacher is R. Levi (A 3).

3. God Elevates Moses

(i) *'Eileh Debarim Zuṭa.* Adduced by this name in *YalShim, Pinḥas*, §776. According to this citation, R. Judah said that in 175 portions the DN precedes the name of Moses; whereas in Num. 27: 16,

[71] For *'ish* as the divine Husband of Israel, see Hos. 2: 18.

[72] On this reading, the *nota accusativa* (*'et*) must be disregarded.

> Moses precedes the (divine) Name—*kivyakhol*, the Holy One, blessed be He, exalted Moses to His Name.

This is a presumptive explanation of the change in precedence; the term *kiv.* marks this theological assertion. It is a weak usage.

E. Other Personalities

1. The *Tzaddiq*

(i) *DeutR 10.3*. The scriptural phrase, 'He who rules justly (*tzaddiq*), he who rules (*moshel*) [in][73] awe of God' (2 Sam. 23: 3) is radically reinterpreted by a redivision of the words.

> What does '*tzaddiq moshel* (in the awe) of God' mean?—(It means that) *tzaddiqim* (righteous persons) rule, *kivyakhol* (like) the Holy One, blessed be He. 'Rule' in what way?—Whatever the Holy One... does, the *tzaddiqim* do.

The term *kiv.* mediates the analogy between the rule of *tzaddiqim* and God. It also marks the exegetical presumption of the comparison, which depends on making the concluding adverb of one clause (*tzaddiq*, justly) into the subject of the second (a *tzaddiq*, righteous person). The sentence is thus construed to refer to human decrees. In the process, the phrase 'awe of God' (*yir'at'elohim*) is transformed from the quality of a just ruler to a quality of God Himself. A series of similar acts performed by God and a *tzaddiq* follows.

IV. GOD AND ISRAELITE HISTORY

A. The Covenant Relation

1. Several Teachings Stressing the Intimate Relationship between God and Israel

(i) *ExodR 33.1*. The presence of God is given to Israel through the Torah itself, by a paradoxical reading of the phrase *ve-yiqḥu li terumah* (Exod. 25: 2). This divine behest that the Israelites 'bring Me a gift' for the building of the Tabernacle is homiletically linked to Prov. 4: 2, 'For I have given you a good teaching (*leqaḥ*), (therefore) do not abandon My instruction (*torah*)'. The homily turns on the fact that the word *leqaḥ* can mean 'purchase' as well as 'teaching', and thus raises the paradoxical possibility that God gave Israel a 'purchase'.

> Now is there a purchase (*leqaḥ*) about which one can say that the seller is sold (along) with it?! Said the Holy One, blessed be He: I sold you My Torah (*torati*)—(and) *kivyakhol* I am purchased with it; as it says, *ve-yiqḥu li terumah*.

Based on reading Prov. 4: 2 as suggesting that God has 'given' (*natati*) Israel a 'purchase' (*leqaḥ*), which is the Torah-instruction, Exod. 25: 2 is construed to teach that with that 'purchase' Israel also 'will acquire' (*ve-yiqḥu*) God Himself (*li*, 'Me') as a 'gift'. This bold theological conclusion is read into the first phrases of the command in Exod. 25: 2, and the term *kiv.* alerts one to interpret the proof-text in a manner consonant with both the homilist's rhetorical query (Now is there a purchase?) and the subsequent divine assertion (I am purchased with it). On this view, *kiv.* does not so much mark a

[73] According to some MSS.

euphemistic weakening of the teaching (which would deprive it of motivation and force), as signal a daring theological interpretation of the ensuing proof-text. The power of the homily lies in the mythic concreteness of the exegesis involved, even if it was deemed necessary to mark its presumptive character.

A variant teaching in *ExodR 33.6* is attributed to R. Berekhia (A 5). Here again normal purchase practices are juxtaposed to divine actions, but without any direct reference to Prov. 4: 2. In this case, the exegetical point is made explicitly: 'But the Holy One, blessed be He, gave the Torah to Israel, and says to them—*kiv*. "(It is) Me (*li*) that you are purchasing (*loqeḥim*)"; thus (it says,) *ve-yiqḥu li terumah* ("and they shall acquire Me... ").' The use of the verb *loqeḥim* indicates that a reference to Prov. 4: 2 has been lost here. As above, the term *kiv*. marks the presumptive relation between the bold *theologoumenon* and its scriptural proof. There would be no sense in underminding the former and then linking it to a proof-text.[74]

(ii) *LevR 30.13 ʾEmor* (MM, 710 f.). In this case, the presence of God is given the nation through the Sanctuary. A homily of R. Judah (bar Ilaʾʿi, T3) transmitted by R. Simeon b. Pazzi (A3) notes that Scripture refers to commands where Israel was asked to 'take' something—for their benefit. On this basis, Exod. 25: 2 is interpreted as a divine request to the people.

> *Kivyakhol* the Holy One, blessed be He, said: Take Me and I shall dwell among you. (Hence Scripture) does not say *ve-yiqḥu terumah* ('And they shall take a gift') but *ve-yiqḥu li terumah*—You are taking Me (namely, 'And they shall take Me as a gift').

The theological assertion is underscored by the specificity of scriptural langauge. The term *kiv*. thus marks the bold statement of God, which is based on a presumptive reading of the proof-text; for were its primary function to qualify this assertion, the effect of the homily would be thereby neutralized or undermined.

The same homily is found in *Tan ʾEmor 17*, though here with the explicit qualification '*dabar qasheh* (a difficult passage) *kiv*.'—marking the boldness of the exegesis.[75] Similarly, in *TanB ʾEmor 24* (p. 98) and Ca.

(iii) *MdRI Yitro 2* (H–R, 208). Emphasizing the covenantal relationship between God and Israel, Exod. 19: 6 is explained:

> 'And you shall be for Me' (Exod. 19: 6)—*kivyakhol* I shall not set up or cause any others to rule (over you) but Me; as it says, 'Behold, the guardian of Israel will neither slumber nor sleep' (Ps. 121: 4).

The point made here is to stress the exclusive lordship and protection of YHWH for Israel; only divine sovereignty shall prevail, according to this divine promise. As this teaching of providence is not unusual, it would be hard to explain the use of the *kiv*. here as qualifying the teaching. One possibility is that it marks the categorical aspect of the use of Exod. 19: 6 here—in contrast to its original function as a result clause consequent upon Israelite compliance with covenantal demands ('If you heed... *then* you shall be for Me'; Exod. 19: 5–6). The exegetical shift is thus to construe v. 6a in

[74] The homily is given anonymously and very tersely in the *Tan Terumah* 3 and *TanB Terumah* 2 (p. 89), in both cases without *kiv*.

[75] For the phrase *dabar qasheh*, see above, p. 153.

apodictic terms, and not as an *apodosis*-clause. Alternatively, *kiv.* marks the emphasis on the exclusivity of God's relationship with Israel (i.e. 'for Me')—a point reinforced by the divine epithet in the proof-text.

2. Mighty Manifestations of Divine Aid

(i) *SongsR 1.9*. Songs 1: 9 is boldly interpreted by R. Akiba (T 2) in terms of God's appearance at the Sea in the image of a mare. This passage is cited and analysed above (pp. 233–4). The term *kiv.* marks the exegetical presumption involved (namely, that the scriptural verse indicates this appearance). Twelve other proof-texts are appended and deemed to indicate the variety of divine manifestations on Israel's behalf. The term *kiv.* accompanies each instance. The whole thrust of the teaching would be destroyed if *kiv.* merely functioned as a euphemistic qualification.

In *MdRI Beshalaḥ 6* (H–R, 112) only the example from Songs 1: 9 is given, in the name of R. Pappius (in debate with R. Akiba). The swift censure of the remark by R. Akiba indicates that the exegetical proposal was taken seriously. In light of this debate structure, where R. Akiba takes a more moderate position in the other cases, R. Pappius may be the original proponent of this bold exegesis.[76]

B. Divine Participation in Miracles, Sorrow, and Joy

1. God and the History of Israel

(i) *MdRI Beshalaḥ 2* (H–R, 186). After Moses built an altar, following the defeat of Amalek (Exod. 17: 15), the speaker of the next phrase *Va-yiqraʾ shemo YHWH nisi* is ambiguous. According to R. Joshua, Moses spoke it (Hence he construed the phrase: 'And he (Moses) called its name (i.e. the altar): "YHWH is my banner" '); but according to R. Eleazar ha-Modaʿi, the speaker was God (hence, he construed it: 'And YWHW called its name (i.e. the altar): "My banner" '). After this, an anonymous midrashic expansion follows. It picks up the term *nes* (banner), but now construes it as 'miracle' (another meaning of this word).

> So also you find (in Scripture) that whenever Israel experiences a miracle—*kivyakhol* the miracle is His (lit. before Him); as it says, 'YHWH is my miracle (*nisi*)'; (and whenever there is) trouble for Israel, (the) trouble is His (lit. before Him); as it says, 'In all their trouble He was troubled' (Isa. 63: 9); (and whenever there is) joy for Israel, joy is His (lit. before Him); as it says, 'I rejoice in your salvation' (1 Sam. 2: 1).

In each of these three teachings, God is presumed to be involved with Israel's fate, by virtue of an exegetical emphasis: in the first case, *YHWH nisi* is construed to mean 'YHWH is my miracle' or '(partakes of) the miracle that befalls me'; in the second, the sense is clearer that God partakes of Israel's trouble;[77] and in the third instance, it would appear that the speaker is midrashically presumed to be God, who says, 'For I (God) rejoice in your (Israel's) salvation.' In all cases, the pertinent phrase is isolated from context and given a new sense. Only in the first case is the hermeneutical proof preceded by the term *kiv.*;[78] and this instance may have been the original supplement,

[76] This is also the structure in an important MS not adduced by H–R; namely British Museum Or 5559 fo. 18. It was published by Z. M. Rabinovitz, *Ginze Midrash* (Tel Aviv: Tel Aviv Univ. Press, 1977), 4–14. For the value of this MS unit, see M. Kahana, *Tarbiz*, 55 (1986), 500, 508.

[77] For this verse, see above, pp. 132–6, and in C, below.

[78] > *Tan Beshalaḥ* 28; and thus also *Midrash Hizhir*, ed. J. Freiman (private printing, 1873), 43.

with the other two subsequently added.[79] The force of the supplement is to make a new theological point based on Scripture; its qualification would weaken this intent.

C. Divine Participation in Egyptian Bondage, Exiles, Return

1. Comprehensive Anthologies of Cases

(i) *MdRI Boʾ 14* (H–R, 51 f.). See the translation and discussion above (pp. 134–9). This collection is the most complete and nuanced of all exempla. Three general categories are used, followed by examples and proof-texts: (1) 'Whenever (*kol zeman*) Israel is enslaved (*meshuʿabadin*)—*kivyakhol* the *Shekhinah* is enslaved (*meshuʿabedet*) with them.'[80] The proof-text is Exod. 24: 10, whose two clauses are said to mark the enslavement and liberation, respectively. (2) 'Everywhere (*be-khol maqom*) that Israel was exiled—*kivyakhol* the *Shekhinah* went into exile with them'; the exiles of Egypt (1 Sam. 2: 27), Babylon (Isa. 43: 14), Elam (Isa. 49: 38), and Edom (Isa. 63: 1) are adduced with proofs.[81] (3) 'And when (Israel) shall return—*kivyakhol* the *Shekhinah* returns with them'; Deut. 30: 3 and Songs 4: 8 are adduced in proof. The exegetical use of the proof-texts is analysed above; the term *kiv.* marks the hermeneutical presumptions about divine participation in Israelite history that are involved.

In (1) Isa. 63: 9 is adduced as another proof-text; but this passage only states that 'He was troubled' in all their troubles, without details. 2 Sam. 7: 23 is also cited, but only the liberation is specified. Both texts are discussed fully above (pp. 139, and 140). Breaking the overall editorial pattern, where the term *kiv.* heads up each subunit, *kiv.* is also mentioned in the bold interpretation applied to 2 Sam. 7: 23.

SifNum Behaʿalotekha 84 (H, 84) contains the same anthology of passages as in 1(i), but only category (1) is introduced by a category designator plus the term *kiv.* (Here the *Shekhinah* is said to be *mishtaʿbedet*.)[82]

(ii) *BT Meg. 29a* is a condensed anthology of traditions about divine participation, in a *beraitha* attributed to R. Simeon bar Yochai (T3).[83] A variant of the rubrics in (2) and (3) occur, but without the term *kiv.* This compilation may be the core form of the bi-polar anthology (exile-restoration) found in the sources. It is notable that late Babylonian tradition has preserved this old collection of materials (unknown as such in EI sources), and associates it with a named EI sage from tannaitic times.

ExodR 15.16. A variant of (2), with other nations introduced (Media and Greece). No comprehensive topic heading is used here. Rather, there is first the statement 'When Israel was enslaved in Egypt, the Holy One, blessed be He, *kivyakhol* went into exile with them'; after this, the other cases are introduced by 'so too'. This example is a later and weakened formulation of (2).

Ostensibly, the topic categories suggest that *kiv.* functions as an overall theological qualifier of the types of divine participation noted. However, the fact that proof-texts

[79] For numerous Geniza variants, see M. Kahana, *Ha-Mekhiltot Le-Parashat ʿAmaleq*, 101. His point (n. 196) that Hannah is speaking about God's salvation tallies with R. Abbahu's teaching in *MidSam* 4.4 (B 5); but it does not explain the radical midrashic point here.

[80] The term *kiv.* >Ox2 and M2; it occurs in *PH* 59.

[81] *Kiv.* >*D*, M2, and *NumR* 7.10.

[82] Lo, *meshuʿabedet*.

[83] Only Egypt and Babylon are mentioned as exiles; only Deut. 30: 3 is given as proof of divine participation in restoration—with the term *melammed* used to narrate the inference drawn from it.

follow, and almost all of these presuppose some midrashic reuse, suggests that the term *kiv.* marks the presumptive scriptural basis ('as it were') of the theological assertions of God's participation in Israelite history.[84] The only exception is Jer. 49: 38, where God explicitly puts His throne in Elam.[85]

The mythic theology found in these teachings presumably preceded the proofs, which now support the teachings with texts requiring midrashic explication. If the term *kiv.* had been primarily employed to qualify the theological statements, their rhetorical impact and proclamatory assertions would be completely undermined, and the function of the scriptural proofs that follow would be inexplicable.[86]

2. Egyptian Bondage and Redemption

In other cases, interpretations of Exod. 24: 10 are presented as part of a series of related midrashic traditions. Three distinct interpretations are found. The first is traced to R. Levi b. Sisi (T5), as reported by R. Berekhia (A5) among others; the second is given by R. Berekhia alone; and the third is by Bar Qappara (T5). See the full explication of this passage in terms of God's participation in Israel's enslavement and redemption above (pp. 136–8).

a. Enslavement and redemption as two poles of divine activity (i) *LevR 23.8 Aḥarei Mot* (MM, 537 f.). The first and third cases both use the formula 'before they (the Israelites) were redeemed', but only in the first case is it preceded by the lemma from Exod. 24: 10a; they then both give the formula 'but after they were redeemed', and follow it with citations from Exod. 24: 10b. The midrashic details are somewhat apocopated or elided in the first case, but more fully articulated in the third one (see below). The use of the formulas in both instances (but not in the second) suggests that this was an original component of the tannaitic rhetoric. Both R. Levi and Bar Qappara are T5. The *Shekhinah* is not mentioned in any of the three cases, the subject being 'the God of Israel' mentioned in the lemma. Only the third case uses the term *kiv.*, but does not cite the whole lemma (presumably because it was adduced earlier).

The third teaching reads as follows:

> Bar Qappara said: Before Israel was redeemed from Egypt—*kivyakhol*[87] it (the brick, *lebeinah*)[88] was inscribed in the firmament; (but) after they were redeemed, it was no longer seen in the firmament. What is the proof?[89]—'And like the purity of the heavens for splendour' (Exod. 24: 10b); namely, when they (the heavens) were cleared of clouds.

[84] Isa. 43: 14 is cited in *MdRI* and *SifNum* with an orthography indicating the midrashic sense (*šwlḥty=shullaḥti*, 'I sent Myself'), not the MT version (*šlḥty=shillaḥti*, 'I sent'). This is a single scribal adaptation to the new 'sense' (H, 83 n. is unnecessarily perturbed).

[85] The language of restoration in v. 39 uses a phrase similar to Deut. 30: 3, but was never used in the midrashic attestations.

[86] In *MZ Songs 2.9* (B, 26), *ad* Songs 2.9 (p. 26), Isa. 41: 25 is uniquely adduced to indicate divine arousal from the north. The passage continues: 'Why does He come from the north?—because when Israel were exiled to the north, *kivyakhol* the Glory was exiled with them to the north.' But here *kiv.* merely suggests the possibility of God's exile to the north from His later arousal from that place. No proof-text is provided, and *kiv.* is used to mark a hypothetical event.

[87] *kiv* > *D*, M2, and Pa.

[88] The opaque reference refers to the specification of the brick in the first case; the second case deals with both the brick and the work implements. See above, p. 187.

[89] Lit. *maʾi taʿamaʾ*.

The term *kiv.* is linked to the first interpretation of the lemma in this cluster; the query *maʾi ṭaʿamaʿ* ('what is the proof?') introduces the scriptural proof for the second half of the teaching. In both instances, the myth is based on an exegetical presumption. The interpretation here is softer than that found in *MdRI* (1(i)). In that case, the word *ke-maʿaseh* could be construed to mean that God's action was 'like the labour' of the Israelites; while here it suggests that God only put an image of the work (something 'like' it) in the firmament, out of sympathetic concern. (Weaker yet is the reference in *SifNum Zuṭa, Behaʿalotekha 35* (H, 267), where the people saw a *zekher lebeinim*, 'a memorial of the bricks'.) Note in this regard that 1(i) refers to the enslavement of the *Shekhinah* 'with' the Israelites; whereas 2(i) mentions neither, suggesting that God remains transcendent while attentive to Israel's plight.[90]

Notably, the first interpretation indicates that R. Levi delivered the teaching in a synagogue in Nehardea; it was still transmitted down to the end of the Amoraic period (A5).

The foregoing cluster of traditions recur (with minor variations) in *JT Sukkah* 4.3, 54c; and *SongR* 4.8, but the term *kiv.* does not occur in these instances.

A striking addition to *LevR 23.8* is found in MSS Ox4 and JT. After the conclusion ('cleared of clouds') it states: '(He is) the God of Israel; but when they were not cleared of clouds—*kivyakhol*, He is not the God of Israel.' The purport of the remark is to introduce the visibility of God after the redemption from bondage and thus expand the midrash. However, the comment paradoxically subverts the original teaching, whose very point was to state that God was active as Israel's God—even doing a manner of brickwork which obscures His appearance.[91]

b. Emphasis solely on the pole of divine redemption or restoration from Egypt. Three proof-texts are critical: (i) *MdRI Boʾ 14* (H–R, 51). The bold rereading of 2 Sam. 7: 23 by R. Akiba (T2) is quoted and discussed above, pp. 139–41. By construing the preposition + pronoun suffix *lakh* in the lemma in a self-reflexive sense (as 'Yourself'; not 'for Yourself'), and by taking the ensuing reference to 'a nation and its God' to indicate God's direct involvement, the sage gave scriptural proof of divine self-redemption with the people from Egypt. Normally the idiom *ʾilmalei sheha-dabar katub* ('if it were not written'), which is also found here, indicates a reinterpretation that does not require any change to the received scriptural spelling or vocalization.[92] Just this is the case at hand. Hence, the term *kiv.* seems pleonastic in this instance; though it still functions in context to underscore the exegetical basis of the interpretation put forth. The force of the term here is to indicate that the theological assertion is found 'as it were' in the written Scriptures.

(ii) *JT Sukkah* 4.3, 54c. R. Akiba explicitly rebuts his interlocutor and stresses that the word *ʾelohav* in the lemma must designate Israel's God, not an idol—for otherwise one would make a 'sacred' designator secular. This brief exchange is a further indication that the adduced interpretation in the passage is the issue here.[93]

[90] For such theological differences, see above, pp. 136–8.

[91] The secondariness of the remark is also indicated by its use of Aramaic. For a weak version of this topos with *kiv.*, see *AgBer* 72 (B, 140).

[92] See p. 140. *Kiv.* occurs in *PH*, 122.

[93] The interlocutor structure seems original here, and is neutralized in *MdRI Boʾ* 14. In this setting Akiba takes the more radical position, *contra* his debates with Pappius (see ibid., *Va-Yehi Beshalaḥ* 6 (H–R, 112f.)). See similarly in *EccR 7.3*.

Notably, the *ʾilmalei* formula is not given in this version; and the term *kiv.* is itself qualified by the word *keʾilu* ('as if'). This usage is a clear pleonism, and suggests that *kiv.* was not perceived by subsequent tradition as qualifying R. Akiba's theology *per se*.

(iii) *ExodR 15.12*. R. Meir (T3; a disciple of R. Akiba) makes the co-redemption explicit. He explained the phrase 'This month is for you (*lakhem*)' (Exod. 12: 1) to mean: 'For me (*li*) and for you is the redemption (*geʾullah*)—*kivyakhol* I am redeemed with you (*nifdeh ʿimmakhem*); as it says, "When You redeemed yourself (*padita lakh*) from Egypt, people and its God" ' (2 Sam. 7: 23).[94] Notably, the phrase following *kiv.* is terminologically linked to 2 Sam. 7: 23, after R. Meir makes his theological point. It thus appears that *kiv.* precedes a supportive supplement to the bold reading of Exod. 12: 1 by R. Meir, and that this presumptive explication of the first teaching is itself reinforced by a proof-text.

It is possible that R. Meir had the full verse in mind when he conceived his midrash of Exod. 12: 1, for the subsequent phrase reads, 'It shall be the first for you (*riʾshon huʾ lakhem*).' One may wonder whether the sage perceived this clause as doubling the first teaching about God's redemption and as asserting that God, the '*Primus* shall be with you' at the redemption. Notably, the term *riʾshon* is a cognomen for God in Isa. 44: 6 and elsewhere. The pronoun *huʾ* would reinforce the point; namely, that 'The First One, *He* shall be with you.'

Precisely this cognomen is explicated in *ExodR 15.1*, where Exod. 12: 1 is cited and commented upon: '*Kivyakhol*, the Holy One, blessed be He, is called "the first (*riʾshon*)"—as it says, "I am (the) first (*riʾshon*) and I am (the) last" (Isa. 44: 6).' In this case, the term *kiv.* marks the reading of Exod. 12: 1 in terms of God. The teaching is anonymous and now heads a cluster of comments marked by the term *riʾshon* known from amoraic homilies on Lev. 23: 40 (but without this prologue; see *GenR* 63.8 (T–A, 687), *LevR* 30.15 (MM, 713), and *PdRK* 28.10 (BM, 416f.)).

c. A Godly Exodus (i) *PesR 21 ʿAseret Ha-Dibrot (A)* (MIS, 110a). Interpreting the lemma, '(I am the Lord, your God) who took you out (*hotzʾeitikha*) of the land of Egypt, from the house of bondage' (Exod. 20: 2),

> Ḥananiah the nephew of R. Joshua says: (The scriptural word *hotzʾeitikha*) is written *hwtzʾtyk*—*kivyakhol* I and you went out of Egypt.

Relying on the orthography involved, Ḥananiah (T2) reinterprets the verb *hotzʾeitikha* (which indicates that God supremely took Israel out of their Egyptian bondage) and implicitly repoints it as *hutzʾeitikha*, 'I was taken out with you' (construing a 1st-pers. *hophʿal* with pronoun suffix); possibly presuming a crasis of *hutzʾeiti* ('I was taken out' (*hophʿal*)) + *ʾitkha* ('with you'; i.e. the preposition *ʾet* plus a pronoun). The term *kiv.* marks this remarkable exegetical presumption, and in that sense qualifies the theological point being construed.

JT Sukkah 4.3, 54c, cites this tradition up to but not including the term *kiv.* It is thus truncated and inaccessible, except for one who would already know this midrash. Presumably, an earlier version of the teaching with *kiv.* plus an explication was edited

[94] MT *goyyim* is cited; as noted (p. 000), the original midrash had the version *goy* ('a people/nation').

out. Had *kiv.* been a true qualifier of the theology, it is unlikely that this opaque redaction would have been necessary.[95]

d. An anthology of redemptions (i) *Tan Aḥarei Mot 12*. In a long catena of texts and interpretations documenting divine participation in Israel's redemption (cited, pp. 151 f.), Exod. 14: 30 is adduced, presumably by R. Berekhia (A5) who gives several related explications based on scriptural orthography. In *TanB Aḥarei Mot 18*, the teacher is R. Meir (T3).

> 'And YHWH saved... Israel.' It is written *wywšʿ—kivyakhol*, when Israel was redeemed, He was redeemed (*nigʾal*).[96]

As above in c, the midrash is based on the received spelling of Scripture. In this case, *wywšʿ* is presumably read as *vayivvashaʿ*, 'He (YHWH) was (Himself) saved with (*ʾet*) Israel'—not as *vayoshaʿ*, 'He saved' them. Once again, an act of divine deliverance is reconfigured as a conjoint event (the particle *ʾet* is read as the preposition 'with', not as a *nota accusativa*). Note also that the concise orthographic point is clarified by a theological paraphrase, as in *PesR 21*. Again, the term *kiv.* functions to mark the remarkable exegetical presumption—and thus characterize the theological assertion being made.[97]

A brief citation of this interpretation from the lost *Midrash Abkir* is preserved by R. Eliezer Ha-Darshan in his *Liqquṭim Mi-Sefer Gemaṭriot* 94a.[98]

> *wywšʿ* (namely, *vayoshaʿ*). Read it *wywšʿ* (namely, *vayivvashaʿ*)—*kivyakhol*, He was saved (*noshaʿ*) with them.

The *qere* (read) tradition is emphasized, not the *ketib* (written) orthography. *Kiv.* marks this midrashic intervention. As elsewhere, an active verb depicting divine redemption is construed to denote God's inclusion in the process.

e. For God's sake (i) *ExodR 30.24*. A series of bold teachings on God's own redemption begins with a comment on Isa. 56: 1, 'For My salvation is soon to come.' In context, this divine proclamation refers to God's mighty act of salvation on behalf of Israel in exile. The language of the proclamation allows the rhetor to make a striking observation.

> 'For My salvation is soon to come' (Isa. 56: 1). Scripture does not say 'your (pl.) salvation', but 'my salvation'. May His name be blessed! If it were not written, it would not be permitted to say it. The Holy One, blessed be He, said to Israel: If you do not have merit (for salvation), I shall do it for Myself (*bishvili*)—*kivyakhol*. All

[95] The verb in the JT version is quoted in *plene*-form also in the *Minḥat Shai*, *ad loc*. The 'Qorban Ha-ʿEdah' gives a *defectiva* version; but if this were original, the midrash would lack any orthographic basis.

[96] R. Meir's point is given tersely and without *kiv.* in *TanB Aḥarei 13*. The exegesis is weakened in *NumR 2.2* and *TanB Bemidbar 10* (B, 9), where after '*kiv.* when Israel was redeemed', the qualifier 'as if (*keʾilu*)' is interpolated. Cf. *Tan Aḥarei 12* (R. Berekhia).

[97] According to *Pesiqta Ḥadita*, as published in *Bet ha-Midrasch*, ed. A. Jellinek (3rd edn.; Jerusalem: Wahrmann Books, 1967), vi. 37 (Cod. Heb. XII, Leipzig Rathsbibliotek), *kiv.* is used with an assertion of God's own salvation. The punctuation *vayošaʿ* is explicated as an *ʾal tiqre* reading, given in the name of R. Abbahu.

[98] Munich 227[10]; cited by A. Epstein from his MS, in 'Yalqut Shimʿoni', *Ha-ʾEshkol*, 6 (1909), 207.

> the time you are there in trouble, I am with you; as it says, 'I am with him in trouble' (Ps. 91: 15)—and I redeem My self (*go'el le-ʿatzmi*), as it says, 'He saw and there was no one (person) and was astonished... so His arm saved him (*va-toshaʿ lo zeroʿo*)...' (Isa. 59: 16). And it also says, 'Rejoice greatly, O daughter of Zion; shout aloud, O daughter of Jerusalem—for behold your king is come for you: a righteous one and saved (*noshaʿ*)' (Zech. 9: 9). It is not written 'who saves', but 'who is saved (*noshaʿ*)'. Truly, even if you do not have good deeds (as merit), the Holy One, blessed be He, does it for Himself (*bishvilo*); as it says, 'For My salvation is soon to come.'

In this remarkable (anonymous) homily, the specification of the personal pronoun suffix 'my' allows the preacher a bold turn: the salvation of the people is done by God, for Himself—even if Israel is without merit. The term *kiv.* hardly qualifies the overall force of the original proclamation, for then the absolute graciousness of this theological pronouncement would be diminished. It rather marks the subsequent exegetical presumption, which transforms the act of divine agency—into an act done by God for Himself. Indeed, the full force of this teaching is spelled out through a series of proof-texts in which the sovereign action of God includes a self-reflexive aspect. The specific phrases and terms used (note especially the term *le-ʿatzmi* and the use of Isa. 59: 16 to refer to God, not Israel) make it clear that the action is an act of divine self-deliverance, and not solely a supreme act of beneficence. In ways unspecified, the act of God's participation in exilic suffering requires His own salvation. The mythic dimension of this teaching is bold in every respect, and presumes to explicate divine prophecies of salvation with respect to God Himself. Particularly notable in this regard are the epexegetical comments (*bishvili*, *bishvilo*, and *le-ʿatzmi*). By this means, the preacher has God Himself concur and underscore his own exegetical presumptions.

D. Divine Participation in Babylonian Bondage, Exile, and Redemption

1. God in Exile

(i) *ME Pet 16* (B 13; *ed. prin.* Pet 15). In a teaching of R. Simeon b. Lakish (A2) about the exile of Israel among the nations, it is recorded that God overheard these people deride His divinity and assert that He has now been punished for His defeat of ancient kings such as Pharaoh, Sisera, and Sennacherib.

> Will He always be a youth?—*kivyakhol*, 'things' have aged; as it says, 'And he went (*va-yabo'*) to the nations among whom they (Israel) came (*ba'u*) and they desecrated His holy Name' (Ezek. 36: 20). Scripture should have said 'they went' (*va-yabo'u*), and you say 'he went'? Rather, *kivyakhol* (this verb indicates) He (God) Himself, as it says, 'He went to the nations'...

In this homily the term *kiv.* occurs twice with respect to the putative senescence of YHWH, after the nations sent Israel into exile. In the first case, it comes after the charge that God is no longer a youth, and introduces the theme of debility with a supporting verse from Ezek. 36: 20. If *kiv.* is not simply used euphemistically in this instance, because of the assertion of divine ageing, it anticipates a verse referring to the desecration of God's Name, which could only happen if He were weak and powerless.[99] In any event, the application of this verse to God in exile (stated at the outset of the homily) needs reinforcement, and this is adduced by means of the odd use of the singular verb *va-yaboʾ* alongside the reference to Israel by the verb *baʾu.*[100] According to R. Simeon, had Scripture intended only to indicate Israelite exile, the verse would have said *va-yaboʾu*; hence we must conclude that God Himself came into exile, as a weakened and exiled God. The term *kiv.* precedes this exegetical application of the singular verb to God Himself; and, at the same time, this explication reinforces the earlier assertion of divine senescence. That is, God has become old and His Name has been desecrated by foreign peoples in the exile to which He now comes—a matter that stands in stark contrast to His vigorous, victorious past. Scripture proves the point, by an exegetical presumption.

R. Simeon's teaching is blunt and may refer to contemporary polemics. In other instances this sage also expresses a theology of divine transformation and weakness (above, p. 170).

(ii) *TanB Behar, 2.* This passage comments on Lev. 25: 35, 'If your kinsman becomes destitute and comes under your authority (*u-maṭah yado ʿimmakh*; lit. and his hand is bent toward you)'. The original rule deals with treatment of a compatriot in economic straits; it is reread as dealing with the Babylonian enslavement of Israel and God's presence with them in exile.

> 'When your hand shall bend' towards Nebuchadnezzar, *kivyakhol* the *Shekhinah* 'is with you (*ʿimmakh*)'.

The legal lemma is cited and its clause reinterpreted: the first phrase is construed as Israel's subjugation to Nebuchadnezzar; the second understands the *Shekhinah* to be the subject of 'is with you (*ʿimmakh*)'. Through this reformulation, a totally new sense is given to the biblical passage. The term *kiv.* here introduces the bold specification of divine involvement in Israel's travail—marking the exegetical presumption, by which God's hand is putatively subjugated along with Israel. The proof-text adduced thereafter is Isa. 43: 14, which was commonly also reread in terms of the *Shekhinah* and its exile (cf. *MdRI Boʾ* 14; see above, p. 139).[101]

2. Israel's Degradation and God

(i) *SongsR 4.2* (end). In the context of comments about Israelite exile and redemption there occurs the following midrash by R. Simeon b. R. Yannai.

> 'Now I shall arise' (Ps. 12: 6). Whenever she (Israel) is wallowing in ash (*ʾefer*)—*kivyakhol*, He is also (*ve-huʾ khen*),[102] as Isaiah said, 'Shake yourself from the dust (*ʿafar*), arise, O captive of Israel' (Isa. 52: 2). At that time, 'All flesh is silent before the Lord' (Zech. 2: 17). Why? 'Because He is aroused from His holy dwelling' (ibid.)

[99] This is the midrashic reading; the plain sense suggests that it is Israelite behaviour that has caused this degredation. See also S. Blank, 'Isaiah 52.5 and the Profanation of the Name', *HUCA* 25 (1954), 1–8.

[100] The LXX, Syriac, Vulgate, and Targum have a plural verb. R. Eliezer of Beaugency says that *va-yaboʾ* 'is like *va-yaboʾu*'!—a deft emendation. Cf. his comment on Ezek. 14: 1, noted by S. Poznanski, *R. Eliezer Mi-Belgantzi: Peirush Yeḥezkel* (Warsaw: Mekize Nirdamim, 1909), i. 58 n. 5.

[101] The term *kiv.* seems attached to this proof-text in the version in *TanNum Behar 1.1*, and Ca.

[102] This reading is underscored by 'Matnot Kehunah'; it was presumably lacking in his MS copy.

The opening scriptural passage (Ps. 12: 6) is a divine assertion, announcing God's decision to requite the needy people. This is understood by R. Simeon as God's own act of self-aroused redemption on behalf of exilic Israel. The *kiv.* clause marks the ensuing *theologoumenon* of divine participation in Israel's suffering. It is reinforced by correlating Isa. 52: 2 and Zech 2: 17. Just as Israel is called upon to shake off (*hitnaʿari*) the dust of degradation (Isa. 52: 2), God's arousal (*neiʿor*) to redemptive action suggests that He, too, has shaken off His sympathetic suffering (Zech. 2: 17). This exegetical correlation works out the theological presumption indicated by the term *kiv.* Possibly the word 'Now' in the lemma indicates for the teacher the transition from the earlier condition of Israelite suffering to the heralded moment of God's arousal.

(ii) *GenR 75.1* (T–A, 878; Lo). The version of this midrash found here is garbled. After citing Ps. 12: 6, it says 'Whenever she is wallowing in ash, *kiv.*' This account depletes the force of a teaching about the divine involvement in national suffering and treats the metaphor of Israel's wallowing in ash as a kind of euphemism. The relationship between Israel's arousal in Isa. 52: 2 and God's arousal in Zech. 2: 17 is thus also without motivation or precedent. However, the versions in Pa and Ox4 have '*kiv.* even He also (*ʾaf huʾ khen*)'.

The tradent in *GenR* is R. Simeon b. R. Jonah.

3. Israel's Bondage and the Arm of God

(i) *PdRK 17.5 Va-Toʾmar Tziyon* (BM, 286f.; Ox1). A tradition of R. Azariah (A5) and R. Abbahu (A3) 'in the name of Resh Lakish' (A2; R. Simeon b. Lakish, as in Ox3).[103] The tradition presumably derives from Tiberias. R. Abbahu studied with R. Yoḥanan, head of that academy, and was a companion of his brother-in-law, R. Simeon.[104]

This teaching is translated and analysed above (pp. 147–9). In the face of the enemy's acts, God empathically binds His arm behind His back. Lam. 2: 3 is the proof-text, marked by *kiv.* The citation originally indicates divine aggression and the withdrawal of aid. Rereading the preposition *mipnei* (as 'on account of', instead of 'before') transforms the verse. The new event is God's concrete imitation of a 'historical' event befalling Judaean soldiers. The mythic realism is direct; but the proof-text needs qualification to mark its new sense (hence the term *kiv.*).

The projected release of God's arm at the end of days reinterprets Dan. 12: 13—but without the term *kiv.* The introductory lemma for the homily is Ps. 137: 5, 'If I forget you, O Jerusalem, let my right hand wither'. This human oath is reread here (implicitly) as a divine asseveration, that indicates God's faithful remembrance of Zion: He will not forget Jerusalem just as He will not forget His arm. *PesR* 31 (MIS, 144b–145a) iterates this tradition and cites Lam. 2: 3, but without *kiv.* God does not explicitly imitate Israel's travail, or speak in the first person. Rather, the teacher says that God's withdrawn arm is 'caused to dwell (*memushkan*)' with the people in exile.[105] However, in this version the interpretation of Ps. 137: 5 as dealing with

[103] In *LamR 2.6* the tradents are R. Azariah (A5) in the name of R. Judah b. R. Simon (A4).

[104] Cf. *SongsR* 1.6

[105] Elsewhere, the arm is 'in bondage (*meshuʿabedet*)'; see p. 148. The use of *kiv.* with the enslaved arm in *MidPs 98.1* (B 1422f.) is apparently extraneous—no proof-text is given there. Notably, the tradent is R. Aḥa (see 4(i) below).

God's oath is explicitly spelled out (this version also suggests the shape or scope of the original homily). In *MidPs* 137.5 (B, 524), Lam 2: 3 is cited as God's response to the Levites' mutilation of their fingers, so that they will not play songs of Zion while in exile (Ps. 137: 5). The withdrawal of His arm is construed in terms of a divine oath, by which God assures the nation that He will 'not forget' Zion. The term *kiv.* does not occur here.

(ii) *PesR 28 ʿAl Naharot Babel* (MIS, 136a). This tradition also regards the withdrawal of the divine arm as an oath, as in *MidPs* 137.5, though now in reaction to the joyous martyrdom of the Levites. The act of asseveration is introduced by the query, 'Is it possible (*kivyakhol*) that He enacted' this oath? And following the citation of Lam. 2: 3, indicating the withdrawn arm, there is a second query, 'Is it possible (*kivyakhol*) that the Holy One, blessed be He, did not restore His arm to its place?' That question is now answered by God's explication of Ps. 137: 5, to prove His good intent (and also v. 6).

These two uses of *kiv.* are most unusual, since the term is employed somewhat like *yakhol*, which is regularly used to introduce hypothetical queries in halakhic discourse. They have thus been contaminated by other rhetorical forms, and indicate nothing of exegetical practice or euphemistic pronouncement. Their value lies solely in the semantic confusion and transformation of usage to which they attest.

4. Divine Bondage and the Exile

(i) *PdRK 13.9 Dibrei Yirmiyahu* (BM, 232)[106] and *ME* (B, 38). This teaching has been translated and discussed above (p. 145). The lemma from Jer. 40: 1, deals with Jeremiah's incarceration in chains on his way into exile; in the reinterpretation, the phrase 'and he (*ve-huʿ*) was bound (*ʾasur*) in chains' is applied to God ('He') Himself by R. Aḥa.[107] The pronoun *huʿ* is taken as a direct reference to the divine.[108] The term *kiv.* introduces the exegetical presumption involved in this bold theological teaching.

(ii) *TanB Tetzaveh, 2* (B, 96). The plain sense of Songs 7: 6 (*melekh ʾasur birehaṭim*, 'A king held captive in the tresses') is uncertain. It presumably indicates the erotic entanglement of the lover (king) with his beloved. In this passage, it is midrashically construed as the divine king saying that He is 'bound (*ʾasur*)' or foresworn to Israel on account of two episodes in which Abraham ran to fulfil a commandment.[109] The term *kiv.* precedes God's application of the verse to Himself. The context is unstated, and possibly indicates God's presence with Israel in exile. The verse is not directly used here as an oath; but this is how it is used in *LevR* 31.4 (MM, 718 f.), *SongR* 7.6, and *Tan Tetzaveh, 6.*[110]

In these last three cases, Songs 7: 6 introduces a statement by God saying that He is 'bound in oath' to Israel, on account of Abraham's deeds. In the first two instances, this oath binds the *Shekhinah*—either to remain in the Temple, and thus not leave it

[106] Minor variants with *kiv.*; cf. Pa.

[107] Presumably, R. Aḥa of Lod (A4), later of Tiberias.

[108] *Huʾ* is considered to be a divine Name in the Tosafot to *BT Sukkah* 45a; s.v. *ve-huʾ*. But see the position of R. Judah in the *Gemara*. Also, cf. above, III.B.4(i).

[109] The word *rehaṭim* is understood as the plural noun 'runnings', and thus related to the Hebrew verb *rutz*. Philologically, *rehaṭim* has a double plural marking (internal *h* and final-*im*).

[110] On a divine oath and the exodus, cf. *LevR* 23.2 (MM 528).

on account of the people's sins, or to dwell with the people in exile.[111] In the last case, *kiv.* marks a divine act of importance to the people.

The term *kiv.* occurs only in the foregoing two *Tanḥuma* versions, and may therefore be a later editorial element.[112] These traditions are anonymous. In *LevR* 31.4 and *SongsR* 7.6, the merit feature is attributed to R. Abba b. Kahana and R. Levi in the first case; R. Levi alone in the second. They are both A3.

E. Divine Suffering, Sorrow, and Mourning

1. Universal

(i) *GenR de-Rabba.* From an Oxford MS published by A. Epstein.[113] Herein a passage from Jer. 30: 6 ('Why then do I see every man (*kol geber*) with his hands on his loins, like a woman in labour? Why have all faces turned pale?') is radically reinterpreted.

> *kol geber . . . kivyakhol,* this (refers to) the Holy One, blessed be He, for all Power (*kol ha-geburot*) is His, yet He suffers for His world.

The scriptural term *kol geber* (every man) is applied here to God (not as 'Man' but as the supreme 'Omnipotent' one; lit. 'all the powers are His'). So, too, is the subsequent image of pain. Such a reading of the verse confirms the explication adduced by Raimundo Martini ('*kol geber* refers to the Holy One, blessed be He'), though without the term *kiv.*; this version occurs in a citation from *MidPs* 20.[114] However, the exegetical application to God is missing from the text of *MidPs* 20 known to moderns (B, 174), and from all MSS.[115] It cannot be determined from Martini's citation whether *kiv.* occurred in the full version known to him. The term *geber* is also applied to God in *BT Sanh.* 98b, with the better reading, 'He who has all Power (*geburah*)';[116] but no reference is made there to divine suffering.

2. For Individuals

(i) *ExodR Shemot* 2.5 (1) (S, 110 f.). An anonymous teaching that interprets the phrase 'I am with him in sorrow (*tzarah*)' (Ps. 91: 15) as God's sharing in Israel's suffering on the basis of His appearance to Moses in the thornbush—'*kiv.* I share (*shutaf*) with them (Israel) in their pain (*tzaʿar*)'.[117] The teaching is elliptical and without exegetical symmetry. It is taught elsewhere that God's participation in Israel's *tzarah* (sorrow) is by appearing in a 'contracted' or 'narrow' (*tzar*) place (i.e. the thornbush). Cf. *Tan Shemot* 14 and *TanB Shemot* 12; but both are without *kiv.*

The biblical verse refers to God as being 'with' Israel as a helper in their sorrow; whereas in the interpretation, pain and constriction are assigned to Him as well.

[111] In the case of *LevR, rehaṭim* refers to the 'Temple'; in *SongsR* it marks the 'tents' of Jacob. In *SongsR* 1.17 *rehiṭeinu* ('our bower') is also interpreted as the Temple.

[112] *Kiv.* also occurs in *Tanḥuma* MS Col4.

[113] *Magazin für Wissenschaft des Judentums* 15, p. 75.

[114] *Pugio Fidei adversus Mauros et Judaeos*, ed. B. Carpzov (Leipzig, 1687), 845. This passage is also adduced as authentic by Lieberman, *Sheqiʿin*, 64. Martini's text also gives the second clause a heavenly referent, since the 'faces' that have turned pale are interpreted as the 'angelic retinue' (*malʿakhei ha-sharet*).

[115] The application of the last part to the angels does occur; *kiv.* does not occur.

[116] A teaching attributed to Rab (BA1), who often engaged in esoteric theology.

[117] In the Jerusalem MS used by Shinan (National and University Library, 240 5977); *kiv.* and *shutaf* are missing in the printed editions.

Presumably the term *kiv.* serves to mark the reinterpretation of *ʿimmo* (be with him) in terms of the verb *shutaf*, and the construal of *tzarah* (sorrow) in terms of the 'narrow place' of the thornbush. In *MidPs* 20.3 (B, 173), *tzarah* (based on Ps. 20: 1) is also applied to God's participation in human suffering (*mishtatfin kebodi*, 'My Glory shares'); but there is no reference to the Egyptian locale and the term *kiv.* does not occur. In view of the link between the lemma, 'He (God) will answer you (*yaʿankha*) on the day of sorrow (*tzarah*)' and the reference to divine suffering, it is possible that the lemma was construed as if it said: 'He will be pained with you (*yeʿunnekha*) on the day of sorrow.'

(ii) *TanB Aḥarei Mot 13*. The twofold occurrence of the phrase *lifnei YHWH* ('before the Lord') in Num. 3: 4, in connection with the death of Nadab and Abihu, is noted and its meaning pondered. The answer given is this:

> The Holy One, blessed be He, said, 'Remove the dead from before Me'; as it is written, 'Draw near and carry out your brethren from before (*penei*) the Sanctuary (*ha-qodesh*)' (Lev. 10: 4). *Kivyakhol*, when Israel is in sorrow, He is also with them; as it is written, 'He is with them in all their sorrows' (Isa. 63: 9).

The logic of the homily is opaque. Presumably, the double occurrence of the phrase *lifnei YHWH* marks the occurrence of the sin and its punishment before God Himself; and the presence of the corpses before God is reinforced by the divine command to remove them. This non-scriptural command functions here as the focus for Moses' otherwise autonomous order to the priests to remove their brethren from the sanctuary. However, the phrase 'from before *ha-qodesh*' was apparently taken in this midrash as an indication of the presence of the corpses before God, the 'Holy One', who was like a mourner whose dead are placed before him. This point is underscored by the *kiv.* clause. The midrash thus introduces a teaching of God's compassion into a scriptural scene of divine wrath and punishment.

(iii) *M. Sanh. 6.5* (Vilna edn., 1908–9; Vienna edn., 1801).[118] At the beginning of the mishnah we read:

> R. Meir said: When a man is sorely troubled (*mitzṭaʿer*), what does the *Shekhinah* say?—*kivyakhol*, 'My head is ill at ease (*qlny*), My arm is ill at ease.'[119]

The teaching of R. Meir (T3) follows mishnah 4, which concludes with a reference to the need to remove a hung criminal 'at once', and the citation of the scriptural proof: 'His body shall not remain all night upon the tree, but you shall surely bury him the same day; for (*ki*) he that is hanged is a curse against God (*ki qillelat ʾelohim taluy*)' (Deut. 21: 23). The final motive clause (beginning with *ki*) is then clarified, 'As if to say, why is he hanged?—Because he cursed (*beireikh*) the (divine) Name, such that the Name of Heaven (God) is profaned.' Following R. Meir's comment, there is a homiletical expansion of this point: 'If God (the Omnipresent, *ha-Maqom*) is sore troubled (*mitzṭaʿer*) at the blood of the wicked that is spilt, how much the more so for the death of the righteous?'[120] The mishnah then returns to the subject of keeping

[118] For other versions, see the discussion below.

[119] I simply cite the phrase 'is ill at ease' from H. Danby, *The Mishnah* (Oxford: Clarendon Press, 1933) 390f., as a basis for the ensuing discussion of the difficult word *qlny* (possible vocalizations and interpretations follow).

[120] On the langauge of this clause, see below.

corpses overnight. It is thus clear that R. Meir's remark is a distinct homiletic unit within the legal discourse.

However, R. Meir's dictum raises questions. The first of these bears on the origin of the formulation itself, since not all MSS and editions refer to the *Shekhinah* or use the term *kivyakhol*. Indeed, the reference to God first appears in the mishnah cited in a medieval MS of the Jerusalem Talmud (*Leiden Scal.* 3; 1289), and the term *kiv.* is first attested in the citation in Tosefot Yom Ṭov (16th c.), ad loc. In addition, there is a problem of meaning, since the verb *qlny* is not immediately understood. The earliest discussion of the term is found in *BT Sanh.* 46a, by Abbaye (BA 4) and Rabba (BA 4). According to the first, the sense is, 'I am not *qal*' (i.e. *qalleini*);[121] according to the second, 'I am *qal*' (i.e. *qallani*). But the exact sense of the element *qal-* is questionable. Following the variant of Abbaye's position in *BT Ḥag.* 15b, it appears that the speaker in the mishnah takes the verb *qalal* to mean 'lightness' in the sense of 'debasement' or even 'contempt';[122] whereas Rabba's position is that the term bespeaks a sense of 'worthlessness'. Variants of these positions recur in the Middle Ages, as found respectively in Rashi (*ad BT Sanh.* 46b) and the Geonim (*ad BT Ḥag.* 15a).[123]

But who is speaking? If the words '*Shekhinah*' and *kivyakhol* are not original, we must wonder at the motivation of R. Meir or those who transmitted his teaching; for it would appear to introduce the cry of despair for a criminal into the mishnah. But even if this is the case, the sense of the phrase 'what does it say?' is puzzling; for to what idiom and why are we so directed? If it is directed to the phrase *qillelat ʾelohim* ('curse of God') in Scripture, then R. Meir would have us think that the cry of despair *qlny* is the criminal's (or hanged one's) curse of God. But if this is so, we are hard pressed to explain the sequel in the mishnah, which speaks of divine pain for the wicked and even more so for the righteous.

It would thus appear from the mishnaic addendum to R. Meir's comment that God Himself is the subject of the sentence; and this is also the import of the variant of Abbaye's remark in *BT Ḥag.* 15a (which says that *qal* is used as a euphemism with respect to divinity).[124] Starting from this point, and noting the verbal link between *qlny* and *qillelat ʾelohim*, we may suggest that R. Meir proposed a midrash on the motive-clause in Deut. 21: 23, construing the phrase as if it meant 'the hanged person is a *qillelat ʾelohim*'. He taught that when a person suffers such a death (i.e. by hanging), God Himself experiences a loss (or depletion) or debasement in His own being, since a person created in His image has endured pain to his limbs. He thus cries *qellani* (meaning 'depleted' or 'debased').[125]

[121] As if a crasis of *qal* / *ʾeini*.

[122] Cf. Nah. 1: 14; 2 Sam. 6: 2. The reading of *qlny* as from *qalon* ('contempt') occurs in the Yemenite tradition in a copy of Maimonides' commentary on the Mishnah in MS Jerusalem 80, 596. In this text, the terms Shekhinah and *kiv.* are absent, but they do occur in MS Jerusalem 40 1336.

[123] *ʾOtzar Ha-Geʾonim*, ed. B. M. Lewin, vol. iv, *Ḥagigah*, pp. 30f. For a full analysis of the term and its occurrence in the MSS, see G. Alon in *ʾAlummah*, 1 (1936), 124–8.

[124] Rabba's comment could also be spoken by God, if we assume that when it says 'I am light' or 'weak' it means 'I (God) am heavy (burdened)' by this death (cf. Alon, *ʾAlummah*, 1 (1936), 125).

[125] The vocalization follows G. Yalon in Ḥ. Albeck, *Shishah Sidrei Mishnah* (Jerusalem: Mosad Bialik, 1953), iii. 188.

Alternatively, God's cry (*qellani me-*) is over a depletion or debasement of (*me-*) the structure (or limbs) of His own being (namely, 'I am weakened in My head', etc.). Such an understanding of the cry would bring R. Meir's midrashic teaching into alignment with a remarkable statement (ultimately also a midrash) of his teacher, R. Akiba. That sage taught: 'Whosever sheds blood (*shofekh dam*), Scripture accounts him as one who has diminished (*miʿeṭ*) the (divine) image. What is the reason? (It says:) Whoever sheds the blood of *ha-ʾadam* (a man), by man will his blood be shed (Gen. 9: 6)' (*GenR* 34.6; T–A 326). R. Akiba was apparently struck by the definite article in the verse, and understood it to be referring to *the* Primordial Adam—namely, the divine Anthropos itself![126]

The mishnaic redactor, as noted, also understood R. Meir's midrash on Deut. 21: 23 as a divine cry; and he shows his secondariness to R. Meir's comment by his use of the term *ha-Maqom* for God (not *Shekhinah*), by his rhetorical expansion of the scope of divine pain for the death of the righteous, and by his reference to spilt blood (*damam . . . she-nishpakh*) here (where hanging is the subject). If the latter expression is merely used idiomatically, it may also tally with R. Akiba's theological dictum. In any event, three layers of composition are evident in mishnahs 4 and 5: (1) the law of hanged criminals, which concludes with a midrashic explication; (2) R. Meir's piece of midrashic theology; and (3) a mishnaic supplement that uses *a fortiori* argumentation.

We may thus conclude that the reference to the *Shekhinah* is original to R. Meir's teaching, and that the term *kiv.* marks the exegetical reading of the words *qillelat ʾelohim* as God's cry '*qlny*.' But even a euphemistic reading of this midrash was apparently too much for some later tradents, who deleted the words '*Shekhinah*' and '*kiv.*' entirely—preferring an incomprehensible solecism to such a bold piece of mythic theology.

R. Meir's theology of a God who 'is sorely troubled' (*mitzṭaʿer*) for members of His people may be related to another midrash by him. In *Sifre Deut.* 319 (F, 365), the phrase 'You forgot the God who bore you (*meḥollalekha*)' (Deut. 32: 18) is explained by R. Meir as referring to 'The God who writhed (*he-ḥal*) for you, who was sorely troubled (*she-nitzṭaʿer*) for you; as it says, "writhing (*ḥil*) like a woman in labour" (Ps. 48: 7).' Presumably the *pollel* form *ḥll* in Deut. 32: 18 ('writhe') was associated with the *qal* stem *ḥwl* and had the double entendre of 'writhe' and 'be ill'. Cf. Jer. 4: 31, where the verbal noun *ḥolah* (a person 'in travail') puns on the word *ḥolah* (meaning an 'ill person'), and is also linked to the adverb *tzarah*, 'trouble'.

(iv) *SifNum 82 Behaʿalotkha* (H, 93). At the end of a collection of teachings dealing with the *kabod* ('honour'; 'glory') which God gives the elders of Israel (H, 92 f.), it is taught that

> The Omnipresent is as sorely troubled (*mitzṭaʿer*) for a singular elder (*zaqen*) as He is for the whole of Israel; as it says 'I was angry at My people, I defiled My heritage (*ḥillalti naḥalati*)'—*kivyakhol*, troubled (*meḥolalim*) for all; but 'upon the aged (*zaqen*) you made your yoke exceedingly heavy (*hakhbadet*)' (Isa. 47: 6).

[126] The language is even stronger in *Tos. Yeb.* 8.7 (TL, *Nashim*, 26), where it says that one who sheds blood 'annuls (*mebaṭṭel*) the image'.

This midrash is a striking reinterpretation of a divine condemnation of Babylon, in which God says that He defiled His people and inheritance in His anger, but they showed no mercy even upon the aged. Read in the light of the initial theological assertion that God is as sorely troubled for the affliction of each elder as for the whole nation, the negative phrase *ḥillalti naḥalati* in the lemma is radically transformed. Guided by the explication '*kiv.* troubled (*meḥolalim*)', the expression of destruction in the lemma is retrospectively understood as expressing God's affliction on behalf of His people (something like *ḥolalti naḥalati*, 'I was troubled for My inheritance'). The final clause is now set off in counterpoint—by God's emphasis on the travail put on 'the *zaqen*'. In context, this undoubtedly refers to the oppression of the elderly in general. But the midrash picks up on this specification of the elderly by a collective noun and reads it as if only one elder is indicated—one who stands out for special emphasis within the larger context of national suffering.[127]

The term *kiv.* bridges the lemma and its explication, and marks the exegetical presumption read into the biblical text. Given the opening reference to divine trouble, there can be no doubt that the word *meḥolalim* must be read in this light. Other versions of this teaching read *meḥullalim* (in the sense of 'defiled') or even *maḥul lakh*—as if God has 'forgiven' Babylon for its actions against all except 'the elder'. But this reading weakens the thematic structure of the teaching and undercuts the exegetical transformation.[128]

3. God Suffers with Israel—General

(i) *BT Giṭṭin 58a.* A teaching of Resh Lakish (A1) on the sorrows of the destruction. An episode of a renowned woman is recited, and this leads to an interpretation of Jer. 6: 26. According to the first clause, the nation (called here 'daughter of My people') is enjoined to mourn in the dust; but the second phrase is interpreted to indicate God's participation in the suffering of individuals. Thus, following the citation 'mourn as for an individual (child),[129] wail bitterly, for suddenly the destroyer is come upon us (*ʿaleinu*)', the sage notes:

> It does not say 'upon you' but 'upon us'—*kivyakhol* upon Me and you has the destroyer come.

The term *kiv.* marks the exegetical presumption whereby the word *ʿaleinu* is interpreted to indicate God's shared suffering with Israel—not Jeremiah's call to the nation to begin mourning in anticipation of the doom to befall it, himself included. Resh Lakish uses the same exegetical emphasis on *ʿaleinu* in *PdRK* 15.4 to teach about God's request that a dirge be recited for His suffering along with that of Israel. See below, 7b(i).

(ii) *SongsR 2.3.* After the qualifying comment 'If it were not written, etc.' R. Reuben goes on to explicate Isa. 66: 16 ('For YHWH is judged through fire') as applying to

[127] Presumably, the reference to the 'exceedingly heavy' yoke which Babylon imposed (*hikhbadeti*) upon 'the elder' encoded for the midrashist the special *kabod* (or honour) which the Lord would account him by suffering on his behalf.

[128] Cf. in the versions found in Lo1 and *Sifre Num Zuṭa* (H, 271), respectively. In the first case, *kiv.* is transformed into the hypothetical *yakhol*; in the second, the term *kiv.* occurs but the whole daring theology is neutralized by the reference to forgiveness.

[129] In the citation, *ʾeibel yaḥid* literally means an 'only child', not an individual sufferer.

God Himself. The term *kiv.* occurs between the qualifying phrase and proof-text—though not in all versions. A full citation and a consideration of parallels is given above (p. 169). Following the qualification, the term *kiv.* sharpens the presumptive aspect of the exegetical teaching.

4. God Suffers with Israel—as His Twin

(i) *SongsR 5.2*. This teaching is translated and discussed above (p. 165 and n. 26). The female is addressed by her beloved as *tamati* ('my pure one') in Songs 5: 2. In the midrash, this designation is reinterpreted as *te'omati* ('My twin'), and understood as God's characterization of His relationship to Israel. The teaching first emphasizes the sympathetic pain felt between twins, and then boldly applies this observation to God's suffering 'with' Israel (Ps. 91: 15) in her times of travail. The term *kiv.* precedes this theological point, which is dependent upon the aforementioned exegetical presumption concerning the noun *tamati*.

The teaching is attributed to R. Joshua of Sikhnin in the name of R. Levi (T5). See the variant in *ExodR* 2.5 (ShR, 111).[130] The teaching of shared suffering also occurs in *PdRK Haḥodesh*, 5.6 (BM, 87f.) and *PesR Haḥodesh* 15 (MIS, 70b), but without *kiv.*[131]

Kiv. is an unstable element in these traditions, and probably a secondary element in *SongsR* (and the later *ExodR*). If it were primary in *PdRK*, it is unlikely to have been removed.

5. God Suffers with Israel—as His Eye

(i) *ME Lamentations 1.16* (B, 88). This remarkable teaching is translated and discussed above (pp. 165f.). God mourns for His damaged eye, which is midrashically interpreted as the destroyed people Israel. The term *kiv.* marks the application of the reinterpreted lemma ('My eye, My eye') to God, after a bold reuse of Zech. 9: 1.

The teaching is attributed to R. Levi (T5). Cf. his teaching adduced in 4a (above).

(ii) *MdRI Beshalaḥ 6* (H–R, 135). In a comment on Exod. 15: 7, praising God for defeating enemies, the commentator stresses that Scripture says 'Your opponents (*qamekha*)', not 'our opponents'. This observation leads to the exegetical proposal that 'Whoever rises (*qam*) against Israel is as if he rises against the Holy One, blessed be He.' The reinterpretation turns on a rereading of *qamekha* as those 'who rise against You' (i.e. God is now the object of the opposition, not the Lord of battles). Among a series of proofs is a list of eleven passages that are said to refer to God, though they contradict the plain sense. The first of these passages, and its interpretation, is based on Zech. 2: 12.

'For whoever harms (*noge'a*) you harms the pupil of his eye' (MT Zech. 2: 12).[132] R. Judah says that it (Scripture) does not state 'pupil of an eye', but rather 'pupil of

[130] The formulation is condensed; the word *tomim* ('twins') is used. The personal pronoun suffix is thus dropped, leaving the exegesis somewhat obscured. The tradent here is R. Yannai (A1).

[131] Also a condensed formulation, referring to the twins as *te'omim*. In these cases, the teaching attributed to R. Yannai interprets *tamati* as *tomyati/teyomati* ('My twin') to teach about Israel's equivalence with God at Sinai—neither one superior to the other.

[132] I give the MT formulation, which triggers the ensuing comment. Remarkably, the citation adduced in the midrash reads 'My eye', thus introducing the very reading into Scripture which the teaching claims was altered for euphemistic reasons. See further below.

His eye' is written—*kivyakhol* the reference is to God, but Scripture speaks euphemistically (*kinnah ha-katub*).[133]

According to R. Judah (b. Ila'ʿi?, T 3), the phrase 'his eye' refers to God's own eye, which is harmed when Israel is harmed. The sage presumes that writing 'My eye' would have been too bold, so a softer formulation is used ('His eye'). He asserts this point on the basis of the written formulation of Scripture; and while the proof itself is weak, the mythic assumption behind it is strong. The term *kiv.* does not, therefore, qualify the reference to God's eye *per se*, since this is precisely the locus of midrashic concern—which would otherwise be left rhetorically inconsequential. It rather serves to indicate the presumptive reading of the third-person pronoun in the text with respect to God. R. Judah's teaching is adduced again in *SifNum 84* (H, 81 f.), though here only eight of the examples of such euphemisms are found. Following it, a teaching by R. Yose is given, which takes 'his eye' to be none other than a human eye.[134]

The list of euphemisms in these tannaitic sources are noted in some later lists as 'scribal corrections' or 'emendations'.[135] This latter idiom first appears in amoraic traditions, where it notably occurs with regard to our passage—according to a teaching by R. Joshua ben Levi (A1): ' "Whoever harms you, harms the pupil of his eye" (Zech. 2: 12). R. Joshua says that this is a scribal correction, (that) was (originally) written "My eye" ' (*ExodR Boʾ* 13.1).[136] There are thus two distinct traditions: one that speaks only of original euphemistic formulations; another that refers to secondary corrections due to divine honour.[137] Notably, the term *kiv.* occurs distinctively in the former cases, thus marking a midrashic construal of the pronoun with respect to God. Alternatively, if the verb *kinnah* (marking the euphemism) actually indicates a change of the pronominal attribution, it would mark a secondary feature, and the term *kiv.* would then relate to the final formulation.[138] Significantly, references to the scribal formulation *ʿeini* ('My eye') not only occur in traditions about corrections, but also in those referring to euphemistic renderings. The lemma quoted in *MdRI Beshalaḥ 6* (H–R, 135) reads *ʿeini*;[139] and the word *ʿeini* is used with the phrase *kinnah ha-katub* in *Tan Beshalaḥ* 16, according to Col3, where the presumption

[133] This passage is repeated as an editorial *Wiederaufnahme* at the end of the list (see ll. 13, 13), before a new subject is taken up.

[134] This source also repeats R. Judah's teaching in *Wiederaufnahme* (pp. 81, l. 16; 82, l. 6).

[135] See the lists and discussion in C. D. Ginsburg, *Introduction to the Massoretic-Critical Edition of the Hebrew Bible* (1897; Ktav Reprint, New York: Ktav Pub. House, 1965), 347–63. W. E. Barnes, 'Ancient Corrections in the text of the Old Testament (*Tiḳḳun Sopherim*)', *JTS* 1 (1900), 387–414, has argued that the tradition of changes is midrashic conceit and not a Massoretic feature. C. McCarthy, *The Tiqqune Sopherim and other Theological Corrections of the Massoretic Text of the Old Testament* (OBO, 36; Fribourg: Universitätsverlag, 1981), basically agrees but allows that Zech. 2: 12 (*inter alia*) is a correction.

[136] So *ed. prin.* (Constantinople, 1512). In Ox the reading is 'it was written with a *yod*' (i.e. *ʿeiniy*, 'My eye').

[137] See Lieberman, *Hellenism in Jewish Palestine* (New York: JTSA, 1962), 26–37). The reading 'My eye' is adduced in *Minḥat Shai ad* Zech. 2: 12, but the author piously rebuts it. See also the 'Matnot Kehunah' commentary at *ExodR Boʾ* 13.1.

[138] Ten of the eleven euphemisms in *MdRI* involve changes in the pronominal suffix.

[139] Cf. also the lemma edited from early texts, *ArCom* iv. 181.

is that it was the original reading.[140] Here, also, *kiv.* marks the mythic interpretation based on the final scriptural formulation.

6. Divine Sorrow

a. God is shattered (i) *MZ Lamentations 18* (B, 58). The lament in Jer. 8: 21, 'Because my people are shattered (*ʿal sheber bat ʿammi*) I am shattered (*hoshbarti*)', is connected with that in Lam. 3: 41, 'My eyes shed streaming water because my people are shattered (*ʿal sheber bat ʿammi*).' This latter lament is explicitly ascribed to God in the midrash; and the one in Jer. 8: 21 is presumed to teach the same thing. The midrash adds:

> If Scripture did not say (this), the tongue that speaks such would have to be cut in pieces; but earlier (generations) have preceded (us in astonishment at this clause); as it says, 'Previous ones are seized in terror' (Job 18: 20).

This powerful teaching of divine shattering is stated concisely, without any qualification. A parable follows about a king who, hearing that his son was shattered by a stone said, 'I am shattered.' The application to God then follows.

> Similarly, the Holy One, blessed be He, said—*kivyakhol* 'because My people are shattered, I am shattered' (Jer. 8: 21).

This version seems to qualify the previous one; but it arguably has been adduced to explicate the full theological force of the initial assertion. Since the application of the parable has God speaking, to regard the term *kiv.* simply as a theological qualifier undermines the rhetorical force of the passage. Alternatively, it marks the midrashic presumption that God is to be deemed the speaker in Jer. 8: 21—with all the ensuing mythic implications. For a similar use of *kiv.* in v. 23, see below, 6b (iii).

b. Sorrow and tears (i) *PesR 29 Bakhoh Tibkeh* (MIS, 136b).[141] A series of passages are adduced to show divine tears at the destruction of the Temple. After a comment about Jeremiah's lament (Lam. 3: 20), the teaching continues:

> *Kivyakhol* (Jeremiah) saw what is written about the glory of the Holy One, blessed be He, 'On that day, the Lord God of Hosts called for crying and lamentation' (Isa. 22: 12).[142] And it also says, 'Therefore I say, "Let Me be, I shall weep bitterly"' (ibid. 4). *Kivyakhol*, the Holy One, blessed be He, said: Just as it is below, so also there is crying above, before Me, concerning what has occurred. *Kivyakhol* there is crying before Me, since I left (*heinaḥti*)[143] My *Shekhinah* (below), as it says, 'This is My Place of habitation (*menuḥati*) forever' (Ps. 132: 14). And she cries, insofar as I have left the glory of My Place of habitation and left her. Therefore, she cries. And

[140] The texts states: "*eini huʾ*—it is (originally) "My eye."' Reference is also made to a 'scribal correction' here, but this seems secondary. The version in *Tan Beshalaḥ* 16, 1 is more hypothetical in nature (i.e. Scripture 'should have said *ʿeini*'—but chose a euphemistic formulation).

[141] The beginning of this section is of the 'Yelammedenu'-type. It only appears in the *ed. prin.* (Prague, 1656).

[142] Possibly construed as 'The Lord God called the (angelic) host to crying', etc. See above, pp. 228–9, and b (ii) below.

[143] Emended to 'I took away' by R. Ephraim Margoliot, in his commentary, 'Zeraʿ Ephraim', printed in the Lvov edn. of *PesR* (1853).

the proof?—That which is said in the passage, 'Cries, she cries (*bakhoh tibkeh*) in the night' (Lam. 1: 2).[144]

The three uses of *kiv.* in this homily appear to be euphemistic; and since they disturb the syntax and sense of the passage, may be secondary additions. This notwithstanding, the primary teaching evokes great mythic pathos. It appears that the word *menuḥati* is used here as a substantive term for God's indwelling presence, the *Shekhinah* (presumably called here 'My Indwelling'). After the destruction, the Holy One leaves this earthly modality of the divine presence and withdraws to heaven. The teaching stresses that there is crying below and on high—and this is taken to be the crying of the *Shekhinah* on earth and the Holy One in heaven. The scriptural proof for this event is the phrase *bakhoh tibkeh* (Lam. 1: 2)—understood here not as a stylistic construction that marks a verbal intensification ('She shall surely cry'), but as a twofold clause: 'He (The Holy One) cries, when She (the *Shekhinah*) cries.'

What is theologically remarkable and unique here is the presentation of God in terms of male (transcendent) and female (immanent) modalities which separated after the destruction—the assumption being that the two were conjoined when the Temple stood. On the formal level, this division integrates different midrashim which alternatively depict the *Shekhinah* remaining on earth after the destruction, and God as ascending to the heavenly world (see above, pp. 157–9). But the result is most striking, and anticipates features found in a variety of later Kabbalistic sources (see pp. 296–9)

(ii) *ME 1* (B, 59). This is a more condensed version of the preceding teaching. Hereby, the phrase, 'Cries, she cries', is explained and applied.

She cries and causes others to cry (*bokhah u-mebakkah*); (meaning,) she cries and *kivyakhol* causes the Holy One, blessed be He, to cry.

In this teaching, various 'others' are presumed to have cried.[145] Arguably, this version does not go as far as b(i) (above), since here it is Zion that cries, not the *Shekhinah*. The use of the term *kiv.* may be secondary here (as also above), and was added to temper the notion that Zion influences God's emotions. Notably, *kiv.* does not occur in the version found in *LamR* 1.23 (D).

(iii) *MZ Lamentations 18* (B, 59). In the context of divine mourning and sorrow, the angels instruct God in the proper praxis—one feature of which is tears. God responds:

I too shall cry day and night, as it is said: 'And I shall cry day and night for the slain of my people' (Jer. 8: 23). Who cries?—*kivyakhol*, the Holy One, blessed be He.

The citation adduced by God is arguably the voice of Jeremiah. Hence, the point is made that God is, 'as it were', the speaker. The term *kiv.* marks this exegetical presumption, whose striking depiction is the very purpose of the teaching. If *kiv.* functioned solely as a euphemistic qualfier, the rhetoric effect would be entirely eviscerated.

(iv) *MZ Lamentations (version 2) 1.20* (B, 142). After the destruction, God determines to remove His presence from Zion. The homily then adds:

[144] The 'passage' refers to the scroll of Lamentations, recited on Tishaʿ be-ʾAb.

[145] On the basis of Isa. 22: 12, first God and the angels were interpreted as crying. In addition, the tears of the heavenly bodies and earthly elements were adduced, with proofs brought from Joel 2: 10 and Jer. 4: 23–4 (B, 60).

> *kivyakhol* the Holy One, blessed be He, cried and said: What have I done that I have caused My *Shekhinah* to dwell below for Israel?

God goes on to lament that He will now withdraw and fears being a laughing stock before the nations. In this case, the term *kiv.* expresses a pious qualification and has no apparent exegetical function.

(v) *MZ Lamentations (version 2) 1:3* (B, 74). In conjunction with divine sorrow and the rejected angelic attempts at consolation,[146] R. Joshua b. Levi states:

> From the day the Temple was destroyed and Jerusalem laid waste, the Holy One, blessed be He, has no joy—*kivyakhol* until the Temple and Jerusalem shall be rebuilt and Israel returned to its midst; as it is said, 'I shall rejoice over Jerusalem and be happy for My people, and the sound of weeping and wailing shall not be heard any more' (Isa. 65: 19).

The use of *kiv.* does not qualify the present divine sorrow, but marks its future cessation on the basis of Isa. 65: 19. In that verse, God's joy is stated explicitly; whereas the end of sorrow, applied in the prophecy to the nation alone, is understood in the midrash as pertaining to God.

R. Joshua b. Levi is A1.

The expression that God 'had no joy' recurs elsewhere with *kiv.*, but only as pious insertions and without any exegetical function. Various reasons are given: (1) the death of the wicked, noted in *MdRI Beshallaḥ 1* (H–R, 118), *MdRS* (E–M, 72), and *Tan Beshallaḥ 10.1*;[147] and (2) because of various considerations bearing on the state of the world, noted in *LevR 20.2 'Aḥarei Mot* (MM, 450), *Tan 'Aḥarei Mot* 21 (also Ca, *Tan Shemini 3*, and *MidPs 148.4* (B, 538)).

(vi) *SER 28* (MIS, 154). In the context of dealing with divine sorrow and tears, the special character of God's feelings is underscored:

> 'My eye must stream and flow with tears' (Jer. 13: 17)—*kivyakhol* there is no being more compassionate for Israel than the Holy One, blessed be He, alone.

The term *kiv.* appears to qualify this concrete assertion of divine compassion. Alternatively, it may mark the presumptive attribution of Jeremiah's human speech to God.

c. God's cry of 'Woe' (i) *PdRK Eicha 15.4* (BM, 251 f.). R. Yoḥanan (A2) likened the successive exiles of the nation to a king who punished and banished his sons. Just as the king lamented in woe on these occasions, so also when God exiled the ten northern tribes He recited the verse 'Woe (*'oy*) to them for they have wandered from Me' (Hos. 7: 13). And subsequently,

> When the tribes of Judah and Benjamin were exiled—*kivyakhol* the Holy One said 'Woe (*'oy*) is Me for My shattering [*shibri*]' (Jer. 10: 19).

In this teaching, the term *kiv.* occurs before the second expression of 'woe' to mark the presumptive transfer of the pronoun (from Jeremiah) to God. There is no reason to employ the term it in the first instance (Hos. 7: 13) since God is clearly the speaker. The same teaching recurs in *ME Pet 3* (B, 4).

[146] Citing Isa. 22: 4.

[147] *kiv.* > *B. Meg.* 10b; this is arguably the original formulation.

R. Yoḥanan's teaching is linked to another by his brother-in-law, R. Simeon b. Lakish. See 7b, below.

(ii) *NumR Naso' 12.7*. An interpretation of the opening word of Num. 7: 1, 'And it was (*va-yehi*) on the day that Moses completed' building the Tabernacle. The meaning of *va-yehi* is midrashically construed as a contraction of *vay hayah*, 'There was (a cry of) woe.' As to who said this,

> R. Abin said, *kivyakhol* the Holy One, blessed be He, said *vay*.

By way of explication, a parable is given of a king who had a contentious wife and had her make him a royal garment—during which time she was preoccupied and did not complain.[148] When she finished, he cried 'Woe', out of concern that she resume her contentious behaviour. In a like manner, we are told, Israel frequently complained in the desert, but ceased to do so when preoccupied with the building of the tabernacle. When they finished, God Himself cried *vay*—recalling Israel's past behaviour and hopeful that she would not resume her complaints. The term *kiv.* thus marks the injection of a divine dimension into the archival notice found in Scripture, underscoring the presumptive nature of the interpretation proposed.

R. Abin is A4.

A related version of the teaching occurs in *PesR 5 Vayehi Beyom* (MIS, 20b), though it is more opaquely rendered. The attribution here is to a R. Abba.

7. Divine Mourning

a. God observes bereavement (i) *LamR 1.1* (D, Vilna). A teaching of R. Naḥman and R. Samuel (A 3) 'in the name of R. Joshua b. Levi' (A1). God asks the ministering angels to teach Him how a human king mourns, so that He could also grieve for His people and Temple. The rites include putting on sackcloth, darkening lamps, going barefooted, overturning beds, and ripping one's robe. The proof-texts given are, respectively, Isa. 50: 3, Joel 4: 15, Dan. 7: 9, Nahum 1: 3, and Lam. 3: 17. After the citation of Dan. 7: 9, regarding overturning the bed ('As I looked on, the thrones were set up (*remiv*)'), the text adds: '*kivyakhol*, which were overturned'.

The term *kiv.* does not occur elsewhere in this teaching, nor in the versions found in *PdRK* 15.3 (BM, 250 f.) and *ME* 1.1 (B, 42 f.).[149] Possibly, *kiv.* marks the fact that the verb *remiv* is used (in the midrash) in its explicit sense ('thrown down'), and not in the applied or figurative sense of setting up furniture (found in Dan. 7: 23). The term is most likely a secondary addition, underscoring the act of divine mourning.

(ii) *Tan Shemini 1*. In this passage we learn that God observed

> seven days of mourning before He brought the flood—*kivyakhol*. And from what passage (can we deduce) that He mourned? (From the fact that it says), 'And the Lord . . . was saddened (*va-yitʿatzeb*)' (Gen. 6: 7), and the meaning of sadness (*ʿatzibah*) is mourning (*'eibel*).

The use of *kiv.* here is loose and disconnected from the exegetical application. As it stands, it appears to be a secondary or euphemistic element. The term does not occur in Ca.

[148] So also, the 'Yad Moshe'.

[149] In *PdRK*, in the name of Bar Qappara (T5); in *ME* in the name of R. Naḥman (A5).

b. God needs lamentation (i) *PdRK Eicha 15.4* (BM, 252). This teaching of Resh Lakish (A 1) follows a related one about divine suffering by R. Yoḥanan, discussed above, 6c (i). The present instruction takes a more radical position, stating that 'after the tribes of Judah and Benjamin were exiled—*kivyakhol* the Holy One, blessed be He, said: "I do not have the strength to mourn them."' God then requests professional mourners, invoking Jer. 9: 16. A bold interpretation of v. 17 follows. It emphasizes the inclusive pronoun 'us' or 'our' used in Scripture in order to mark the fact that the keeners mourn for God as well as for the people.

This teaching is translated and discussed above (pp. 170–1). The term *kiv.* appears to be euphemistic here; since it does not occur with the explanation of v. 17, where such words as *ʿaleinu* (us) are interpreted in an inclusive sense. Withal, it proleptically sets up the ensuing exegesis. A similar interpretation of *ʿaleinu* occurs in *BT Giṭṭin* 58a, in another teaching by Resh Lakish. In that case, however, the term *kiv.* does occur and marks the transition from the specific scriptural term *ʿaleinu* to its explication with reference to both God and the people.

ME Pet 3 (B, 4) gives the same teaching.

8. Divine 'Sleep'

In striking contrast to the dominant motif of divine participation in Israel's historical suffering, a number of sources portray an apparent divine disengagement from protective care—compared to sleep—during which time Israel hopes in and evokes God's arousal. This activation of divine power will result in a positive new era for Israel, and an end of their enemies and oppressors.

a. During Israel's suffering (i) *Tos. Soṭah 13.9* (TL, 234; MS Vienna 46). According to *M. Maʿaser Sheni* 5.15, Yoḥanan the High Priest abolished three things—one of which were the 'Awakeners' (*meʿorerim*). The list in *Tos. Soṭah* 13.10 is different, and the reference in 13.9 simply says: 'These are the Levites, who recited on the (Temple) dais, "Arise, Why do You sleep, O YHWH?" (Ps. 44: 24).' The specific time and purpose is not indicated.[150] Instead, an exegetical teaching is given by R. Yoḥanan b. Zakkai.

> And does He sleep? Is it not already stated, 'Surely He shall neither slumber nor sleep' (Ps. 121: 4). Rather (understand it): Whenever Israel is in sorrow and the nations of the world are at ease—*kivyakhol*, 'Arise, why do You sleep?'

R. Yoḥanan resolves the contradiction between Pss. 44: 24 and 121: 4 by means of a metaphorical interpretation. The term *kiv.* marks the shift to the more figurative undertanding of God's withdrawal and arousal. Indeed, its present function as an epexegetical ligature is clear from the formulation in the Erfurt MS (TL, 233), where the term *kiv.* is absent and the verb 'they recite' occurs. This version gives the recitation an exhortative tone that is much stronger and more concrete. Moreover, following the initial condition ('When Israel is in sorrow'), the Levitical recitation assumes a somewhat time-bound character.[151]

[150] See the full discussion above, pp. 177–8.

[151] The version in *BT Soṭah* 48a has the same effect. It, too, is without the term *kiv.*; but instead of the ligature 'they recite' we have 'for that reason it was said'. Presumably, this shift is due to the redactors' sense that since reference to the abrogation of the Awakeners is mentioned earlier, the recitation is a thing of the past.

(ii) *JT Soṭah 9.11, 24a* offers a version that is set within the context of activities of Yoḥanan the High Priest, but does not indicate a reform against the Awakeners; and the teaching on Ps. 44: 24 is given anonymously. The first part is basically like the toseftan passage, where a textual contradiction is raised. However, in this case, another verse is added:

> Why then does Scripture say, 'The Lord awoke like one who sleeps' (Ps. 78: 65)? Rather (understand it): *kivyakhol*, as if He sleeps when Israel is in sorrow, etc.

Hereby a different rhetorical strategy was followed. By introducing Ps. 78: 65 with its simile ('like one who sleeps') the redactor has prepared for a qualified reading of the divine sleep mentioned in Ps. 44: 24. Now the sleep is deemed entirely figurative. The added qualifier *keʾilu* ('as if') shows just how a later scribe wanted the term *kiv.* to be taken.

Use of the sleep motif in connection with the topos 'When Israel is in straits and the nations at ease' provides a sharp contrast with those teachings where this topos is used to introduce God's participation in Israel's travail (e.g. *PdRK 17.5* (D.3(i))).[152]

R. Yoḥanan b. Zakkai (T1) is explicitly the teacher of the midrash only in the toseftan version, MS Vienna 46. He is mentioned in JT as reporting the deeds of Yoḥanan the High Priest; hence, he could be construed as speaking the midrash there, as well.

b. Before the Redemption (i) *MidPs 59.5* (B, 303). The lemma discussed is Ps. 59: 6, 'O You, YHWH, God of Hosts, God of Israel, bestir Yourself (*haqitzah*) to bring all the nations to account; have no mercy on any treacherous evildoer.' This exhortation is explicated as follows:

> (It is) because in this world the Holy One, blessed be He, makes Himself as one who sleeps. And why?—Since it is not time that they (i.e. Israel) be redeemed; as it is said, 'And He awoke (*va-yiqatz*) as one who sleeps' (Ps. 78: 65). But in the future, when the end (*ha-qetz*) shall come—*kivyakhol*, the Holy One, blessed be He, is aroused (*neiʿor*); as is said, 'Bestir Yourself to bring all the nations to account.' At that time, 'Have no mercy on any treacherous evildoer.'

The term *haqitzah* (in the lemma), *va-yiqatz* in the citation, and *ha-qetz* in the reference to future time establish the temporal coordinates of this midrash (present plea; present reality; future time). The terms are used to indicate that God in the present makes Himself 'as' one who is asleep. He is thereupon evoked by the imperative *haqitzah*—meaning here both, 'bestir Yourself' *and* 'bring about the end'. The term *kiv.* mediates this double sense for the verb. The semblance of divine sleep serves as an indication of divine absence in this world; and it provides the metaphorical basis for hope in God's immediate engagement with the enemy.

This teaching also occurs in *YalShim* §777; but it is > in various MSS, and in the *ed. prin.* (Venice, 1546).

(ii) *MidPs 78.18* (B, 356). A condensed paraphrase of b(i), though God's future arousal is as if from a wine-stupor.

[152] Discussed above, pp. 147–50. Cf. also M, 3.2, p. 45 (with *kiv.*); and similarly in *Batei Midrashot*, ed. A. Wertheimer (Jerusalem: Ketav Ve-Sefer, 1980), ii. 103.

(iii) *MidPs 121.3* (B, 505f.). An expansion of earlier traditions, with proofs why there can be 'neither sitting nor sleeping on High'. Having established this point, the query is then posed:

> But what (is the meaning) of 'Let Your guardian not slumber'? Just that: *kivyakhol*, it is from the afflictions that befall Israel in the world that the Holy One, blessed be He, sleeps.

In this version, the lemma (Ps. 121: 3) is taken to mean that although God 'sleeps' and is disengaged from the troubles of the world, *loʾ yanum ve-loʾ yishan*—He will neither slumber nor sleep in the world to come. The force of the term *kiv.* is thus apparently to mark this exegesis. This construal of the verb in the future sense (rather than as a present conditional) adds a further exegetical dimension to the meaning of Ps. 121: 3.

V. GOD AND HUMAN ACTION

A. Gracious Kindness and Forgiveness

1. God 'Forgets' Sin

(i) *PdRK Ki Tissaʾ 2.7* (BM, 26f.). The homily links the verse that immediately precedes this lection, dealing with atonement (Exod. 30: 10), with the opening injunction of this unit: 'When (*ki*) you raise up (or, count, *tissaʾ*)... the Israelites' (ibid., v. 12). Exod. 30: 10 thus serves to establish the overall thematic focus of the homily; whereas v. 12 deals with the specific issue of concern. The scriptural citation adduced (v. 12) does not, however, follow the MT spelling *tsʾ*, but has *tsh*—a consonantal cluster that may be read *taššeh*, 'lend'. This latter reading is then midrashically tallied with the same verb in Deut. 24: 10 (dealing with loans). On the basis of this hermeneutical revision of Exod. 30: 12, Moses is presumed to have addressed God as follows:

> 'When Israel has merits (for atonement), let them alone'; but when they do not have such merit—*kivyakhol* lend them credit (*hinnasheh*) once a year, so that the Day of Atonement will come and provide atonement, 'For by means of (lit. "on"; *ba-*) this day atonement shall be made for you' (Lev. 16: 30).

The homily boldly transforms a divine rule dealing with counting into an appeal of intercession by Moses. The term *kiv.* marks the midrashic reading of the written orthography of Scripture known to the homilist and its application to an appeal for divine grace. It is unlikely that the term *kiv.* functions here to qualify God's ability to grant merit, for this would undermine the entire force of Moses' request. It would also contradict a feature of normative rabbinic theology; indeed, elsewhere God is asked to forgive unilaterally, if necessary, without the precondition of human repentence (cf. *BT Yoma* 86a).

The MT spelling *tissaʾ* is found in *MhG Ki Tissaʾ* (M, 641), but the verb *taššeh* is implied since the teaching invokes God to 'forgive them—*kivyakhol*, once a year'. In *TanB Ki Tissaʾ* and *YalShim Ki Tissaʾ* (§ 386), neither *tissaʿ* nor *taššeh* occurs. None the less, a trace of the older sense may still be preserved insofar as God tells Moses to 'go do it' (*zekofʾoto*; i.e. the act of atonement) immediately. Significantly, the verb *zakaf* is often used by the ancient rabbis to refer to the establishment or erection of a loan (cf.

SifreDeut. 34; *BT Metzi'a'* 72a). However, in these two cases Moses does not act as an intercessor on behalf of Israel; and the term *kiv.* does not occur.

(ii) *PdRK 25.2 Seliḥot* (BM, 381). In the context of extended explications of the divine attributes in Exod. 34: 6–7, the term *nose' 'avon* ('forgives sins') is taken up. Among the interpretations, we read:

> R. Ḥuna (taught) in the name of R. Abbahu—*kivyakhol*, there is no forgetting (*shikheḥah*) before Him; yet for Israel He becomes forgetful. What is the proof? 'Who is a God like You, *nose' 'avon* and passing by transgression' (Micah 7: 19).

In this terse teaching, *nose'* is midrashically construed as *nošeh*, 'forgetting' (cf. Gen. 41: 51); and the second phrase of the proof-text from Micah is assumed to reinforce the point. The use of the term *kiv.* here is somewhat opaque, since it qualifies the fact that God does not forget, but does not qualify the more radical point. One must therefore prefer the version in *JT Sanh. 10.1, 27c*, where *kiv.* immediately precedes the words 'yet for Israel' (and also *JT Sheb. 1.6, 33c*). While the term may be taken as offering a qualification here, as well, it may more likely mark the midrashic presumption attributed to God (i.e. that He forgives Israel). The midrash is spelled out in the version in *JT Sanh.* There after the query concerning the proof, we have the clause: '*nosheh 'avon* ("He forgets sin")—but the text writes *nose'*.' But as this explication interrupts the query from the proof itself, it may be secondary or misplaced. By comparison, *PdRK* is remarkably (and perhaps intentionally) laconic. Another variant occurs in *MidPs 32.2* (B, 242).

R. Ḥuna here is presumably R. Ḥuna b. Abin (A4). He received the teaching from R. Abbahu (A3). The same tradents appear in *JT Sanh* (R. Abbahu) and *MidPs* (R. Ḥuna in the name of R. Abbahu).

(iii) *Midrash Ḥaser Ve-Yater.*[153]

> Every (occurrence of) *nose'* (forgiving creatures) is written with (the letter) *shin.* Why? Whereas forgetting occurs among humans, with regard to the Holy One, blessed be He, (it says) 'Who is a God like You, who forgives (*nose'*) transgression?' (Micah 7: 19). Why (is it written) with a *shin*? (To teach) that even though there is no forgetting with Him—*kivyakhol*, He causes the transgressions of Israel to be forgotten.

This formulation specifies the orthographic issue, and agrees with the theological content noted in (i)–(ii). The term *kiv.* marks the exegetical presumption.

2. God Forgives the Repentant

(i) *MdRI Beshalaḥ 3* (H–R, 166). In connection with a discussion about the meaning of the manna, described 'as hoar frost' (*ka-kefor*),

> R. Ṭarfon says, It only came down upon the hands of those who gathered it (*ha-'osfim*).[154] '*ka-kefor* upon the earth'—*kivyakhol* God stretched forth His hand and received the prayers of our ancestors who lay in the dust of the earth; and He

[153] Text printed in *OM*, i. 195b; repr. from A. Berliner, *Pletath Soferim* (Breslau, 1872), 36 ff. (Hebrew section).

[154] With Ox2 and M2; H–R with *D* reads *ha-'ofsim* (presumably a metathesis of the *s/f*). The emendation of I. Löw to *'iskufim*, 'thresholds', in 'Lexicalische Mizellen', *Festschrift zum siebzigsten Geburtstage David Hoffmanns* (Berlin, 1914), 199 f., is unjustified.

thereupon brought down the manna for Israel. As it says, 'Then He has mercy upon him, and decrees: "Redeem him from descending into the Pit; for I have obtained a ransom (*kofer*)" ' (Job 33: 24).

R. Ṭarfon (T2) teaches that the manna that descended upon Israel was given in response to the prayers of the ancestors. He apparently construes the scriptural phrase *ka-kefor* as *ke-kippur* ('as a ransom' or 'as an atonement').[155] That is, the prayers resulted in divine forgiveness and atonement and culminated in the physical gift of the manna. Alternatively, God receives the *kofer* (ransom) of intercessory or supplicatory prayers of the dead ancestors—and the complaining people receive *kippur* (atonement) and the gift of manna in return. On either reading, the term *kiv.* would seem to mark the bold theological meaning given to *ka-kefor* rather than serving to qualify God's reception of intercessory prayer.

MdRS (E–M, 110) has a similar reading.[156]

3. God Overlooks Sin

(i) *PdRK 24.13 Shubah* (BM, 370). A condensed exposition of Job 11: 11 is preserved.

R. Issaḥar of Kefar Mandi interpreted 'For He knows false men, He sees iniquity but will not consider it' (Job 11: 11). It is man's way in the world to heap up piles and piles of transgressions; but if he repents—*kivyakhol*, 'He sees iniquity but will not consider it'

In this teaching the two phrases of the verse are exegetically transformed. According to the plain sense, the opening assertion of divine providence is reinforced by a rhetorical query: 'And if He sees iniquity, will He not consider it?' R. Issaḥar transforms the two phrases into a dramatic contrast: in the first part, God knows human iniquity; but the second part boldly indicates God's merciful overlooking of transgressions, if a person has repented. The term *kiv.* marks this exegetical presumption in which standard theology is taught through a hermeneutical rereading of the verse. It is unlikely that the term *kiv.* simply qualifies standard rabbinic theology about divine mercy.

The version in *MidPs* 5.8 (B, 54) is without *kiv.* and provides a fuller explication of the dynamic of human repentence and divine mercy. However, as only the second phrase of Job 11: 11 is cited, the radical rereading is obscured, and the quoted unit fits in with standard theology. The absence of the full exposition would explain the absence of the term *kiv.* in this case.[157]

B. Prayer and Intercession

1. God to Himself

(i) *MidPs 76.3* (B, 341). On the verse 'And His booth was in Shalem (*va-yehi be-shalem sukko*), and His dwelling in Zion' (Ps. 76: 3).

155 This construal of *ke-kofer* is presumed by the gloss of the Gaon of Vilna: 'This teaches that the sins of Israel were atoned for (*nitkapperu*)'. See *'Efat Tzedeq'*; and cf. *'Birkat Havetzib'*.

156 However, it reads *ha-'ofsiyim*—an even more incomprehensible version of *D* (see n. 154).

157 The reference to this teaching in *JT Rosh Hashanah* 1.3, 57a is apocopated, and without the exposition.

R. Berekhia said: From the beginning of the creation of the world, the Holy One, blessed be He, made a booth (Temple) in Jerusalem—*kivyakhol* He would pray in it (thus): May it be (*yehi ratzon*) that My children do My will (*retzoni*) so that I do not destroy My House and Shrine... And when it was destroyed He (would) pray in it, May it be favourable before Me (*yehi ratzon milefanai*) that My children repent so that I may hasten the building of My House and Shrine. Indeed, *yehi be-shalem sukko*.

In this exposition, the Temple is projected back to the creation and God prays for the obedience of His children—so that His Shrine should not be destroyed. The term *kiv.* marks the transition betwen the prologue of the primordial Temple and God's ongoing prayer. Presumably, then, *va-yehi be-shalem sukko* was triply instructive. In the first instance, the lemma was taken to mean 'His booth (Temple) was in Shalem (i.e. Jerusalem)'—from the beginning of creation. However, on the basis of the two cases of God's prayerful petition (*yehi*), we may understand that the lemma was understood as stating God's hope that His Temple 'be' whole (*shalem*) in Zion—namely, that it *remain* complete, and not be destroyed; and (after the disaster) that it *become* complete once again. In these two cases, *va-yehi* would have been construed as the optative: *viyhi*, 'may it (the Temple) be'. In the first case the appeal invokes obedience, lest the Temple be destroyed; in the second it invokes repentance, that the Temple be rebuilt.

Hence the power of the exposition is not only the divine prayer itself, but the reinterpretation of the lemma *as* a divine prayer. The term *kiv.* marks this exegetical presumption.

The version of R. Berekhia's exposition of Ps. 76: 3 in *GenR* 56.10 (T–A, 608) is abbreviated and adapted to other purposes. In it, R. Berekhia (A5) taught in the name of R. Ḥelbo (A4) that God built a booth in Shalem in the time of Abraham, and prayed therein that this patriarch might see the building of the Temple. The daring thrust of the *MidPs* version does not occur in this case, and the lemma is given an unremarkable application. The term *kiv.* is not used.

2. God and Moses

(i) *DeutR 3.15*. The subject is Moses' entreaty of divine favour after the sin of the Golden Calf (Exod. 32: 11). Moses is portrayed as telling God that he knows of His love for Israel and desire for someone to speak on their behalf. R. Simeon (ben Pazzi? A3) offers a parable of a king who argued with his son and cried out, '*haniḥah li* (leave me be) that I may kill my son'—but really wanted someone to intercede on the son's behalf. This is applied to Israel's sin and God's wrath.

Thus the Holy One, blessed be He, said to Moses: '*haniḥah li* that I become angry against them and destroy them' (Exod. 32: 10). Whereupon Moses thought, Am I holding (*tofes*) onto the hand of the Holy One, blessed be He, that He said 'leave Me be'?—*kivyakhol* He is requesting someone to speak on their (Israel's) behalf. Hence, immediately thereafter, 'Moses entreated YHWH' (ibid., v. 11).

This striking homily tries to contextualize the sequence of actions in vv. 10–11. The divine divine cry *haniḥah li* is deemed puzzling to R. Simeon. Why would God request Moses to let Him destroy Israel *before* Moses did anything to prevent this? (In the homily, this point is thematized by Moses' deliberation when he construes the phrase *hanihah li* as read concretely—as if God asked Moses to leave Him alone!) Moses thus draws the conclusion that *hanihah li* is, in fact, a divine request whereby God says: 'Assuage Me' or 'Calm Me down (by speaking on the people's behalf) lest I get angry, etc.' The term *kiv.* marks this presumptive reinterpretation of God's command as a bold request. Moses' supplication follows.

DtRL 'Eqeb 1.15. (SL, p. 90) has the same tradition.

In *BT Ber.* 32a, R. Abbahu (A3) interprets *hanihah li* to be God's command to Moses to 'let go' of him, since Moses was 'holding' (*tofes*) onto Him as one holds onto a garment. (The term *kiv.* is not used here, since the contextual meaning of the term is not transformed, but only read more concretely.) In *DeutR 3.15* R. Simeon uses this motif, but rejects it in favour of a request by God for Moses to calm His wrath.

C. Human Action and Divine Effect

1. Doing God's Will (General)

a. Affects divine protection (i) *MdRI Beshalah 5* (H–R, 134). An anonymous interpretation of Exod. 15: 6, where the phrase 'Your right hand (*yeminkha*), O YHWH' is followed by a second reference to God's 'right hand' in the next bi-colon. This is explained:

> When Israel does (*'osin*) the will of the Omnipresent,[158] they make (*'osin*) the left (hand) a right (hand); as is stated, '*yeminkha YHWH, yeminkha YHWH*' twice. But when Israel does not do the will of the Omnipresent, *kivyakhol* they make the right (hand) a left (hand); as it says, 'He put His right hand (*yemino*) behind Him' (Lam. 2: 3).

Doing the commands of God affects His protection of Israel. This is part of a varied theology of the powerful effects of human action.[159] The term *kiv.* only appears in this teaching to mark the negative pole, as is common in midrashic teachings of this type.[160] From a hermeneutical standpoint, the second proof-text is more presumptive than the first, and this may explain the occurrence of *kiv.* here. However, this term is not well attested in texts and MSS (> MH, Ox 2, *YalShim*, and *MdRS* (E–M, 84)). It is also frequently absent in the other examples of this type (see below). *Tan Beshalah 15* is like *MdRI*.

(ii) ibid. (H–R, 134). A teaching of the preceding type. It states that when Israel obeys God, He does not sleep (proved by Ps. 121: 10); but when they do not,

> *kivyakhol* He does sleep, as it says, 'YHWH was aroused like one who had been sleeping' (Ps. 78: 65).

The term *kiv.* occurs only in the negative position, which is also the one with the bolder and more presumptive exegesis (the positive position simply reaffirms Scripture). However, the term is missing in many MSS, and is thus an unstable element. It may therefore be used here as a euphemistic qualification of God's inactivity.

158 For this term, see Urbach, *The Sages*, 66–9.

159 See above, pp. 173–90; and further on in this section. This theurgical theology is thus, presumably, at least tannaitic in age.

160 In addition to 1.a(i), see below for other examples (1.a(ii–v); b(i); c(i); d(i–iii); e(i); 2.c(i–iv); e(i)).

(iii) *Midrash Panim ʾAḥeirim* (*B*) (B, 74).[161] The reference to the 'sleep of the king' in Est. 6: 1 is identified allegorically with 'the sleep of the Supreme King of kings, the Holy One, blessed be He'.[162] And on the substantive issue, the query is posed:

> And is there sleep on High? Rather (understand it thus): When Israel sins, *kivyakhol* He makes Himself like one who sleeps; as it says, 'Arise, why do You sleep?' (Ps. 44: 24). But when Israel does the will of the Omnipresent, 'Behold, the Guardian of Israel neither slumbers nor sleeps' (Ps. 121: 4).

Like the preceding case, this teaching sees the 'sleep' topos in conjunction with Israel's observance of the commandments. As in other cases of this type, the term *kiv.* is in the negative position[163] though in this instance it occurs first, not second. However, the fit between the topos and the proof-text in the first part is weak; a citation from Ps. 78: 65 (with its simile, 'like one who has been sleeping' would have been more fitting, given the statement that God makes Himself 'like one who sleeps' (see (ii) above).[164]

(iv) *SifNum 157, Maṭṭot* (H, 211). Another teaching of the previous type. It states that when Israel obeys, God fights for them;[165] but when they do not,

> *kivyakhol* He fights against them; as it says, 'He turned into their enemy, He fought against them' (Isa. 63: 10).

The term *kiv.* is found only in the second position;[166] and it may be a scribal addition here, since it is hermeneutically extraneous. Scripture makes the case explicitly—even stating that the change is due to disobedience. The term *kiv.* does not occur in *MdRI Beshallaḥ* 5 and *Tan Beshallaḥ* 15

The idea that whenever Israel does God's will, He aids them, but when they do not, He is their enemy, is presented in *SifNum* 157 as a theological principle (*kelal*) and adduced in connection with the lemma, 'Yet they (the females) are the very ones who, at the bidding of Balaam', led the people astray (Num. 31: 16). According to the homily, Balaam counselled the Midianites to lead the Israelites into perversity as the only way to destroy them—for he said that if Israel sinned their God would be angry and punish them Himself. After the principle, the midrash repeats the point with another proof-text: 'Moreover (if Israel disobeys God), they make the Merciful One cruel; as it says, "YHWH became an enemy and destroyed (*billaʿ*) Israel" (Lam. 2: 5). This verse alludes to the opening lemma from Num. 31: 16, and suggests that the name Balaam (Hebrew, *bilʿam*) was interpreted as an allusion to the fact that it was God Himself who 'destroyed them' (*billeʿam*; i.e. the Israelites) for their sins.

This second proof (and the summary principle) was carried over to the list in *MdRI Beshalaḥ* 5, where it seems extraneous.[167] Hence the entire unit about God becoming

[161] In *Sifrei de-ʾAgaddeta ʿal Megillat ʾEster*, ed. S. Buber (Vilna: Romm, 1886).

[162] Cf. *BT Meg.* 15b, in the name of R. Tanḥum: 'The sleep of the King of the world'.

[163] See above, n. 160.

[164] I have translated *yashein* differently, in these cases, to bring out the temporal modalities implied.

[165] Here, 'does His will', not 'does the will of the Omnipresent', as in (i) and (ii).

[166] See n. 160.

[167] It is the only use of this rhetorical type with a second proof.

an enemy is probably secondary there, and its primary example concerning God's right hand in *MdRI* (C.1a(i)) was subsequently supplemented by an anthology of similar types.

(v) *MdRI Beshalaḥ 4* (H–R, 130). On the lemma 'YHWH is a man of war' (Exod. 15: 3), the midrash compares a human warrior to God.

> With respect to a (human) warrior (*gibbor*) in the province—when an arrow departs from his hand, he cannot retrieve it; but the Holy One, blessed be He, is otherwise. When Israel does not do His will—*kivyakhol* a decree departs from Him; as is said, 'When I whet[168] (*shannoti*) My flashing sword' (Deut. 32: 41). (But if) they repent, I immediately retrieve it; as is said, 'My hand lays hold of judgement' (ibid.).

This teaching utilizes an analogy in order to laud God, who is both just and merciful—in response to human behaviour. As is common in this midrashic type, observance and non-observance are juxtaposed, with the term *kiv.* in the negative position (here given first).[169] The midrash utilizes the theme of the sword of justice as a metaphor for a decree (*gezeirah*; something 'cut'); and most probably construes *shannoti* as meaning God's 'change' from mercy to judgement.[170] The second phrase is correspondingly also given a new sense. According to the plain sense of the passage, the two *stichoi* comprise a complementary parallelism. In the midrash, the second one is interpreted as denoting God's return to mercy and restraint.[171] Altogether, the biblical image of God as a divine warrior is thoroughly transformed.

The term *kiv.* marks the allegorical reading of Deut. 32: 41. It does not occur in *MdRS* (E–M, 82).

b. Affects divine protection or withdrawal (i) *SifDeut 355 Ve-Zoʾt* (F, 422). An anonymous tannaitic midrash deals with Deut. 33: 26, 'There is none like the God of Jeshurun,[172] Who rides through the heavens to help you, through the skies in His majesty.' In the teaching, the last two clauses are not construed as a synonymous parallelism, lauding the mighty warrior Lord in heaven, but as two aspects of divine providence which respond to Israelite behaviour.

> When Israel is upright[173] and does the will of the Omnipresent, 'He rides through the heavens to help you'; but when they do not do His will, *kivyakhol* 'and in His majesty, (the) skies'.

The term *kiv.* occurs only in the second part of this rhetorical figure, which regularly indicates a negative consequence.[174] The first part uses Scripture in a straightforward manner, whereas the second part is the product of exegesis. In it, the reference to God's 'majesty' (*gaʾavato*) is boldly construed as Israel's rebellious 'pride', which results in God's withdrawal to the heights of heaven as an act of

[168] Cf. Saadia, Rashi, and Rashbam. [169] See above, n. 160.

[170] Namely, 'If I change'. The particle *ʾim* is thus construed as introducing a conditional clause (if), not a temporal one (when).

[171] In *SifDeut* 331 (F, 380 f.), the first phrase denotes the swiftness of punishment; the second, the fact that due process will be done.

[172] For the bold midrashic treatment of this phrase, see my *Exegetical Imagination*, 57–9.

[173] The adjective *yesharim* plays on the people's name *Yeshurun* (Jeshurun).

[174] See n. 160.

punishment and rejection.[175] The term *kiv.* marks this hermeneutical presumption; otherwise, its function is opaque.[176]

c. Affects divine strength or weakness (i) *LamR i.6, 33* (*D*, Vilna). Two teachings are given for Lam. 1: 6, 'And they went without strength (*belo' koaḥ*) before the pursuer'.

(1) R. Azariah said in the name of R. Judah b. R. Simon: When Israel does the will of the Omnipresent (*Maqom*), they increase (*mosifin*) strength (*koaḥ*) in the *dynamis* (*geburah*) on high;[177] as it is said, 'We shall make strength (*ḥayil*) in God' (Ps. 60: 14). But when Israel does not do the will of the Omnipresent, *kivyakhol* they weaken (*metishin*) the great strength (*koaḥ gadol*) on High; as it is said, 'You have forgotten (*teshi*) the Rock who bore you' (Deut. 32: 18).[178]

(2) R. Judah b. R. Simon said in the name of R. Levi b. R. Ṭarfon: When Israel does the will of the Holy One, blessed be He, they increase strength in the *dynamis* on High; as it is said, 'And now, let the strength (*koaḥ*) of YHWH be made great' (Num. 14: 17). But when Israel does not do the will of the Holy One, blessed be He, *kivyakhol* they weaken the great strength on High, and they also go 'without strength before the pursuer'.

In these two similar traditions about increase or decrease of the divine *geburah*, the term *kiv.* occurs only in connection with the second, negative consequence[179]—even though the positive positions are equally bold. It should be noted that the proof-texts in positive positions presume no midrashic changes. By contrast, the negative consequences in (1) presume the reading *teshi* (from the stem *nšy*, 'forget') as if it were from *twš* ('weaken', as in *metishin*);[180] hence in this instance *kiv.* marks an exegetical presumption. Oddly, the term *kiv.* in (2) appears separated from the proof-text, which is now adduced as a plain sense reference to the flight of Israel (Lam. 1: 6). This doubling of the negative consequences (for God and for Israel), and the appearance of the term *kiv.* only in connection with the divine effect (note that the second consequence is set off by a 'they also' clause), gives the teaching about divine weakening an apparent euphemistic dimension.

These two traditions are also found in *PdRK 25.1 Seliḥot* (BM, 380) with various differences. One will note that the teaching in *PdRK* 25.1 (1) and *LamR* 1.6 (1) have the same tradents as *LamR* (1), but that the *PdRK* unit focuses on 'the righteous' (not Israel), and uses Num. 14: 17 as the proof-text.[181] In addition, teaching (2) in *PdRK* gives a variant version of the father of R. Levi (referred to here as Parṭa'),[182] and uses

[175] My interpretation of this phrase here differs from that found in *Exegetical Imagination*, p. 60, where I suggested that God's Majesty ascended to the heights. For this latter view, see R. David Pardo, *Peirush Sifre de-Bei Rab, ad loc*; repr. with an edition of *Sifre* (Jerusalem: Lev Sameaḥ Institute, 1990), iv. 317.

[176] The term *kiv.* is a stable feature in the MSS.

[177] Regarding the *dynamis* as the divine Power or Might, see above, p. 180 and n. 82.

[178] Translating the lemma according to the plain sense; see further, below.

[179] As customary with this rhetorical form; cf. n. 160.

[180] A by-form of the term *tšš*.

[181] Also the terminology is more terse, stating only *geburah*—without the words 'on High'. In *LamR*, 'on high' is written with slight variations (*ma'alah/ma'alan*).

[182] The two names (Ṭarfon/Parṭa') are apparently scribal metatheses of each other.

Ps. 60: 14 as the proof-text in the positive first part. These are not substantial differences. By contrast, it is notable that *PdRK* (2) cites Lam. 1: 6 solely in connection with a decrease in divine strength. This results in a different conclusion from the one noted earlier in *LamR*. Rather than suggesting different consequences for God and Israel, one is led to the conclusion that 'Israel went before the pursuer' into exile because there was 'no strength' in the divine *dynamis* to protect her. If this is correct, the term *kiv.* in *PdRK* (2) marks this strong midrashic presumption about God's impotence. By contrast, *LamR* (2) shows a weakened use of the proof-text—linking it solely to Israel's exile.[183]

The overall relationship between *LamR* and *PdRK* is fairly complex, and leads to ambivalent and complicated conclusions.[184] The present instance is a case in point, and it is arguably best to regard the two pair of traditions as two variations of a common type—with each one evincing primary exegetical features along with secondary scribal adjustments. For example, among its primary features *LamR 1.6* has two symmetrical traditions about Israel's actions; and preserves the older DN *Maqom* (Omnipresent) in (1).[185] On the other hand, the formula *koaḥ geburah* (strength of the *dynamis*) has been expanded by the word 'on High' in (1) and (2); and the conclusion to (2) refers to both God *and* Israel, thereby breaking the symmetry of the rhetorical structure (dealing with the effects of human behaviour upon God).

For its part, *PdRK 25.1* has a symmetrical structure in the second portion; and does not have the word 'on High' in either teaching. These are its primary features. On the other hand, teachings (1) and (2) evince asymmetrical elements, insofar as (1) speaks only about the deeds of the righteous and (2) only about those of Israel. This variation is undoubtedly due to the impact of the opening rhetorical sequence of the pericope, which refers to the triad Moses—the Righteous—Israel. Were *PdRK* the primary version overall, the reference to the righteous would presumably have been carried over to *LamR*; moreover, the conclusion to *PdRK* speaks about exile and redemption—a topic that is irrelevant to its purposes, but is entirely befitting *LamR*. One may therefore conclude that a version like that preserved in *LamR* influenced the incorporation of the exilic features now found in *PdRK*, but without either its stylistic expansions or its theological softening.

R. Azariah is A5; R. Judah b. R. Simeon (ben Pazzi) is A4. No R. Levi with either patronymic is known. If the name Ṭarfon is original, it is first attested by the Ṭanna R. Ṭarfon (T2) and possibly related to the Greek name Tryphon.

d. Affects divine realm in heaven (i) *SifDeut 346, Zo't* (F, 403). A comment on the phrase 'together (*yaḥad*) the tribes of Israel' (Deut. 33: 5) evokes a comment on the benefit of national unity, which by implication establishes God as King in Jeshurum (the beginning of the lemma). The comment uses the phrase *'aguddah 'aḥat* ('one band'), and this language is correlated with Amos 9: 6, 'Who (God) builds His

[183] The formulation in *ME 1.6* (B, 70) is even weaker. In it, the second position states: 'But when they anger Him, "they go without strength before the enemy".' This revision aligns the passage with more normative rabbinic theology about the sovereignty of God.

[184] See Jos. Abrahams, *The Sources of the Midrash Echah Rabba* (Dessau: H. Neubürgen, 1881 (doctoral diss., Leipzig)), 45–59.

[185] On the antiquity of this epithet, and variants in the MSS, see Urbach, *The Sages*, 67 f., 77.

chambers in heaven and establishes His vaults (*ʾaguddato*) on earth'[186]—presumably to make the same point. Rabbi Simeon bar Yochai (T3) then explicates the theological import of this verse (and its reiteration of the effect of national unity upon God) by a parable about how separate boats can provide the basis for a residence to be built upon them, if they are lashed together. This parable is then applied it to Israel:

> When they do the will of the Omnipresent, He builds His upper chambers in heaven; but if they do not do His will, *kivyakhol* 'He establishes His vaults on earth.'

This application is puzzling, since the second half of Amos 9: 6 should make a negative point—as is common in this rhetorical type, where the term *kiv.* appears in the second position.[187] R. David Pardo tellingly observed that the language here is 'garbled', and went on to reconstruct the meaning on the basis of the opening (anonymous) comment on Deut. 33: 5. There the ideal of national unity is referred to by the noun *ʾaguddah* ('group, band') and divisiveness by its plural form *ʾaguddot*.[188] The teaching would thus be that when Israel collectively does God's will, God's realm is exalted above,[189] but not when the nation is religiously disobedient (and fragmented).

Following Pardo's lead, we may say that the scriptural word *ʾaguddato* (in Amos 9: 6) was understood to allude to this negative effect. On this basis, the term *kiv.* marks the midrashic presumption in which *ʾaguddato* was construed to refer to disobedient 'divisions' or 'groups' separate from God on earth. Negative or divisive behaviour by Israel was thus presumed to impede the establishment of God's realm (kingship) on high.[190]

In both *Tan Behaʿalotkha 11.2* and *MidSam 5.15* (B, 62) only the positive first part is given, regarding Israel's obedience. The term *kiv.* is found in both phrases, but now functions merely as a euphemism regarding the effects of Israelite action upon God's upper realm.

(ii) Ibid. (F, 404). At the end of a series of proofs connected to R. Simeon's teaching (above, d(i)), the establishment of the divine throne in heaven is also linked to human action (unspecified, but contextually joined to doing the will of God). The teaching states:

> 'I have raised my eyes to You, who dwell in the heavens (*ha-yoshbi ba-shamayim*)' (Ps. 123: 1). Were it not for me, *kivyakhol* You would not dwell (*yosheb*) in the heavens.

The relationship between the plain sense and its midrashic transformation is unclear. Presumably, the shift from a human acknowledgement of God's heavenly transcendence to a constitutive act of divine enthronement is based on construing the old genitive ending *-i* in *ha-yoshbi* (who dwell) as a self-referential pronoun suffix

[186] 'Vaults' is a figurative rendition for something like the 'bond' of heaven; cf. the Akkadian term *markas šamê* ('bond of heaven') in *CAD, M*, i. 283, 4a. This cognate phrase was noted by S. Paul, *Amos* (Hermeneia; Minneapolis: Fortress Press, 1991), 280 n. 77.

[187] See above, n. 160. [188] See his *Peirush*, iv. 288.

[189] It is not certain if the verb *boneh* in the midrash means that God or Israel 'builds' up the divine realm.

[190] *NumR 15.18* uses *kiv.* and specifically refers to the establishment of the divine throne 'on high'.

uttered by the speaker, such that it means 'who dwell on my account' (namely, God 'is enthroned' in heaven 'through my agency'). The term *kiv.* marks the exegetical explication of the genitive ending in the lemma as the pronoun 'me' (*'ani*), and with it the great presumption that affects divine sovereignty.[191]

(iii) *MZ Songs 1.1* (B, 9). In a discussion of songs recited by the angelic host, it is said that the angels spoke of God's glory (in Isa. 6: 8) in order to indicate (*inter alia*) that:

> If His nation does not enthrone Him on earth, *kivyakhol* He has no kingdom in the highest heavens.

The passage goes on to indicate that when Israel recites the *Shemaʿ*-prayer below, proclaiming divine sovereignty there (Deut. 6: 4), they give the angels permission to proclaim His sovereignty above (Isa. 6: 2).[192] This is a lapidary use of the term *kiv.*, transparently euphemistic, and does not mark any exegetical feature.

MZ Songs 3.11 (B, 30) gives a more expansive version of this topos (also with the term *kiv.*). Just prior to that reference, Songs 3: 11 is used to introduce a lapidary formulation of crowning God with the crown of kingship (also with *kiv.*). See similarly in *AgSongs* 3.1 (SS, 34).

e. Affects the divine Name (i) *MdRI, Beshalaḥ 3* (H–R, 128). Commenting on Exod. 15: 3, R. Simeon b. Eleazar (T4) taught:

> When Israel does the will of the Omnipresent, His Name becomes great (*mitgaddel*) in the world; as it says... (Josh. 5: 1 and 2: 10–11 are cited, respectively); but when they do not do His will—*kivyakhol* His Name is desecrated (*mitḥallel*) in the world; as it is said, 'But when they came to these nations,[193] they caused My holy Name to be desecrated (*vayiḥallelu*)...' (Ezek. 36: 20–3).

This is a tannaitic teaching of the 'When Israel does the will' type, with positive-negative valences; and as is common to this form, only the negative implication has *kiv.*[194] However, in this instance the proof-text from Ezek. 36: 20–3 states the point of desecration explicitly and no midrashic interpretation is involved. Hence, the term *kiv.* qualifies neither the content nor the exegesis; it was presumably added to conform to the general rhetorical type.[195] Notably, *kiv.* is not found in Ox2, M2, and YalShim; nor in MdRS (E–M, 80). The topic of enhancement and desecration of the divine Name focuses here on God's reputation. This is different from the substantive effect upon the divine Name found elsewhere (see 2a below).

2. Doing God's Will (Specific Acts)

a. Affects the divine Name (i) *LevR 23.12 Aḥarei Mot* (MM, 548). At the conclusion of a homily dealing with the effect of adultery on the changed characteristics of

[191] The style here is different from the rhetorical form found elsewhere in this series, which sets forth both positive and negative consequences of human action. Here, too, the second position contains a negative valence (cf. n. 160).

[192] This issue is part of a larger liturgical and thematic topos; see overall A. Green, *Keter: The Crown in Early Jewish Mysticism* (Princeton: University Press, 1997), *passim*. Again, the negative valence is in the second position.

[193] Lit. *vayyabo'*, 'When he came'; this verse was understood elsewhere to refer to God's participation in exile. See above, p. 155.

[194] See n. 160 for other examples.

[195] The proof-texts of the first part have no relationship to the key word, and are out of order (they are similar in content).

an embryo, a supplement by R. Isaac considers the effect on God.[196] In one version, that effect is not on God's image in the embryo, but on the divine Name itself, and the minuscule letter *yod* in the verb *teshi* (*tšy*) in the scriptural lemma (Deut. 32: 18) marks this diminution. See the analysis above (pp. 188–9).[197] The term *kiv.* introduces the reference to this divine effect. For a different midrash on the incompleteness of the divine Name because of evil, see 3a(i) below.

b. Affects divine power (i) *Tan, Naso' 4.* In this version of the impact of adultery on the embryo, the teaching is given in the name of R. Isaac;[198] and the effect is on the image of God in the unborn child (whose face is changed from that of the woman's husband to that of her paramour). The teaching opens with the forceful assertion that the adulterer weakens 'the power (*koaḥ*) of the *Shekhinah*'. This point is then developed. The proof-text from Deut. 32: 18 is introduced by *kiv.*, so that the meaning of the phrase *tzur yeladekha teshi* is not, literally, 'You have forgotten (*teshi*) the Rock that bore you', but:

> A minuscule *yod* (occurs, indicating that) you have weakened (*tashash*) the hands (*yedei*) of the Artisan.

In this case, God (the Rock, *tzur*) is interpreted as the Artisan (*tzayyar*) and the act of Israel's forgetting is midrashically transformed into a weakening of the hands of God. The term *kiv.* marks this midrashic presumption, which includes understanding the minuscule letter *yod* as signalling a weakening of divine power ('the hands (*yedei*) of God') because of adultery.[199]

Another version of the act of divine transformation occurs at the end, in the name of R. Abbahu (A3). Hereby there is a pointed reference to the changing of the 'signs' (*sammanim*) of the embryo's appearance:

> What does the Holy One, blessed be He, do?—*kivyakhol* He goes back and changes the original form of the husband's image into the image of the adulterer. Indeed, 'He hides (*seiter*) his face' (Job 24: 15).

The term *kiv.* marks the general theme of divine transformation together with its proof-text. Specifically, a verse stating that an adulterer has masked or hidden his face by an act of nightly stealth is midrashically construed to suggest that 'He (God) has changed (*satar*) his face (i.e. of the embryo).' Alternatively, He has changed the image of the embryo into the face of the adulterer. Either way, *kiv.* underscores the bold exegetical presumption. The first half of Job 24: 15 (about the adulterer at twilight) also occurs at the beginning of *LevR 23.12*, but in this version the second half of the verse is used to refer to God who dwells in 'the hiddenness' of the world and sees all acts. Hence the passage is thus construed to mean that 'He who dwells in hiddenness puts His face' (namely, providential regard) to observe the acts of humans. The term *kiv.* does not occur with this more routine theology of divine omniscience.[200]

196 Presumably, R. Isaac Nappaḥa (A3)

197 This addition is > in *Tan Naso'* 4.

198 In *LevR* 23.12 the teaching is traced to R. Levi b. Parṭa, through R. Judah b. Simon.

199 In *NumR Naso'* 9, R. Isaac's opening assertion about weakening the power of the *Shekhinah* is preceded by *kiv.*; this usage appears to be a euphemistic addition.

200 Two other uses of *kiv.* occur at the beginning of *Tan Naso'* 4; but both seem to be euphemistic supplements, without any exegetical import or function.

c. Affects the covenantal relationship (i) *LevR 23.9 ʾAḥarei Mot* (MM, 538). Basing himself on a digest of Lev. 18: 2–3,

> R. Ishmael taught, 'Do not follow the practices of the land of Egypt or land of Canaan'—'I (*ʾani*) am YHWH, your God'; otherwise, *kivyakhol* I am not (*ʾaini*) YHWH, your God.

In this formulation of Scripture, R. Ishmael (T2) condenses v. 3 ('Do not follow', etc.) and shifts the divine formula ('I am YHWH, your God') from before the exhortation in v. 2 to its conclusion. This transposition serves a rhetorical end, and allows R. Ishmael to contrast the positive 'I am' (*ʾani*) with the counterpoint, 'I am not' (*ʾaini*). The midrashically revised formula is preceded by the term *kiv.*, which marks both this exegetical innovation and its bold theological implication.[201]

(ii) *SifDeut 346, Ve-Zot* (F, 403 f.). In a series of teachings linked to an opening midrash attributed to R. Simeon b. Yochai (T3) on Amos 9: 6,[202] and dealing with the overall theme of the effect of Israel's behaviour and convenantal commitment upon God, we read:

> 'You are My witnesses—declares YHWH—and I am (*ve-ʾani*) God' (Isa. 43: 12). When you are My witnesses I am (*ʾani*) God; but when you are not My witnesses, *kivyakhol* I am not (*ʾaini*) God.

This teaching has rhetorical and exegetical features similar to (i) (above). Here also the term *kiv.* marks the homiletical point. This extraordinary midrash is also found in *PdRK 12.6, Ba-Ḥodesh* (BM, 208), where it is explicitly linked to the Tanna R. Simeon b. Yochai. However, the final phrase, '*kiv.* I am not (*ʾain ʾani*) God' obscures the exegetical point and daring evident in *SifDeut 346*. The result is that *kiv.* appears to serve a more euphemistic function. The term is used in the negative position.[203] Theologically speaking, this teaching marks a limit case for God's dependence upon humans.

(iii) *SongsR 1.4*. In a homily on Torah and its effects, Hos. 4: 6 is explained in a striking way.

> 'Because you have forgotten (*va-tishkaḥ*) the Torah of your God, I too (*ʾaf ʾani*) shall forget (*ʾeshkaḥ*) your children' (Hos. 4: 6). Said R. Aḥa: 'I, too'—*kivyakhol* I too am forgotten (*be-shikheḥah*).

In R. Aḥa's transformative exegesis, the result clause is not God's action against Israel, but His being forgotten by them. He puts his emphasis on the finals words *ʾaf*

[201] Variants of the positive first part of this teaching (also using Lev. 18: 2–3) occur in *MdRI, Yitro* 6 (H–R, 222 f.) and *Sifra, ʾAḥarei Mot* 13.3—both times in the name of R. Simeon bar Yochai. The version from the school of Akiba lacks R. Ishmael's bold conclusions. Note the use of *kiv.* in the negative position; see n. 160.

[202] The beginning of this unit is given above, C.1.d(i). These teachings are incorporated into a comment on Deut. 33: 5, which provides a rhetorical inclusio. Amos 9: 6 comes first, as it has a verb tally with the comment on Deut. 33: 5.

[203] Two other teachings in this series (citing Exod. 15: 2 and Deut. 32: 3) follow this contractive rhetoric; here, too, *kiv.* marks only the negative application. Neither instance involves any apparent exegetical dimension, and *kiv.* serves a purely rhetorical and euphemistic function (i.e. to qualify the assertions that without human praise or proclamation, God or His Name would be somehow diminished). Note the use of *kiv.* in the negative position; see n. 160.

ʾani, and indicates his hermeneutical intent by using *be-shikheḥah* to explain *ʾeshkhaḥ*. This latter was thus presumably construed as a *nipḥʿal* reflexive (i.e. *ʾishakaḥ*, be forgotten). In the version of this exegesis found in *MidPs* 8.4 according to the *ed. prin.*, (Venice, 1546), and Ro1, the teaching is attributed to R. Ḥiyya and the exegetical point is clarified: '*Kivyakhol*, I also am forgotten (*mishtakeaḥ*), for the children used to bless Me.' In the Buber edition of *MidPs* 8.4 (B, 77), this same phrase occurs; but instead of a named sage, it says, 'the Holy One, blessed be He, said'. The comments in *MidPs* appear to be epexegetical and secondary. In all cases, the term *kiv.* marks the bold transfer of the effect from Israel to God, mediating between the proof-text and the comment.[204]

The names R. Aḥa and R. Ḥiyya are undoubtedly scribal variations but it is difficult to assert which is original, or which Aḥa or Ḥiyya is meant.

(iv) *Tos ʿAbodah Zarah 5.5* (Z, 466). Quoting Lev. 25: 38, 'To give you the land of Canaan, to be for you as a God', the following rhetorical assertion is made:

> Whenever you are in the land of Canaan, I am a God for you; (but whenever you are) not in the land of Canaan, *kivyakhol* I am not (*ʾaini*) a God for you.

This unit exploits the two phrases of the lemma, construed in conditional terms. Indeed, the idiomatic phrase *lihyot lakhem leiʾlohim* ('to be your God') is now read in concrete terms which stress the resultative nature of the phrase. The word *kiv.* marks the inversion and qualifies the negative implication. No special exegetical aspect is adduced at this point; and *kiv.* evidently serves only a euphemistic function.[205]

d. Affects the divine attributes (i) *NumR Shelaḥ 17.3*. In a homily Deut 1: 45 is cited and explicated.

> 'Again you wept before YHWH, but YHWH would not heed your cry' (Deut. 1: 45)—*kivyakhol*, you have made the Attribute of Judgement as if it were (*keʾilu*) cruel. R. Samuel b. Naḥman said that they made the Attribute of Judgement as if it were cruel.

This teaching, given twice, reacts to the failure of supplication to move God. The remark is apparently based on the fact that the divine name YHWH is used here, and although it normally denotes God's merciful presence, no mercy occurs in this proclamation. This example is one of several cases where divine judgement occurs with the Tetragram and is explicated by R. Samuel b. Naḥman as denoting a change in divine providence. See discussion above (pp. 183–4). The term *kiv.* seems to qualify the theological assertion, and is likely a secondary addition.

e. Affects divine judgement (i) *PdRK 5.13 Ha-Ḥodesh Ha-Zeh* (BM, 102f.). In a teaching of R. Hoshaʿyah, reference is made to the determination of a human court regarding the dates of Rosh Hashanah—a decision is accepted by God Himself, who then convenes His court. A reason is proposed on the basis of Scripture:

> 'For it is a law for Israel, a judgement (*mishpaṭ*) for the God of Jacob' (Ps. 81: 5). If it is not a law for Israel—*kivyakhol* there is no judgement for the God of Jacob.

[204] See n. 160

[205] Z is based on MS Erfurt; *kiv.* also occurs in *D* and MS Vienna (Heb. 20; in list of A. Schwartz (1925) N 46).

The striking exegetical point of R. Hoshaʿyah turns on transforming the positive parallel clauses of the lemma into a conditional sequence. The sage does not do this directly, but by rereading the clauses as a negative condition followed by a negative result. The term *kiv.* marks the bold theological implications of his reinterpretation—calling attention to the implications if Israel does not determine the date of the holiday. Indeed, the sage's 'reason' goes so far as to suggest that if Israel does not actually establish the date, God does not bring His judgement upon the world. The implications clearly exceed the point that human calendration is decisive for the Jewish festival year.[206]

This teaching also occurs in *JT Rosh Hashanah 1.3*. R. Hoshaʿyah is the teacher here as well. He is presumably R. Hoshaʿyah Rabba (A1, even though the teaching in *PdRK* opens with *teni*, a verb that regularly marks a tannaitic tradition). The version in *MidPs* 4.4 (B, 43f.) is an elaborate rendition; and although Ps. 81: 5 is adduced, the negative implication is not, and thus *kiv.* is also absent. In this form, the theology is quite unremarkable.

f. Divine augmentation (i) *BT Baba Batra 10a*. In a succinct teaching, R. Yoḥanan (A2) asks, 'What is the meaning of *malveh YHWH ḥonen dal* (Prov. 19: 17)?' He answers thus:

> If it were not written in Scripture, one could not say it—*kivyakhol* 'And the borrower is slave to the lender (*ʾish malveh*)' (Prov. 22: 7).

The teaching seems opaque. It answers the meaning of one verse with another, which it presumes to be clear. But this is hardly the case. The relationship between the passages is all the more puzzling if Prov. 19: 17 simply means that 'YHWH lends to one who is generous to the poor', as one might assume from the parallel phrase (namely, 'and his good deed He will repay him').

It would appear that R. Yoḥanan intends a bolder point, and even takes Prov. 19: 17 as saying that, 'One who is generous to the poor person makes a loan to YHWH'. For if he merely meant the plain sense, what is the purpose of the rhetorical question? This suspicion is strengthened insofar as the sage adduced a bold qualifier ('If it were not written') before the seemingly innocuous citation Prov. 22: 7—which is is offered to explain the first passage! On this logic, we may assume that R. Yoḥanan rereads the second verse to mean, paradoxically, that 'a slave makes a loan to a lender (i.e. God)'. Only such a theological presumption would allow one to bring the two passages into alignment, which is R. Yoḥanan's exegetical purpose. The term *kiv.* marks the bold exegetical presumption offered here about divine augmentation.

In *LevR* 34.2 (MM, 774f.), R. Yoḥanan's brother-in-law, R. Simeon b. Lakish (A2) offered a similar interpretation of Prov. 19: 17. However, in the tradition of his teaching presented there, he simply says, 'it is the (normal) way for the borrower to become a slave of the lender', and then adduces Prov. 22: 7. While R. Simeon's explication is both without the clause 'If it were not written, etc.' and the term *kiv.*, it is nevertheless clear from his comment that he is inverting the sense of Prov. 22: 7—and thus also rereading Prov. 19: 17 in a radical manner. Hence R. Simeon's laconic version confirms the foregoing explanation of R. Yoḥanan's exegesis, although it completely conceals the bold reinterpretation. It is not hard to assume that this

[206] As usual, the term *kiv.* is in the negative position; see n. 160.

condensation is the work of an editor, who fully perceived the radical force of R. Simeon's remark.

Both *Tan Mishpaṭim 15* and *TanB Mishpaṭim 6* (B, 85) are later reflexes of the teachings just noted. In the first case, R. Tanḥuma cites Prov. 19: 17 and clarifies it with the remark: '*Kivyakhol*, he makes a loan to YHWH'; in the second, a fuller comment is given: 'Whosoever lends to a poor person, *kivyakhol* it is as if (*ke*ʿ*ilu*) he makes a loan to the Holy One, blessed be He.' In both instances, the term *kiv.* marks an exegetical reuse of Prov. 19: 17. But given the absence of Prov. 22: 17 in these cases, the teachings (especially the second) tend to have a more rhetorical character.

(ii) *MZ Songs 1.15* (B, 21). Applying the opening words of the verse to acts of charity, the word *ra*ʿ*ayati* ('my darling') is identified with the 'community leaders' (*parnasim*). This leads to a general point:

> When you sustain (*mefarnesim*) the poor, I deem it favourable on your behalf, *kivyakhol* (as if it were possible) you are sustaining Me.

The term *kiv.* is used in a lapidary way here, as part of the formulation itself. The strong exhortation is thus qualified with regard to the divine effect; see similarly in *AgSongs 1.15* (SS, 27 f.).

There is no exegetical justification for this bold teaching. The one that follows is instructive in this regard, and shows how the point could be developed. The term *kiv.* does not occur, but the teaching is itself qualified at the end.

> 'Behold you are fair, my darling' (Songs 1: 15). The Holy One, blessed be He, says to Israel: You are sustaining Me; as it said, 'My sacrifice and My food' (Num. 28: 2). Is it possible (*yakhol*) that He eats and drinks? Scripture therefore says *le-*ʾ*ishai* (lit., 'for My fire-offerings'), (to teach that) you (should) give (gifts) to persons (*le-*ʾ*ishim*). If so, why is 'My food' stated?—(To teach that) though you give to persons, I regard (or: credit) you *as* sons who sustain their father.[207]

3. Existence of Amalek

a. Affects the divine presence (i) *PdRK 3.16, Zakhor* (BM, 53). In connection with Exod. 17: 16, regarding the existence of Amalek,

> R. Berekhia (said) in the name of R. Abba bar Kahana: Whenever the seed of Amalek exists in the world—*kivyakhol* as if (*ke*ʾ*ilu*), a wing (*kenaf*) covers the divine Face; (but when) the seed of Amalek is destroyed from the world, 'then your Teacher will no longer be concealed (*yikkanef*), and your eyes shall see your Teacher' (Isa. 30: 20).

The evil deeds of Amalek result in the occultation of God's presence, presumably by a wing of the seraphic host (cf. Isa. 6: 1–20); but in the future, when the evil nation will be destroyed, this situation will change. Then all will see God—called here 'your Teacher' or Guide. The assertion of covering, as with a wing, anticipates the proof-text that refers to the end of God's concealment (indicated by a verb that alludes to the covering of a wing). The term *kiv.* marks this exegetical instruction overall; though, in

[207] These teachings are unique. In *SongsR* 1.15 the emphasis is on various human deeds and commandments, but nothing affecting God.

point of fact, it is not directly conjoined to the proof-text from Isa. 30: 20, which marks the positive pole of the teaching. Indeed, such a placement gives the term a euphemistic tenor. In consequence, other tradents felt that further euphemistic augmentation was necessary; hence the term *keʾilu*. Both *kiv.* and *keʾilu* recur in the versions found in *PesR 12 Zakhor* (MIS, 51a) and *TanB Ki Tetzeʾ 18*.

R. Abba b. Kahana is A3; R. Berekhia is A5.[208]

b. Affects the divine throne and Name For this teaching and the interpretation of scriptural orthography, see above (pp. 189–90). The term *kiv.* occurs only in *PesR 12 Zakhor* (MIS, 51a),[209] but not in parallel passages (see a(i)). It is apparently secondary and added for symmetry with the previous instruction (a(i)).

4. Existence of the Wicked

a. Affects the divine throne (i) *YalShim §754*. Using the standard trope, the following teaching is given in the name of R. Mesharshiʾa:

> Whenever the wicked exist in the world—*kivyakhol*, the Holy One, blessed be He, does not sit upon His throne.

This point is proved by proof-texts from Hag. 2: 25 and Dan. 7: 9. But these accounts of an eschatological upheaval of the thrones of the nations do not fit the point. This appears to be a weak use of the topos.[210]

5. Curse Against Israel

a. Affects God (i) *AgBer 66* (B, 131). In a striking teaching about the close relationship between God and Israel, it is reported in the name of R. Judah b. Pazzai that

> When Balak sent for Balaam to curse Israel, Balaam said: What are you doing? If you want to injure (*liggaʿ*) the Holy One, blessed be He, who is 'with them' (consider the analogy of)[211] two persons who are bound (*medubbaqim*) one to another. If someone should smite one of them, is it not as if (*keʾilu*) both are smitten? (So, similarly) *kivyakhol*, the Holy One, blessed be He, is bound (*medubbaq*) to Israel. (Hence,) if I curse them, *kivyakhol* I injure (*nogeʿa*) Him; as it is said, 'How can I curse (*mah ʾeqob*) whom God has not cursed (*loʾ qabah*)?' (Num. 23: 8).

In this teaching, Balaam uses an analogy to suggest the intimate bond between God and Israel. The first occurrence of the term *kiv.* simply adduces a pious qualification to the bold notion. The second instance seems to function likewise. However, it will be noted that the plain sense of the proof-text does not seem to justify the rhetorical point made by Balaam; for according to the plain sense, one cannot curse Israel, the beloved of God. Hence one must assume that the verse was construed to mean: How could I curse (Israel) without (also) cursing God? This remarkable reading is signalled by the term *kiv.*, which marks the *theologoumenon* and hints that the proof-text must be understood in accord with its point.

208 In *PesR 12* only R. Abba is mentioned. 209 Before the phrase 'whenever'.

210 Weaker yet is the use of the trope in *OM* (i. 19b) regarding Esau, where the point is made that so long as they practise idolatry, God's kingdom is not complete. The formulation is entirely lapidary; there is no proof-text provided. Also regarding Edom, cf. *AgBer* 58 (B, 116).

211 The text is lacunose; I have reconstructed it *ad sensum*.

This is a unique tradition. R. Judah b. Pazzi is R. Judah bar Simon (A 4), the son of Simeon b. Pazzi.

D. Human Denial of Divine Power

1. At the Conquest

(i) *JT Taʿanit 4.5, 68d.* In the contexts of negative statements by the spies,

> R. Simeon b. Lakish said, They spoke words against (God) on High: 'For he (the enemy) is stronger *mimmennu*' (Num. 13: 31). They said, *kivyakhol* He is not able (to defeat) them.

The formulation is compact. R. Simeon construes the phrase in Num. 13: 31 to indicate the spies' denial of divine power. He thus takes the pronoun suffix in *mimmennu* to refer to God ('than Him'), not the spies themselves ('than us'). The term *kiv.* marks this presumptive deviation from the plain sense ('than us'), and the application of *mimmennu* to God. Indeed, this is its signal function; for were *kiv.* to be a euphemistic qualifier, the teaching of R. Simeon would make no sense.

In the two variants of this bold teaching found in *BT Soṭah 35a* and *BT ʿArakhin 15b*, the exegetical device attributed here to R. Ḥaninah b. Pappa is more clearly specified. After quoting from Num. 13: 31, it is stated: 'Do not read *mimmennu* but *mimmennu—kivyakhol*, the master of the house is not able to remove his utensils from it.' The effect of making the *ʾal tiqre* (do not read *x*) construction helps the reader see that nothing is changed in the text itself, but only that the pronoun suffix is construed differently.[212] The statement about the impotence of the owner of the house (God) goes further than the laconic statement attributed to R. Simeon. The version of the teaching in *NumR Masaʿei 23* offers a conflation of the versions of R. Simeon and R. Ḥaninah. It is anon.

R. Simeon b. Lakish is A2; R. Ḥaninah b. Pappa is A3.

2. In Acts of Theft

(i) *BT Baba Qama 79b.* Discussed below (VI.C.2(i)).

3. Near the Redemption

(i) *BT Sanh. 97a.* Among various comments offered concerning when the Messiah, son of David, would come, there is an interpretation of Deut. 32: 36 ('YHWH will judge His people ... When He sees that their might is gone, and neither bond nor freeman is left (*ve-ʾefes ʿatzur ve-ʿazuv*)'). This passage is construed to mean that the divine judgement will come when the people lose all hope in salvation. To reinforce the point the final phrase is invoked, but with a surprising twist:

> *Kivyakhol*—there is neither a supporter nor helper for Israel.

Since the opening plain sense of the passage indicates that God will bring the salvation when hope is lost among persons, one must wonder what is indicated by this comment. Surely it cannot be that Israel has no warriors to help, since that would

[212] See Rashi, *BT Soṭah* 35a, s.v. *mimmennu*. In *BT ʿArakhin* 15b, the Tosafists (s.v. *ʾal*) adduce another opinion that claimed that the letter *nun* had a *dagesh forte* only in the second (midrashic) one, but reject this as invalid.

make the comment redundant. Rather, the term *kiv.* alerts us to a more radical theological reading; namely, that the redemption will not come until the people themselves despair of God's salvation. This is the bold and presumptive interpretation of Scripture marked by the term *kiv.*[213]

VI. GOD AND JUSTICE

A. Divine Rewards and Justice

1. Positive (Reward)

(i) *ExodR 25.8 Beshalaḥ.* Among a series of teachings on heavenly bounty, Isa. 33: 16 is variously adduced. The following is included:

> 'He dwells on high (*huʾ meromim yishkon*)' (Isa. 33: 16). As it is written, 'For YHWH, your God, brings you to the good and spacious land (*ʾaretz*)' (Deut. 8: 7),[214] to see the table prepared in the Garden of Eden; as it says, 'I shall walk before YHWH in the lands of the living' (Ps. 116: 9)—*kivyakhol,* He sits above the partriarchs, and the patriarchs and all the righteous are in it (*be-tokho*); as it says, 'and they followed at Your feet (*tukku le-ragleykha*)' (Deut. 33: 3).[215] And He distributes to them portions (from the Edenic table on High)...

In this teaching, Isa. 33: 16 operates on two levels. It first indicates the human being who shall dwell on high, in 'Eden'. Such a reading extends the plain sense of the passage (vv. 15–16), in which the righteous are promised divine security—not destruction. Now the deserving ones may anticipate a heavenly dwelling—a point reinforced by an allegorical transposition of Deut. 8: 7 to refer to an entrance into a divine realm.[216] However, the teaching abruptly shifts to a second level. The term *kiv.* marks a rereading of the initial lemma in terms of God's own supernal dwelling. The shift in subject is clearly indicated, since the first-mentioned righteous are now (along with the patriarchs) said to be 'in it'—this being Eden—and below the one seated 'on High'. However, the proof-text introduced to reinforce the 'indwelling' of the patriarchs and the righteous in Eden is surprising; for the citation from Deut. 33: 3 does not simply support the fact that these persons are 'in' Eden, but that they are at the feet of God. Presumably, the phrase *ve-heim tukku le-ragleykha* was construed to mean 'they are in it at Your feet' (reading *tukku* as *tokho*).[217] In one stroke, therefore, both theological

213 This point was perceived by Rashi, who comments on the term *kiv.* used here as indicating 'as if one could say *this thing* against God (*kelapei maʿalah*)'.

214 The copyist has mistakenly conflated Deut. 8: 7, which only has 'to the good land', with the phrase 'to the good and spacious land' from Exod. 3: 8.

215 The verb is unknown; this translation follows Saadia and Kimḥi, who construe the phrase contextually. Ibn Ezra takes *ragleykha* metaphorically ('your ways'). For the use of the *lamed* to indicate a noun (*namely*, according to), see 1 Sam. 25: 22. In the midrash, it expresses locality.

216 The divine bounty of sustenance in the midrash is undoubted influenced by the end of v. 16. Cf. also the comment in 'Ḥiddushi ha-Radal', s.v. *kivyakhol,* where v. 17 is also adduced. In linking the vision of God to the eating below the divine feet, R. David Lurie (Radal) may have had Exod. 24: 10–11 unconsciously in mind.

217 Reading the difficult verb *tukku* in terms of an entrance underlies Rashi's comment, though in his point of entering the protective 'shade' of divinity he seems to have been influenced by Targum Onkelos.

assertions at the end (God dwells above; the patriarchs and righteous are below Him at His feet) are supported by the proof-text.[218] At the same time, the image of God's dwelling in heaven also receives a new emphasis, since He is exalted high above those partaking of a heavenly reward.

The term *kiv.* marks the presumptive rereading of Isa. 33: 16 in terms of God's exalted dwelling in a heavenly paradise (Eden), where His faithful assemble at His feet for their reward.

(ii) *ExodR 21.3 Beshalaḥ*. The lemma from Exod. 14: 15 in which God asks Moses 'Why do you cry out to Me?' serves as the basis for teachings about God's response to humans in this world and the next. With respect to one 'who does the will of the Omnipresent and directs his heart in prayer', we learn that God answers them in this world and similarly rewards them in the next.

> And (with respect to) in the world to come, 'they speak (*medabberim*) and I shall hear' (Isa. 65: 24). And what do they speak? Each stands and causes his study (*talmudo*) to be heard (*mashmiʿa*)—*kivyakhol* He sits and listens among them;[219] as it is said, 'Then (*ʾaz*) those who revere YHWH were talking with one another (*nidberu*); YHWH has paid attention and heard (*va-yashmaʿ*)' (Mal. 3: 16)[220]...

In this scenario God attends to the study of the righteous in heaven. This application of the scene of speaking to the world to come presumably derives from a construal of the word *ʿod* in the phrase *ʿod heim medabberim* (Isa. 65: 24) to mean 'they shall yet (or again, in the future) speak' (not: 'while they are still speaking').[221] The term *kiv.* marks the shift from a prognosis of human speech in heaven to God's attention to heavenly study by humans, and marks the exegetical presumptions involved. Just as the particle *ʿod* is presumably the key to the use of Isa. 65: 24 as prophesying a future hearing by God of human speech, it appears that the particle *ʾaz* triggers the application of Mal. 3: 16 to the world to come. This usage of the particle is a standard rabbinic trope, asserted most famously in the principle 'In some instances *ʾaz* indicates the past; in others, the future to come' (*MdRI Beshalaḥ* 1).

The term *kiv.* does not occur with Isa. 65: 24, and its reinterpretation as a prophecy of future divine hearing; it is only found in connection with the more dramatic scenario of divine activity putatively supported by Mal. 3: 16.

2. Negative (punishment)

(i) *MidPs 52.2* (B, 283). In a teaching against *lashon ha-raʿ* ('slander'), the principle is given that such speech leads to heresy. According to R. Yose, this point is proved by (the sequence of phrases in) Ps. 12: 15 ('They say, "By our tongues we shall be mighty... who can be our lord?"'). The divine response follows:

[218] In his commentary 'Peirush Maharzu', R. Zeev Wolf Einhorn makes a similar observation; the link between *tukku* and *tokho* is also noted.

[219] *D* (Vilna) reads *mashmiʿa* ('makes Himself heard'); but I have emended to *ve-shomeʿa* ('and listens') following 'Ḥiddushei ha-Radal', who correctly notes the formulation 'I shall hear' (*ʾeshmaʿ*) in Isa. 65: 24 (cited earlier in the homily) and the use of the *qal*-form in the proof-text itself. See similarly in 'Ḥiddushei ha-Rashash'. This is the commentary of R. S. Strashun.

[220] The last phrase is not cited in *D*, but it is obviously central to this teaching.

[221] The midrash does not explicitly cite *ʿod*; but its exegetical importance is clear and was pointed out by the Rashash (cf. n. 219, above).

Kivyakhol, the Holy One, blessed be He, cries out against 'the masters of the tongue', 'Who will arise with Me against the evildoers (*merei'im*)?' (Ps. 94: 15). Who is able to stand against them, and who will?—Gehinom. But Gehinom says, 'I am not able to stand (against them).' The Holy One, blessed be He, says to it: 'I am above and you are below.' And (Scripture) says, 'The sharpened arrows of a warrior, with hot coals of broom-wood' (Ps. 120: 4).

The passage is compact and dense. At the outset, God cries out in judgement against the slanderers. The term *kiv.* marks this transition and the presumptive application of Ps. 94: 15 to a divine response against those engaged in evil speech. God answers His own (rhetorical) query by noting Gehinom; but this embodiment of hell-fire claims insufficient power. The divine response and the subsequent proof-text leave the result opaque. The issue is clarified in *BT 'Arakhin* 15b, where we are told that 'R. Ḥisda said in the name of Mar 'Uqba, Whosever speaks slander, the Holy One, blessed be He, says (about him) to the Prince of Gehinom: I shall be against him above and you shall be against him below, (and together) we shall judge him.'[222] Thereupon, Ps. 120: 4 is cited and allegorically applied to this topic: the arrows are slanders, the hero is God, and the hot coals are Gehinom. Presumably the word *shenunim* (sharpened) was midrashically construed to mean a 'doubled (judgement)'. This would explain the formulation of the conclusion (*we* shall judge him); but nothing is stated in the received tradition.

Given this striking and expansive version of the tradition, it is clear that *MidPs 52.2* means to indicate that God responds to Gehinom's refusal by indicating that the two of them would conjointly punish the slander. The citation from Ps. 120: 4 bears on this point, though not in any way that could be construed form this version alone.

MidPs 12.2 (B, 106) is an even more condensed and opaque version of this teaching (hence *MidPs* 52.2 was explicated first).[223] Nevertheless, the citation from Ps. 12: 5 shows that this is the primary locale for the peculiar conflation of traditions kept separate in *BT 'Arakhin* 15b (namely, the distinct teachings about the link between slander and heresy and the scenario of divine judgement). Moreover, after God's response to Gehinom ('I am above', etc.), the citation from Ps. 120: 14 given here is apocopated—*ḥitzei gibbor shenunim*. But this brief citation is sufficient to show that the verse was adduced to indicate a conjoint punishment. Read in the light of the Talmudic explication, these three words refer to the slanders, to God, and to the two powers that will bring punishment, respectively.

The teaching in *BT 'Arakhin* 15b is not introduced by the query in Ps. 94: 15, and the term *kiv.* does not occur there. In the two versions in *MidPs*, the term marks the shift to a divine response to slanders, and thereby provides a bridge between distinct traditions.[224]

R. Yose (b. Zimra) is A1 (his tradent is R. Yoḥanan; A2); Mar 'Uqba is BA2 (his tradent is Ḥisda; BA3). *MidPs* thus combines EI and Babylonian traditions, preserved on the same page of the Talmud.

222 This teaching is separate from the one about the link between slander and heresy, which is given earlier as a teaching of R. Yoḥanan in the name of R. Yose b. Zimra, in a different form.

223 The term *kiv.* occurs in the same position in the teaching.

224 The formulation in the Talmud shows a common epigrammatic style; the formulations in *MidPs* evince a more dramatic dialogue.

(ii) *MidPs 12.3* (B, 107). Commenting on Ps. 12: 5 ('Because of the plundered poor and the groan of the needy, I shall now arise, says YHWH'),

> R. Yudan said, The punishment for robbing the poor is greater than the sin of the generation of the Flood. Regarding the generation of the Flood, it is written, 'YHWH sat (enthroned) at the Flood' (Ps. 29: 10)—*kivyakhol*, He exacted punishment against them while seated; and hereby (it is written), 'I shall now arise', (meaning that) He does not exact punishment against them except while standing.

R. Yudan interprets Ps. 29: 10 to refer to the physical position of God during acts of judgement. He does this to emphasize God's arousal against those who harm the poor. The term *kiv.* marks the presumptive interpretation of Ps. 29: 10, and thus does not qualify the act of divine punishment *per se*.[225]

B. God and the Courts

1. Divine Warning to the Judges

(i) *Tan Shofeṭim 7*. In the context of the warning in Deut. 16: 19 ('Do not bend judgement'), advice is given to the judges. Specifically, they are told to act with great trepidation, because

> *Kivyakhol*, they judge on behalf of the Holy One, blessed be He; for just this did Jehoshephat say to the judges: '(Consider what you do,) for you judge not on behalf of man (*le-ʾadam*), but *le-YHWH* (lit. on behalf of the Lord)' (2 Chron. 19: 6).

At first glance this teaching seems to be a weak, lapidary use of the term *kiv.*, which piously qualifies what is already stated explicitly in Scripture. Similarly, in *TanB Shofeṭim 6*. However, this concise formulation may conceal the more radical implication that the phrases *le-ʾadam* and *le-YHWH* in the proof-text were construed to mean that the judges judge man and God Himself (not simply on His behalf). That this reading is not out of the question is indicated by the explicit teaching of R. Ḥama b. R. Ḥaninah (A2) that follows. Having 2 Chron. 19: 6 in mind, he says, 'If it were not written in Scripture, one could not say it: one of flesh and blood (a human judge) judges his Creator. Hence the Holy One, blessed be He, said to the judges, exact trepidation upon yourselves as if you are judging Me.'

On this basis, the difference between the first anon. teaching and the second by R. Ḥama is not one of content but of form, the second one being more epexegetical and specific. *Non liquet*.

2. Divine Presence and Absence

(i) *ExodR 30.24 Mishpaṭim*. In connection with Exod. 21: 1 ('And these (*ve-ʾeilleh*) are the laws'), the following is taught:

> 'These also (*gam ʾeilleh*) are by the wise: to be partial in judgement is not good (*bal ṭov*)' (Prov. 24: 23 ... What is *bal ṭov*?—When the judge sits and gives true judgement, *kivyakhol*, the Holy One, blessed be He, leaves the highest heaven and causes His *Shekhinah* to dwell near Him; as it says, 'When YHWH raised up judges for them, YHWH was with the judge' (Judg. 2: 18). And when He sees him being

[225] Use of Ps. 29: 10 to indicate God's seated judgement at the Flood also occurs in *ExodR* 17.4; but the term *kiv.* does not occur.

partial, *kivyakhol*, He causes His *Shekhinah* to depart and ascend to heaven . . . as it says, 'Because of the plundered poor and the groaning of the needy, I shall now arise, says YHWH' (Ps. 12: 5).

This teaching opens with a verbal tally between Exod. 21: 1 and Prov. 24: 23 (the word *ʾeilleh*),[226] and this serves as the basis for introducing the ensuing teaching against partiality. As to the meaning of *bal ṭov*, we first are told that God descends to be with the judge who administers truthfully. The term *kiv.* precedes this idea and the presumptive transformation of Judg. 2: 18. Correspondingly, we further learn that when there is partiality in judgement God leaves the judge and ascends. As in the first case, the term *kiv.* precedes this notion and the presumptive application of Ps. 12: 5.

But what is *bal ṭov*—in light of this teaching? It can hardly simply mean that partiality is 'not good', for this would be a banal instruction and not explain the central motif of divine presence and absence. One might therefore conclude that when God ascends to heaven in the face of injustice, this is 'not good' for people.[227] But this view also moralizes the point, and is a weak explanation of the divine movement. Hence, it would seem that the phrase *bal ṭov* means that when there is partiality in human courts, God is no longer there; i.e. *bal ṭov* means that God, 'the Good One',[228] is 'not' on earth. This would be the bolder reading, that takes into account the divine consequences of human injustice.

In both instances here, the term *kiv.* marks bold theological assertions and the striking uses of scriptural proof-texts brought to support them.[229]

C. Deceit of God as a 'Theft'

1. At Sinai

(i) *Tos Bab Qama 7.9* (TL, 31). In the context of types of theft (beginning 7.8), it is said that

> When Israel stood at Mt. Sinai, they sought to deceive God;[230] as is said, 'All that YHWH has said, we shall do and we shall hear' (Exod. 24: 7)—*kivyakhol*, He was deceived by them.

This use of the term *kiv.* merely serves as a pious comment, qualifying the assertion that God was deceived. It is probably a scribal addition.

2. During Acts of Theft

(i) *BT Baba Qama 79b*. In the context of a query as to why the penalty for theft is greater than robbery, the answer of R. Yoḥanan b. Zakkai is that it is an act of affrontery against the Creator:

> *Kivyakhol*, he (i.e. the thief) makes the eye below as if it cannot see . . .

[226] See also the 'Peirush Meharzu'. [227] Cf. the 'Ḥiddushei ha-Radal'.

[228] For this designation, note the eulogy *ha-ṭov veha-meiṭiv*, 'The Good One, who does good' (*M. Ber.* 9.2; *J. Ber.* 9.2, 13d; and the discussion in *GenR* 13.15 (T–A, 124)). Ṭov is one of the seventy names of God at the beginning of *Midrash Lekaḥ Ṭov* on Song of Songs, by R. Tuvia b. Eliezer, ed. A. Grünhut (London, 1909), 5.

[229] Notably, the term *kiv.* does not appear in *MidPs* 12.3 (B, 107), but this may be because the teaching is structured around the two parts of Ps. 12: 5, and thus the teaching seems more of a sharpened reiteration of the biblical verse.

[230] Lit. 'they sought to steal, *daʿat ha-ʿelyonah*'.

This text is problematic. Given the opening comment about the thief's offence against God, and the proof-texts (from Isa. 29: 15; Ps. 94: 7; Ezek. 9: 9), that deal with assumptions and statements that God cannot see human acts, it is likely that 'the eye below (*maṭah*)' is a euphemistic substitute for 'the eye above (*maʿalah*)' (of God).[231] The term *kiv.* serves a euphemistic function here, qualifying the rabbinic assertion. It is therefore probably a scribal addition.

VII. OTHER: PIOUS AND LAPIDARY USES

In this section are collected all other examples of the term *kivyakhol* that have neither been studied nor mentioned in Sections I–VI above. In different ways, they show usages at variance with the patterns and functions considered earlier. For example, (1) in many cases the term *kiv.* is used in a purely lapidary sense, piously added to references concerning God or His activities. These instances simply qualify the *theologoumenon* involved and render it a theological possibility. Such usages are notably extraneous when they occur in the second part of a parable, at the point when the figure is applied to God (e.g. 'Thus *kivyakhol* the Holy One'; or 'such (is the case) *kivyakhol* (regarding) the Holy One'). Proof-texts are either absent or irrelevant in these cases. By contrast, (2) another cluster of examples adduces the term *kiv.* solely in connection with the proof-text. In effect, such uses simply qualify an explicit statement made about God in Scripture—without further explication. Such usages are manifestly extraneous and secondary. Finally, (3) a number of examples actually apply the term *kiv.* to the people Israel. Such uses diverge totally from the preponderant occurrence of the term with respect to God's personality or actions in the Midrash.

The ensuing examples are merely listed, without evaluation. The categorization is designed to facilitate correlation with the materials presented above.

I. Primeval Events
   - A. Creation: *MdRI Yitro* 7 (H–R, 230); *ExodR* 23.1; *TanB Bereshit* 11; *PesR* 42 (MIS, 175a); ibid. 46 (MIS, 187b); *OM* I. 67 (col. 2)
   - B. Eden: AgBer 22–3 (B, 48)
   - C. Flood: *TanB Bereishit* 36; *Tan Noaḥ* 4

II. God and History
   - A. Events
     1. Egypt: During Bondage: *ExodR* 15.15; 18.7; *NumR* 2.6; *PesR* Add 2 (MIS, 196b); at Deliverance: *MidPs* 114.6 (B, 473)
     2. At the Sea: *DtL* 1.8 (SL, 87)
     3. At Sinai: *ExodR* 28.1
     4. Temple: *MdRI Beshalaḥ* (H–R, 150); *SER* 28 (MIS, 50); *OM* IV. 281 (col. 2)
   - B. Personalities
     1. Adam: *Tan Shemini* 2; *SER* 8 (MIS, 185)
     2. Patriarchs and Matriarchs: Adam, *AgBer* 28 (B, 57f.); Jacob, ibid. (B, 108); Rachel, ibid. (B, 104).

[231] The designation *maʿalah* is itself a periphrastic reference to God in old rabbinic discourse. Cf. *GenR* 53.14 (T–A, 572).

3. Moses: *ExodR* 18.1; *TanB Shemot* 18; *DeutR* 1.2; *DtRL Ve'etḥanan* (SL, 49)
4. Righteous: *AgBer* 50 (B, 100); *PesR* 2 (MIS, 5b); *SER* 18 (MIS, 97)

C. God and Israel (Helper, Guide, Protector, etc.)
1. Special Relationship: *GenR* 18.5; *DeutR* 2.15; *LamR* 3.20; *EstR* 7.10; *Tan Vayishlaḥ* 28; *Tan Vayiqra'* 4; *DtRL Re'eh* (SL, 95); *DtRL 'Eqev* 12 (SL, 113); *AgSongs* (SS, 40)
2. God Does Not Abandon Israel: *TanB Beshalaḥ* 15; Seeks Intercession: *PesR* 33 (MIS, 150b)
3. Loves the Land of Israel: *SifDeut* 40 (F, 80)
4. Redemption: *OM* I. 226 (col. 1) = *BhM* VI. 87 (*Mid. Yelammedenu*)

III. God and Human Behaviour

A. Divine Providence
1. Inaction: *MidPs* 10.5 (B, 94f.); Action (Victory): *PesR* 9 (MIS, 32b)
2. Mercy: *MidPs* 86.7 (B, 374f.); Compassion: *AgBer* 47 (B, 94); *SER* 18 (MIS, 89); Attends Needy: ibid. 19 (B, 37)
3. Judgement: *SifDeut* 326 (F, 377); *MidPs* 10.5 (B, 94f.); ibid. 30.3 (B, 234); ibid. 75.2 (B, 338)
4. Immanence: *Tan Ki Tissa'* 27; *Tan Be-Midbar* 13; *Tan Naso'* 12
5. God as Source of Life: *AgBer* 35 (B, 69); Desires Life/Repentence: *PesR* 44 (MIS, 182b)

B. God Responds to Prayer: *ExodR* 23.8; 29.9; 42.5; 43.1

C. Sinful Behaviour: *Tan Va-yeitzei'* 5; *RuthR Pet* 7; Idolatry: *MidPs* 97.2 (B, 422); Improper Use of DN: *Tan Va'eira'* 1; God's Response: *Tan Balak* 11; Mistreatment of Parents: *SER* 24 (MIS, 134)

D. God is Misled: *Tan Qedoshim* 8

IV. God and Parables

A. Term *Kiv.* Qualifies Application to God
1. With Formula 'Thus (*kakh*) *kiv.* said the Holy One': *NumR* 21.2 (*Pinḥas*); *NumR* 23.11 (*Masa'ei*); *Tan Be-Midbar* 20 (*TanB* 23); *Tan Pinḥas* 11 (*TanB* 2)
2. Without Formula: *ExodR* 20.11; *NumR* 11.26 (*Shelaḥ*); *TanB Shelaḥ* (Addendum 7)

B. Term *Kiv.* Qualifies Parable Itself: *NumR* 16.27 (*Shelaḥ*)

V. Term *Kivyakhol* and Humans

A. Applied to Israel: *Tos Soṭah* 14.5; *LevR* 23.6; *SongsR* 2.9; 4.12; *Tan 'Emor* 16; *MidPs* 20.3 (B, 173); ibid. 18.20 (B, 147); ibid. 81.5 (B, 367); *SER* 18 (MIS, 107); ibid. 28 (MIS, 148)

VI. Other

A. *Kiv.* and Allegory: Divine Body: *AgBer* 59 (B, 118); Attributes: *OM* II. 484 (col. 2) = *BhM* III. 188 (*Mid. Tadshe*, 20)[232]

B. Desecration of DN: *Mid. Yelammedenu* (*ad* Gen. 1: 1).[233]

[232] Cf. A. Berliner, *Beiträge zur Jüdischen Alterthumskunde* (Vienna: Lippe, 1887), vol. i, p. xxxix.

[233] See MS fragment published in *Batei Midrashot*, i. 141 (no. 'b'). A related tradition occurs in *GenR* 1.12 (T–A, 10f.), to teach divine humility; it is > *kiv.*

Conclusions

I. 1. The hundreds of occurrences of the term *kivyakhol* in rabbinic sources (classical and early medieval), and the diversity and inconsistency of these textual versions (in MSS and in printed editions) make claims of authenticity hazardous and final determinations of limited value.[234] Moreover, due to the impact of scribal factors, there is no clear progression over time of increased or decreased use of the term in the evidence at hand. Early sources (like the Tosefta, among tannaitic ones) evince examples of routinized or lapidary usages characteristic of later midrashic compilations (like *AgBer*, *PesR*, and *MidPs*)—though certainly not in the same degree or manner. Even the best manuscript evidence for certain works does not yield consistent results. Certainly in most comparative cases, one may presume that the absence of the term *kiv.* indicates the more authentic version of the teaching at hand (though not necessarily the more authentic version overall). But this does not mean that the term is always or only a secondary qualification, for certain stylistic conventions and hermeneutical patterns suggest otherwise (see II. 1–2, below).

Moreover, there is no way to get completely behind the manuscript evidence in which the term *kiv.* is a consistent feature. One is therefore obliged to understand the usages as they occur, and cautioned to eschew putative reconstructions in most instances. This was the procedure adopted above—with the main weight placed on hermeneutical, thematic, and rhetorical factors. Nevertheless, the evidence at hand is nettlesome, insofar as the occurrences of the term *kiv.* appear to undermine or qualify the very theological assertions being made. This factor cannot be excluded entirely or in specific instances, and the term would then mark the exegete's own hesitation in making bold theological assertions. This being so, one must wonder at the status of the teaching itself; the role of scriptural proofs adduced to justify it; and the implication of the use of *kiv.* before a biblical citation. These factors must be included in any comprehensive estimation of the phenomenon.

I. 2. Analysis of the data reveals three characteristic features (in different combinations): (*a*) a *theologoumenon* (usually highlighting bold anthropomorphic and anthropopathic elements); (*b*) the term *kivyakhol*; (*c*) a scriptural proof-text. Two patterns are most typical: (1) the term *kiv.* is incorporated into the theological assertion, and followed by a citation formula (like 'as is said') and a verse from Scripture (unqualified); and (2) the theological assertion (itself unqualified) is followed by the term *kiv.*, after which occur the citation formula and a proof-text. The first of these patterns is the more frequent; the second sometimes includes an exegetical observation before the term *kiv.* (see below).

The combined occurrence of the three above-noted features is significant for understanding the meaning and function of the term *kiv.* in its various contexts. If there were only the *theologoumenon* plus *kiv.*, there would be little doubt that the term

[234] Note, for example, the following: *kiv.* in *MdRI Boʾ* 14 (H–R, 51, l. 10), and also in *D*, but > Ox1, M2, *YalShim*; *kiv.* in *MdRI Boʾ* 14 (H–R, 51, 1. 18), but > *D*; however, in *MdRI Beshalaḥ* 5 (H–R, 134, l. 3), *kiv.* only in *D*. The inconsistency is also evident in parallel teachings. Thus, for example, *kiv.* in *MdRI Boʾ* 14 (H–R, 54, ll. 5, 7), but > in *SifNum 84, Behaʿalotekha* (H, 83, ll. 5, 7); and the opposite, *kiv.* in *SifNum 157 Maṭṭot* (H, 211, l. 20), but > in *MdRI Beshalaḥ* 5 (H–R, 134, ll. 10–11).

serves to qualify the content of the assertion (as especially in late collections); whereas if there were only *kiv.* plus proof-text, one might suppose that the term seeks to qualify the boldness of Scripture—thus implying a more figurative apprehension of the biblical phrase. However, the evidence shows that *all three* elements are standard.[235] This raises the following questions. In what sense does the term *kiv.* qualify the *theologoumenon*, when these are followed (and justified) by an unqualified proof-text? And in what sense does the term *kiv.* qualify the proof-text, when these are preceded by an unqualified *theologoumenon* making a bold claim? And finally, what is the bearing on both queries of the fact that there is a marked disjunction between the assertion of the *theologoumenon* and the plain sense of the proof-text?

I. 3. Taking the foregoing factors into account, the following proposal is offered. The term *kivyakhol* marks a presumptive possibility of meaning ('as in/by the possibility'): when incorporated into the *theologoumenon*, it qualifies that assertion insofar as it is based upon an exegetical possibility presumed of the cited Scripture; and when it precedes the proof-text, the term indicates that the preceding theological assertion is based upon an exegetical presumption concerning the cited Scripture's plain sense. Hence the role of the proof-text is crucial. It both justifies and qualifies the exegetical theology proposed.

On this understanding, *kiv.* is taken as having distinct rhetorical and hermeneutical functions in the contexts where it occurs. This does not obviate the possibility that with regard to pattern 1 the word *kiv.* introduces a tone of pious qualification to the *theologoumenon*; but the present argument is that this occurs within a broader hermeneutical awareness of the presumptive nature of the exegetical theology involved. With regard to pattern 2, the term *kiv.* pointedly marks a hermeneutical presumption. Over time, the different uses melded, and the term was perceived to be a pious qualifier and adduced by scribes in more indiscriminate ways. Increased usage of the term was undoubtedly affected by rationalistic suspicions of *midrash ʾaggadah* in Geonic times, and as part of internal self-censorship in the face of Karaite critiques of rabbinic midrash and its bold anthropomorphic theology. This notwithstanding, some occurrences undoubtedly reflect older and possibly authorial conventions (see below).

II. 1. In addition to the aforementioned three-part hermenutical structure, several interrelated stylistic patterns recur. (*a*) A pattern used in connection with divine participation in Israelite history characteristically makes the general assertion that 'wherever' or 'whenever' Israel is in exile/straits, God is with them. The term *kiv.* occurs before the divine reference. Proof-texts are adduced to support this positive situation, but their exegetical import is only implied and must be deduced. (*b*) Another pattern is used in connection with Israelite observance and its effect upon God is binary ('If Israel does/does not do God's will'). The term *kiv.* occurs only in the negative part, after the introit ('If Israel') and before the proof-text regarding divine diminishment whose exegetical import is only implied. (*c*) A similar binary pattern (if/if not) is used in connection with certain deeds or proclamations by Israel and their effect upon God. Here, too, *kiv.* only occurs in the negative part before a statement

[235] For the weakening of this structure, see Sect. VII above.

which exegetically inverts the positive assertion of the proof-text. In these cases, the exegetical procedure is made somewhat transparent. (*d*) A pattern is used regarding evildoers or evil nations, stating that 'whenever' (or, as long as) they exist, a divine feature or aspect is not complete. The term *kiv.* occurs in these negative cases, before the statement of divine consequences which explicates the cited proof-text. Finally, (*e*) the formula 'whenever *x* is said, (this means) *kiv. y*'. This hermeneutical formula is clearly explicative, and the term *kiv.* marks the point.

It will be noted that the term *kiv.* occurs in the first four patterns ((*a*)–(*d*)) in conjuction with a negative situation. In all, this is deemed a positive feature of God's sympathetic involvement; in the other cases, negative behaviour has a diminishing effect upon God. One may therefore claim that in patterns (*b*) and (*c*) the term *kiv.* is used to qualify the negative consequence—even though in (*b*) (especially) the positive consequence is also bold. However, it will also be observed that the proof-texts used in the positive parts either intensify the plain sense of Scripture (in (*b*)) or simply reiterate it (in (*c*)). Only in the negative part is a bold exegetical rereading of the proof-text required for an understanding of the relation between the proclamation and the citation. This suggests that a hermeneutical function for the term *kiv.* is also involved in such instances.

The regularity of the pattern (despite much thematic diversity) suggests that the placement of the term *kiv.* in the negative position is an old and fixed convention. Latter scribes never tamper with it.

II. 2. In structural pattern two (*theologoumenon* followed by *kiv.* + proof-text), an exegetical condition or procedure is sometimes noted (before the term *kiv.*), thereby setting up the basis for the presumptive rereading of Scripture that underpins the theological assertion. Among the conditions mentioned is an emphasis on the written text ('*x* is written'; or 'not *x* is written but *y*'). In this way, either the form of the written text is stressed in order to support a reconstrual of it; or to highlight the written form (*ketib*) over its traditional recitation (*qere*); or even to underscore an orthographic or stylistic oddity in received Scripture. Among the procedures used is the exegetical injunction: 'Do not read *x* but *y*.' Here a new recitation is the key to the new theology, although this does not necessarily mean that a different articulation is involved; for sometimes all that is involved is a different emphasis (e.g. of an ambiguous pronoun suffix). Occurrences of *kiv.* in these instances suggest secondariness; but in some cases the reference to a technique may itself be a later clarification incorporated into the text. Each instance must be assessed with its variants. At all events, the term *kiv.* now signals to the reader that a bold rereading of Scripture is required in order to understand the use of that verse as a proof for the preceding *theologoumenon.*

III. 1. Many teachings with *kiv.* are transmitted anonymously. The problems of attributions notwithstanding, a review of the evidence indicates several striking clusters of named traditions. One is a group of tannaitic traditions attributed to R. Meir and R. Simeon b. Yochai (both T3; both students of R. Akiba); a second cluster is amoraic traditions attributed to R. Yoḥanan and R. Simeon b. Lakish (both A2); a third group is attributed to R. Abbahu and R. Samuel b. Naḥman (both A3);

and a fourth bundle of traditions is linked to R. Berekhia (A5), who transmitted or reformulated earlier teachings and delivered newer ones. All the foregoing traditions overlap but also exceed the mythic teachings of these masters discussed in Part II.

III. 2. The above evidence also highlights the occurrence of bold anthropomorphic theologies in certain schools and chains of disciples. Thus one master–disciple chain is centred around R. Akiba. A second chain begins with R. Yoḥanan (b. Nappaḥa), who taught first in Sepphoris and later at Tiberias. His close disciple and associate there was R. Simeon b. Lakish. R. Abbahu was also a student of R. Yoḥanan. R. Samuel b. Naḥman (a student of R. Jonathan b. Eleazar) studied in Tiberias and his main student and tradent was R. Ḥelbo (A4), who taught R. Berekhia.[236] Midrashic traditions linked to the term *kiv.* were thus associated with EI masters,[237] and especially those with a connection to Tiberias. Further generalizations are more allusive, and the evidence dictates caution. Nevertheless, the great number of traditions associated with A3–4 masters is a matter of particular note.

[236] R. Jeremiah (A4) is also affiliated with these late chains of tradition, and was an authority of the school of Tiberias.

[237] This exegetical theology was apparently not developed in Babylonian academies (although such theology was preached there by EI sages; cf. *LevR* 23.8 (MM, 573)).

SPECIAL ABBREVIATIONS FOR APPENDIX 2

AgBer	*Aggadat Berei'shit*, ed. S. Buber (Vilna: Romm, 1891)
AgSongs	*Aggadath Shir Hashirim*, ed. S. Schechter (Cambridge: Dell, 1896)
anon.	anonymous
AnOr	Analecta Orientalia
ArCom	*Arukh Completum*, ed. A. Kohut (Vienna: Menorah, 1926)
B	Solomon Buber
b.	*ben*; *bar* (son of)
BhM	*Bet ha-Midrasch*, ed. A. Jellinek (3rd edn.; Jerusalem: Wahrmann Books, 1967)
BM	*see PdRK*
Ca	MS Cambridge 1212
Col1	MS Columbia 64
Col2	MS Columbia 81
Col3	MS Columbia 205
Col4	MS Columbia 262
D	*Defus* (printed edn.)
DE	*Massekhet Derekh 'Eretz Zutta ve-Pereq ha-Shalom*, ed. D. Sperber (3rd edn.; Jerusalem: Tsur-Ot, 1994)
DH	*Midrasch Tannaim zum Deuteronomium*, ed. D. Z. Hoffmann (Itzkowski: 1908–9; repr. Jerusalem, 1984) = *Midrash Tannaim*
DN	Divine Name
DtRL	*Midrash Debarim Rabba*, ed. S. Lieberman (Jerusalem: Wahrman Books, 1964)
ed. prin.	*editio princeps*
EI	*Eretz Israel* (land of Israel)
E–M	*see MdRS*
F	*see* SifDeut
H	*see* SifNum
H–R	*Mechilta D'-Rabbi Ismael*, ed. H. S. Horovitz and I. A. Rabin (Jerusalem: Bamberger & Wahrman, 1960) = *Mekhilta de-Rabbi Ishmael*
Jer	MS Jerusalem 245
JTSA	Jewish Theological Seminary of America
kiv.	*kivyakhol*
Lo	MS London (British Museum Add. 27, 169)
Lo1	MS London (British Museum Add. 16, 406)
LXX	Septuagint
M	*Midrash ha-Gadol* (on Exodus), ed. M. Margulies (Jerusalem: Mossad HaRav Kook, 1967)
M	Mishnah
M1	MS Munich 97

M2	MS Munich 117
MdRI	*Mekhilta de-Rabbi Ishmael*, ed. H–R
MdRS	*Mekhilta d'-Rabbi Šimʿon b. Jochai*, ed. J. N. Epstein and E. Z. Melamed (Jerusalem: Hillel Press, 1955) = *Mekhilta de Rabbi Simeon bar Yochai*
ME	*Midrash 'Eicha* (Lamentations), ed. S. Buber (Vilna: Romm, 1899)
MH	*Midrash Ḥakhamim* (MS of V. Aptowitzer; cited in F, H; H–R)
MH1	*Midrash Ḥakhamim*, abbreviated version (MS of A. Epstein; cited in T–A)
MhG	*Midrash ha-Gadol*
MidPs	*Midrash Psalms (Shoḥer Tov)*, ed. S. Buber (Vilna: Romm, 1891)
MidSam	*Midrash Samuel*, ed. S. Buber (Cracow: J. Fischer Press, 1893)
MidTan	*see* DH
MinY	Minḥat Yehudah (commentary of J. Theodor in T–A)
MIS	Meir Ish Shalom
MM	*Midrash Wayyikra Rabbah*, ed. M. Margulies (Jerusalem: Wahrmann Books, 1966) = *Vayiqra' Rabbah* (*Leviticus Rabbar*)
MZ	*Midrash Zuṭa*, ed. S. Buber (Berlin: Itzkowski, 1894)
OM	*'Otzar Midrashim*, ed. J. D. Eisenstein (New York: Eisenstein, 1915)
Ox	MS Oxford 147 (Neubauer Cat.)
Ox1	MS Oxford 151 (Neubauer Cat.)
Ox2	MS Marshall Or 24 (Oxford Bod.)
Ox3	MS Oxford 2334-11 (Neubauer Cat.)
Ox4	MS Oxford 2335 (Neubauer Cat.)
Pa	MS Paris 149
Par	MS Parma (de Rossi 261)
PdRK	*Pesikta' de-Rav Kahana*, ed. B. Mandelbaum (New York: JTSA, 1962)
PesR	*Pesikta' Rabbati*, ed. M. Ish Shalom (Vilna: Kaiser, 1880)
Pet	Petiḥta' (proem)
PH	*Peirush Ha-'Aggadot le-R. 'Azriel*, ed. I. Tishby (Jerusalem: Magnes Press, 1982)
PN	Personal name
PRE	*Pirkei de Rabbi Eliezer*, ed. M. Higger (in *Ḥoreb*, 8 (1944), 82–119; 9 (1946–7), 94–166; 10 (1948), 185–294)
R	Rabba
rd.	read
RH	*Rabbeinu Hillel*, annotated commentary on the *Sifre*
Ro	MS Rome (Vatican 32)
Ro1	MS Rome (Vatican 76)
S	*see ShR*
SER	*Seder Eliahu Rabba*, ed. M. Ish Shalom (Vienna: Achiasaf, 1904; 3rd printing, Jerusalem: Wahrmann Books, 1969)
ShQ	*The Shiʿur Qomah: Texts and Recensions*, ed. M. S. Cohen (Tübingen: J. C. B. Mohr, 1985)
ShR	*Midrash Shemot Rabba, Chapters I–XIV*, ed. A. Shinan (Jerusalem–Tel Aviv: Dvir Publishing House, 1984)

SifDeut	*Sifre on Deuteronomy*, ed. L. Finkelstein (2nd edn.; New York: JTSA, 1969)
SifNum	*Siphre D'Be Rab*, ed. H. S. Horovitz (Jerusalem: Wahrmann Books, 1966)
SL	*see* DtRL
SS	*see AgSongs*
St	MS Stuttgart (Orient 32)
T	Tanna (followed by generation number)
T–A	*Midrash Bereshit Rabba*, ed. J. Theodor and Ch. Albeck (2nd printing; Jerusalem: Wahrmann Books, 1965) = Theodor–Albeck
Tan	Tanḥuma
Tg. Jon.	Targum Jonathan (to the Prophets)
TL	*The Tosefta*, ed. S. Lieberman (New York, JTSA: 1955–88)
Tz	Tzefat-Safed (MS of Bibliothèque de l'Alliance Israelite)
var.	variant
Y	MS Yemen (MS of E. Adler; cited in T–A)
YalShim	*Yalkut Shimʿoni*
Yeb.	Yebamot
Z	*Tosephta*, ed. M. S. Zuckermandel (Trier, 1882; NE, Jerusalem: Wahrmann Books, 1970)
>	missing; absent

SELECT BIBLIOGRAPHY
(MONOGRAPHS AND ARTICLES)

AHN, G., '"Monotheismus"—"Polytheismus": Grenzen und Möglichkeiten einer Klassifikation von Gottesvorstellungen', in Manfried Dietrich and Oswald Loretz (edn.), *Mesopotamia-Ugaritica-Biblica: Festscrhift für Kurt Bergerhof* (Kevelaer and Neukirchen-Vluyn: Butzon & Bercker and Neukirchen, 1993), 1–24.

ALBREKTSON, B., *History and Gods: An Essay on the Idea of Historical Events as Divine Manifestations in the Ancient Near East and Israel* (Lund Gleerup, 1967).

ALTMANN, A., 'A Note on the Rabbinic Doctrine of Creation', *JJS* 7 (1956), 195–206.

—— 'Symbol and Myth', *Philosophy*, 20 (1945), 162–71.

APTOWITZER, V., 'Licht als Urstoff', *MGWJ* 72 (1928), 363–70.

ASSMANN, J., *Moses the Egyptian* (Cambridge, Mass.: Harvard University Press, 1997).

—— 'Die Verborgenheit des Mythos in Ägypten', *Göttinger Miszellen*, 25 (1977), 7–43.

—— BURKERT, W., STOLZ, F., *Funktionen und Leistungen des Mythos: Drei altorientalische Beispiele* (OBO 48; Freiburg: Universitätsverlag, and Göttingen: Vandenhoeck and Ruprecht, 1982).

ATTRIDGE, H., and ODEN, Jr., R., *Philo of Biblos: The Phoenician History* (CBQM 9; Washington, DC: Catholic Biblical Association of America, 1981).

AVISHUR, Y., *Studies in Hebrew and Ugaritic Psalms* (Jerusalem: Magnes Press, 1994).

BAINES, J., 'Myth and Literature', in Antonio Loprieno (ed.), *Ancient Egyptian Literature: History and Forms* (Leiden: E. J. Brill, 1996), 361–77.

BALENTINE, S., *The Hidden God: The Hiding of the Face of God in the Old Testament* (Oxford: Oxford University Press, 1983).

BARBOUR, I., *Myths, Models and Metaphors: A Comparative Study of Science and Religion* (San Francisco: Harper & Row, 1974).

BAR-ILAN, M., 'The Hand of God: A Chapter in Rabbinic Anthropomorphism', in Gabrielle Sed-Rajna (ed.), *Rashi 1040–1990: Hommage à Ephraim E. Urbach* (Paris: editions du Cerf, 1993), 321–35.

BARR, J., 'The Meaning of "Mythology" in Relation to the Old Testament', *VT* 9 (1959), 1–10.

—— *The Semantics of Biblical Language* (Oxford: Clarendon Press, 1961).

—— 'Theophany and Anthropomorphism in the Old Testament', *Congress Volume, Oxford* (SVT 7; Leiden: E. J. Brill, 1960), 31–8.

BARTON, G., 'Tiʾamat', *JAOS* 15 (1893), 1–27.

BIANCHI, U., *The History of Religions* (Leiden: E. J. Brill, 1975).

BLUMENBERG, H., *Work on Myth* (Cambridge, Mass.: MIT Press, 1985).

BOGATYREV, P., and JAKOBSON, R., 'Die Folklore als eine besondere Form des Schaffens', in *Donum Natalicium Schrijnen* (Nijmegen–Utrecht: N. V. Dekker & Van de Vegt, 1929), 900–13.

BOYARIN, D., *Intertextuality and the Reading of Midrash* (Bloomington: Indiana University Press, 1990).

BRISSON, L., *Plato the Myth Maker* (Chicago: University of Chicago Press, 1999).

BUBER, M., 'Myth in Judaism', in Nahum Glatzer (ed.), *On Judaism* (New York: Schocken Books, 1967), 95–107.

BURKERT, W., 'Oriental and Greek Mythology: The Meeting of Parallels', in Jan Bremmer (ed.), *Interpretation of Greek Mythology* (London: Routledge, 1988), 10–40.

—— *The Orientalizing Revolution: Near Eastern Influence on Greek Culture in the Early Archaic Age* (Cambridge, Mass.: Harvard University Press, 1992).

—— *Structure and History in Greek Mythology and Ritual* (Berkeley and London: University of California Press, 1979).

CAGNI, L., *The Erra Epic* (Malibu: Udena Publications, 1977).

CANICK, H., *Mythische und historische Wahrheit* (Stuttgarter Bibelstudien, 48; Stuttgart: Verlag Katholisches Bibelwerk, 1970).

CAQUOT, A., 'Le Leviathan de Job 40,25–41,26', *RB* 99 (1992), 40–62.

—— 'Sur quelques démons dans l'Ancien Testament (*Reshep, Qeteb, Deber*)', *Semitica*, 6 (1956), 53–68.

CASSIN, E., *La Splendeur divine: Introduction à l'étude de la mentalité mésopotamienne* (Civilisation et Société, 8; Paris and The Hague: Mouton & Co., 1968).

CASSIRER, E., *The Philosophy of Symbolic Forms*, ii: *Mythic Thought* (New Haven and London: Yale University Press, 1955).

—— *Sprache und Mythos* (Studien der Bibliothek Warburg, 6); trans. Susanne Langer as *Language and Myth* (New York: Harper & Brothers, 1946).

CASSUTO, U., 'Chapter iii of Habakkuk and the Ras Shamra Texts', in *Biblical and Oriental Studies* (1st pub. 1938; Jerusalem: Magnes Press, 1975), ii. 12.

—— 'The Israelite Epic', in *Biblical and Oriental Studies* (Jerusalem: Magnes Press, 1975), ii. 80–102.

CHARBONNIER, E., LaB., 'The Logic of Biblical Anthropomorphism', *HTR* 55 (1962), 187–206.

CHARLESWORTH, J. (ed.), *The Old Testament Pseudepigrapha* (New York: Doubleday & Co., 1985), i–ii.

CHAZE, M., 'De l'identification des patriarches au char divin: Recherche du sens d'un enseignement rabbinique dans le Midrash et dans la Kabbale prézoharique et ses sources', *REJ* 149 (1990), 5–75.

CLAPHAM, L., 'Mythopoeic Antecedents of the Biblical World-View and their Transformation in Early Israelite Thought', in Frank M. Cross, Werner E. Lemke, and Patrick D. Miller, Jr. (edd.), *Magnalia Dei: The Mighty Acts of God: In Memory of G. E. Wright*, (New York: Harper & Row, 1976), 108–19.

CLEMEN, C., *Die Phönikische Religion nach Philo von Byblos* (MVAG 42.3; Leipzig: J. C. Hinrichs Verlag, 1939).

COHEN, N., 'Shekhinta Ba-Galuta: A Midrashic Response to Destruction and Persecution', *JSJ* 13 (1982), 147–59.

COHEN, P., 'Theories of Myth', *Man*, 4 (1969), 337–53.

COLLINS, A., *The Combat Myth in the Book of Revelation* (Harvard Dissertations in Religion, 9; Missoula: Scholars Press, 1976).

Collins, J., *Daniel* (Hermeneia; Minneapolis: Fortress Press, 1993).
——'Stirring up the Great Sea: The Religio-Historical Background of Daniel 7', in A. S. van der Woode (ed.), *The Book of Daniel in the Light of New Findings* (Leuven: University Press, 1993), 121–36.
Collon, D., 'The Smiting God: A Study of a Bronze in the Pomerance Collection in New York', *Levant*, 4 (1972), 111–34.
Colpe, C., 'Zur Neubegründung einer Phänomenologie der Religionen und der Religion', in Hartmut Zinser (ed.), *Religionswissenschaft: Eine Einfüring* (Berlin: Dietrich Riemer, 1988), 131–54.
Conrad, D., 'Der Gott Reschef', *ZAW* 83 (1971), 157–83.
Cooper, A., 'PS 24: 7–10; Mythology and Exegesis', *JBL* 102 (1983), 37–55.
Cooper, J., *The Curse of Agade* (Baltimore: Johns Hopkins University Press, 1983).
Cross, F., *Canaanite Myth and Hebrew Epic* (Cambridge, Mass.: Harvard University Press, 1973).
Dahl, N., and Segal, A., 'Philo and the Rabbis on the Names of God', *JJS* 9 (1978), 1–28.
Daiches, S., 'Talmudische und midraschische Parallelen zum babylonischen Weltschöpfungsepos', *ZA* 17 (1903), 394–9.
Dalley, S., 'Bel at Palmyra and Elsewhere in the Parthian Period', *ARAM* 7 (1995), 137–51.
——*Myths from Mesopotamia: Creation, the Flood, Gilgamesh, and Others* (New York: Oxford University Press, 1989).
Davies, G., 'An Approach to the Problem of Old Testament Mythology', *PEQ* 88 (1956), 85–91.
Day, J., *God's Conflict with the Dragon and the Sea* (Cambridge: Cambridge University Press, 1985).
Delitzsch, F., *Babel und Bibel: Ein Vortrag* (Leipzig: J. C. Hinrichs, 1903).
——*Zweiter Vortrag über Babel und Bibel* (Stuttgart: Deutsche Verlags-Anstalt, 1903).
de Moor, J., 'Rapiʾuma-Rephaim', *ZAW* 88 (1976), 323–45.
——*The Seasonal Pattern in the Ugaritic Myth of Balu* (Leiden: E. J. Brill, 1971).
Detienne, M., *The Creation of Mythology* (Chicago: University of Chicago Press, 1986).
Dobbs-Allsopp, F., *Weep, O Daughter of Zion: A Study of the City-Lament Genre in the Hebrew Bible* (Biblica et Orientalia, 44; Rome: Pontifical Biblical Institute, 1993).
Dolezel, L., 'From Motifemes to Motifs', *Poetics*, 4 (1970), 55–90.
du Mesnil du Buisson, R., 'Le Bas-Relief du Combat de Bel contra Tiʾamat dans le Temple de Bel à Palmyre', *Les Annales Archéologiques Arabes Syriennes*, 26 (1976), 83–100.
Durand, J.-M., 'Le Mythologeme du Combat entre le Dieu de l'Orage et la Mer en Mésopotamie', *MARI, Annales de Recherches Interdisciplinaires*, 7 (1993), 41–61.
Durr, L., *Die Wertung des Göttlichen Wortes im Alten Testament und im Antiken Orient* (MVAG 42.1; Leipzig: J. C. Hinrichs Verlag, 1938).
Eissfeldt, O., *Baʿal Zaphon, Zeus Cassius und der Durchzug der Israeliten durchs Meer* (Halle: Niemeyer, 1932).

ELBAUM, Y., 'Rhetoric, Motif, and Subject-Matter—Toward an Analysis of Narrative Technique in Pirke de-Rabbi Eliezer', *Jerusalem Studies in Jewish Folklore*, 13/14 (1991–2), 99–126 (in Hebrew).

ELIADE, M., *Cosmos and History: The Myth of the Eternal Return* (New York & Evanston: Harper & Row, 1963).

—— *Myth and Reality* (New York and Evanston: Harper & Row, 1963).

ELSTEIN, Y., 'Liqra't Ṭematologia shel Sifrut ʿAm Yisra'el: Perespeqṭivot u-Baʿayot', *Proceedings of the Tenth World Congress of Jewish Studies* (Jerusalem: World Union of Jewish Studies, 1990), ii. D, 51–8.

—— and LIPSKER, A., 'The Homogeneous Series in the Literature of the Jewish People: A Thematological Methodology', in Frank Trammler (ed.), *Thematics Reconsidered: Essays in Honor of Horst S. Daemmrich* (Amsterdam: Rodapi, 1995), 87–116.

EMERTON, J., 'The Origin of the Son of Man Imagery', *JNES* 9 (1958), 225–40.

EYALI, M., 'Ha-'El Ha-Mitztaʿer Be-Tzaʿaram shel Yisra'el', in Sarah Heller-Wilensky and Moshe Idel (edd.), *Mehqarim Be-Hagut Yehudit* (Jerusalem: Magnes Press, 1989), 29–50.

FASCHER, E., 'Dynamis', in *Reallexicon für Antike und Christentum*, ed. Theodor Klauser (Stuttgart: Hiersemann, 1959), iv.

FEUCHTWANG, D., 'Das Wasseropfer und die damit verbunden Zeremonien', *MGWJ* 54 (1910), 539–52, 713–29; and 55 (1911), 43–63.

FISHBANE, M., *Biblical Interpretation in Ancient Israel* (Oxford: Clarendon Press, 1985).

—— *The Exegetical Imagination: On Jewish Thought and Theology* (Cambridge, Mass.: Harvard University Press, 1998).

—— *The Garments of Torah: Essays in Biblical Hermeneutics* (Bloomington: Indiana University Press, 1989).

—— 'Some Forms of Divine Appearance in Ancient Jewish Thought', in Jacob Neusner, Ernest Frerichs, and Nahum Sarna (edd.), *From Ancient Israel to Modern Judaism: Essays in Honor of Marvin Fox* (Atlanta: Scholars Press 1989), ii. 261–70.

FLUSSER, D., and AMORAI-STARK, S., 'The Goddess Thermuthis, Moses, and Artapanus', *JSQ* 1 (1993/4), 217–33.

FRANKFORT, H., 'God and Myths on Sargonid Seals', *Iraq*, 1 (1934), 2–29.

—— and FRANKFORT, H. A. (edd.), *The Intellectual Adventure of Ancient Man: An Essay on Speculative thought in the Ancient Near East* (Chicago: University of Chicago Press, 1946).

GALLI, B., 'Rosenzweig Speaking of Meetings and Monotheism in Biblical Anthropomorphisms', *JJTP* 2 (1993), 219–43.

GASTER, T. H., *Thespis: Ritual, Myth and Drama in the Ancient Near East* (Garden City, NY: Doubleday & Company, 1961).

GINSBERG, H. L., 'The Arm of YHWH in Isaiah 51–63 and the Text of Isa 53: 10–11', *JBL* 77 (1958), 152–6.

GINZBERG, L., 'Anthropomorphism and Anthropopathism', *The Jewish Encyclopedia* (New York and London: Funk and Wagnells, 1901), 621 f.

—— *Legends of the Jews* (1909–28; 12th impression, 1962; Philadelphia: The Jewish Publication Society, 1962), i–vi.

GLADIGOW, B., 'Strukturprobleme polytheistischer Religionen', *Saeculum*, 34 (1983), 292–304.
GOLDIN, J., 'Not by Means of an Angel and Not by Means of a Messenger', in *Religions in Antiquity: Essays in Memory of Erwin Ramsdell Goodenough* (suppl. to *Numen*, 14; Leiden: E. J. Brill, 1968), 412–24.
GOLDZIHER, I., 'Proben muhammedänischer Polemik gegen den Talmud', *Jeschurun* (ed. Koback), 8 (1872), 76–104.
GOODMAN, L., 'Mythic Discourse', in Shlomo Biderman and Ben-Ami Scharfstein (edd.), *Myths and Fictions* (Leiden: E. J. Brill, 1993), 51–112.
GRAF, F., *Greek Mythology: An Introduction* (Baltimore: Johns Hopkins University Press, 1993).
GREEN, A., *Keter: The Crown in Early Jewish Mysticism* (Princeton Princeton University Press, 1997).
——'Shekhinah, the Virgin Mary, and the Song of Songs: Reflections on a Kabbalistic Symbol in its Historical Context', *AJS Rev.* 26 (2002), 1–52.
GREEN, M., 'The Eridu Lament', *JCS* 30 (1978), 127–67.
——'The Uruk Lament', *JAOS* 104 (1984), 253–79.
GREENSTEIN, E., 'The Snaring of Sea in the Baʿal Epic', *Maarav*, 3 (1982), 195–216.
GRUPPE, O., 'Geschichte der klassischen Mythologie und Religionsgeschichte, während des Mittelalters im Abenland und während der Neuzeit', in *Lexicon der griechischen und römischen Mythologie*, ed. W. H. Roscher, suppl. (Leipzig: B. G. Teubner, 1921).
GUNKEL, H., *Schöpfung und Chaos in Urzeit und Endzeit: Eine Religionsgeschichtliche Untersuchung über Gen 1 und Ap Joh 12* (Göttingen: Vandenhoeck & Ruprecht, 1895).
GWALTNEY, Jr., W., 'The Biblical Book of Lamentations in the Context of Near Eastern Lament Literature', in William W. Hallo, James C. Moyer, and Leo G. Perdue (ed.), *Scripture in Context*, ii: More Essays on the Comparative Method (Winona Lake, Ind.: Eisenbrauns, 1983), 191–211.
HAAS, V., 'Die Dämonisierung des Fremden und des Feindes im Alten Orient', *Rocznik Orientalistyczny*, 41.2 (1980), 37–44 (anniversary volume dedicated to Rudolf Ranoszek).
HAENCHEN, E., 'Das Buch Baruch: Ein Beitrag zum problem der christlichen Gnosis', *ZTK* 50 (1953), 123–58.
HALBERTAL, M., ''Ilmalei' Miqra' Katub 'Iy 'Efshar le-'Omro', *Tarbiz*, 68 (1998–9), 39–59.
——and MARGALIT, A., *Idolatry* (Cambridge, Mass.: Harvard University Press, 1992).
HANDY, L., *Among the Hosts of Heaven: The Syro-Palestinian Pantheon as Bureaucracy* (Winona Lake, Ind.: Eisenbrauns, 1994).
HARREY, Z., ' "Gadol Kokhan shel Nivi'im", ʿIyyun be-Moreh Nebukhim Ḥeleq I Pereq 46', *Daat*, 37 (1996), 53–61.
——'She'elat 'Iy-Gashmi'ut ha-'El 'Etzel Rambam, Ra'bad, Qresqes, ve-Shpinozah', in Sara Heller-Wilensky and Moshe Idel (edd.), *Meḥqarim be-Hagut Yehudit* (Jerusalem: Magnes Press, 1989), 63–78.

HASSAN, I., 'The Problem of Influence in Literary History: Notes Towards a Definition', *Journal of Aesthetics and Art Criticism*, 14 (1955), 66–76.

HAZAN-ROKEM, G., *Web of Life: Folklore and Midrash in Rabbinic Literature* (Stanford, Calif.: Stanford University Press, 2000).

HEHN, J., *Die biblische und die babylonische Gottesidee* (Leipzig: J. C. Hinrichs, 1913).

HEIDEL, A., *The Babylonian Genesis* (Chicago: Phoenix Books, 1963).

HELD, M., '*mḫṣ/*mḫṣ* in Ugaritic and Other Semitic Languages (A Study in Comparative Lexicography)', *JAOS* 79 (1959), 159–76.

HELK, W., *Die Beziehungen Ägyptens zu Vorderasien im 3. und 2. Jahrtausend v. Chr.* (Wiesbaden: Harrassowitz, 1962).

HELLER, B., 'La Chute des anges: Shemhazai, Ouzza et Azael', *RÉJ* 60 (1910), 202–12.

HENDRICKS, W., 'Structure and History in the Semiotics of Myth', *Semiotica*, 39 (1982), 131–65.

HERMANN, S., 'Die Naturlehre des Schöpfungsberichtes: Erwägungen zur Vorgeschichte von Genesis 1', *TLZ* 86 (1961), 413–24.

HERMANN, W., 'Jahwes Triumph Über Mot', *UF* 11 (1979), 371–7.

HEUZEY, L., 'Dragons sacrés de Babylone et leur prototype chaldéen', *RA* 6 (1906), 95–104.

HIEBERT, T., *God of My Victory: The Ancient Hymn in Habakkuk 3* (HSM 38; Atlanta: Scholars Press, 1986).

HIRSCH, H., 'Die "Sünde" Lugalzagesis', in *Festschrift für Wilhelm Eilers* (Wiesbaden: Otto Harrassowitz, 1967), 99–106.

HIRSCHFELD, H., 'Mohammedan Criticism of the Bible', *JQR* OS 13 (1900–1), 222–40.

HONKO, L., 'Der Mythos in der Religionswissenschaft', *Temenos*, 6 (1970), 36–67.

HORSTMANN, A., 'Der Mythosbegriff vom Frühen Christentum bis zur Gegenwart', *Archiv für Begriffsgeschichte*, 23 (1979), 7–54, 197–245.

IDEL, M., *Absorbing Perfections: Kabbalah and Interpretation* (New Haven and London: Yale University Press, 2002).

—— *Kabbalah: New Perspectives* (New Haven: Yale University Press, 1988).

—— 'Meṭatron—He ʿarot ʿal Hitpatḥut ha-Miṭos be-Yahadut', in *ʾEshel Beʾer-Shebaʿ*, iv (*Miṭos Be-Yahadut*), ed. Ḥaviva Pedayah (Jerusalem: Mosad Bialik, 1996), 29–44.

—— 'Quelques remarques sur la place du symbolisme dans la Kabbale', in Jean Petitot and Paolo Fabbri (edd.), *Au Nom du sens, autour de l' œuvre d'Umberto Eco* (Paris: B. Grasset, 2000), 185–212.

—— 'Rabbinism versus Kabbalism: On G. Scholem's Phenomenology of Judaism', *Modern Judaism*, 11 (1991), 281–97.

—— 'Sexual Metaphors and Praxis in the Kabbalah', in David Kraemer (ed.), *The Jewish Family: Metaphor and Memory* (New York: Oxford University Press, 1989), 197–224.

JACOBS, I., 'Elements of Near Eastern Mythology in Rabbinic Aggadah', *JJS* 28 (1977), 1–11.

JACOBSEN, T., 'The Battle between Marduk and Tiʾamat', *JAOS* 88 (1968), 104–8.

JACOBY, A., 'Der Baum mit den Wurzeln nach oben und den Zweigen nach unten', *Zeitschrift für Missionskunde und Religionswissenschaft*, 43 (1928), 78–85.

JACOPIN, P.-I., 'On the Syntactic Structure of Myth, or the Yukuna Invention of Speech', *Cultural Anthropology*, 3 (1988), 131–59.

JEREMIAS, J., 'Golgotha und der heilige Felsen', in *Angelos: Archiv für neutestamentliche Zeitgeschichte und Kulturkunde* (Leipzig: Eduard Pfeiffer, 1925), 74–128.

JOËL, M., *Blicke in die Religionsgeschichte zu Anfang des zweiten christlichen Jahrhunderts* (Breslau: Schottländer, 1880).

JONAS, H., *Gnosis und spätantiker Geist* (pt. 1, Die mythologische Gnosis; Göttingen: Vandenhoeck & Ruprecht, 1934).

——'Myth and Mysticism: A Study of Objectification and Interiorization in Religious Thought', *Journal of Religion*, 49 (1969), 315–29.

KAHANA, M., 'Mahadurot Ha-Mekhilta' de-Rabbi Ishma'el le-Shemot bi-Re'i Qeṭa'ei ha-Genizah', *Tarbiz*, 55 (1987), 399–524.

KAPELRUD, A., 'Mythological Features in Genesis Chapter 1 and the Author's Intentions', *VT* 24 (1974), 178–86.

KASHER, M., 'Ha-Zohar', in Y. Maimon (ed.), *Sinai: Sefer Yovel* (Jerusalem: Mosad Ha-Rav Kook, 1957), 40–56.

KAUFMANN, Y., 'The Bible and Mythological Polytheism', *JBL* 70 (1951), 179–97.

——*Toledot ha-'Emunah ha-Yisra'elit* (1937; 6th printing, Jerusalem and Tel Aviv: Mosad Bialik & Devir, 1964), I–IV.

KEARNS, R., *Vorfragen zur Christologie* (Tübingen: Mohr–Siebeck, 1982).

KING, L., *The Seven Tablets of Creation* (London: Luzac & Co., 1902).

KINGSLEY, P., 'Ezekiel by the Grand Canal: Between Jewish and Babylonian Tradition', *JRAS*, 3rd ser. 2 (1992), 339–46.

KIRK, G., *Myth: Its Meanings and Functions in Ancient and Other Cultures* (Berkeley and London: University of California Press and Cambridge University Press, 1970).

KISTER, M., 'Haddithū 'n banī isrā'īla wa–lā–ḥaraja: A Study of an Early Tradition', *IOS* 2 (1972), 215–39.

KITTAY, E., *Metaphor: Its Cognitive Force and Linguistic Structure* (Oxford: Clarendon Press, 1987).

KNOHL, I., and NAEH, S., 'Milu'im ve-Kippurim', *Tarbiz*, 62 (1993), 17–44.

KOCH, K., 'Wort und Einheit des Schöpfergottes in Memphis und Jerusalem', *ZTK* 62 (1965), 251–93.

KÖNGÄS, E.-K., and MARANDA, P., 'Structural Models in Folklore', *Midwest Folklore*, 12 (1962), 133–92.

KORPEL, M., *A Rift in the Clouds: Ugaritic and Hebrew Descriptions of the Divine* (UBL 8; Münster: Ugarit-Verlag, 1990).

KRAMER, S., 'The Lamentation over the Destruction of Nippur', *Acta Sumerologica*, 13 (1991), 1–26.

——*Lamentation over the Destruction of Ur* (AS 12; Chicago: University of Chicago Press, 1940).

——'BM 98396: A Sumerian Prototype of the *Mater-Dolorosa*', *EI* 16 (1982), 141–6.

——'The Weeping Goddess: Sumerian Prototypes of the *Mater Dolorosa*', *BA* 46.2 (1983), 69–80.

KUHN, P., *Gottes Selbsterniedrigung in der Theologie der Rabbinen* (Munich: Kössel, 1968).

——*Gottes Trauer und Klage in der Rabbinischen Überlieferung* (Leiden: E. J. Brill, 1978).

LAMBERT, W., 'The Cosmology of Sumer and Babylon', in Carmen Blacker and Michael Loewe (edd.), *Ancient Cosmologies* (London: George Allen & Unwin, 1975), 42–62.

——'A New Look at the Babylonian Background of Genesis', *JTS*, NS 16 (1965), 285–300.

——'Ninurta Mythology in the Babylonian Epic of Creation', in Karl Hecker and Werner Sommerfeld (edd.), *Keilschrift Literaturen: Ausgewälte Vorträge der XXXII Rencontre Assyriologique Internationale (1985)* (Berliner Beiträge zum Vorderen Orient, 6; Berlin: Dietrich Reimer Verlag, 1986), 55–70.

——'Old Testament Mythology in its Ancient Near Eastern Context', *SVT* 40 (1986), 124–43.

——'The Reign of Nebuchadnezzar I: A Turning Point in the History of Ancient Mesopotamian History', in W. S. McCollough (ed.), *The Seed of Wisdom: Essays in Honor of T. J. Meek* (Toronto: University of Toronto, 1964), 3–13.

——and MILLARD, A., *Atrahasis: The Babylonian Story of the Flood* (Oxford: Clarendon Press, 1969).

LAMBERTON, R., *Homer the Theologian: Neoplatonist Allegorical Reading and the Growth of the Epic Tradition* (Berkeley: University of California Press, 1989).

LANG, G., 'Dead or Alive? Literality and God-Metaphors in the Hebrew Bible', *JAAR* 62 (1994), 524f.

LÉVI-STRAUSS, C., *Structural Anthropology* (New York and London: Basic Books, 1963).

——'The Structural Study of Myth', in Thomas Sebeok (ed.), *Myth: A Symposium* (Bloomington: Indiana University Press, 1958), 81–106.

LEWIS, T., '*CT.* 33–34 and Ezekiel 32: Lion Dragon Myths', *JAOS* 116 (1996), 28–47.

L'HEUREUX, C., 'The Ugaritic and Biblical Rephaim', *HTR* 57 (1974), 265–74.

LIEBERMAN, S., *Hellenism in Jewish Palestine* (New York: The Jewish Theological Seminary of America, 1962).

——'Raymundo Martini and the Alleged Forgeries', *Historia Judaica*, 5 (1943), 87–102.

——*Sheqiʿin* (2nd edn.; Jerusalem: Wahrmann, 1960).

LIEBES, Y., 'De Natura Dei: On the Development of Jewish Myth', in his *Studies in Jewish Myth and Jewish Messianism* (Albany: State University of New York Press, 1993), 1–64, 151–69.

——'Miṭos Le-ʿumat Semel ba-Zohar uba-Kabbalat Ha-ʾARI', in *ʾEshel Beʾer-Shebaʿ*, iv (*Miṭos Be-Yahadut*), ed. Haviva Pedayah (Jerusalem: Mosad Bialik, 1996), 192–209.

——'Response to Shalom Rosenberg', *Jewish Studies*, 38 (1998), 181–5.

——*Torat ha-Yetzirah shel Sefer Yetzirah* (Tel Aviv: Schocken, 2000).

——'Yahadut Ve-Miṭos', *Dimui*, 14 (1997), 6–15.

——'Zohar ve-ʾEros', *ʾAlpayyim*, 9 (1994), 67–119.

—— 'Ha-Zohar ke-Renesans', *Daat*, 46 (2001), 5–11.
LINCOLN, B., *Theorizing Myth: Narrative, Ideology, and Scholarship* (Chicago: University of Chicago Press, 1999).
LIPIŃSKI, É., 'Juges 5, 4–5 et Psaume 68, 8–11', *Bib.* 48 (1967), 185–206.
LIPSIUS, R., *Der Gnostizismus, sein Wesen, Ursprung and Entwicklungsgang* (Leipzig: Brockhaus, 1860).
LISZKA, J., *The Semiotic of Myth: A Critical Study of the Symbol* (Bloomington: Indiana University Press, 1989), part 4.
LOEWENSTAMM, S., *Masoret Yitzi'at Mitzrayim Be-Hishtalshelutah* (Jerusalem: Magnes Press, 1967).
—— 'Miṭos ha-Yam be-Kitvei 'Ugarit ve-Ziqato 'el Miṭos ha-Yam ba-Miqra'', *EI* 9 (1969), 96–101.
—— 'Raʿadat ha-Tebaʿ be-Shaʿat Hofaʿat YHWH', in *ʿOz le-David* (David Ben-Gurion Festschrift), pub. by the Israel Bible Society and the World Jewish Bible Society (Jerusalem: Kiryat Sepher, 1964), 508–20.
LONGMAN III, T., *Fictional Akkadian Autobiography: A Generic and Comparative Study* (Winona Lake, Ind.: Eisenbrauns, 1991).
L'ORANGE, H., *Studies in the Iconography of Cosmic Kingship* (Oslo, 1953).
LOTMAN, J., and USPENSKIJ, B., 'Mito, nombre, cultura', in Jurij M. Lotman y Escuela de Tartu, *Semiotica de la cultura* (Madrid: Ediciones Cátedra, 1979), 111–35.
MCDANIEL, T., 'The Alleged Sumerian Influence upon Lamentations', *VT* 18 (1968), 198–209.
MARÓT, K., 'Die Trennung von Himmel und Erde', *Acta Antiqua Hungarica*, 1 (1951–2), 35–63.
MARTIN, R., *The Language of Heros: Speech and Performance in the Iliad* (Cornell, NY: Cornell University Press, 1989).
MAUL, S., ' "Wenn der Held (zum Kampfe) auszieht" . . . Ein Ninurta-Eršemma', *Or.* 60 (1991), 312–34.
MAUSS, M., *Œuvres: Representations collectives et diversité des civilisations* (Paris, 1969), ii.
MAYER, W., 'Ein Mythos von der Erschaffung des Menschen und des Königs', *Or.* 56 (1987), 55–68.
MAYS, H., 'Some Cosmic Connections of *Mayim Rabbîm*', *JBL* 74 (1955), 9–21.
MEEKS, W., 'Moses as God and King', in J. Neusner (ed.), *Religions in Antiquity: Essays in Honor of E. R. Goodenough* (Leiden: E. J. Brill, 1968), 354–71.
MENSCHING, G., *Die Religion: Erscheinungsformen, Structurtypen und Lebensgesetze* (Stuttgart, 1959).
MICHALOWSKI, P., *The Lamentation over the Destruction of Sumer and Ur* (Winona Lake, Ind.: Eisenbrauns, 1989).
MILIK, J., *The Books of Enoch: Aramaic Fragments of Qumran Cave 4* (Oxford: Clarendon Press, 1976).
MILLAR, F., *The Roman Near East 31 BC–AD 337* (Cambridge, Mass.: Harvard University Press, 1993).
MILLER, P., 'Fire in the Mythology of Canaan and Israel', *CBQ* 27 (1965), 256–61.

MONDI, R., 'Greek Mythic Thought in the Light of the Near East', in L. Edmunds (ed.), *Approaches to Greek Myth*, (Baltimore: Johns Hopkins University Press, 1990), 142–98.

MOORE, G., 'Daniel viii. 9–14', *JBL* 15 (1896), 193–7.

MORGENSTERN, J., 'The Mythological Background of Psalm 82', *HUCA* 14 (1939), 29–126.

MUFFS, Y., *Love and Joy: Law, Language and Religion in Ancient Israel* (New York: The Jewish Theological Seminary of America, 1992).

MÜLLER, H.-P., 'Gott und die Götter in den Anfängen der biblischen Religion: Zur Vorgeschichte des Monotheismus', in Othmar Keel (ed.), *Monotheismus im Alten Israel und siener Umwelt* (Biblische Beiträge 14; Schweizerisches Katholisches Bibelwerk, 1980), 99–185.

MÜLLER, M., *Lectures on the Science of Language*, 2nd ser. (New York: Scribner, Armstrong, 1873).

MUNZ, P., *When the Golden Bough Breaks: Structuralism or Typology?* (London: Routledge & Kegan Paul, 1973).

MUSSIES, G., 'The Interpretatio Judaica of Serapis', in M. J. Vermaseren (ed.), *Studies in Hellenistic Religions*, (Leiden: E. J. Brill, 1979), 189–214.

NAEH, S., '*potērion encheiri kyriou*: Philo and the Rabbis on the Powers of God and the Mixture in the Cup', *Scripta Classica Israelica*, 16 (1997), 91–101.

NEMOY, L., 'Al Qirqisani᾿s Account of the Jewish Sects and Christianity', *HUCA* 7 (1930), 317–97.

NESTLE, W., *Vom Mythos zum Logos: Die Selbstenfaltung des griechischen Denkens von Homer bis auf die Sophistik und Sokrates* (Stuttgart, 1940).

ODEN Jr., R., ' "The Contendings of Horus and Seth" (Chester Beatty Papyrus No. 1): A Structural Interpretation', *HR* 18 (1978–9), 352–69.

—— 'Method in the Study of Near Eastern Myths', *Religion*, 9 (1979), 182–96.

OPPENHEIM, A., 'Akkadian pul(u)ḫ(t)u and melammu', *JAOS* 63 (1943), 31–4.

PAGE Jr., H., *The Myth of Cosmic Rebellion* (SVT 65; Leiden: E. J. Brill, 1996).

PÉPIN, J., *Mythe et allégorie: Les Origines grecques et les contestations judéo-chrétiens* (2nd edn.; Paris: Études augustiniennes, 1976).

PETTAZZONI, R., 'The Formation of Monotheism', *Essays on the History of Religions* (Leiden: E. J. Brill, 1954), 1–10.

—— 'Monotheismus und Polytheismus I. Religionsgeschichte', in H. Gunkel and L. Zscharnack (edd.), *Die Religion in Geschichte und Gegenwart* (Tübingen, 1930), iv. 185–91.

—— 'The Truth of Myth', in *Essays on the History of Religions*, 11–23.

PHILIPPSON, P., *Geneologie als Mythische Form: Studien zur Theogonie des Hesiod* (Symbolae Osloenses Fasc. Supplet. VII; Oslo: A. W. Bro/gger, 1936).

PINES, S., 'Ha-᾿El ha-Kabod veha-Mal᾿akhim lefi Shiṭah Te᾿ologit shel ha-Me᾿ah ha-Sheniyah la-Sefirah', *JSJT* 6.3–4 (1987), 1–14.

PODELLA, T., 'Der "Chaoskampfmythos" im Alten Testament: Eine Problemzeige', in Manfried Dietrich and Oswald Loretz (edd.), *Mesopotamica-Ugaritica-Biblica: Festschrift für Kurt Bergerhof* (Kevelaer and Neukirchen-Vluyn: Butzon & Berker and Neukirchen, 1993), 283–329.

POHL, A., 'Die Klage Marduks über Babylon im Erra-Epos', *HUCA* 23.1 (1950–1), 405–9.

PORTER POOLE, F., 'Metaphors and Maps: Towards Comparison in the Anthropology of Religion', *JAAR* 54 (1986), 411–57.

PREUS, J., 'Anthropomorphism and Spinoza's Innovations', *Religion*, 25 (1995), 1–8.

PROPP, V., *Theory and History of Folklore*, trans. Ariadna Y. Martin and Richard P. Martin; ed. with introd. and notes Anatoly Liberman (Minneapolis: University of Minnesota Press, 1984).

QUINE, W., *Word and Object* (Cambridge, Mass.: MIT Press, 1960).

RAGACS, U., 'The Forged Midrashim of Raymond Martini—Reconsidered', *Henoch*, 19 (1997), 59–68.

RAWIDOWICZ, S., 'Saadya's Purification of the Idea of God', in his *Studies in Jewish Thought*, ed. Nahum N. Glatzer (Philadelphia: The Jewish Publication Society, 1974), 246–68.

REEVES, J., *Jewish Lore in Manichaean Cosmogony: Studies in the Book of Giants Traditions* (Cincinnati: Hebrew Union College Pres, 1992).

ROBINSON, H., 'The Council of Yahweh', *JTS* 45 (1944), 151–7.

ROSENBERG, R., 'The God Sedeq', *HUCA* 36 (1965), 161–77.

ROSENBERG, S., 'Miṭos ha-Miṭosim', *Jewish Studies*, 38 (1998), 145–79.

RUBENSTEIN, J., 'From Mythic Motifs to Sustained Myth: The Revision of Rabbinic Traditions in Medieval Midrashim', *HTR* 89 (1996), 146–58.

RUDOLPH, K., *Gnosis* (New York: Harper & Row, 1983).

SAGGS, H., *The Encounter with the Divine in Mesopotamia and Israel* (London: Athlone Press, 1978).

SAPERSTEIN, M., *Decoding the Rabbis. A Thirteenth-Century Commentary on the Aggadot* (Cambridge, Mass.: Harvard University Press, 1980).

SARNA, N., 'The Psalm for the Sabbath Day (Psalm 92)', *JBL* 81 (1962), 155–68.

SCHÄFER, P., 'Daughter, Sister, Bride, and Mother: Images of the Femininity of God in the Early Kabbalah', *JAAR* 68 (2000), 221–42.

—— *et al.* (edd.), *Synopse zur Hekhalot-Literatur* (Tübingen: Mohr–Siebeck, 1981).

SCHIRMANN, J., *The Battle Between Behemoth and Leviathan According to an Ancient Hebrew Piyyuṭ* (Proceedings of the Israel Academy of Sciences and Humanities; Jerusalem: Sivan Press, 1970), iv, no. 13, pp. 327–69.

SCHMIDT, W., 'Mythos im alten Testament', *Evangelische Theologie*, 27 (1967), 237–54.

—— *Die Schöpfungsgeschichte der Priesterschrift* (Neukirchen-Vluyn: Neukirchener Verlag, 1964).

SCHNABEL, P., *Berossos und die babylonische-hellenistiche Literatur* (Leipzig, 1923).

SCHOLEM, G., 'Jaldabaoth Reconsidered', in *Mélanges d'histoire des religions, offerts à Henri-Charles Peuch* (Paris, 1974), 405–21.

—— 'Kabbalah and Myth', in *On the Kabbalah and its Symbolism* (New York: Schocken Books, 1960), 87–117.

—— *Major Trends in Jewish Mysticism* (New York: Schocken Books, 1941).

—— *On the Mystical Shape of the Godhead: Basic Concepts in the Kabbalah* (New York: Schocken Books, 1992).

SCHOLEM, G., *Origins of the Kabbalah*, ed. R. J. Zwi Werblowsky; trans. Allan Arkush (Philadelphia and Princeton: The Jewish Publication Society and Princeton University Press, 1987).

—— 'Das Ringen zwischen dem biblischen Gott und dem Gott Plotins in der alten Kabbala', in his *Über einige Grundbegriffe des Judentums* (Frankfurt am Main: Suhrkamp, 1970), 9–53.

SCHWEID, E., 'Bein Ḥoqer le-Mefaresh Filosofi shel ha-Miqra'', in Michal Oran and Amos Goldreich (edd.), *Massu'ot: Studies in Kabbalistic Literature and Jewish Philosophy in Memory of Prof. Ephraim Gottlieb* (Jerusalem: Mosad Bialik, 1994), 414–28.

SEBEOK, T. (ed.), *Myth: A Symposium* (Bloomington and London: Indiana University Press, 1965).

SÉD, N., 'Les Traditions secrètes et les disciples de Rabban Yohanan be Zakkaï', *RdHR* 184 (1973), 49–66.

SEELIGMANN, I., 'Menschliches Heldentum und Gottliche Hilfe—Die doppelte Kausalität im alttestamentlichen Geschichtsdenken', *TZ* 19 (1963), 385–411.

SMITH, J. Z., *Drudgery Divine: On the Comparison of Early Christianities and the Religions of Late Antiquity* (Chicago: University of Chicago Press, 1990).

—— *Imagining Religion. From Babylon to Jonestown* (Chicago: University of Chicago Press, 1982).

SMITH, M., 'The Common Theology of the Ancient Near East', *JBL* 71 (1952), 135–47.

SPERBER, D., *Magic and Folklore in Rabbinic Literature* (Tel Aviv: Bar-Ilan Press, 1994).

STADELMAN, R., *Syrisch-Palästinensiche Gottheiten in Ägypten* (Leiden: E. J. Brill, 1967).

STAUDACHER, W., *Die Trennung von Himmel und Erde: Ein vorgriechischer Schöpfundsmythus bei Hesiod und den Orphikern* (diss.; Tübingen: K. Bölzie, 1942).

STERN, D., *Midrash and Theory: Ancient Jewish Exegesis and Contemporary Literary Theory* (Evanston: Northwestern University Press, 1996).

STERN, S., 'Attribution and Authorship in the Babylonian Talmud', *JJS* 45 (1994), 28–51.

STROUMSA, G., 'Polymorphie divine et transformations d'un mythologème', *VC* 35 (1981), 412–34.

STUMMER, F., *Sumerisch-akkadische Parallelen zum Aufbau alttestamentlicher Psalmen* (Paderborn: Verlag von Ferdinand Schoeningh, 1922).

TATE, J., 'Plato and Allegorical Interpretation', *Classical Quarterly*, 23 (1929), 142–54.

TURNER, T., 'Narrative Structure and Mythopoesis: A Critique and Reformulation of Structuralist Concepts of Myth, Narrative, and Poetics', *Arethusa*, 10 (1977), 103–64.

URBACH, E. E., *The Sages* (Cambridge, Mass.: Harvard University Press, 1987).

USENER, H., *Dreiheit: Ein Versuch Mythologischer Zahlenlehre* (Bonn: Carl Georgi, Universitätsbuchdruckerei, 1903).

VAN BUREN, E., 'The Dragon in Ancient Mesopotamia', *Or.* 15 (1946), 1–45.

——*Symbols of the Gods in Mesopotamian Art* (AnOr 23; Pontificium Institutum Biblicum, 1945).

VAN DER VALK, M., 'On *Apollodori Bibliotheca*', *Revue des Études Grecques*, 71 (1958), 100–68.

VERNANT, J.-P., *Myth and Society in Ancient Greece* (New York: Zone Books, 1988).

WALCOT, P., *Hesiod and the Near East* (Cardiff, 1966).

WAUGH, L., 'Marked and Unmarked: A Choice Between Unequals in Semiotic Structure', *Semiotica*, 38 (1982), 299–318.

WEINFELD, M., *Deuteronomy and the Deuteronomic School* (Oxford: Clarendon Press, 1972).

——'Divine Intervention in War in Ancient Israel and in the Ancient Near East', in H. Tadmor and M. Weinfeld (edd.), *History, Historiography and Interpretation: Studies in Biblical and Cuneiform Literature* (Jerusalem: Magnes Press, 1983), 120–47.

——'Ha-ʾEl ha-Boreiʾ be-Bereishit 1 ube-Nebuʾat Yeshayahu ha-Sheni', *Tarbiz*, 37 (1967–8), 105–32.

——'Kuntillet ʿAjrud Inscriptions and their Significance', *SEL* 1 (1984), 121–30.

——' "Min ha-Shamayim Nilḥamu": Hitʿarbut Gufim Shamaymiyim be-Qerab ʿim ha-ʾOyeb be-Yisrael ube-Mizraḥ ha-Qadum', *EI* 14 (1968), 23–30.

——'Yesodot Niqbiyim be-Teʾurei haʾElohut ha-Yisraʾelit', *Beth Miqra*, 40. 143 (1995), 348–58.

WEST, M., *Early Greek Philosophy and the Orient* (Oxford: Clarendon Press, 1971).

——*The East Face of Helicon: West Asiatic Elements in Greek Poetry and Myth* (Oxford: Clarendon Press, 1997).

WOLFSON, E., *Along the Path: Studies in Kabbalistic Myth, Symbolism, and Hermeneutics* (Albany: State University of New York, 1995).

——'Hebraic and Hellenic Conceptions of Wisdom in Sefer ha-Bahir', *Poetics Today*, 19 (1998), 147–76.

——*Sprache, Eros, Dasein: Kabbalistische Hermeneutik und poetische Einbildungskraft* (Berlin and Vienna: Philo Verlagsgesellschaft, 2002).

——*Through a Speculum that Shines: Vision and Imagination in Medieval Jewish Mysticism* (Princeton: Princeton University Press, 1994).

YAHALOM, Y., *Piyyuṭ U-Metziʾut Be-Shalhei Ha-Zeman He-ʿAtiq* (Tel Aviv: Hakibbutz Hameuchad, 1999).

ZAKOVITCH, Y., "Ani ve-Rokhev ʿal Ḥamor (Zech. 9: 9–10)', *The Messianic Idea in Jewish Thought* (Jerusalem: Israel Academy of Sciences and Humanities, 1982), 7–17.

ZANK, M., 'The Rabbinic Epithet *Gevurah*', in *Approaches to Ancient Judaism*, NS, xiv, ed. Jacob Neusner (1998), 83–168.

GENERAL INDEX*

Aaron 45, 47, 67, 76, 152; *see also* Priest
Abba (R.) 370
Abba b. Kahana (R.) 209, 360, 388–9
Abba Yose (R.) 335
Abbahu (R.) 102, 147, 151–3, 195–6, 269, 343–4, 358, 377, 384, 400–1
Abbaye (R.) 362
Abin (R.) 344–5, 370
Abraham 73, 171, 247–8, 269, 334, 337–40, 359, 376; *see also* Patriarchs
Abraham Saba' (R.) 343
Abulafia, Todros ben Joseph (R.) 266
Academies 95, 194–8, 231; *see also* Mythmaking; Tradition
  Babylonian 95, 163, 194, 196–8, 203
  Palestinian 95, 112, 163, 183, 194–7, 203
Adad 20, 45–6, 83
Adam 88, 289, 396
Addu 33
Agade 160, 163
Aha (R.) 158, 196, 248, 359, 385–6
Aḥa b. Ada (R.) 312
Aḥa b. Jacob (R.) 316
Aḥa b. 'Ulla (R.) 194
Akiba (R.) 135, 138–42, 162, 195–6, 233–4, 239, 350, 353–4, 363, 400–1
Al Qirqisani, Jacob 149, 254
Alfonsi, Petrus 254
Amalek 189–90, 239, 388; *see also* Enemy; Nations
Ammi (R.) 151–3, 168, 196–7
Amora (R.) 257
Amos 170, 225
Anat 33, 49
Angels 132–3, 136, 171, 217, 228–9, 246, 257–8, 261, 273, 298–9, 321, 340–1, 369; *see also* Divine Messengers, Retinue
Anthropomorphism 3–11, 40, 52–4, 62, 66, 69, 81–3, 325–6, 328, 398–401; *see also* Anthropopathism; Arm/Hand; Divine, Anthropos
  Age 171–2, 232, 238, 356–7
  Embodiment 165–7
  Eyes 98, 165–6, 170, 224, 365–6, 396
  Face 52–3, 82, 224, 236, 384
  Feet 38, 52, 55, 77, 117, 135–7, 201, 204, 210, 224, 391–2
  Hair 261–5, 270–1
  Memory 44, 66–9, 83, 150, 162–4, 224, 298, 323, 358–9, 373–4
  Sitting 71, 189, 373, 393–4
  Sleep 177–9, 371–3, 377–8
  Standing 393
  Tears/Weeping 14, 96, 98, 159, 163–7, 170, 172, 197, 222, 254–5, 293, 298–300, 321–4, 367–70
  Voice 47, 52–3, 65, 73, 84, 98, 104, 225, 260–1,
Anthropopathism 3–11, 230, 235, 325, 328, 398–401; *see also* Anthropomorphism; Divine/God; Human Beings
  Compassion 14, 42, 44, 68–9, 149, 229, 232, 246, 329, 361, 369, 373–5, 397; *see also below* Sympathy
  Mourning 162–4, 170–3, 191, 197, 222, 228–9, 261, 293, 361, 364, 365, 368, 370–1
  Personality 5, 14, 32, 63, 68–9, 81, 100, 172, 179, 181, 191, 239, 293, 310
  Sorrow 14–15, 160, 162–73, 197, 222, 225, 255, 285, 293, 309, 321–4, 363, 367–70
  Suffering 110, 132, 134, 154, 159, 160, 164–7, 174, 197, 215, 226, 272, 293, 297–8, 356, 360–7

* Indices prepared by Steven D. Sacks

INDEX OF SCRIPTURAL AND OTHER SOURCES

HEBREW BIBLE

SELECTED HEBREW TERMS